W9-ABR-540

Acclaim for VISIONS OF JAZZ

"*Visions of Jazz: The First Century* is a massive attempt to encompass the music from its earliest beginnings . . . the essays are superbly written, manifest examples of the manner in which the best writing about jazz combines historical perspective, social insights, and musical understanding."

—Don Heckman, *Los Angeles Times*

"Gary Giddins is that rarest of jazz critics. He feels the music as deeply as the artists who make it, and he writes as expressively and with the same depth and breadth as his stellar subjects perform and compose. . . . He writes with such insight, wit, and vigor that one need not be an aficionado [to be] swept up by the power of his prose and the skill of his narrative essays."

—George Varga, *San Diego Union-Tribune*

"Effectively a popular history of the United States through music."

—Ian Thompson, *The Daily Telegraph* (London)

"Giddins brings to the table an impeccable ear, encyclopedic tastes, a reporter's gift for detail and a scholar's knowledge of jazz history and the urban sprawl of American culture—all filtered through a strikingly eloquent and witty prose style."

—Mark Stryker, *Detroit Free Press*

"To say that Gary Giddins is a great jazz critic is no more useful than saying Ruskin wrote well about art or that Johnson was a darned good lexicographer. Giddins is an essayist and thinker capable of astonishing erudition, insight, and sensitivity, but first and foremost he's a breathtaking stylist, whose suppleness of tone and flexibility of line here elucidate the most American of musical forms in a way that—gently, unobtrusively—swings."

—Rick Moody

"Titans roamed the land and plied the rivers . . . Giddins limns them all incisively and often poetically. [His] passion and commitment burn through *Visions of Jazz* like a hot, blue flame."

—Don Asher, *San Francisco Chronicle*

"Finally, under one roof, is the conclusive evidence of jazz's centrality in our complicated national narrative and of Gary Giddins's supreme mastery of his topic."

—Ken Burns

"The most penetrating, persuasive and engagingly personal overview of the music. . . . Whatever the next century has in store, this century of jazz couldn't receive a better sendoff."

—Lloyd Sachs, *Chicago Sun-Times*

"Though his greatest gift is a knack for translating musical experience into concrete prose (e.g., first listening to Gerry Mulligan is like 'trying to climb a glass wall'), Giddins is also a consummate historian and fearless contrarian."
—*Publishers Weekly*

"As jazz celebrates its centenary, Giddins has given it, and those who love it, the perfect birthday present."
—Andrew Vine, *Yorkshire Post* (Leeds)

"His fascination and ardour show through on every page, and the reader will find that these 'Visions of Jazz' continue to illuminate his or her own, long after they have closed the book."
—*The Economist*

"Accessible, informative and entertaining . . . beautifully turned phrases. . . . Just great!"
—Brian Case, *Time Out*

"[Giddins's] phenomenal appetite for the sound of the new will give all but the most blinkered reactionary an appetite for the unknown. But above all, the overwhelming strength of this book is that it also makes you want to listen afresh to music that you thought you knew well."
—Clive Davis, *Washington Times*

"Jazz-loving listeners with no technical knowledge of the music might fear being overwhelmed by the author's close analysis, but they would be wrong . . . Giddins's aim is to transmit enjoyment."
—George Melly, *The Times* (London)

"Dazzling intellectual range and finely honed writing. . . . Jazz creativity is examined against a backdrop of racism, economic depression, political paranoia and democratic experimentation."
—Norman Weinstein, *Pulse*

"His knowledge of the subject is prodigious and his tastes wide-ranging. What is more, he writes clear, unpretentious English. . . . I can think of few other writers who would be up to the job . . . and I know of no one who has written better on Sinatra or Billie Holiday. Giddins's writing is full of insights and ideas."
—Dave Gelly, *Jazz-Wise*

"A monumental work . . . Giddins has become a master of the lightning insight, the unexpected connection (his use of literary analogies is particularly apt). . . . This is an important book, one that any serious student of jazz will want to own."
—Kirkus Reviews

Visions of Jazz

Visions of Jazz

THE FIRST CENTURY

GARY GIDDINS

OXFORD
UNIVERSITY PRESS

Jessamine County Public Library
600 South Main Street
Nicholasville, KY 40356
(859) 885-3523

OXFORD
UNIVERSITY PRESS

Oxford   New York
Athens   Auckland   Bangkok   Bogotá   Buenos Aires   Calcutta
Cape Town   Chennai   Dar es Salaam   Delhi   Florence   Hong Kong
Istanbul   Karachi   Kuala Lumpur   Madrid   Melbourne   Mexico City
Mumbai   Nairobi   Paris   São Paulo   Singapore   Taipei   Tokyo
Toronto   Warsaw

and associated companies in
Berlin   Ibadan

Copyright © 1998 by Gary Giddins

First published by Oxford University Press, Inc., 1998

First issued as an Oxford University Press paperback, 1999

Oxford is a registered trademark of Oxford University Press

All rights reserved. No part of this publication may be reproduced,
stored in a retrieval system, or transmitted, in any form or by any means,
electronic, mechanical, photocopying, recording, or otherwise,
without the prior permission of Oxford University Press.

Library of Congress Cataloging-in-Publication Data

Giddins, Gary.
Visions of jazz : the first century / Gary Giddins.
p.   cm.   Includes index.
ISBN 0-19-507675-3 (Cloth)
ISBN 0-19-513241-6 (Pbk.)
1. Jazz musicians—Biography.   2. Composers—Biography.
3. Jazz—History and criticism.   I. Title.
ML385.G53   1998   781.65'092'2—dc21   [B]   98-12199

781.65
GIDD

5 7 9 10 8 6

Printed in the United States of America
on acid-free paper

3 2530 60623 6378

FOR LEA, DEBORAH, AND ALICE
AND FOR SHELDON MEYER

AND IN MEMORY:

LEO GIDDINS
AND
WALTER CLEMONS
ROY ELDRIDGE
GIL EVANS
DIZZY GILLESPIE
MEL LEWIS
GERRY MULLIGAN
SARAH VAUGHAN
MARTIN WILLIAMS

Cornetist to Queen Victoria Falls Dead on Hearing Coney Island
Jazz Band.   —headline (1926), The New York Times

Jazz is the expression of protest against law and order, the bolshevik
element of license striving for expression in music.
                              —Anne Shaw Faulkner, Ladies Home Journal

The "jazz mania" has taken on the character of a lingering illness
and must be cured by means of forceful intervention.
                              —Boris Gibalin, Izvestia

What a terrible revenge by the culture of the Negroes on that of the
whites!   —Ignace Paderewski

Jazz opposes to our classical conception of music a strange and subversive chaos of sounds . . . it is a fashion and, as such, destined some
day to disappear.   —Igor Stravinsky

Jazz is only what you are.   —Louis Armstrong

Contents

Visions of Jazz

Introduction

Shortly after I began writing about jazz, in the early '70s, I had the occasion to visit a formidable English jazz historian. We had hardly crossed his threshold when he asked me, "What kind of jazz do you like?" That was the first time the chronic riddle had been put to me, and I have no better response now than I did then, when, shrugging my shoulders, I replied, "Anything good." With a harrumph worthy of a Dickens or Austen dramatization, he proclaimed, "I *know* what I like." And what would that be? Came the resounding reply, "The '20s!"

The '20s—culture by the decade. A panel of jazz experts representing its various eras and movements might conceivably be reduced to a pandemonium of such proclamations: "The '50s!" "The '40s!" "The '60s!" "The '30s!" "The '90s!" Well, not the '90s. Or they might thunder favorite genres: "Swing!" "Dixieland!" "Free jazz!" "Modern!" "Fusion!" No, not fusion. But you get the idea. For most of this century, the jazz audience has been atomized into frequently warring satellites. One could interpret jazz schismatics as a tribute to the music's diversity and the speed with which it evolved from neighborhood socials to worldwide sovereignty. Or one could mock the miserable churls who lack our exquisitely liberal sensibility.

Even the deep solace of prejudice has its shoals. As the formidable jazz expert walked me back to the sitting room where his wife was preparing a tray of tea and lemon biscuits, I recognized Tommy Dorsey's big band in full sway. I must have cocked my head, because before I could say a word, he griped, "Oh, I have to play that for the missus."

As jazz saunters past its one hundredth anniversary (an indeterminate date that stems from the 1890s, when the New Orleans trumpeter Buddy Bolden led the first band universally regarded as an identifiable jazz ensemble), it has waxed too much history for concise assessment and too little for time-filtered consensus. Fans who confidently recited the tidy record of a traditional to swing to bop chronicle that tied each generation to the next have given way to fans intimidated by an increasingly tangled epic; they don't know much about it, but they like what they know. Jazz has been taken up by the academy at a time when only the academy can keep track of it, and the university imprimatur is people's exhibit number one that jazz is approaching its marble-bust era.

Excoriated at its birth and mocked or neglected during many of its most glorious eruptions, jazz at the outset of its second century faces the more perilous future of respectability and disinterested acceptance. Big money has moved in, the sort that goes to institutions, not musicians: government money, which is to say tax money, and corporate money, which is to say tax-deductible money. Some of it trickles down to artists, chiefly to those who play by institutional rules.

The entrepreneur George Wein, who invented the annual jazz festival, recently said, "There are probably 2000 jazz festivals now. It's a reaction against rock—*jazz* is a good word and cities will give money to subsidize jazz festivals, and now schools will subsidize them. They won't subsidize rock festivals. They'll subsidize a folk festival or a blues festival occasionally. But just mention jazz and there's money there. Maybe not a lot—maybe just 10,000 bucks for concerts, maybe 30,000. But whatever it is, the money's there."

Sounds good, no? Yet many ruefully recall a vanished age when what we now call classical music was a vital, transfiguring, seductive, and galling art, often improvised, that spoke to people's lives and kept them on their toes. It was also popular. Then the institutions took over and retailored it into a malleable craft and fixed repertory, easily channeled from one orchestra to another, for the amusement of the upper middle-class shopper out on a cultural excursion, the fat-cat subscriber whose seasonal boxes entertain clients and friends, and children who eat their spinach. True, an active contemporary music field flourishes downtown and on campus, but who cares? Name five composers under forty. All right, three. The louts who rioted at the debut of *Le Sacre du printemps* now seem quaintly admirable in their concern. In the age of the Three Tenors, when superstar virtuosos record themes from Oscar-winning movies (a task previously left to studio hacks), the concert series subscriber may be identified by a lobotomized grin.

Is this the future of jazz?—a repertory dominated by the tastes of dilettantes, a morbid obsession with the saintly dead, a horror of innovation? As someone who has long fought for the acceptance of repertory jazz (the establishment of institutional orchestras that interpret and re-interpret classic scores), I do not think so. But I worry about the marginalization of creative musicians who don't abide by institutional concerns and have been ostracized as "nonjazz" to keep them at the gates. A jazz classicism that can keep alive the music of Ellington and Basie and Lunceford and Gil Evans, yet fails to coexist with the most vital of jazz traditions—its inventiveness, irreverence, and canny involvement with other musics and life as we live it—will produce a dozen lovely plaster busts for home or school and a gorgeously ornate headstone.

In *Rhythm-a-Ning* (1985), I posed the under-forty question as it related to jazz. "Few educated Americans can name even five jazz musicians under the age of forty," I confidently asserted, and got no arguments. That is perhaps not as much the case today, though I imagine once you leave major urban centers and stipulate that Kenny G and US3 do not count, the average respondent will go blank after mentioning a Marsalis brother or two and maybe Joshua Redman, Kenny Garrett, or Diana Krall, none of whom can individually pack a concert hall. Yet jazz is enjoying an upsurge in popularity, as always in periods of consolidation when the audience is replenished until a new pathfinder unsettles the status quo and frightens it away.

It isn't fashionable to point out that this is a fallow era. The *New York Times* recently designated the '90s "a jazz renaissance." But if we compare the present period to, say, 1960, we may want to tighten our hyperbole. Every assessment of the present era begins with a litany of able musicians in their twenties and thirties. The roll of active musicians under the age of forty in 1960 included Miles Davis, Sonny Rollins, John Coltrane, Stan Getz, Charles Mingus, Sarah Vaughan, Carmen McRae, Horace Silver, Ornette Coleman, Erroll Garner, Cecil Taylor, Milt Jackson, Randy Weston, Lee Konitz, Cannonball Adderley, Ray Brown, J. J. Johnson, Gerry Mulligan, Jackie McLean, Paul Chambers, Bill Evans, Dinah Washington, Max Roach, Roy Haynes, Jim Hall, Wayne Shorter, Wes Montgomery, Paul Desmond, Jimmy Heath, Zoot Sims, Oscar Peterson, Chet Baker, Booker Ervin, Elvin Jones, Art Farmer, Thad Jones, Phil Woods, Gene Ammons, Sam Rivers, and Eric Dolphy. No one dubbed that period a renaissance. When the goods are delivered, special pleading isn't necessary. I do not mean to wring a nostalgic sob, but to underscore the cyclical history of jazz—1960 wasn't even that great a year.

Cycles and cycles within cycles are the meat of the matter. One could argue that jazz is a music based on cyclical motion, a strictly defined chorus, usually twelve or thirty-two measures, repeated until a musical statement has been made. Cycles are fomented by radical evolutionary movements, each of which contains the seeds of its own destruction. One example: during the ferment of jazz activity in the '40s, when modern jazz, or bebop, was born, the intoxicating harmonic ingenuity of Charlie Parker and Dizzy Gillespie blinded sympathetic fans from recognizing the antiharmonic implications of George Russell's modal composition, "Cubana Be/Cubana Bop," written for Gillespie's orchestra. In a day when Thelonious Monk's clattering minor seconds and rhythmic displacements were dismissed as the fumblings of a charlatan, Russell's work was appreciated as something of a sui generis novelty.

Russell codified the modal approach to harmony (using scales instead of chords) in a theoretical treatise that he says was inspired by a casual remark the eighteen-year-old Miles Davis made to him in 1944: "Miles said that he wanted to learn all the changes and I reasoned that he might try to find the closest scale for every chord." His concept, published as the *Lydian Chromatic Concept of Tonal Organization*, is based on a perfect cycle of fifths generated by the Lydian mode, which sounds more complicated than it is. Russell was exploring relationships between chords and scales that would foster a fresh approach to harmony. Davis popularized those liberating ideas in recordings like *Kind of Blue*, undermining the entire harmonic foundation of bop that had inspired him and Russell in the first place.

George Russell is not in this book. He's in good company. Clifford Brown, Benny Carter, Earl Hines, Sidney Bechet, Johnny Hodges, Bix Beiderbecke, Teddy Wilson, Gil Evans, Bessie Smith, Bing Crosby, Fletcher Henderson, Henry "Red" Allen, Art Ensemble of Chicago, Albert Ayler, Ben Webster, Jack Teagarden, Jimmie Noone, James P. Johnson, Woody Herman, Wardell Gray, Charlie Christian, Mary Lou Williams, Teddy Edwards, Clark Terry, Tadd Dameron, Mildred Bailey, Lennie Tristano, Anthony Braxton, Cedar Walton, Red Norvo, Tony Williams, Serge Chaloff, and Illinois Jacquet, along with most of those already mentioned in the class of 1960, and many others, are major figures in jazz and personal favorites of mine and are not in this book, at least to the degree that their accomplishments merit. Nor are popularizers like Paul Whiteman, Dave Brubeck, and Wynton Marsalis, or such peripheral galvanizers as Claude Debussy, Igor Stravinsky, Louis Jordan, Earl Bostic, and Ray Charles. The most glaring absence of all is that of the entire jazz world beyond the borders of the continental United States. I set American jazz as my parameter in an attempt to make this work manageable, and the inclusion of a chapter or two on Django Reinhardt, Stan Hasselgard, Ted Heath, Lars Gullin, Albert Manglesdorff, Svend Asmussen, Evan Parker, Bengt Hallberg, Martial Solal, Willem Breuker, Han Bennink, Peter Brötzmann, Dino Saluzzi, Pierre Dorge, the Danish Radio Band, Junko Onishi, Mike Westbrook, Ian Shaw, or numerous others could not help but suggest an egregious sort of tokenism.

On the other hand, this book enfolds a number of suspicious characters who tend to be discounted, patronized, or relegated to the footnotes in most critical or historical discussions of jazz. My intention is to present a canvas of the music over time in a tableau of innovators, journeymen, precursors, and sidesteppers, all of whom suit my purposes on at least two levels: each of the artists discussed generates a distinct musical vision, a personal expression that, large or small, is unique and ultimately matchless; and each embodies, for me, an idea that, in a critical or literary sense, evokes something of the singularity and magic of the jazz phenomenon.

The marble-bust era entails two responses to the unmanageable past. First, the weeding out of minor figures in a vain attempt to cram all the big guns into a single semester, a concert subscription series, a five-foot shelf of CDs, or a late-night commercial that guarantees the masterworks of *every* jazz giant for $19.95—plus every vocalist if you act right now. Even the orthodox genesis of Great Men—King Oliver begat Louis Armstrong who begat Roy Eldridge who begat Dizzy Gillespie who begat Miles Davis—has to be winnowed for these hot-spot surveys. Oliver goes because pre-electric records are hard to hear, then Eldridge because he isn't famous enough. But jazz is primarily a performer's art and resists the funneling of time as strenuously as it does facile evaluations. Classical music is content with its busts, and the occasional resurrection rarely takes hold for long (Alkan anyone? Fanny Mendelssohn?) But individuality in jazz is subtly asserted. A minor player may have only a few good solos or a few good notes, but if they express something found nowhere else, they are treasurable and they sustain our interest.

The most pleasurable experiences in jazz include countless fugitive passages, some not much longer than a few seconds—an inspired eight-bar variation in an otherwise leaden recording, a sensational voicing for the brasses in an otherwise routine arrangement. Everyone venerates and assimilates the masters. But the odd personalities that bloom in their shadows, like flowers fracturing an urban pavement, should be valued no less. One example: Frank Newton (1906–54) is a relatively minor figure, little known except to ardent enthusiasts. A trumpet player with an unmistakable style and sound, he exerted marginal influence (a poor criterion for measuring achievement) and recorded a small body of work between 1929 and 1946. Yet anyone who fails to ferret out such performances as "Please Don't Talk About Me When I'm Gone" (1937), "The Blues My Baby Gave to Me" (1939), "Sweet Georgia Brown" (1941, an after-hours duet with Art Tatum), or "Lullaby of the Leaves" (1944, a Mary Lou Williams session) is missing a remarkable artist, whose solos Charles Fox once astutely described as "devious, even faintly subversive." Armstrong, Ellington, and Parker are gods. But Newton is one of a thousand worthy angels.

The second inclination is the opposite of the first: a worship of minutiae, the necessary adjunct of publish-or-perish academia. As a generation of educators is encouraged to specialize, a circle will be closed: it will be a mark of distinction and not of parochialism to be an expert on, say, the '20s! Prepare yourself for monographs on "Frank Teschemacher and the Ambiguity of Pitch" or "Contrasting Plectral Tonalities in the Musical Integration of Freddie Green and Walter Page." Quiz to follow.

Jazz is too capacious, generous, and lively an art to surrender to either approach, for in the end both—concise survey and minute specialization—tend to encourage a listener's digest with most of the good parts missing. Professional listeners, not least, are vulnerable to received and unreflecting wisdom and have been known to pay lip service to the vaunted jazz tradition when they can't distinguish "Snake Rag" from "Stock Yards Strut," Fats Navarro from Red Rodney, or Art Tatum from Cecil Taylor. I hasten to note that some such critics can relate Miles Davis to Stockhausen or David Murray to Sly Stone with an authority and insight I sadly lack. We are all of us, to one degree or another, overwhelmed. The technocracy discards nothing. New generations of musicians and critics inevitably compute new matrices of influence. In 1997, trumpet solos as devious and subversive as Frank Newton's could be heard in the playing of Hugh Ragin, Dave Douglas, and Nicholas Payton, to choose three entirely different visions.

Small wonder that spoilsports emerge who want to establish more exclusive laws of jazz immigration. Unlike Ellington, who reveled in diversity and abhorred restrictions, the guardians of musical morality are appalled by such latitude (Sartre's phrase, "to freedom condemned," comes to mind) and mean to cleanse jazz of impurities transmitted through contact with the European classics, American pop, new music, and other mongrel breeds. But this is merely what Walter Benjamin called "processing of data in the Fascist sense." If jazz ceases to interact with the musical world around it, will inbreeding bring it down? What's to become of a music that once epitomized play and is now flaunted as culture with a capital *K*?

The one truth about jazz of which I am certain is that it incarnates liberty, often with a perversely proud intransigence, merging with everything and borrowing anything, yet ultimately riding alone. Unlike pop, it doesn't measure success with sales charts. Unlike classical, it isn't, as yet, certified by a state-subsidized ladder of achievement. Jazz does what it wants when it wants and pays the price of commercial marginality. Not a bad thing, independence, which is what hooked many of us on art and jazz in the first place. Still, good fences make good neighbors and fat endowments so independence will always be under siege.

Louis Armstrong and others got laughs when they told the little old lady, "If you don't know what it is, don't mess with it." The line was funny because everyone did know what jazz was, in a general sort of way. It was raucous and swinging and fun—not corny like pop or solemn like longhair. Now if you don't know what it is, nobody will laugh at you because no one else knows either. Ellington wrote of jazz many years ago, "I don't know how such great extremes as now exist can be contained under the one heading." The word has become so commodious with "great extremes" that its boundaries are no more secure than those of baroque or romantic or classical. Indeed, having secured after a hundred years its place at the banquet, the meaning and pull of jazz may be said to flow backward as well as forward.

Borges famously argued that Hawthorne is a changed and perhaps deepened writer in Kafka's world—that, in effect, Kafka seems to have influenced Hawthorne because he has so thoroughly influenced our reading of him. In that spirit, can anyone in a world remade by jazz fail to hear a harbinger of swing in the uncanny rhythmic figure Beethoven introduces in the arietta of his thirty-second piano sonata (op. 111)? In a remarkable two-minute episode, he switches to a twelve-beat rhythm, implying an unmistakable backbeat in alternating thirty-second and sixty-fourth notes, an augury made all the more explicit by a melodic and harmonic content that suggests (for example, the major to diminished harmonic change at III 14) the first phrase of "Muskrat Ramble." Beethoven was also an impassioned improviser who knew heavy blues. But, of course, he had nothing to do with jazz.

Yet one remembers it was written of Ellington in 1932 and 1943 that he had betrayed and abandoned jazz, so I tend to keep the door open. The same has been written more recently of Cecil Taylor. Several other performers, whose relationship to jazz is admittedly tangential, now seem a lot more relevant than they did in the past. A mere thirty years ago, jazz tradition had no truck with Paul Whiteman, Ethel Waters, or Louis Jordan. Yet several Whiteman performances (Bill Challis's "Lonely Melody," for one cunning example) are now recognized as marvels of '20s jazz orchestration, and the profound impact of Waters and Jordan is taken for granted. One may acknowledge their divergent roles and still celebrate their importance, not to mention the pleasure of their company. Thirty years from now, it will be a rare jazz expert who fails to value the relevance of James Brown or Jimi Hendrix.

Musical innovations begin with the voice, which conjures up sounds later developed instrumentally, and end with the voice, which simplifies and popularizes instrumental convolutions. But singers are often shortchanged in jazz chronicles, no matter the pedigree, and when acknowledged are not infrequently acclaimed *in spite of* the songs they interpret. It seems preposterous at this remove to feign indifference to songwriters as varied as Irving Berlin, W. C. Handy, Jerome Kern, Spencer Williams, George Gershwin, Richard Rodgers, Harold Arlen, and Hoagy Carmichael, along with the milieu in which they and their colleagues worked, when without them jazz harmonies would have evolved a lot less quickly from the rudimentary chords of "Muskrat Ramble."

I have organized my material under eight general headings that might apply to the evolution of any art. My intention was to get away from the temporal and generic groupings—the King Oliver begat Louis Armstrong rendition. I have no quarrel with it, nor with the idea of jazz as a distinct art with a consistent body of work and decisive parameters. My quarrel is with absoluteness and certainty. Inevitably, the musicians I examine tend to fall in line with their contemporaries, but the relationships seem to me more fluid this way. In several instances, an artist is treated out of his or her usual bracket for reasons I trust are made evident. Armstrong and Ellington recur throughout this book in sort of a simulation of their abiding power to guide and regenerate jazz at every turn, no less so posthumously. My groupings make for strange bedfellows and equally strange separations. Fats Waller and Spencer Williams were friends and frequent collaborators, yet I offer Waller at the fount of jazz and Williams as a precursor not only because the older Williams was quite obviously not a jazz player, but because his songs imply and help generate the inventiveness ultimately realized by Waller, Armstrong, and others. Spike Jones is an example of a performer who has little to do with jazz, yet could not exist in a jazzless world; he is here as a reminder that the common coin of jazz, swing, is a delicate thing easily provoked to lunacy. That discovery was as much an element of modernism as that of Jones's contemporary, Charlie Parker, who showed that swing contains multitudes. Everyone has his or her vision of jazz, and this is mine.

PART ONE

Precursors

1 ❖ Bert Williams/Al Jolson
(Native Wits)

Almost every aspect of American music during the past seventy years, the modern era, is prefigured in the flurry of activity documented in recording studios between 1923 and 1927. In that intense period of innovation and realignment, musicians of color assumed nearly absolute aesthetic dominance over all the musics yet to be embraced by the academy. Most of our assumptions about rhythm, instrumentation, articulation, improvisation, and presentation were formulated; and for the first time, a significant body of enduring masterworks was preserved on record. While Bessie Smith heralded the image of the blues diva, Ethel Waters, drawing on the same tradition, desentimentalized and refashioned theater songs. King Oliver and Louis Armstrong of New Orleans conjured jazz in Chicago, while Fletcher Henderson and Don Redman, of Georgia and West Virginia, orchestrated it in New York.

By the time Duke Ellington issued modernity's coup de grace with his 1927 triumph at the Cotton Club, four/four rhythms with accents on the downbeats were ubiquitous. It remained only for a few white acolytes to spread the word to the majority population, a mission successfully adopted by associates of Paul Whiteman and Red Nichols—among them Bix Beiderbecke and Pee Wee Russell, Bing Crosby and Mildred Bailey. Never mind that most of them were far removed from the mainstream or that not until the mid-'30s did swing make the world safe for improvisation. That's commerce and sociology. The musical seeds were sown and cultivated in the '20s, and the culture never looked back except to indulge a rather remote nostalgia.

As a result, the premodern era—the first two decades of the century—is lost to neglect, ignorance, and embarrassment. Beclouded as it is with blackface minstrelsy and unseemly ethnic humor, not to mention two-beat rhythms with accents on the up beats, we tend to cringe before that dark, distant, unswinging past. The first generation of jazz critics was as loathe to deal with it as the first generation of rock critics was to track the pop roots of rock and roll, preferring the partial patrimony of blues and country. Each instance perpetuates the idea of the new music as a revolutionary cudgel and denies the evolutionary facts. The distinct commercial nexus of music and comedy that defined minstrelsy and vaudeville and laid the groundwork for movies, records, cabaret, theater, radio, and television is largely unmapped. Of the early musical idioms, the only ones infrequently reexamined above ground are marches, operettas, and especially ragtime.

Bert Williams and Al Jolson are two dominant figures of the dark age who require periodic excavation, an effort rewarded by the enduring pleasures of their undeniably compelling talents. Now, Jolson is famous enough: he is enshrined in cultural history for *The Jazz Singer* (for several years, he was absurdly associated with that hot new music he could only sentimentalize) and because he lived long enough to enjoy a stunning postwar comeback. After thrilling to his threat "You ain't heard nothin' yet!" in *The Jazz Singer* and suffering through his lament "Sonny Boy" in *The Singing Fool* (a dreadful concoction that, benefiting from the first film's publicity and the increased number of theaters wired for sound in 1928, remained the top grossing film until *Gone With the Wind*), audiences dropped him. Bigger than life on stage, he was strangely stilted, wired, monstrous on screen. It took Larry Parks in *The Jolson Story* (1946) to do what Jolson couldn't—tone down his feverish theatricality with a stylized elegance suitable to a more intimate medium. With Parks handling the semaphore, Jolson is still found irresistible by children of all ages. Yet the degree to which our own experience of the man himself, in movies or on records, differs from that of his contemporaries, who unanimously proclaimed him the greatest of all entertainers, is evidence that we live in a different world. Indeed, the bizarre figure of Jolson, with outstretched arms and blackened face, falling to bended knee, lips quivering as he recollects old mammy, voice barking out melodies that just will not quit, has become music's counterpart to the mad woman in the attic.

Bert Williams, the patron saint of African American entertainers, has not fared so well, having died in 1922, at forty-seven, though it is unlikely Vitaphone would have been much use to him had he lived. He passed away in a season when a new generation of black performers who didn't wear burnt cork and were ashamed of those who did began to replace him in the affections of younger audiences. In one of those telling coincidences, like Ethel Waters ending her era as a recording artist on the afternoon Billie Holiday began hers, Williams died as Louis Armstrong made his way from New Orleans to Chicago. Armstrong greatly admired Williams, but he was knocked for a loop by Bill Robinson, who beguiled audiences north of Mason-Dixon with his manly grace and natural color. Williams, a light-skinned man, was a whopping success in the nation's most glamorous revue, the Ziegfeld Follies, but the price he paid was the continuance of minstrelsy's blackface caricature.

Williams never had the chance to spearhead his rediscovery. Dimly remembered today, he deserves better. W. C. Fields called him "the funniest man I ever saw," and Eddie Cantor wrote of him, "As a performer, he was close to genius. . . . Whatever sense of timing I have, I learned from him." Even before Jolson conquered Broadway, the uncanny figure of Williams, in his tattered top hat and tails, almost always covered in cork, held the key to entertainment's mansion, especially in his many years as a Follies headliner, singing, after a fashion, mocking comic monologues. Of the many minstrels on the Great White Way, Williams alone could not rub off every indication of his plight as a well-paid second-class citizen. While white minstrels spoke of the liberating influence of blackface, Williams expressed a loathing for its restraints.

In 1822, an English music-hall performer named Charles Matthews was visiting America, observing Negro music and dialect. He got the idea of blacking himself up and becoming an interpreter of "Ethiopian" melodies. Robert C. Toll, in his 1974 history *Blacking Up*, pinpoints that moment as the beginning of minstrelsy, the most widespread and influential medium for American popular culture in the nineteenth century.

Minstrelsy is said to have died at the hands of vaudeville, but it was a death in form, not spirit. Its images abound in contemporary life, from the indelible memory of Tim Moore's Kingfish to the caricatures of *National Review*. The Aunt Jemima–Uncle Ned darkies, solicitous of massa and scornful of the abolitionists who would wreck their joyful plantations, were implanted in the American mind to such an extent that even black minstrels in the Reconstruction years were expected to enact the familiar stereotypes memorialized by minstrel composers like Stephen Foster. There was triple-edged irony here: minstrelsy provided unprecedented opportunity for gifted black performers, among them Bert Williams and Ma Rainey, but only if they could adapt the ludicrous precepts of white "Ethiopian imitators"; the blacks were so good, so "authentic," that white minstrel troupes were soon put out of business; the minstrel form was then replaced by a new kind of entertainment nourished by Tin Pan Alley tunesmiths who had found their initial success by appropriating black styles like ragtime or the cakewalk.

Williams's firsts are legendary: first major black recording artist (1901); star of the first successful black Broadway musical, *In Dahomey* (1903); the only black artist to headline the *Ziegfeld Follies* (1910–19); the first to be featured in a film (1910). Yet little has been written of him (he obfuscated details of his life in interviews), and his art is little recalled, except for one song, "Nobody," which has been revived in tribute to him by several entertainers, including Bing Crosby (on radio and record), Bob Hope (*The Seven Little Foys*), and Avon Long (*Bubbling Brown Sugar*). He made about seventy-five records—Victor signed him a year *before* Caruso. Yet except for a Folkways compilation produced in conjunction with Ann Charters's 1970 biography, *Nobody*, few records have been available, and they whet the appetite. "The Moon Shines on the Moonshine" (1919) is typical, his rusty baritone emerging with sly animation in a satirical song about prohibition, while the rolling rhythms of "You Can't Get Away from It" (1914) prefigure swing.

By way of explaining his penchant for speaking his songs, Williams claimed to have mistreated his voice when touring in minstrel shows. The lamentable sound of battered 78s combined with his monologist's style makes for tough going. But Columbia and Victor ought to clean up and issue its Williams recordings or give the masters to companies willing to do so. (Most are public domain anyway.) Let's finally hear the original Elder Eatmore sermons that Louis Armstrong imitated in the '30s and a decent recording of the send-up "I Want To Know Where Tosti Went" (which captured the high-versus-low-art interaction of the vaudeville era) and his many other parlando observations on American manners before and after the First World War.

A lively, personal echo of Williams is offered in the extraordinary concert tape of Eddie Cantor's *Carnegie Hall Concert*, and there hangs a tale. In 1962, Audiofidelity issued an LP that purported to document Cantor's March 21, 1950, Carnegie Hall concert. Thirty years later, Cantor's grandson, Brian Gari, learned that the album was really recorded in a studio in 1960; he then found the concert lacquers from the actual concert in his aunt's closet. Perhaps the live performance was shelved because Cantor occasionally leaps off-mike when singing. But the music is less evocative than the recitation, an expansive and moving reminiscence of a career that began in 1910. Cantor begins by recalling "a much more pleasant day without the H-bomb, Senator McCarthy [the audience titters nervously], or other evil things that want to destroy mankind" and goes immediately into "There's No Business Like Show Business," followed by vivid recollections of Williams and Jolson, along with Fanny Brice, W. C. Fields, and Will Rogers. They were a circle of outsiders and walking oxymorons: blackfaced Negro, Jewish darkie, womanly baby, comical misanthrope, cowboy philosopher. Cantor celebrates Jolson's genius and Williams's humanity, as if they balanced an equation. Cantor roomed with Williams, and three decades later he yearns to strike a blow against prejudice by underscoring a bond of decency. For Williams, genius could never be enough.

In the '70s, after the Broadway opening of *Bubbling Brown Sugar*, in which Avon Long (best remembered for his Sportin' Life in the first revival of *Porgy and Bess*; you can see him briefly in the Doris Day vehicle *Romance on the High Seas*) incarnated Bert Williams, I requested an interview. We met at Sardi's, where he entertained me with anecdotes, reclining in his chair, sculpting elaborate figures in the air with long, expressive fingers—until I asked him whom he had most admired when starting out. "Eddie Cantor," he said. I grimaced and asked if he wasn't offended by the blackface. He sat up and asked heatedly, "Do you think black people are stupid?" "Of course not," I sputtered. "Well," he crowed, resuming his reclining position and fixing me with a cunning smile, "don't you think *we* can appreciate genius, too?" It was Long who allowed me to look anew at a generation of performers I had reflexively rejected.

Of them, Jolson remains the most difficult to come to terms with, a fact only slightly exacerbated by the opinion of all who knew him that he was a crazed egomaniac. (See Herbert G. Goldman's 1988 biography, *Jolson: The Legend Comes to Life*, for the gory details.) Aldous Huxley went on a rampage against jazz because he believed the hype that configured Jolson as "the jazz singer." Jolson bought the hype, too, and is said to have boasted that he invented black entertainment; he besieged Gershwin for the part of Porgy. And it is no use trying to separate Jolson—the enduringly hypnotic performer who wears down your defenses with a nearly violent energy, daring you to remain indifferent—from the traditions of burnt cork. He was emboldened and genuinely inspired by the black mask. Even in his '30s movies, made long after his career had peaked, he is never more electrifying or natural than when playing black.

In Jolson, theatrical show-biz schmaltz was mated with an irresistible vitality—maudlin sentiment was the flip side of snappy eye-rolling rhythms. He had much in common with Elvis Presley: each came from lower-class, culturally alienated environments (immigrant Jewish and southern poor white); each was something of a rebel (Jolson, the son of a cantor, left home in adolescence to travel the country singing in music halls and Presley, also from a religious family, found himself in Negro blues); each was an obsessive mother lover; each chose to live in isolation at the peak of his career. In *Feel Like Going Home*, Elvis's contemporary, Jerry Lee Lewis, tells Peter Guralnick, "I loved Al Jolson, I still got all of his records. Even back when I was a kid I listened to him all the time." Elvis's first record for the Sun label, "I Love You Because," was a thinly disguised rewrite of a melody that rebellious Asa Yoelson sings repeatedly during the first half hour of *The Jolson Story* (released when Presley was eleven), a song called "When You Were Sweet Sixteen." What would Jolson have made of a white boy, with a pompadour as high as a Negro conk, bumping like a stripper and singing "Heartbreak Hotel" on national television? He probably would have been a lot less shocked than many of his contemporaries. For Jolson's pelvis swiveled much the same way, as can be seen in his performance of "Toot Toot Tootsie" in *The Jazz Singer*.

Bert Williams performed in blackface at least as often as Jolson and considered it a vulgar, repressive disguise, a racist formality from which he could not escape. Nor could the society. Minstrelsy was a commonplace in the movie musicals of the '40s; in the '50s, a vogue for recreating genuine minstrel shows was reflected in theater and on records. When the nostalgic pleasure for minstrelsy could no longer be justified, the flag of cultural scholarship was raised as the new excuse. During the presidential election of 1992, it was reported that thirty years earlier President Bush's brother Jonathan had hoped to "revive" the minstrel era, combining "Negro talent along with the blackface components." As recently as 1989, news circulated of a producer's desire to mount a Broadway musical based on the apogee of Negro stereotypes, *Amos 'n' Andy*. How can one overstate the importance of minstrelsy in coming to grips with America's racialist past and present? In the most demotic of the popular arts, a theatrical tradition was born in town and country alike based on the premise of racial disdain, in which parodic intent was confused with sincere imitation and in which many of the finest practitioners were African American. Many celebrated minstrels thought they were playing Negro roles: Mr. Bones and Jim Crow as alternatives to Othello or Aida, all of them Ethiopian (exotic) types. The most ardent defenders of the idiom compare minstrelsy with commedia dell'arte, and they have a point if one overlooks the dehumanizing force of racial mockery.

Still, for some, for Jolson, it unleashed a core vitality, underscoring what Goldman calls a "mysterious, somewhat macabre appeal," as in the whiny madness of his 1912 recording "That Lovin' Traumerai." Driven but stiff, reluctant to lower his wattage to the requirements of a recording booth, he was a very different performer in the beginning (a tenor and not the baritone he became) than the warmhearted singer of his postwar comeback. Jolson may have little to do with jazz, though his "When the Grown Up Ladies Act Like Babies" (1914) is undeniably jazzy, complete with vocal breaks. But he helped create the singer as matinee idol, popularizing the vernacular emotionalism and rhythmic zeal that underscore so much of what was to follow. His forty years in front of microphones (detailed in Larry F. Kiner and Philip R. Evans's *Al Jolson: A Bio-Discography*, 1992) defines a huge and peculiarly inbred repertoire, ranging from the traveling minstrel show to theaters, then broadening to film and radio, expanding its trappings every step. He was abetted by the songwriting factory that preceded—in musical sophistication if not chronology—the fabled generation of Berlin, Kern,

Rodgers, and Porter. The best writers of that predawn era were originals who had the zeitgeist by the tail: Walter Donaldson, DeSylva-Brown-Henderson, James Monaco, Kalmar and Ruby. Like Jolson, they mapped out a genesis of sentimental debauchery ("keep away from bootleg hooch/when you're on a spree/take good care of yourself/ you belong to me"), mother worship, and limitless optimism. This was the big bang of show business excess, vulgarity as a measure of our native wit.

2 ❖ Hank Jones/Charlie Haden (Come Sunday)

Mendelssohn's oratorical music, especially the *Lobgesang* Symphony, hangs precariously in nineteenth-century religious repertory, in part because it so clearly reveals the convert to Christianity keeping faith with Jewish themes. His hymns have it both ways, rendering ambiguous mention unto the son but reserving the full measure of praise for the father, who is exalted specifically for the gifts of enlightenment and liberation and not just for being merciful and glorious. Mendelssohn would never have heard Negro spirituals, which weren't performed in Europe until thirty years after his death, but surely he would have responded to the parity between the Old and New Testaments they embody. Here was an entire people claimed by Christendom who needed no prompting to see that King Jesus the redeemer had better not ride too far without General Moses the liberator.

"Go Down Moses," an obvious example, would suit any seder and, as a piece of music, beats the Passover anthem "Da-yenu" by a country mile or a desert sea. Considering how indifferently Jews, who practically invented the modern pop song, have fared with hymns, one wonders why they haven't borrowed from other ex-slaves with a cannier ear for the pentatonic scale. In pop, of course, they have. One of Jerome Kern's breakthrough songs, "Look for the Silver Lining," written for but dropped from a 1919 show and resurrected a year later in *Sally*, is often praised for its hymnlike melody; according to his biographer, Gerald Bordman, the comparison pleased Kern, who "loved to play hymns and hoped his music reflected his pleasure." That he had a particular hymn in mind has not been suggested, to my knowledge, but with the 1995 release of *Steal Away: Spirituals, Hymns and Folk Song* (Verve), a magically affecting album by Hank Jones and Charlie Haden, it is difficult to believe he didn't enjoy more than a fleeting acquaintance with "My Lord, What a Morning."

But then the relationship between the sacred and secular in American music has always been shadowy, rarely developing beyond an assortment of adaptations that reduces the spiritual to a kind of fuel. It provided the basis for blues at the turn of the century, for the antiphonal orchestrations of the swing era, for various soul movements in jazz at midcentury. If sacred music, black and white, has inspired composers as diverse as Kern, Duke Ellington, Charles Ives, Aaron Copland, and Virgil Thompson, it has also generated much of the breakout pop that followed the war, from Louis Jordan's choir-driven call-and-response novelties to Ray Charles's substitution of "baby" for "Jesus" and all that followed.

Yet where are the great or not-so-great liturgical works that draw on that perennial idiom—where are the gospel-derived tries at a *Lobgesang*, let alone a Missa Solemnis or B Minor Mass? For all the countless jazz church services, including several outsized works ranging from Ellington's ecumenical sacred concerts to Dave Brubeck's mass and oratorio, the pickings are improbably slim. Ellington successfully introduced the concept of pageantry in his church music, built on the idea that instrumental virtuosity was a gift from God that, suitably displayed, would serve as a reverent offering in return. But Ellington's three religious works are structurally open-ended, with old and new pieces tailored to specific personalities, and we have yet to experience how that music might be reconstituted into a compelling canvas in the absence of his own magnetism. Perhaps the most fervent work of religious devotion in jazz is John Coltrane's *A Love Supreme*, and that, too, seems inseparable from the musician who created it.

For all their incalculable influence, spirituals remain most potent in their purest form. A little religion goes a long way in the secular world, about one "He's Got the Whole World in His Hands" (1958, Mahalia Jackson) or "Oh Happy Day" (1969, Edwin Hawkins Singers) per decade on the pop charts. Which is one reason *Steal Away* works as well as it does: shorn of lyrics and pyrotechnics, it mines a program of melodies—including some of the most familiar in all of music ("Nobody Knows the Trouble I've Seen," "Swing Low, Sweet Chariot")—with a quiet, studied lyricism that relocates them in the secular world in general and the jazz world in particular. I don't believe anyone made a record before quite like Haden's and Jones's, though it is bound to remind some people of the boom in spirituals in the '50s.

The album's subtitle is significant: the respectable idiom of the spiritual needs to be distinguished from the raucous tradition of gospel performance, though both presumed themselves to be under eternal attack by the devil's music. The archetype of the rebellious son who rejects his parents' religious calling for the Great White Way was popularized as a Jewish fable in the '20s, but it was more lastingly a black story (the movie *St. Louis Blues*, a purported biography of W. C. Handy, is really an all-Negro version of *The Jazz Singer*), where imprecations to separate the two have never completely faded. In the '50s, bluesman Big Bill Broonzy claimed to be scandalized by Ray Charles. A few years later, Little Richard made a compelling gospel album when he forsook rock and roll and then returned to what little Mammon he had at his disposal, but he couldn't do both—he couldn't do nationally what, say, Count Basie and Jimmy Rushing could do provincially, barnstorming the Southwest of the late '20s, playing buckets of blood Saturday night and churches Sunday morning.

The more genteel tradition of spirituals and hymns had a different sort of pedigree. From the time the Fisk Jubilee Singers began concertizing in the 1870s in the North and then in Europe, the "sorrow song," in W. E. B. DuBois's phrase, became associated with the dignified Negro and his low estate. As great trained voices like those of Paul Robeson and Marian Anderson performed spirituals in recitals, the political solemnity was underscored. (At a political benefit featuring Robeson and Charlie Parker, Robeson sang "Water Boy," and Parker, who grasped the limits of solemnity, came onstage with a glass of water.) But the liberal pieties associated with spirituals quickly gave way in the '40s, and more so in the '50s, to something far more patronizing.

After years of white as well as black performers harmonizing Negro hymns and work songs with anthropological brio, the songs began to take on a childlike and sometimes childish character. No longer the utopian dreams of tolerance and justice, they were co-opted by the right to symbolize the conviction that the American dilemma was nothing more than some Swedish egghead's paranoia. Until Louis Armstrong got angry and told Eisenhower to take a flyer into the fiery pit, he and Mahalia Jackson made middlebrows feel comfortable about their melting-pot pieties. When Armstrong appeared on one of the great kitsch album covers of the '50s, for his Decca collection of spirituals, few recalled his earlier recording of "Goin' to Shout All over God's Heav'n," in which the choir sang about "hebben" and Armstrong adamantly growled, "hea-VEN, hea-VEN." The folk movement of the early '60s brought renewed interest in spirituals, but with an unmistakable air of noblesse oblige. Nearly twenty years before, in the musical no one would produce on Broadway (*Jump for Joy*), Ellington wrote, "*Green Pastures* is just a technicolor movie." Yet as Kennedy took office, white elementary school teachers continued to declare *Green Pastures* an authentic portrait of black culture.

Maybe it was inevitable that jazz musicians would rediscover the repertory of spirituals, given the hard bop revival and its original impetus in church-derived chords and backbeats, and the '90s produced several examples. Nat Adderley, brother of Cannonball, the patron saint of the soul-hymn movement, issued two entertaining albums to mark the connection: *Good Company* (Challenge), with Cannonball's "Sermonette" and some of altoist Antonio Hart's best recorded work up to that date, and the more spirited *We Remember Cannon* (In + Out), with Nat's own "Work Song" and the increasingly resolute altoist Vincent Herring. Herring also appears on Carl Allen's *Testimonial* (Atlantic) with an all-star contingent of newcomers, including Cyrus Chesnut, Nicholas Payton (more assured here than on his own Verve debut), Mark Whitfield, Christian McBride, and Kevin Mahogany. It's a well-played, conventional set that derives its distinction from themes loosely associated with Sunday morning, including Ellington's supreme contribution to the American hymnal, "Come Sunday." Short of outright parody—for example, Dizzy Gillespie's "Swing Low, Sweet Cadillac"—hard bop is one way to cut the deacon down to size.

Steal Away is something different. Charlie Haden, whose many previous recordings have an autobiographical edge, produced the album, undoubtedly recalling his family band apprenticeship in the Bible Belt. His looming, sonorous, shivery bass tone always seems to have a hellhound on its trail and so works perfectly here. But the more particular triumph belongs to Hank Jones. In a career of more than fifty years' duration, this stands as one of his most seductive yet understated recordings. It's hard to imagine another pianist pulling it off. Only a musician of exceptional maturity would be inclined to hold his technique at bay in theme statements that draw their power from basic harmonies, foursquare rhythms, and a stately resolve to honor the unadorned ingenuity of simple melodies. With his inimitable touch, ringing the keys like chimes, and his cunning use of dissonance and altered changes, he gets to the core of each piece, though the real magic is often in the transition to the second chorus, when he swings into time for improvisations that sustain the initial aura while probing a still deeper level.

The material is fearlessly obvious, with only a few less well-known titles among the very famous ones, which include "Danny Boy," an ingenious choice that recalls the many links between Irish American and African American music in the nineteenth century, and "Wade in the Water," a certifiable hard bop chestnut. "Abide with Me," recorded by Monk in solidarity with the William Henry Monk who wrote it, is heard in a medley that concludes with "Amazing Grace." They even reclaim "We Shall Overcome." The unadorned first chorus sounds like something a rural church pianist might intone on an old upright, but after a brief bass transition, Jones embarks on a solo that reminds us that we're dealing with a musician of transcendent worldliness, modernist cool, and dry wit.

This isn't one of those albums that wants to get your flesh all bumpy with unbridled hosannahs. It's subtle and sober without being dusty and politic, solemn but never somber, performed with a purity beyond the reach of the kind of pianist who can't resist flashing over the keys to cover a lapse in thought. It's gentle, deep, and often starkly beautiful, and it underscores a fundamental ingredient in the spiritual life of jazz.

3 ❖ *Louis Armstrong/Mills Brothers (Signifying)*

Just as Civil War battles and the politics of Reconstruction are rehearsed ceaselessly by buffs and historians, the power plays between slave and master have also remained vestigially alive at the end of the twentieth century, with this difference: they are secretly preserved, chiefly in popular songs handed down through generations increasingly deaf to their meaning. Subverted into neutralized meal for children (like much nineteenth-century American literature, for that matter), those songs, which once gladdened and even changed people's hearts, are now presumed to be opaque if not downright nonsensical. They are as invisible as the black bards who wrote so many of them. On the other hand, Stephen Foster, whose music embodied the widespread belief that former slaves spent the rest of their lives longing for the resumption of slavehood, remains a popular brand name, like Uncle Ben's and Aunt Jemima's.

One of the first songs I can remember learning well enough to sing was "Jimmy Crack Corn," or "The Blue-Tail Fly" (its real name); not for twenty years or so did I realize it wasn't a nonsense song, a kids' song, but an expression of glee at a slaveowner's death. What makes the song chilling is that massa isn't made out to be wicked; he isn't characterized at all, except as massa—reason enough to crack corn in celebration of his demise. A blue-tail fly got him, as the singer details in a series of verses, each followed by the chorus of merriment ("Jimmy crack corn and I don't care/My massa's gone away"). We don't know for sure where he's gone until the end, when his epitaph is sung. The song was popular in minstrel shows of the 1840s and has been handed down for a hundred and fifty years, transformed into a campfire song for white middle-class kids. Perhaps "A Hard Rain's Gonna Fall" will be redis-covered in the next century as a cautionary ballad about the need to put on your galoshes.

These thoughts are prompted by listening to the long-neglected sides, eleven in all, recorded by the Mills Brothers and Louis Armstrong for Decca between 1937 and 1940. The most reverberant are two numbers originally released together on a very successful 78 recorded at their first encounter—a politically astute response to the pastoralism that became rife in the recording industry of the '30s and continued into the early '60s. In the long, irreverent history of black performers signifying atti-tudes that went over the heads of white audiences, this is one of the most ironic pop records ever released. The songs were James A. Bland's "Carry Me Back to Old Virginny" (1878) and Benjamin R. Hanby's "Dar-ling Nellie Gray" (1856).

Part of the disc's power lies not in the talents of the performers, but in how they were perceived by audiences. The Mills Brothers, the most enduringly successful male quartet in American pop music and one of the first black groups to win international acceptance, made the leap from tent shows to New York via a triumphant radio stint in Cincinnati in 1929. Soon they were touring the country, recording prolifically (team-ing up with such white stars as Bing Crosby, the Boswell Sisters, and Al Jolson), and appearing in films and on network radio. With only one change in personnel (brother John, Jr., died and was replaced by their father), they recorded a chain of hits over thirty years, then kept on as a trio for another fifteen, after John, Sr., retired at age seventy-four. Their biggest hit, the weirdly fetishist "Paper Doll," was the third biggest hit of the '40s, after "White Christmas" and "Rudolph, the Red Nosed Rein-deer" (and was later mugged in a noted essay by the semanticist turned right-wing bureaucrat, S. I. Hayakawa). They had velvety voices, impec-cable diction, dreamy harmonies, supple time, and—especially in their early, more jazz-oriented years—a remarkable gimmick: they imitated instruments (trumpet, trombone, sax, tuba) so well that they subtitled their act Four Boys and a Guitar to stress the cleverness of their mimicry. When they muted their vocal brass effects, their riffs suggested the El-lington band. But straight as they were honest, they allowed their later work to be subsumed in a blandness that bespoke too many chic night-clubs and hacked-out arrangements.

Louis Armstrong, on the other hand, was always a renegade, even when he acceded to the same idiocies in material and setting. He could telegraph with a growl or a rolling of his eyes his independence, confidence, and security. If the Mills Brothers were heroes in the black community for their talent and success, Armstrong (whose music influenced theirs, as it did every black band and vocal group to come along in the '30s) was venerated for all that plus an indomitable will and irreverence. As the embodiment of jazz, he made jazz the embodiment of individual signifying; the singer, not the song, was what counted, or as Trummy Young used to chant, " 'Taint What You Do (It's the Way That You Do It)." There's no better example than the material Armstrong rendered with the brothers Mills.

By 1937, seventy-two years after the Civil War, songs of the nineteenth century had long since become a staple of recording sessions not only because they appeared to tame black performers into a new kind of servility—singing pro-slave lyrics for liberal record producers on the grounds that they were true folk material—but because they were free, having escaped into public domain. One might reasonably assume that the lyrics of "Carry Me Back to Old Virginny" and "Darling Nellie Gray" had lost their bite if not their meaning, and indeed no one seems to have commented on the strangeness of black performers recording them, of black and white audiences buying them, of what Armstrong did with them. Yet though the lyrics of both songs are as explicit as those of "The Blue-Tail Fly," I haven't been able to find a single reference to them in the past sixty years of pop or jazz commentary. This despite the fact that it was a major seller, putting the Mills Brothers back on the charts after a troubled three years during which John, Jr., died. Its popularity contributed to the state of Virginia's decision to adopt "Carry Me Back to Old Virginny" as the official state song in 1940, a decision hotly contested in 1997.

What kind of song is it? A nostalgic minstrel expression of mourning for the Old South, for massa and the plantation. The melody is hauntingly beautiful, and the structure—thirty-two bars, AABA—surprisingly modern. The Mills Brothers sing it exactly as written, including the line "There's where this old darkie's heart does long to go" and the stupefying release:

> There's where I labored so hard for dear ol' massa
> Day after day in the fields of yellow corn
> No place on earth do I love more sincerely
> Then old Virginny, the state where I was born.

Armstrong, whose first entrance serves to introduce a scat figure that propels the piece immediately into double time, attacks the song with creative relish, but he makes a couple of seemingly casual changes in the offensive lines that make all the difference in the world. In the first case, he sings (twice, both times accommodating the loss of sibilance with a rhythmic adjustment), "There's where the [not 'this'] old darkie's heart longs to go." In the release, he changes "dear ol' massa" to "old master," carefully enunciating the consonants. (When Ray Charles recorded the song in 1960, he obviated the problem by changing the first line to "That's where this heart of mine yet longs to go" and omitted the release, replacing it with a new chorus about finding freedom in death.) Perhaps Armstrong's most able signifying comes at the end of the first eight bars of his thirty-two-bar solo, an unmistakable trumpet call—to freedom in life. If the flip side had been a similar piece or an ordinary ballad, the record would—despite Armstrong's saves—have limited meaning. But "Darling Nellie Gray" was one of the most powerful abolitionist songs of the 1850s; published only four years after *Uncle Tom's Cabin*, it is widely credited with changing people's minds on both sides of the Mason-Dixon Line.

Only sixteen bars and five lines long, crooned nostalgically by the Mills Brothers, then swung with candid effervescence by Armstrong, it is a Kentucky slave's lament for his lover, sold or traded like a prize sow: "Oh, my poor Nellie Gray/They have taken you away." If the choice of material alone didn't counter the sentiment of the A side, the job was done by Armstrong: his tender solo; utterly engaged vocal, made the more dramatic by syncopations (especially in the second of two surviving takes); caressing, virtuoso fills behind the quartet; interpolated remark before the close ("Now, boys, what do you know about this?"); second chorus alteration of the line "I'm sitting by the river and I'm weepin' all the day" to "I'm sitting by the river and I'm all in a shiver"; and extended scat cadenza.

The whole endeavor is heightened by the irony of authorship. The composer of the Virginia state song, the celebrated minstrel and tunesmith James Bland (he wrote "In the Evening By the Moonlight" and "Oh Dem Golden Slippers" as well), was black. "Darling Nellie Gray" was composed by a white twenty-two-year-old minister, Benjamin Hanby, to aid the abolitionists. His tune spurred heavy black sales of the record in the summer of 1937, but did anyone comment back then on the curiosities of the disc? It's difficult to know what contemporary black reviewers thought since black newspapers have yet to be fully gleaned for the valuable anthologies they could undoubtedly produce. White critics, then as now, paid it no mind. Jazz critics hated the idea of Armstrong working with a silky pop group, which is one reason the sessions have been incompletely reissued in the United States, while that strange breed of folklorists who trekked into the Alabamy veldt in search of folk Negroes ignored city ones as ersatz. Yet most of the Armstrong-Mills material is uncommonly interesting: three Irving Berlin gems; a wry novelty about the WPA's impact on the Puritan work ethic ("Sit Down and Smoke While You Joke, It's Okay—the WPA"); Don Redman's gently lubricious "Cherry"; the scat-filled call to dancers, "Boog It," with its descriptive verse ("You do like shinin' a window/But you ain't got no window/So you just picture a window/and Boog It!—slow and easy"); and most pungent of all, Stephen Foster's outrageous and eternal "The Old Folks at Home."

They did the Foster song at the same session as the other minstrel tunes and coupled it with the turn-of-the-century ballad, "In the Shade of the Old Apple Tree." With a few alterations, Armstrong could distance himself from "Carry Me Back"; with his natural élan, he could restore the emotion to "Darling Nellie." What in heaven's name could he do with Foster's recalcitrant song, in which free darkies sadly roam the dreary world, "longin' for the old plantation and for the old folks at home," except burlesque the hell out of it? No sooner does the quartet croon it straight than he suddenly turns the performance into a mock church service, entering like a deacon ("Now brothers!"), impaling every phrase on the precision of his caricature: "That's where *my* heart turns, *Yowsah!* ... Know one thing? My heart am still *longin'* for the old plantation ... Hallelujah, hallelujah ... Oh, darkies!" He ends speaking, "Well, looka here, we are far away from home," and adds with devastating menace, "Yeah, man." Rasped with implacable finality, that phrase buries the song and the maudlin pastoralism that kept it alive. Few whites, however, in or out of the academy, wanted to hear what old Deacon Satchmo was signifying. Here once again was evidence that, as Pope wrote of Homer, Armstrong's art "is like a copious nursery which contains the seeds and first productions of every kind, out of which those who followed him have but selected some particular plants."

4 ❖ *W. C. Handy*
(Birth of the Blues)

W. C. Handy called his autobiography *Father of the Blues*, and his patriarchal status is no less sound than that of George Washington's as father of the country in which the blues was born. Not to suggest that the blues was invented all at once in August of 1912, when W. C. Handy elected to publish his "Memphis Blues." We are unlikely to learn precisely when, where, or how the blues was first codified as a musical form. Indeed, Handy's tune was actually performed by him three years earlier. Nor was it the first song to use the word *blues* in the title. Yet as the first blues to create a stir with its publication, "Memphis Blues" triggered the widespread recognition of a new idiom. As issued that autumn by two shady white publishers identified by Handy in his autobiography as X and Z, his song hastened the prevailing codification of the twelve-bar blues form, and its national acceptance, if as nothing more than a stylish musical fad. The song originated in 1909 as part of a campaign for Memphis Mayor E. H. Crump, a reformist whose cause Handy inexplicably espoused by portraying him as a regular pol and none too bright.

Imagine hearing this lyric at a rally today, sung by the candidate's *supporters*:

> Mr. Crump won't 'low no easy riders here
> Mr. Crump won't 'low no easy riders here
> We don't care what Mr. Crump don't 'low
> We gon' to bar'l-house anyhow—
> Mr. Crump can go and catch hisself some air!

"Luckily for us," Handy recalled in his 1941 memoir *Father of the Blues*, "Mr. Crump himself didn't hear us singing those words. But we were hired to help put over his campaign, and since I knew that reform was about as palatable to Beale Street as castor oil, I was sure those reassuring words would do him more good than harm." In true blues fashion, the song was infinitely pliable: Handy gladly accepted a check to perform the same lyric with a name change for Crump's opponent, one Walter W. Talbert. By the time Crump was elected, the piece had established a following for itself and for Handy's band in the dance halls of Memphis.

He faced two problems in getting it published. The first was easily resolved—what with Crump in charge, a change in the lyric was mandatory. The lyric, as published in 1912, included this prophetic verse:

> I'm goin' down the river, down to the river, goin' to
>   take my rockin' chair,
> Goin' to the river, goin' to take my rockin' chair.
> Blues overtake me, goin' to rock away from here.

The second obstacle was more considerable, according to Handy; no one wanted to publish a song made up of twelve-bar strains; "every reputable American publisher of popular music gave the 'Memphis Blues' the go-by," he wrote. In the days when sixteen-bar strains were the norm, Handy's tune was considered to "lack completeness." The disreputable publishers X and Z finally brought out the song in 1912, denying him royalties and incurring a lawsuit by Handy that took decades to resolve in his favor. It was an immediate hit. Almost instantly the word *blues* replaced the word *rag* in hit songs, soon to be replaced in turn by *jazz*. By that time, however, the twelve-bar blues was the most constant form in jazz, infinitely malleable and invulnerable to all fashion and caprice. It would be sustained anew after the midcentury by the advent of rhythm and blues and rock and roll.

Handy, who became a legend and a wealthy man as a result of a song he crafted in 1914, "St. Louis Blues" (the most frequently recorded song in America during the quarter century between the two world wars, and one that combines twelve- and sixteen-bar strains, as well as tango and two-beat rhythms), is often regarded less as a composer than as gatherer-arranger-publisher. To be sure, he was a businessman first and last. Yet it was Handy who organized the elements of the blues with compositional ambition, joining diverse refrains and focusing primary attention on melody. His best songs are intractably melodic, far more so than the typical three-chord/three-line stanzas encountered among most performers of the '20s, rural or urban. Not unlike Irving Berlin and his "Alexander's Ragtime Band," Handy was able to crystallize the musical moment—Fitzgerald refers to his "Beale Street Blues" as an emblematic tune in *The Great Gatsby*.

Handy was candid about what he brought to "Memphis Blues": melody, popularization, a degree of personal expression. Whether he did, in fact, compose the melody or merely notated it from memory, he undoubtedly preserved a trove of blues melodies that were uncommon and durable enough to ensure the validity of the copyrights he held on them. Despite the title of his memoir and the assumptions of a dazed media, he never pretended to father the blues as a musical form. The twelve-bar chorus and the elegantly simple harmonic structure (tonic, subdominant, dominant seventh) that goes with it were, Handy wrote in regard to "Memphis Blues," "already used by Negro roustabouts, honky-tonk piano players, wanderers and others of their underprivileged but undaunted class from Missouri to the Gulf, and had become a common medium through which any such individual might express his personal feelings in a sort of musical soliloquy."

If this sounds like primping by the popularizer who brought his people's folk music to the gentry at Carnegie Hall (he marked "Memphis Blues" tempo di blues), it should be noted that he took his roots seriously enough to approve commandments in the 1949 edition of his landmark 1926 *Blues: An Anthology* that were designed to encourage correct—that is, ethnic—interpretations. "For a while at least," Abbe Niles absurdly advised in the notes to that edition, "the white man should play them exactly as written—that his subsequent embellishments (if any) may be in character." Handy himself suffered for the blues. He and not Al Jolson was the archetypal "jazz singer," the son of a deacon who demonized him for playing the devil's music. Jelly Roll Morton was similarly disavowed by his family for trafficking with black jazzmen in uptown New Orleans.

With a start like that, it's small wonder Handy spent much of his life demanding respect for his music. He got it, too. He conquered Carnegie Hall in 1928, at fifty-five, and when he died thirty years later, Handy had achieved a paternalistic approval rating rivaled only by George Washington Carver and Ralph Bunche—in two years, his image was on a postage stamp. By then, the blues were ubiquitous. Mainstream pop singers no longer felt compelled to record them, as their novelty value had long since worn out, though one could still spot aberrations on the order of *Eydie Gormé Sings the Blues*. Few of the selections on such albums would actually be blues, but rather pop songs with blue titles, for example, "The Birth of the Blues," "Blues in the Night," and "Blue Moon." At an '80s lecture at New York University, Martin Williams addressed a group of musicologists and educators on the blues, dissecting the twelve bars and showing how they had been treated by various artists. When he finished, a distraught academic complained about his emphasis on structure, "Isn't the blues just a feeling?" Williams said, "Only in the sense that sonata is just a feeling."

Yet by the time of Handy's death, hardly a jazz record was released that didn't have at least one true blues. The chords had become highly sophisticated, sometimes to the point of virtually disguising the tonic-subdominant-dominant relationship (an especially favorite ploy of Miles Davis's, for example, "Sippin' at Bells," "Israel," "Footsteps"). But the twelve-bar stanza remained every improvising musician's training ground, and very often the material with which he eventually proved his maturity—Coleman Hawkins and Dizzy Gillespie became great blues players in their middle years. Then, too, in the '60s, the burgeoning popularity of urban blues (Muddy Waters and Howlin' Wolf finally began to break the race barrier, and B. B. King would soon follow) and rural blues (Son House, Skip James, and Mississippi John Hurt were pressed into harness and Columbia rediscovered its Robert Johnson records) kept the basics alive. Rock and roll represented the ultimate popularization, especially in the blues-with-a-bridge variant—three blues choruses spelled by an eight-bar bridge, successfully employed by Lester Young in his "D. B. Blues," but used constantly in the '50s (dozens of times by Fats Domino alone) and achieving renewed prominence in the Beatles' "Can't Buy Me Love."

The miracle of the blues is its endurance, which is probably inseparable from its elemental logic and its strenuous integrity. Almost anyone can be led to a piano and taught to hammer out the rudiments of a blues chorus. It takes only a matter of minutes to learn. Yet pianists who are great virtuosos in other idioms have spent years shoveling one blues chorus after another without getting close to a genuinely creative or satisfying blues. American born and bred, the blues is quintessentially American in form and function. It epitomizes progress and transition. Unlike the symphony, sonata, or concerto, the blues has no beginning, middle, or end. It is a building block; the number of blocks, or choruses, required to complete the building is usually decided on the spur of the moment. Not only have millions of such choruses been played without exhausting the form and its possibilities, but the fact of its constancy has underscored the challenge of keeping it meaningful. The blues remains the outer domain of musical exploration. You enter every chorus at peril, tempted by cliché and banality. Yet when you negotiate the trip perfectly, whether a single stanza or a whole series of them finessed with expeditious turnbacks, nothing in art is more satisfying.

5 ❖ *Irving Berlin* (*Ragging the Alley*)

Six years before the American dream of empire sent doughboys "over there," a benign and more lastingly successful invasion had already been spearheaded by Irving Berlin. He led the charge with a song—"Alexander's Ragtime Band"—that had little to do with ragtime and everything to do with ragtime audacity, alerting Europe to hot times in the colonies. His lyric, supported by deft melodic interpolations, referred to the ragging of military music and minstrel songs, old forms made new. "Come on and hear," it declared, promising a music "so natural that you want to go to war"—an unhappy phrase that, in the wake of two world wars and Viet Nam, Berlin changed to "so natural that you want to hear some more." He quickly followed it with "Everybody's Doing It Now," and everybody was. In 1913, Europe was ready to look the gift horse in the mouth. Berlin accepted an invitation to visit England on a vaudeville tour, billed grandly if inaccurately as the King of Ragtime.

The night before he opened in London, in a panic to present new material, he wrote "That International Rag," and with his usual dispatch addressed the phenomenon of the new music:

> What did you do, America?
> They're after you, America.
> You got excited and you started something.
> Nations jumping all around.
> You've got a lot to answer for.
> They lay the blame right at your door.
> The world's gone ragtime crazy from shore to shore.

In the chorus, he explained how all Europe lost its dignity while dancing to "a raggedy melody full of originality," the latter phrase employing
a triplet that Berlin felt gave the song its memorable "punch." At the
time of his death, on September 22, 1989, four months after his 101st
birthday, both songs were no longer protected by copyright, a rare if not
unique instance of a composer forced to witness the loss of his own work
to the public domain. How difficult that must have been for the crusty
old tycoon, who owned his songs as completely as the law allowed. He
had outlived much of the world he helped create. As Armstrong was to
jazz or Griffith to film or Joyce to fiction or Balanchine to dance or, for
that matter, Scott Joplin to ragtime, Berlin was the progenitor of modern
song—the agent of transition, who shaped the diverse strains of a fading
era into the representative art of a new one and made himself that new
art's premiere practitioner.

The nature of Berlin's accomplishment is such that the more closely
you scrutinize it, bringing to the job however much doubt and skepticism
you think necessary for the probing of so massive a reputation, the more
miraculous it seems. His work embodies as comprehensive and diverse
a marriage of high and low culture as we've seen in any sphere of the
seven lively arts and shows no sign of fading away. That he never received a Pulitzer Prize or election to the American Academy of Arts and
Letters is fair indication of how confusing and perhaps threatening the
canny raffishness, demotic eloquence, accessible beauty, and unembarrassed universality of his music is to the benighted Europhiles who continue to lay wet blankets on native fires. To the extent that our lives are
measured in song, we live in the Irving Berlin Era.

As paradigm, Berlin served double duty: besides producing a catalogue of songs so diverse it strains credulity to ascribe them to one soul,
he embodied the most frequently told yet jealously guarded saga in
American entertainment. As early as 1915, the year D. W. Griffith premiered *The Birth of a Nation*, a columnist writing in *Music and Theater
Gossip* proposed Berlin as the ideal subject for a six-reel movie. Imagine
a biography of the world's most famous songwriter told in flickering
silence. The columnist had been inspired by the premiere of Berlin's first

revue, *Watch Your Step*, often cited as the first Broadway score by a single composer. At the close of that evening—which presented Vernon and Irene Castle dancing to "The Syncopated Rag," a splashy number (seventeen pages of music) called "Opera Burlesque," and a new kind of song, "Play a Simple Melody," in which complementary melodies and lyrics were counterpoised—the audience cheered, "Composer! Composer!" Berlin, who refused Hollywood's many importunities to film his life, was not yet twenty-six.

Berlin's grasp of common taste was absolute in the decades before rock, when we embraced music with the earnest felicity of a people seeking in popular culture a reflection of our best instincts, hopes, and illusions. An indication of how durable his command was between 1910 and the mid-1950s can be adduced by the fact that "Play a Simple Melody" achieved its ultimate success and a gold record for Bing and Gary Crosby thirty-six years after *Watch Your Step*. Even the most benighted members of a generation weaned on Top-40 radio and unacquainted with the seductive powers of Kern, Gershwin, Arlen, Rodgers, Ellington, and Porter can't help but know Berlin songs, if only the most sentimental of them. Like Stephen Foster's antebellum arias, they have grown as anonymous as folk songs, from "White Christmas" and "Easter Parade" and "There's No Business Like Show Business" to "Blue Skies" and "Always" and "God Bless America."

The bare bones of his story rattle with all the phrases once beloved of backstage musicals and grade-school teachers: melting pot, rags-to-riches, hard work and dedication, Mr. Show Business, entertaining the troops, God bless America. Israel Baline was one of eight children born to Cantor Moses Baline and his wife, Leah, near the Siberian border. Like many impoverished Russian Jews terrorized by pogroms, the family sold its possessions and journeyed from Temun to the Baltic coast, where ships were bound for America. Twenty years later, Berlin's idol, George M. Cohan, got a laugh paying tribute to him with the line, "Irving Berlin is a Jewboy who named himself after an English actor and a German city." Everyone in the business had heard the true story of how a printer mistakenly changed Baline to Berlin in setting the type for his first song (1907): "Marie from Sunny Italy" by I. Berlin. The young man, presented with a liberating initial, renamed himself *Irving* because he thought *Israel* pretentious. By then he had seen a good deal of show business from the bottom up.

Berlin was eight when his father, with whom he had sung in synagogue, died. His siblings were already at work in sweatshops, and now he, too, got a job, selling papers after school. He began hanging around Bowery

beer houses, and his mother was mortified when he announced his ambition to become a singing waiter. We can only imagine the mixture of
daring, ambition, tenacity, and dislocation that propelled him at fourteen
to leave home and school, to sleep in basements and hallways, while
searching for places to sing. He had no musical background other than
the synagogue, and his voice was high and reedy, though he could project it well enough. For a while he accompanied a blind street singer,
then went solo. The popular songwriter Harry Von Tilzer got him a job
reprising songs from the balcony of Tony Pastor's Music Hall on Fourteenth Street. At eighteen, he finally got his singing-waiter job at a saloon
in Chinatown called Pelham's Cafe, where a black ragtime pianist named
Lukie Johnson also worked. Berlin was in an ideal setting for soaking
up every kind of ethnic song—black, Jewish, Irish, Italian—as well as
the highly sentimentalized Tin Pan Alley product. After hours, he learned to pick tunes on the black keys of the piano and wrote parody lyrics
of songs by Cohan and Von Tilzer. "Marie of Sunny Italy," written at
the behest of his boss in a season when Italian songs were hot, earned
him thirty-seven cents and was well worth it; the man who later chided
a lyricist for rhyming "apples" and "Minneapolis" was in youth satisfied
with "queen"/"mandolin" and "beauty"/"suit me."

Still, within two years Berlin was scoring minor hits, writing lyrics to
Ted Snyder's music as well as his own, and finding unknown but talented people to sing them. "Next to Your Mother, Who Do You Love?"
was introduced at a Coney Island cafe by Eddie Cantor; "Sadie Salome
Go Home," a Yiddish dialect song, was the first comedy number ever
performed by a burlesque singer named Fanny Brice. People paid attention when he altered "Spring Song" with syncopation and came up with
"That Mesmerizing Mendelssohn Tune." When the up-and-coming Cantor added "My Wife's Gone to the Country (Hooray!)" to his vaudeville
act and a recording was made by Arthur Carter, 600,000 copies of sheet
music were sold, earning Berlin $12,000 and a commission for new lyrics
(he wrote 100 different verses) from the *New York Evening Journal*. He
moved his mother and siblings to a larger apartment.

From that point, despite a series of tragedies and even occasional periods of writer's block, Berlin's career appears to have rolled along with
the speed and certainty of a locomotive. Nearly every year between 1910
and 1954 saw the introduction of an important Berlin song. Those songs
circled the globe as ambassadors of the American temperament; accelerated and in some instances engendered the careers of singers, dancers,
and bandleaders; became emblematic of their native turf. One thinks of
the parallel impact Louis Armstrong was to have on jazz. The differences
between them are interesting but not very revealing: one black, ebullient,

true to the aesthetic of improvisation, unwilling to be bothered by the demands of business; the other Jewish, reclusive, a stickler for detail, obsessed with promotion. The similarities are more intriguing: Two of the most influential figures in American music were set on their ways with backgrounds of grinding poverty and minimal education. Fueled by genius and a resolute work ethic that left no time for self-congratulations or complacency, they claimed the world.

In 1910, Berlin sang two of his songs in a show in Boston, while the great vaudeville star Nora Bayes introduced three more in her own show. Fanny Brice won a coveted position with Zeigfeld's Follies and asked Berlin for material; his "Dance of the Grizzly Bear" and "Goodbye Becky Cohen" secured her stardom. He would later write several show-stoppers for the Follies, including "Woodman, Woodman, Spare That Tree" and "Ephraham Played Upon the Piano" for the master of comic pathos, Bert Williams; "You'd Be Surprised" for Cantor (his only million-selling disc); and the most delectable of chorus-line themes, "A Pretty Girl Is Like a Melody." Meantime, he'd also written a two-step without a lyric, which, in Berlin's words, was "a dead failure" that lay unpublished for six months. Berlin described what happened next in one of the several interviews he gave in and around 1915:

> One day a social organization, the Friars, got up a club show and asked me to sing a song in it. I hastily wrote a lyric, silly in the matters of common sense, and sang it—"Alexander's Ragtime Band"—at the performance. It turned out to be what the vaude-villians call "a riot," both here and in Europe. No one was more flabbergasted that I was at the smashing hit it made. I humbly began to study my own song, asking myself, "Why? Why?" And I got an answer. The melody . . . started the heels and shoulders of all America and a good section of Europe to rocking . . . Its opening words, emphasized by immediate repetition—"Come on and hear! Come on and hear!"—were an *invitation* to "come," to join in, and to "hear" the singer and his song. And that idea of *inviting* every receptive auditor within shouting distance to become a part of the happy ruction—an idea pounded in again and again throughout the song in various ways—was the secret of the song's tremendous success.

That's probably as good a rationale as any. From the moment the deep-voiced ragtime singer Emma Carus belted it in Chicago, "Alexander's Ragtime Band" was a popular sensation. Within weeks, Al Jolson adopted it for Dockstader's Minstrels, and Helen Vincent and Sophie Tucker installed it on the vaudeville circuit. Though he hadn't written a true rag, Berlin was promptly dubbed "the rag king," and he was besieged for more of the same.

Gilbert Seldes recognized the song as a "crystallization" of a hustling new spirit waking in the new world and ready for export. Not least, Berlin's melody served as an oblique conduit for the rhythmic excitement of black music, even though his song has relatively little rhythmic interest. All the syncopations are in the verse, where eleven out of sixteen measures begin with a rest—a device used by Joplin in the first three strains of "Maple Leaf Rag" and later adapted by Gershwin for his ballad "The Man I Love." The ABAC chorus has nothing to do with ragtime (unlike the countermelody of "Play a Simple Melody," which does capture ragtime's lilt), but the interpolated fragments—the bugle call in measures eleven to twelve, "Swanee River" in measures twenty-seven to twenty-eight—give it symbolic value as a bridge out of the nineteenth century. The song's harmony is twice congruent with the blues: in its use of a minor third and in a key change (C to F) from verse to chorus—the standard blues modulation of a fourth. In *American Popular Song*, Alec Wilder credits it as the first successful pop song with two keys.

To many observers, the song crystallized black music and little else, and rumors circulated charging Berlin with stealing it from a black composer: Lukie Johnson was suspected, but he emphatically denied having anything to do with the song. Berlin dared claimants to step forward and take the credit. No one did. Scott Joplin, however, privately complained to his wife, publisher, and aquaintances that Berlin stole "Alexander's Ragtime Band" from a rag written for his unpublished opera *Treemonisha*. On hearing Berlin's hit, Joplin claimed he revised the passage, destroying any evidence he may have had to back up his grievance. Berlin did have access to the opera—he and Snyder operated from the same brownstone as Joplin's publisher. Joplin's biographer, Edward A. Berlin, has pointed to a similarity between the verse in Berlin's song and the "Marching Onward" section of Joplin's schottische, "A Real Slow Drag," the opera's rousing climax.

Yet songs with similar melodic ideas are hardly uncommon, and the most that can be said in favor of Joplin's assertion is that a melody of his might have lodged in Berlin's brain along with a thousand others. The accusation of plagiarism is plainly absurd. "Alexander" was not a fugitive from ragtime, but rather a contrary creation designed to do away with the complexity and gentility that had turned ragtime into polite salon music several years earlier. The song's melodic strength is characteristic of many Berlin songs and not of Joplin's rags. The important point is that New York's Lower East Side may not have produced an economic or cultural melting pot, but it did produce a musical stew (not unlike New Orleans's gumbo) in which ethnicities rose to the top, affirming the rise of the underclass musical styles that would dominate American music in the twentieth century. Joplin himself was not immune to the cross-cultural assimilations taking place in the neighborhood. Edward A. Berlin also points out that the last work Joplin published, "Magnetic Rag" (1914), is distinct in having two minor-key strains with "a distinct Hebraic cast," reflecting his own exposure to Yiddish theater.

Berlin recognized that of all the ethnicities competing for a songwriter's attention, African American traditions were the most resilient. In time, he moved away from them, but between 1911 and 1916, his rhythm songs speeded recognition of black styles beyond that of spirituals. The influential black bandleader James Reese Europe teamed up with Vernon and Irene Castle to popularize the turkey trot, a dance perfectly suited to "Everybody's Doing It," and in 1919, Will Marion Cook provided Europe with a taste of genuine African American music when he took his Southern Syncopators Orchestra (with Sidney Bechet) overseas. But Berlin's triumphant tour had paved the way, exemplifying one of the earliest manifestations of the increasingly symbiotic relationship between Jewish and black musicians. The synergy between cantorial singing and African American music—the minor third, pentatonic scale, expressive vocalisms, spare harmonies, improvisation—were widely noted. Just as Berlin absorbed the spirit if not the letter of ragtime ("You know, I never did find out what ragtime was," he told Max Morath), Kern assimilated spirituals, Gershwin and Arlen the blues, and Rodgers jazz. What Berlin carried abroad was authentic Americana, and it opened the door.

The previous year, Berlin had married twenty-year-old Dorothy Goetz, and they honeymooned in Cuba during an outbreak of typhoid. She succumbed to the disease and died shortly afterward. Berlin expressed his grief in a song utterly unlike anything he'd written before, a waltz called "When I Lost You." Though rarely sung today, it was as integral to his development as a songwriter as the so-called rags. Here the influence of Cohan, who called it "the prettiest song I've ever heard in my life," is unusually apparent: measures five and six are borrowed from "45 Minutes to Broadway." Yet as the first ballad of lost love by the composer who eventually produced "All Alone," "What'll I Do," "How About Me?" "Remember," "How Deep Is the Ocean?" and "They Say It's Wonderful," among many others, it represented a personal and professional breakthrough. Enormously popular (more than two million copies of sheet music were sold), it has been called the first modern love ballad, though "My Melancholy Baby," also written in 1912 (by Ernie Burnett, who had no other hits), must share pride of place.

Love ballads, a staple of minstrelsy and vaudeville, had rarely displayed original melodies or interesting harmonies and tended to be grievously sentimental. Two years after "When I Lost You," Kern's "They Didn't Believe Me" brought decisive and unmistakable sophistication to the form. (Kern's arresting use of a triplet in that song was almost certainly influenced by "That International Rag," which was popular in England when Kern lived there.) Even so, it was Berlin and not his successors who wrote the largest number of durable ballads, several of them tied to his publicized courtship of the telegraph heiress Ellin Mackay, who married him against her father's wishes in 1926. Grace Moore introduced many of those songs in the Music Box Reviews and said she felt like a singing telegram, carrying Irving's laments to Ellin. They included "All By Myself," "The Song Is Ended," and "Always." At the same time, he turned out rhythm hits that encapsulated the talents of specific performers: "Heat Wave" for Ethel Waters, "Puttin' on the Ritz" for Harry Richman, "Shaking the Blues Away" for Ruth Etting, "Blue Skies" for Belle Baker, and others. He even provided Zeigfeld with a festive account of the country that filled him with deepest remorse, "I'll See You in C-U-B-A."

To many, however, Berlin was still known as the ragtime man, and if the world was dancing or spooning to his melodies, there were any number of critics who disparaged what they construed as American vulgarity. The same insensibility that dismissed jazz as whorehouse music repudiated Berlin's suspicious popularity, especially when Berlin cheerfully affirmed the suspicions. "The mob is always right," he said, "A good song embodies the feelings of the mob and a songwriter is not much more than a mirror which reflects those feelings." When apprised of a composer who said his songs must please him first, Berlin told Max Wilk, "*I* write a song to please the *public*—and if the public doesn't like it in New Haven, I change it!" As Wilder admiringly demonstrates, what is wholly personal in Berlin is his honest eclecticism, lucidity, and wry wit—his faith in song, his determined populism.

Yet Berlin was never entirely the primitive or weathervane he made himself out to be. His work set standards in every idiom of popular songwriting. More than most of his contemporaries, he consistently avoided the standard AABA form (in part because he came to maturity before that form was codified), and his melodies and harmonies are often challenging, even as they reveal an incomparable instinct for the anthem—the melody that gnaws at the listener, indicating an irreducible level of tuneful expression. This is the man, after all, who wrote the most famous American patriotic song since "The Star-Spangled Banner," the most popular Christmas song since "Silent Night," and the only universally recognized Easter song.

Since Berlin could play the piano only in F-sharp (he used a transposing piano to shift keys, as Cohan and other self-taught songwriters did) and required arrangers to prepare his scores (he would dictate his harmonies through trial and error), derogatory rumors continued, always implying that his music was funneled to him from unknown Negroes. The charges were not intended as compliments to black music; quite the contrary. An interview Berlin gave the *New York Herald* in 1912 was bannered with the news that he had made $100,000 in just three years of songwriting. Berlin, the writer huffed, "has 'ragged' more money from the public's unsentimental pockets than possibly all the writers of real poetry since the days of Thomas Chatterton put together."

The reporter concluded with comments on "boosting," an early form of payola: "To have a song introduced by a popular Broadway star may require quite a payment to the idol of the footlights. The songwriter depending on personal suasion will wait at the rear entrance of theaters and buttonhole the noted black face comedian or the pretty lass of the twinkling toes to interest them in a new song." In truth, players were beating a path to Berlin. "Success," he explained, "depends on the trick of putting in what we call 'the punch'—that's a swinging melody [this in 1912] or a sudden twist which will make an impression on the public mind." But will such songs live? "I think so. At least they'll live 10 years—that's long enough for me."

Berlin collaborated with Justus Dickenson in 1915 on an article for *The Green Book* magazine, "Words and Music (How They Are Written)," in which he expounded at length on his craft. Some songs were written in white heat, but most required "torments and tortures." He continued, "So many of my songs are written under pressure that I can't trust to what is called inspiration. I have an expensive publishing and selling organization almost wholly dependent upon me for a product." He attributed his success to the fact that he wrote words as well as music, as though that were simply the most efficient thing to do. "I sacrifice one for the other. If I have a melody I want to use, I plug away at the lyrics until I make them fit the best parts of my music, and vice versa." His primary concern, he said, was phrasing, " 'Easy to sing, easy to say, easy to remember and applicable to everyday events' is a good rule for phrasing."

Melodies, Berlin suggested, should go up on an open vowel (A, I, O) because ascending on a closed vowel (E, U) "makes enunciation difficult." He believed the rules of marketing were the essence of successful songwriting and that you couldn't succeed if you weren't also a performer of your songs. A lifelong insomniac, he wrote chiefly between eight in the evening and dawn. "When I work in the daytime, I pull down the window-shades and work by artificial light, strumming away by ear in the key of F-sharp, or using a transposing keyboard." Nothing is more emblematic of Berlin's influence on modern song than his belief in short verses and long choruses, the opposite of the nineteenth-century approach. He was warned that "Alexander's Ragtime Band" wouldn't succeed because the chorus was too long, but he argued that short choruses "don't carry enough sustained interest." He concluded, "I know rhythm. Therein is one of the great qualities, for rhythm is a big part of any one-octave song. It's the swing. When I get the swing, songs come easy."

Five years later, in 1920, he gave *The American Magazine* his "nine rules for writing popular songs": (1) The melody must be in the range of the average voice; (2) The title must be strong and effectively planted in the song; (3) The song must be "sexless," or suitable to performers of both sexes; (4) It should have "heart interest"; (5) It must be original in "idea, words, and music"; (6) "Stick to nature—not nature in a visionary, abstract way, but nature as demonstrated in homely, concrete, everyday manifestations"; (7) A lyric should strive to be "euphonious," with lots of open vowels; (8) Keep it "perfectly simple"; (9) "The song writer must look upon his work as business, that is, to make a success of it, he must work and *work*, and then WORK." It goes without saying that Berlin violated all those rules, excepting the last.

He was already a legendary character. In 1918, the year Bartók wrote *Bluebeard's Castle* and Stravinsky *A Soldier's Tale*, Berlin was inducted into the army and conceived the idea for a show that would star 350 soldiers, called *Yip! Yip! Yaphank!* The highlights were his songs "Mandy" and "Oh, How I Hate to Get Up in the Morning!" which had its genesis in his insomnia. Berlin withdrew one song from the show because he deemed it too shameless a flag-waver. It lay in his files until 1938, when Kate Smith asked him for a song to sing on her Armistice Day radio show. He dug out the twenty-year-old reject, "God Bless America," and realizing he had another blockbuster, albeit one ill-suited to his capitalist ethics, assigned all future royalties to the Boy Scouts, Girl Scouts, and Campfire Girls. His other contribution to the Second World War, the show *This Is the Army*, reunited many of the *Yaphank* doughboys. During each war, his reputation became iconic. In 1919, when he parted with

Ted Snyder to open his own publishing house, "Irving Berlin Week" was proclaimed across the nation.

Berlin and producer Sam H. Harris (Cohan's partner for many years) opened the Music Box in 1921—it remains the only theater ever built in New York to exhibit the music of one composer. Berlin wrote four annual reviews, with such numbers as "Say It With Music," "Everybody Step," "Pack Up Your Sins" (the wittiest of his contrapuntal songs), and "The Schoolhouse Blues." Oddly, some of his best songs of the period, including the ballads for Ellin Mackay and "Lazy," were not written for the Music Box and had to be interpolated into the shows when they became hits. In 1925, he wrote the score for *The "Cocoanuts"*, starring the Marx Brothers. In 1927, he became the only composer to score an entire edition of the Ziegfeld Follies and also wrote "Russian Lullaby," "The Song Is Ended," and "Blue Skies," which made its way to Hollywood and the first musical film, *The Jazz Singer*, starring Jolson.

For Jolson's fourth and arguably best film, *Mammy*, a recreation of the world of minstrels directed by Michael Curtiz, Berlin wrote "Let Me Sing and I'm Happy," a song that served Jolson and his fading generation of entertainers as astutely as "There's No Business Like Show Business" would eventually embrace the larger aesthetic. A ballad from the same film, "To My Mammy," creaked along with a flat melody but had an idea in the lyric that Berlin would make memorable two years later in one of his finest songs, "How Deep Is the Ocean?" Back on Broadway, in *Face the Music* and *As Thousands Cheer*, he unveiled "Soft Lights and Sweet Music," "Supper Time" (a forceful lament about the aftermath of a lynching), "Let's Have Another Cup of Coffee," "Heat Wave," and "Not for All the Rice in China." Two other songs of the early '30s were reworked from material he had previously rejected—"Say It Isn't So" and "Easter Parade" (the last originally sported the title "Smile and Show Your Dimple").

The best of Berlin's original film scores was the 1935 Fred Astaire and Ginger Rogers vehicle, *Top Hat*, which produced five instant classics: "Isn't This a Lovely Day?" "No Strings," "Top Hat, White Tie, and Tails," "The Piccolino," and, best of all, "Cheek to Cheek," which was equally daring in melody and words. The music begins with the opening strain of Chopin's *Heroic* Polonaise, here relieved of all heroism, and includes not one but two releases. The lyric begins midsentence ("Heaven, I'm in heaven") and swallows its own tale after the second release ("The charm about you will carry me through to . . . /Heaven"). *Top Hat* was Berlin's personal favorite among his film scores, not least because it was the highest-grossing musical film to date. His second score for Astaire, *Follow the Fleet*, is almost as strong and includes "Let's Face the

Music and Dance," "I'd Rather Lead a Band," "I'm Putting All My Eggs in One Basket," and a siren call to free spirits (as sung by Ginger), "Let Yourself Go."

By the late '30s, Berlin had matured into one of the most consistently creative of lyricists, rivaled only by Cole Porter as a words-and-music man. Yet this aspect of his gift has often been overshadowed by the diversity of his melodies and his penchant for unusual song forms. In a 1938 interview in the *New York Times*, he said, "The words of a song are all important, for the melodies linger on, but it is the words that give the song freshness and life." That same month, in the *New York Journal American*, he showed how he wrote songs at his "trick" piano. "I'm a little like a poet who can write verses that people like, but who can't parse the sentences in his poems. Well, he isn't worried. Any high school kid can parse." Berlin probably enjoyed acting the musical rube; he certainly no longer felt impelled to share the nine rules of successful songwriting.

His songs were everywhere. Long after minstrelsy, vaudeville, and the Follies bit the dust, his catalogue was renewed not only by top pop stars, but by generations of innovative jazz artists: Louis Armstrong's "Marie," Bing Crosby's "Waiting at the End of the Road," Billie Holiday's "I've Got My Love To Keep Me Warm," Mary Lou Williams's "Blue Skies" (commissioned by Ellington), Coleman Hawkins's "Say It Isn't So," Lee Wiley's "Some Sunny Day," Teddy Wilson's "This Year's Kisses," Art Tatum's "Isn't This a Lovely Day," Roy Eldridge's "The Song Is Ended," Fats Waller's "Mandy," Sarah Vaughan's "Cheek to Cheek," Betty Carter's "Remember," Jimmy Rushing's "Russian Lullaby," Ray Charles's "Alexander's Ragtime Band," Sonny Rollins's "There's No Business Like Show Business," John Coltrane and Johnny Hartman's "They Say It's Wonderful," as well as songbook albums by Ella Fitzgerald, Billy Eckstine and Sarah Vaughan, Connee Boswell, and Tony Bennett, among others. More surprisingly, Berlin was the only golden age songwriter whose work frequently turned up in the early years of rock and roll: the Ravens's "Marie" and "White Christmas," the Isley Brothers's "How Deep Is the Ocean?," Sammy Turner's "Always," Lloyd Price's "Blue Skies."

His triumphs continued with alarming regularity: *Holiday Inn* (in which Bing Crosby introduced "White Christmas," thereafter the best-selling record of all time), *Easter Parade*, *Blue Skies*, and *White Christmas* in Hollywood; *This Is the Army*, *Miss Liberty*, and *Call Me Madam* on stage. Yet even by those lofty standards, one venture stands above the rest, exemplifying his untutored virtuosity. *Annie Get Your Gun* (1946) is built on an ingenious premise devised by Dorothy Fields, locating the birth of American entertainment in Wild West shows of the fin de siècle. The book traces the romance of sharpshooters Annie Oakley and Frank Butler, stars of the Buffalo Bill touring company. That might seem a slim peg on which to hang genesis, yet it contains the parallel truths and illusions of the American West and the show business in a setting of genuine spectacle. Buffalo Bill once rounded up the legends of the West for a road show; *Annie* brought the show to Broadway.

Annie Get Your Gun was originally intended for Jerome Kern, but Kern died late in 1945. The show was then offered Berlin, who had just turned down a request from the Shaw estate to adapt *Pygmalion*. Despite the stipulation that his name would not be billed above the title (a spot reserved for Rodgers and Hammerstein, the producers), he hesitated briefly—complaining he couldn't write hillbilly music—before accepting. But no one else could have tackled so handily the commonsensical comic drama of forthright people with limited education and a God-given gift to do what comes naturally. Berlin was ideally suited to enlarge upon the theme of feminist moxie, a subject he had treated in his early songs, and to distill the voracious theatricality of showbiz.

The success of Rodgers and Hammerstein musicals in the '40s helped bring about the end of the revues that were Berlin's stock and trade, and restored coherent texts of the sort that had made Kern's *Showboat* a milestone of the '20s. Berlin accepted the challenge with extraordinary vigor; hardly a melodic refrain or lyric in *Annie Get Your Gun* fails to deliver something unusual and memorable. With Ethel Merman at her outlandishly brassy best (Berlin, who insisted she play Annie as a precondition of his participation, had her kid "pretty" singing in "Anything You Can Do"), the show was a model of Tin Pan Alley savvy, an unaffected pageant by and about self-made entertainers.

In Kern's hands, *Annie* might have been a classier act with love songs approaching the operatic and a showstopping inquiry into the vicissitudes of trouping. One cannot imagine Kern writing "Anything You Can Do" (one of the best of Berlin's many comic songs) or "There's No Business Like Show Business"; nor can one imagine his excellent lyricist Dorothy Fields creating verses as forthright as Berlin's. And no other songwriter capable of writing those numbers could also be expected to come up with such purebred ballads as "They Say It's Wonderful" and "I Got Lost in His Arms" or the waltz "The Girl That I Marry" or those remarkably sunny soliloquies "You Can't Get a Man with a Gun" and "I Got the Sun in the Morning" or the loony pseudo-folksong "Doin' What Comes Naturally," which is fitted with a dual-release to break up the nattering main melody. *Annie* is all pretense, greasepaint, and costume, a point Berlin emphasizes brazenly in the score's most inspired coup, that peremptory round of theatrical grit, "There's No Business Like Show Business"—an entr'acte that he almost pulled because the producers looked ambivalent in rehearsal. Here, for once, a songwriter tells the truth about the vain, insecure people on stage and those others in the audience, "the butcher, the baker, the grocer, the clerk," who are jealous because they never get any applause.

Berlin continued to compose throughout the '50s. Early in the decade, he reunited with Merman for a stage hit inspired by the career of Washington hostess Perle Mesta. *Call Me Madam* introduced the ballad "It's a Lovely Day Today" and the best known of his contrapuntal songs, "(I Wonder Why) You're Just in Love," which was an emergency replacement for "Free," a tricky canon of a song that died on the road. Outfitted with a new lyric, "Free" was reborn as "Snow" in *White Christmas*, the top-grossing movie of 1954. Though beset by a pedestrian script that sentimentalizes the Second World War, *White Christmas* offered, in addition to a reprise of the title song and several Berlin chestnuts, his last great score, complete with singular song structures and whimsical lyrics, notably "Count Your Blessings," "The Best Things Happen While You're Dancing," "Sisters," "Love, You Didn't Do Right By Me," "Gee, I Wish I Was Back in the Army" (a three-chorus lyric plus a swing-time finish), and a minstrel production number that parodies minstrel conventions— eschewing, for the first time, blackface—while partaking of their raucous satisfactions, thereby closing a circle in the songwriter's long career.

After the unsuccessful stage show *Mr. President* in 1962, Berlin, always leery of the obligations of celebrity, dodged the glare of public life. He wrote seven songs for a projected MGM musical (never filmed) and offered his last published effort, "I Used to Play by Ear," on a 1968 television show celebrating his eightieth birthday. After that, silence. Alienated by the pop music of the '60s and depressed by diminished interest in his own kind of song, he now kept his music to himself, reversing with a vengeance his stand as dedicated populist. "I'll continue to write them," he told Michael Freedland, "because songwriting is not just a business with me. It's everything."

Toward the close of an open letter to Berlin published in *Town and Country* in 1954, Bing Crosby wrote:

Many times I have come to the studio, apathetic, dispirited, unhappy with my work, and after five minutes listening to you demonstrate a song in your something less than adequate demifalsetto, your arms waving and your eyes sparkling, I am back in action again. The material is always good, I know, but it's your enthusiasm that's so infectious and I've just got to go along with you, not only on your birthday, but every day.

That same infectiousness, as communicated in the material itself, led John Alden Carpenter to predict in the '20s, "I am strongly inclined to believe that the musical historian of the year 2000 A.D. will find the birthday of American music and that of Irving Berlin to have been the same."

6 ❖ Spencer Williams
(The Bard of Basin Street)

Anyone familiar with jazz or blues recordings of the '20s and '30s has come across the name Spencer Williams numberless times in parentheses following a song title. Of the many black songwriters who flourished in the years of the Harlem Renaissance, Williams was among the most enduringly successful. Yet little is known about him. Indeed, he shares an anonymity with most of his compatriots, who have disappeared from public memory even as their songs wax in fame to the point where they seem less the product of individual (copyrighted) artistry than part of that eternal, hazy region known as Public Domain.

Most listeners will likely recognize the names of the white composers now embedded in a Golden Age pantheon that generally admits of only three African Americans (W. C. Handy, Duke Ellington, and Fats Waller). Yet other songs of universal distinction are so completely sundered from their authors that people are invariably surprised to learn that they were written by black composers and lyricists. Consider the renown of the following and the obscurity of their makers: "Sweet Georgia Brown" and "Sugar" (Maceo Pinkard); "If I Could Be With You" (James P. Johnson and Henry Creamer); "Charleston" (Cecil Mack and James P. Johnson); "Shine" (Ford Dabney and Cecil Mack); "Way Down Yonder in New Orleans" and "After You've Gone" (Henry Creamer and Turner Layton); "The Darktown Strutters' Ball" and "Some of These Days" (Shelton Brooks); " 'Tain't Nobody's Business If I Do" (Clarence Williams and Porter Grainger) and "Baby, Won't You Please Come Home?" (Charles Warfield and Clarence Williams).

The repetition of names is no accident, for many belonged—as did the baronial Fats Waller and his favorite lyricist, Andy Razaf—to a circle of prolific writers who were helped and on occasion filched by the most energetic and independent black publisher of the era, Clarence Williams (no relation), whose Harlem-based Clarence Williams Music Publishing Company (CWMPC) almost monopolized that precious turf ignored by white publishers, the blues. No one in his clique got around better than Spencer Williams, who, like Clarence and jazz itself, made the journey from New Orleans to Chicago to New York. A catalyst who was present at the birth of numerous careers, Spencer Williams is estimated to have produced about two hundred songs, nearly half of them published by CWMPC. It's impossible to envision the map of early jazz without them.

Williams's songs propelled the early careers of Louis Armstrong, Bessie Smith, Fats Waller, Fletcher Henderson, Frank Teschemacher, Duke Ellington, and Jack Teagarden, among many others. He also knocked out dozens of blues, usually risqué, that were accounted hits for the finest twelve-bar singers of the era. He was the man who helped launch Josephine Baker's international career, and it was his first collaboration with Clarence Williams, "Royal Garden Blues," that Darius Milhaud interpolated in *La creation du monde*. Imagine the jazz discography without "Basin Street Blues," "I've Found a New Baby," "I Ain't Got Nobody," "Squeeze Me," "Everybody Loves My Baby," "Tishomingo Blues," "Papa De-Da-Da," "Shim-Me-Sha-Wabble," "I Ain't Gonna Give Nobody None of My Jelly Roll," "Mahogany Hall Stomp," and "Careless Love"—each with music or words or both by Spencer Williams.

Yet although he died relatively recently (in Flushing, New York, in 1965), little has been written about him, and much of that is contradictory. One problem is that he spent nearly thirty years living the life of a country squire in Europe; another is that the machinations of CWMPC often obscure who did what to which song. We must also contend with the obfuscating neglect that is too frequently the harvest of songwriters in a music obsessed with performance and improvisation. Here, culled from diverse sources, are some presumably reliable facts.

Williams was born in New Orleans, probably on October 14, 1889. He later claimed the address to have been the notorious Basin Street, which he so successfully transfigured in song ("The band's there to meet us/ Old friends to greet us/Where all the light and the dark folks meet/This is Basin Street!") that thousands of tourists descended on New Orleans looking for it, to the chagrin of the city fathers who ordered all evidence of its existence destroyed in the mid-'40s (they didn't want the town acclaimed merely as the nation's most musicalized red light district.) Williams was apparently orphaned young, for by the time he was seven or eight he was placed in care of his aunt, the fabled madam Lulu White, whose business establishment, Mahogany Hall, he likewise immortalized. There he began to mimic the piano playing of Tony Jackson and

Albert Cal and to compose his first tunes. Other relatives then arranged for him to live in Birmingham, where he was raised through adolescence and at which time he probably discovered the tiny Gulf Coast town of Tishomingo, about which he would write:

> To resist temptation, I just can't refuse
> In Tishomingo, I wish to linger
> Where they play the weary blues.

In 1907, he arrived in Chicago and earned his living as a Pullman porter while playing piano in San Souci Park and at various nightclubs. Among the many New Orleans musicians he met there was the younger Clarence, an imposing entrepreneur, pianist, and songwriter, who had toured as a blackface minstrel after running away from home, then opened a cabaret on Rampart Street and set himself up, or so he claimed, as the first black song publisher in New Orleans. By the time they met, Spencer had already written two of his most popular songs, "I Ain't Got Nobody," a hit record for Marion Harris in 1917, and "Tishomingo Blues," which Abbe Niles, in his notes to the 1949 edition of W. C. Handy's *Blues: An Anthology*, describes as a national hit in 1917, with impressive sheet music sales. Spencer and Clarence published their first collaboration, "Royal Garden Blues," an instant classic, in 1918. Later that year, they set up shop in New York.

Willie "The Lion" Smith once called Clarence the first big New Orleans influence to hit New York and credited him with giving a start to James P. Johnson, Fats Waller, himself, and everyone else who had a song title with the word *blues*. Spencer immediately hit it off with Waller: one of his first assignments was to write a decorous lyric to a melody that Fats had adopted from a bawdy old ditty called "The Boy in the Boat." The adaptation, "Squeeze Me," became Waller's first hit, though Clarence claimed the credit. Maybe the credit didn't matter much. The First World War was over; despite the threat of Prohibition, a fever for partying was in the air and Harlem was the place to be. With blacks now involved in publishing and recording, and with the Broadway stage welcoming black revues, work was plentiful and so was money.

Still, competition for publishing rights was fierce, especially when white publishers saw the profits to be made. Jack and Irving Mills signed up more than a dozen black songwriters, Spencer among them. There were disappointments and a misstep along with the triumphs. In January 1922, Williams collaborated on a revue that was admired by many and criticized by many others for stepping beyond the conventions of minstrel stereotypes. *Put and Take* opened at Town Hall and was selling out nightly when it was mysteriously pulled, presumably in response to racial pressures. That same month, Lucille Hegamin introduced Spencer's "Arkansas Blues" at a blues singing contest at the Manhattan Casino that was attended by Governor Miller, future Mayor LaGuardia, Caruso's widow, and Irene Castle. Hegamin came in second to Trixie Smith, who sang an original. Later that year, Spencer was in trouble, perjuring himself on behalf of his friend Perry Bradford, who had been sued for publishing a tune owned by someone else. Bradford served four months for suborning perjury; Williams walked.

But opportunities advanced unabated. For Handy, Spencer wrote lyrics to a tune that became a blues standard, "Careless Love"; for Clarence, he contributed two pieces that became benchmarks in the careers of Louis Armstrong and Sidney Bechet, "Papa De-Da-Da" and "Everybody Loves My Baby." On the historic day in 1924 when Armstrong made his first recordings with the Fletcher Henderson orchestra, two of the three tunes were Spencer's, "Poor House Blues" and "Thunderstorm Blues" (Waller and Razaf wrote the third). Armstrong, who made a point of recording songs by African-American writers, would soon ensure the classic stature of "Basin Street Blues," "Mahogany Hall Stomp," and "I Ain't Got Nobody."

Henderson, too, became a major associate. He had the keys to the studios, and he regularly accompanied Bessie Smith, who recorded at least eighteen of Spencer's songs, among them "Nobody Can Bake a Sweet Jelly Roll Like Mine," "Cemetery Blues," "Ticket Agent, Ease Your Window Down," "What's the Matter Now," "I Want Ev'ry Bit of It," and "Moan You Mourners," as well as the perennial hits, "I Ain't Got Nobody" and "Careless Love." Bessie represented the crest of a huge blues wave. In 1924 and 1925 alone, Spencer's songs were recorded—all with Henderson accompaniments—by Ethel Waters ("No One Can Love Me"), Clara Smith ("West Indies Blues" and "Shipwrecked Blues"), Hazel Meyers ("Pipe Dream Blues"), Rosa Henderson ("Low Down Papa"), George Williams and Bessie Brown ("I Can Do What You Do," "Cheatin' Blues," and "She's My Sheba, I'm Her Sheik"), Bessie Brown ("Mississippi Delta Blues"), and Maggie Jones ("Box Car Blues" and "Western Union Blues").

The beauty was not just the conviviality of round-the-clock boozy partnerships and the near certainty of lucrative record sales, but the potential for a comprehensive attack on the marketplace. That was what friends were for. "Everybody Loves My Baby" hit the ground running in 1924 in recordings by Clarence, Fletcher, and a Red Nichols–Adrian Rollini group, underscoring the popularity of Spencer's music with white players. For that matter, "Shim-Me-Sha-Wabble" became a proving ground for white clarinetists in recordings that featured Leon Rappolo,

Frank Teschemacher, Benny Goodman, and Don Murray, among others. "Basin Street Blues" was the first big hit for Glenn Miller and Jack Teagarden (in 1931), in a version that inserted a verse that soon became a standard if uncredited part of the song, and it remained Teagarden's signature theme for life. Everyone, white and black, recorded "I've Found a New Baby," first Clarence and Fletcher and Ethel Waters, then McKinney's Cotton Pickers, Joe Venuti and Eddie Lang, Sidney Bechet, Chicago Rhythm Kings, Frank Newton, Pee Wee Russell, Dickie Wells, George Wettling, Teddy Wilson and Lester Young, Benny Goodman, Django Reinhardt and Stephane Grappelli, Bud Freeman, Erskine Hawkins, Lionel Hampton, Bing Crosby, Harry James, James P. Johnson, Art Hodes, and more. It was the first tune recorded by Kenny Clarke in 1938 and the first recorded by Charlie Parker, with Jay McShann in 1940.

Even the theater opened up. Frank Schiffman chose Spencer to work with Waller on a new revue at the Lafayette called *Tan Town Topics*. From that show came the song that briefly eclipsed the earlier "Squeeze Me" and established Waller for the first time as a composer of hit songs. "Senorita Mine" is all but forgotten today, but Clarence was determined to make it work for them after his name was added to the credit line. Though Fats never recorded the song (because he resented Clarence's imposition?), Clarence issued four versions—by Eva Taylor, Bessie Brown, Blue Grass Foot Warmers, and Savoy Bearcats—within three months, boosting its popularity in 1926.

Schiffman was so pleased he teamed the two again for a second revue, *Junior Blackbirds*, but Spencer had time only to leave a few written notes. A wealthy socialite had hired him to compose the music for a show intended for a tour of Europe in 1925. When Ethel Waters outpriced herself in the starring role, Spencer suggested a chorus girl he admired in Eubie Blake and Noble Sissle's *Shuffle Along*, Josephine Baker. He would remain in Europe for the next three years. *Revue Nègre* debuted to extraordinary accolades at the Theater des Champs Elysées and later played Brussels and Berlin.

In London, in 1926 Spencer met a singer named Pat Castleton, whom he would marry ten years later. He was intoxicated by the lack of discrimination and lack of Prohibition and by the generous admiration of the European musicians and audiences. He played piano at Bricktop's, alternating with Leslie Hutchinson, the cabaret pianist and singer who performed simply as Hutch and, on one occasion, entertained at a party for the Prince of Wales. No sooner did he return home than Ellington recorded the definitive version of "Tishomingo Blues." In 1929, the *Chicago Defender* announced Spencer was back "doing his stuff on Broadway, NY, with headquarters in the Clarence Williams office." He was listed on the CWMPC books as "Manager of Bands and Orchestras." He performed on a series of oddball recordings, including four selections by Phil Pavey, a yodeler; vocal duets with guitarist Teddy Bunn; and four sessions of ribald vocals with guitarist Lonnie Johnson, accompanied by pianist James P. Johnson.

What happened next is unclear. According to jazz historian John Chilton, Williams was arrested, tried, and acquitted in 1931 for the stabbing death of Hal Baquet, the brother of clarinetist George Baquet. No mention of this incident can be found in most other reference works or in a 1954 *Ebony* profile of Williams or in his *New York Times* obituary. But such an experience may have encouraged him to return to Europe. In 1931, he and Waller and Razaf worked on a new fall show at Connie's Inn, featuring Don Redman, the Mills Brothers, Snake Hips Tucker, and Baby Cox (remembered for her growl vocal on Ellington's "The Mooche"). Afterward, Williams convinced Waller to join him for a European vacation. As they were broke, they locked themselves up at Spencer's place one weekend in the summer of 1932 and wrote twenty-seven songs (no hits), which they sold to buy passage on the *Ille de France*.

That August they played all the cafés in Paris for drinks and sport. But Waller worried about not having a return ticket and, as Spencer told it, he disappeared from a café one night and left for the States without a word. Spencer stayed on. He had friends and a steady income from song royalties. He himself was royalty: he escorted Josephine Baker to a party Bricktop threw in honor of Duke Ellington in 1933. Decades later, French pianist Alain Romans would tell Chris Goddard:

> Spencer had a big round face like sunshine. He was always smiling and had a little cigar. He and Fats were very funny people. They used to call us white musicians "ofays" and they called themselves "spades." And when they didn't want us to know what they were talking about they would use jive.... A lot of the white musicians—Americans—wouldn't play with them. They recognized that they were good musicians but they wouldn't play with them.

Williams eventually moved to England, marrying Pat Castleton (the *Times* obit gives her name as Agnes Bage) and settling in Sunbury-on-Thames, near London; they had two daughters, Della and Lindy. A 1936 newspaper interview with Waller by Joseph Mitchell reported, "Mr. Williams now lives in London, and is prospering. He is a writer for a French magazine published by Hugh [*sic*] Panassie."

When Waller made his triumphant European tour in the summer of 1938, he wired Williams, who met him at Victoria Station before his appearance at the Palladium. Spencer found him a flat, where they spent a day writing a song called "A Cottage in the Rain," and took him around at night. At his famous recording session on pipe organ, Fats introduced a new piece by his friend, "Pent Up in a Penthouse," possibly the last Spencer Williams tune recorded. When Fats left for Paris, where he showed his wife the haunts he and Spencer had visited six years earlier, word that he had recorded spirituals on a pipe organ preceded him, and he was invited to play the organ at Notre Dame—a high point in his short life.

Spencer and his family remained in England until 1951, when they relocated to a suburb of Stockholm and took over a large three-story house. When *Ebony* caught up with him in 1954, he was recovering from an eye operation, which enabled him to read "some of those terrible clauses in some of my song contracts." He told the reporter that his mother had been part Polish, his father a Trinidadian, and that he had been married earlier to blues singer Lizzie Smith. He expressed impatience with the sort of protest blues popularized by Josh White: "Listen, these lyrics are silly. If you got a grouse against white folks don't sing about it. Get up, go out, and kick 'em in the teeth. The blues are strictly entertainment. There's nothing sophisticated about them. Keep 'em simple all the time." Williams told the magazine he continued to write songs "morning, day and night," but evidently none were successfully published or recorded. Three years later, in 1957, he brought his family to the United States and into a house on Newburg Street in the St. Albans neighborhood of Queens. He died there, after several years of failing health, on July 14, 1965, at seventy-five.

7 ❖ *Ethel Waters* # *(The Mother of Us All)*

Ethel Waters had been living in California for some time when she died there on September 1, 1977, but the obituary sent out by the Los Angeles office of the Associated Press was perfunctory and misguided. In one paper, it bore the headline "ETHEL WATERS DIES 80 AND PENNILESS" and claimed, "She made an art form of singing the blues." The same thing had been said of her in 1921, when she cut her first big records with mostly blues-tinged material; the journalistic sophism that makes all black singers blues singers is apparently deathless. The *New York Times* did better, even beginning its story on the front page, yet

neglected her singing in favor of her Broadway and Hollywood successes, furthering the prevailing notion that she is a historical figure remembered chiefly for her acting.

Waters's singing has long been in eclipse, although many of her records have been reissued periodically. If you were born after the Second
World War, you probably remember her as Berenice Sadie Brown in
Member of the Wedding; you may dimly recall her television series, *Beulah*;
and you may have been aware that she was a frequent participant in
Billy Graham's crusades. But before that she was a radiant jewel of the
"jazz age"—a brilliantly witty, sassy, and subtle singer of pop songs—
and one of the most fascinating aspects of her career is that the vaudeville trouper and the evangelist in her continually vied for dominance.
Much of her art seems to have been forged in extreme rebounds between
a bitter rebelliousness that she traced back to her loveless childhood and
a refined gentility that she once girlishly coveted in the much admired
white ladies of vaudeville. As an actress, she faced down the conflict
between her spiritual and secular selves; and as a singer, she recognized
her ambivalence about being black.

It isn't difficult to understand why she's treated peripherally in his-
tories of American music. She was not a jazz signer, though she influenced many jazz singers and a few jazz musicians (Bix Beiderbecke was
an enraptured fan); nor was she a blues singer, though she had an unprecedented impact on popularizing the blues among white audiences.
So it's not surprising that jazz and blues writers have concentrated on
Bessie Smith while cursorily acknowledging Waters's coequal influence
in the '20s. Contemporary pop writers, on the other hand, confine themselves to rock; lineages, when they are bothered with at all, are traced
to blues and country roots at the expense of the pop tradition itself. As
a result, that tradition is forever being recycled as unevaluated nostalgia.

Waters, in many respects, was the mother of modern popular singing,
the transitional figure who combined elements of white stars such as
Nora Bayes, Fanny Brice, and Sophie Tucker with black rhythms, repertoire, and instrumentation. If this sounds analogous to an idea included in countless essays written about Elvis Presley, the comparison is
unavoidable. Presley adapted a black aesthetic to a white image; Waters
adapted white theatrical styles to a black image. Presley made rhythm
and blues a workable form for whites; Waters opened the world of high-
toned white entertainment to blacks. She was a source of inspiration for
black singers who had no inclination toward the blues and for black
comics and actors who had little affinity with the characterizations inherited from minstrelsy (as exemplified by Butterbeans and Susie and

Bert Williams, the only black performers to get top billing in a white theater before Waters). She was equally inspiring to white singers who wished to sing jazz, blues, and pop but lacked the burnished sonorities of Bessie Smith or Ma Rainey. They admired her unpretentious but finely tuned dramatic style, her energy, and her perfect phrasing. By the late '20s, she had developed such rigorous standards for the delivery of pop songs that even Sophie Tucker, older by twelve years, paid her for singing lessons. Waters's influence, whether direct or indirect, is discernible in the work of numerous vocalists of varied styles, including Bing Crosby, Adelaide Hall, Mildred Bailey, Ivie Anderson, Lee Wiley, Bill Kenny, Lena Horne, Una Mae Carlisle, Connee Boswell, Frances Wayne, Pearl Bailey, Mel Tormé, Bobby Short, Barbra Streisand, and Maria Muldaur. Along with Crosby and Louis Armstrong, she is the defining influence on American popular singing, and she preceded both of them.

The ease with which she made the transition from a blues-oriented repertoire to Tin Pan Alley even had its effect on such individualists as Bessie Smith and Billie Holiday. Although Waters began recording two years before Smith, Bessie was the older and more established performer; yet it was almost certainly Waters's phenomenal success that encouraged Bessie to record as much pop material as she did. I suspect, too, that the popularity of Waters's 1928 "My Handy Man" fostered Smith's 1929 "Kitchen Man" session, as well as countless other double-entendre blues records. (Andy Razaf was commissioned to write both of those songs, and Smith's rolled "r" in the "Kitchen Man" verse was as unusual for her as it was characteristic of Waters.) Billie Holiday attributed her style exclusively to Bessie and Louis Armstrong, but it is Waters we hear on the first Holiday record, "My Mother's Son-in-Law." And there is an unmistakable harbinger of Billie's mature style in Waters's 1928 "My Baby Sure Knows How To Love"—listen to the way she phrases the lines "He plays my ukelele / Likes to strum it daily." There's little doubt that Billie found her "Love is like a faucet / It turns off and on" chorus (from "Fine and Mellow") in Waters's 1923 "Ethel Sings 'Em."

Waters did not much care for genuine blues singers; she called them "shouters" and was thrilled to eventually earn the epithet "the Ebony Nora Bayes," for Bayes—the composer of "Shine On, Harvest Moon," who billed herself as "The Greatest Single Woman Singing Comedienne in the World"—never, in Waters's words, "gave out with any unladylike shouts and growls." Yet Waters boasted in her vivid and unsparing autobiography, *His Eye Is on the Sparrow* (1951), of her own vulgar tongue, violent disposition, and lonely toughness. Born October 31, 1896, the illegitimate child of a thirteen-year-old rape victim, she grew up in the red-light district of a suburb of Philadelphia. She suggests her childhood ambivalence over color in describing the way she mistreated her step-sister: " 'Yaller dog' and 'yaller puppy' were my favorite names for Genevieve. But I'd warn her, 'I'll kill you if you ever say I'm dark. Don't you ever dare say I'm blacker than you.' " A practiced thief and gang leader, she discovered religion when her grandmother enrolled her in a Catholic school for black and white kids. She was astonished by the nuns' patience and especially by the fact that you could call them "sister"—a common term of familiarity in black neighborhoods—instead of "ma'am." Significantly, like Crosby, her best subject was elocution.

Buffeted between the warmth of her religious citadel and the brutish world of her childhood, fiercely proud of her blackness yet envious of sophisticated white women, Waters somehow synthesized these contradictions in her art. Her worldly cynicism led her to parody the very performers she idolized; her imagination and sincerity enabled her to adapt their talents to a modern sensibility. Of course, the same contradictions were operating at large when she began touring the southern black vaudeville circuit as Sweet Mama Stringbean and when she was given the chance to record. By 1920, when Mamie Smith became the first black woman singer to record, blues singers had long been tempering their music with musical and showmanship borrowings from minstrelsy—not because they wanted to reach white audiences (which was largely unthinkable), but to express their own aspirations in the emerging show business climate. There was another motive: at a time when record companies were threatened with boycotts if they recorded black singers, compromises were unavoidable.

In 1921, the clarity of Ethel Waters's diction, the lilting gaiety of her voice, and the relative whiteness of her style impressed the ambitious Harry Pace, cofounder with W. C. Handy of Black Swan records. The company was more ambivalent about blackness than Waters was. A 1923 ad read: "Only bona fide Racial Company making talking machine records. All stockholders are Colored, all artists are Colored, all employers are Colored. Only company using Racial Artists in making *high class* song records. This company made the only Grand Opera Records ever made by Negroes. All others confine this end of their work to blues, rags, comedy numbers, etc." There was a discussion over whether Waters would sing popular or classical numbers, but she knew exactly what she wanted to do and what kind of accompaniment she needed. Her first sides, "Down Home Blues" and "Oh Daddy," sold 500,000 copies in six months and brought the company out of the red. More important, the record sold to blacks and whites alike; she was acclaimed "Queen of the Blues," though the record was a vivacious minstrel-like interpretation of the blues, complete with a spoken chorus à la Jolson. The Black Swan house pianist was Fletcher Henderson, then a chemistry student with classical leanings. Waters made him study the piano rolls of James P. Johnson, and his accompaniments improved markedly (hear him on Bessie Smith's "Any Woman's Blues"). Henderson organized a band to accompany Waters on a tour of the South, where they became the first blacks heard on Southern radio. Following the tour, she was advised to make it on "white time," while Henderson abandoned chemistry to start a regular band (which debuted at the Nora Bayes Theater).

Those early collaborations are wonderfully eager and spirited—Waters was more the scintillating entertainer out to kill the audience than the jazz singer inviting the audience into her own emotional sanctum. She was inclined to tell the story rather than swing the song; by jazz standards, she often didn't swing at all (though she swing's like mad on some records, like "Heebie Jeebies"), but her rhythmic sensitivity and buoyancy were acute. There's a touch of Al Jolson on "Oh, Joe, Play That Trombone"; the brightness with which she invests the line "I'm goin' down to the levy" on "One Man Nan" and the polished bravura of "Sweet Man" are her own; "Georgia Man" is replete with minstrel histrionics, but the phrasing is impeccable and that high note in the middle of the first chorus is still exciting.

In 1925, she replaced the legendary Florence Mills at the Plantation Club and introduced "Dinah"; in 1927, she appeared in a Broadway revue, *Africana*. She made her first film in 1929, playing herself in *On with the Show*—here we can appreciate her compelling stage presence as she sings "Birmingham Bertha" and (dressed as a cotton picker) "Am I Blue?"; she's beguiling and timeless. The jazz age was in full gear, though jazz itself was still underground. Ballrooms sprouted all over the country, and everyone wanted to foxtrot to the syncopated sounds of Paul Whiteman and the like. Black music, however diluted, best captured the sensual stance of rebellious youth; traditionalists found it a heart of darkness, and accused it of undermining the nation's morals. Without meaning to—the divisions in her temperament mirrored the divisions in the nation—Waters played both sides against the middle. She was irrepressibly erotic at one moment and abundantly high toned the next. She was now recording for Columbia, and her accompaniments varied from lone pianists to studio orchestras. Her theatrical characterizations matured as she perfected a conversational delivery in which the subordinate notes in a phrase were half-spoken and half-sung. She became an expert parodist, occasionally dropping quick-witted asides from the corner of her mouth. She "took off on" Ethel Barrymore on "You Can't Do What

My Last Man Did" and Rudy Vallee on "You're Lucky to Me." On the hilarious "Come Up and See Me Sometime," she begins as Waters and concludes as Mae West.

Sometimes it's difficult to tell when she's kidding and when she's playing it straight. One presumes she was hamming it up on "When Your Lover Has Gone," with its stressed vowels, rolled consonants, and cracking voice, but there are ballad performances from 1929–30 that are simply dreadful. The subtlety of her diction and intonation is such that her attitude toward a song sometimes seems to change from line to line. In a recording of "My Special Friend Is Back in Town," she strikes a dazzling balance between singing, talking, and joking and recalls, in her comedic personality and assurance, Fanny Brice. Ironically, her last session for Columbia took place on November 27, 1933, with the accompaniment of Benny Goodman's band; that same afternoon, Goodman recorded a couple of titles under his own name that introduced an eighteen-year-old Billie Holiday. Waters had dominated pop singing in the early '30s—even Bessie Smith had fallen out of favor—but the Holiday debut foreshadowed the coming of the great jazz singers who would make Waters's own records date prematurely. Broadway was beckoning.

Waters's career is rather neatly packaged in decades—she was a recording star in the '20s, a Broadway actress and personality in the '30s, a film star in the '40s, and the architect and victim of her own myth in the '50s. Her earliest Broadway performances were in musical revues, but even then she thought of acting as something deadly serious. She would not accept roles she couldn't relate to or admire. The ambivalences she resolved as a sophisticated chanteuse stormed into open combat when she mounted the stage. In a sense, the theater for her became a churchlike edifice, and she was never frivolous in it, whether belting the showstopper "Heat Wave" in *As Thousands Cheer* or emoting "Stormy Weather" in the *Cotton Club Show of Spring, 1933*. "Your imagination can carry you just so far," she wrote. "Only those who have been hurt deeply can understand what pain is or humiliation. Only those who are being burned know what fire is like. I sang 'Stormy Weather' from the depths of the private hell in which I was being crushed and suffocated." She turned down *Porgy and Bess* because it wasn't "quite true to life to me," but she jumped at the chance to play Hagar in the 1939 *Mamba's Daughters*, her first dramatic role. In Hagar—"a lumbering, half-crazy colored woman with a single passion: seeing that her beautiful daughter Lissa has a better life than she's known"—she recognized her mother: "All my life I'd burned to tell the story of my mother's despair and long defeat." Waters was the first black actress to star on Broadway, and the highest-paid woman in show business. She considered opening night the most important in her life, "except for when I found God."

Her Hollywood experience was less fulfilling, at least in the beginning. Whatever her talent, she was black, so she was relegated to playing cooks and maids. In her middle forties and having gained too much weight, she was equipped to move in on the Mammy monopoly controlled by Louise Beavers (more than sixty films between 1929 and the early '60s) and Hattie McDaniel (thirty-eight films between 1934 and 1949), who had recently won an Oscar for portraying the super-Mammy in *Gone with the Wind*. The situation was worse for young, attractive, light-skinned women since Hollywood would not allot them love-interest roles, unless the story concerned a doomed mulatto; with people like Jeanne Crain and Mel Ferrer playing light-skinned Negroes, not even those parts could be counted on. For young, dark-skinned actresses, the situation was hopeless. Waters, in just a handful of basically stereotypical roles, made a crucial difference.

She played opposite Paul Robeson in a segment of *Tales of Manhattan*, which Robeson considered so vile that he left Hollywood, never to return. In 1943, she re-created her role in the stage hit *Cabin in the Sky*, after demanding that the part be rewritten to suit her religious convictions. Waters did full justice to the best songs in the elegant Vernon Duke–John LaTouche stage score—"Taking a Chance on Love," "Cabin in the Sky"—as well as the great ballad written especially for the film (lyrics by E. Y. Harburg), "Happiness Is Just a Thing Called Joe." Symbolically reenacting the polarities of her personality, she outprays and outsings and then outvamps and outdances everyone in the picture (no mean feat in a cast that included Lena Horne and John Bubbles). Yet the set was a stormy one. She earned the reputation for being "difficult" and was, she claimed, blacklisted from Hollywood for the next six years— the nadir of her career. During that bleak time, she sang occasionally, but Ella Fitzgerald had come on the scene and Waters felt inferior. She ached for another dramatic role. In 1949, Hollywood responded to postwar moralizing with no less than four it's-all-right-to-be-a-Negro movies: *Home of the Brave, Lost Boundaries, Intruder in the Dust,* and *Pinky,* the story of a light-skinned girl passing for white. John Ford was to direct; and Ward Bond, an old fan of Waters, recommended her for the part of the girl's grandmother.

During the enforced years away from Hollywood, Waters came to understand the extent to which she was caught between two cultures. Her hotel room became "like the walls of a cell," and she spent more and more time in Harlem—"But I quickly learned there are great disadvantages when you are prominent and try to live in a humble place. . . . All I wanted was to be with the kind of people I'd grown up with, but I discovered you can't go back to them and be one of them again, no matter how hard you try." Shortly before getting the offer to do *Pinky*, she was asked to star in the Broadway production of Carson McCullers's *Member of the Wedding*. She assumed both roles with a vengeance. McCullers had to assure her personally that she could interpret the character of Berenice as she chose, and John Ford was replaced by Elia Kazan on *Pinky* because of his disagreement with her concept of the part. (Darryl F. Zanuck was quoted as saying, "Ford's Negroes were like Aunt Jemima characters.")

Pinky was a timorous social-conscience movie, but there was nothing half-stated about Waters. She played Jeanne Crain's grandmother, a laundress, with urgency and the suggestion of infinite personal reserve. If the Mammy figure had been cartoon simple in the Beavers-McDaniel films, Waters exposed the long-repressed complexities behind the mask. As Donald Bogle suggests in his book *Toms, Coons, Mulattoes, Mammies, & Bucks*, she used this part and the one in the film version of *Member of the Wedding* to demolish one of Hollywood's iron-clad clichés.

Before *Member* was filmed, she signed for a television season as Beulah, the happy domestic originated by McDaniel on radio and subsequently taken over from Waters by Beavers. She also published *His Eye Is on the Sparrow*, which became a best-seller. In it, she emerged as a tough survivor of mythic resilience: cantankerous, naturally gifted, suspicious, deeply religious, ungiving, loving, smart, naive, vulgar, refined—a tangle of paradoxes cut through only by her mother's love (which arrives climactically on the last page). Some who read it cried when they saw her performance of Berenice Sadie Brown in *Member*, certain that she was playing herself. To a degree, she was; Berenice's relationship with the white girl, Frankie, parallels Waters's relationship with her grandmother. "All my life I been wanting things I ain't been getting," Berenice/Waters says stoically and you can no more imagine the part played differently than you can Brando's Terry Molloy in *On the Waterfront*. In this crowning achievement, she once again gave us both sides of Ethel Waters—the spiritually comforted, infinitely patient earth mother and the earthier, comfortless woman whose best years had passed.

But America extracts great prices from its mythical figures, and Waters's decline was cruel. Having turned the Mammy caricature into a figure of strength and depth, while still offering the broadest shoulders ever made to dry white tears, she found herself in a cul-de-sac. She didn't make another film for seven years, when she played Dilsey in an idiotic version of Faulkner's *The Sound and the Fury*. Worse, there had been the humiliation of appearing on a TV quiz show, *Break the Bank*, in a widely publicized attempt to win the money she owed in back taxes. From being earth mother she became queen for a day. There was a final one-woman show on Broadway and a memorable role as a jazz singer in an episode of *Route 66* on television, but her forty-year career in the lively arts was pretty much over. The church, which had provided her only solace as a girl, became a haven to her again, and she began years of touring with Billy Graham; her second volume of autobiography, published in 1973, is called *To Me It's Wonderful*.

Yet the records are still there, as are the movies, though infrequently shown, and the first book continues to be reprinted. Through them, especially the records, she shows that popular art can survive the fashions that spawn it and triumph over those that dismiss it. The records fairly sparkle with her talent, with her knowing, seductive wisdom.

8 ❖ *Bunk Johnson/George Lewis (Pithecanthropus Jazzman)*

With a flourish of unlikely trumpets, the polar opposites in a long-ago musical feud seemed fully revitalized when two albums were released in the spring of 1990, one from prewar New Orleans and the other from contemporary Paris. On the right, we had Bunk Johnson, who died in a blaze of contention in 1949; on the left, Dizzy Gillespie, who at seventy-two was still fast as a rattlesnake and twice as resourceful. The oddly synchronous appearance of *Bunk Johnson: The King of the Blues* (American Music) and *Max + Dizzy: Paris 1989* (A&M) was a compound irony with manifold interest.

The music world first learned about both men in the '40s and was parted in two, resulting in a fracas that came as close to civil war as jazz could stand. In the same year that John Birks "Dizzy" Gillespie joined Cab Calloway's band, 1939, writers Bill Russell and Fred Ramsey, Jr., while researching their influential book *Jazzmen*, learned that the legendary and unrecorded William Geary "Bunk" Johnson was forgotten but not gone. During the next four years, Russell helped Johnson get new teeth and a trumpet and recorded him, creating in 1944 the American Music Company to release his Johnson records and to make more. As

Russell recorded Johnson, Gillespie fell in with the nest of radicals, including Charlie Parker, hiding out in the Earl Hines band. In 1944 Gillespie led the radicals into the Billy Eckstine band as music director.

For the next five years, Johnson and Gillespie were jazz's oil and water. The old man from New Iberia, who claimed to have played with Buddy Bolden and was consequently declared the missing link between the dawn of jazz and its sanctification in King Oliver, became the King Lear of jazz revivalism. Bunk was past his prime, irascible when drunk, and fanciful in his recollections; nor was he untouched by modern times—records and radio had long since penetrated Louisiana's veil. But he offered to shed light on a prematurely dark history, and one can readily understand those who scrutinized him with anthropological zeal. The stories he spun were entrenched in jazz history, repeated as gospel as recently as 1994 in Bill Russell's posthumously published *New Orleans Style*. Russell makes no mention of fellow New Orleans scholar, Donald M. Marquis, who conclusively disproved them in his book, *In Search of Buddy Bolden*, in 1978.

Bunk said he was born in 1879, only two years after Bolden, which would have made them fifteen and seventeen respectively at the time Johnson swore he worked with him. Marquis believes Bunk was born as much as ten years later and could not have played with Bolden, who was not known to use a double-cornet lead. But Johnson may have heard him and undoubtedly heard a great deal about him. Some of Bunk's recollections ring true, including his description of the ensemble and a repertoire that included "St. Louis Tickle," "Didn't He Ramble," and "Lazy Moon." He provided Russell with a typical assessment of Bolden's gifts: He couldn't read, but he could play in any key, "execute anything." He had "everybody in the city of New Orleans real crazy and standing on their heads." This comports with the usual hyperbole, including the anonymous reverie, "On a clear night, you could hear Bolden's cornet for fourteen miles." Clark Terry recalled an encounter when Duke Ellington, who never came within fourteen hundred miles of Bolden, was in the grip of Boldenmania and claimed, "He used to tune up in New Orleans and break glasses in Algiers!" Bolden had become the John Henry of jazz, and here was Bunk, insisting the tales were true, or close enough.

Yet even if he didn't bear witness to God's covenant with an undoubtedly brilliant musician, who was said to have created jazz by virtue of his inability to read a score, and even if he wasn't the embodiment of the Southland's inviolate music before northern mercantilists compromised its native purity, Bunk Johnson had undoubted presence and a personal style. Gillespie, in those years, reinvented jazz in his own irreverent image. His was the call of liberation for a postwar wised-up black America. The revivalists, mostly white intellectuals who thought even swing a debasement of true black jazz, found in Johnson a rallying point for their idea of authenticity. The modernists belittled Johnson's technical shortcomings, as well as the requited nostalgia surrounding his apotheosis. "Moldy figs," as the reactionaries were dubbed, dismissed Gillespie and associates as clowns and anarchists. Both sides took it on the chin in 1949: Johnson died, between the ages of sixty and seventy, and Gillespie's band went bankrupt.

As revealed in his collected letters, James Jones started writing his short story about Johnson in 1950 while awaiting the publication of *From Here to Eternity*. "The King" appeared five years later. Key names were changed (common courtesy in fiction before docudramas), but it was a faithful rendering of the facts surrounding Johnson's comeback and the attendant excitement among young jazz fans, and it included an astute evaluation of his music:

> This trumpet sounded as if a man whose reflexes had forsaken him was fumbling and choking to get half-remembered things in his head out through the mouth of his horn. And to complete it, there was not a single original phrase in the whole collection of sides. The numbers were all traditional old New Orleans numbers, and the trumpet's treatments of them were the same old trite treatments, solos so ancient they had beards, so hackneyed we all knew every note before it came out of the horn. And yet, with all the faults and blunderings, you couldn't deny that there was power in the trumpet, a strong emotional power, that hit you hard.

You can't help but wonder if Jones didn't discern his own writerly vices and virtues in Johnson's music. In any case, he'd have been surprised to learn that the revered recordings Johnson made for the American Music Company would be out of print within two years and remain scarce (except in Japan) for more than thirty. Johnson's name was kept alive through the '50s and early '60s when his former sidemen (most notably clarinetist George Lewis) enjoyed international acclaim as the beacons of New Orleans traditionalism. The oft-heard phrase "from Bunk to Monk" indicated a sweeping approach to jazz. Yet the controversy simmered, especially after Don Marquis debunked much of the foundation of jazz history as supplied by the aptly named Bunk. With his best records out of print, Johnson receded once again into the mists of legend. The fact that some of his lesser performances—the album on Columbia, the Blue Note session with Sidney Bechet—remained in print didn't help his case.

But in 1990, Bill Russell, then eighty-five and ailing (he died two years later), entrusted his catalog to George H. Buck, Jr., the leading entrepreneur of traditional jazz records. Retaining the name American Music, Buck released a series of CDs. Not too surprisingly, Russell's notes insist on the 1879 birth date and include a number of acerbic comments sure to rankle hot-tempered veterans of the bop wars. The rest of us can attend the music on *The King of the Blues*, which lives up to many of the claims made for it and perhaps justifies the grand title given that initial album. Johnson was surely *a* blues king, if not *the* blues king—poetic license in the choice of an article is not unacceptable. These sides, superbly recorded during one week (July 29 through August 4) in 1944, were remastered with characteristic care by Jack Towers and Don Jarvis. They have a weight and purpose all their own—primitive to the point of effrontery, yet uncannily poised and compelling.

Johnson was no Oliver, let alone an Armstrong. His best phrases on "Dippermouth Blues" come directly from Oliver's own solo, glued by a pet lick Johnson can't seem to shake. But the tempo is vital and the direction is sure and forthright. Bunk's tone is surprisingly mellow, even cool, just as witnesses to the young Bunk frequently contended. Even with false teeth (Russell and the other revivalists put his dental bills where their mouths were), his timbre is unmistakable, as are his sustained notes and his plaintive lyricism—for example, the embellishments he chances after the clarinet solo on "C. C. Rider." That's as hoary a blues line as you can name, but Johnson gives it life. The rhythm on that selection and several others is strictly thump-thump-thump-thump, and sometimes the wind instruments veer out of tune, but you don't mind—a rhythm section that stomps as heavily and as faithfully as this one can't help but emphasize the down and dirty essence of swing.

Jim Little's tuba (bonded with bassist Alcide "Slow Drag" Pavageau, banjoist Lawrence Marrero, and drummer Baby Dodds) is especially winning; he floats the ensemble. Bunk's seven-piece band (George Lewis and trombonist Big Jim Robinson share the front line) affirms much of what the avant-gardists of the '60s reclaimed for themselves; pitch deviation can be pleasing when the context is emotionally honest. George Lewis, an inspired primitive, is heard to advantage: his solo on the nine-minutes-plus "Midnight Blues" is luscious—the elements are mundane, but the flow and sensibility are undeniable. Even singer Myrtle Jones, with her hair-trigger vibrato, spices the groove on two tracks. But it's Bunk's show, and you can hear why he made converts instead of fans.

He pumps the blues as though more than a paycheck were hanging in the balance.

After Johnson, the most venerated of the New Orleans stay-at-homes was Lewis, who recorded so often and on so many labels he must be accounted as much a part of the '50s jazz scene as Miles Davis or Sonny Rollins. He became the living symbol of the revivalist movement after Johnson's death, but even before that, he was fawned over by the figs, presented as living testimony to what jazz was like before it lost its virginity to Tin Pan Alley and other musical swains. Purity was highly valued in the '40s, with all those servicemen returning after two years or more. And Lewis was a perfect conduit: A true gentleman, sincere and well-spoken, a dedicated professional, a musician who believed in his calling and found no need to prevaricate. None of that protected him from becoming the punch line in one of the '40s more surreal presentations.

The great but willfully parochial folklorist Alan Lomax and others gathered around the clarinetist at a New York radio station in the mid-'40s, assuring listeners they were about to hear something truly unblemished by the miscreants of modern music, as though Lewis—who was born in 1900, one year after Ellington, one year before Armstrong—had not only remained in his hometown of New Orleans, but had been kept under glass. Then he began to play the blues with his shapely old-time reedy tone. The revivalists, who never deigned to tune in popular radio broadcasts, didn't know it, but their man was playing phrases borrowed from Woody Herman, whose "Woodchopper's Ball" and other blues records had been on the charts since 1939. Lewis, like any good musician, used whatever pleased him, and probably thought he'd make a better impression if he demonstrated he was up-to-date. Lomax and company didn't have a clue, of course, and proceeded to offer the notion that had Louis Armstrong remained in New Orleans, he might very well be playing in the manner of George Lewis.

Lomax was always a regressive defender of old ways, though he mellowed enough in later years to enjoy the accomplishments of such new-fangled idioms as gospel, albeit regretting the displacement of improvised spiritual harmonies. His reluctance to place his research in the context of a larger historical canvas is problematic in his indispensable autobiographical history, *The Land Where the Blues Began*, published in 1993, in which he fails to trace the origins of songs beyond his own discovery of them (some were pop hits he would have recognized had he delved deeper into his car radio) and perpetuates myths long since discounted—including the one about Bessie Smith dying because she was refused admission to three hospitals. Such oversights are the price of being a hedgehog. The rewards are the unearthed human resources, as no one knew better than Lomax, whose father, John, had brought Leadbelly north with a fervor worthy of Frank Buck or Carl Denham.

Inevitably, the Lomax prize and Bill Russell's prize would have to meet, and they did at a concert, issued on disc in the American Music series as *Bunk & Leadbelly at New York Town Hall 1947*. The meeting was uninspired, not least because the singer's idea of rhythm never jells with that of the band; the jazzmen leave him alone for most of his three selections. But Bunk had lost his limited powers that night, and his notes are muffled and pained. The producers did him no favor by replacing his own band with an all-star ensemble including virtuoso clarinetist Edmund Hall and the young pianist Ralph Sutton. Virtuosity and primitivism are ill-matched in the best of times. Those who admired Bunk and Lewis were not looking for flash.

As Bunk declined, the more responsible Lewis answered the desire for an Arcadian jazz, uncomplicated and folksy in ways all but antithetical to jazz as an evolving art. The hipsters, in their peremptory dismissal of the guy who cranked out Woody Herman licks, missed a rare musical disposition, fragile in its limitations but powerful in its conviction. Lewis became an international success, recording for the top independent labels, including Riverside, Blue Note, and Verve; touring Europe and Japan; and telling his story in a popular biography (by novelist Ann Fairbairn writing as Dorothy Tait). Ridiculed by modernists for his imprecise intonation and crude phrasing, he was taken up by postmodernists for his expressive inflections and artless simplicity.

Lewis found himself at the head of the last great revival of New Orleans jazz as performed by black musicians born in the first decade of the century. That most of those musicians were not good enough to have made the northward trek instigated by Morton and Oliver is probably besides the point. By 1960, antiquarianism had its own dominion, and Lewis, who had never been remotely connected to the jazz mainstream, was as exotic as any other representative of a folk culture not long for this world. What he lacked in technical aplomb he made up in feeling, unlike those accomplished but often robotic luminaries beloved of well-heeled tourists, Pete Fountain and Al Hirt.

He surrounded himself with a marvelously colorful crew of adequate players, neighborhood celebrities who enjoyed their increasing renown and made their audiences feel at home: Big Jim Robinson, whose tailgate trombone made every note a glissando; Alcide "Slow Drag" Pavageau, the spirited bassist and senior member, who thumped the strings so hard they cracked against the wood like gunshots; Emanuel Sayles, one of three banjoists in the circle (with Lawrence Marrero and George Guesnon), who used Lewis as a sideman with his Silverleaf Ragtimers and favored endlessly repeated polyphonic theme statements; Joe Watkins, whose easygoing drumming matched his surprisingly silky vocals; Alton Purnell, by contrast a down and dirty singer, and Joseph Robichaux, two pianists who unfailingly pounded four chords per measure; and trumpeters Kid Howard, Alvin Alcorn, and Kid Thomas Valentine, all sputterers, but feisty.

One of Lewis's best and least-known recordings was a ten-inch album recorded by Joe Mares for his Southland record label in 1954, an especially ripe year for Lewis. In those twenty or so minutes of music, the richness of his low bleeding sound was perfectly captured, in part because he was recorded close-up, with a quartet as well as the larger ensemble. Watkins croons "St. Louis Street Blues," an adaptation of Louis Armstrong's "Melancholy," and Alton Purnell wails charming versions of "Darkness on the Delta" (later recovered by Thelonious Monk) and "Louisian-i-a." On "Over the Waves" (or "The Singing Clarinet") and "Red Wing," Lewis imparts his patented arpeggios, up and down the scale, but with brio and poignance. Unhappily, the American Music series compromised those selections in a production that incarnates thoughtless reverence. *Bands, Trios & Quintets* combines the Southland sides with a previously unreleased concert with Lewis at his worst—out of tune and floundering ("Jingle Bells" insults his memory)—while omitting Lewis's touching and evocative speech at the close of the Southland album, and crediting Purnell with Watkins's vocal. Bill Russell would have been aghast.

Another strangely illuminating volume in the series is *George Lewis with Red Allen: The Circle Recordings.* Allen was the last of the genuinely great figures to emanate from New Orleans in the '30s, and his vitality (plus Paul Barbarin's pulsing drums) on four selections spurs Lewis and Big Jim to heights that must have surprised even them. They play as though eager to please him, moving beyond their workaday phrases. When Alvin Alcorn takes over from Allen, the ensemble settles into a tighter groove—it's like a homecoming, as Lewis returns immediately to the haven of his preferred licks. Revivalists, like all true believers, take an awful lot for granted, but they demand little. By the time Lewis died in 1968, it was evident that his career was the most important by-product of the Bunk Johnson episode. Neither he nor Bunk represented jazz before the expulsion from the garden, but they did conjure a piquant interlude in which jazz could be reimagined as a community music, untouched by ambition or genius.

PART TWO

❖

A New Music

9 ❖ *Jelly Roll Morton (Red Hot Dandy)*

We can only surmise why Jelly Roll Morton, whose date of birth was lately certified through baptismal records as October 20, 1890, insisted he was born five years earlier. Beyond the usual reasons (a few extra years may have got him into the bordellos, honky-tonks, and pool halls to which he escaped from his stuffy, disapproving family), an 1885 birth date made his famous claim of having single-handedly invented jazz in 1902 seem a tad more plausible. Even the imperial Jelly might have hesitated at issuing so grand a claim on behalf of his twelve-year-old self. At seventeen, though, he was a man of the world: Who could say what peaks the strutting teenage minstrel, pianist, hustler, pimp, and incipient composer wouldn't have dared? Of course, even given the 1890 date, he was a mature thirty-three when he initially found access to a recording studio and three years older than that when he carried out the Red Hot Peppers sessions that underpin his reputation.

The consensus on the Peppers within the international jazz community has hardly wavered in the sixty years since the New Orleans revivalists, abetted by Alan Lomax and the Library of Congress, spurred their resurrection. By the middle '60s, after Martin Williams helped reinterpret them for modernist holdouts, their acceptance was virtually uncontested. Few musical opinions are now as broad based as the one that places those records—made only a few months before Duke Ellington issued the first broadsides ("East St. Louis Toodle-oo" and "Black and Tan Fantasy") that would date them irretrievably—at the pinnacle of the once luminescent and soon faded glory of New Orleans jazz. The conviction abides despite three inconvenient hurdles: the pinnacle was achieved not in New Orleans, but in Chicago; the music has been out of print for long stretches, encouraging the acceptance of received wisdom; and controversy about the man himself continues to seethe. The purple prose to which many of Morton's admirers have been given has not helped his case with those who, willing to concede Morton's talent, blanch (still!) at his egoism.

Comparison with Orson Welles is instructive: Morton came to Chicago ready to venture everything, to bend the rules and recreate the idiom. And that's what he did. His version of New Orleans jazz is far richer, craftier, and more cultivated than anything he encountered in the bayous, which may help to explain why rapid stagnation banked the fires of traditional jazz, as less adventurous musicians were content to copy Morton, King Oliver, and Louis Armstrong and a once admirable music was reduced to the precincts of tourism, complete with moniker (Dixieland), costume (straw boater and garter belt), and snacks (peanuts and beer). By the time Morton completed his epochal 1926–28 records, polyphony was on hold—Armstrong had put the soloist in the limelight and squared the beat, and Ellington had introduced melodies and voicings that supplanted the idylls of the South with the cosmopolitanism of the North. Confronted with such subversion, Mr. Jelly scrambled, embracing several musical fashions but unable to find the right cut of cloth for his genius before he faded away.

When Welles couldn't get his films financed, he turned to autobiography and self-immolation. Morton, his reputation in tatters, famed, like Welles, as much for his bragadoccio (the 1902 tale was one of many) as for his skill, was likewise the subject of interminable biographical probing. Welles's last barely released works were self-referential documentaries (*Filming Othello* is a little seen marvel, the documentary as personal essay). The last great works of Morton's career were interviews, recorded at the piano in the Library of Congress's Coolidge Auditorium. The punch line is this: like those of Welles, most of Morton's aesthetic theories and claims—notwithstanding his birth date and the birth date of jazz—were posthumously validated. He had, in fact, been everywhere he claimed, and at the right time: New Orleans; San Francisco; Chicago; and Richmond, Indiana, home of Gennett Records, where, with the New Orleans Rhythm Kings, he precipitated one of the first racially mixed recordings. The infamous business card that claimed for him the invention of jazz was, like most of his bragging, more of an exaggeration than a downright lie. He did prove to be, after all, the catalyst who transfigured ragtime and minstrelsy into a new music that adroitly weighed the respective claims of the composer and the improviser—in a word, jazz.

Morton's accomplishment, scarcely less impressive than the one he vaunted, was to establish jazz as a pancultural bouillabaisse. He redefined the playing field in his use of diverse ethnic spices ("if you can't manage to put tinges of Spanish in your tunes," he advised, "you will never be able to get the right seasoning, I call it, for jazz") and his plenary borrowings from pop, folk, and the academy—not that Morton would have considered opera, a musical form to which, as a New Orleans Creole of color, he was practically born, academic. Caught between the French tutorial traditions to which his family aspired and the enchantment of blues improvisation emanating from the poor black quarter uptown, he was impeccably positioned to avoid the hazards of high art/low art snobbery. Morton soaked up Italian opera, military brass bands,

French quadrilles, Latin habaneras and tangos, and all the other sounds he found on his travels through the South (Biloxi was a hotbed of blues), the West (he was a hit in Los Angeles as early as 1917), and the Midwest (although he did regret missing the piano competition at the St. Louis Exposition). By the time he returned to Chicago in 1923, he was a walking treasury of the nation's musical byways, which he integrated into a music of his own. He was the first of the "workshop" composers, prefiguring Ellington, Mingus, and Muhal Richard Abrams.

Morton wrote some of the loveliest ("The Pearls," "Frog-i-more Rag") and trickiest ("King Porter Stomp," "Pep") works for piano in the American repertory. Few pianists (Dick Hyman is one) can do justice to them, which says more about Morton's alleged primitivism than any amount of debate. Morton was a product of ragtime and not of Tin Pan Alley. His compositional procedure was by nature formal and compound—a piano opus was a succession of strains, varied and complementary, not a stand-alone song fit for variations. But he was also grounded in the blues, those elemental twelve- and sixteen-measure sonatas that in the New Orleans style of his youth were rooted in riveting bass patterns and seductive moods. He sought to modify ragtime's parlor propriety with the suggestive rhythms and the spacious harmonies of the blues; he sought to enrich blues with the gaudy melodies and thumping euphoria of ragtime. His stimulating cross-rhythms, ringing overtones, skillful syncopations, and steady bass could make of the blues a pianistic showcase ("Fat Meat and Greens") or an inspired evocation ("I Thought I Heard Buddy Bolden Say").

But he was too ambitious, too prolific, and too talented to limit himself even to the unlimited vagaries of the blues. Though by no means a virtuoso, Morton was good enough to play the knuckle-busting music he wrote, and the standards he had to meet were those of ragtime. "Grandpa's Spells," which he recorded as a solo piano piece in 1923 and later adapted for the Red Hot Peppers, is essentially a rag tricked up with a stomp episode. Its structure, following a four-bar intro and with a four-bar transition preceding the stomp, is AABBACCA (each letter represents a sixteen-bar strain). Formally, it could almost pass for a Joplin rag, though Joplin preferred four strains. But the crashing accents of the stomp (C) announce a change that is decisively underscored by the final sixteen-bar embellishment of the A strain—a jazz chorus.

"King Porter Stomp" is a famously transitional piece that Morton claimed to have written in 1902, the year he elected for genesis. He said he submitted it to Joplin and won his approval. It combines ragtime structure with a stomp episode that became anthemic in the swing era when Fletcher Henderson turned it into a big band riff chorus. Morton himself did not adapt it for his recording ensembles, but he did arrange one of the most melodious of his stomps, "The Pearls," which began life as an ABACC piano solo, initially recorded in 1923. In that performance, the stomp aspect is muted, yet the piece demonstrates a rapprochement with Tin Pan Alley in combining two sixteen-bar strains with a closing thirty-two bar chorus. When he rerecorded it as a piano solo in 1926 (the same year he arranged it for the Red Hot Peppers), he added a pronounced fourth-beat stomp in B and freely embellished the final choruses.

By the time of the first Peppers session, in 1926, Morton was a seasoned musician who could order, edit, and transform various musical elements and influences with unequivocal conviction. His insistence on hiring three clarinets to play the trio strain of "Dead Man Blues" or obtaining a Klaxon horn for an effect on "Sidewalk Blues" typifies the certainty with which he conceived each piece. Yet the records were not initiated as an end in themselves. Melrose Publishing, which had made a pile with Morton's "Wolverine Blues" and owned the rights to many of his other songs, figured recordings by a band would boost their sheet-music sales and urged Victor to sign him. Though they never performed outside a studio, the Red Hot Peppers were billed as "The Number One Hot Band." In those insuperable sessions, Morton consolidated his instincts for formalism and spontaneity, and fused the racial divisions that marked his adolescence—educated Creoles of color in his own neighborhood and self-taught blacks uptown. He hired homeboys from both communities.

Morton scored first time out. "Black Bottom Stomp" is an exuberant example of his ability to fully exploit seven musicians while dodging disarray. The opening strain, blaring with daring mirth, suggests military pomp filtered by irony and typifies his gift for highly rhythmic melodies. It consists of four four-bar figures that imitate the call-and-response of a preacher and his congregation, the rhythm varying between a Charleston stop-time (for the preacher) and a stable four/four. The second strain, which animates the improvisations, combines an eight-bar blues and a twelve-bar blues and is dramatically heightened by the inclusion of two-bar breaks ("it's always necessary to arrange some kind of spot to make a break," he counseled). In the closing episode, he employs one of his favorite devices for increasing tension: the ensemble states the theme, then repeats it exactly, except for the addition of trombone smears and a break.

That device is achieved with greater subtlety in "Dead Man Blues," as a clarinet trio plays a charming theme alone and then again with the mild shading of a trombone. In the best of the Peppers, Morton makes you aware of the unique properties of each instrument: the tailgate glissandi of the trombone, the sparkling snap of the trumpet, the prettiness of the clarinet, the brazen rhythms of the banjo. "Dead Man Blues" is Morton's interpretation of the traditional New Orleans funeral, which he traced to scriptural injunction: Rejoice at the death and cry at the birth. In case the listener fails to appreciate his intentions, which in 1926 would have been more than likely in most parts of the country, he opens the performance with vaudeville dialogue to set the scene. A somber march, condensed from the hymn "Flee as a Bird to the Mountain," leads to the helium-light first strain—as graceful an example of New Orleans polyphony as exists on record. You can almost see the Grand Marshal prancing nimbly with his gaily colored parasol at the head of a funeral procession. The second strain is written for solo trumpet, and the third for clarinets, which leads to a reprise of the ensemble episode.

Other high-water marks are "Sidewalk Blues," which employs stop-time (the articulation of some beats and not others), ensemble turnbacks (junctures between choruses or segments of choruses), another twice-told trio (this time enhanced by Morton's piano), and an automobile horn; "The Chant," a New Orleans Rhythm Kings tune dressed up in Charleston rhythms, wacking cymbals, a brass riff with clarinet counterpoint, and ensemble breaks; and "The Pearls" and "Grandpa's Spells," vivid orchestrations of pieces written for piano. Morton brought controlled euphoria to composed jazz, as Oliver and Armstrong had to improvised jazz. In "Smoke House Blues," he fills what should have been a piano break with the lament, "Oh, Mr. Jelly!" as though notes could never fully express his feelings.

Yet for all its bite and pleasure, Morton's music was out of sync with '20s New York. He was not averse to infecting records with hokum and sentimentality, but he wasn't much good at condescension. Ultimately, he took up the gauntlet dropped at his feet by Henderson and Ellington and Webb and enlarged his unit, succeeding where Oliver had failed in adapting the New Orleans style to a big band. The results are uneven, yet fascinating. "Sweet Anita Mine" is a soufflé for twelve musicians, marred by a tacky clarinet solo, with a transitional passage for reeds that shows he had been listening to Frank Trumbauer. On "New Orleans Bump," he effectively acknowledged the jungly timbres that were packing them in at the Cotton Club. "Burnin' the Iceberg" is more indigenous, a roaring blues that, after two stop-time choruses, changes into a sixteen-measure theme heightened by repetition and textural alterations. The bubbly octet "Little Lawrence" boasts a catchy harmonic pattern that moves from major to minor and jaunty solos by an impressive crew, including Ellington's first trumpet star, Bubber Miley. And there is more: "Mr. Jelly Lord," with Johnny and Baby Dodds; "Mournful Serenade," a quartet based on Oliver's "Chimes Blues"; "Ponchartrain," something of a sequel to "Dead Man Blues"; and "Blue Blood Blues," an important outing for clarinetist Albert Nicholas. Yet by 1930, Morton was considered out of date, and Victor threw in the towel.

One aspect of Morton's talent, his singing, was all but ignored in the days of the Peppers, as though he considered it unworthy, a holdover from vaudeville. He was an outstanding jazz singer, by turns dramatic and touching and flamboyant. But except for an explosive minstrel-like foray on "Doctor Jazz" (the "Roll Over Beethoven" of its day), Morton hardly sang at all until the last, desperate phase of his life. This is part of the enduring Morton mystery. After Victor declined to renew his contract, he vanished from records and public view for eight long years. Did he have no inkling and was there no one to tell him that singing might have transformed his cycle of hard luck, that singing was a more respectable response to changing tastes than joyless farce?

Not until the final act, when, unlike Welles, Morton was barely acknowledged in his own business, did he casually record unforgettable vocal performances of "Winin' Boy," "Sweet Substitute," "I Thought I Heard Buddy Bolden Say," "Mamie's Blues," "Mr. Jelly Lord," and others as good, either for General, a tiny label later acquired by Commodore, or the Library of Congress, which released its tapes years after his 1941 death. (He also recorded a few vocals during his brief comeback at Victor in 1939, but they tend to be less effective.) Morton's disappearance in the '30s has never been satisfactorily explained.

What demons pushed him off the map? Surely, it wasn't just the specter of bobby-sox aesthetics. Yet that's what many cranks argued: "cheap commercial music" was the culprit, according to Rudi Blesh, who insisted that "printed scores are not a part of jazz." Never mind Morton's own scores, which were notated down to the bass lines. The '30s were years in which Armstrong, Ellington, Fats Waller, Cab Calloway, and Ethel Waters enjoyed unprecedented success. A man with the performing abilities of Morton as bandleader, pianist, and singer should have been able to negotiate his way through that crest in black entertainment. The success of "King Porter Stomp" alone ought to have revived his fortunes to the point where he could at least finance a band and get decent work. By all accounts, the problem seems to have been one of character—his and that of onlookers who enjoyed seeing him brought low. The stubborn, loudmouthed dandy with diamond tooth and stickpin was due for a comeuppance. Jelly was temperamentally unsuited to the era, and no one helped him turn the corner.

❖ ❖ ❖

Morton's stock has of necessity risen and fallen according to the availability of his music. The reputation of no figure of comparable importance has been quite so vulnerable to the impulses of one record company. The Morton revival didn't begin to transcend the true believers until 1959, when RCA issued a compilation (billed on the jacket as "Dixieland Jazz") of sixteen Morton masterpieces, *The King of New Orleans Jazz*. They made one mistake by inadvertently including the "wrong" take of "Dead Man Blues," but even that was fortuitous. The alternate, though marred by a flawed trumpet solo, achieves a buoyancy in the ensemble passages beyond that in the master take. In the '60s, the fine RCA-Vintage series released most of the remaining Victors in entertaining and non pedantic sets that juxtaposed the ludicrous and the sublime.

By the mid-'70s, however, the Red Hot Peppers were available only as multi volume chronological imports from RCA's French operation. His music was then in the forefront of jazz repertory, thanks to Dick Hyman, Bob Greene, and Martin Williams's office at the Smithsonian, but Morton himself was largely invisible, except for the 1923 piano solos collected on Milestone. The Commodores and Vocalions were in and out of print in a flash, and the Library of Congress series remained a rare collector's item. One of the most enterprising and genuinely witty minds in American music was once again out of the loop. His name is rarely mentioned by critics who came of age in the '70s and '80s.

At the close of 1990, to honor a centennial that was otherwise shamefully ignored, Bluebird (RCA) issued *His Complete Victor Recordings*, a handsomely packaged set of five compact discs that includes the seventy-four titles he recorded between 1926 and 1930 and during his brief return in 1939, as well as thirty-eight alternate takes. This should have done the trick, but the potential significance of the release was undermined by technological caprice. The label and producer relied on a digital process developed by Sonic Solutions called NO NOISE, which produced quiet surfaces at the expense of musical vitality. Like so many other CDs issued in that period (RCA and Columbia were the worst offenders), the high and low frequencies were deleted along with the static, and the music was cramped in airless midrange. The presentation was particularly disappointing because the producer, Orrin Keepnews, was a prominent figure in the Morton revival of the '50s and '60s.

The Bluebird discs reduce Morton's music to the echoes of a metallic ghost. The sad irony is that the original Victor sound was exceptionally good for its time, unlike, say, the 1923 King Oliver Gennetts, which demand of the listener great patience, if not a trained ear. This particular desecration was simply one of the most heartbreaking among many in the rush to speed digitally processed product to the stores. Numerous musicians, from Louis Armstrong to Miles Davis, were treated as ingloriously. But they had long since achieved unwavering recognition. Morton, having fallen between the cracks, was now lost in the grooves. The ambience of his music was gone along with the pulsing rhythmic bottom of bass or tuba. The swelling and decaying shhhhhhh! of the cymbal sounded like a pot falling on Formica, and the piano might as well have been covered by a blanket.

Just how detrimental the sound is was made clear by the simultaneous release of the Morton Victors on a small English label called JSP, supervised by an exacting engineer, John R. T. Davies, whose exemplary work is a model for reprocessing archival jazz. A comparison of the JSP and Bluebird CDs was a terrible revelation of how critical an engineer's input can be in properly reproducing music that we who are not audiophiles tend to think of as immutable. The JSP edition, poorly distributed Stateside, became an instant collector's item, while Bluebird—despite great leaps in digital technology (even at Sonic Solutions)—declined to rectify its fiasco.

Alan Lomax's Library of Congress interviews with Morton were also in limbo. In 1990, an independent American label, Solo Art, issued the first of eight promised volumes (remastered by the meticulous Jack Towers with speed and pitch corrections by John R. T. Davies), but was enjoined from continuing by legal issues. Four years later, Rounder Records won the rights to release the Library of Congress recordings and elected to release four CDs, excerpting all the musical fragments without the commentary they are meant to illuminate. A few new selections (once considered too risque for home listening) are included, but the absence of Morton's guff and wisdom is deeply disappointing. As of 1998, this matchless historical document, financed by tax dollars, has been generally unavailable for almost four decades.

Why is it important? Under Lomax's eager prodding, Morton keeps up a march-like vamp on the piano while ruminating on his past. He is so compelling an anecdotalist, you don't mind his pontificating. After declaring that he wrote the first stomp, he says he doesn't know what *stomp* means, but that he coined the term. His famous demonstration of how "Tiger Rag" evolved from a French quadrille is an essential music lesson (as are his displays of the evolution of "Maple Leaf Rag" and the ways in which Verdi's *Miserere* was made to serve the purposes of jazz). Best of all, he sings "Mr. Jelly Lord," "The Jelly Roll Blues," and "Alabamy Bound" in his thick, whiskey-stained drawl, sustaining an incomparably langorous tempo that delineates a world that disappeared long ago but seems bracingly familiar all the same.

10 ❖ King Oliver
(Working Man Blues)

To anyone for whom the music of King Oliver is a source of continuous and deepening delight, the disproportionate attention paid to his historical and mythic station rather than to his art is puzzling and frustrating. But not entirely surprising. The acoustic recording techniques in use during the year of Oliver's most consequential records, 1923, were better at capturing sounds than reproducing them. The question of his genius became a matter of faith, sworn to by sympathetic and imaginative listeners undaunted by surface noise or primitivism. The first obstacle ought to disappear. Digital remastering, cautiously executed, can work miracles, as Thomas G. Stockham, Jr., proved with Caruso recordings two decades older than Oliver's, and as Jack Towers, John R. T. Davies, Robert Parker, and others have demonstrated with classic jazz recordings (alas, only for small independent labels). In time, they will surely remaster all of Oliver's important music; Parker's first two CD compilations show how dramatic the improvement in texture and clarity can be—his transfer of "Dippermouth Blues" is so vivid you may feel, as I did, that you are hearing the real Oliver for the first time.

The primitivism issue may be harder to dispel, as it became ingrained in the very rhetoric that worked to establish Oliver's importance in jazz history. He is chiefly famous for two things: he was Louis Armstrong's mentor (since the '50s, his records have often been reissued under Armstrong's name), and he led the first black New Orleans ensemble to triumph up north in clubs and on records. One can applaud those achievements without feeling obliged to penetrate the hiss and crackle of a Neanderthal's 78s. Yet the Oliver admirer is surprised that anyone would want to talk about his music in terms of obligation. The essence of his relatively small, flawed body of work is a rollicking, plangent, sensuous collectivization of musical wills that not even Armstrong could replicate. As a cornetist, his impassioned playing reaches us across the decades, conveying a solitary dignity, a pain and urgency, even as it spurs his cohort to action.

Joseph Oliver was born on Dryades Street in New Orleans in 1885, or so it is generally believed. Most of the facts have been disputed: a plantation outside the city has been proposed as his place of birth, and his birth date has on extremely slim evidence been estimated at one to eight years earlier. While still in his midteens, he lost his left eye, presumably in a brawl. He started on trombone, switched to cornet, and was touring with a brass band by the turn of the century. About that time, he was heard by Dr. Edmond Souchon "blasting the heavens and shaking the blackberry leaves in funeral parades through the fringes of his neighborhood." He worked in numerous marching and cabaret bands, including one led by Kid Ory, who billed him as King Oliver—a sobriquet he was said to have earned a few years before when he cut Freddie Keppard one night in Storyville. At the request of bassist Bill Johnson, who had left New Orleans for California in 1909 but found a more auspicious climate for jazz in Chicago in early 1918, Oliver went north. Within two years, he was leading one band at the Dreamland Cafe until 1 A.M. and a second band at the Pekin Cabaret till dawn.

After a two-year sojourn with Ory in California, where work proved increasingly hard to find, he returned to Chicago and on June 17, 1922, introduced his Creole Jazz Band at the Lincoln Gardens Cafe, a large balconied ballroom with a revolving cut-glass ball that refracted the light. By now Oliver had been playing more than twenty years. He knew the importance of surrounding himself with disciplined musicians, and with one exception his recruits were Orleanians: Bill Johnson, his original sponsor in Chicago; trombonist Honore Dutrey, who had become asthmatic in the navy; and the Dodds brothers, Johnny on clarinet and Baby on drums. The original pianist, Bertha Gonsoulin, was replaced in the fall by Memphis-born Lillian Hardin. A week or so after opening night, Oliver wired New Orleans for a second trumpeter, his one-time apprentice, Louis Armstrong. Commentators have argued over Oliver's motive. Did he feel the need to compensate for his own failing powers or to reproduce the double-cornet lead of Bill Johnson's 1918 band (in which Freddie Keppard is said to have briefly played) or to keep Little Louis from the competition? One has only to listen to the records to *know* why. It made momentous musical sense. The band was a sensation, and its most widely noted effects were double-cornet breaks, seemingly improvised on the spot, yet played in perfect unison.

Young musicians, black and white, sat openmouthed as they listened to the Creole Jazz Band. They were impressed by its deep blues feeling, its rhythmic vitality, and its refusal to stoop to the barnyard antics popularized by the Original Dixieland Jazz Band. In *We Called it Music*, Eddie Condon wrote about the first time he heard Oliver's band:

> Oliver lifted his horn and the first blast of "Canal Street Blues" hit me. It was hypnosis at first hearing. Everyone was playing what he wanted to play and it was all mixed together as if someone had planned it with a set of micrometer calipers; notes I had never

heard were peeling off the edges and dropping through the middle; there was a tone from the trumpets like warm rain on a cold day. [Bud] Freeman and [Jimmy] McPartland and I were immobilized; the music poured into us like daylight running down a dark hole. The choruses rolled on like high tide, getting wilder and more wonderful. Armstrong seemed able to hear what Oliver was improvising and reproduce it himself at the same time. It seemed impossible, so I dismissed it; but it was true.

Armstrong, in the original typescript of his autobiography, wrote that those impossible breaks began the first night he arrived in Chicago:

We cracked down on the first note and that band sounded so good to me after the first note that I just fell right in like old times. Papa Joe really did blow that horn. The first number went down so well we had to take encore, that was the moment Joe Oliver and I developed a little system whereby we didn't have to write down the duet breaks. I was so wrapped up in him and lived his music that I could take second to his lead in a split second.

The impact of the Dodds brothers was also great. Born in 1892, Johnny had studied clarinet with the legendary tutor Lorenzo Tio, Jr., although his artistic inspiration was Sidney Bechet. He toured the South with Kid Ory between 1911 and 1917, played the riverboats with Fate Marable, and worked with Oliver in Chicago as early as 1919. He had neither Bechet's virtuosity nor Jimmie Noone's polish, but he was a compelling bluesman with a stinging tone. Though upright, sober, and proud in his personal life, he was nicknamed Toilet by musicians who admired his earthy conception. In the best of his solos with Oliver, such as "Canal Street Blues" and "Dippermouth Blues," his every note is fire. He's everywhere on the Creole Jazz Band records, spinning lattice work through the ensemble or shaping vertigenous breaks. He could be surprising, too: his whispy second break on "Weather Bird Rag" has been called a parody of white Dixieland clarinetists; his breaks on "Alligator Hop" are so genteel some critics have argued it isn't him at all.

It's difficult to grasp the contribution of Warren "Baby" Dodds to Oliver's band since on records he was forced to use woodblocks and tone down his style so as not to disturb the delicate equipment. Seven years Johnny's junior, he was widely considered the best of the New Orleans drummers, idolized by Dave Tough and Gene Krupa, and rivaled only by Zutty Singleton. Armstrong wrote of his role in the Creole Jazz Band, "To watch him play, especially when he beat on the rim of his bass in a hot chorus, he sort of shimmied when he beat with his sticks. Oh! Boy that alone was in my estimation the whole worth of the price of admission." Little of that comes through on Oliver's sides, but you can hear his slashing cymbal spur the climax on Armstrong's "Willie the Weeper," and his press rolls enliven Bechet's "Save It, Pretty Mama." On a Folkways album recorded in 1946, Dodds demonstrated the distinction between playing a two-beat with Oliver and four/four with Armstrong. Jo Jones recorded a rollicking homage to Baby's "shimmy" beat on his survey *The Drums*.

If King Oliver's skills as a cornetist earned him his title, his untitled apprentice reluctantly usurped him. More than anything else, Armstrong's own work on records from 1925 make the older man's tone and phrasing sound antiquated. Oliver's contemporaries didn't see it that way, and to be sure, he had a profound impact on the next generation of jazz trumpet players, not only through his world famous disciple, but in his innovative work with mutes. The "jungle style" as developed in the Ellington orchestra via Bubber Miley reflected Oliver's way with a plunger; the Harmon company even manufactured a mute in the '20s designed to replicate Oliver's wa-wa sound—it would provide a link between him and such modernists as Harry Edison and Miles Davis. Indeed, the wa-wa effects created for keyboards and guitars in the rock era can be traced to Oliver's plaintive style.

Yet Oliver's cornet was never particularly imposing in isolation. We can hear his instrument most clearly in his accompaniments to blues singers and in electrically recorded collaborations with Jelly Roll Morton and Eddie Lang, but, putting aside his rapid physical decline (he suffered from pyorrhea, a gum disease), little in his conception beyond the singularity of his timbre compels our admiration in an era dominated by Armstrong and Beiderbecke. That's hardly the case with the Creole Jazz Band recordings. Here he is every inch a king, no more supplanted by the beneficiaries of his invention than they are by subsequent innovators. His fierce muted lead, the eloquently modulated and often imploring breaks, need no apology. It isn't simply that he was in better health in 1923, but that for the only year of his benighted recording career he had a band that perfectly complemented his impulses as an instrumentalist.

Oliver could play solo riffs with biting power, but that was a secondary gift: what he could do better than any one else was drive an ensemble that specialized in improvised polyphony. Holding to a steady, impervious tempo at which several instruments simultaneously riffed with abandon, yet didn't trip one another up, he created a music that is at once the apex of traditional New Orleans style and so far beyond its norm that there is little to compare with it. The Creole Jazz Band seems to float in the air, a great hovering hydra playing all the instruments in perfect accord. Oliver's cornet provides more than just the lead; remove it and the heart and depth are gone—through him all the forces of the ensemble find just proportion, each chorus multilayered but uncluttered. The same cornet style that may wither in the relatively naked settings of duets and blues singers glows with a dark audacity in the Creole Jazz Band. Oliver's stately tempos additionally underscore his alert authority.

In April of 1923, Oliver brought the band to the Gennett Studios in Richmond, Indiana, to record nine sides. Later that year, they recorded eight more titles for Gennett, of which four were approved for release; twenty for the OKeh Company in Chicago, of which nineteen were released, and five for Paramount. The masters for unissued performances, including numerous alternate takes, were destroyed. The Creole Jazz Band survives in just thirty-seven performances. They are not especially diverse in form, based for the most part on strains of twelve and sixteen measures, from basic blues to pop chord progressions, in a handful of keys— usually C, F, B-flat, E-flat, A-flat. Perhaps the most startling of the Gennetts is "Working Man Blues": Oliver stepped right up to the recording device for his final chorus, which consists mostly of three-note phrases punched against the second beat of each measure. Also noteworthy are the two double-cornet breaks and the measures immediately following them, where the unison phrases disperse.

By far the most famous of Oliver's solos is "Dippermouth Blues"— three choruses, each pinned to a simple riff figure, exemplifying Oliver's vocalized intonation. That solo was imitated for two decades and was orchestrated for Fletcher Henderson's band as "Sugar Foot Stomp." "Working Man" and "Dippermouth" were recorded again for OKeh, and the second, faster version of the latter, in which Oliver's solo is preceded by a chorus of Armstrong's lead cornet, was probably the most popular of Creole Jazz Band records, enjoying brisk sales in January 1924.

Armstrong's first solos are heard on the Gennetts, and though they are negligible by the standards he was to set two years later, they constitute one of the most astonishing debuts in recording history. One needn't have a trained ear to be taken aback by his readings of the trio strains on "Froggy Moore" and especially "Chimes Blues." He doesn't improvise at all, but the declamatory tone and rhythmic dash are unmistakable, unlike anything recorded up to that time. His best playing with Oliver came at the OKeh sessions in his breaks on "Tears," which prefigure his mature phrasing, and his full chorus and coda on the majestic "Riverside Blues." The celebrated double-cornet breaks figure in "Snake Rag," "Where Did You Stay Last Night?" "Buddy's Habits," and perhaps the two finest examples of sustained ensemble propulsion,

"Chattanooga Stomp" and "I Ain't Gonna Tell Nobody." No less notable is the cornet counterpoint on "Mabel's Dream"; Oliver's dynamic lead during the last episode of "Sweet Lovin' Man"; the clarinet theme (played by Buster Bailey, according to Laurie Wright's research) on "Camp Meeting Blues," which was to be refurbished by Ellington as "Creole Love Song"; and the twice prophetic "Jazzin' Babies Blues," with its riffs that anticipate early midwestern territory bands and an Oliver solo that begins with a five-bar episode retained by Armstrong in his 1928 "Muggles." Among the band's last recordings for Paramount are two takes each of "Mabel's Dream" and "Southern Stomps" and a more incisive version of "Riverside Blues."

The Creole Jazz Band fell apart in 1924, but Oliver continued as a leader, though he attempted to modernize his later bands along the lines of the New York orchestras. In 1926, he introduced the ten-piece Dixie Syncopators, with three saxophones—his sidemen included such prominent straddlers of the '20s and '30s as Kid Ory, J. C. Higginbotham, Luis Russell, Barney Bigard, Albert Nicholas, Omer Simeon, and Johnny St. Cyr. Journeyman Bob Shoffner replaced Armstrong. Though the organic unity of the earlier group was sacrificed to written arrangements (the best are by saxophonist Billy Paige), the leader's vividly recorded cornet offers several epiphanies: his lead on "Snag It," the jubilant ride out on the lively if dated "Deep Henderson," his re-creation of the much celebrated "Dippermouth Blues" solo on "Sugar Foot Stomp," his deft vocalized solo on "Wa Wa Wa," and his brief, amiable invention on "Doctor Jazz." On the other hand, versions of "Farewell Blues," "West End Blues," "Lazy Mama," and "Speakeasy Blues" are arid, joyless attempts to catch up with the times. Two memorable cuts from 1928, "Aunt Hagar's Blues" and "I'm Watchin' the Clock," seemed to suggest the possibilty of a comeback, but the trumpet solos were actually played by Andy Anderson. From that point on, Oliver, his gums decaying and in constant pain, would delegate many solos.

By the time he traveled to New York in 1927, Oliver was king in name only. He worked the newly established Savoy Ballroom for a while, until Luis Russell left the band and took several musicians with him. Oliver organized pickup groups for a while, but at forty-three he was losing his teeth and suffering from a weak heart. He recorded for RCA in 1929 and 1930, usually with ten or twelve pieces, but in attempting to assimilate the Harlem style, he vitiated the rhythmic drive of his own music. The records are undistinguished, though a glimmer of the old verve can occasionally be found: his second sixteen measures on "I'm Lonesome Sweetheart," his counterpoint to Clinton Walker's tuba on "What You

Want Me To Do?" the cuffing riffs of "Struggle Buggy." The highlight of the RCAs is provided not by Oliver, but by Ellington trumpeter Bubber Miley, who expanded Oliver's work with mutes and showed what he could do on "St. James Infirmary."

Oliver couldn't play at all by 1935, though he continued to lead bands for two more years. Ailing and embittered by his own bad judgment (he turned down the 1927 job at the Cotton Club that made Duke Ellington famous), he finally settled in Savannah, Georgia, where he found work as a poolroom janitor and ran a fruit stand. He was broke but not yet broken when Armstrong, passing through Savannah with his orchestra, ran into him. In the '60s, Armstrong recalled the incident for Richard Merryman:

> He was standing there in his shirtsleeves. No tears. Just glad to see us. Just another day. He had that spirit. I gave him about $150 I had in my pocket, and Luis Russell and Red Allen, Pops Foster, Albert Nicholas, Paul Barbarin—they all used to be his boys—they gave him what they had. And that night we played a dance, and we look over and there's Joe standing in the wings. He was sharp like the old Joe Oliver of 1915. . . . A little time after we left Savannah, the owner of a bar, an old fan, give Joe a job as a flunky cleaning up—emptying those cuspidors like the ones he used to tap his foot on. And pretty soon he died [in 1938]—most people said it was a heart attack. I think it was a broken heart.

11 ❖ *Louis Armstrong*
(The Once and Future King)

I'd rather hear Louis Armstrong play "Tiger Rag" than wander into Westminster Abbey and find the lost chord.
                                        —Edward, Duke of Windsor

I agree with that.

                                        —Louis Armstrong

If the twentieth century has proven to be the American era in music—an assessment made with increasing frequency and growing confidence—it can also be characterized as the Armstrong era. In the decade before the Second World War, through the visionary genius of Louis Armstrong—whose place in jazz Dizzy Gillespie described as "unimpeachable"—a new music asserted itself in all its native glory. It changed the cultural direction of America and took possession of the world. To be sure, Irving Berlin had colonized Europe with "Alexander's Ragtime Band" in 1911, and Will Marion Cook's Southern Syncopated Orchestra had demonstrated in 1919 that, as conductor Ernst Ansermet famously predicted, African American music might be the "highway the whole world will swing along tomorrow." But Berlin and Cook belonged to the musical theater, which is where their influence was primarily assimilated. Armstrong defined an art that stood apart from its precursors. He didn't depend on spirituals or plantation songs or dance bands or country blues or the music hall to herald the much anticipated music of a newfound land, an analogue to the Brahmin mandate for an American literature. He was the thing itself, the transfiguring agent, the artist, the maker of masterworks that could withstand generations of shifting tastes and critical scrutiny.

He did not come from the most respectable of families; indeed, he and his music laughed in the face of Brahmin rectitude, not to speak of Brahmin education. Armstrong was the culmination of a hidden musical phylogeny that developed in the relative isolation of a cultural outland, black and southern. More specifically, he was the product of thirty years of musical customs unique to New Orleans that weren't tagged as *jazz* until they were successfully expurgated, tricked-up for laughs, and brought north by the white Original Dixieland Jazz Band in 1916. King Oliver arrived in Chicago three years later and installed his Creole Jazz Band at Lincoln Gardens in 1922, bringing that exuberant group-based style of improvised music to its highest plateau. All that was missing was the beacon of individuality: the artist who, incarnating the music's power, would continue a trajectory that had already taken it from picnics, funeral parades, and honky-tonks to fancy northern clubs with art deco appurtenances and overpriced drinks; the artist who would restructure the music according to the lights of his own imagination, thereby opening it to the imaginative powers of anyone who fell under its sway.

When Oliver cabled Armstrong to join him, he augured the end of his reign and the beginning of something he could scarcely have imagined and was unable to adapt. The timing was propitious. Numerous blacks relocated to Chicago to take advantage of the accelerated job market, guaranteeing an audience for migrating musicians. An improvised music thrives on technology, and Armstrong's apprenticeship ended just as electrical recording replaced the primitive acoustic method. (In part because Oliver's best recordings are acoustic, they partake of that primitivism, which is set in bold relief by Armstrong's radiantly recorded performances.) His arrival also coincided with the introduction of sound films, the triumph of live radio, and the coming of age of songwriters who retired moon/June and mother's-broken-heart bromides in favor of a poetic, knowing, grown-up verse that merited the interest of willful interpreters. Though deeply influenced by Oliver and inclined to hire his colleagues from the Creole Jazz Band, Armstrong's remaking of jazz and pop was total.

He manifested the rhythmic gait known as "swing," transformed a polyphonic folk music into a soloist's art, established the expressive profundity of blues tonality, demonstrated the durable power of melodic/harmonic improvisation, and infused it all with an irreverent wit—for to enter the world of Louis Armstrong is, as Constance Rourke wrote of Whitman, "to touch the spirit of American popular comedy." None of which should detract from the most prominent of Armstrong's strengths: he was a prodigiously gifted trumpet player. His famous "satchelmouth" provided him with the perfect equipment—strong teeth and leathery lips. He was not a virtuoso in the conventional sense in that he did not play the conventional trumpet repertory. Yet the unrivaled brilliance of his sound, complemented by his economical style, transformed the instrument's timbre and range not only in jazz, but in symphony orchestras and dance bands. He popularized the trumpet's upper range and unknowingly set in motion a revised model for the mastery of playing lead in a brass section. His career was in its early stages when musicians began to covet his authenticity and power, mimicking his personal manner; pundits routinely likened him to Gabriel. Philharmonic orchestras that once favored concision now used a heavier vibrato (the conductor Maurice Peress recalled that when he studied trumpet his teacher made the students listen to Armstrong records). Miles Davis said, "You know you can't play anything on the horn that Louis hasn't played—I mean even modern." Twenty years later Hannibal Marvin Peterson came to the same conclusion, "There's nothing on the trumpet that doesn't come from Louis Armstrong. Yeah, you could say there's nothing in jazz that doesn't come from him." Twenty years after that, Nicholas Payton echoed the sentiment: "He's the father of us all, regardless of style or how modern we get."

Seventy-five years after Armstrong made his first records, his stature is more secure than it was during his lifetime, when his enormous popularity engendered self-righteous fulminations. The serpent in the garden was his gregarious desire to please, which was misconstrued as a penchant for compromise. He was pilloried for enlarging the indigenous jazz repertory to include pop songs and for dividing his energies between

trumpet and voice. He never fit the paradigm of the serious artist, refusing to disown the blue jokes or refine his repertory or reduce the
mugging. To the original true believers, "West End Blues" was one
thing, "You Rascal You" quite another—though even the purists were
amused to learn that during his tour of Europe in 1933, he dedicated the
latter to the British crown, "This one's for you, Rex."

The anxiety began with his singing, which Fletcher Henderson forbade during the year Armstrong played in his band. Small wonder—
this was the age of boyish tenors, Irish tenors, cloying tenors, all sweet-
voiced and depressingly sincere. Armstrong's confidence in his vocal
powers (he finally persuaded Henderson to give him a brief scat break)
is interesting to contemplate, as it was initially more radical than his
trumpet, consisting of intensely rhythmic guttural effusions. Armstrong
is often credited with having invented scat (singing improvised nonsense
syllables), but the custom had long been established in New Orleans. Yet
he did far more than popularize the practice: he added scat's moans and
riffs to the palette of conventional song interpretation, employing them
to underscore emotion and rhythm and meaning. Ultimately his influence on popular and jazz vocal styles was no less sweeping than his
impact on instrumentalists.

Still, for several years no one shared his conviction concerning the
charms of his gravel pit of a voice. In attempting to explain Armstrong's
hold on the singers of his generation, Rudy Vallee acknowledged the
"utterly mad, hoarse, inchoate mumble-jumble that is Louis' 'singing',"
but insisted that "a subtle musical understanding and keen mind are
being manifest." He went on to identify "I Surrender Dear" as Armstrong's masterpiece—a curious choice in that it was a cover of Bing
Crosby's huge hit, a reciprocating homage to one singer who, unlike
Vallee, grasped and adapted Armstrong's innovations. Yet if Crosby was
the first to transmit—with his smooth and tranquil baritone—Armstrong's exemplary time, phrasing, and swing, Armstrong soon learned
to make his own singing accessible, revealing a wellspring of feeling that
required no intermediary.

By 1936, when Crosby brought him to Hollywood to appear in *Pennies
from Heaven*, Armstrong's popularity on stage, records, and radio was
immense, and with his tough-guy manager Joe Glaser pulling strings, he
used his renown to shatter racial obstacles while spreading the gospel of
jazz. Yet his demeanor was so at odds with highbrow prescriptions about
the way an artist is supposed to conduct himself that many of his admirers wished him to be more decorous. In several early reviews, admiring and critical, he is characterized as something of a monster—sa-

cred or profane or both. He has the face of a gargoyle, the daring of Prometheus, the glint of Satan, the energy of a demon. As the most popular Negro of any provenance in Western musical history to that point, and as an African American just two generations removed from slavery, Armstrong was an undeniable symbol of the age in which American music would rival and eventually trump that of Europe and Russia.

Yet he never abandoned a joyful and even roguish disposition that resembled the comic archetype Constance Rourke delineated in *American Humor* as the Negro minstrel, a role that remained a viable strain in black entertainment well into the twentieth century. Armstrong reveled in the role of entertainer, and in refusing to give it up, he defied and redefined Edwardian notions of art, artistry, and artists. His music was recognized immediately, albeit by a happy few, for a spirituality that shivered the nervous system and focused the mind in a manner reminiscent of Bach. And yet he remained stubbornly funny, bawdy, available, human. Audiences who expected to see the genius of the Hot Fives wear the mantle of a traditional concert artist were put off by what they perceived as coarseness. Here was the only figure in musical history—high or low, Western or other—whose singing was as influential as his musicianship, proving twice over that improvisation can yield not just the authority but the perfection of composition. So why was he playing to the groundlings?

Armstrong's transcendence of stereotypes continues to bother those who catch the spiritual uplift but mourn the absence of a suitably solemn presentation: James Lincoln Collier analyses the monster as a self-hating victim of racism; Gunther Schuller, discerning critic though he is, wishes America had given Armstrong an "honorary pension (as Finland did with Sibelius) to live out his life in dignity . . . without the need to scratch out a living as a good-natured buffoon, singing 'Blueberry Hill' and 'What a Wonderful World' night after night." But separating Armstrong the exalted musician from Armstrong the impish stage wag censures a magnanimous artist for the pitiful purpose of satisfying an outmoded appeal to "Kulchur," while underestimating the absurdist humor that informs his genius. His ability to balance the emotional gravity of an artist with the entertainer's communal good cheer helped demolish the Jim Crow/Zip Coon/Ol' Dan Tucker stereotypes prominent in the '20s. Thus he perpetuated the positive qualities of Rourke's Negro minstrel, which were respectfully mimicked by antebellum white minstrels as portraits of native humor, while undermining negative images prolonged by Reconstruction minstrels as demeaning caricatures. In their place he installed the sexy, stylish, African American black joker-artist whose music's undeniable splendor projects an equally undeniable spirit of freedom. Not the least significant measure of his luster is the continuing reluctance to tackle him whole. He endures as an outsized figure.

Spontaneous invention is the soul of jazz. The jazz musician doesn't view improvisation as optional, like a cadenza or a missing part. Nor is it the first step toward a completed score, as it was for Bach, or a spellbinding feat of audience manipulation, as it was for Beethoven, or an adventure in indeterminacy, as it is for twentieth-century new-music classicists. Improvisation is the jazz musician's richest form of expression. His object is to extemporize a perfect musical statement—predetermined song structures may provide the groundwork, but the substance of the solo is the measure of the artist. "If you don't feel it, you can't get it," Armstrong said. He illustrated his point with a music that seemed instinctive, seemed to embody whatever he was feeling and hearing at the moment. He accomplished this in part with expressive techniques such as half-valved effects, slurred notes, burnished glissandi, and fast tonguing. These were so effective that on one occasion doubters examined his instrument in search of trick valves and on another accused him of playing a slide trumpet. But Armstrong's powers were far more than the sum of his technical abilities. His dramatic and rhythmic talents were of a piece with an internal editor that permitted him to reshape songs to maximize their effectiveness. It is often said that he could make commonplace melodies worthy and worthy melodies vital, but he could also make commonplace melodies vital, from "West End Blues" to "Sittin' in the Dark" to "Jubilee." In the words of his British biographer, Max Jones, Armstrong infused his songs with "distinctive and ardent qualities that enchant or disturb a listener."

Armstrong's improvisations required more elbowroom than he could find in the traditional New Orleans ensemble. As no one before him had imparted as much contagious impiety and emotional poignancy, it was perhaps inevitable that he would be the one to refashion the ensemble around his own diverting personality. In effect, he changed jazz from a collective idiom, in which embellishments are conceived and limited by a group mentality, to a soloist's art with mutable boundaries tailored to the strengths of each player. Before Armstrong, jazz was relatively controlled, as folk musics are. After Armstrong, jazz had a life of its own that no one, try as they might (they did, they still do), could restrain. He made ur-modern, modern, supermodern, postmodern, and neomodern jazz inevitable. His vision, in effect, activated and accelerated what we loosely call "the jazz tradition." Yet at the same time, that vision—soaring, beautiful, racy, ironic, impetuous, mercurial, gleaming—separated him from contemporaries and successors whose inspiration and reach were less celestial. His musical universe, like Bach's, is complete and sovereign.

If the Armstrong trumpet soars, the Armstrong voice belongs to a more earthly realm. He transcended bad songs with so little effort that they all but disappear into the amplitude of his individuality. Although he became an emphatic interpreter of lyrics (his Porgy is a stark example), he was also capable of using the words of a song as musical conveniences, conveying no more meaning than scat syllables. Put another way, Armstrong didn't merely sell a song; he sold himself selling the song. The same could be said of most great vocal stylists, from Al Jolson to Ray Charles, but no one else made the verbal meaning of a song as subordinate to spontaneous musical impulses. Implicit in the liberties Armstrong took, and in the rise of jazz itself, is the assumption that musicians are superior to the songs they perform—a radical stance by classical principles, where a performance is evaluated by its fidelity to the text. In jazz, performance *is* the text.

Consequently, the crux of many jazz masterpieces is the degree of tension between the improviser and his material. This is especially true when the performer has been induced to record inferior songs, but also applies to great songs and compositions: the performer essaying Thelonious Monk's " 'Round Midnight" in the wake of a thousand versions must make something new and personal of its too familiar melody. By decisively illuminating the huge gap between jazz feelings and pop bromides, Armstrong introduced the notion (if not the lingo) of "Hip" and its negative face, "Corn." Hip is witty and daring. Corn is meretricious and safe. Hip, because it is honest and takes risks, may withstand passing fashions. Corn incarnates those fashions. Armstrong's rough and aberrant croon was ideal for making the case. In teaching America to swing, he liberated its vernacular voice—a bruising, teasing, gravel-throated everyman-voice that had been largely confined to the church, the backwoods, and the blues.

Armstrong was born in the poorest section of New Orleans, on a dark block of wooden ramshackle houses called Jane Alley, between Perdido and Gravier Streets, on August 4, 1901. His father left at once; his mother went to work in a nearby red-light district, leaving him in the care of his paternal grandmother until he was old enough to go to school, at which time he moved in with his mother, his younger sister, and a round of "stepfathers." From earliest adolescence, Louis helped to put food on the table, taking whatever odd jobs he could find in a district so ridden

by violence and vice that it was known as "the Battlefield." He might
have been sucked into its venomous whirlpool had his mother not had
relations in Boutee, a sugarcane community about seventy miles west of
New Orleans. Frequent trips to those sunny fields eased the hunger that
was a constant companion on Jane Alley, firmed his ties to his mother,
and opened his eyes to a gentler life and a more generous society. He
was also fortunate in winning the affection of an immigrant Jewish family, the Karmofskys, who fed him; taught him songs (they "instilled in
me singing from the heart"); put him to work selling junk, rags, and
coal; provided him with his first instrument, a tin horn; and enabled him
to buy his first cornet when he was eleven. He credited music and maternal affection with seeing him through the worst years, and somehow
he emerged relatively unscathed.

Louis had been singing in a street quartet when, in 1912, he became
enamored of the musicians who played on the stoops of the honky-tonks
in order to draw a crowd—he was especially taken with King Oliver.
For a while he was in danger of succumbing to the Battlefield. He
dropped out of school, quit working for the Karmofskys, picked through
bins of discarded produce, sold stolen newspapers, hustled coal to pros-
titutes, and begged musicians for pointers. In the early hours of January
1, 1913, he took a dare and fired six blanks from his stepfather's .38 into
the air. Collared for disturbing the peace, he was remanded to the Colored Waif's Home under the direction of Captain Joseph Jones, a former
cavalry officer and esteemed educator. It was the turning point in his
young life. Here he learned music, starting out on tambourine and drums
and progressing to bugle and cornet. After his release in 1914, he began
to sit in with his musical heroes when he wasn't shoveling coal or un-
loading boats. According to Pops Foster, he played only blues at first,
but under the tutelage of Kid Ory and especially Oliver, his talent quickly blossomed, and by 1917 he was playing most of the local repertoire.

A year later, when Oliver left New Orleans, Louis replaced him in
Ory's band, took a job with Fate Marable, whose Jazz Syncopators played
the Mississippi steamers, married a hot-tempered prostitute named Daisy, and adopted a retarded cousin whom he cared for all his life. That
same year, probably to disguise the fact that he was underage, he secured
a draft card that made him out to be a year older than he was. The birth
date he submitted—July 4, 1900—would become an ineradicable part of
jazz lore, a presentiment of the ambassadorial status he achieved. The
riverboats were floating ballrooms that employed the best southern musicians of the day and spread the music of New Orleans as far north as
St. Paul and Davenport, where Bix Beiderbecke is said to have first heard
Armstrong. Among his bandmates were Baby Dodds, Pops Foster, John-

ny St. Cyr, and a mellophonist named David Jones who helped him with his reading.

Armstrong was earning a reputation, and musicians traveled far to see if it was deserved. On one occasion when the riverboat docked in New Orleans, Louis learned that a young trombonist had hitchhiked from San Antonio to meet him. He idealized that first encounter with Jack Teagarden: "He was from Texas, but it was always, 'You a spade and I'm an ofay. We got the same soul. Let's blow'—and that's the way it was." He was beginning to write his own tunes, though his lack of business sense occasionally cost him credits and profits. He sold a tune called "Get Off Katie's Head" to two publishers who added a lyric and changed the title to "I Wish I Could Shimmy Like My Sister Kate," cutting him out of the copyright. He is also said to have written "Muskrat Ramble," which Kid Ory appropriated. When he wasn't working on the paddlewheels, Louis played in parades, at fairs and picnics, and in the honky tonks—dodging fights, bullets, and knives. He once attributed his '50s success with "Mack the Knife" to his intimate knowledge of outlaws as sinister as anything in Brecht.

In 1921, Fletcher Henderson heard Armstrong while touring the South with Ethel Waters and tried to lure him to New York. Louis begged off, saying he didn't want to leave his band, but he was ready to leave a year later, when his idol King Oliver wired him to come to Chicago. On the afternoon of August 8, he played a funeral with the Tuxedo Jazz Band, packed a small bag, grabbed a trout sandwich his mother fixed, and caught the evening train. The Armstrong discography begins with King Oliver's Creole Jazz Band recordings, made between April and December of 1923, which capture his declamatory tone and rhythmic dash in the trio sections of "Froggie Moore" and "Chimes Blues" and display at least a glimmer of the contrapuntal jousting between Oliver and Armstrong, as on "Mabel's Dream." In February 1924, he married the band's pianist, Lillian Hardin, who saw a greatness in him that he was slow to recognize himself. He could stand his ground among the transplanted good old boys of New Orleans, but he was none too sure about heading off on his own. Lil realized that he was overly devoted to Oliver and reluctant to leave. But she pressed him, and later that year he accepted an offer from Henderson.

The slick New York musicians initially treated him as a rube—compared to Henderson's well-schooled players and sartorial sharpies, he must have seemed laughably country. Coleman Hawkins could play anything, and Don Redman was the most prominent of the young black dance band arrangers. And Louis? He was the guy who blew full blast through a pianissimo marking during rehearsal, and when Henderson asked why he ignored the *pp* marking said he thought it meant "pound plenty!" The musicians didn't laugh long. With his heady rhythms and blues locutions, Armstrong triggered a massive reconsideration. He found New York a backwater of ornamental virtuosity; he left it a swinging cosmopolis. In the best tradition of Rourke's minstrel, the hick proved to be a trickster. Everyone he touched was transformed. Out went the plodding time and showy overstatement. Don Redman admitted, "I changed my style of arranging after I heard Louis Armstrong." He wasn't alone. Duke Ellington recognized Armstrong's might as the binding ingredient necessary to propel his music, too. On Paul Whiteman's side of the tracks, Bill Challis was stumping to feature the Armstrong-inspired Bix Beiderbecke in his arrangements and not the corn of the far better known (and paid) Henry Busse.

The evidence of his influence on Henderson is well documented in a comparison of the band's records made before, with, and after Armstrong. His driving theme statement on "Everybody Loves My Baby" is the only savory element in a desultory performance. The brasses can barely keep up with his sterling phrasing on "Copenhagen" and "Shanghai Shuffle." He made about forty records with Henderson, including "One of These Days" (a stirring solo) and Redman's orchestration of Oliver's "Dippermouth Blues," retitled "Sugar Foot Stomp," an opportunity for Armstrong to pay homage to his mentor. It was chiefly Henderson's refusal to let him sing that prompted him to quit the band after fourteen months. By then, the conversion process was fairly complete. Everything about Armstrong smacked of authenticity. In a day when many of the top young black musicians distanced themselves from the blues as a vestige of plantation days, medicine shows, and overdressed hot mamas, he reminded them how potent and varied and alchemical a language the blues could be. He radiated soul, energy, beauty.

Armstrong's recording activities in New York were not confined to Henderson. A wonderful series with the Clarence Williams Blue Five combined the raggy swing of southern vaudeville with the sweeping exuberance of a lean, New Orleans style ensemble and paired Armstrong with the one man who briefly seemed his equal as an improviser, soprano saxophonist and clarinetist Sidney Bechet. Four years his senior, Bechet was a far more sophisticated man, having left New Orleans in 1914. Except for a spell in 1916 when he returned to play with Oliver, Bechet worked throughout the United States before touring Europe with Will Marion Cook in 1919 (it was he who most excited Ernst Ansermet) and winning acclaim on his own in London and Paris—all this before Armstrong had taken the train to Chicago. His charged sound and trumpet-like phrasing complemented Armstrong's slashing articulation, and on one occasion—the Red Onion Jazz Babies' version of "Cake Walking Babies from Home"—Bechet nearly routs Armstrong, something no one, not even Bechet, would ever do again. The finest of the Blue Fives include a faster version of "Cake Walking Babies from Home"; "Papa De-Da-Da," an example of Armstrong's note bending and call-and-response interplay with the reeds; and the pièce de résistance, "Everybody Loves My Baby," an exceedingly rare example of his using a plunger mute in homage to Oliver.

Armstrong was also a prolific accompanist to blues and pop singers, most famously Bessie Smith, with whom he made nine sides, including an enchanting interpretation of "St. Louis Blues." He said of their work together, "She'd always have the words and tune in her head, and we'd just run it down once. Then she'd sing a few lines, and I'd play something to fill it in, and some nice, beautiful notes behind her. Everything I did with her, I *like*." Also notable are his three numbers with Ma Rainey and her Georgia Jazz Band (actually a group drawn from the Henderson orchestra) and two sessions with Bertha "Chippie" Hill, whose vivid style and good tunes ("Lonesome Weary Blues" and "Low Land Blues") inspired him. The singers he worked with were an uneven lot of blues, vaudeville, and nightclub performers. Among the best were Sippie Wallace (whose brother, Hersal Thomas, a talented blues pianist who died at seventeen, appears with them on "Special Delivery Blues"), Hociel Thomas ("Deep Water Blues" and "Sunshine Baby" with Hersal Thomas and Johnny Dodds), Maggie Jones ("Good Time Flat Blues"), Clara Smith ("Shipwrecked Blues"), Margaret Johnson ("Changeable Daddy"), and Eva Taylor ("You Can't Shush Katie"). Yet Armstrong was never more ingenious than in backing the worst, like the incomparably hapless Lillie Delk Christian, whose "Too Busy" is an epiphany of cross-purposes. She chirpily slogs through the first chorus without the remotest hint of swing, but after an instrumental passage in which Armstrong, Earl Hines, and Jimmie Noone pinch themselves awake, Armstrong sneaks up on her with an impromptu scat vocal that rattles her into action.

On November 12, 1925, in Chicago, Armstrong embarked on the most influential recording project in jazz, perhaps in American music. Over the next three years, he produced the sixty-five sides (not including those by singers or similar bands in which Armstrong appeared as a sideman) generally known as the Hot Fives and Hot Sevens. If Armstrong had put music aside after the December 12, 1928, session, he would not have exerted the full measure of his charisma as a singer; would not have recorded the dozens of nonpareil big band performances; would not have enjoyed the pop hits and movies; would not have matured and mellowed over time into an even more expressive instrumentalist and singer; would not have achieved international renown; would not even have earned the nickname Satchmo. But he would still be the most eminent figure in jazz history.

Like the Creole Jazz Band, the Hot Five—Armstrong, Johnny Dodds, Kid Ory, Lil Armstrong, Johnny St. Cyr—was made up of musicians who, excepting the Memphis-born and university-trained Lil, hailed from New Orleans. Unlike Oliver's group, the original Hot Five and its successors existed only to make records; they are not known to have played a single engagement before an audience. For most of that period, Armstrong earned his bread as a featured performer with orchestras: Erskine Tate's pit band at the Vendome Theater and Carroll Dickerson's dance band at the Sunset Cafe. In the relative privacy of Chicago's OKeh studio, Armstrong directed a measured yet rapid assault on jazz practices, supplanting group embellishment with solo improvisation, two- and four-bar breaks with entire ad-lib choruses, and the multiple refrains of ragtime with theme and variations patterned on the blues and songs.

OKeh was founded in 1916, and two years later led the other labels in capitalizing on the Original Dixieland Jazz Band craze, recording another white band, called New Orleans Jazz Band (all the members were from New Orleans except music director and pianist Jimmy Durante). But in 1920, OKeh broke the color line in recording Mamie Smith and was besieged with orders from black communities. The company started a subsidiary, OKeh Race. It installed state-of-the-art acoustical recording equipment, hired Clarence Williams as music director, and became the leading purveyor of jazz, blues, and gospel records over the next decade. Armstrong's OKehs instantly made the rounds among musicians and were avidly collected by young white enthusiasts, many of whom had already been drawn to the music by Oliver, the New Orleans Rhythm Kings, and other benchmark bands. But the primary audience was in black areas, where the records were stocked in all kinds of stores and quickly sold. As Doc Cheatham recalled, "You were very lucky to find one of Louis's records." The loyalty of the so-called race market encouraged OKeh to record him as frequently as possible.

The Hot Five got off to a cautious start at the first session, completing three releasable numbers: Armstrong's solo on "My Heart" is built on a lick that prefigures by five years the pop song "Them There Eyes," "Yes I'm in the Barrel" opens with an attention-getting riff before moving into tempo, and his best solo of the day is on "Gut Bucket Blues." But the genial introductions he provides for each of the musicians is even more striking. Imagine the formal, dignified King Oliver doing such a thing! Even speaking, the cadences of his voice project a promiscuous self-confidence. He is a man in charge of his talent and of the world in which it thrives—adult, secure, generous. Of the two pop geniuses working in America in the '20s, Charlie Chaplin and Louis Armstrong, Chaplin celebrated the Little Man, but took care to distinguish his own gentility from the everyman he invented; Armstrong insisted he *was* the Little Man—and the equal of any Big Man.

The group came into its own at the highly productive second session, which occasioned a major double-sided hit in "Muskrat Ramble" and "Heebie Jeebies." The former became an immediate Dixieland standard (so enduringly popular that a rock-and-roll version was done in the early '60s), but the performance is more a rousing consolidation of the New Orleans style than a flight to new ground. "Heebie Jeebies" is another story entirely, though once again Armstrong makes the difference with his voice, not his trumpet. Indeed, the journeyman performance has little to recommend it until he bursts forth in a torrent of staccato grunts and groans in no known language. This isn't the smooth oo-bop-sh'bam or shooby-dooby-do of postwar lounge scat, but a volcanic throat-clearing:

> Eh, eef, gaff, mmff, dee-bo, deedle-la-bahm,
> Rip-rip, de-doo-de-doo, de-doo-de-doo, da-de-da-da-do,
> Ba-do-de-do-do-doo, ba-ro-be-do-be-do, dat. . . .

Armstrong liked to tell how his scat vocal was nothing more or less than an instance of quick thinking—the lead sheet slipped to the ground and he bopped to save the take. Considering his unsuccessful struggle with Fletcher Henderson for a chance to sing, one suspects that if the sheet music did fall, he knocked it off the stand. In any case, he got the response that he and surely no one else anticipated. Scat was on the map and not only did his many admirers want to follow suit, but they wanted his voice as well. As Earl Hines noted, musicians were sticking their heads out of windows trying to catch colds to sound like Louis.

Yet "Heebie Jeebies" was not the crown of the session. "Cornet Chop Suey," which Armstrong later said he wrote on a staircase during an outing in Chicago, represented a more significant breakthrough, with its exciting sixteen-bar episode of stop-time breaks and beautifully phrased eighth-note figures replete with melodic ideas that were copied for years to come. From the martial cadences of his intro, Armstrong is the whole show—the soloist triumphant. The other instruments are no longer front-line partners, but a second-line backup. The number was a warning and a warm-up.

The masterpiece of the Hot Fives was recorded twenty months later, after the Hot Sevens, by which time he was an old hand in the studio. "Struttin' With Some Barbecue" is built on a major seventh in the manner of the 1959 bossa nova classic, "Samba de Orpheus." Armstrong's twelve-bar intro, based on a two-bar ascending riff, precedes a traditional theme statement, but his hallelujah chorus (the object of several modernist homages) stops tradition in its tracks: urged on by offbeat banjo accents, he unveils a dazzling cache of devices—rips, triplets, a breathless glissando—before arcing climactically over the ensemble.

On three pieces, the Hot Five is augmented by the pioneer guitarist Lonnie Johnson. Known in later years as a blues singer (his "Tomorrow Night" was the best-selling r & b record of 1948), Johnson was greatly admired by the most advanced jazz musicians in the '20s. Ellington drafted him to play a rollicking counterpoint to Baby Cox's homage-to-Armstrong vocal on "The Mooche." He also helped ignite the Chocolate Dandies, backed many singers from Clara Smith to Martha Raye, and recorded spellbinding duets with the white guitarist Eddie Lang, who renamed himself Blind Willie Dunn for the occasion. Johnson plays a key role on Armstrong's "I'm Not Rough," shadowing the three trumpet choruses with trills, providing the sole accompaniment for the vocal, and bearing down in the final passages with fourth-beat accents. His startling twelve-bar solo is made up entirely of evenly articulated triplets (a strangely prophetic ploy because it was the overdubbing of a vocal choir and adamant triplets that made "Tomorrow Night"—a modest seller in its initial version—a megahit). He seems to spur Armstrong to a greater level of abandon, one that nearly upsets the band's balance on the lamely rural (despite the title) "Savoy Blues."

Then there is "Hotter Than That," based on a strain of "Tiger Rag" and rich with astonishments. After an eight-bar introduction, Armstrong revels in the theme, bursting into a break at bar fifteen, the melodic content of which appeared in many guises over the next decade (the Ink Spots sing it on "Java Jive"). What should have been Armstrong's second break (bars thirty-one to thirty-two) functions instead as a relay point to introduce Johnny Dodds. Armstrong in turn takes up the relay from Dodds, only this time he sings a rhythmically devious scat chorus, upping the ante with cross-rhythms in bars sixteen to twenty-six—his finest vocal to date. He then sings two-bar exchanges with Johnson's guitar, foreshadowing the voice/clarinet interchange on "West End Blues." A piano transition and trombone solo provide a brief lull before the storming climax, a trumpet break and solo in which Armstrong parses twelve high Cs over seven bars. The pacific conclusion is a reprise of two-bar exchanges between trumpet and guitar.

❖ ❖ ❖

In early 1927, the bandleader Carroll Dickerson was fired from the Sunset Cafe, and Armstrong inherited the job. Fronting his first band in a major club, he now felt he had more clout in drafting the orchestra's ace musicians, among them Earl Hines, for his records. But he moved carefully. For three sessions in May, he made a few changes: he added Pete Briggs's tuba and Baby Dodds's drums and replaced Kid Ory with John Thomas. This was the Hot Seven, and its eleven recordings exhibit a substantially richer texture and—is it possible?—a more inventive and assured Armstrong. The overpowering "Potato Head Blues," its intrepidly military theme evoking the brass band roots of New Orleans jazz, is the band's monument. A charged Johnny Dodds solo and a banjo break set up Armstrong's electrifying stop-time chorus (propelled by the band's first-beat accents on alternate bars)—a celebration of self that borders on arrogance, yet never sacrifices the emotional urgency of the moment. His syncopations are spellbinding, his lead work in the final chorus ecstatic. A hot seller for OKeh, "Potato Head Blues" exemplified a level of musicianship that must have awed even King Oliver.

Bold solos by Armstrong and Dodds on "Wild Man Blues," a collaboration between Armstrong and Jelly Roll Morton, relegate the ensemble to a supporting role. "S.O.L. Blues" and "Gully Low Blues" are alternate versions of the same piece (the former was suppressed until 1940 because of its risque lyric and shit-out-of-luck acronym), each distinguished by Armstrong's mighty descending arpeggios—a motive that would reappear at the acme of "West End Blues." Dodds plays an impassioned solo at the outset of "Weary Blues," a prelude to a tortuous takeoff by Armstrong that lifts him into unexpectedly high ground, from which he drives home a dynamic finish. Baby Dodds earned his keep on "Willie the Weeper," goading the final chorus with his cymbal. "Twelfth Street Rag" renovates a piece that must have seemed innocuously raggy even in 1927. "Melancholy" has an eloquent melody, not unlike "I Ain't Got Nobody," that New Orleans revivalists were singing thirty-five years later as "St. Louis Street Blues."

For nearly a century, American music had made its way pell mell with martial airs, sentimental ballads, secularized psalms, and rhythm numbers that accented the first and third beats of the measure. The mixture was as rigidly informal and predictable as the comic sketches, melodramas, and minstrel turns that sufficed for American theater—and, as such, was equally unfocused and unassimilable. American black music, much acclaimed in the years following Reconstruction, when spirituals were concertized in northern halls and ragtime resounded from middle-class parlors, won international attention as an indigenous folk music. Trained composers on both sides of the Atlantic took note. But with the arrival of jazz, and particularly with the release of Armstrong's Hot Fives and Sevens, a few people realized that an art music was brewing in America—something that demanded attention in its own right, not simply as source material for symphonic modernists. At last someone had fulfilled the promise Ernst Ansermet divined in 1919, when he compared Bechet to "those figures [of the seventeenth and eighteenth centuries] to whom we owe the advent of our art." America's unshakable place on the world's musical stage was now assured.

An indication of Armstrong's preeminence in 1927 was the appearance of two highly innovative books issued by a Chicago-based music publisher: *Louis Armstrong's 125 Jazz Breaks for Cornet* and *Louis Armstrong's 50 Hot Choruses for Cornet*. "Hundreds of jazz cornetists," the Foreword asserted, "have adapted the Armstrong style of playing." The publisher faced three ways of assembling the books: He could commission transcriptions of Armstrong solos taken from his recordings, but that might involve copyright complications and would produce a limited number of solos. He could commission written solos and breaks in the Armstrong manner, but that would undermine claims to authenticity, and it is unlikely anyone in 1927 could have credibly performed the task. He could hire Armstrong himself to record new solos and farm them out for transcription, and that's what he did do. The implication was not insignificant, in that it virtually erased the distinction between music that was improvised and music that was composed: the solos were created exclusively to be turned into a printed text to be interpreted by other musicians. Witlessly, the publisher destroyed the recordings. But the transcriptions (the Swedish trumpeter Bent Persson has recorded them all) show the copiousness of Armstrong's imagination as he tossed off variations on dozens of tunes he never otherwise recorded.

In 1928, Armstrong made a record that more than any other has come to symbolize the ascendancy of the new American music, especially in its thrilling and totally improvised introduction. "West End Blues" begins with a clarion call-to-arms—a bewitching, fantastical, rhythmically headlong cadenza that, in Gunther Schuller's words, "served notice that jazz had the potential to compete with the highest order of previously known expression." The keening momentum of that passage cannot be precisely notated because note values are subtly altered by Armstrong's embouchure technique and extremely supple phrasing. The piece itself is an unusually banal King Oliver blues, but Armstrong refashions the twelve-bar theme into a varied and emotionally charged performance. Each chorus differs from its neighbors: a sober trombone solo accompanied by woodblocks; enchanting exchanges between clarinet and voice; a dreamy salon-style piano solo; and, ultimately, Armstrong's resplendent return on trumpet, holding one note for four measures and then caroming into a series of fervent descending arpeggios. The concluding rubato piano and clop cymbal sign-off is at best a stoical anticlimax. Few composers have imparted as much emotional and formal pleasure in three minutes.

"West End Blues" was part of a series of recordings made in 1928 that is often regarded as Armstrong's peak. Although the new band continued to record as the Hot Five or Savoy Ballroom Five, it invariably numbered six of seven musicians and most of them were not in the same league as Armstrong's earlier associates. Certainly Fred Robinson, Jimmy Strong, and Mancy Cara were unequal to Ory, Dodds, and St. Cyr. On the other hand, drummer Zutty Singleton (a New Orleans veteran whose playing experience would eventually range from Jelly Roll Morton to Charlie Parker) surpassed Baby Dodds. More significantly, the Pittsburgh-born pianist Earl Hines—whose broken chords, linear improvisations, and "trumpet-style" octave phrasing liberated jazz piano from the exacting conventions of ragtime and stride—stimulated Armstrong more than anyone since Oliver. The others no longer mattered. In addition to working with Hines at the Sunset, Armstrong had recorded with him under the leadership of Johnny Dodds and with the frightful Miss Christian. The best of their collaborations are the bedrock of modern jazz, that is, jazz utterly unbound by the traditions of New Orleans.

"Muggles," in a way, is as radical as "West End Blues" and the daddy of the tens of thousands of jazz records that consist exclusively of solos, though few can match its drama. This despite the plodding trombone and clarinet solos that claim the first third of the performance and serve only the didactic purpose of illustrating the chasm between Armstrong and the average players he was resigning to history. What it lacks in organizational esprit, it makes up in Armstrong's crowning invention, combining a twenty-four-bar rhythm fantasy and an electric twelve-bar blues. His runway is a four-bar break that has about as much in common with the preceding solos as a twenty-megabyte laptop has with Univac. For the next five bars, he alternates between two pitches (A and C), and in the following seven, he employs only the C and its octave; yet the tension he establishes is enthralling. Burnishing a slow blues as the ultimate payoff, he skids into half-time with a four-bar transition that sets up a chorus built almost entirely on the expressive power of seventh chords.

"Weather Bird" is another milestone, the only Armstrong-Hines duet and the prototype for countless duets and other off-the-cuff skirmishes.

Where classical duets are cooperative and usually unbalanced (one player has the lead role), this one is a competitive, impolite, and occasionally hilarious joust between the master and his most obstreperously talented disciple. Extreme liberties are taken with the three-strain rag and meter as Armstrong and Hines jab and feint—in one passage they size each other up with one-bar exchanges—ever vigilant and ever swinging. Armstrong wins because he swings harder and is faster on his feet. Hines contributes a fanciful accompaniment to Armstrong's vocal on "St. James Infirmary," and interplay between the two heightens the largely prosaic "Skip the Gutter." Hines switches to celeste for an oracular rendition of "Basin Street Blues," a dramatic vignette in which the trumpet emerges softly from the hushed ensemble, serenely attains full bloom, then disappears in favor of a scat vocal that cuts deeper than the song's words ever could.

On several selections, a seventh musician was added, the arranger, songwriter, and saxophonist Don Redman. "Save It, Pretty Mama" is one of Redman's best known tunes and this version is memorable for a gilded Hines solo and one by Redman played in the Armstrong style (something he didn't have to read *50 Hot Choruses* to absorb). "Heah Me Talkin' To Ya" has supple work by all, but here Armstrong is relatively tranquil. Redman also appears on Alex Hill's inventively arranged "Beau Koo Jack," notable for the whiplash trumpet breaks. "Tight Like That," however, is by far the most stirring result of their work together, engendering one of Armstrong's most expansive and scrupulously designed improvisations. The prelude incorporates some disarmingly risqué banter that recurs before each trumpet chorus, an absurdly lewd counterpoint to Armstrong's imperturbable majesty. His smoldering theme statement is followed by Hines's variations on it. At his return, Armstrong begins the first of his three architectonic choruses with a solemn scene-setting motif (E-natural to B-natural) played five times. His two subsequent choruses also turn on sturdy motifs (the third on an indelicate World War I jingle), each beginning at a higher interval than the last and heightening the parallel intensification in range and excitement.

The Armstrong-Hines recordings marked the end of that phase in Armstrong's career when he could confine himself to the province of jazz qua jazz. Never again would a coterie of enraptured fans be able to claim him for their own. In 1929, he went to New York and first night out played with Luis Russell's band at the Savoy Ballroom. The next morning, he fronted a blues jam organized by Eddie Condon, producing "Knockin' a Jug," Armstrong's first studio encounter with Jack Teagarden (Eddie Lang and Joe Sullivan were also present) and one of the first generally acknowledged integrated recordings. That afternoon, he front-ed Luis Russell's nine-piece band, with Condon and Lonnie Johnson sitting in, and recorded two important sides. Spencer Williams's "Mahogany Hall Stomp," named after Lulu White's Storyville establishment, captures the New Orleans spirit and offers a compelling view of Armstrong the structuralist: the first of his three muted choruses consists of short, rhythmically displaced phrases; the second is one full-moon note held for ten measures; and the last is a five-note riff played six times. It's so efficient you want to scream (and some critics have), but it's also wondrously effective.

The second piece that afternoon put Armstrong on a whole new course. "I Can't Give You Anything But Love" was his first pop song in the company of an orchestra that does little more than parade the chords as a scrim, leaving him free to reshape, kid, and personalize—yet never undermine—the material. For all the guttural asides, he makes of Dorothy Fields's strapped Lothario a true and amorous romantic. Ethel Waters, who along with Armstrong and Crosby shaped the modern delivery of pop songs in the '20s and was the first of the three to make a mark, recorded an imitation of his vocal solo, a salute from one who knew. To the reactionaries, Armstrong's embrace of the songwriting factory was a compromise—as if jazz could, any more than Mozart, be kept pure and untouched by the rest of the world. Far from compromising his music, he opened its maw, allowing it to ingest anything that was nourishing, anything that kept it fit, current, and flexible.

That summer he led Carroll Dickerson's band in Harlem and appeared on Broadway in *Hot Chocolates*, introducing Fats Waller's "Ain't Misbehavin' " with such vitality that he was taken out of the pit and presented on stage. The recorded version was a milestone hit, confirming the widespread acceptance of his unorthodox voice (which in the '30s grew quite mellow) and paving the way for dozens of records that made jazz adaptations of pop songs acceptable. At the same session, he recorded his stunning rendition of another Waller gem, "Black and Blue," transforming a lament about a dark-skinned gal longing for her lighter-skinned man into a powerful statement about racism (the reed section swoons in commiseration; this is the performance Ralph Ellison invokes in the prologue of *Invisible Man*). Armstrong was Waller's finest interpreter, excepting Fats himself: two of his most transcendent performances in the '50s, when his timbre took on a satiny and ever more suggestive sheen, were of "Black and Blue" (filmed at a concert in Accra, in Africa) and "Blue Turning Gray Over You" (on the album *Satch Plays Fats*). He was also the defining interpreter for Spencer Williams ("Everybody Loves My Baby," "Basin Street Blues," "I Ain't Got Nobody") and for Hoagy Carmichael ("Star Dust," "Georgia on My Mind," "Rockin' Chair," "Lazy River"). In setting the stage for the mainstream acceptance of jazz, he laid the foundation for the swing era, which has been described as orchestrated Louis.

For seventeen years, until 1946, when he returned to a small-group setting, Armstrong would be heard almost exclusively as the featured performer with big bands, his voice and trumpet emblematic of the jazz sound and spirit. During his first trip abroad in 1932, he netted a permanent nickname when a reporter mangled one of his boyhood monikers, Satchelmouth, and called him Satchmo. Things were not always easy: he survived life-threatening managerial warfare, a marijuana bust, the rise of the big bands, the death of the big bands, the seductions of bop for his white fans and of r & b for his black fans, right-wing boycotts (after he insisted that Eisenhower take action in Little Rock and refused to tour as a cultural ambassador until he did), left-wing accusations of Tomism (which he defied with greater mugging), the hegemony of rock and roll (which he hurdled with the miraculous "Hello Dolly"), and the diminishment of his chops (though never of his bell-clear tone). He stayed on the bus, performing hundreds of one-nighters year after year, never asking for any special due because a new art had sprung to life in his image, a new way of thinking about and playing music. Though there were many who chided him as old-fashioned and commercial, no one seriously contested his unimpeachable stature. The last of the New Orleans trumpet kings was, as Bing Crosby observed, "the beginning and the end of music in America."

12 ❖ *Duke Ellington*
(Part 1: The Poker Game)

In its originality, scope, and abundance, Duke Ellington's music has no rivals in jazz, and few outside of jazz. Ellington is often called America's greatest composer and just as often ignored entirely in discussions of American music, an indication of a separatism that continues to vex the nation's cultural habits. The question of how he measures up to his contemporaries in the European tradition is one I'll leave to academics, but Ellington's own ambivalence about the word "jazz" is worth noting. He tried to rid himself of it as early as the late '20s, blaming it in part for the tendency of commentators to interpret his use of improvisation, dance rhythms, and blues tonalities as evidence of nonseriousness. Like Mozart, he wrote music specifically designed for dance and concert and, again like Mozart, fudged the distinction between the two by the originality and consistency of his vision.

Not surprisingly for a man whose favorite accolade was to proclaim an artist "beyond category," Ellington insisted, "I don't believe in categories of any kind." Yet in transcending boundaries he alienated many of the listeners he initially attracted. He took critical lumps every decade or so from pundits who judged his latest work a decline from the masterpieces that a few years earlier had also been decried as failures. Ellington was furious with lexicological critics who persisted in trying to lash him to the latest definition of jazz, then thundered in condemnation when he wriggled free. He would have been disgusted to find the very snobbery used against him now perpetuated by guardians of jazz at cultural shopping malls, who are as determined to protect jazz from foreign influences as the high-art mandarins were to defend the sanctity of "serious" music. Ellington defined jazz loosely ("an American idiom with African roots") or not at all: "*Jazz* is only a word and has no meaning. . . . I don't know how such great extremes as now exist can be contained under the one heading."

Still, if Ellington's music stands apart, it is entirely rooted in what we recognize as jazz principles and usually (but by no means always) exhibits some or all of the standard characteristics: an equation of composition and improvisation, robust rhythms, dance band instrumentation, blues and song frameworks, blues tonality. Jazz is primarily a music of improvisation, and improvisers of genius—Armstrong, Parker—were able to recast it in their own idioms. But no instrumentalist has experimented as constantly and variously over so long a period of time as Ellington did with his orchestra or dared as substantial a body of through-composed work. Calling Ellington a bandleader is like calling Bach an organist, which, of course, is precisely how they were known to their contemporaries. Ellington was, in fact, his orchestra's composer, arranger, conductor, pianist, talent scout, entertainer, agent, nursemaid, and advocate. He bristled at condescension of any kind, particularly the sort that disguised racial sociology as music criticism. In his response to a patronizing article by Winthrop Sargeant, Ellington confessed he was made to feel "badly" at the suggestion that "jazz doesn't encompass such emotions as tragedy, romantic nostalgia, wonder, delicate shades of humor, et cetera." He continued, "Most of all, I was struck by Mr. Sargeant's concluding statement, that given a chance to study, the Negro will soon turn from boogie-woogie to Beethoven. Maybe so, but what a shame!"

Ellington produced many conventionally notated scores as well as numerous sketches (the bass part for one piece, passed from bassist to bassist for years, consisted of four bars jotted on a cocktail napkin). But even the most fastidious of scores can not fully convey Ellington's music: a virtuoso ensemble might interpret a score flawlessly and yet muddle it beyond recognition. For one thing, swing cannot be notated, and—more germane to Ellington's distinctive genius—neither can the range of idiosyncratic timbres and styles that are as integral to his art as his autodidactic approach to harmony. Ellington did not compose music in the solitude of his own inspiration, but rather incorporated the specific skills ("the tonal personalities") of the musicians he hired. As he wrote in 1942:

> I regard my entire orchestra as one large instrument, and I try to play on that instrument to the fullest of its capabilities. My aim is and always has been to mold the music around the man. I've found out that it doesn't matter so much what you have available, but rather what you make of what you do have—finding a good "fit" for every instrumentalist in the group. I study each man in the orchestra and find out what he can do best, and what he would like to do.

In the same period, he told an interviewer, "You can't write music right unless you know how the man who'll play it plays poker."

He was able to tailor his music to the man because he recognized early on that a trumpet solo by Cootie Williams was a very different animal from a trumpet solo by Arthur Whetsol. In jazz, an instrument does not predicate an ideal sound from which, once mastered, individuality may flower. As Buddy Tate once observed, the jazz musician's individual sound is far more important than the instrument's innate qualities and may even precede orthodox mastery. Ellington crafted a score as though he were casting the roles in a drama—offering a "Concerto for Cootie," not a concerto for trumpet. When Johnny Hodges died, Ellington's sister Ruth asked him who would replace the incomparable saxophonist; he replied, "No once can replace him." Because he wrote intuitively and pragmatically, he happened upon many of the sounds we now identify as Ellingtonian with the kind of impetuous creativity associated with improvisation. Imagine the scene at a recording studio: The musicians are assembled, and the parts of a new score have been distributed. The band plays it through, and the Maestro begins to call out alterations: in bar six, third trumpet should flat the A-natural; in the second release, the bass trombone will play in tandem with the reeds; in the last chorus, the violin solo will continue another eight bars. By the time he has honed the piece to his satisfaction, and the recording made, the result is significantly different from the original manuscript.

Over time, Ellington might continue to make changes, large and small, so that the basic arrangement might appear in a dozen different recorded versions. Which is the correct one? The issue of correctness (as opposed to comparative excellence) is as spurious here as in a discussion of various blues improvisations by Johnny Hodges. In those many instances where Ellington and his copyists failed to incorporate the alterations in a master score, the records are the only incontestable documents of the finished work. As a result, the secrets behind many of Ellington's most colorful effects died with him and his musicians, forcing subsequent bands to rely on the unscientific practice of transcription. When Mercer Ellington took over the orchestra after his father's death, he tried in vain to simulate the train whistle effect produced by the reeds in "Daybreak Express," ultimately admitting defeat and using a slide whistle. Ellington's cryptic orchestrations—exemplified in the first chorus of "Mood Indigo," voiced for straight-muted trumpet, plunger-muted trombone, and clarinet—prompted Andre Previn's observation: "Stan Kenton can stand in front of a thousand fiddles and a thousand brass and make a dramatic gesture and every studio arranger can nod his head and say, 'Oh, yes, that's done like this.' But Duke merely lifts a finger, three horns make a sound, and I don't know what it is."

Ellington could not have assessed the poker-playing habits of his musicians so completely had he not been able to maintain their loyalties. No other composer in history had his own orchestra for half a century or commanded comparable dedication from as many celebrated musicians. I emphasize composer to distinguish Ellington from other bandleaders whose long-running organizations were fueled by staffs of arrangers and the unlimited supply of published music. Almost all of Ellington's best-known work was composed and arranged by himself or in collaboration with members of his orchestra, except in the years 1939–67, when he enjoyed a fabled partnership with his brilliant aide de camp, Billy Strayhorn. Because of his great success as a songwriter (an especially notable achievement, as Ellington's songs, unlike those of, say, Arlen, Gershwin, and Porter, rarely enjoyed the commercial send-off of a hit movie or stage production), he was able, in effect, to play both roles in the time-honored relationship between artist and patron. He was court composer and prince of the court, subsidizing the band through the royalties he accrued from his hits. His reward was an orchestra constantly at his beck and call—an orchestra consisting of great musicians who devoted years, in some instances lifetimes, to the interpretation of his music. He paid his musicians well and permitted a good deal of laxity; but when precision was required, precision was delivered. Whether he was battling a deadline for an aspiring suite or amusing himself with a bauble, he could hear the results—and revise them—immediately.

In "The Mirrored Self," Ellington wrote, "I live in the realm of art and have no monetary interests." Yet his art was hardly monastic. He might have used his royalties to retire from the road and write music in comfort and at leisure. But then he wouldn't have been Duke Ellington, for very little in his music suggests comfort, leisure, or isolation. He wrote for people in the midst of people, shrewdly assessing responses in ballrooms and concert halls. His energy was staggering. Ellington traveled his country and the world as few artists in any medium ever have, from slick dance halls, buckets of blood, and farm towns to palaces, cathedrals, and the way stations of the fine arts. He wrote about it all, frequently on the spot, his music a programmatic record of his experiences. Consider the energy required not only to keep a big band on the road and stable, but to compose in all the off-hours, fulfilling commissions as well as the copious challenges he set for himself. Even in his last years, prized as an international resource, Ellington stayed on the road, playing for dancers at a 4-H Club in Iowa one night and debuting his concert of sacred music at San Francisco's Grace Cathedral the next.

During the Strayhorn years, he was able to delegate much of the work, but as if to prove to himself that his energy and inspiration had not flagged, he became more prolific than ever when Strayhorn died. Ellington didn't create for posterity, or so he insisted, but we can hardly doubt that he trusted in posterity's good taste. Certainly, he was in no rush to get all his music before the public. He spent a great many hours, at his own expense, recording music, some of which remained unreleased for more than two decades after his death. His legacy is immense: some fifteen hundred copyrighted pieces, including swing instrumentals, ballads, production numbers, concertos, portraits, suites, symphonic works, piano solos and piano-bass duets, ballets, spirituals, a television musicale, blues, movie scores, oratorios, sacred concerts, novelties, musical comedies, two unfinished operas (one, *Queenie Pie*, was completed posthumously), and arrangements of standard material ranging from Tchaikovsky to the Beatles. By no means were all his endeavors successful, but the unexampled bond between Ellington and his band encouraged him to try everything.

Edward Kennedy Ellington was born in Washington, D.C., in 1899 to a middle-class family that encouraged his talent for music and art. He is said to have garnered his nickname as a child by virtue of his regal bearing, though the banjoist Elmer Snowden—whose dislike for Ellington colored the accuracy of his memory—has said that he was more widely known in the early days as "Cutie." In any case, Snowden's assertion that Ellington became Duke only after arriving in New York is demonstrably untrue: one of Ellington's early D.C. bands was called the Duke's Serenaders. As a teenager, Ellington's poster painting attracted attention and won him a scholarship to study art at Pratt Institute. "I didn't take advantage of it," he wrote, "because I was already involved in what was just beginning to be called jazz. I told myself that kind of music couldn't last, that I'd give it another year, and then maybe next year go and pick up my scholarship." Instead, he pursued the stride pianists who frequently visited D.C. and were breaking with the formalism of ragtime in favor of a more percussive, freer style of piano music. Ellington listened well. His first piece, "Soda Fountain Rag," written at fourteen and never recorded by him, was much indebted to James P. Johnson's "Carolina Shout," which, like many other aspiring pianists of his generation, Ellington taught himself to play by slowing down the roll on the family pianola and placing his fingers on the depressed keys.

As a high school senior, Ellington bought a large ad in the Yellow Pages for a five-piece band that included saxophonist Otto Hardwicke, who played C-melody sax at the time, and trumpeter Arthur Whetsol, the group's de facto disciplinarian. Within a year, he had enough local jobs to send out several bands, and in 1920, he recruited drummer Sonny Greer (who also sang), trombonist Juan Tizol, and Elmer Snowden, who, doubling as business manager, briefly took control of the group and brought it to New York in 1923. The chanteuse and club owner Bricktop, quite taken with the handsome Ellington, helped get the band a few weeks work at Baron Wilkins' Inn. There followed a long residency at the Hollywood Club, which after two incidents of insurance-motivated arson was rebuilt as the Kentucky Club. A succession of chockablock events prepared him for his first major triumph. Bubber Miley replaced Whetsol, who left to study medicine (he rejoined Ellington in 1928 and remained nine years), and trombonist Charlie Irvis was added, developing the brassy, menacing, vocalistic sound that was soon to become the band's trademark. Snowden's departure allowed Ellington to resume leadership of the band, called the Washingtonians. Irving Mills, who in Ellington's ironic account was attempting to corner a monopoly on the blues by purchasing lead sheets at $15 or $20 a pop, became a Kentucky Club habitué and eventually assumed management of the band.

The most remarkable aspect of the recordings Ellington made between 1924 and 1926 is how little indication they give of what was to come. In some respects, the first session (recorded November 1924 for Blue Disc) is the most rewarding: the two titles, "Choo Choo" and "Rainy Nights," are Ellington originals, and the spirited performances are firmly in the prevailing New York manner, which consisted of unison passages and solos that made the six-piece group sound larger than the polyphonic ensembles of Oliver and Morton. Ellington's feeling about "Rainy Nights" can perhaps be adduced by his failure to copyright it until 1973: it is shamelessly sentimental and light years from the captivating "Black Beauty" (1928), to which it bears a slight resemblance. "Choo Choo" is another story: the first of Ellington's train songs, it boasts an attractive melody that elicits a memorable stop-time chorus from the assured Miley, as well as rigorous section work and technically adept if dated tonguing by Hardwicke. The eight selections recorded by the Washingtonians between 1925 and 1926 (for Pathe and Gennett) are not Ellington compositions, yet the addition of several guest musicians put him in front of a big band for the first time. "If You Can't Hold the Man You Love" (trombonist Jimmy Harrison is the singer) has a trumpet duet with a rhythmic figure that presages the doo-wat-doo-wat riff of "It Don't Mean a Thing" (1932) and "You've Got Those 'Wanna Go Back Again' Blues" introduces the train whistle effect that culminated in "Daybreak Express" (1933). "Animal Crackers" and "L'il Farina" are indifferently executed vaudeville tunes (Ellington's stride solo on the former strides right out of his hands), notable only for Miley's inventions and Hardwicke's wrestling with a bass sax.

We can only speculate about how Ellington progressed from those inauspicious beginnings to his first milestones, recorded in November 1926 and throughout 1927. But it helps to remember his insistence on knowing a musician's poker-playing habits. In this instance, the player is Bubber Miley, a South Carolina-born trumpeter who heard King Oliver in Chicago in 1922 and developed his style accordingly. Miley, who would remain with Ellington for five years, debuted on records with him a month or so after Louis Armstrong first recorded with Fletcher Henderson. Whether he was thinking along similar lines or was merely quick in assimilating the example of Oliver's key disciple, Miley was of inestimable value in bringing a rugged blues-based swing to the Ellington band. Though somewhat stiff with an open horn, Miley was exceptionally deft with mutes (probably surpassing Oliver), and his poetic and almost macabre directness of expression, quite unlike Armstrong's brawny majesty, was ideally suited to Ellington's theatrical muse.

Miley inspired Ellington to craft a series of evocative settings for him, employing Miley's own compositional ideas. Each of four remarkable pieces for which they share composer credit draws power and a sense of mystery from the contrast between Miley's growly trumpet and Ellington's neat scaffolding. On "East St. Louis Toodle-oo," recorded several times between 1926 and 1928 and meant to evoke a popular ragtime dance called the todolo, Miley's urgent solo and the somber, almost weeping figure Ellington scored for the reeds and tuba combined to introduce a new sound in American music. Thoroughly distinct from the orchestral blueprint of such predecessors as Bill Challis or Don Redman, it was audacious and strangely carnal, and became the band's first theme song—reprised in the '30s and again in the '50s (minus the pixieish trio for reeds). "The Blues I Love To Sing" and the enduringly popular "Creole Love Call," two very different approaches to the blues, offer the wordless singing of Adelaide Hall, scored like an instrument, low down in the former and operatic in the latter. Most arresting of all is "Black and Tan Fantasy," which counterpoises a characteristic twelve-bar blues by Miley with a flouncy sixteen-bar melody by Ellington. Miley's contribution (black?) was based on a spiritual he said he learned from his mother, and Ellington's (tan?) was written in the music hall and ragtime traditions of the '20s. As the two strains merge in a climactic funeral march, the piece seems to embody Ellington's comment on the black and tan clubs that dotted Harlem in that period and were vaunted as an answer to segregation. The clubs disappeared, but the "Fantasy" remained a staunch and much revised number in Ellington's book.

On December 4, 1927, Ellington began an engagement at the Cotton Club that, nothwithstanding interruptions (tours, a 1930 movie), lasted more than three years, certifying his prominence in New York and—through the club's radio transmissions and international reputation—the world. Writing in support of erotic revues and sundry dancers, he perfected a wry, insinuating music in which canny instrumental voices were blended into an intimate and seductive aggregate. Many thought Ellington's music as salacious as the dancing. But whether heard as saucy, wry, or something else entirely, it offered a fresh and daring musical language. In contrast to Paul Whiteman's elephantine, if graceful orchestra, which had dominated music written for dance band instrumentation for most of the decade, Ellington's band was contained and incisive and exceedingly personal. Whiteman conjoined several aspects of American popular music into a brightly contemporaneous model. Ellington tapped into something deeper and previously unexplored, unshackling shadowy characters like "The Mooche" and flaming-youth injunctions like "Rockin' in Rhythm."

Ellington was the first American composer to acknowledge as legitimate subjects racial pride—in contradistinction to Tin Pan Alley's countless coon songs—and sex without romance—in contradistinction to Tin Pan Alley's effusions of virginal romance. He was a revelation: not a

composer who borrowed from jazz, as Gershwin did, but a jazz composer—one of enormous vitality and wit, not to mention a gift for sensuous melodies, an ingeniously original grasp of harmony, and a predilection for seesaw rhythms that reflected a lingering love of stride piano.
Two pieces show especially well Ellington's ability to deploy stride in
orchestral writing. "Jubilee Stomp," based on James P. Johnson's "Victory Rag," echoes Ellington's own stride solo and Miley's break in the
striding rhythms that ground the ensemble. "Black Beauty," the first
portrait in what grew to be a gallery honoring African American performers, is dedicated to Florence Mills and captures her fleeting stardom
in the most enchantingly beautiful melody ever conceived in the stride
idiom. Ellington recorded it as a piano solo and in a full-blown orchestration.

As the familiar cast of Ellingtonians began to take their places, Miley and
Hardwicke were on the way out. Each was prone to alcoholic benders
that kept them off the bandstand for days at a time. When Ellington
heard Johnny Hodges, Hardwicke's days were numbered, but he was
cautious about replacing Miley, whose growling had long incarnated the
band's soul. Cootie Williams was not a plunger-mute player when Ellington first heard him, but Ellington somehow intuited that he might
become one, and Miley was out in 1929. Miley toured Europe with Noble
Sissle's band, and on his return was associated with Leo Reisman, a
white bandleader (because of segregation, Miley was sometimes forced
to play behind a screen), and Roger Pryor Dodge, the dancer and critic
who wrote a pioneering essay on Miley and Ellington ("Harpsichords
and Jazz Trumpets") for *Hound & Horn* in 1934, two years after Miley
died of tuberculosis at twenty-nine. Miley recorded prolifically in the
mid-'20s, usually in pickup bands or with singers, but his own sessions
consist of six trumpet-organ duets in 1924 and six sides at the helm of a
musty dance band built around singers. Aside from his work on King
Oliver's "St. James Infirmary" and Reisman's spooky version of "What
Is This Thing Called Love?" his recorded work outside the Ellington fold
displays little depth or surprise. Miley was the first in a line of artists
who achieved great heights with Ellington yet faltered on their own.

For Ellington, who prized frazzled originality over faceless virtuosity,
Miley had confirmed the kind of musician he wanted: individual, flexible, idiosyncratic. The history of the Ellington band involves an astonishing array of musicians, most of whom were unknown until Ellington
hired them, gauged their capabilities and foibles, and tailored his writing
to emphasize their best features. The Ellington paradigms were inducted
early. In 1926, to replace Charlie Irvis, he raided Elmer Snowden's band

for Joe "Tricky Sam" Nanton, Miley's foremost disciple and one of Ellington's most expressive voices over the next twenty years. Nanton engendered a tribe of introspective plunger-mute specialists in the trombone section. In the '20s, he was the band's sole trombonist, and his nuanced snarls and moans conveyed rue, violence, and whimsy, as on "Jubilee Stomp," "Black and Tan Fantasy," "Stevedore Stomp," "The Blues with a Feelin'," "Harlem Flat Blues," and "The Duke Steps Out."

Also in 1926, bassist Wellman Braud, from New Orleans, and clarinetist Rudy Jackson, from Chicago, were recruited from a New York stage band. Braud remained eight years, but Jackson, who created the clarinet trio in "Creole Love Call," was soon replaced by the ebullient New Orleans clarinetist Barney Bigard, who stayed fifteen years. Braud, an expert at slapping the strings, was sure at any tempo and worked well with the mercurial, rocking drummer, Sonny Greer, who presided over the Ellington rhythm section for twenty-five years. Braud's versatility allowed Ellington to write prominent parts for arco bass, voiced with the winds as in "The Blues I Love To Sing" (as Hardwicke overlays a soprano sax improvisation) and "The Blues with a Feelin'," or sly pizzicato figures as in "Flaming Youth," where Braud employs the bow in the theme statement before plucking a pattern that switches between eight and four beats to the bar.

Even in an era of such dazzling clarinetists as Benny Goodman, Artie Shaw, Pee Wee Russell, Edmund Hall, and Irving Fazola, Barney Bigard was a standout musician, who sustained the robust qualities of New Orleans in the genial reediness of his tone, especially in the sultry chalumeau register—he insisted on using the outmoded Albert system of fingering, which is said to produce a larger sound. Unlike European clarinetists, who aim for a pure, light timbre, jazz clarinetists have sought a more natural tone that acknowledges the sliver of wood closing the mouthpiece and the wooden body of the instrument itself. Bigard favored a stout, purring vibrato and broad, piping effects; he relished sprightly tempos, but could also mine a slow blues. Yet it wasn't his improvisational skill that secured his place in jazz history. Left to his own devices, Bigard tended to be a showy and sometimes incoherent soloist. He flourished with Ellington because, like so many of his band mates, he needed the discipline of a composer to channel his talent. Ellington took his measure from the start, convincing him to concentrate on clarinet instead of tenor sax, which he had played with Luis Russell and King Oliver. Their most material collaboration may not have been entirely consensual: in 1930, Ellington expanded a melancholy fragment Bigard liked to play into a song and orchestration that epitomizes jazz for many people, not least because of Ellington's poetic title, "Mood Indigo." Though Bigard's best known performances with the band followed in the '30s and early '40s, not least as nominal leader and featured player in one of Ellington's chamber groups, he had a prominent role from the moment he entered the picture, in 1928, as on "The Mooche," "Tiger Rag," "Saturday Night Function," "Wall Street Wail," and "Jungle Jamboree."

The most durable Ellington recruit of 1926 or any other year was the preeminent baritone saxophonist, Harry Carney, who was sixteen when he was hired for a one-nighter near his hometown of Boston and stayed until his death forty-seven years later. Matched only by Count Basie's guitarist Freddie Green in the duration of his service to one leader, Carney is one of jazz's monuments: a modest, unassuming man, rarely heard outside the Ellington fold, acclaimed for his radiant sound (he completely dominated the baritone until the arrival of his most gifted disciple, Gerry Mulligan), immaculate technique (he was ideally sonorous in every range of the horn), and awesome consistency (he served unfailingly as the orchestra's bedrock). As a soloist, Carney was a devotee of Coleman Hawkins, who with characteristic generosity gave him the lion's share of a 1944 recording, "Three Little Words"—the record Carney most prized. As a section man, Carney's impact on the Ellington band is incalculable.

The quality that most immediately distinguishes the Ellington sound is the baritone sax voice leading (most reed sections are voiced with alto on top and baritone on the bottom). A light must have glimmered in Ellington's head when he heard Carney, for the recordings show he lost no time in making him the heart of the orchestra. "If he wasn't in Duke's band," Miles Davis said, "the band wouldn't be Duke." Carney's round sound, appealingly grainy and utterly imperturbable, was matched by an instinctual gift for phrasing—the other saxophonists followed his lead. He also played clarinet and alto sax, and in two respects presaged developments in the postbop avant-garde: he made extensive use of bass clarinet, an instrument otherwise ignored until the advent of Eric Dolphy, and he introduced to jazz the Zen-like discipline of circular breathing (inhaling through the nose while exhaling through the mouth), a technique largely ignored until the advent of such musicians as Roland Kirk, Roscoe Mitchell, and Arthur Blythe. Best remembered for the baronial resonance with which he imbued the orchestra, Carney was a sturdy soloist, who blossomed in the '30s as he absorbed the influence of his boyhood friend, Johnny Hodges. But he was forceful from the start, as on "Doin' the Voom Voom," "Cotton Club Stomp," "Breakfast Dance," and "Ring Dem Bells."

Another significant pact of 1926 was the contract signed by Ellington and Irving Mills in October. It remained in effect for thirteen years, and though Ellington ultimately sued for his release he was quite explicit about Mills's contributions to the band, which included the historic engagement at the Cotton Club, record contracts, motion picture deals, European tours, acceptance into ASCAP, and several victories over Jim Crow. It was Mills, Ellington wrote, who "insisted that I make and record only my own music." It was also Mills who insisted on playing boy crooner on a few records, initiated ventures of doubtful dignity, and cut himself in as co-composer on dozens of Ellington songs. Undoubtedly, the initial Cotton Club engagement was the key point in Ellington's career. It enabled him to double the size of his band, encouraged his daring prolificity, and internationalized his name and music. The tremendous range of material he had to produce for the Cotton Club shows forced him to stretch his resources way beyond that of any other band. In addition, he had the inestimable experience of working with top-flight choreographers, songwriters, performers, set designers, and the other professionals involved in putting on those slick and sexy revues. The Washingtonians had given way to Duke Ellington and His Kentucky Club Orchestra, now succeeded by Duke Ellington and His Cotton Club Orchestra, eventually to become Duke Ellington and His Famous Orchestra. Mills helped make him a celebrity, but Ellington's musical progress during the next few years owed no less to the induction of two musicians who soon became the most popular of his soloists, Johnny Hodges and Cootie Williams.

Hodges, nicknamed Rabbit, was the most beloved performer in the band after Ellington and shared with Benny Carter the mantle of leading alto saxophonist in the prebop era. A devout romantic with a sound that cuts like a knife and yet spreads like butter, Hodges was a stunningly lyrical player who required few notes to make a powerful and lasting impression in any musical situation. He was detached in manner and invariably looked bored on the bandstand, but as soon as he lodged his mouthpiece in the corner of his mouth, he produced a sexy, fluorescent sound that tinged the orchestra and billowed into every corner of the room. Charlie Parker admiringly dubbed him, "Johnny Lily Pons Hodges," and people otherwise indifferent to jazz were attracted to his songful, epigrammatic improvisations. Though enormously influential, especially on such colleagues in the Ellington reed section as Harry Carney and Ben Webster, he eluded imitators.

Raised in Boston, Hodges worked briefly with Chick Webb and Lucky Roberts before Ellington signed him in May of 1928. After less than three weeks at the Cotton Club, he was featured on two immensely appealing

Ellington records: W. C. Handy's "Yellow Dog Blues" and Spencer Williams's "Tishomingo Blues," playing soprano sax on the former and alto on the latter. On the basis of those solos, he seems to have been born fully formed, but Hodges himself described his style as an amalgamation of what he learned from Sidney Bechet, who personally motivated him, and Armstrong—likely sources for his wasteless elegance and peerless glissandi. His affection for Bechet was further reflected in his devotion to the soprano sax, an instrument he helped keep alive through the early '40s, when he decided to concentrate exclusively on alto.

Hodges was one month short of his twentieth birthday when he recorded "Tishomingo Blues," and yet he is not only a confident soloist but a dominant voice in the ensemble, investing the reed section with a luxurious texture. Playing an instrument that had little pedigree, Hodges displays the timbre and rhythmic control of a master. His teamwork with Bigard and Carney demonstrates the kind of unison attack that can make written figures feel vitally unstudied. Ellington cleverly transformed the sixteen-bar blues theme, adding an eight-bar intro that mixes descending chromatic chords, sustained whole notes, and Hodges's pungent fills. The first two choruses accommodate two-bar exchanges between Nanton and Bigard, who gets off a firecracker arpeggio in the second chorus. Louis Metcalf's trumpet solo is accompanied by the reeds, which hum a different chord in each measure. Hodges's alto is backed only by the rhythm section: elegant and restful, he begins with a cogent four-bar phrase, pauses, and then builds to a patented glissando. Bubber Miley's solo is filled with growls and upward rips, followed by a fanciful written chorus in which Hodges's luster tethers the reeds. The whole band stomps the final chorus, permitting the altoist a few quicksilver breaks.

"Yellow Dog" is something of a companion piece: solos by Miley, Nanton, and Metcalf, splashy writing for the bonded reeds, a beguiling Ellington intro, and a Hodges chorus, this time on soprano over stop-time rhythm. Perhaps the most impressive of his early forays on soprano is "Cotton Club Stomp," where he sails through the turnbacks—a familiar tactic in the late '30s, but an adventurous one in 1929. All of Hodges's early solos are vivid and include many Ellington landmarks. "The Mooche," an occult theme that Bechet later tackled with great success, was recorded in several Ellington versions, of which the most inventive includes a wordless vocal by Baby Cox and a guitar solo by Lonnie Johnson. In "The Blues with a Feelin'," Hodges's architectural soundness and economy on soprano suggest Armstrong rather than Bechet. He is sandwiched between Miley and Nanton in "Flaming Youth" (Ellington never tired of juxtaposing Hodges's gleaming saxophone with the gnarling muted brasses) and is cocomposer of the trim "Rent Party Blues," a blues in name only, as it combines a thirty-two-bar song and a secondary sixteen-bar theme. In time, Hodges would front the best of Ellington's chamber recordings and inspire Strayhorn's luminous concertos ("Day Dream," "Isfahan," "Blood Count"). Except for a five-year sabbatical in the early '50s, he served Ellington until his death in 1970.

Charles "Cootie" Williams was hired at seventeen, recommended by Hodges, with whom he had played in Chick Webb's band. If Ellington had selected him as Miley's heir, he apparently didn't tell Williams. But Nanton, who learned the secrets of the plunger and its altered pitches from Miley, passed them on to Williams, who soon surpassed everyone else in the realm of growling brass. Williams brought something else to the band, however—a devotion to Armstrong that gave Ellington's music a thrust and power Miley could not supply. As Ellington began to feature him with increasing frequency, Williams subtly transformed the band, intensifying its swing with the radiant clarity of his open horn and the precision of his muted yelps. The passage in "Mississippi Moan" where Williams is backed by the ensemble's lamentations sounds uncannily like an Armstrong recording. On Ellington's version of Don Redman's "Paducah," a glint of Williams's individual buzz cuts through his appropriation of Armstrong's blues attack; it is more distinct in "Black and Blue," Ellington's flawed rendition of a Fats Waller song that became an Armstrong masterpiece.

The one thing Williams could not do as well as Ellington might have liked was sing, though in the manner of the clarinet-voice duet on Armstrong's "West End Blues," Ellington provided a few chase choruses for Williams to vocally answer Hodges's alto, as on "Ring Dem Bells" and "Sweet Chariot." On the latter, he is far more imposing in a riveting instrumental exchange of choruses with Nanton, holding one jewel-like note with true Armstrongian élan. The mute, however, underscored his originality. He developed it to a degree where he could manipulate the plunger so subtly you could barely detect its use. More often he used it with a dynamic strength bordering on vehemence. In 1936, Helen Oakley (Dance) wrote, "Cootie has a conception of savagery and force on the instrument that cannot be equalled. His work with the wa-wa mute is more expressive than speech." And so it often seemed—alternately delicate and aggressive, frequently humorous, always recognizable. Like Hodges, he was brought to the fore in hundreds of works and became so associated with Ellington that when Benny Goodman hired him away in 1940, the irrepressible Raymond Scott marked the event with a recording, "When Cootie Left the Duke." "He'll be back," Ellington is alleged to have said at the time; twenty-two years later he was. The irony of Williams's career is that while his most celebrated performance is the endlessly analyzed "Concerto for Cootie" (Ken Rattenbury's dissection in his *Duke Ellington Jazz Composer* is the most exhaustive of several), he was best known in his last dozen years with the orchestra not for an improvisation, but for his febrile interpretation of a solo his interim successor Ray Nance created on the 1941 "Take the A Train." Williams played it thousands of times, but always made it sound rudely up-to-date.

The players were seated, the cards dealt, and the pot grew mountainous. The Depression was as good to Ellington as it was to Fred and Ginger, Bing Crosby, Rodgers and Hart, Busby Berkeley, and everyone else who helped shake the blues away. If racism circumscribed his potential, and it surely did, he appeared not to notice. He was delighted when in 1930 the band was brought to Hollywood to appear in *Check and Double Check*, the blackface Amos and Andy movie: true, the light-skinned guys, Barney Bigard and Juan Tizol, had to blacken up, and Whiteman's Rhythm Boys (with Crosby) had to appear off camera while Ellington's bandsmen mimed the vocal, and the film was bloody awful. But Ellington knew that black communities all over the United States would have the opportunity to see him, and they did. He didn't have much chance in the movies—he was suave, sophisticated, sexy, and smart, everything desired in a white performer but not in a black one. But it didn't matter. In 1932, he wrote "It Don't Mean a Thing (If It Ain't Got That Swing)"; three years later, white America figured out what he meant and reserved network radio hookups and magazine covers for white bandleaders. But it didn't matter. In 1938, Carnegie Hall put out its welcome mat for jazz, and Benny Goodman took his bows; Ellington wouldn't crack that barrier for another five years. But it didn't matter. Nothing mattered but the music, which poured as if from an open tap. Nothing daunted him, nothing got in his way. The swing era went belly up, but he continued for another thirty years, as if it had been no more than a blip in time.

As noted, his independence was in part secured by his discovery in 1931 with "Mood Indigo" that he could write a genuine commercial blockbuster hit. In the world of Mickey Rooney and Judy Garland movies, big bands may have run the gamut from Whiteman to Tommy Dorsey, but in life, mechanical or songwriting royalties were a lot more lucrative than royalties from record sales. Like almost all the great songwriters of his generation, Ellington's pop muse was reliable from the early '30s into the early '50s, when the public turned first to white-bread novelties and later to rock and roll. He didn't write nearly as many songs as those who did nothing else (although the staying power of his best songs has been surprisingly steady, especially for someone who devoted relatively little time to the craft). Few would challenge Alec Wilder's assertion that among songwriters Ellington scarcely belongs in the company of Jerome Kern, who along with Irving Berlin virtually invented the modern popular song.

And yet: a study of the respective catalogs of Ellington and Kern (who wrote more than twelve times as many songs as Ellington), undertaken in 1997, with a view toward compiling every song that could by the widest latitude be considered an enduring standard, produced unexpected statistics. Given a few songs that provoke arguments as to whether they are merely famous (perhaps because of a classic movie or record) or actually performed by present-day singers, the number for Kern was between thirty and thirty-five, that for Ellington between thirty and thirty-four. The Ellington list includes "Sophisticated Lady," "Solitude," "In a Sentimental Mood," "Caravan," "I Let a Song Go Out of My Heart," "I Got It Bad and That Ain't Good," "Prelude to a Kiss," "In a Mellow Tone," "All Too Soon," "Rocks in My Bed," "I Didn't Know About You," "Don't Get Around Much Anymore," "I'm Beginning To See the Light," "I'm Just a Lucky So and So," "Jump for Joy," Come Sunday," "Do Nothin' Till You Hear from Me," and "Satin Doll."

Beyond the pop realm, it was evident by the mid-'30s that Ellington perceived jazz not as a limitation, but as a springboard for a new music. "Duke Ellington enlivened the whole period," Roger Pryor Dodge wrote, "His music sounded more like jazz *composition* than popular tune arrangement." Constant Lambert called him the finest composer of popular music since Johann Strauss, and Percy Grainger proclaimed him the only original mind in American music. Yet few critics kept up with Ellington. When in 1932 he hired the great trombonist Lawrence Brown, he was pilloried for hiring a musician who sounded "white." His cachet was greatly enhanced by his European tour of 1933, when he performed in Paris, at the London Palladium, and elsewhere in the United Kingdom. But for all the cheering that accompanied his return to the Cotton Club, he was disparaged as pretentious by critics when he attempted to breach the tyranny of the 78 r.p.m. disc in his extended work, "Reminiscing in Tempo," written in memory of his mother. All this, the accolades and aspersions, took place years before he wrote his most sumptuous instrumental miniatures, suites, and tone poems. In truth, he was just getting started. If he could survive the blandishments of celebrity, he could survive anything.

13 ❖ *Coleman Hawkins (Patriarch)*

My memory of the few times I saw Coleman Hawkins remains so vivid, after thirty years, that it continues to color my understanding of his music. By 1966, he had already embarked on the intractable downward spiral that culminated with his death on May 19, 1969, at sixty-four. But as a young enthusiast making three trips to the Village Vanguard to catch a bill that paired his quartet with that of Sonny Rollins, I was blissfully unaware of anything but appearances. Not that my observations were detached. I knew RCA Vintage's Hawkins compilation, *Body and Soul,* and his Opera House recording with Roy Eldridge, so while I was excited about seeing Rollins, in Hawkins I fully expected to see a god. And I did. The grizzled full-bearded patriarch still looked sharp and slightly forbidding, even if he had receded a bit into his tailored, gray silk mohair. He gazed over the crowd with sad but alert eyes, his tight-lipped smile implying bemusement and perhaps disdain. When he greeted someone between sets, his voice was stately and deep, a match for his sound on tenor. He exuded dignity.

Still, I found his music more complicated and less rewarding that week than Rollins's, which, with its rhythmic change-ups, medley-style juxtapositions, and expressive techniques, offered easy points of entry. Hawkins's evenly stamping choruses, brazen with crisscrossing arpeggios, demanded closer inspection, and although his bitingly aggressive phrasing and huge sound carried me along, I didn't know the language well enough to comprehend the details.

At another 1966 performance, a concert at Philharmonic Hall called "Titans of the Tenor" (Hawkins, Rollins, Zoot Sims, John Coltrane), Hawkins in his only selection produced the evening's most memorable note—the first he played. He bent the mike into the bell of his horn and delivered himself of a weighty, gruff suspiration that filled the hall, established the tone and tempo of his performance ("In a Mellow Tone"), and underscored his primacy—you sensed immediately that no one else could make such a sound. A decade later, Rollins told me he was initially attracted to Hawkins's image of "a big man playing a big horn." That, of course, is Rollins's own image. Hawkins, at five feet eight inches, wasn't nearly as big, but his carriage and the nature of his music suggested elevation as well as invincible will.

Jon Hendricks once introduced Hawkins as "the man for whom Adolphe Sax invented the saxophone," an engaging way of saying that Hawkins was not only the indomitable emperor of the tenor, to a degree that no other jazz musician has ever dominated an instrument (even Armstrong had an early rival in Bix Beiderbecke), but that he established its legitimacy in contemporary music. The saxophone was introduced some sixty years before Hawkins's birth and was occasionally used in symphonic music by Berlioz, Bizet, Richard Strauss, and Ravel, among others. Yet when Hawkins began playing, it was still regarded as an undisciplined poor relation to other reed instruments.

The saxophone's most indulgent audience and most resourceful practitioners were found in vaudeville, where virtuosi made hay by imitating the sounds of barnyard animals or by playing two or three saxophones at once. The most successful of those wizards was the instrumentalist, composer, and tinkerer, Rudy Wiedoeft. During the very years Hawkins was creating his style, Wiedoeft brought the instrument's lip-smacking tendencies to a zenith with scrupulously articulated novelty performances (he favored titles like "Saxophobia," "Saxemia," and "Sax-O-Phun"), in which every note was emphasized with a rapid flickering of his tongue against the reed. Wiedoeft specialized in the alto sax, an instrument he helped design; other musicians transferred his headlong staccato rhythms to tenor, baritone, bass, and C-melody saxes as well. His was the "correct" approach.

Small wonder, then, that the first jazz saxophonist of consequence was Sidney Bechet, who played soprano as though it were a more ardent and powerful cousin to the clarinet. The obscure C-melody briefly had some adherents, at first because young players with little schooling thought it would save them from having to master transposition and later because its most famous specialist, Frank Trumbauer, created the illusion of a flexible, highly lyrical instrument with sweeping range. In fact, the C-melody was a recalcitrant monster in anyone else's hands, sounding more like a groggy tenor eternally slipping out of pitch. Bechet's brilliance and Trumbauer's skill notwithstanding, the saxophone's pedigree in early jazz was as elusive as in the symphony. Coleman Hawkins changed all that. He gave the tenor saxophone character and sensibility, with his hearty virile timbre, legato fluency, and impassioned drive. Before Hawkins, no one thought the tenor was capable of much passion. Perhaps the first indication of his genius was the decision he made at age nine to play it. He had already studied piano and cello, and in 1913 not even Wiedoeft had caught the public fancy. We may never know what inspired him or how he came to recognize the potential cello-like sonority in his chosen instrument.

During the more than ten years he starred with the Fletcher Henderson orchestra, Hawkins occasionally played saxophones other than tenor.

But he disliked having to double, and as soon as he had the clout, he refused to do so. In later years, when his primacy on tenor was universally conceded, he took satisfaction in expansive displays of modesty. "People always say I invented the jazz tenor," he said. "It isn't true. There was Happy Caldwell in Chicago and Stump Evans out of Kansas City. They were playing like mad . . . why, gangs of tenors would be coming into New York all the time from bands on the road. They used to wake me up out of my bed to come down and cut people." Elsewhere he spoke of "a whole lot of ofays playing tenor, even when I was just beginning."

Such protests must be taken lightly. Hawkins was notorious for carving his opponents in jam sessions, and he was a professional for more than a decade before any of them were capable of making contributions of their own. The musicians he names were all born within a year of Hawkins. Evans died young and recorded little, rarely on tenor. Caldwell and another saxophonist he mentioned, Prince Robinson, were formidable technicians whose earthy intonations and decorative styles may have rivaled Hawkins in the '20s, but by the early '30s, their music seemed stillborn since neither had mastered the legato control that brought the tenor out of vaudeville and into the heart of jazz. If there were any other tenor saxophonists, ofay or not, who could seriously match Hawkins's prowess, music chroniclers failed to take note. Bud Freeman offered an alternative approach, but made few converts. Hawkins's constituency among musicians preceded his public following by several years. The teenage Ben Webster was hooked on his "punch and drive," despite the distorting tinniness of primitive recordings, and preferred it to the style of his traveling companion, Lester Young. Young, the first important tenorist who wasn't stylistically beholden to Hawkins and the only one to best him in a cutting session, also acknowledged his preeminence.

For an innovator of Hawkins's stature, his early years are surprisingly obscure. In the absence of a serious biography (John Chilton partially filled the gap in 1990 with *The Song of the Hawk*), tales and suppositions became entrenched as fact. Hawkins himself gave good, generous interviews (Riverside Records issued two volumes of recorded discussions with him), but he may have fudged his birth date, and he was vague about other aspects of his apprenticeship. The generally accepted birth date is November 21, 1904. Hawkins was known to give later dates, historians suspect an earlier one. There's a paradox here. The 1904 date makes Hawkins seem fairly precocious in his deportment and independence, as well as in his instrumental skill and knowledge of theory. It means he was working at twelve, studying composition at Washburn College at sixteen, touring at eighteen, and starring with the first important black jazz orchestra at twenty.

By the standards of his art, however, Hawkins was hardly a prodigy. He may have dazzled musicians from the start, but not until 1929, at twenty-five, did he achieve a breakthrough of lasting significance. Indeed, there is a tendency to view Hawkins's beginnings as slow and deliberate when compared with that of Louis Armstrong, whose genius was evident as soon as he recorded. Yet Armstrong was twenty-four when he introduced the Hot Five; had he started recording in 1919, his apprenticeship might seem gradual, too.

Hawkins was born in St. Joseph, Missouri, about fifty miles north of Kansas City, to Will Hawkins, an electrical engineer, and his wife Cordelia, a teacher, who taught the boy piano from the age of five and bought him a tenor at his request for his ninth birthday. It's worth remembering that, though he left as a young man, Hawkins was very much a product of the Midwest. We tend to think of him as a cosmopolitan easterner because of his long tenure with Fletcher Henderson and the Roseland Ballroom, not to mention his tastes in clothes, cars, brandy, and modern classical music. As a boy, he visited Kansas City, where he heard Stump Evans, and boarded in Chicago, long before King Oliver arrived. The territory he soon abandoned would within a dozen years nurture many of his most important disciples, among them Ben Webster, Budd Johnson, Dick Wilson, Herschel Evans, and Buddy Tate, as well as Lester Young and Charlie Parker.

A question arises: Did the aspects of the Hawkins style that influenced all those saxophonists, except Young, derive from Hawkins's associations with Missouri, or, as Martin Williams wrote, was "this so-called Southwest tenor style . . . first expounded by Coleman Hawkins in a New York recording studio"? We don't know enough about his early years to be certain. Even his association with Washburn College, in Topeka, is hazy since the college has no record of his having attended. Perhaps he audited classes unofficially. In any case, he quickly displayed an uncommonly solid foundation in theory, which, combined with his technical mastery of most single-reed instruments, his competence on piano, and his devotion to music, assured him of a career.

In 1921, Mamie Smith, a quasi-blues singer with a florid style who made the history books as the first black woman to make records, heard Hawkins in a Kansas City theater. She hired him for her ensemble, the Jazz Hounds, and a year later he joined her in New York. Although he toured and recorded with her, his ticket east is important mostly because it facilitated his meeting with Fletcher Henderson, who was about to launch a "colored" answer to Paul Whiteman's behemoth semijazz band. As Hawkins posed with Henderson's start-up group in a photograph taken in 1922, we can assume they had an understanding: when the bandleader presented his band formally and found a place to work, Hawkins would be part of it. In 1923, Henderson recorded a piece by his chief arranger, Don Redman, called "Dicty Blues," a clunky but impetuous treatment of the New Orleans style as performed in Chicago by King Oliver, complete with a piano motif borrowed from Oliver's "Chimes Blues" and jagged, reedy improvisations by Hawkins. Most of the early black innovators—Armstrong, Bechet, J. C. Higginbotham, Johnny Hodges—used a pronounced vibrato, and Hawkins attributed his initial success to a "heavier tongue" and the roomy sound it produced.

Armstrong came east in 1924 to play with Henderson, and his impact on New York proved incalculable. Hawkins may have joined with the other musicians in chiding the rube for his dress, manners, and slack reading. He nonetheless recognized in Armstrong the answer to his own stylistic problems. Armstrong brought with him a contagious respect for the blues that implied economy of expression and emotional directness. Even more to the point, he brought swing to music—a rhythmic gait that balanced tension and release, and offered a way out of the slap-tongue, jerky phrasing that had been the saxophone's fate. Armstrong's vision, which became jazz's vision, demanded a cessation of tonguing in favor of legato flexibility. Hawkins was smart enough to heed the siren call, and he had the technique to pull it off.

Two years later, he unveiled the fruits of his discovery in Henderson's recording of Redman's "Stampede," a busy matrix of complex riffs and hardy solos that sounds starchy and unswinging now, but was widely imitated by territory (midwestern) musicians in its day. Despite a shimmering passage for reeds, a rousing trumpet solo by Rex Stewart, and a more lyrical one by Joe Smith, the highpoint is a thrusting chorus by Hawkins, spurred by the brass section. For the first time, the tenor sax leaps out of the band and jabs and punches with the dynamism of a trumpet. His notes are overarticulated, but his phrases are logical and proceed from the piece's harmonies rather than from the melody. This solo mesmerized musicians around the country, including Webster, who made it the model for his emerging style. Buddy Tate switched from C-melody to tenor after hearing it. Roy Eldridge transposed it to trumpet in order to perfect what he called his "tenor style." As dated as the performance is, Hawkins's vitality, coherence, and unfailingly bright tone abide.

Hawkins recorded prolifically, not only with Henderson and Redman, but with singers Bessie Smith (his clarinet is audible in the ensemble on her "Alexander's Ragtime Band"), Clara Smith, Ma Rainey, Rosa Henderson, Bessie Brown, Edna Hicks, Ozie McPherson, and Hannah Sylvester. Judging from the few tracks that have been reissued, I assume the body of this work throws little light on his development. Hawkins's reputation in New York was growing steadily, and though Prince Robinson and Happy Caldwell were much admired, his dominion over the tenor was unchallenged. Hawkins's personal style was also noted: the impeccably tailored suits and rakish hats, the big cars, worldly manners, manly good looks, and a vast store of knowledge in sundry areas.

Although the tenor sax seemed to exist exclusively in Hawkins's image, the alto saxophone made a dashing leap into the spotlight in 1928 when its yin and yang appeared in the persons of Johnny Hodges and Benny Carter. Each unveiled a performing style of undoubted maturity—Hodges's impassioned drive, Carter's cool lyricism. In early 1929, not a single tenor saxophone solo on record could equal the maturity of Bechet's soprano on "Cake Walking Babies," let alone Hodges's alto on "Tishomingo Blues." By early 1930, that was no longer the case. Hawkins had established for all time the stature of the tenor during two weeks in November with a handful of solos that require no apologies. The first evidence of his heightened skill was heard on sessions by a Redman unit, McKinney's Cotton Pickers, especially "Miss Hannah" and "Whenever There's a Will, Baby." One week later, he produced a monumental solo as a guest of the Mound City Blue Blowers, an integrated, seven-piece pickup band organized by Red McKenzie, including the magical clarinetist Pee Wee Russell.

The first side was an uptempo blast, "Hello, Lola," in which Hawkins's tremendous energy is undermined by his chugga-chugga rhythmic patterns and rasping tone. The flip side is a benchmark. "One Hour" is based on James P. Johnson's song hit, "If I Could Be With You One Hour Tonight"—the title was presumably altered to emphasize the originality of the improvisations. Though the melody is never actually stated, it informs each of the solos. From the very beginning, a six-measure introduction by Hawkins, the record is gripping in a way that was utterly new for jazz. Hawkins had discarded, at least for the time being, the staccato articulation and quarter-note/eighth-note rhythms that had been endemic in his playing.

Here was the tenor as we know it today, a warmly rhapsodizing instrument capable of shaping each note for maximum impact. After a laboriously atavistic chorus by McKenzie, playing a comb wrapped in tissue paper, Hawkins uses a pickup measure to launch his solo, which he propels with a legato drawl and the two-note descending figures (a flatted fifth in the second measure) that would become emblematic of his style. He has everything under control—rhythm, intonation, melody, harmony, even the suspenseful romanticism (note the tension-building arpeggios in measures nine and ten) that remains at the core of the modern ballad style. Flawlessly conceived and executed, it carries the listener along with the force of its logic and character. More than the first entirely successful tenor solo, it's the first distinguished ballad improvisation in jazz. Hawkins's single chorus, only eighteen measures, consolidated the impulse to improvise at slow to medium tempos on the chords of familiar songs.

"One Hour" also marked the beginning of a decade in which Hawkins would extend his influence across Europe and reestablish himself at home with "Body and Soul," the most celebrated of all tenor saxophone performances. Weeks after the Mound City Blue Blowers disc was released, the first of many homages to Hawkins appeared: a decent imitation by one Castor McCord on "Dismal Dan," a record by the trumpeter, adventurer, and con-man Jack Purvis. It may have been Purvis's most successful if unintended con because for nearly fifty years many experts insisted it *was* Hawkins. The Henderson orchestra continued to enjoy the real Hawkins's inspiring abilities for four more years.

If several of Hawkins's recordings with Henderson are over-embroidered, most of them confirm his steady bearings: even his recognition of deficiencies (rhythmic sameness, a sentimental streak, a penchant for the ornate) and the determination to overcome them. The steps he took can be tracked in Henderson's Columbia records: "Chinatown," "Hot and Anxious" (on clarinet), "Blue Moments," "Honeysuckle Rose," "It's the Talk of the Town," and "I've Got To Sing a Torch Song"; and in Henderson's parallel RCA sides: "Sugar Foot Stomp," "Strangers," "I Want To Count Sheep," and "Hocus Pocus"—Hawkins's marvelous parting shot with the band, a canny Will Hudson arrangement that has the reeds dancing with Ellingtonian grace against stop-time brass chords and the master strutting through his chorus with disarmingly effortless poise. Hawkins's interest in modern composition is manifest in the rhythmically hypnotic "Queer Notions," a piece he wrote for Henderson employing augmented chords and whole-tone scales. But modernism informs most of what he plays as well—I suspect many of his solos sound strikingly advanced at century's end because they are so deeply, personally alive with singular details, lunar howls, stamping savoir faire. A quintessential American memento of 1932 is Henderson's "Underneath the Harlem Moon," which begins with lustrous statements by Hawkins and Rex Stewart, setting up a vocal about how darkies were born to guzzle gin. The irony is exquisite: a song depicting black people as pleasure-seeking morons, brought to life by a black orchestra running over with musicianship so urbane—so predictive of the then unimaginable swing era—that no white band could hope to lay a glove on it.

Hawkins was much in demand, recording with Benny Carter's Chocolate Dandies, a small Benny Goodman combo, and the little remembered Spike Hughes orchestra and enlivening every session. For his first date as a leader, in 1933, he instigated a series of memorable performances with trumpeter Henry "Red" Allen (another Henderson alumnus) that, though tainted by poor material, found Allen shuffling off the influence of Armstrong and Hawkins affirming his many strengths, especially on "Heartbreak Blues." His follow-up session of tenor-piano duets with Buck Washington was ponderous. But his reputation was now international, and in the fall of 1934, the English bandleader Jack Hylton invited him to tour Europe. Hawkins sailed with the expectation of staying a few months, unprepared for the size and enthusiasm of the crowds that greeted him in every city. He stayed five years.

Along with Benny Carter, who embarked on a three-year tour of the continent in 1935, Hawkins lifted the level of European jazz, establishing abroad as he had at home a paradigmatic approach to the tenor. His style was mimicked for decades to come. After triumphant tours of England and France, he parted company with Hylton when the bandleader headed for Germany and went to Amsterdam instead. His recordings with Theo Masman's Ramblers were extravagantly praised by European critics, but though they document his increased warmth and mastery, they are compromised by stilted arrangements and vocals—Hawkins himself often overstates his case like a guest trying too hard to please. He was more himself, charged and sure, in outstanding encounters with the great Belgian guitarist, Django Reinhardt.

On the eve of the war, Hawkins's homecoming was slightly mitigated by the changes that had taken place in jazz while he was gone. He had made it a point of keeping up through records, and in an interview in Europe expressed admiration for Ben Webster, who had taken his chair with Henderson. The primary change, however, was the long-delayed acceptance of Lester Young. Hawkins had succumbed to Young during a fabled all-night jam session in Kansas City, and Henderson had briefly hired him as Hawkins's replacement, until band members protested, for the specific crime of not sounding like Hawk. Hawk had a heavy stalwart attack, while Young was light and airy; Hawk tagged every chord in a harmonic procession, while Young favored a compressed melodicism borne on the higher harmonic intervals; Hawk clamped down on rhythm, Young floated over it. Hawk wasn't in the least fazed by Young (they were mutual admirers), but the jazz world anticipated a show-down.

It never came. Hawkins cut the skeptics off at the knees the first time he returned to an American recording studio. The session was hardly propitious. It presented the eager but largely faceless nine-piece ensemble that Hawkins had brought into Kelly's Stables a week earlier to indifferent response and, excepting a ballad to showcase singer Thelma Carpenter, featured unmemorable material. In truth, Hawkins worked hard on the originals, "Meet Doctor Foo" and "Fine Dinner," which were obviously intended to show off his talent for modish composition, in the manner of "Queer Notions." His solo on "Foo," spurred by scored interjections at the turnbacks, is vigorous, and the ensemble episode after the piano on "Dinner" is almost boppish in its open harmonies and is followed by a good shout chorus. On the ballad, "She's Funny That Way," Carpenter's nuanced vocal is cradled througout by the ensemble, and Hawkins contributes a busily masterful yet subtly romantic solo. Yet the selections are strangely vague and unprepossessing for a return foray after five years.

Legend has it that near the end of the session, with three masters in the can, the producer induced a reluctant Hawkins to play "Body and Soul," one of several tunes he used to spell the band at Kelly's Stables. His hesitation was decidedly unfeigned. Earlier that year, Chu Berry—another supposed rival—had enjoyed success with a version of the song with a searing, long-meter extrapolation by Roy Eldridge, a good friend and inveterate Hawkins fan. What's more, Hawk had just worked with Berry (and Ben Webster) at a Lionel Hampton session. He didn't need a pissing contest. More to the point, he had no arrangement, and the idea of the session was to promote his band. Artists often low-rate what comes most easily. But he agreed—one take, no need to rehearse.

Well . . . launched by Gene Rodgers's impromptu piano intro, he moves in on the melody, his tone smooth as worn felt, his tempo brisk and mildly aggressive. After two fleeting measures, something happens: "Body and Soul" all but disappears. Lifted on a surge of inspiration, Hawkins extends the song's initial phrase into steep melodic arcs of his own invention—spiraling figures of varied length that advance with the assurance and deliberation of a taut story. Miraculously, he maintains the conceit through two full choruses and a coda, never touching down on Johnny Greene's melody. It's an improvised rhapsody, profuse with ideas, yet disciplined by the logic of his imagination and rhythmic authority, accruing dynamic tension phrase after phrase before gliding back to earth in a sudden yet satisfying finish. On top of that, the record was a tremendous hit.

If Hawkins's "Body and Soul" isn't the single most acclaimed improvisation in jazz's first hundred years, it is unquestionably a leading contender. Nothing was changed by it. Hawkins's station had long since been established, and Lester Young's time was at hand no matter what. At least one critic professed not to understand the hoopla—Hawkins played like that all the time, he made fifty records as good, didn't he? Not quite. What elevated "Body and Soul" was its purity, its perfection; here, in one spellbinding improvisation, was the apogee of everything Hawkins achieved thus far, an uncompromising example of his gift, a work of art. In his own way, he demonstrated what Lester Young was also in the process of demonstrating: a scheme to penetrate the presumed boundaries of conventional harmony. And he did it with his patented arpeggios, compensating for the absence of identifiable melody with his drive, warmth, and coherence. The public approbation was significant, if puzzling. The record was a sophisticated abstraction of a popular song, yet Hawkins's variations were embraced to the degree that he had to memorize them to satisfy clubgoers, who insisted he play the famous solo, not a fresh improvisation.

For years, handbills advertised his appearances using "Body and Soul" as a come-on, and long after the handbills vanished, audiences demanded it of him. Sometimes he played the recorded solo, sometimes a new solo, sometimes both—the original variations and then variations on the variations. The record took on a life of its own. Benny Carter orchestrated it, Eddie Jefferson put lyrics to it. The song itself became a challenge to every tenor saxophonist who followed Hawkins. And they all took a shot at it, from Lester Young and Ben Webster to Dexter Gordon and Stan Getz to Sonny Rollins and John Coltrane to David Murray and Joshua Redman. Hawkins himself continued to develop the material beyond the routine of nightly performances. In 1948, he adapted the harmonic framework for "Picasso," the first piece conceived for unaccompanied saxophone.

The '40s were a remarkable time for Hawkins. If Young provided a stylistic basis that facilitated the thinking of the modernists, it was Hawkins who actually stepped onto their playing field and used his clout to get bebop a hearing. Not that his influence was chiefly promotional: Charlie Parker grew up in the shadow of Young, but was no less drawn to Hawkins's method—his first significant recording is a radio transcription of "Body and Soul" with a liberal citation from the 1939 record. In 1944, egged on by Budd Johnson, Hawkins marked the end of a two-year AFM recording ban with two sessions that teamed advanced swing thinkers and exuberant modernists, including Dizzy Gillespie and Max Roach. They premiered important pieces by Gillespie ("Woody'n You") and Hawkins ("Disorder at the Border"), as well as a gloriously fresh take on "Body and Soul," called "Rainbow Mist." Hawkins was by far the most eminent of the prebop monarchs to embrace the new jazz.

The previous year, Hawkins had participated in two sessions for a fledgling independent, Signature, in violation of the ban. When the records were released, they unveiled a masterful version of "The Man I Love" that is something of a companion piece to the 1939 "Body and Soul." In both performances, Hawkins improvised two choruses that turned the harmonic patterns of familiar songs into blueprints for inventions that barely graze the melodies they were designed to support. But where the former was a ballad, "The Man I Love" is played fast in long meter (each measure doubled in length), and where the ballad was treated as a sonata for tenor sax, "The Man I Love" finds Hawkins's imperious autonomy and wit preceded by two relatively orthodox solos.

After an eight-bar intro by drummer Shelly Manne, pianist Eddie Heywood states Gershwin's melody in a clever paraphrase, with functional motifs and a dryly percussive attack. Oscar Pettiford picks up from him midway through the second chorus, pacing his two- and four-bar phrases with vocal gasps on the first beat of appropriate measures—it's one of the preeminent bass solos up to that time. Then Hawkins enters, regally. Although jouncing firmly on the beat, he continuously alters his phrases rhythmically and dynamically. His sound is huge, but not monolithic, and after a couple of bellicose growls, he storms through the second release as though possessed by the amazing fertility of his ideas. Despite the rhythm section's relentless harmonic underpinning, Hawkins is untouched by the gravity of Gershwin's tune—he is agog with inspiration.

Hawkins is no less irreverent but slighly less inspired on "Get Happy" and "Crazy Rhythm." The most compelling contrast is afforded by "Sweet Lorraine," in which Hawkins plays nothing *but* the melody; like a loving parent, he embellishes each measure yet never threatens the song's integrity. "How Deep Is the Ocean" is less successful, partly because Manne wields his brushes like two-by-fours, but primarily because Hawkins gets mired in gushy tremolos, fussy tone, and limpid figures— still, the sentiment is *his* sentiment, not Irving Berlin's. The famous "Stumpy" returns Hawkins to the summit with a riff theme based on "Whispering." He succeeds Bill Coleman's tart trumpet solo with a terrific blast that sounds as if he were shredding his reed in the process.

He had nothing to fear from modern jazz; his best records were timeless. Yet times change, audiences are fickle, and jazz patriarchs are often more honored in the breach than the observance. By 1960, Hawkins was often characterized as "mainstream," a polite way of saying that he was no longer in the mainstream. Yet while he continued to perform frequently and often glowingly with musicians of his own generation— maintaining long alliances with Roy Eldridge, Ben Webster, and Benny Carter, among others—he insured his musical contemporaneity in nourishing a close relationship with the modernists. He gave Thelonious Monk his first exposure on records in 1944, performed his music, and served as a sideman on the 1957 Monk album that paired him and John Coltrane. Over time Hawkins encouraged and hired Miles Davis, Fats Navarro, J. J. Johnson, Howard McGhee, Allen Eager (a disciple of Lester), Bud Powell, and Ron Carter. He worked almost exclusively with modern pianists, including Tommy Flanagan, Ray Bryant, and Barry Harris. He aquitted himself with enormous intelligence and skill in his 1963 recording with Sonny Rollins, backed by a Paul Bley rhythm section.

In those same years, Hawkins recorded worthy reunions with Pee Wee Russell, Henry "Red" Allen, and Shelly Manne, as well as a charming high-noon encounter with Ellington (a small band, alas). He recorded with string orchestras, riffing a lick Count Basie wrote for him ("Feeding the Bean") against a musty "Mademoiselle de Paree" and romancing "La Vie en Rose" with great ardor. At a spirited 1957 collaboration with Ben Webster, the two achieved an understated rapture on "La Rosita," and Hawkins thundered at full throttle on two originals: "Maria," a blues riff with a bridge, in which he varies his accents with slurs and double timing, and "Blues for Yolanda," in which he times reed-chomping squeals to the second beat of each of four measures in the third chorus.

He was at his assertive best on an unreleased television pilot foolishly compromised by showbiz jive and the prototypical cute but untalented singer. When finally allowed to play, Hawkins impatiently takes the bull by the horns and holds on chorus after chorus. Roy Eldridge, waiting for his turn, laughs in astonishment, his look of radiant admiration reflecting the delight and wonder that Hawkins engendered throughout his career. Cannonball Adderley liked to tell of a young saxophonist who complained to him that Coleman Hawkins made him nervous: "I told him Hawkins was *supposed* to make him nervous! Hawkins has been making other sax players nervous for forty years!"

14 ❖ Pee Wee Russell
(Seer)

A quarter century after his death, Pee Wee Russell is as much a conundrum now as when he was alive. The contradictions in his life and music ran deep. Born to the upper middle class, he preferred the hardships of the road. A confirmed loner, he was virtually helpless without the ministrations of friends and especially his wife of twenty-five years, Mary Russell. A lifelong alcoholic, he took a rigorous view of jazz improvisation. It shouldn't be necessary to encumber his deeply plaintive music with biographical footnotes, yet the music itself is so riddling that it's impossible not to wonder what manner of man made those crafty, sorrowful solos.

Russell's music was never quite what it seemed. For most of his long career, he was portrayed as a Chicagoan or Dixielander, though his connections to Chicago were few and he expressed loathing for Dixieland. A master of subtle and varied timbres, he perfected a style that caused timid listeners to question his technique—he was not infrequently mocked. A resolute improviser, he was that rare jazzman who could make a compelling statement out of written melody. Profoundly introspective, he spent much of his life with conventional musicians in conventional settings.

Unsurprisingly, critical opinion was sharply divided about Russell. Even an art that prizes originality as much as jazz can get flustered when the genuine article appears. "You have to be in the sun to feel the sun. It's that way with music, too," Sidney Bechet—a Russell admirer—advised. To those who could feel the warmth of Russell's deliberations, he was not only a peerless clarinetist but something of a seer. Kingsley Amis called him "the greatest lyric poet since Yeats"—an overstatement (Lester Young was Yeats's successor), but a typical one. Russell was frequently esteemed as a jazz poet because he could intimate compassion and mother wit concisely and in disparate surroundings. Yet he troubled many. One critic described his "rhapsodizing" as "musical nonsense set forth in phlegmy rasping 'spit' and 'growl' tones" and "a kind of sad and childish piping." History has come down enthusiastically on Russell's side, but his music retains the power to disturb. Only his uniqueness has never been in question. Russell never took jazz or his role in it lightly. His every improvisation was conscientious and daring; even his ensemble playing suggests simmering anarchy. Like any true seer, he was intransigent.

He was born Charles Ellsworth Russell in Maplewood, Missouri (a suburb of St. Louis), in 1906, the only child in a family with southern and Cherokee Indian roots. When he was six, the family moved to Muskogee, Oklahoma, where his father modestly prospered in oil, and where Charles began an unsuccessful regimen of music lessons, first on piano, then on drums and violin. One night his father took him to a dance at the Elks Club, where as steward he had arranged for a quintet from New Orleans to perform. The twelve-year-old boy was transfixed by clarinetist Alcide "Yellow" Nunez, best remembered for his recordings with the Louisiana Five, but also a charter member of the Original Dixieland Jazz Band. Russell convinced his parents to buy him a clarinet and persuaded a local pit-band musician to give him lessons. Determined to master the instrument and blessed with perfect pitch, he learned quickly and was able to accept a job that summer. When he sneaked out of the house to play on a riverboat, his father became the first of many authority figures who vainly attempted to discipline him.

Russell was enrolled at Western Military Academy in St. Louis, from which—thirteen months later—he was expelled. The following year, Russell crashed the University of Missouri, informally auditing music classes. He studied clarinet with a member of the St. Louis Symphony, traveled occasionally to Chicago to hear Johnny Dodds and Jimmie Noone ("there's a man influenced everybody . . . we all listened to Jimmie," he said), and worked on steamboats, in tent shows, and with local bands.

His most important association of that time was with Herbert Berger, who hired the fifteen-year-old boy for his Coronado Hotel Orchestra and dubbed him Pee Wee. (Russell grew to more than six feet, but stayed lean enough to sustain the nickname.) Berger would later arrange for Pee Wee's recording debut on a few sessions in 1922 and 1924 (no solos), but first he invited him to join him in the notorious border town of Juarez, Mexico. When Russell's parents surprised him by permitting him to go, he concluded they didn't love him, and he never lived at home again.

Pee Wee's Mexican experience got off to a calamitous start when a drunken altercation—he was already a heavy drinker—landed him three nights in jail. Yet he became a favorite in Juarez, and he settled in the Southwest for well over a year, spending several months in Houston with the legendary and influential pianist Peck Kelly, whose band included another fledgling, Jack Teagarden. Returning to St. Louis at the height of Prohibition and mob rule, Russell found a job with the Arcadia Ballroom Orchestra, working side by side with Frank Trumbauer and Bix Beiderbecke, who became his closest friend. Red Nichols lured him to New York in 1927 with the promise of recordings. On their first outing together, Russell took honors on "Ida," dramatically transforming an otherwise humdrum performance with his spirited, riff-laden twelve-measure solo. He played on numerous recordings after that and, in 1929, became one of the first jazzmen to perform an accomplished solo on film when he performed "Ida" in a one-reeler produced by the Vitaphone Company, featuring Nichols and his Five Pennies, among them the singing banjoist Eddie Condon.

Occasionally, Russell accepted money jobs with sugary commercial bands (he doubled on alto, tenor, soprano, and bass clarinet with Paul Sprecht's orchestra), but he preferred to play in Boston with his friend Bobby Hackett or with Louis Prima's extroverted combo in a two-year residency that took them from the Famous Door in New York to the one in Los Angeles. His fate was sealed, however, in 1937, when Nick Rongetti opened a nightclub in Greenwich Village called Nick's, devoted to a brand of music that was subsequently tagged Chicago-Dixieland or Condon-style (after his first bandleader) or Nicksieland. Russell's unpredictable approach to his solos alternated fierce growls with plaintive mewing and achingly tender sighs. He juxtaposed lithe melodies that seemed to abandon the ground beat with earthbound blues riffs and mesmerized the crowd at Nick's. Russell's facial contortions—eyes shut tight, mouth shuddering—underscored the emotional resolve behind his every note.

Russell was as quiet and sad and intent as a circus clown. Eddie Condon soon recognized him as a drawing card and stamped him in the role of buffoon. When *Life* made the photogenic Pee Wee the centerpiece of its 1938 article on jazz, he became something of a celebrity. Conn Instruments signed him for endorsements. And after years as a sideman on recordings by Nichols, Beiderbecke, the Mound City Blue Blowers, Condon, Billy Banks, Hackett, Teddy Wilson, and others, he was finally offered a recording date of his own. But Pee Wee Russell's Rhythmakers, an admirable, largely black octet, was a one-shot deal. The die had been cast, Russell's status as a supporting character confirmed. He remained a part of Nick's house band for nine years, despite frequent sabbaticals to play with Bobby Hackett's orchestra, the Summa Cum Laude cooperative, James P. Johnson's group at the Pied Piper Club, and a band of his own in Boston. He enjoyed little marquee value as a recording star until the late '50s.

Yet his fame mounted in the '40s, largely the result of his regular appearances on Eddie Condon's Sunday afternoon broadcasts from Town Hall. Few realized how much he resented his role as a clown or how bored he had become with Condon's limited approach and repertoire. He once remarked that the only good thing about Nick's was meeting Mary there; they married in 1943. By the late '40s, Russell was peering out from an alcoholic haze that subsumed whole weeks, then months. He left Mary in 1948 and went on the road with a trio he formed with pianist Art Hodes.

Two years later he turned up in San Francisco, weighing seventy-three pounds. On New Year's Eve 1951, he collapsed on the bandstand and was taken near death to the charity ward at San Francisco County Hospital. He was hospitalized nine months, suffering from alcoholism, malnutrician, pancreatitis, and cysts on his liver. When Louis Armstrong and Jack Teagarden visited his bedside, *Life*'s Wayne Miller took a startling photograph of them looking anxiously at the ailing Russell: sunken cheeks, eyes closed, boils on his face and neck. A benefit concert, headlined by Armstrong and Teagarden, took place in San Francisco; others followed in Chicago and New York. Russell survived, but he continued to drink. He returned to Mary and to Condon.

Friends noted a change in his personality—he became more assertive. So did his music. After a triumphant appearance at the first Newport Jazz Festival in 1954, Russell began appearing in unlikely modernist settings, including a concert (later a TV appearance) with Jimmy Giuffre. Despite his continuing allegiance to Condon, he now preferred younger musicians and entered into a mutually satisfying association with the thirty-year-old traditional trumpet player, Ruby Braff. Recordings with Braff led at long last to Russell's own 1957 recording session and many that followed.

The central dilemma Russell had to face in his music was his inability to function as an effective leader. Although he wrote a handful of memorable pieces in his later years, he was unable to establish a band that suited his unique improvisational gifts. He was invariably at the mercy of musical directors, none of whom devised ideal settings for him. It is something of a miracle that Russell managed to refine and modify his style over time while working almost exclusively in an orthodox milieu. That is not to say he was always at loggerheads with the Nicksielanders; he recorded many of his most witting and accomplished performances— "Serenade to a Shylock," "A Good Man Is Hard to Find," "Embraceable You," and "The Eel," among others—in their company.

But he needed a way out of the confines of a music that had become predictable to the point of suffocation, and his associates were more discouraging than enthusiastic. His playing had the effect of a hermetic vision probing nervously within the conventional polyphony of the Condon bluster. "I'm not a Dixieland clarinetist," Russell protested. "Why, I couldn't even play 'High Society' correctly if I had to. Oh sure, maybe I'd stagger through it because I've heard it so often. But that's about all."

Yet neither was he a true modernist—bop and cool held no allure for him.

Russell was most relaxed, most natural, with a mainstream rhythm section and perhaps one or two forceful soloists on the order of Coleman Hawkins, Buck Clayton, Vic Dickenson, and Bobby Hackett. Only in that kind of setting was he fully in control. His breakthrough sessions of 1957 and 1958, recorded for the soon defunct labels Stere-o-craft and Counterpoint (reissued in part by Xanadu on *Over the Rainbow* in 1982), capture Russell and his rhythm sections at precisely the moment when he was rebelling against Chicago-Dixieland's strictures. Three musicians on the 1957 date—Nat Pierce, Steve Jordan, and Walter Page—had worked with him in the Ruby Braff Octet. Drummer George Wettling was a talented Condon veteran, responsive to Russell's asymmetrical phrasing. On the fast numbers, he and Russell sound as though they are engaged in duets—among the highlights are Wettling's weird two-bar cymbal break at the close of "I'm in the Market for You," his use of press rolls to spur Russell's second chorus on "I Would Do Anything for You," and the jolting climax he spurs on "Exactly Like You."

Russell's ballad playing, one of the glories of jazz, is another instance of his incongruity. He resolved to make every solo an unpremeditated search, expressive and beautiful—a purpose he shared with fewer players than one might think, among them Roy Eldridge, Lester Young, and Lee Konitz. Russell was never content to thread the chord changes, and he often panicked players on the bandstand by venturing so far beyond the harmonic parameters of a song that no one thought he'd find his way back. Sometimes he didn't. Yet this same artist was no less devoted to undiluted interpretations of written music. Perhaps only Johnny Hodges could surpass him at creating emotionally and intellectually satisfying performances that stick to the melody. The 1957 session included two takes of "I'd Climb the Highest Mountain," lovely examples of Russell's ability to personalize a song, in this instance an old favorite that he had played with Beiderbecke in the mid-'20s and that he would record in a still more deliberate and spartan interpretation in 1963 for the album *Ask Me Now*.

The 1957 session was also notable for the introduction of two Russell originals, the hauntingly attractive "Pee Wee's Song" and "Muskogee Blues," which finds him moving with sly ingenuity from the lower to middle register. The one Russell composition that became a bona fide classic was introduced at the 1958 date for Counterpoint, "Pee Wee's Blues," a tune he would perform on numerous occasions. The shy, halting quality of the melody is arresting and not easily forgotten, but the success of the piece probably derives from the way it codifies his style as an improviser. Russell's approach to the blues was never obvious, and his initial version of "Pee Wee's Blues" created a curious tension between his unearthly exposition, gliding intrepidly out of the low chalumeau register, and Nat Pierce's funky accompaniment.

By the late '50s, Pee Wee was looking beyond traditionalism altogether. Jazz was now under siege from a new avant-garde, and two of its most unlikely and inadvertent heroes were Russell and Henry "Red" Allen, who had recorded together as early as 1932. Both men had long been pigeonholed as mainstreamers of a particular sort. Yet the instrumental mannerisms that sounded eccentric in the context of traditionalism were deemed prophetic in the age of New Music, where expressive technique and idiosyncratic pitch is valued as a means of breaking with convention. Trumpeter Don Ellis proclaimed Red Allen an icon of the New Music, and Coleman Hawkins said of Russell: "For thirty years, I've been listening to him play those funny notes. We used to think they were wrong, but they weren't. He's always been way out but they didn't have a name for it then."

Hawkins and Russell first recorded together in 1929 with a recording unit called the Mound City Blue Blowers. That session produced a milestone in "One Hour," in which Hawkins established the tenor saxophone as an instrument capable of great feeling. No less individual was Russell's chorus, his percussive articulation clipping and growling every note for maximum impact and providing an affecting contrast with Hawkins's lavish melodies. In 1961, they were reunited for *Jazz Reunion* (Candid). The album isn't perfect—Nat Pierce's arrangements are curiously dry—but Russell and Hawkins are. At the time, their careers were like opposing diagonals. Russell had only recently begun a regular schedule of recording, while Hawkins was in the studios on an almost monthly regimen. Russell was at the outset of an extended last hurrah; Hawkins, who would outlive Russell by three months, was edging toward a period of decline. Here, they inspired each other.

On their remake of "One Hour," still played as sixteen-measure choruses with two-measure tags, Hawkins charges in with his unmistakable, virile authority, biting the higher notes, unraveling begrudging arpeggios as though the song were a blues, and double-timing against the chords in his second chorus. Russell's solo is not the impeccable construction of his 1929 chorus, but there is greater generosity of feeling, a nearly serendipitous lyricism—the tenacious yearning for beauty that increasingly came to characterize his music. On "All Too Soon," he complements Hawkins's certitude with a wise and weary caution that suddenly transforms itself into a wailing tempest—Russell's Ariel responding to Hawkins's Prospero. He is at his best on two blues. On "Mariooch," his inquiring, strangled tones are flawlessly captured; he begins his second solo with his anthem, "Pee Wee's Blues," and concludes it with a smoky calculation and asperity that might have translated to Miles Davis's trumpet. On "28th and 8th," his ratchety sound would cut your fingers off if you could touch it, though in a reversal of his usual procedure he ends with rustic chalumeau.

Overall, *Jazz Reunion* and Russell's 1960 quintet session for Prestige (with Buck Clayton and Tommy Flanagan) are more satisfying than the self-consciously modern quartet Russell fronted a couple of years later, yet that collaboration—with valve trombonist Marshall Brown—represented another personal triumph. A journeyman musician and high school teacher, Brown was a martinet who served as music director for the pianoless foursome designed to bolster Russell's standing as a modernist. The idea was sound enough, but Brown was the wrong man to make it work. According to Russell's friends, the clarinetist was less offended by Brown's martial personality than by his insistence on writing out every head and all of his own solos. Yet the idea was fascinating: old pop songs and new jazz pieces by Thelonious Monk, John Coltrane, and Ornette Coleman, played in a spare contemporary style. Dull as Brown's playing was, the quartet's austerity provided a brave new context for Russell.

On the first album, *New Groove* (Columbia), recorded in 1962, Russell surprised critics with his diverse transformations, ranging from George Jessell's impossibly maudlin "My Mother's Eyes" to Coltrane's "Red Planet" (better known as "Miles' Mode"), which has a twelve-tone row for a theme. His rousing interpretation of the latter is an impetuous, woolly ride, yet always coherent and persuasive. One of the most adventurous albums of its day and generally well reviewed, *New Groove* sold poorly and was dropped from the label's catalog before the year was out, never to be reissued.

As a result, *Ask Me Now*, a follow-up recorded four months later (in April 1963), wasn't released until 1966, by Impulse, which put a deceptive date ("Recorded 1965") on the label copy. A tamer session in some respects, it, too, underscored Russell's predilection for Coltrane: he tears into "Some Other Blues" as though impatient for the arranged part to end and the revelry to begin. The album's emotional peak is his slow translucent reading of "I'd Climb the Highest Mountain." At the 1963 Newport Jazz Festival, the allegedly reconstructed Russell was invited to sit in with Thelonious Monk's quartet, hardly a meeting of minds, but he did improvise seven punchy choruses on "Blue Monk."

Russell continued to appear on occasion with Condon (their Far East tour in 1964 was a great success, producing a decisive recording of "Pee Wee's Blues"), but his own records wore an entirely different garb: a

1966 collaboration with Earl Hines put him amid a band of Ellington alumni and Coltrane's drummer, Elvin Jones (*Once Upon a Time*); a live recording later that year with Red Allen boasted a rhythm section with Steve Kuhn and Ornette Coleman's bassist, Charlie Haden (*The College Concert*); best of all, a 1967 big band venture with Oliver Nelson, *The Spirit of '67*, produced exceptionally personal renderings of "Memories of You," "Ja-Da," "I'm Coming Virginia," and "A Good Man Is Hard to Find"—the latter notable for his ingenious pickup after a fervent Phil Woods solo. Those three albums were recorded for Impulse, a label that promoted "the new wave of jazz."

It was a heady period for Russell, who additionally found the energy to pursue another art, oil painting. Though he never held a paintbrush before 1965, when Mary put one in his hand and told him to paint, he achieved immediate attention as an adept and color-savvy technician in the manner of Stuart Davis, an old acquaintance of his. But Russell's renaissance was short-lived. Mary died in 1967, and he never got over it. Three weeks after playing the 1969 presidential inaugural ball, Russell died in a hospital in Alexandria, Virginia. Intransigent to the end, he had been caught trying to sneak a pint of vodka into the hospital.

One song repeatedly marked the last and, in many respects, best decade of his career, the adaptable "Pee Wee's Blues." He recorded it with a 1959 swing octet, the 1962 pianoless quartet, the 1964 Condon quintet, the 1966 *College Concert* rhythm section, and the 1967 Oliver Nelson big band. In each instance, he showed how deeply—and with what imagination and skill—he could reach beyond the surface of a twelve-bar blues to uncover a poetry that existed only in the moment. His achievement exists apart from the neat categories of musical history and fashion. "For poetry makes nothing happen," Auden reminded us, "it survives."

15 ❖ Chick Webb (King of the Savoy)

The story of William Henry Webb, nicknamed Chick for his small size, seems to cry out for novelistic scope and nuance. His musical accomplishments were diverse: he was the first great drummer of the swing era, the leader of a fiercely competitive and innovative orchestra, a pacesetter for dancers during the golden age of ballroom dancing, and a nurturer of talent whose fabled generosity was rewarded when he discovered and groomed Ella Fitzgerald. But the nearly unconquerable King of the Savoy Ballroom was also a dwarfed hunchback, mangled by spinal tuberculosis, who lived most of his short life in pain and died within a year of his first major commercial success. He overcame staggering obstacles with a tenacity that awed other musicians, and he did it with élan, never asking for or requiring handicap points. He was as much adored by dancers as by musicians, and no one dared patronize him.

Chick Webb's story wouldn't exercise so powerful a spell if the contrast between his imposing reputation and atrophied frame didn't find a correlative in his music. He may well have been the first jazz drummer to convey complicated emotions, at least on records. Even today, despite half a century of virtuoso band drummers who surpassed and refined his technique, Webb's rattling breaks and solos are astonishing. Those who heard him live insist that records hid his genius, but there is nothing remotely like the feeling of a Webb break—a pealing explosion in which each stroke has the articulation of a gunshot. Fast and disciplined, he was attuned to his soloists and spurred them with flashing cymbals or emphatic shuffle rhythms. He orchestrated the components of his traps like an arranger, meshing the sound of his huge bass drum with bells, blocks, and rim shots, punctuating the airless rumble with choked swipes at two cymbals that swayed before him on gooseneck hangers. Writing in 1939, Charles Edward Smith observed, "Listening to the drums, you got a sense of percussive build-up, to the blood as well as to the ear, but you also came to understand that a drummer was, after all, a musician playing tones." Webb didn't solo frequently, but when he did, he was ferocious. At the Savoy, his drums were nailed to a movable stand; on tour, he often needed assistants to bolster them against his attack.

Unfortunately, there's no filmed record of Webb in action. His band appeared in a 1929 short, *After Seben*, but he's out of camera range. Numerous drummers who saw him, however, never forgot him; they describe him in grandly romantic terms. Enthroned over his traps, which included a twenty-eight-inch bass drum with pedals built to accommodate his stunted legs, he is said to have conveyed a wry magnificence, dominating all the accoutrements with a winning lopsided smile, leaning into the hardware while hands and feet pumped rhythms and counter-rhythms. Those who learned from him include Buddy Rich, Gene Krupa, Sid Catlett, Jo Jones, Dave Tough, Cozy Cole, and Panama Francis. Ronald Shannon Jackson says he studies Webb's records for inspiration. Krupa remarked, "When he really let go, you had a feeling that the entire atmosphere in the place was being charged. When he felt like it, he could down any of us."

Bandleaders also loved him, sometimes too well. Webb had an extraordinary ear for talent, and his band was raided in the years when he was known only in Harlem. Fletcher Henderson hired away trumpet players Bobby Stark and Cootie Williams, and Duke Ellington grabbed twenty-year-old Johnny Hodges. Ellington later said that Webb came to him and offered Hodges because he "would be better in our band where he would have more freedom of expression" and played broker for Williams, who had left Webb for Henderson. Webb reportedly told Ellington, "He was with me for a while, but he's too much for me. Fletcher heard him and hired him but that style don't fit Fletcher's band . . . for you he'll be a bitch!"

If that sounds magnanimous even for the saintly Webb, it undoubtedly reflects his gratitude to Ellington for starting him as a bandleader in 1926, a position he accepted with some reluctance at first. Ellington later wrote that when he was in residence at the Kentucky Club, someone came in wanting to hire a band; the Maestro assembled a small group and dubbed Webb the leader. "As a drummer, Chick had his own ideas about what he wanted to do. Some musicians are dancers, and Chick was," recalled Ellington, who went on to elaborate the importance of that equation: "The reason why Chick Webb had such control, such command of his audiences at the Savoy Ballroom, was because he was always in communication with the dancers and felt it the way they did. And that is probably the biggest reason why he could cut all the other bands that went in there."

All but one. Ten years after the Kentucky Club episode, Webb was the undisputed King of the Savoy, but in March 1937 he did battle with the Ellington band and was trounced. According to Teddy McRae, a Webb saxophonist and arranger, Webb saw Sonny Greer tuning his drums before the melee and said, "What is he tuning up for? I'm gonna kill him before he gets started. And he did." But his band was demolished. "I can't take it," Webb told trombonist Sandy Williams during a break, "this is the first time we've ever really been washed out." Webb and Williams recorded a few days later with several Ellington musicians (including Cootie Williams) as The Gotham Stompers; on "My Honey's Lovin' Arms," he showed how he might have sparked the Ellington rhythm section.

Webb's most celebrated battle came three months later, and it, too, was a rout, only this time Webb regained his crown. From 1931 on, Webb was admired by many white bandleaders—including Paul Whiteman—who knew they couldn't raid a black band. Benny Goodman got around that by appropriating the orchestrations of Webb's gifted saxophonist-violinist-arranger-composer Edgar Sampson, creator of several of the era's anthems. The early Goodman hits that didn't come from Fletcher

Henderson's book came from Webb's, including "Don't Be That Way," "Stomping at the Savoy," "Blue Lou," and "If Dreams Come True," all by Sampson. Goodman's appearance at the Savoy opposite Webb on May 11, 1937, was bound to be tense, especially since his drummer, Gene Krupa, was the most highly publicized percussionist in the country.

Helen Oakley Dance, who covered the event, reported that nearly 10,000 people showed up, half of whom were turned away at the door, causing a traffic tie-up that lasted all night. Mario Bauza, Webb's lead trumpeter, recalled the little man giving the band a pep talk: "Tonight we got to make history. Our future depends on tonight." The verdict rendered by the teaming crowd as well as representatives of *Down Beat* and *Metronome* was unanimously decided in Webb's favor. According to Dance, the climax came when Webb followed Goodman with one of Goodman's own hits, "Jam Session," and "blew the roof off the house." Earlier in the evening, Krupa had stood, facing Webb, and bowed down in respect.

Chick Webb's birth date has been variously given as 1902, 1907, and 1909, but the latter seems to be widely accepted now, which puts him in an increasingly long column of precocious jazz musicians who made themselves out to be older. He was born in Baltimore and raised by his grandfather after his father and later his mother moved out. He is said to have started teaching himself drums at three, eventually arranging batteries of tin cans, pots, and stacks of magazines. At eleven, he earned enough money as a newsboy to buy a set of traps and was soon playing in the Jazzola Band on a riverboat on Chesapeake Bay, along with guitarist John Truehart. Three years later—when Webb was fifteen—the two arrived in New York, where the segregated band scene was dominated by Paul Whiteman and Fletcher Henderson. Webb convinced Tommy Benford to give him lessons and hustled for chances to play. Eventually Bobby Stark recommended him for a job with a group led by Edgar Dowell, and he began to earn a reputation. At first people made a point of coming to see him because of the way he looked. That began to change with the gig Ellington set up in 1926, which lasted five months. In Truehart, Stark, Hodges, and pianist Don Kirkpatrick, Webb had the nucleus of an important band. He soon added other musicians, including Mario Bauza and saxophonist Elmer Williams, and emerged as a tutor to drummers of both races who came to hear him in Harlem. Defensive about his band, he invited cutting competitions and invariably charmed his victims. Still, the Webb band was barely making it and remained unknown beyond a coterie of musicians.

Webb's luck began to change in 1931 when he was booked into downtown dance halls as well as the Savoy. He toured with *Hot Chocolates,* the show that made Louis Armstrong a star, and his band backed Armstrong when the great man resumed recording after his European tour of 1932. Webb's snare work is in evidence on "Hobo You Can't Ride This Train," and his eleven-piece band rips through the climactic riffs on "You'll Wish You'd Never Been Born," which opens with an enchanting Armstrong cadenza that anticipates his solo on "Laughin' Louie." By that time, Webb had recorded a couple of sessions on his own. In 1929 he appeared on disc as the Jungle Band, hewing to the Fletcher Henderson–Don Redman style on "Dog Bottom," but mining Ellington's shadowy terrain on "Jungle Mama." A session under his own name followed in 1931, around the time be began the first in a series of long residencies at the Savoy; on that date, he introduced Benny Carter's "Blues in My Heart" and a version of "Heebie Jeebies" with a benchmark trombone solo by Jimmy Harrison and a promising tenor sax solo by Elmer Williams.

During the next three years, Webb stubbornly refined his band and found an orchestral style of his own. By the time he recorded in January 1934, he had assembled a rigorous unit with efficient jazz soloists and some of the hottest arrangers of the day, including Edgar Sampson, whose earliest contributions included "If Dreams Come True," "Stomping at the Savoy," and Webb's theme song, "Let's Get Together." Soon Webb hired Wayman Carver, the first jazz flutist and (aside from Albert Socassas, who was really a classical player) the only one of consequence for nearly twenty years. The unison sound of Carver's flute and Chauncy Haughton's clarinet, especially in Webb's small unit (Chick Webb and His Little Chicks), was startling. Neither man swung very hard, but they could project a daunting string of sixteenth notes with radiance and they pointed up the diversity of Webb's band. By the time Benny Goodman kicked off the swing era with his triumph at the Palomar Ballroom in Los Angeles in 1935, Webb had one of the most distinctive bands in New York—his arrangers included Van Alexander, Charlie Dixon, and Dick Vance. But like Henderson's, it couldn't break nationally. Webb and Henderson watched as their records caused small ripples, while cover versions by the Goodman orchestra caused tidal waves. Goodman even had his name added as composer. In the movie *The Benny Goodman Story,* you can watch Goodman compose Sampson's "Don't Be That Way."

Most of Webb's records were in the Henderson tradition, which massed reeds and brasses in antiphonal call-and-response. Yet the band's audacious attack, primed by Webb's prodding rhythms, rim-shot turnbacks, and explosive breaks, gave the arrangements a unique kick. In some of the band's best choruses, reeds and brasses collude like overlapping shadows. The band's stately, almost arhythmic side, as reflected in the Carver-Haughton passages, made for beguiling contrast. His soloists have been grievously underrated—among them trombonist Sandy Williams (spotlighted on "Organ Grinder's Swing"); trumpeters Stark, Bauza, and Taft Jordan (who came closer than most to capturing the Armstrong might); and saxophonists Sampson, Hilton Jefferson, Elmer Williams, and Teddy McRae. With John Truehart and John Kirby, Webb had one of the better rhythm sections of the '30s ("That Rhythm Man" is a good example). In 1934, he finally discovered a musician who grabbed the public; unlike Hodges, Cootie, or Sampson, this one didn't get away.

In 1934, the teenage Ella Fitzgerald won a talent contest at the Apollo Theater trying to sing like Connee Boswell. At Benny Carter's suggestion, Webb agreed to give her a tryout and was hooked. He became her legal guardian, bought her clothing to perform in, and remade his band around the voice he predicted would be heard for decades. From the summer of 1935, she was featured on almost all his recording sessions and quickly attracted a following. The band began to tour, working some of the better hotels and picking up radio airtime. In 1938, Van Alexander orchestrated a novelty tune Fitzgerald had worked up from a nursery rhyme to entertain Webb during a hospital stay. "A-Tisket A-Tasket," recorded in May and powered by Webb's offbeat accents, was one of the biggest hits of the decade—the biggest Ella, who had just turned twenty, would ever have. Within months she was billed as "the first lady of swing." Lena Horne recently recalled, "A whole generation of us girl singers went looking for that yellow basket." Webb found himself a commercial property, and to the dismay of many of his supporters, made the band increasingly subordinate to his singer.

Helen Oakley Dance, who was hired as his publicist, has pointed out the painful irony in Webb's sudden celebrity. He had fought extraordinary odds for a decade to assemble a great band, and now, just when swing was at the height of its popularity, he was playing it safe. Some thought he knew his time was running out and wanted to secure a foothold for Ella. In any case, the accusation wasn't entirely fair: Webb made many of his finest instrumental recordings during the Ella years, including Benny Carter's feature for drums, "Liza," as well as "Harlem Congo," "Spinning the Web," and "Clap Hands! Here Comes Charlie." Some of his best work is heard on such peerless Fitzgerald sides as "Cryin' Mood" (in which Webb seems to levitate the orchestra), "My Heart Belongs to Daddy," "Undecided," "Pack Up Your Sins and Go to the Devil," "Holiday in Harlem," "Shine," and "My Last Affair."

Almost from the time "A-Tisket A-Tasket" topped the charts, Webb was in chronic pain; the tuberculosis worsened and pleurisy developed. He was in and out of hospitals and on at least two occasions collapsed on the bandstand. He was in John Hopkins Hospital in Baltimore for a couple of days before the end came. According to Dance, he lifted himself from the pillows, said, "I'm sorry, but I gotta go," and was gone. If the 1909 birthdate holds, he was just thirty years old. Ella sang "My Buddy" at the funeral, and the pallbearers and honorary pallbearers included Fletcher Henderson, Benny Carter, Al Cooper, Duke Ellington, Gene Krupa, Cab Calloway, and Jimmie Lunceford. A couple of months later, Count Basie paid homage with a cover of "Clap Hands! Here Comes Charlie." Fitzgerald returned Webb's loyalty by fronting the band for two more years, with Teddy McRae and Eddie Barefield as music directors, and then went out as a single. In 1947, a recreational center in Baltimore was named in his honor. Three years later, "A-Tisket A-Tasket" was certified as a gold record.

16 ❖ Fats Waller
(Comedy Tonight)

Fats Waller, one of the most enduringly popular figures in American music, is a state of mind. Jazz has always claimed him (what idiom *wouldn't* claim him?) and yet he spent most of his abbreviated career cavorting through, and contributing to, the Tin Pan Alley canon—applying a determined jazz accent, perhaps, but with the sui generis detachment of a free-floating institution. He wasn't witty, if that word is taken to imply a kind of humor too subtle to engender belly laughs—he was funny. He was also bigger than life, Rabelaisian in intake, energy, and output. His greatest joy was playing Bach on the organ, but he buttered his bread as a clown, complete with a mask as fixed as that of Bert Williams or Spike Jones. It consisted of a rakishly tilted derby, one size too small, an Edwardian mustache that fringed his upper lip, eyebrows as thick as paint and pliable as curtains, flirtatious eyes, a mouth alternately pursed or widened in a dimpled smile, and immense girth, draped in the expensive suits and ties of a dandy.

A ripe sense of humor is indigenous in jazz. It's a music quick to enlist whatever barbs can best deflate pomposity and artificiality. But jazz has not always been rich in humorists, though one can point to a few in any given period. Those in the postwar era include Dizzy Gillespie, Clark

Terry, James Moody, Jon Hendricks, Jaki Byard, Lester Bowie, Willem
Breuker, the Jazz Passengers, and Waller's druggy disciple, Harry "The
Hipster" Gibson. Humor was more extensive in the '20s and '30s, when
Prohibition, the Depression, and the insularity of a new and predominantly black music conspired to create an undercurrent of protective irreverence. Accustomed to a place on the outside looking in, jazz took
pleasure in skewering anything that made the mainstream feel safe and
smug. It was a time when Fats Waller could count on a laugh by inter-
rupting a particularly suave solo with the rumination, "Hmm, I wonder
what the poor people are doing tonight."   ·

Musicians, singers, and other entertainers created countless songs
about bathtub gin, drugs, sex (of every variety), and other subjects un-
suitable for Judge Hardy and his family, and invented slang—a new
kind of signifying—to get it over. As late as the mid-'60s, Cab Calloway
could cheerfully invite Ed Sullivan's audience to hi-de-ho with him on
the joys of cocaine. Jazz recordings offered euphemisms so arcane (example, women's genitals: barbecue, paswonky, the boy in the boat) that
no postgraduate course in ebonics could have brought them all to light.
They slipped through broadcasting codes and around censors. The real
measure of jazz grit in those years, however, was the way it stood up to
the conventions of pop culture. Encumbered with the dreariest products
of the songwriting factory, the stuff Alec Wilder *didn't* write about, musicians were obliged to transcend or annihilate the material. Waller did
both with dog tunes Victor forced on him at one session after another;
but his comic ebullience also informed his serious side, girding his exacting piano pieces and peerlessly swinging ensembles.

Waller's primary influence was James P. Johnson, the songwriter and
grandmaster of the Harlem school of stride piano. The term "stride" is
descriptive and refers to the movement of the pianist's left hand, which
upholds the rhythm while swinging side to side, from distant bass notes,
played on the first and third beats of the measure, to close chords in the
octave below middle C, played on the second and fourth beats. Stride
was a social music, powerful enough to surmount the din of a rent party
and vigorous enough to encourage dancing. It was also a competitive
music, a specialist's art. The best players were fine composers, but stride
was malleable: they could stride pop songs or classical themes, just as
an earlier generation of pianists could rag them. Stride per se never had
a large audience. It was bypassed during the boogie-woogie rage and
overlooked by all but a few in the years of bop. Of its key practitioners,
only Waller achieved real commercial success, and then only because of
his wisecracks. Had he done nothing but pursue his art as a pianist, he
might be no better known than Johnson, Luckey Roberts, Willie "The

Lion" Smith, Donald Lambert, Willie Gant, or other Harlem-based keyboard professors, who took themselves pretty seriously. The complaint aimed at Waller is that he didn't take himself seriously enough.

He was perversely inspired by kitsch, for example, the 1913 saloon tearjerker, "The Curse of an Aching Heart," which Fats leaps upon at breakneck tempo, with all the fake operatic bravado he can muster, somehow ending up with a splendid vehicle. Billie Holiday, who was also held in chancery by song pluggers, could transform the maudlin horror "It's a Sin To Tell a Lie" into an arresting and winsome love song—shaping the phrase, "I love you, yes I do, I love you," with a plaintive candor that turns frivolity into urgent revelation. For Waller, the song is simply ludicrous and must be skewered, shaken, and swung, especially that "I love you" line. An outsider like Spike Jones could make fun of rhythm itself, but not Waller. Pop was his cross, swing his salvation.

A local celebrity while still in his teens, Waller died unconscionably at thirty-nine, spurring the long debate as to how his genius might have been better realized had he lived to compose, perform, and record in more salubrious circumstances. But how much poorer we would be without the comic legacy, by far the predominant part of his more than 500 recordings. The idea that the full breadth of his gift was heard only in private after-hours settings or before a pipe organ doesn't quite comport with his boisterous personality. In the decades following his death, he was exhaustively acclaimed as a songwriter, in tribute albums by Louis Armstrong and Dinah Washington, among others, as well as the revue *Ain't Misbehavin'*. He was, indeed, after Ellington, the most successful songwriter to emerge from the heart of jazz. Supremely confident of his capabilities, he was known to trade songs (including a few that became standards) for hamburgers. He wrote them in minutes and improvised an entire instrumental suite in less than an hour. Yet only in the records, especially when he debunks other people's songs, are we encouraged to partake of the saucy leer, the fey hand movements, the metronomic time, the offhanded virtuosity, and nasal pitch-perfect voice.

Waller divides his vocal range for effect: middle octave for straight swinging variations, lower notes for rude asides, higher ones for feminine mockery and cries of encouragement to the band. Yet the miraculous thing about his comedy is that it is never an end in itself (unlike, for example, recordings of Jimmy Durante, who used his raggy piano chops purely as an adjunct to his clowning). Humor enabled Waller to sweep up the musical debris of the day, but also allowed him to inflect it with his own exuberance. Jazz in the swing era was frequently an alchemical art. Waller's musicianship complements his most abusive remarks. Significantly, he neglected to record some of his own best songs.

As the only stride pianist to achieve true stardom, Waller influenced generations of pianists drawn to the ideal articulation of his lateral left hand and the delicate refinement of his right. Duke Ellington's piano style was grounded in stride and so were many of his best compositions. Art Tatum once observed, "Fats, that's where I come from," and it is probably true that Waller's early blues instrumentals, notably "Blue Black Bottom" and "Numb Fumblin'," represent the most imperious blues technique in jazz piano until Tatum. Teddy Wilson expanded on Waller's broken tenths, and Count Basie began as a Waller-mimic and then edited his style down to its essentials. Thelonious Monk and Bud Powell occasionally employed Wallerian mannerisms, and most postmodernist pianists who turned to stride as a means of levitating their performances (Jaki Byard, Muhal Richard Abrams, Dave Burrell, Stanley Cowell, Hilton Ruiz) chose Waller as their point of departure. James P. Johnson demonstrated more imagination in his bass figures and greater concern with developing stride as a basis for large-scale composition, but Waller's rhythmic gait, matchless clarity, and joie de vivre were irresistable.

Waller's instrumental compositions are as rewarding as his songs, among them "Stealin' Apples" (a staple of jam sessions), "Whiteman Stomp," "A Handful of Keys," "Clothes Line Ballet," "Viper's Drag," "Smashing Thirds," "Fractious Fingering," "Alligator's Drag," and the largely improvised *London Suite*. A couple of them were orchestrated for big bands; the rest are charming piano pieces. His more famous songs include the endlessly recast "Honeysuckle Rose" and the abiding "Ain't Misbehavin'," as well as "Squeeze Me," "(What Did I Do To Be So) Black and Blue," "I've Got a Feeling I'm Falling," "Blue Turning Gray Over You," "I'm Crazy 'Bout My Baby," "Keepin' Out of Mischief Now," and "Ain'tcha Glad." He was fortunate in his stellar lyricist, Andy Razaf, a master of double entendre and original imagery, and in his insuperable interpreter and faithful advocate, Louis Armstrong. Waller himself was a gifted leader of small ensembles, able to whip musicians into a frenzy with shouts of encouragement and the rhythmic brawn of his piano.

Thomas Wright Waller was born in New York in 1904, the son of a clergyman. His mother played piano and organ and supervised his musical education. At fifteen, shortly before her death, Waller began playing professionally; he could always find work accompanying silent movies, a discipline that spurred him to cultivate the standard devices of melodrama. Those wary tremolos, ominous bass walks, and "Spring Song" epiphanies were later employed by Waller in his commentaries on pop songs. Sometimes, as in "Russian Fantasy," they *are* the song. At eighteen, he recorded his first piano pieces, "Muscle Shoals Blues" and "Birmingham Blues," both heavily indebted to James P. Johnson. For the next few years, he worked in various theaters, backing singers as well as movies, absorbing the latest fancies in Broadway musicals (he adored Gershwin), and assimilating the teachings of Johnson and, at Gershwin's urging, Leopold Godowski. As Johnson's heir apparent, he was in constant demand for all kinds of recording sessions—vaudevillian Juanita Stinette Chappelle, the Elkins Negro Ensemble, Porter Grainger, and a would-be singer (and nephew to the queen of Madagascar) who changed his name from Andreamenentania Paul Razafinkeriefo to Andy Razaf. But Waller was more at home with blues divas, among them Alberta Hunter, Rosa Henderson, Sara Martin, Hazel Myers, Maude Mills, and, though he never recorded with her, Bessie Smith.

By the 1926–27 season, Waller had made important contacts on Broadway and in jazz, and his career forged ahead. He took over the piano chair when Fletcher Henderson recorded his "Henderson Stomp" and "Whiteman Stomp," a pointed reference to the kings of a racially divided music; completed twenty-three piano rolls; and recorded a dozen pipe organ solos. At a session by the Louisiana Sugar Babes, his pipe organ was combined with James P. Johnson's piano. The payoff came in 1929, when he wrote three solid hits for the revue *Hot Chocolates*: "Black and Blue," "Sweet Savannah Sue," and the showstopper that secured Armstrong's reputation in New York, "Ain't Misbehavin'." That same year, RCA invited Waller to record several of his works for piano. At twenty-five, he was widely respected as a major young talent. Few could have imagined the strange turn his career was about to take.

The Depression slowed him down for three and a half years, during which he recorded very little, though memorably with Jack Teagarden, Pee Wee Russell, and vaudeville headliner Ted Lewis. But he kept busy. He played with several bands, collaborated with Spencer Williams on a show at Connie's Inn, accompanied Williams to France for a few weeks, accepted a great deal of radio work, including a long residency as staff pianist for a station in Cincinnati, and made occasional performance tours. In 1931, he recorded two solo numbers for OKeh, "Draggin' My Heart Around" and "I'm Crazy 'Bout My Baby," that suggest something of his bubbling potential as an entertainer. Yet three years would pass before he had another session under his own name. This time, in May 1934, he was under exclusive contract to Victor and at the helm of a sextet billed as Fats Waller and His Rhythm. In the first seconds of the farcical "A Porter's Love Song to a Chambermaid" (written, apparently with him in mind, by Johnson and Razaf), a new Fats was born—in J. R. Taylor's words, "the gargoyle Fats, spouting pianistic filigree while regarding the world through a mocking mask of bowed lips and swooping eyebrows." His success was immediate, but it should be noted that almost all his best songs were composed before his incarnation as court jester.

Waller's hundreds of Rhythm sides present a problem for the listener, especially when they are issued in complete and sequential boxes rather than sensibly edited anthologies. Although the songs range from top-of-the-line to mind-shattering swill, the delivery tends to follow a pattern and the vocal asides ("my, my," "well, alright then," "one never knows, do one?") wear thin over too large a helping. Yet the energy level rarely flags. Waller is always center stage, exhorting soloists when they dally and charging the rhythm section with his thumping left hand. He is surrounded by a crew of talented, eager second-tier musicians. Trumpeter Herman Autrey (a skillful Armstrong man), saxophonist Gene Sedrick (merry if a bit wheezy), and trombonist Floyd O'Brian (melodic and slick) are almost always pleasing. On two sessions, Fats is availed of Bill Coleman's bright, masterful trumpet, and guitarist Al Casey is almost always around to beef up the rhythm. On those first dates, Waller's piano sparkles on "I Wish I Were Twins," "Do Me a Favor," "Have a Little Dream on Me," and "I Ain't Got Nobody."

Within a year, the material started to get really gruesome. That Waller can get as much as he does from "My Very Good Friend the Milkman" is miraculous; even he is stopped cold by "You're the Cutest One." He's ebullient on "Lulu's Back in Town" (hear him crank the engine during Autrey's solo); seductive on "Sweet and Slow"; stately on the straight rendition of "I'm Gonna Sit Right Down and Write Myself a Letter," one of his most admired recordings; irascible on "There'll Be Some Changes Made"; and suitably disrespectful on "Brother Seek and Ye Shall Find." He has his share of good period pieces ("Dinah," "Truckin'"), but none of them are Waller originals. He recorded far too often to sustain his creativity, but the gems are luminous: "I Can't Give You Anything But Love" (with Una Mae Carlisle as straight woman), "Until the Real Thing Comes Along," "Hold Tight" (a lyric of Joycean complexity having to do with sex or constipation or both), "If I Were You," "Beat It Out," "Blue Turning Gray Over You" (one of his prettiest originals), "Christopher Columbus" ("the crew was making merry," he sings, then mutters "so Mary went home"), "Don't Let it Bother You" (ah, if only he could have had a shot at the '80s' similarly constituted "Don't Worry, Be Happy"), the remake of "I'm Crazy 'Bout My Baby," and dozens more. On a 1937 session, he uses steel guitar and sends up the "Sweet

Leilani" craze with "Neglected," yet is maddeningly respectful of "Why Do Hawaiians Sing Aloha?"

Recording alone at the piano, he could betray frustration and a perfunctory attitude, even to the point of clumsy execution, as on the plodding blues "My Feelings Are Hurt." But such instances are rare. He was a born pianist with a distinctive attack and usually imperturbable. "Handful of Keys" is based on little more than a scale, but it is the embodiment of Harlem stride and boasts what is probably the single most imitated lick in the entire idiom. "I've Got a Feeling I'm Falling" is a lesson in voice leading with the left hand. "Numb Fumblin' " is a blues of exquisite finesse. "Valentine Stomp" and "Smashing Thirds" perfectly embody his clean, strutting, virtuoso control, varied bass lines, deft variations, and compositional imagination. All of these performances date from 1929; some that followed are more impressive: "African Ripples" deals playfully with Gershwin harmonies, "Clothes Line Ballet" wittily alternates between impressionism and stride, "E Flat Blues" is paced with the certainty of a metronome and the solicitude of a prayer.

Waller learned to heighten popular songs with an emotional texture rare in stride, yet devoid of the sentimentality that intrudes in the music of other stride pianists, for example that of Willie "the Lion" Smith. In addition to reharmonizing chords, he employs an eight-to-the-bar boogie framework to make the rhythms edgier. "Georgia on My Mind" is perhaps the peak example of his transfigurative powers, closely followed by "Tea for Two" (with shades of mock-classicism, boogie, and stride), "Basin Street Blues," "Keepin' Out of Mischief Now," "I Ain't Got Nobody," and a startling, sinuous "Ring Dem Bells." He recorded a fastidious if compressed version of James P. Johnson's "Carolina Shout" and a parodistic survey of "Honeysuckle Rose ("a la Bach-Beethoven-Brahms-Waller"). Some of his most intriguing solo work was recorded not for Victor, but at 1939 radio broadcasts that found him performing nineteenth-century spirituals and minstrel songs with a combination of nostalgic relish and blustery impatience—he takes the melodies seriously, but not the words, which he whimsically attacks as though telling outrageous stories.

During his European tour of 1938–39, he recorded spirituals on organ, popular songs with an English edition of his ensemble, stodgy duets with Adelaide Hall, and the six movements of *London Suite*, which is stiff in parts ("Bond Street," "Limehouse"), but also unforced ("Piccadilly"), lovely ("Chelsea"), stately ("Soho"), and even grand ("Whitechapel"). He was hugely successful everywhere and was soon summoned to Hollywood, where he appeared in three features. Yet for all his renown,

Waller had a difficult time of it. A vindictive ex-wife was always trying to put him in jail (sometimes successfully) for unpaid alimony. The movie parts were patronizing and unrewarding, and his attempt to organize a big band in 1942 failed. Despite the money he made for Victor and others, he was stymied in his aspirations as organist and composer, constrained by the buffoonery that made him famous. In June 1943, however, he enjoyed a Broadway hit in *Early to Bed* (lyrics by George Marion, Jr.)—not his best work, but his song "The Ladies Who Sing with the Band" stopped the show nightly and it stayed the season. Waller died the following December, on a train en route from Hollywood to New York. With his last words, he unknowingly played one final joke on the gulf between black vernacular and white inference. The train had departed Chicago for Kansas, when Waller's manager, Ed Kirkeby, said, "Jesus, it's cold in here!" Fats agreed, "Yeah, hawkins is sure blowin' out there tonight," using a term common among black midwesterners for a bitter winter wind. In his biography of Waller, Kirkeby created the widely repeated legend that Fats went out contemplating Coleman Hawkins.

PART THREE
❖
A Popular Music

17 ❖ Benny Goodman
(The Mirror of Swing)

It won't do to consider Benny Goodman, who died in his sleep on the afternoon of June 13, 1986, at seventy-seven, exclusively as a jazz musician. The emotions conjured by his name are unique to those few who transcend the specifics of talent and come to represent an era. If he wasn't the king of a musical idiom called swing, he was surely king of the swing era, an agreeable focus for Yankee pride at a time when music counted not only for art, entertainment, and sedative, but as a balm with which to weather terrible storms. Goodman will be remembered for his contributions to jazz, which are manifold, and he occupies an impressive historical niche as the first musician to enjoy hugely successful careers in three discrete fields (jazz, pop, and classical). Yet in his time Goodman was also a blessed and seemingly eternal presence in media culture who, through an unofficial contract between artist and public, reflected the nation's new vision of itself in the arts—earthy, democratic, and home-grown and, at the same time, refined, virtuosic, and international.

The enormous sense of loss that attended his death was animated in part by the realization that an age had passed, and not just a musical one. (Other swing era titans survived him, including the great progenitor Benny Carter, the great rival Artie Shaw, and the great crooner Frank Sinatra, who inadvertently helped supplant big bands in the public affection.) Goodman came to prominence when America was making major discoveries about the nature of its cultural life and proved an exemplary figure for national preening. He was in all important respects distinctively American, purveying an undeniably American music with at least the tentative approval of academics and the Europhile upper crust, into whose circles he married. His connections put him in Carnegie Hall (a big deal in 1938) five years before Duke Ellington. The public took comfort in him, too. He was white, but not too white, which is to say Jewish, but not too Jewish; and serious, but not too serious, which is to say lighthearted, but sober. At the height of the Depression, he had perfect credentials for entertaining a suffering, guilt-ridden nation: one of twelve siblings born to penniless Russian immigrants in Chicago, Goodman received his first clarinet at ten, in 1919, and had a union card three years later.

Everyone knows this story, or a version of it. As the favorite fable of the '30s, it was internalized by Depression-bred children who went on to dramatize it for stage, screen, and radio countless times into the late

'50s, and occasionally ever since. It's told of Berlin, Gershwin, and Jolson—and with appropriate variations in ethnicity—of Armstrong, Sinatra, Handy, Jim Thorpe, and Elvis Presley. Until Vietnam and the civil rights era, it was standard grammar school indoctrination, combining the American dream with melting pot diversity, cheerful tolerance, and a ready willingness to brave new frontiers. If nations were judged by the lies they told about themselves, this one just might guarantee salvation. Small wonder, then, that when an individual appears worthy of the crown, we bow our heads in gratitude. With few exceptions, however, only performing artists and athletes are able to pull this particular sword from the stone.

Few Americans have handled the role of cultural icon as well as Goodman. For more than fifty years, he endured as one of the nation's favorite images of itself. Several weeks before his death, a few musicians were sitting around trading anecdotes about him, causing one to remark, "At any given time, somebody somewhere is telling a Benny Goodman story." Those stories are rarely kind, usually having to do with his legendary cheapness, absentmindedness, mandarin discipline, rudeness to musicians, and various eccentricities. But they never dented his media image, nor were they meant to. Americans usually come to resent the entertainers they've deified, yet Goodman remained virtually unblemished. Any real skeletons that may have resided in his closet rattled in peace. It isn't hard to understand why. Everyone could feel good about Goodman. You could send him anywhere, from Albert Hall to Moscow, and rest assured that he would comport himself with quiet dignity and spread Americanism in a manner the world would take to heart. Had he worn striped pants and a top hat, he could not more naturally have embodied everything America wanted to believe about its promise of tolerance and opportunity, those democratic underpinnings insufficiently embraced at home but glamorized for export to the rest of the world.

The *Time/Life* history of all things would have us believe that Goodman helped the country unwind with a new and thrilling music, which is true only in the sense that Columbus discovered America. The music wasn't new, and some of the country had already unwound to it. Goodman, like Elvis twenty years later, adapted black music for white tastes. He toned it down, cleaned it up. Unlike Presley, he was willing to take risks with his celebrity. Perhaps he was so socially unconscious that he didn't realize the implications of those risks. In any case, with the politically astute critics John Hammond (his future brother-in-law) and Helen Oakley spurring him on, Goodman hired Teddy Wilson virtually at the moment he achieved commercial leverage. They first recorded together in the summer of 1935 at two sessions produced by Hammond—the first in support of Billie Holiday, the second the debut of the Benny Goodman Trio. A year later, after the success of his big band, Goodman took Oakley's suggestion to take Wilson on the road, and a bulwark of racism was fatally breached.

Goodman was proud of his musical origins, as witness his many tributes to Fletcher Henderson, whose reputation was fading when Goodman and Hammond conspired to revive it. Henderson's arrangements provided the original Goodman orchestra with a style and remained Benny's favorite music to play (he especially loved Henderson's arrangement of "Somebody Loves Me") until the end of his life. Beyond the vagaries of race, however, Goodman's stellar musicianship indemnified him as an honorable standard-bearer for the art suddenly thrust into his hands. He was, this above all, a nonpareil clarinetist; a bandleader who innovated chamber-sized ensembles; and the sponsor who introduced (again with the help of the ever alert Hammond) numerous great players, arrangers, and singers.

With his unpretentious air and perpetually puzzled look, his amiable stage manner and nearly country-boy shyness, his strangely aristocratic inflections despite a tendency to mumble, and his unmistakable obsession with music/work, he was all that central casting could ask as the hero of the most celebrated parable in American music. The fabled night during which Goodman was transformed from mere musician to looming eminence is an elaborate morality play, involving the genesis of the swing era, the ascendancy of mass-market technology, the hero's conflicting feelings about race, and semirugged individualism. Goodman's rise is not unlike the touchingly grotesque Hollywood version of *Moby Dick* (called *The Sea Beast* and starring John Barrymore and Joan Bennett), played out as a road story with a happy ending for an agreeably ambivalent Ahab.

Goodman was a twenty-six-year-old fledgling bandleader when he embarked on a promotional cross-country tour in the summer of 1935. Despite six months of weekly appearances on the *Let's Dance* radio program; a library of arrangements by Fletcher Henderson, Edgar Sampson, Benny Carter, and others; and a band that included Bunny Berigan, Jess Stacy, and Gene Krupa, Goodman had cause for misgivings. Big band jazz was still far removed from the mainstream; talented jazz players of Goodman's generation were obliged to work in stuffy ballrooms, playing bland dance music and novelties to earn a living. Jazz was something you played after hours or sneaked into arrangements as a condiment when no one was looking. Indeed, shortly before leaving New York, Goodman was fired from the Roosevelt Grill for not playing "sweet and low," as he later recalled. Reaction was no better on the road west, and after three dismal weeks at Elitch Gardens in Denver—where he was nearly fired for playing pieces that went on too long and for not offering waltzes, comedy, and funny hats (Kay Kyser was packing them in down the street, Goodman was drawing flies)—his bookers suggested he cancel the ensuing engagements in California.

He refused. Tour's end was to be the Palomar Ballroom in Los Angeles. But first there was a Monday night in Oakland, and Goodman was astonished to find the place nearly filled; it reminded him that one reason he had been able to finance the tour was the report of interest in his records in California. Still, he knew the Palomar was a more imposing room, and chastened by the experience in Denver, Goodman decided to open with stock arrangements and sugary ballads. He continued in that vein for an hour with no response, but by the second set he had made up his mind that if he was doomed to failure he would go down honorably. He called for the Henderson charts and counted off "Sugar Foot Stomp." The crowd roared with approval. He couldn't believe it. *This* was what they had come to hear, the good stuff. The young audience stopped dancing and pressed against the bandstand. On that night, August 21, 1935, the swing era was born because on that night middle-class white kids said yes in thunder and hard currency. Goodman stayed at the Palomar for two months, then moved on to Chicago, his hometown, where he played six months at the Congress Hotel.

It's a good story, and variations on it have been told many times since with different protagonists. *The Buddy Holly Story* offered an almost verbatim reenactment, as the discouraged rock and roller opens a set with country favorites, before—pride of purpose coming to the fore—switching to rock and roll. Inherent in every retelling are two paradigmatic twists in the Goodman saga. First, the influence of technology: The mystery of California's enthusiasm was solved when Goodman and his booking agent, Willard Alexander, realized the impact of network radio. Through *Let's Dance*, Goodman's music had been relayed around the country by fifty-three stations, with the necessary allowance for different time zones. In New York, he was heard from 10 P.M. until 1 A.M., playing the tame band arrangements of the day. For the Los Angeles market, he had to perform two additional hours, on a five-hour program that began at the outset of prime time, 7 P.M., and finished around midnight. To fill the larger time slot, he drew on the very jazz numbers that cost him his job at the Roosevelt Grill. He had no way of knowing he was nurturing an audience on the West Coast with every Saturday night broadcast.

The second twist was racial: From the days of antebellum minstrel shows to the present, the point at which indigenous American music becomes pop culture is the point where white performers learn to mimic black ones. Many of Goodman's biggest hits were virtual duplications of records that Fletcher Henderson and Chick Webb had recorded months, even years, before. Ellington's band had been declaring "It Don't Mean a Thing If It Ain't Got That Swing" for three years before Goodman reached California, and territory bands had spread the sound of swing throughout the Midwest by 1930. Louis Armstrong's success on records opened the door for everyone. Even before that, the Original Dixieland Jazz Band and its imitators caused sensations in Chicago and New York, helping to usher in the jazz age, with Paul Whiteman reigning as surrogate for the real thing. In one form or another, jazz had been skirting America's consciousness for nearly twenty years before Goodman's triumph—a point he acknowledged (at Irving Kolodin's instigation) in performing the medley, "Twenty Years of Jazz," at the January 1938 Carnegie Hall concert.

Goodman himself learned jazz from those musicians, white and black (notably clarinetists Leon Rappolo and Jimmie Noone), who had left New Orleans for Chicago during the teens and early '20s. His borrowings have been held against him. But given the colonialist iniquities of the period—especially the fact that network radio hookups were closed to blacks—and the emotional prejudices directed at the very foundations of African American music (the puritanical distrust of heady rhythms, at least until they were distilled by white precision and decorum), it's no good blaming the symbol of racial favoritism for racism itself, especially when that symbol took an activist stand against it. As Milt Hinton observed, Goodman's contribution to dismantling the color barriers was "a daring, daring thing."

Yet by the mid-'60s, when race was a central issue in discussions about jazz, Goodman was often dismissed as though his stature in jazz was as spurious as that of Whiteman. The King of Swing hyperbole, an astoundingly effective public relations ploy in its day, had become an albatross, as had the invidious 1955 movie ("Here, Fletcher, hold my clarinet") *The Benny Goodman Story*, which, frequently broadcast, was a real source of embarrassment to him and did nothing to improve his reputation for insensitivity. The racial animus, matched by envy and personal resentment, not least in the ranks of musicians who had suffered under his withering stare (known as "The Ray" by bandsmen) or who despaired at never getting the chance, resulted in a barrage of contentious carping.

Easy to understand why: in the '60s, Goodman was still exhibited as the representative jazz artist for the home viewing and arts center audiences, while Ellington continued on the road playing one-nighters as he composed and recorded the most extensive body of music ever produced by an American. Musicians of John Coltrane's generation remained relatively unknown to the general public. As late as 1975, a leading classical music critic challenged me with the assertion that Goodman was a more important composer than Ellington. When I told him Goodman didn't compose at all, he was incredulous. Goodman himself had no trouble penetrating the delusions of reputation. I once asked him if he actually composed any of the several riff tunes for which he is co-credited. "Oh, maybe one or two, but I doubt it," he said. At the other extreme, the director of Jazz at Lincoln Center told a *New York Times* writer in 1997 that Goodman's music didn't merit performance because he didn't write anything. So it goes.

Goodman, like all icons, is an easy target. In the '60s, I heard a jazz musician acknowledge him as a great clarinetist who should stick to the classics since he couldn't really improvise, and a classical musician groan that Goodman had murdered Mozart but was a genius in jazz. (In the '90s, the same has been said of Wynton Marsalis.) Other forms of damning praise saluted him as a popularizer or as an ambassador. Even Bud Freeman, who presumably had no racial or high-versus-low-art axes to grind, put a weed in his bouquet. After describing Goodman, at thirteen, as having "the technique of a master and a beautiful sound to go with it" and recalling the "thrill" of working with him in 1928, he concluded, "I don't mean to imply that he's a creative player; but he certainly is a masterful player." I've heard people who ought to know better argue that Goodman never surpassed his early idol, Jimmie Noone, which is like saying that Louis Armstrong never surpassed King Oliver. In truth, Goodman's instrumental style is so much his own that you can recognize it almost immediately. His playing may ultimately have done more to sustain his reputation than his work as a bandleader. In the latter capacity, Goodman demonstrated an irreproachable taste in arrangers, but he offered little that was genuinely new until the '40s, when he reformed his band to play the modernist music of Eddie Sauter and Mel Powell. As a clarinetist, he was his own man.

Goodman's victory at the Palomar meant that jazz would no longer be the property of the impassioned few. It now emerged from the underground jam sessions to engulf even the ballroom pioneers—the Whitemans and Pollacks and Reismans—who had tried to limit jazz to an occasional solo or effect. Following the examples of Henderson, Ellington, and Webb, Goodman played music that was jazz from start to finish. He upended the music business. Yet as a major white star, he had to pay the usual price; he was required to water down the original brew. On the surface, that meant recording nearly as many pop vocals as jazz instrumentals; the result was essentially popular music with jazz interpolations (or fusion, as it's known today). Even in this regard, he went his own way. In addition to his regular pop singers, including Martha Tilton and the very talented Helen Forrest, he recorded with authentic jazz singers—Ella Fitzgerald, Jimmy Rushing, Maxine Sullivan, and others. The same little-known studio player who presided over Billie Holiday's first record in 1933 would launch Peggy Lee's career in 1941.

Goodman always kept his balance, refusing to allow his celebrity to dictate essential musical decisions. When he broke all records at New York's Paramount Theater in 1937 and faced the kind of shrieking adulation that was then new to American entertainment, he would sit placidly, waiting for the audience to finish its performance before he started his. By introducing trios, quartets, and other small groups in addition to the big band, he even made the fans sit still for chamber jazz. Yet subtler indications of musical dilution were apparent, reflecting Goodman's stringent personality and insistence on precision. He often seemed more concerned with unison execution and projection than with the spirited abandon that typified not only the best black bands but his own early work as a sideman. Paradoxically, his rigidity was a primary reason for his success.

Goodman's soloists didn't compare with those in the Henderson orchestra, but his fastidious ensemble could sometimes get more value from a Henderson arrangement than Henderson's relatively unwieldy band did. If some of Goodman's records are anemic copies of Henderson's ("Wrappin' It Up," for instance) others ("Blue Skies," "Sometimes I'm Happy") are exemplary interpretations, which is undoubtedly one reason Henderson enjoyed writing for him. Despite his apprenticeship in hot jazz, Goodman had a preternatural understanding of what a mass audience would accept. Were the dancers discomfited by brutal tempos? Goodman simmered them down. He knew how to inject just the right touch of excitement into a performance.

Consider his hit version of Edgar Sampson's "Don't Be That Way," originally recorded by Chick Webb. Webb took the tempo way up and climaxed the performance with an explosive eight-bar drum solo. Goodman modified the tempo, streamlined the ensemble parts, introduced a famous fade-down in volume, and reduced the climax to a two-bar drum break by Gene Krupa that, because of its sudden intrusion, jolted the jitterbugs. (Coda: Years later, Krupa's formidable replacement, Dave Tough, completed a performance of "Don't Be That Way" with an extended break that awed everyone in the band but left the audience cold. He asked Goodman to give him another chance in the second show. This time he imitated Krupa's relatively simple outburst, and the crowd cheered.) Still, he put together a terrific repertory of swing anthems, drawing on many of the best writers of the day, kept his competitive edge (he once made the mistake of challenging Armstrong, who cut him so badly at their first concert that Goodman left the tour and had himself hospitalized for rest), and never slackened in his quest for perfection.

If Goodman was primarily a popularizer of big bands, he was an innovator of small ones. The Benny Goodman Trio was conceived when Goodman heard Teddy Wilson play "Body and Soul" at a party given by Red Norvo. Shortly afterward, in the summer of 1935, Goodman, Wilson, and Krupa recorded four sides for RCA. The combination of clarinet, piano, and drums was by no means new (Goodman had heard others, notably Jelly Roll Morton, use it during his adolescence), but Goodman greatly increased its flexibility and made it the foundation for several variations. A year later in California, he was advised to visit a disreputable sailors' hangout called the Paradise Cafe to hear the entertainment—one Lionel Hampton. Goodman returned the next night with Wilson and Krupa to jam and had no trouble convincing Hampton to join them on the road.

The small groups were a popular draw at Goodman's shows, and although Wilson and Hampton were billed as special attractions rather than as members of the orchestra, their presence paved the way for integrated bands. Krupa went the distance when he left Goodman to start his own band and allowed his star soloist, Roy Eldridge, to sit in his trumpet section. (Integrated audiences came later.) The chamber groups also gave Goodman the opportunity to indulge himself as a clarinetist on wistful ballads ("The Man I Love," "Moonglow") and flashy stomps ("Runnin' Wild," "China Boy") and rekindled the spark of his earlier playing. They gave him the chance to work with favorite musicians without regard to race. In the big band, Goodman's soloists tended to mimic the great stylists assembled by Henderson, especially Coleman Hawkins and Eldridge. Only Goodman himself bested his opposite number, Buster Bailey, in the Henderson band, though arrangements tended to limit the size and scope of his solos. With the small group, which grew to a sextet by 1939, he could stretch out in the company of the incomparable guitarist Charlie Christian, trumpeter Cootie Williams, whose temporary defection from Ellington wowed the music community (Goodman also tried, unsuccessfully, to snare Johnny Hodges), and, on records, Count Basie. Before long, other bandleaders introduced chamber groups, including Webb, Ellington, Artie Shaw, Woody Herman, and Tommy Dorsey.

If the combo recordings as a whole stand up better than those by the big band, which today suffer needlessly from the idiot obsession with reissuing complete works in chronological order, the generous playing time accorded the leader is a major reason. On the orchestra's pop sides, his clarinet is often the only solace: in the course of a conventional arrangement worsened by a dire vocal, Goodman's blistering clarinet flashes to the fore and creaky sentiments are momentarily banished. Goodman was a hot player whose adroit blues choruses distinguished him almost from the start during his days in Chicago. His command of every register enabled him to contrive a style of high drama and earthy swing. A student of the Chicago Symphony's Franz Schoep as well as of jazz clarinetists, he never allowed technique to vitiate the rhythmic charge of his music. Artie Shaw had a prettier tone, Barney Bigard a fatter one, but Goodman was unfeigned and lusty. He could growl with bemusement or ardor, according to mood, and when he really let go, leaning back on his chair, feet flailing the air, or hopping around on one leg, he could make anyone's heart beat a little faster. Goodman's rhythmic gait was unmistakable; his best solos combined cool legato, a fierce doubling up of notes, and the canny use of propulsive riffs.

He displayed some of those gifts as early as 1926, when he first recorded, still under the influence of Jimmie Noone. A year later, when Goodman was eighteen, an English publisher issued *Benny Goodman's 125 Jazz Breaks for the Saxophone and Clarinet*—this in 1927, when only the more widely known Louis Armstrong received parallel treatment. Had Goodman retired in 1935, he would be remembered now for his rigorous solos on numerous records by Ted Lewis, Adrian Rollini, the Joe Venuti–Eddie Lang Orchestra, Red Nichols, the Charleston Chasers, and others. At his best, he was able to sustain a similar excitement all his life. Forty years after the kingdom of swing had been gentrified almost beyond recognition, he could still provoke the crowd's roar. In 1985, as an unbilled performer at a tribute to John Hammond, he provided the highlight of the Kool Jazz Festival. It was anything but a middle-aged jazz audience that cheered him on when he came out and played "Lady Be Good" with George Benson, and then—seated, both legs levitating—layered climax after climax on "Indiana." Up to that point, the young white-blues crowd had greeted every jazz performer with impatient demands for the man of the hour, blues guitarist Stevie Ray Vaughan. When Goodman finished, that same crowd was on its feet.

When my review of that concert appeared, Goodman's assistant told me the Old Man was pleased and surprised by it since he'd gotten it into his head—I can't imagine why—that I considered him outmoded. How could anyone think that? Goodman kept his faith until the end and ultimately mirrored not only a chapter in America's cultural history, but the spirit at the core of a music that can only be enfeebled when nostalgia gets between musician and audience. In 1975, I visited Goodman at his East Side apartment. He had been practicing Gounod's Petite Symphony when I arrived, and I asked him if he preferred improvising or playing written music. "Gee," he said, "I enjoy both. Listening to music is emotional. Sometimes you like something a lot and another time you hate it. The whole goddam thing about jazz is emotional. I like to feel the excitement. If it doesn't come out as a wild endeavor—wild with restraint—it doesn't have it." Goodman had it in 1926, and he had it sixty years later.

18 ❖ Jimmie Lunceford
(For Listeners, Too)

Jimmie Lunceford's music redeemed the sentimental excesses of the swing era with dynamic two-beat rhythms, bravura arrangements, and an overall charm that managed to appear calculating and ingenuous at the same time. His was a musical world onto itself: whimsical yet disciplined, flashy yet innovative. Because Lunceford's showmanship lent itself to fey singers and a stock of novelty songs from minstrelsy, vaudeville, and Tin Pan Alley, his recordings may require a stronger taste for irony than those of Henderson, Ellington, or Basie. But in its originality, the Lunceford band stands with those three as one of the most influential orchestras of the '30s.

Lunceford compensated for his seeming lack of profundity with his own "three Ps": Punctuality, Precision, and Presentation. He had the nattiest looking band of the day, with smartly uniformed musicians waving derby mutes and tossing their instruments into the air, but he never succumbed to the cynical party-hat conviviality of such cornpone hacks as Kay Kyser. On the contrary, he used his three Ps to augment the elements of hard jazz: fervent swing, audacious writing, heady solos. To these he added the suggestion of a Panglossian conviction that the music he celebrated (American music in all its motley) was as good as music could be. He made art out of commercial slickness.

Unlike the other figures associated with distinct big band styles, he had little direct impact as composer, arranger, or instrumentalist. In assigning authorship of the Lunceford sound to Lunceford, we are merely acknowledging his captaincy of the ship—the regal-looking commander with the baton. Perhaps this isn't fair. Jazz has upset several accepted notions of Western music, most especially what a composer does and how his role is defined. The distinction between composition and improvisation is blurred by composer-performers like Louis Armstrong or Lester Young, who produced comprehensive musical styles without much recourse to paperwork. Similarly, a jazz bandleader (unless hired strictly for show because of a pretty face or famous name) does some of the work of a composer in selecting talent and delegating responsibility. Lunceford's sound may have reached its apogee in the writing of his most gifted arranger, Sy Oliver, but the fact remains that neither Oliver (notwithstanding several famous arrangements he later wrote for Tommy Dorsey), nor Trummy Young, Joe Thomas, Willie Smith, and Jimmy Crawford, not to mention lesser luminaries such as Eddie Wilcox, Paul Webster, and Eddie Tompkins, would ever again create as memorable a body of work as they did under his authoritarian rule. He knew what he wanted and how to get musicians to give it to him.

Lunceford was born in Missouri in 1902 and attended high school in Denver, where he studied with Wilberforce J. Whiteman, Paul Whiteman's father. He graduated Fisk University along with Eddie Wilcox and Willie Smith, and enrolled at New York's City College for further study. Lunceford had been playing alto sax professionally for several years and was becoming proficient on the other reeds, as well as guitar, trombone, and flute, though he rarely played at all after founding his orchestra. He formed the Chicksaw Syncopators in 1929 while teaching high school in Memphis and recorded two sides for Victor (on which he probably played trombone). It wasn't until a Northeast tour, culminating in a residency at the Cotton Club in January 1934, that he began to acquire a national reputation. By that time, the man chiefly responsible for giving the Lunceford sound shape and substance was Sy Oliver.

Born in Michigan in 1910 and raised in Ohio, Oliver was the son of two music teachers who groomed him in the three areas he successfully pursued: arranging, trumpet playing, and singing. After apprenticeship with the territory bands of Zack White and Alphonso Trent, he submitted a few arrangements to Lunceford because he'd been impressed by the orchestra's attention to detail. Lunceford recruited Oliver for the band when the young man arrived in New York in 1933. Oliver's impact has occasionally been disputed, mostly by Oliver himself. It is certainly true that the band displayed something of its characteristic esprit before he joined up. One of his predecessors, Eddie Wilcox, was a gifted arranger who was particularly admired by the Lunceford musicians for the way he scored the saxophones. Oliver was quick to point out that people often credited him with Wilcox's work. Yet when Oliver referred to himself as merely "the band's Boswell," insisting, as he did in a 1946 interview with George T. Simon, that he "couldn't write, it's just that those guys played so well," he was being modest to a fault.

Oliver gave the band its distinctive charm, establishing unpredictability—in instrumental juxtapositions and tempos—as a modus operandi. His writing crowded a variety of ideas and techniques in close quarters, including unison trombone smears and trumpet shakes, staccato passages, baritone sax voice leading in the reed section, and a vital bass line. Whereas Henderson and Basie occupied a treble ground, the Lunceford band, like Ellington's, pulsated with bass. It was Oliver who insisted on the illusory two-beat rhythm (the music was usually written in four but executed so as to emphasize the backbeat) that became Lunceford's primary trademark. The two-beat was especially effective at medium tempos, and dancers loved it.

Oliver consistently came up with imaginative voicings and startling call-and-response passages between the soloists and the ensemble. During his six years with Lunceford, he also proved to be a modestly appealing singer and trumpet soloist. But he was not much of an improvisor; his muted solos were patterned after those of Bubber Miley (in the Ellington band), and years later he admitted to writing them out in advance. Almost all the band's major soloists contributed arrangements as well, notably Wilcox (piano), Willie Smith (alto), Joe Thomas (tenor), and the very influential Eddie Durham (trombone, guitar). Many of them sang, often in trios, though the ballad crooning was usually entrusted to saxophonist Dan Grissom, whose demifalsetto earned him the epithet Dan Gruesome.

Among musicians and rival bandleaders, who were invariably among Lunceford's greatest admirers, there is widespread agreement that his records, which often used abridgements of the arrangements heard in ballrooms, fail to capture the band's magic. This prejudice surely reflects a longing for the visual excitement of the band and for the sustained rhythmic grooves, which were not only curtailed but accelerated to accommodate the three-minute running time of the 78 r.p.m. record. Only two souvenirs of the band's stage finesse exist: a Vitaphone short from 1936 and a fleeting appearance in the 1941 feature, *Blues in the Night*. But notwithstanding swing-era banalities and stratospheric crooning, the recordings are by no means negligible.

Lunceford recorded two numbers for Columbia in 1933 that the label failed to release for nearly thirty-five years; one of them, "Flaming Reeds and Screaming Brass," represents the best of Wilcox's early arrangements and suggests how accomplished the band had become at the time Oliver entered the picture. The eight sides Lunceford recorded for Bluebird in early 1934 suffer from generally weak material, but are indicative of what was to come—the ensemble punch on Will Hudson's riff-crazy "Jazz-nocracy," Wilcox's scoring for the trumpets on "Sweet Rhythm." The most interesting selection is Oliver's arrangement of "Swingin' Uptown," the first Lunceford record that sounds like a Lunceford record. In the first chorus, baritone saxophonist Earl Caruthers leads the reeds in counterpoint to the solo clarinet, and surprises abound in the intricate interplay between band and soloists. Bluebird executives weren't paying attention, however. The recently formed Decca Records was, and from 1934 through 1938, Lunceford turned out a string of savory hits for the upstart label.

At first, it had to work through its influences—the ersatz Armstrongian climaxes on "Rose Room" and "Runnin' Wild"; the undistinguished renderings of Ellington vehicles, including an adaptation of "Mood Indigo" that verges on parody. Two Oliver charts, "Dream of You" and "Stomp It Off," exploit the band's dynamics and nuances, but the real highlights come from Wilcox: the brass tuttis after the vocal on "Jealous," the ensemble chorus on "Sleepy Time Gal," and a let's-introduce-the-fellas novelty (compare Louis Armstrong's "Gut Bucket Blues," Andy Kirk's "Git," Slim Gaillard's "Slim's Jam") called "Rhythm Is Our Business" that enjoyed blockbuster sales. The fellas include the great drummer Jimmy Crawford, who shapes many a Lunceford climax, and Joe Thomas, a fine Hawkins-inspired tenor saxophonist with a darker sound, modifying his predilection for melody with an undercurrent of subdued violence.

By 1935 and 1936, the Lunceford-Oliver bounce begins to hit its stride, alchemizing a strange jumble of songs with disarming humor and ostensible simplicity. The material ranges from the mildly uninspiring ("Four or Five Times," "Avalon," "My Blue Heaven") to the extremely uninspiring ("Swanee River," "Organ Grinder Swing," "On the Beach at Bali-Bali"); most if not all chosen by Oliver and covered with moss. The outstanding arrangement is Oliver's transformation of "Organ Grinder Swing" into an off-the-wall fantasy in which the colors change every eight measures, from growl trumpet and vamping baritone sax to celeste and woodblocks to guitar and clarinet, and so forth. In 1937, the pioneering critic Hugues Panassie described it as "a pearl" to be prized for its "radically different" (slow) tempo, as well as its "marvelous use of contrasts," which produce "the most perfect balance, the most supple rocking you can imagine." The public agreed—it was one of the best-selling records of 1936.

Lunceford didn't rely entirely on Oliver. For one thing, the singers—Oliver, Grissom, a trio patterned after Paul Whiteman's Rhythm Boys—

were never too far from the mike. Eddie Durham, a veteran of the territory bands who later helped develop the Count Basie band, wrote several tidy arrangements in the Kansas City vein, surpassing himself with the steady build-up in "Running a Temperature" and the muted brass passages in "Pigeon Walk." Eddie Wilcox displayed his effectiveness with saxophones on "Honest and Truly," and Willie Smith borrowed Oliver's approach for an outrageous five-alarm adaptation of "Put On Your Old Gray Bonnet." But Oliver's unabashed wit was something else. His concoctions weren't comical: they were not conceived to poke fun at dire songs, as Fats Waller did. He clearly enjoyed vivid and unsophisticated melodies, and his subtle subversion of them allowed the audience to share his enjoyment and feel superior at the same time. He rendered harmless the idiocy of "On the Beach at Bali-Bali" by meeting it head-on, enlivened "Swanee River" through meticulous caprice, desentimentalized "Coquette" with buttery reeds fortified by brass alarums and cool trombone chords.

In "For Dancers Only," another huge hit, Oliver bypassed the generic thirty-two-bar song form in favor of an eight-bar chorus that is unceasingly altered, with unison stutter phrasing, high-note trumpet (by Paul Webster), dramatic drumming, and mounting riffs that heighten the tension throughout. In the third chorus, a second theme is introduced, widely known as the "Christopher Columbus" passage, after Fletcher Henderson's famous record. Yet by all accounts, Oliver sketched the piece before Henderson's record was released. The number was a highly popular showpiece. Gerald Wilson, who joined the band long after it had become a staple in the book, once recalled it as the piece that initiated him into Lunceford performing rites. "The brass would play a series of triplets," he said, "then we'd all throw our horns up in the air and twirl them before we resumed playing." During a show at Loew's State in New York, his trumpet sailed up, up, and away, and nearly crowned a member of the audience.

Oliver's adaptation of the traditional song "Annie Laurie" is one of his supreme creations, an orchestration that manages to exemplify the band's colloquial two-beat style and penchant for ripe melody, while incorporating the rigors of virtuoso ensemble work and ingenious solos. In addition to exemplary work by Crawford, Thomas, and the gleaming brasses, it served to introduce the Lunceford band's most talented star, trombonist and vocalist James Osbourne "Trummy" Young, who announces his arrival with a daring entrance, snorting like a raging elephant. Formidable in every detail, it has a thrilling close, complete with flash-fire trumpet figures and descending saxophone arpeggios (Armstrong's influence is fully assimilated), and swings like mad. Oliver arranged "Margie" as a feature for Young, who had come to Lunceford from Earl Hines's band; he is equally assured as soloist and vocalist, setting the stage for his ultimate collaboration with Oliver, " 'Taint What You Do (It's the Way That You Do It)," an axiomatic benchmark of the '30s. As a singer, Young was indebted to Armstrong, with whom he would perform from 1952 to 1964 as a member of the All-Stars, but he had a breezy unaffected appeal of his own. As a trombonist, he was an original, leavening a brash blustery attack with mocking humor.

" 'Taint What You Do" came about during the band's sojourn with Columbia Records in 1939 and 1940. Oliver was becoming disillusioned with Lunceford's martinet manner, but he continued to contribute, singing eloquently on "Time's a Wastin' " and setting the brasses to swoon on "Ain't She Sweet." Joe Thomas's lusty saxophone skillfully states the head of "Cheatin' on Me," and he delivers the entirely unexpected and splendidly imaginative vocal chorus on Oliver's quasi-Dixieland arrangement of "Baby Won't You Please Come Home," an indispensable recording. But the end was dawning: Tommy Dorsey had a yen for the Lunceford sound, too, and he hired Oliver, who soon had the Dorsey band hopping to a two-beat rhythm. The 1940 "I Wanna Hear Swing Songs" serves as the transitional selection since the melody is by Oliver and the arrangement is by his replacement, Billy Moore; it opens ruggedly with the theme, no intro, and is tightly voiced.

Moore, one of the most undervalued orchestrators of the era, also wrote the modernistic "Bug Parade" and a definitive version of Mary Lou Williams's "What's Your Story, Morning Glory?" (from whence the pop hit "Black Coffee" was plagiarized). He brought a novel sensibility to the band and, in later years, was himself hired by Dorsey as well as Charlie Barnett before moving to Europe, where he toured as music director and pianist for the Delta Rhythm Boys. "Belgian Stomp" is a prime example of his work, revealing exceptional foresight in form and substance. No two choruses are alike, and each eight measures of the theme are different (the trumpet figures in the second eight are unmistakably boplike)—it's the kind of thing Charlie Parker later achieved in "Confirmation."

A remarkable new member of the band was twenty-year-old trumpeter Snooky Young, who recorded his most famous solo at his first session with Lunceford, on "Uptown Blues," a head arrangement given over to Willie Smith and two penetrating and dramatic choruses by Young, who went on to redefine the role of the lead trumpet in orchestral jazz, eventually taking over that chair in the *Tonight Show* orchestra under the direction of Doc Severinson. Amid all the new blood, Eddie Durham rose to the occasion with the most provocative arrangement of his career, "Lunceford Special," a fiesta of displaced accents with a roaring high-note windup. Willie Smith created his most accomplished solo on a two-part head arrangement of "Blues in the Night."

Another twenty-year-old addition was the arranger and trumpet player Gerald Wilson, whose influence as composer and leader of his own orchestra would be felt well into the '70s. Initially hired to take over Oliver's seat in the brass section, he presented two arrangements in 1941 that had other arrangers scratching their heads for years to come. "Hi, Spook" fuses Oliver's flair for contrast with Wilcox's affinity for reeds and employs a stratospheric trumpet part. As the arrangement is too intricate to cut, Lunceford counted off a slightly rushed tempo for the record, sacrificing some of its potency. Wilson's mischievous style is in evidence from the outset: a thirteen-bar intro, followed by an apparently orthodox chorus structure that turns out to have an eleven-bar release and a thirteen-bar finish. The equally vibrant "Yard Dog Mazurka" has a sixteen-bar intro, played initially on drums, in which the baritone sax links figures played by the brasses. Mirroring the intro, the first chorus is also split, between reeds and brasses. A six-bar riff extension sets up the second chorus, and a four-bar transition leads into a sultry vamp that continues into the third chorus; Trummy Young solos and Paul Webster rigs the finale. Highly advanced, it represents quite a turn from the four-square swing and inviting melodicism of the Oliver years.

Yet by this time the band was beginning to fall apart. The musicians rebelled at Lunceford's low wages and balked at having to play the old charts. Grueling one-nighters were no longer fun, especially when musicians were denied paid vacations. Lunceford persevered through the war, but one by one the key members left him. A few surviving broadcasts and V-discs from 1944 and 1945 reveal the band as more progressive than most, but its identity was failing and times had changed. The swing era was approaching oblivion when Lunceford died in Oregon in 1947 of a heart attack while signing autographs. For more than a year, Eddie Wilcox and Joe Thomas attempted to assume the reigns of leadership, but without Lunceford the band succumbed to mediocrity. Though he occasionally returned to music, Thomas eventually entered his family's undertaking business. Even so, he kept the Lunceford book in the basement of his Kansas City home until his death in 1986; there wasn't much call for it. Two years later, the American Jazz Orchestra prepared two concerts of Lunceford's music, but by then the book had been burned like so many old newspapers.

If Lunceford's reputation had faded, the impact of his sound endured. Dorsey upheld it, of course, and Gerald Wilson brought aspects of it into the Dizzy Gillespie band of the '40s, further developing the style in his own orchestra. Stan Kenton founded his first band on the Lunceford of "Bug Parade" and especially "Yard Dog Mazurka," which he appropriated in his "Intermission Riff." Billy May recorded one of the earliest jazz repertory albums in tribute to Lunceford and extended his sonic boom into countless studio session of the '50s. Tadd Dameron, who briefly wrote for Lunceford ("It Had To Be You"), adapted his trademark voice leading by baritone sax and trumpet. Basie's post-1954 band was jokingly referred to as his Lunceford band for its startling precision, particularly the unison shakes and smears. (When Basie had first come east in 1936, he was defeated by Lunceford in a battle of the bands. "We just weren't ready for Jimmie at the time," he observed, "his band was too rugged for any of us.") Of the soloists who entered the band toward the end, Freddie Webster proved to be a crucial influence on Miles Davis, who adapted his meditative trumpet tone and calm whole notes; and Kurt Bradford was the teacher of Arthur Blythe, who popularized his plummy alto saxophone timbre in the '80s, thirty years after it had gone out of style.

One bandleader who failed to recapture the Lunceford spirit was Sy Oliver. After his highly successful tenure with Dorsey, he freelanced arrangements, organized a series of bands, and served as music director at a couple of labels, including Decca—a rare breakthrough for a black musician in the '50s. Although he created several memorable settings (notably Frank Sinatra's *I Remember Tommy*), his later work was too long on pop and too short on antic wit. He was a member of the New York Repertory Company, but incurred the wrath of critics for interpreting Ellington, Henderson, and others with his patented two-beat rhythm. Until shortly before his death in 1988, he led a polished band at New York's Rainbow Room, where tempos and dynamics were adjusted to accommodate dancers old enough to have heard Lunceford in his prime. Witnessing those infinitely genteel evenings, it required effort to remember that when Oliver's two-beat was young it buttressed some of the most inventive and idiosyncratic music ever conceived for a big band. Hearing it today on records, the Lunceford sound summons forth a mirage of the past—a world without Depression or war, and rife with inspired lunacy, boundless energy, and immeasurable optimism.

19 ❖ Count Basie/Lester Young (Westward Ho! and Back)

Count Basie inspired a curious hyperbole. Musicians in and out of his band claimed he could make one note—struck on the piano in his matchless way—swing. Now, a solitary note hangs in the air like a floating leaf and can no more engender rhythmic momentum than the leaf can engender a tree. Yet the unshakably succinct orchestra leader, who conducted from the piano with his eyes and those momentous piano tones, gave the illusion he could do just that. He had an uncanny knack for playing a near-staccato note in a way that fueled the orchestra and revved it up. His sidemen often noted that the orchestra didn't quite sound like Basie's band in his absence. During rehearsals, they would run down a piece until it was polished and slick. Then the Chief would arrive and take his place, and the same piece came alive; even a chart that had seemed pedestrian suddenly felt cogent and trim.

Basie is the easiest pianist to mimic badly—you can learn a couple of Basie licks in minutes, even if you've never previously touched a piano— and almost impossible to imitate well. Virtuoso tricks are readily absorbed by virtuoso hands, but Basie's genius was a result of timing, and in this respect he was as inimitable as Jack Benny. It takes more equanimity to accept silence than to fill it up, more self-confidence to sacrifice conventional technique than to shore it up. Basie pared down Fats Waller's plush style to its skeletal essentials, consisting of little more than triplets, punctuations, bass transitions, and boogie-woogie fragments. The trick was knowing where to put them and how to make them chime. Basie mastered the spaces between beats. "Time won't stand beating," the Mad Hatter cautioned Alice. "Now, if you kept on good terms with him, he'd do almost anything you liked." Basie and Time were on excellent terms. He never failed to set the right tempo, then grooved with it like a lover.

How deceptively simple the Basie magic was: blues riffs, medium tempos, spare piano interjections. And yet with every beat, every dynamic burst, you knew that what you were hearing was incomparable. "Jazz is an art of the young, and it is a young art in itself," he remarked in his later years. "The progressive force of change will always fall chiefly into the hands of the young in mind and body." Of course, he left a pretext for himself and his comrades in adding, "The true disciple of jazz remains young at heart." He knew; he was proof. He had trudged out of Kansas City in 1936 with a ragtag band whose imprecision was countered by exuberant spontaneity, educated swing, and innovative soloists, especially Lester Young, who floated over time like an eagle gliding through the Grand Canyon. When the era of the paladin improviser ended in the '40s, he rebuilt the band as an orchestra first and a school for soloists second. This time his band epitomized precision.

The elegance of the later band emanated from the leader's economy, his pretense that what he did was too basic to require comment. Like Jack Benny, who got his biggest laughs by staring into the middle distance, or Bill Robinson, who appeared most at ease (arms akimbo, torso unmoving) dancing confounding rhythms, Basie charmed his audience by seeming to exert no effort at all. Tranquil and frog-eyed, he conducted his ensemble with a flicker of the brow, an encouraging nod, a solitary chord placed squarely on the beat, a fillip in the bass, a tinkle in the treble, a lone note that conveyed information about rhythm and harmony and who knows what else. After a day on the band bus, I asked a few of the musicians how they interpreted his keyboard interjections. Curtis Fuller said, "It means he's on top of you every second, he knows what you're up to all the time." Basie's rhythm-section interludes ostensibly spell the orchestra's perfervid attack with rest periods. Yet they, too, invariably sustain the tension. In Basie's music I hear, as Albert Murray might put it, the hand-clapping elation of a Southern Baptist church stylized into a sophisticated art. Basie put it more bluntly. Asked by a *60 Minutes* commentator what his music meant, he said, "Pat your foot."

When Basie died in 1984, a few months short of his eightieth birthday, a chunk of American musical history receded into the past. Woody Herman, who started his band in the same year that Basie's took flight, 1936, was now the last great swing era bandleader on the road, and he would be gone in three years. Basie and Herman and their compatriots left a massive library for repertory companies, revivalists, and students to examine and reconsider. But in the absence of traveling concert-dance bands bringing the immediacy of a new and vital music into every neighborhood ballroom and auditorium, the music itself became academic. Certainly a career like Basie's seems unlikely to recur: fifty-five years of recording, forty-eight years at the helm of his own orchestra. Today a musician goes on the road to generate interest in records that may ultimately free him from the road. We may well ask what kept him out there, rolling to the piano in a wheelchair during his last three years. Some who knew him well said he had to work to pay off gambling debts. Some who knew him better said he incurred gambling debts as an excuse to keep working. In any case, Basie's music is not the sort that can be made in your room or at an isolated event in a coliseum. It's a music of process and constancy. Take it for granted until it no longer exists, then marvel that it ever did.

William Basie was born in Red Bank, New Jersey, in 1904 and studied drums before taking up the piano. Fats Waller, only three months his senior, was Basie's boyhood idol and encouraged him to sit on the floor and study his pedal technique as he played organ in theaters. Before he was out of his teens, Basie was accompanying films in Harlem and working with variety acts. Touring with singer Gonzelle White and her vaudeville troupe in 1925, he was stranded in Kansas City. He decided to stick around, picking up work in movie theaters, accompanying performers, hitchhiking to neighboring cities, often with Jimmy Rushing—they played blues on Saturday night and spirituals in church the next morning. By 1928, he was with one of the hottest of the southwestern territory bands, Walter Page's Blue Devils; a year later, he joined Bennie Moten's band. The records he made with Moten capture his ability to play spirited stride piano, his solos bristling with the same ingenuous enthusiasm that prompted his anomalous scat vocal on "Somebody Stole My Gal." In later years, Basie showed he could still summon his powers—the 1977 "Trio Blues" is a delirious example—but he made his mark by discarding technique.

Basie is the one major figure in jazz to realize his individuality by playing less. He reasoned that his piano got in the way of his streamlined band: the fewer notes he played, the more heft each of them packed. Kansas City converted him from the lush New York style to a midwestern austerity, and his baptism was almost certainly engineered by Walter Page, his boss in the Blue Devils and his bassist from 1936 to 1942. When Page switched from tuba to bass in 1926, he found that a straight-four walk made the rhythm more fluid while buoying the soloists. Previous rhythm sections were locked into the rigid alternation of tuba on the one and three, and drums on the two and four. Page ironed out the beat. His 1929 record "Squabblin' " is the first instance of Basie piloting a rhythm-section interlude, as opposed to a solo with support from bass and drums. During that period Jo Jones, who credited Page with teaching him drums (but also absorbed the work of such advanced drummers as Alvin Burroughs, A. G. Godley, and Walter Johnson), perfected the "sizzling cymbal," making the beat something supple and vibrating instead of a rigid thump on the bass drum. By the time Basie brought his own nine-piece ensemble into Kansas City's Reno Club, he and Page and Jones had perfected the rhythmic entr'acte. When he added Freddie

Green's guitar a year later, having set out for Chicago with an expanded group, the beat was even more pronounced, unified, and spacious.

Basie was explicit about the importance of his All-American Rhythm Section:

> I've always built my band from the rhythm section to the tenors, then on to the rest, for the living pulse of a band is naturally the rhythm section. The piano can create a mood but it can also join forces with the guitar, bass, and drums to become a power unit that drives and motivates the entire outfit. The result should be "solid" but also flexible; there must be control that is not confined.

Basie's rhythm section was his greatest innovation, the finest foundation of its kind. Leveling offbeat accents in favor of a resolute four/four, it floated the band. Nothing in music can quite match those moments in Basie's '30s recordings when Jo Jones tattoos the hi-hat and the other All-Americans go into action. By then, streamlining was evident in every aspect of the band.

The idea of dividing the dance band into sections akin to the traditional New Orleans front line—replacing trumpet, trombone, and clarinet with multiple trumpeters, trombonists, and reeds and supplanting polyphony with an orchestrated call-and-response between the sections—probably originated in the East with Don Redman and Fletcher Henderson, achieving special grace in the arrangements of Benny Carter. During his five years with Bennie Moten, Basie saw how choruses of riffs could generate enormous excitement, as on Moten's "Blue Room." Moten's rhythms mined the traditional two-beat. He offered something of a transition from Jelly Roll Morton's raggy embellishments in his recordings of "The Jones Law Blues" and "Milenberg Joys" to the spare efficiency of Basie in more advanced recordings like "Moten's Swing" and the dazzling "Blue Room." Basie's piano was apparently more conventional with Moten than it had been with the Blue Devils. On Moten's records, he exhibits the expected influence of Waller ("Prince of Wails"), plus the asymmetrical phrasing of Earl Hines ("Small Black," "Rit Dit Ray"). But nothing was lost on him regarding the minimalist building blocks of blues riffs, to which he added a crucial difference.

After Moten's death in 1935, Basie brought his own band into the Reno Club and was soon joined by several of Moten's best men. In that context, playing eight- and twelve-hour nights (a situation in which written arrangements, even had they been abundant, would not have gone far), he devised and perfected a method of producing ad-lib arrangements—head arrangements—on the bandstand. To the degree that Basie was an arranger, he arranged by goading and editing—goading his musicians into producing musical ideas that could be transfigured into sectional riffs and editing them for maximum effect in setting off his soloists. As trombonist Dickie Wells recalled, Basie would play a phrase aimed at the trumpets, which they picked up and repeated in unison; he followed with a contrasting figure for the saxophones (Basie was one bandleader who didn't put much stock in clarinets) and then a third for the trombones. In all those hours of playing and jamming, countless phrases were offered, rejected, modified, and accepted in what rapidly became a common language. He made the blues a disarming flatland of infinite possibility.

Riffs were also drawn from other bands (a common practice): an analysis of Basie's '30s recordings reveals several borrowings from Henderson, Ellington, and others. His theme song originated one night as Basie was finishing a piano solo and motioned to altoist Buster Smith to start up a riff. Smith led the reeds in a Don Redman figure (from "Six of Seven Times"); Hot Lips Page instigated another for the trumpets, and Dan Minor produced one for the trombones. The full band roared a walloping finish, and by evening's end, a new piece was in the band's repertory. Basie's men called it "Blue Balls" until Basie was asked the title on a radio broadcast. Noticing the time, he said, "Oh, that's the 'One O'Clock Jump'." After they recorded it in 1937 and Buck Clayton prepared a transcription, "One O'Clock Jump" become a written arrangement for the first time.

The live remotes, broadcast from the Reno Club over W9XBY, ended Basie's Kansas City sojourn. John Hammond chanced to hear one on his car radio in Chicago, traveled to the Reno, and ultimately helped Basie enlarge the ensemble to a full-sized orchestra and arranged for a tour that would take the band, with much fanfare, from Chicago to New York. George Simon's comment was typical of the critical reaction: "If you think that sax section sounds out of tune, catch the brass!" The poor reception confirmed Basie's suspicion that head arrangements weren't good enough for the big time. Jo Jones remembered him calling them "old hat." That diffidence belied the scrappy excitement of the band, which brought Hammond to his door in the first place. Still, Basie had no more than twelve written arrangements, an astonishing shortfall by eastern standards. Fletcher Henderson pitched in by offering him a batch from his own stock, but Basie's Kansas City approach prevailed. The consensus soon changed in his favor.

Hammond planned to sign him to one of the labels in the Columbia tribe, but Decca's Dave Kapp allegedly tricked Basie into thinking he represented Hammond and signed him to Decca for two years. Determined to record Basie first, Hammond brought a five-piece group into the studio to make four sides, released pseudonymously as Jones-Smith Incorporated (after Jo Jones and trumpeter Carl Smith). The impact of those records was immediate, and semirevolutionary on at least three counts: Lester Young's solos finished Coleman Hawkins's decade-long unchallenged hold over the tenor saxophone; the Basie-Page-Jones unit redefined the rhythm section; and the totality of the performances brought to jazz an expansionist élan, supple and almost giddily liberated. Ten years after Louis Armstrong codified jazz as a soloist's art and Duke Ellington unlocked its singular compositional textures, Basie and his men embodied an audacious widening of the canvas.

Countless westerners and midwesterners had contributed to jazz, but most of those who went east were assimilated by the East, as Bix Beiderbecke was in Paul Whiteman's band and Hawkins in Henderson's. New Jersey's kid from Red Bank sounded like the Wild West with his loose-limbed abandon. At a time when Benny Goodman was declared king of swing for popularizing the well-made arrangements of Henderson, Benny Carter, and Edgar Sampson, Basie challenged the necessity of conventional writing, let alone Ellington's impressionism or Lunceford's inexorable two-beat. Personally, Basie and his crew were sweet-faced, sweet-talking introverts, but musically—as demonstrated at the Jones-Smith Incorporated session—they were cutthroats. Young's two-chorus solos on "Lady Be Good" and "Shoe Shine Boy" assert one of the most dynamic debuts in the history of records (he was twenty-seven, an advanced age for a newcomer). His windblown inventions combine vigorous riffs and piquant melodies, surfing the registers of the tenor, honking and crooning lean probing tales as narratively precise as a Hemingway story. Young's solos are high points, but there are no low points: Carl Smith, who left Basie in 1937 and spent much of his career in South America, plays with incisive flair; Jimmy Rushing, somber on "Evenin' " and ebullient on "Boogie Woogie," attains the front rank of band singers; the rhythm section, charged by Jo Jones's cymbals, is electric. The big band Deccas clinched the assault on Eastern conventions.

Basie was the first bandleader to popularize a reed section with two tenors. In Herschel Evans, he had one of the Southwest's most distinctive respondents to Hawkins; his darkly romantic tone ("Blue and Sentimental") and red-blooded authority ("Doggin' Around," "Every Tub") complemented Young's insuperably logical flights. Evans mined the ground beat, Young barely glanced at it. Heard back-to-back in such performances as "One O'Clock Jump" and "Georgiana," they define the range of the tenor in that era—they are as distinct as if they were playing different instruments.

The trumpet section offered a similarly contrasting twosome. Buck Clayton was hired in 1936 as a replacement for Hot Lips Page, a rugged bluesman. His warm and golden tone modulated Armstrong's drama with a reticent lyricism that could be celebrational ("Jumpin' at the Woodside"), playful ("Dickie's Dream"), or inscrutable ("Good Morning Blues"). He provided sensitive bookends for Young's solo on "Easy Does It" and a driving resolution to "Jumpin' at the Woodside." Clayton occasionally used a cup mute, but left most of the muted work to Harry Edison, whom Young nicknamed "Sweets" for the insinuatingly nasty tone he produced. Edison brought a crafty and even caustic wit to the band in elliptical solos played with a tight edgy timbre ("Blow Top," "Jive at Five"). His twelve-year tenure began in 1938, and when he left, his grasp of obbligato and dynamics made him an ideal singers' accompanist—Nelson Riddle used him whenever possible on sessions by Sinatra and Nat Cole. Of Basie's trombonists, the most distinctive was Dickie Wells, who had a rambunctious style and used his slide to whine and chortle salty speechlike solos ("Panassie Stomp," "Dickie's Dream," "Taxi War Dance").

Eddie Durham, who came to Basie after a stint with Lunceford and later wrote for Glenn Miller, played trombone and electric guitar, but his primary importance lay in his hand-tailored arrangements, which went a long way in anchoring the Basie style. He wrote "Topsy," voiced so that the saxophone lead is passed between altoist Earle Warren and both tenors, which alters the ensemble texture (in 1958, "Topsy" was a Top 40 hit for drummer Cozy Cole), and also "Swinging the Blues," "Out the Window," and "Time Out." His "Good Morning Blues" is a splendid example of Jimmy Rushing's integral role in the band (twenty-six of the fifty-seven Deccas have vocals, five by Helen Humes, the rest by Rushing). It opens with Clayton emerging from a dark, minor-key ensemble passage, as if in a dream. Basie follows with a sunny chorus in a major key before Rushing sings three merrily impudent choruses—"Good morning blues, blues how do you do? / Baby, I feel all right but I've come to worry you"—backed by a discreet piano obbligato. The band riffs proudly in the last chorus, rolling over the beat. Cryptic, growling, smoke-filled effects used here are heard in other Basie-Rushing sides ("Evil Blues," "I Left My Baby"), but the singer was also featured on pop tunes, notably "Exactly Like You," which Rushing cheerily makes his own with an ascending glide in his first eight bars.

Hammond did not leave the Basie musicians entirely to the ministrations of Decca. In January 1937, he began using them—as he used the key sidemen in other orchestras—for small band sessions run by pianist Teddy Wilson and featuring Billie Holiday. The chord Young struck with Holiday proved every bit as profound as the one with Basie: the musical romance between the two has no real parallels, though numerous record producers and performers have attempted to replicate their telepathic communion. At their first session together, they recorded the masterful "I Must Have That Man," establishing an emotional solidarity that is almost embarrassingly intimate. They became great friends (she dubbed him "Pres," as in president of all the tenor saxophonists, and he called her "Lady Day"), but not lovers—though they sound as if enmeshed in a lofty, irrevocably doomed love. Though often exultant ("Me, Myself and I"), they are more often bound by a predictive melancholy. Their most privileged moments are uncanny duets that begin as singer-with-accompaniment and become operatic collaboration: two equal voices riding out the night ("A Sailboat in the Moonlight").

Young's work with Holiday complements his work with Basie. He is invariably characterized as having a light, cool, gravity-free style, but he also introduced to jazz a carnal earthiness that prefigures modern notions of funkiness. With Basie, he mixes it up for the dancers and gets way down, mooing and honking; with Holiday, he is ever the gentleman, and far more revealing of the delicacy that became more pronounced in later years. Exceptions exist (his solo on Holiday's "When You're Smiling" is a riot of good cheer), but not enough to refute the rule. In time, his alcoholism and her heroin addiction would tear them apart. But before that happened, he would break with Basie, who was succumbing to easternization.

The 1939 band that recorded under Hammond's supervision had undergone one major personnel change with the death of Herschel Evans and the recruitment of Buddy Tate, another inventive southwestern tenor. Many other musicians had come and gone in the ten years Basie had been involved with big bands, but this adjustment in the reed section signaled the sea change to come. Evans had been a major figure in the band, and Tate got his coveted seat in part because he could play Evans's key solos and approximate his big sound (and because Young endorsed him). It was the last time Basie attempted to replace a star soloist with a soundalike. He was coming to realize that a band couldn't be dependent on famous soloists because if you lost them you were sunk. The antidote to such dependency was a book of arrangements that put more emphasis on the ensemble, as keyed to the magical Basie rhythm section. At first, the suggestion of a drift in purpose was discreet: busier charts and more covers of tunes associated with other performers (Goodman's "And the Angels Sing," the Ink Spots' "If I Didn't Care"). The important thing was that the band got stronger, the recordings more impressive.

Many of Young's most inspired performances emerged in 1939 and 1940. One could hardly ask for a better example than the intoxicating "Taxi War Dance." It's a head arrangement without a theme and everything about it is distinctive. Basie begins with four bars of boogie-woogie, extended another four bars with the addition of a band riff. Except for that riff, the first half of the record could be by a small ensemble—rhythm section plus two soloists. Young dances in with a fast paraphrase of the first four notes of "Old Man River," which he repeats as a springboard into a bluesy melody of his own, more than compensating for the absence of a written theme. His chorus is a grid of contrary melodic fragments, each complete in itself and rhythmically invincible, that ultimately makes perfect sense. He disguises completely the origin of the harmonic pattern—Ann Ronell's ballad, "Willow Weep for Me." After a two-measure boogie-woogie transition, Dickie Wells also plays a full and trenchantly expressive chorus. Now the ensemble enters to kick off two choruses in which it plays no more than a four-measure (six-notes) call, eliciting four-measure responses from tenor saxophone, Buddy Tate in the first chorus and Young in the second (notice his final response, a series of "funky" C-sharps and C-naturals varied by alternate fingering). In each instance, Basie claims the bridge for the rhythm section. The piece ends with a round-robin of two-measure breaks by Basie, Young, bass, drums, and ensemble.

This sort of thing was a revelation to musicians who were coming of age in the early '40s, as close to a house rebellion as jazz experienced in the period before bop. Within five years, a flood of Young acolytes would all but dominate the tenor. Basie may have been leaning toward more elaborate arrangements, but for the time being he retained the spontaneity of Kansas City in a string of stunning recordings, most spotlighting Young ("Rock-a-Bye Basie," with Tate, is a notable exception): "Pound Cake" (fifteen years later, Young's improvisation was scored for the Woody Herman band as "Blues Groove"), "I Left My Baby" (Rushing's peak, with Young's support and an ominous climax of orchestral riffs), "Tickle Toe" (a Young original and a candidate for the most exhilarating of all his recordings with Basie), "Song of the Islands," "Dickie's Dream," "Lester Leaps In," "Blow Top," "Louisiana," "Broadway," and "Five O'Clock Whistle." But Young was becoming impatient with life as a sideman. Thanks in part to Hammond, he had become a star away from Basie on records with Holiday and at historic Carnegie Hall extravaganzas hosted by Benny Goodman and Hammond himself (*Spirituals to Swing*), where he unveiled an alluring and typically individual approach to the clarinet. Fed up with endless rehearsals (a new twist for a band that used to make it up on the bandstand), busier arrangements ("It's Sand Man," "Ain't It the Truth"), and endless touring, he left.

Young had always been a loner. Born in 1909 and raised in Mississippi across the river from New Orleans, he spent most of his youth traveling with the Young Family Band, headed by his father, Willis, a Tuskegee-trained musician. His brother, Lee, a noted drummer, recalled Lester's early fascination with the C-melody saxophone virtuoso Frank Trumbauer, famed for his light sound and melodic style. Trumbauer was not really a jazz player, though he partnered Bix Beiderbecke on the latter's finest records, but he offered an alternative to the prevailing technique of heavy vibrato and staccato tonguing. "Anything Frankie Trumbauer could play, Lester could play it," Lee said. In 1939, when Basie played a homecoming date in Kansas City, Trumbauer dropped by to hear the band, and Buddy Tate, who also admired him and had met him as a boy, introduced the two men; Young was deeply moved by Trumbauer's praise. By that time, Lester had been on the road for twenty years, from the age of ten. He feuded with his father while in his teens and ran off, taking jobs with various bands throughout the Midwest and Southwest, impressing musicians as early as 1929 with his unique style.

In 1934, while playing a Little Rock date with Basie, Young received a telegram from Fletcher Henderson, offering him Coleman Hawkins's vacated chair. To New York ears, his sound was foreign, disturbing, and wrong. Henderson's musicians mocked him, and Leora Henderson (Fletcher's wife) asked him to study Hawkins's recorded solos to learn how to play correctly. Henderson had no alternative but to let him go. But first he assembled his reed section and told them that though they had made Lester's stay in the band untenable, he was a finer musician than any of them and some day they'd know it. The day came two years later with Basie's ascent. Young's initial acceptance may have been crimped by his lone-wolf attitude, his peculiar way of doing things in and out of music. He had heavy-lidded eyes and a skewed smile, and hid his red hair under a distinctive pork-pie hat, its flat brim shading his pale eyes. He had a hesitant way of walking and spoke a personal lingo that was much imitated in later years. He was passive yet competitive, ingenuous yet wily, shy yet cocksure. A disastrous experience in the army devastated him and his music, ultimately (with the help of drink) shortening his life. But by the mid-'40s, he was second only to Charlie Parker as the most widely mimicked of saxophonists. His influence could be heard in the music of Dexter Gordon, Illinois Jacquet, Stan Getz, Zoot Sims, Wardell Gray, Al Cohn, Gerry Mulligan, Gene Ammons, Allen Eager, Paul Quinichette, Brew Moore, and many others. Reaching for a novel adjective in 1949, Leonard Feather wrote that Young "symbolized the gradual evolution from hot jazz to 'cool' jazz." He epitomized cool.

His time in the army is invariably blamed for the change in Young's music from youthful radiance to a vulnerable lyricism. At the end, his playing was often marred by physical weakness related to his alcoholism, but the bounding line between young Pres and old Pres isn't so clear. Shortly after his induction in October 1944, Young was sentenced to a detention barracks for five years—reduced to one—on a charge stemming from his admission on a routine form that he smoked marijuana. The DB was located in Georgia, and he is said to have been abused and beaten. When he returned to recording in October 1945, for Aladdin, he began the session with "DB Blues," a triumphant performance that combines haunting melodic phrases with jump licks in the then fresh blues-with-a-bridge format (three twelve-bar blues choruses arranged like the A sections in a song, with an eight-bar bridge based in this instance, but not always, on "rhythm" changes). The record indicates nothing of self-pity or creative diminishment. On the equally classic "These Foolish Things," from the same session, he bypasses the song's cloying melody in favor of a tender composition of his own, prefiguring by two years Charlie Parker's similar treatment of "Embraceable You." If Young and his music had changed, the upshot was hardly the total disintegration many commentators claimed to hear as they dismissed his postwar work.

Young had grown more retiring and distrustful, hiding behind the affectations of the homosexual and the junkie, though he was neither. Musically, he focused more on dynamics, shifting from whispered triplets to bruising shouts, and introspective ballads. Yet indications of change were apparent in recordings he made in 1944, *before* the army, for Keynote, Commodore, and Savoy. These are among his most accomplished and revealing performances, and they display the exaggerated legato, increasingly asymmetrical phrase endings, and darker tone associated with his later years. The Savoy sessions recorded in the spring with the Basie rhythm section are indicative: the affecting "Blue Lester" is cast in a rueful mood that is virtually Hebraic (not unlike Cole Porter's "My Heart Belongs to Daddy") and his languorous but shapely chorus and a half on "Ghost of a Chance" suggests the emotional qualities associated with his '50s ballads. What would Charlie Parker's "Koko" have sounded like if Savoy hadn't issued the second take of "Circus in Rhythm" (in which Young concludes his solo with the bridling riff Parker exclaimed in his masterpiece)? The postwar "Crazy Over J-Z" sounds more like early Pres than the prewar "Jump, Lester, Jump." Even the 1943 Signature recordings Young made with Dickie Wells (excepting "I Got Rhythm") offer a slackening in his rhythmic impetuousness and soulful expressiveness as compared to the 1956 Verve album with Teddy Wilson, where Wilson's eloquence and Jo Jones's shimmering cymbal raise Young to creative heights, by turns forceful ("All of Me"), elemental ("Pres Returns"), and wistful ("Taking a Chance on Love").

Young was permitted an isolated—and televised—moment of glory when he was reunited with Billie Holiday in 1957 on *The Sound of Jazz*. Those who recall his single-chorus, thirty-nine-second blues solo on Holiday's "Fine and Mellow" tend to remember it as a mere handful of notes, a reflection of its impeccable form. The solo is so solidly constructed that, after you've heard it a couple of times, it becomes part of your nervous system, like the motor skills required to ride a bicycle. Young was not expected to play much on that live broadcast. He had appeared, ailing and remote, in the CBS studios three days earlier to perform on the album that would be issued weeks later as a memento of the show, and only his backup for Jimmy Rushing had any spark; his solo on the Holiday number presaged a few ideas in the TV version, but was flat and weary.

Nat Hentoff, who with Whitney Balliett selected the players for *The Sound of Jazz*, has recalled that Young was told he could play his one TV solo seated if he preferred. But when it was his turn, following a chorus by Ben Webster, Young rose to his feet and the unprepared cameraman had to pull back to get him in view. Young was visible for all of twenty seconds, all he needed to steal the show. Director Jack Smight underscored the moment by cutting away from him to the one image that justified the discontinuity. He noticed Holiday was responding to Young's solo with a medley of facial expressions—swinging her head, moistening her lips, arching her brow, nodding in final accord—that seemed to illuminate and even anticipate Young's every note. The Sunday afternoon television audience, which had no way of knowing the two had not spoken to each other in years, heard a musician improvise a solo of immense beauty and saw or at least surmised the deep waters of a profound friendship that was not yet the legend it would become after 1959, the year each of them died.

After Young left his band, Basie enjoyed nearly forty-five years of accolades and triumphs. The changes in his band were relatively mild through 1948. Young, for example, was replaced by Don Byas, another outstanding tenor saxophonist, albeit one in the Hawkins lineage, who climaxed his career with a series of stellar recordings in 1945, then decamped for Europe, where his abilities sadly withered. With the hiring of Illinois Jacquet in 1945, Young's influence was restored in a modernized context—more honking, less lyricism—reflective of a period when Lionel Hampton and Louis Jordan dodged every manifestation of gentleness with the more raucous pleasures of r & b. One of the curiosities of jazz history is that the most commercially successful record Basie ever made was not, as many people assume, "Every Day" (with Joe Williams) or "April in Paris," but an uncharacteristic 1947 cover of the r & b novelty "Open the Door, Richard!" He continued to engage great players (Vic Dickenson, Lucky Thompson, Shadow Wilson), but in the year of his big hit, the band was becoming staid and perhaps bored; two of his brightest discoveries—Clark Terry and Paul Gonsalves—delivered on their promise not with Basie, but under Duke Ellington's appreciative gaze. Big bands were on the way out. The exuberant, gas-guzzling behemoths no longer mirrored the strangely bleak optimism of the times—an era of Rodgers and Hammerstein musicals and film noir, of freedom singing and communist hunting. Ellington, buttressed by his songwriting royalties, survived, but few others did.

Basie's band was much admired by the progressive modernists who turned jazz on its head in the '40s. Charlie Parker, who apprenticed himself at the Reno Club by studying Basie and his men (especially Lester Young and Buster Smith), had once longed to play with the orchestra. Buddy Tate related the sadly comical story of his attempt to get Parker into the band. When he recommended him, Basie assured Tate, "When I need a lead alto I'll call him." On an off-night in Boston, they went to hear Parker, but as Tate remembered, "It was the worst night Bird ever had": He wore oversized suspenders and his pants reached midway between his knees and shoes. Basie remarked, "I'd like to use him, but he looks so bad." Tate retorted, "Half the guys in the band look bad until you put a uniform on their ass," at which point Parker vomited on the microphone. Basie slowly turned his head to Tate, who said "Basie, don't say anything because I've got nothing to say." The alto job went to Tab Smith.

By 1950, when Basie could hold out no longer and he reduced the orchestra to a septet, bop was too much the language of jazz to ignore. He fostered the common denominators between swing and bop, hiring Wardell Gray, Clark Terry, and Buddy De Franco. A few years later, he called Parker and Gillespie "the finest thing in the world that could happen because everything has to change," and added, presumably with irony, "It must have been wonderful to be pioneers like they are." When he did return full-force in 1952, his band was the reverse image of the one that straggled out of Kansas City with its arrangements locked in its collective cranium. He designed the most irreproachable virtuoso ensemble ever to work the dance band idiom. With arranger Neal Hefti supervising a new book and drummer Gus Johnson sparking the gleaming rhythm section, Basie retained the old foundation of twin tenor soloists (Frank Wess and Frank Foster), twin trumpet soloists (Thad Jones and Joe Newman), and powerful trombonists (Benny Powell and Al Grey). They were all first-rank musicians, but they weren't innovators and they weren't the key attraction—the orchestra was. Basie hired the best section players in the business, and in publicizing his intention to lead a writer's band, he attracted the best arrangers, most of whom had no place else to go except the commercial studios.

"I wanted those four trumpets and three trombones to bite with real guts," he said, "but I wanted that bite to be just as tasty and subtle as if it were the three brass I used to use." He achieved that and more. His brasses were celebrated worldwide for their ability to play perfect unison shakes and decays. He continued to blue-pencil everything out of an arrangement that wasn't essential and left plenty of space for rhythm-section interludes. When the ensemble locked gears, it had the force of a steam engine, and audiences gasped with pleasure. The range between shaking fortissimos and barely audible sighs was new—not as new as the band of 1936, but Basie's '50s band was every bit as au courant as the revitalized Sinatra or the songbook Ella, both of whom he regularly backed, along with numerous other singers, from Bing Crosby to Jackie Wilson. When "Every Day" went through the roof, Joe Williams proved to be a bigger attraction than Jimmy Rushing. The swing era was history, but Basie was in flower. Along with Ellington, Herman, and Kenton, he kept the game alive.

Neal Hefti, a Woody Herman alum, crafted an icily romantic sound for the band in such pieces as "Softly with Feeling," "Cute," and "Girl Talk." In the enduring "Li'l Darlin'," he tested the band's temporal mastery with a slow and simple theme that dies if it isn't played at exactly the right tempo. Basie never flinched. Soon the band was an arranger's workshop, drawing on talents in and out of the fold, including Ernie Wilkins, Frank Foster, Frank Wess, Benny Carter, Quincy Jones, Buster Harding, Wild Bill Davis, and Thad Jones, who along with Gil Evans and Bill Holman was one of the most imaginative and influential writers to come along in the '50s. (Jones expanded on his work with Basie in the great band he and Mel Lewis formed in 1965.) Basie had a jazz band, a commercial band, a singer's band, a dancer's band, a concert band—an institution. He had come far from the hissing cymbals, minor-key piano vamps, growly brasses, and shining solos of the '30s, but at its best, as in the 1959 Birdland recordings or the live '70s Pablo albums, it was uniquely fine, lustrous. The fundamental principles remained unchanged. Basie knew if he had your foot, your heart and mind would follow.

20 ❖ Jimmy Rushing
(Swinging the Blues)

If there is a black actor as fat, funny, gracious, and utterly serene as Jimmy Rushing, a great film could be made about the Oklahoma nightingale. The animating nerve would be less the plot than the character and the elated sense of well-being that he and his music so effortlessly conveyed during the forty-plus years of his largely sub-rosa career. The story would be centered in Kansas City, when he teamed with stranded New Jerseyan, Bill Basie, and together hit numerous small towns, playing buckets of blood on Saturday night and churches on Sunday morning. Rushing and Joe Turner shared a nearly equal renown in Kansas City, which they helped colonize on behalf of the blues, and Turner was Rushing's only rival as progenitor and king of all the blues shouters. But they ended up with curiously different legends.

Turner journeyed from K.C., where he often sang while tending bar, to New York's Cafe Society in 1938 in the company of his boogie-woogie compatriot Pete Johnson. The long affiliation with eight-to-the-bar cadences sustained him right through rhythm and blues and rock and roll, which honors him as a forebear, though his best records were the swing sessions he recorded for Atlantic in the '50s (especially *The Boss of the Blues*). Rushing's association with Basie delivered greater rewards in the '30s, lifting both of them out of the Reno Club and into the nub of the swing era in 1936. By the time they were ensconced on Fifty-second Street, Rushing was sufficiently prominent to inspire a pop song, "Mr. Five by Five"—"He's five foot long and five foot wide." For nearly fifteen years, he remained Basie's key singer, and just about every record they made together is classic—not only the lofty, often intensely poetic blues like "I Left My Baby," but even trite songs perhaps no one else could have polished to so durable a shine like "Georgiana."

Yet the association with swing led to more swing, and that meant consignment to the mainstream. Rushing became a cult favorite rather than a genuine star. He was admired by the community of musicians and recorded in the best of circumstances throughout the '50s, under

John Hammond's aegis for Vanguard and under Irving Townsend's for Columbia. He was a perennial hit at festivals, invariably making new fans as he rocked from side to side and raised out-choruses to fevered pitch. Yet without a "Shake, Rattle and Roll," he had little chance of breaking out of the jazz and blues ghetto and into the rhythm and blues zeitgeist. This was not merely a matter of circumstance. Rushing and Turner were both shouters, albeit of different sorts. Turner's brusque, edgy phrasing and ragged tones were suited to the new music; Rushing's quenched and expressive phrasing and riper tones were not. Moreover, Turner's vocal attack remained stable, while Rushing's radiant pipes— almost supernaturally gorgeous in the '30s when he assmiliated Bing Crosby's mordents into his gleeful tenor—grew husky and eventually strident.

It wasn't an issue for him. Rushing was a man comfortable with himself and his music. In the late '60s, record producers tried to extend his audience with darker blues albums that, in their reliance on long and occasionally inferior instrumental solos, were merely tedious. Yet his small audience was loyal; even when he was dying of cancer in the '70s, he made the trip every weekend from his Queens home to the stage of the Half Note on Hudson and Spring Streets and, seated with microphone in hand, rocked the joint. His last, much esteemed album, *The You and Me That Used To Be* (RCA), was a significant record in its day. Despite modest sales, its all-star cast (Zoot Sims, Budd Johnson, Ray Nance, Al Cohn) helped spur the mainstream revival, and the material—not a blues in the bunch—returned Rushing to his musical roots. He may have sounded like the Oklahoma earth, but he was bred in the pop songs of the '20s, and not the least of his contributions to music was an uncanny ability to stamp with a noble luster and resolute swing such numbers as "Exactly Like You" or "When I Grow Too Old To Dream."

Rushing's relatively marginal standing is harder to accept today. With all the reissuing CBS has done in the past couple of decades, it has never compiled the irresistible collection that would gather all the Rushing-Basie sides. (In the '70s, English Decca collected the earlier Rushing-Basie Deccas, an anthology never released here.) In the '80s, Columbia put out a two-disc set containing about half of the material Rushing recorded for the label in the late '50s; that splendid sampling enjoyed modest sales, the remaining selections abided in the vaults. Just as well. Rushing's Columbias are so good—the cover art, concepts, and sequencing as well as individual selections—they ought to be released exactly as conceived. That was eventually done with one of the albums, in a CD reprise of the 1959 *Rushing Lullabies*. It wears its age lightly, as perfect things do.

By 1959, Rushing's voice had hardened, losing the sonorous purity yet retaining much of the opulence of the '30s. The edge was attractive, rough but supple; the time and energy remained incomparable, the out-choruses peaking at a near swoon level. Of all the Columbias, *Rushing Lullabies* was on the face of it the least conceptualized. Primarily a blues set (seven blues, four pop standards), it is perhaps the most completely satisfying album Rushing ever made under his own steam. Nested in a sextet of empathic musicians, including two companions from the Basie orchestra of the '30s, tenor saxophonist Buddy Tate and drummer Jo Jones, Rushing is in an ideal setting. The inspired ensemble breathes around him as one, like a pipe organ. The whole album unwinds with engrossing charm: the selections varied in tempo and form, the obbligati smartly divided among the players, the rhythm section champing steady with much of its power held in reserve, the authority of the singer absolutely persuasive.

Perfection? Consider the opening blues chorus by Ray Bryant, played over Sir Charles Thompson's stop-time organ, a twelve-bar marvel that slips with pealing inevitability into Rushing's entrance on his old collaboration with Basie, "You Can't Run Around." Taken at a slow, bleeding tempo you rarely hear anymore, because it requires a lifetime's confidence to pull off, the piece builds incrementally as Rushing, backed by guitarist Skeeter Best, lifts each chorus to a slightly higher plateau and climaxes with the caressing tenor of Tate, who has rarely played with greater feeling and efficiency than on the three sessions that went into this album. The second blues, one of two collaborations by Rushing and Julia Lee (a far more neglected mainstay of the Kansas City restoration), is "Say You Don't Mean It," taken medium fast and clamped to the earth with a vigorous bass walk by Gene Ramey. Thompson also solos, and for some listeners his Basie-influenced organ may come as an unpleasant diversion—it's the sound of skating rinks. But his solos follow a sensible if invariable pattern (chorus of riffs, chorus of single-line improvisation), and his presence in binding the ensemble gives the album much of its glow.

On numbers in which Rushing is featured throughout, like the slow blues "Did You Ever," his accompanist changes with each chorus, progressing from Bryant to Tate, who enters urgently whispering as Rushing cries, "So long, so long," the reed audibly fluttering in the wind. On numbers in which the players get to solo, they are allotted one or two choruses, enough for a fully cogent statement. Bryant usually provides his own bass lines, though at times, as on "I Cried for You," he is a modernist Teddy Wilson, orchestrating his statement with grand gestures. Skeeter Best, an elusive musician with only a handful of recordings, has his finest solo on that one as well; he plays with a high steely sound that prefigures country-music session man Hank Garland's lone jazz album as well as early George Benson. Other blues numbers include an old cautionary oddity, "Pink Champagne"; "Good Rockin' Tonight," made famous by Wynonie Harris; and a sixteen-bar jewel called "Three Long Years" that avoids the expected repeat strain in the lyric.

Rushing is a percussive singer, who ascends beyond the ensemble yet anchors it with his accents. "Have a little pity, don't make me cry," he sings: the first time, *cry* is a distinct two syllables; the second time it's one, but *make* is wrenched with a distinct turn. Similarly, on "I Cried for You," he stomps the out-chorus with the line, "that's one thing you learnin'," sacrificing grammatical niceties (which he elsewhere exemplifies) because "you lear-nin' " produces three neatly stressed beats. Each of the pop pieces is taken way up. Rushing soars on the final release of "Deed I Do," goading the ensemble to step up its pumping for the last eight bars, and then adds a coda. "I Can't Believe That You're in Love with Me" is faster still and boasts exceptional two-chorus solos before Rushing returns, alighting on a cloud.

But even that one is a warm-up for the closer, the album's masterpiece, Irving Berlin's "Russian Lullaby." The famous melody has a double lineage, in folk music and in a Tchaikovsky ballet, but had never before been treated as a flat-out stomp. This version begins with just the drums, soon joined by organ and voice as Rushing chants, "Rock, rock, rock." When he attacks the melody, the rhythm section is particularly spry, collectively underplaying its strength. Jo Jones is presiding here, and through the solos that follow—lilting Bryant, steady Best, expansive Thompson—he holds the furnace at a low and even flame. Then the magisterial Tate dances on stage, eminently relaxed as he stokes the burner; now Jones's sticks are hitting harder, and you can almost see his Cheshire Cat smile widening in response. Rushing's return is stunning, a full-dress assault that drives exuberantly into a second chorus with Tate and Bryant and everyone else adding to the mix.

Nothing could follow it, except the other Columbia Rushing albums— most notably *The Odyssey of Jimmy Rushing, Esq.*, which has his once celebrated voice-and-piano lament for Depression-era hookers, "Tricks Ain't Walkin' ." On the original LP of *Rushing Lullabies*, nothing did follow the Berlin stomper; on the CD, we have the dubious gift of a short bonus track, an ersatz gospel throwaway called "The Road of Love," not previously released or missed, though not unpleasant. Still, after hearing it once, you may find yourself reaching for the remote after "Russian Lullaby" so as to meditate in peace on the glory of Jimmy Rushing and friends. For a visual supplement, reflect on the farewell image described by those who attended his final recording session. After warmly bidding everyone in the control room good-bye, Rushing threw his coat over his shoulders, doffed his hat, and strolled down the corridor twirling his cane, the graceful exit of a portly Chaplin.

21 ❖ *Roy Eldridge* *(Jazz)*

Through much of its history, jazz made avid converts with the simple promise of undying excitement, whether maximized by throbbing rhythms, bloodcurdling high notes, violent polyphony, layered riffs, hyperbolic virtuosity, fevered exchanges, or carnal funk. Yet excitement often gets a bum rap from those converts who, having mined the music's deeper recesses, suspect all crowd-pleasing gestures of vulgarity. At bottom, the distinction between the two is subtle but clear: if you like it, it's exciting; if not, it's vulgar. If you're cold to a musician's impassioned yowling, that passion will seem awfully dim if not aimless, and since crowds more than individuals thrive on excitement, your response to musical rabble-rousing may depend on your willingness to get lost in a crowd. The showiest expressions of passion frequently border on outright pandering, but immoderation of that sort is a healthy symptom—it tends to proliferate in a milieu where authentic excitement also flourishes.

No one more ably personified that excitement than the indefatigably competitive Roy Eldridge, a paradigm of the music's volatility and joy, whose trumpet electrified the jazz skies of five decades, transforming its fevers with generosity, cunning, and unconstrained elation. He incarnated the love of playing and asserted the highest personal standards of excellence. No one was more esteemed by his peers: Elmer Snowden dubbed him "Little Jazz" in the early '30s. The *Little* referred to his size and was later dropped, but the moniker that equated him with jazz itself stuck. So the unthinkable happened when, after suffering a stroke in 1980, Eldridge was forced to put down his horn. For the next nine years he tried to maintain his career by singing, occasionally playing piano and drums as well. He often turned up as a member of the audience in clubs and concert halls, peppery and alert as ever. But Eldridge was now an artist deprived of his art. Had he been a less zealous musician, he might have been permitted to resume playing. But his doctors knew he was incapable of reining in his emotions, and Eldridge himself knew that if he had to contain his ardor every time he played, the battle was already compromised, which is to say lost.

His music, more than most, seizes the moment, imbuing the air with a risk that marries passion, bravado, and disdain for easy answers to the problems of improvisation. In his hands, the trumpet was an exceedingly personal instrument, scarred with the same gravel that characterized his singing and driven by the same impetuousness and humor that leavened his conversation. His high notes—some of them plums; others, wild crested cries—are always recognizable, as are the low, rasping asides, the arching figures that paraphrase melody while turning the chords inside out, the straight-to-the-belly riffs, and the perfect time. Eldridge embodied jazz's indulgence in the pleasure principle. Even his ballads are cautiously ecstatic, the outcome of inspiration and a daredevil predilection for harmonic substitutions.

Much of Eldridge's music is superbly preserved on records, but his infectiously combative presence, captured in a handful of film clips, is largely a thing of memory. Here is one such memory from early 1977, when Lester Bowie of the Art Ensemble of Chicago stopped in at Jimmy Ryan's, where Eldridge led the house band: Visiting musicians were always welcome to sit in, though to hear Eldridge tell it, you'd think he was under constant siege. Bowie had dropped by the previous week, just to listen, and when he was introduced to Roy as a fellow trumpet player, the older man gave him the fish-eye and issued the cryptic challenge, "Be ready." On the night Bowie returned, instrument in hand, I arrived early and found Roy in conversation with Dan Morgenstern. The sight of two critics perked his antennae. Roy said, "I hope he *does* come tonight, he picked a good night." A few moments later, he asked, "Is he coming to get me or as a social call?"

"Well, I think he's bringing his axe."

"Then he isn't coming to socialize."

Bowie and writer Stanley Crouch arrived shortly before Roy ascended the stage for "Let Me Off Uptown." Afterward, Roy announced a trombone feature and walked over to Bowie, warding off pleasantries with the complaint, "This is a bad night for me." Bowie commiserated, pointing to his own teeth—he'd been to the dentist that afternoon, he said. Bowie unpacked his horn for the second set. Seeing his approach, Eldridge switched to flugelhorn. A big-tipper's request for "Bei Mir Bist Du Schoen" could not be ignored. Bowie didn't know the tune, but he showed off his good ear in a convincing solo capped with one of those pinched-nerve squeals that Eldridge probably invented. Roy, in turn, produced pear tones in a melodic middle-range solo—no shouts.

After another request, "Black and Blue," Eldridge introduced Bowie to the audience and turned the stage over to him. He played "Now's the Time," punctuated with dynamic tremolos and bruising hollers. Clarinet and trombone solos followed, and then Roy returned to blow a dozen or so choruses, building them with patience and agility, the sound of his flugelhorn turning from burnished gold to fiery red. For the out-chorus, he switched to trumpet, riffing high while Bowie's fat middle-register filled in the chinks.

"Yeah, I knew he was gonna build up to the trumpet," Bowie mused at intermission. He observed of Eldridge's conversational style, "It's not about playing time—he'd just be talking." Roy walked over and said, "I'm not even warmed up yet."

"Then I better get out of here quick," Bowie replied.

"I haven't even played a ballad yet. I want to *cry*," Roy said, the adrenalin now flowing freely. Turning to me and referring to something I'd once written about him, he added, "It's like you said. After twelve, I get dangerous."

"What was that first tune we played?" Lester asked.

During the next set, they played ballads, and though Bowie earned spirited applause for a "Misty" that contrasted rapid note flurries with low-register tones, Eldridge elicited shouts with "The Man I Love" as he climaxed his melody inversion with lusty, pleading deliberation. They finished the evening with a nod to Louis Armstrong, "Chinatown," in which the wily Eldridge played an abridgment of Armstrong's original solo and restored peace to the kingdom.

Much has been made of the existential side of playing jazz: the falling-through-space dilemma of seizing the moment and the fragility of the final work, an improvised solo. Records document those solos, just as scores document sonatas, and can, in turn, be made into scores, though notation can't reproduce breathing, tone, and attack. Many Eldridge solos are sturdy enough to withstand transcription and interpretation—as Budd Johnson demonstrated when he arranged Eldridge's 1953 "The Man I Love" solo for a trumpet quartet. Yet Eldridge's playing is inseparable from the man. His solos are etched with slurs, tremors, and cries that can't be transcribed, and truth to tell, not even the records can convey the thrill of seeing this charismatic little man, bent back at the waist, his trumpet grasped with both hands and aimed straight ahead, the notes climbing, thickening, ratcheting upward and out.

He was born in Pittsburgh, on January 30, 1911, and played his first paying gig six years later at a neighborhood New Year's Eve party that found him asleep most of the time. His mother was an untrained pianist who played overtures and accompaniments at movie theaters; his brother Joe, a skillful alto saxophonist, violinist, and arranger, tutored him on trumpet. At fifteen, Roy left home to play in a touring show. Stranded, he joined the Greater Sheesley Carnival Band (he played trumpet, drums, and tuba), got stranded again, and finally worked his way back to Pittsburgh. That was in 1926, about five years before he was exposed to the decisive influence of Louis Armstrong. In the preceding years, he listened mostly to Red Nichols and to saxophonists. "I got that job on the carnival," he said during a conversation in the '70s, "because I could play Coleman Hawkins's chorus on 'Stampede' on the trumpet, which was unheard of then."

Eldridge's originality springs in part from the saxophone techniques he brought to the trumpet—the agility and speed, the idea of playing on the harmonies of a song, as perfected by Hawkins and Benny Carter. In 1928, he went to Detroit as a member of Fletcher Henderson's Dixie Stompers, directed by Horace Henderson, but his brother Joe convinced him to leave the band so he could teach him harmony. "He kept me on track," Roy explained, "and it eventually came out in the way I played." He reeled off the saxophonists he played with: "first Charlie Lee, and then when I got to New York there was Chu Berry, Ike Quebeck, Ben Webster, Lester Young, Hawk, Prince Robinson." Hawkins's influence was especially profound, but Eldridge didn't get to know him until Hawkins's return from Europe in 1939. "He told me he liked my playing from some records he heard in Europe. He was saying, 'Man, this cat ain't playing harsh like the rest of them cats. He's kind of playing more or less like a saxophone, lot of legato things, playing changes.' But he didn't realize that I was playing some of his stuff, and Pres's and Chu's."

One trumpet player Eldridge admired was Rex Stewart, and it was after a competition with Stewart that he began playing high notes. "I had a battle with Rex when he was with Fletcher's band. I screamed a G at the end of my chorus and he came back and screamed a B-flat. Man, I almost cried. I couldn't get that note out of my head, and so I practiced and practiced until I could play up there, and then down. You see, I was never a screamer, I always played *music* up there. Two years later, when I met Rex, it was a different story." Eldridge's confidence was dampened when Chick Webb told his brother Joe, "Roy's fast but he ain't saying nothing." At that point, he began listening to jazz's primary storyteller, Louis Armstrong—absorbing his logic, directness, passion, high-note flourishes.

By the mid-'30s, Eldridge was established as the most vital young trumpet player in New York, with a flashy, voluble style that rampaged freely through three octaves, rich in harmonic ideas and impervious to the fastest tempos. His broadcasts from the Savoy Ballroom with Teddy Hill's band were picked up all along the Eastern Seaboard; one dazzled listener was John Gillespie, who heard them on his aunt's radio in Cheraw, South Carolina, and considered them the transforming experience of his life. He later dubbed Roy "the Messiah of our generation." In 1935, Eldridge made a memorable showing on Teddy Wilson's "Blues in C-sharp Minor" session, even singing the vocal on "Mary Had a Little Lamb." The next year he and bandmate Chu Berry reawakened the Henderson band. By 1937, he was in Chicago leading his own combo at the Three Deuces, with brother Joe and Scoops Carey on saxophones and Zutty Singleton on drums. The exhilarating nightly 1 A.M. broadcasts were avidly followed by musicians, who began appropriating his tunes. The Three Deuces group made only a few studio recordings, among them two explosive landmarks in the coming-of-age of a new jazz generation, "Wabash Stomp" and "Heckler's Hop." The surviving broadcasts find him issuing none too subtle challenges to King Louis himself: "Minor Jive" is a variation on "King of the Zulus," but played faster and higher; his virtuoso renditions of "St. Louis Blues" and "Body and Soul" are enchantingly flamboyant. The last was successfully recorded with Berry, in a widely imitated double-time arragement.

The decade preceding the emergence of bebop was rife with frantic trumpeters. After the war, honking tenor saxophones would assume the role of crowd pleaser, but in the '30s and early '40s the trumpet still ruled, and while many practitioners pursued the course of lyrical composure (Buck Clayton, Bobby Hackett, Bill Coleman, Harry Edison, Billy Butterfield, Doc Cheatham), others (Eldridge, Henry "Red" Allen, Bobby Stark, Hot Lips Page, Charlie Shavers, Rex Stewart, Harry James, Shad Collins) strove for an agitated, coruscating approach. If they were more likely to overstep the bounds of good taste, the payback was in the increased risks they took. In one way or another, Armstrong fathered both groups of trumpeters, but the one aspect of his music that proved inimitable was his fatted sound, shaped and effulgent. Eldridge, the most rugged and compelling of his heirs, never had a pure or golden tone. His sound was always underscored by a vocal rasp, an urgent, human roughness—as if carving a path in the throat before bursting forth in grateful release—that gives his music its immediacy. His high notes often suggest spontaneous, even unbidden explosions of feeling that, instead of climaxing a solo, set up blistering parabolas of melody.

If any doubts about his generational preeminence remained, they were put to rest in May 1940 by his technically and imaginatively stunning solos at a Chocolate Dandies recording session with Carter and Hawkins on "I Surrender Dear" and "I Can't Believe That You're in Love with Me." That breakthrough was confirmed a year later when he joined Gene Krupa's orchestra and recorded a string of flash-fire concertos, including

"Rockin' Chair" and "After You've Gone." His association with Krupa, a gentle man who would not countenance segregation, began at a recording date in 1936. Krupa wanted to send Eldridge to school to study arranging. That wasn't for Roy.

> So finally he called me to do a split-week in Providence and it went so good, he asked me to join the band. Originally, I wasn't *in* the band, I was like an act—like Lionel and Teddy were with Goodman. But I insisted on playing in the section. It'd take a year to tell all the dues I paid. Oh, Jesus, you're so great on the bandstand—now you come off, man, and in some places you can't get a hamburger. It was rough, baby. And we didn't go south!

Sometimes, Eldridge took over on drums, when Krupa conducted or rested, and he frequently sang, scoring his and the band's biggest hit in a duet with Anita O'Day, the incredibly lusty "Let Me Off Uptown."

Eldridge's trumpet solos are the primary reason for the enduring fascination of Krupa's band. Of those solos, "Rockin' Chair" is in a class of its own, and he regarded it as his best recording ever, though insisting he was "blind drunk" when he made it. He recalled:

> I knew what I was doing on "After You've Gone," but "Rockin' Chair" was something else. I'd been playing some first parts, second parts, solos, and I thought the date was over, because Basie was waiting to come in and record. So Gene said, 'Let's try "Rockin' Chair," and I said, "Try it now?" We only made two takes of it, and I actually cried. I said, "Please don't put that out." And then I forgot about it. About two months later, Ben Webster was playing Las Vegas, and he called me to have breakfast with him. He said, "Man, I got a record I want you to hear." So we went to Vegas, had breakfast, and he played a couple of records, and then he played "Rockin' Chair." I said, "Who's that? It's not Louis, it's not Diz." I didn't recognize it was me until it got to the chorus and then I flipped. There really isn't a flaw in it.

Despite the racial abuse, he agreed to try another white band and joined Artie Shaw's orchestra in the mid-'40s. For more than a year, he sparked the big band and Shaw's combo, the Gramercy Five, while recording with his own band for Decca. Though determined to fight segregation in the music business, Shaw could no more protect Eldridge from the realities of life on the road than he could Billie Holiday or Hot Lips Page, and eventually Roy got fed up. Still, he tried again with Benny Goodman for a 1950 tour of Europe. Bitter and confused, he decided to stay in Paris, where he was lionized for eighteen months, writing a newspaper column, singing the blues in French, and worrying about the implications of bop. "Bop had me hung up for a while. The thing I didn't dig the most was the kind of time that was carried on. I still like the bass pedal, that's what I think it's there for." Shortly after he came home, he told a reporter, "As long as I'm in America, I'll never work with a white band again," and was branded a communist in the most extreme instances of a general drubbing in the press.

But the '50s proved a satisfying and fruitful time for him. He signed with Verve records and toured the country with Norman Granz's Jazz at the Philharmonic, singeing the climaxes of those highly popular staged jam sessions. He recorded prolifically with his prewar colleagues, including Lester Young, Teddy Wilson, Ben Webster, Vic Dickenson, Benny Carter, and especially Coleman Hawkins, with whom he developed a close alliance that brimmed with humor, rivalry, and unembarrassed love. Under the aegis of JATP, they made an album at the Chicago Opera House with three members of the Modern Jazz Quartet that plays as a succession of climaxes. But Eldridge also crossed the generational lines, recording duets with Gillespie and working frequently with Oscar Peterson. On one of Eldridge's best albums, *Dale's Wail*, Peterson plays organ and cagily controls the dynamics on the title tune as Eldridge sustains a jubilant tension over nine choruses. On the same album, Eldridge produced his definitive reading of "The Man I Love," interpolating two references to Lester Young in a performance that marries startling confidence, crying emotion, and insouciant swing.

The '60s were less responsive to the old titans. Eldridge toured with Ella Fitzgerald for a couple of years and spent eight weeks with Count Basie's band, playing section parts for the first time in more than twenty-five years. His own groups employed the now graying bop players, like saxophonist Richie Kamuca and trombonist Kai Winding, who weren't having an easy time of it either. He was still a terror at jam sessions: the peaks of *Loose Walk*, a 1972 concert with Al Grey, Eddie Davis, and the Basie rhythm section, are his twelve-chorus solo on the title number (a Sonny Stitt blues) and his single chorus of "I Surrender Dear." In the blues, his solo begins as an exchange of single pitches with Basie, goes off into a flurry of weird quotations ("We Want Cantor," "Yankee Doodle," "Mop Mop"), builds to a piping climax, then settles back into cadences hammered out like the stakes of a picket fence. In the ballad, he defies harmonic expectations before he's out of the first eight bars, turns the release into an expansive melody (the tempo is daringly slow), fires up the last turnback, simmers into a coda and cadenza. In 1970, he was given a rare opportunity for an old lion—a bandstand of his own. For the next ten years he ran the show at Jimmy Ryan's, taking requests through midnight, then—as musicians arrived to pay homage—turning on the juice.

One example of Eldridge's spirit: Billie Holiday's "Fine and Mellow," on the 1957 *The Sound of Jazz* TV show. Eldridge and Holiday were old friends (he played on her first three dates with Teddy Wilson and on several later ones). Nevertheless, in a circle of soloists that included Hawkins, Young, Webster, Dickenson, and Gerry Mulligan, he was the only one to play two choruses instead of one. Coming last to the plate was a familiar challenge to him, but in that context, a second chorus could be interpreted as a presumptuous mistake if it wasn't stupendous. It was, it is. The turnback is a wrenching high-note wheeze that demands a follow-through; the final cadences are paced with depth and drama.

One example of his sensibility: the 1981 tribute to him at Town Hall. Ella Fitzgerald agreed to make an unbilled appearance toward the end of the concert. She arrived much earlier than we anticipated, and I explained to her that we wanted to keep her out of sight until the surprise. In her eagerly cooperative, girlish way, she suggested hiding behind the musty red velvet back curtain, and before I could demur she stepped behind it, creating a mummylike projection. As Roy completed his vocal on "Kidney Stew," I gingerly poked at the great lady, who had been standing in the dark for ten minutes. The audience cheered as she walked out on stage, and of course, Roy thought it was for him. With each step she took, the applause got louder. Roy looked radiant—he turned to Budd Johnson and shrugged his shoulders. As the cheering waxed, he realized something was up and turned around. When he saw her, his tears flowed instantly. They embraced, and sang together, less like two old pros than like neophytes discovering the pleasure of their voices.

One example of his wit: a night at Jimmy Ryan's. After the first intermission, a woman produced a lamb's tongue (a dollar tip) and requested "New Orleans Function," better known as "Didn't He Ramble." Clarinetist Joe Muranyi volunteered that he knew it. The woman stipulated that she wanted all three parts. "You're getting a little deep now," Eldridge advised, but he conferred with his musicians and reported to her, "Yeah, we got it covered. Now we go behind the cotton curtain." As Muranyi played the dolorous lament, Roy groaned, "Have mercy." The house fell out. When music is as genuinely cathartic as it was for Little Jazz, fake passion makes for delicious burlesque.

22 ❖ *Ella Fitzgerald*
(Joy)

When Ella Fitzgerald was singing at her peak—in good voice, with good song, arrangement, and accompaniment—nothing in life was more resplendent. An evangelist of swing, she inspired devotion that bordered on blind and elated trust. Like other performing artists safely ensconced in the pantheon, she offered the illusion of perfection in a context of free-ranging individuality. We defer to that illusion in part because the failings of such performers remind us that in art, unlike the rest of life, our accomplishments ultimately abrogate our shortcomings. She was the finger-snapping oracle who envisioned all of humanity "trucking on down the avenue/without a single thing to do." One of a handful of preeminent jazz performers who were held tight to the public's bosom, Ella Fitzgerald taught us something vital about joy, as Billie Holiday taught us something vital about pain. Each was possessed of a certainty.

Fitzgerald's long career was rich in paradox. Her pop and songbook records notwithstanding, she was determinedly a jazz singer, yet could not sing the blues, tending to embroider them into a numb banality. An irreproachable connoisseur of ballads, she had little talent for histrionics. A product of the swing era, which served up her biggest hit, she soared to far greater celebrity with bebop-inflected scat singing. She was a black singer who named the white Connee Boswell as her primary model. She was a respectful interpreter of pop songs, who could caress them with sensual dedication, and an inspired embellisher, who could deconstruct them as though the lyrics had no more meaning than nonsense syllables. She did not make hit records, but worked exclusively in the world's great concert halls. Exceedingly shy off-stage, she was bold to the point of impudence in the rapture of music. Large-boned and plain-looking, she personified a jazzy glamour—showbiz royalty, the unassailable First Lady of Song.

In the beginning, no one would have thought to characterize her as a lady, first or otherwise. Ella was too much the lively young girl, precocious but vulnerable, looking for a little yellow basket. "A-Tisket, A-Tasket," which she developed from a children's song and recorded with Chick Webb in 1938, remained unaccountably the best-selling disc of her career. Her ability to survive that early success is significant; most big band singers who owed their popularity to novelty songs did not. Fitzgerald's story has been told often, if elliptically—considering her fame, one marvels at how assiduously she protected her privacy. She was born in Newport News, Virginia, in or around 1918, and taken to an orphanage in Yonkers, New York, after the death of her mother in the early '30s. In 1934, Benny Carter heard her at an amateur contest at Harlem's Apollo Theater and recommended her to several influential men in the music business, including Fletcher Henderson and John Hammond, who were unimpressed. The dwarfed drummer and bandleader Chick Webb agreed to audition her and was bowled over. He became Ella's legal guardian even as he reorganized his trailblazing orchestra around her unfledged teenage voice. At Webb's death, a year after "A-Tisket, A-Tasket," Fitzgerald affirmed her loyalty by fronting the orchestra for two years before beginning her career as a single.

Like her mentor, Ella signed with Decca Records, where she made more than 300 sides (about 40 of them as vocalist with the Webb orchestra). Except for a couple of sessions with Teddy Wilson and Benny Goodman, all the records she made between 1935 and 1955 were for Decca, an indentureship rivaling that of the company's main attraction, Bing Crosby. The first half of her career was as much a reflection of the aesthetics of Jack Kapp, who created the label and believed that the middle of the road was where all music should converge, as it was of her extraordinary rapport with the musical fashions of the Depression and war years. Though she would achieve her greatest renown in the affluent society of the '50s, Ella was made for the era of Little Orphan Annie.

Despite Fitzgerald's emphatic rhythmic genius, Kapp appears to have been at loose ends at how to market her, and many of the Deccas are egregiously meretricious, prefiguring her exploitation albums of the late '60s and after (for example, Ella sings country, Ella sings the Beatles). Fitzgerald's sessions were too often burdened with contemptible material and intrusive vocal choirs, though she excelled at Decca's unique penchent for duets. Kapp encouraged a policy in which his artists would appear on recordings together, integrating jazz and pop, and generating encounters as inspired as Louis Armstrong and the Mills Brothers and as contrived as Bing Crosby and Jascha Heifetz. Like Crosby, Ella was amenable, productive, and flexible—the challenge of working with artists she admired stimulated her reflexes. But her career became mired in the enforced versatility.

It's tempting to speculate about the kind of records Ella might have made for Columbia in those years, when John Hammond's policy was to present Billie Holiday in small instrumental groups made up of the most gifted swing musicians in town, usually under the leadership of Teddy Wilson. Early in 1936, she did record two sides with Wilson. "All My Life" is a pleasantly nostalgic ballad, enunciated with a clarity worthy of Ethel Waters, though the sensibility is relatively naive. "My Melancholy Baby" swings steadily on the beat and is enhanced by good-natured embellishments. Whereas Holiday personalized a song by inflecting every phrase, Fitzgerald conveyed a purer approach, less idiosyncratic and sometimes less discerning. Benny Goodman was so impressed with her that he used her as a replacement for Helen Ward in June of the same year. She gave "Goodnight My Love" a well-phrased but stuffy reading, yet "Take Another Guess" unveiled the girlishly swinging Ella, though her vocal projection was thick and clouded, not yet fully formed. In those years, she accented long-vowel sounds with increased vibrato and broke words into staccato syllables to stress rhythmic impact. She put more faith in melody and rhythm than in lyrics.

By the end of 1936, she was emerging as a kind of swing mascot, singing many tunes with the words "swing" or "swinging" in the title. One of them, "Organ Grinder's Swing," was made at the first session under her own name—accompanied by a contingent from the Webb band, the Savoy Eight—and proved to be prophetic. It was a childhood novelty and it led to several others, including "Betcha Nickel," "Chew-Chew-Chew," and, of course, "A-Tisket A-Tasket." Of greater importance, it showed her off for the first time as an aggressively deft scat singer. In the final chorus, riffing the phrase, "Oh, organ," she outpaced the band. For her third session, Decca teamed her with the Mills Brothers, an indication of the label's confidence in her growing success. She was not yet twenty.

Her voice matured greatly during the next couple of years, though her naive, on-the-beat determination abided. More often than not, the material was pitiably weak, but if Fitzgerald could not transcend it as Holiday effortlessly did, she could uplift it with her expressive, trumpet-like delivery—for example, "If You Should Ever Leave" or "Dipsy Doodle." On the last, she sounds entirely oblivious to the song's abysmal words. She could raise temperatures on a worthy swinger like Irving Berlin's "Pack Up Your Sins and Go to the Devil" or fashionable band numbers like "If Dreams Come True" and "Rock It for Me," but also betrayed an awkwardness in those years, a bumptious quality exacerbated by the dire novelties that threatened to become her trademark.

The sensual lilt in her voice became more pronounced in 1939 in such memorable readings as "Don't Worry About Me" and "If I Didn't Care." With "Stairway to the Stars," her characteristic approach to ballads was codified: the first chorus was reasonably straight, the second was an exercise in swing time as she transfigured the key melody into a contagiously rocking riff. Yet her improvisations were often predictable; you can get a fair idea of how much she grew by comparing "Stairway" with "Soon," recorded in 1950. Once again, a forthright chorus is followed by a rhythmic one, but the voice has flowered into the very embodiment of swing phrasing, luscious and fluid.

The '40s were undoubtedly the period of Fitzgerald's most uneven recordings, a reflection of an in-between dilemma that defined the era. Swing was losing its magic, and bop was little more than an underground workshop. Decca coupled her with the label's other black artists: Louis Armstrong, Louis Jordan, the Ink Spots, the Delta Rhythm Boys, Sy Oliver, Bill Doggett, the Mills Brothers (again), and others. These accounted for some of her most successful records of the decade, musically and commercially, especially as compared with the numerous ballads she sang in collusion with lumbering studio orchestras and vocal choirs directed by Gordon Jenkins. Frequently, she overcomes the overblown settings, but the dim arrangements irrevocably date the recordings. Ella's thick delivery had now metamorphosed into a light and pristine style, fully at home in the greater spaciousness of her range. But too often her own superficiality matched the material and made her sound like a brilliantly equipped hack.

Yet a new Fitzgerald was emerging—the queen of scat, the first lady of song. Her 1945 "Flying Home" was an all-scat performance that established her among jazz modernists. She wasn't born of bop, like Sarah Vaughan, but she was thoroughly accepted into the fold. With her ear and technique, Ella was not likely to be intimidated by a flatted fifth; on the contrary, she was now in her twenties, and the new sounds of Charlie Parker and Dizzy Gillespie were a welcome source of inspiration. She thrived on it, roaring through a lexicon of bop licks on "Lady Be Good," which became one of her most requested and enduring showpieces, and on the more imaginative "How High the Moon," where she followed a straight chorus with a variation compiled equally of phrases from swing and bop.

Fitzgerald's ballads, too, reflected her enhanced improvisational powers. She revealed a knack for altering the character of a dull phrase by raising a key note by the interval of a sixth. She continued to develop her mastery of portamento, with which she would rise or fall to the proper note or, more intriguingly, begin with the written note and slide into a more colorful interval. She meshed beautifully with the Mills Brothers on a serene and enticing "I Gotta Have My Baby Back"; displayed wonderfully airy high notes on "I've Got the World on a String"; exhibited an incomparable and unexpected richness of voice on the Martha Raye novelty, "You'll Have To Swing It." Given the fullness of her recording schedule, Fitzgerald could be drearily impersonal even with attractive material (as on "I Wished on the Moon," 1954), but when she was committed to a song ("It Might as Well Be Spring," 1955), she was luminous.

The culmination of Fitzgerald's two-decade association with Decca quietly appeared in the form of twenty selections with pianist Ellis Larkins (eight Gershwin titles in 1950 and a mixed bag in 1954). Never before had she achieved and sustained the sensuousness of the first encounter with Larkins, producing what was essentially her first songbook. Never had those familiar Gershwin melodies and Gershwin words taken on so voluptuous a glow. Her command of the material, measure by measure, is enthralling, and if those matchless readings of "Soon," "Someone to Watch Over Me," "I've Got a Crush on You," and "How Long Has This Been Going On?" point the way to her future, they also define a pinnacle of achievement in that quickly fading vocal style born of the big bands.

The gloried monument of popular song that Fitzgerald personified after she signed with Norman Granz's Verve Records coincided with the rise of TV and hi-fi, both of which she conquered. Along with Frank Sinatra, another reconstituted big band singer who had survived his own hell of constricting ballads and demeaning curios, she found her true recording medium in the long-playing album. At the peak of her success in the '50s, her new label didn't even try to invade the singles market. Fitzgerald was a concert and festival artist, and there was something déclassé, something smaller than life, about jukebox fodder. And Ella was nothing if not outsized and thoroughly liberated, whether shaking up Germany in her blond wig or wailing with the boys at Jazz at the Philharmonic. When, during her hair-raising 1957 concert recording of "Lady Be Good," she begins to riff, "I want to rock/I want to roll," she isn't just acknowledging the fad many of her contemporaries assumed or hoped would disappear with the new year, but making common cause with the latest wrinkle in a rhythmic fabric that underpinned her entire aesthetic. She was now unstoppable, the soul of swing, her rhythmic panache indemnifying her against cliché.

Still, her ballad singing, girded however subtly by rhythmic cunning, exhibited the fullest measure of her accomplishment. In ballads, we could best experience the luxuriousness of her instrument, its warmth and generosity and range—her technical resources, which were extravagant. In command of nearly three octaves, she was a mezzo-soprano with the auxiliary assets of a contralto who additionally displayed an unembarrassed appetite for falsetto and an arsenal of buzzes and growls. (She was one of Louis Armstrong's most astute impersonators.) Yet it was never Fitzgerald's reach that won our hearts, but the emotional energy that directed her musical choices, an energy that will seem wanting only to those who consider joy less rewarding than woe.

For there is no denying Fitzgerald's limitations as an interpreter of songs that express complicated attitudes of sorrow and regret. She had her share of troubles, but in music she was free of them. Her stilted performance in *Pete Kelly's Blues* indicated an inability to step into any character other than her own, though when she sang in that movie one was quick to overlook her line readings. For all the beauty of her Gershwin renditions, she could not match Armstrong's powerful sensitivity when they teamed in *Porgy and Bess*. Louis and Ella enjoyed a productive musical relationship that peaked with their 1957 duets, a discourse on timbre and texture by turns epic ("Autumn in New York" has the interaction of a one-act play) and uproarious ("Stompin' at the Savoy" has the reciprocity of an inside joke). She could match and even trump his every rhythmic jolt, but the role of Bess underscored her dramatic limitations, as did her unhappy attempts at blues singing, where she often masked the idiom's candor in distracting ornamentation.

The true Ella was upbeat or serene or both (what a shame she never recorded an album with Erroll Garner). This was true even of her most penetrating ballads: they are wistful, but rarely distraught. Her "Someone To Watch Over Me" is radiant, but her "Lush Life" is glibly inattentive. She brought a heady commitment to songs that speak of pleasure, but she was not a singer to cry over her absinthe.

The modern American song, as opposed to the European style, inhabits the lower registers. Except for Verdi, the baritone's friend, opera venerates the higher range and allocates supporting roles to altos, baritones, and basses. Even if you've never heard opera, you have heard of a handful of tenors and sopranos: Caruso and Pavarotti, Callas and Price. In American pop and jazz, the baritone has ruled since the mid-'20s when Bing Crosby sang with Paul Whiteman and was celebrated for his virility and naturalness. The tenors he displaced were soon considered effete and affected. The rare exceptions proved the rule: Louis Armstrong began as a tenor, but his leonine growl subsumed the issue; Jimmy Rushing brought operatic fervor to the blues; Tony Bennett once confessed to singer Mary Cleere Haran (with a smile), "I'm a tenor trying to be a baritone."

Our stellar women singers have also sung from deep in the chest (a quality especially strong in Connee Boswell, Ella's first influence) and carried that same earthy resonance into the higher notes, making up in rhythmic and intonational continuity what is lost in purity of voice. Sarah Vaughan, perhaps the most brilliantly equipped of American vocalists, was often referred to as operatic because of her comprehensive range (more than four octaves), but there was nothing operatic in her articulation, which took much of its impetus from the lusty trombone-cello timbre of her lower notes.

Fioritura doesn't exist in American vernacular singing, but melisma does, with its aching, breathless, rumbling blues notes and arching howls. American ornamentation isn't used for the sake of virtuosity alone, but as an expressive device of walloping immediacy. Surely one reason Ella Fitzgerald was celebrated as the first lady of song for half a century (this was no king-of-swing gimmick) is that she so thoroughly embodied the American style. Some observers were disarmed by her seemingly guileless technique, which perhaps they associated with her "girlish" quality. Frank Sinatra, our man in bel canto, once expressed reservations about her phrasing. You can hear her breathe, he complained. Of course you can. Her breathing is the mechanism that incites her interpretations. For Sinatra, the lyric governs the melodic line; Fitzgerald put her money on rhythm. Sinatra would have us forget the body that houses the voice; Ella reminds us of the body's function.

Nowhere is the totality of her spell more apparent than in the remarkable song books. Verve collected them as *The Complete Ella Fitzgerald Song Books*: a cloth-covered red box with a matching 120-page book and all eight volumes (sixteen discs in their original garb, but miniaturized). They have done for Ella what Oxford did for the *Oxford English Dictionary*, only without the requisite magnifying glass, producing a kind of musical Limoges box, its tiny wonders to be examined with bemused astonishment.

Armstrong and Crosby and Astaire and Holiday and Sinatra each had an incalculable impact on the canon of modern song. But Fitzgerald erected the pantheon. After Norman Granz pried her out of her Decca contract, they went to work on a quite lavish examination of the great songwriters, one of the boldest achievements of the LP era. The first honoree was Cole Porter, whose stock consequently soared, even as his talent and the world that produced it began to disappear. As an example of the series' impact, consider that Irving Berlin requested inclusion after the Rodgers and Hart collection was issued. As an example of its prescience, consider how close the series' canonization is to that of Alec Wilder and James T. Maher in the 1972 *American Popular Song*.

Those who insist that Fitzgerald failed to make the most of sophisticated lyrics should go back to the Porter set: no one has done better by the upper-crust mockery and minor-key irony of those songs—certainly not Mabel Mercer, who embraced many of the affectations. When the eight collections were recorded, between 1956 and 1964, singers frequently updated lyrics and altered pronouns to suit the performer's gender. The one misstep in the venture is Fitzgerald's cursory gloss on Larry Hart's "Manhattan," the lyric that made him famous. Her updated verse, "And *My Fair Lady* is a terrific show they say," simply can't compare with the tart reference in the original to *Abie's Irish Rose* (an expressed hope that "our future babies" will see it close), and she omits other classic rhymes ("Greenwich"/"men itch") as well.

Yet throughout the Rodgers and Hart volume, Fitzgerald affirms Hart's preeminence among lyricists even as she mines for all they are worth the ingeniously jazzy, endlessly appealing melodies Rodgers had in him before he tailored his art to the ponderous musings of Oscar Hammerstein II. Hart brought out his soul, and does the same for singers. An alcoholic, depressive, four-foot-eleven, Jewish homosexual who died at forty-seven, thinking *Oklahoma!* was the promised land, Hart always avoided the obvious. He wrote love songs for people who didn't expect to be loved, like "My Funny Valentine": "Is your figure less than Greek/Is your mouth a little weak/When you open it to speak/Are you smart?" Don't answer, just be mine. Fitzgerald understands Hart wonderfully well, knows, or appears to know, about "ordering orange juice for one," love with and without "dizzy spells," and the blessed absence of people ("Who needs people?"). She makes the most of the "Little Girl Blue" who is as "merry as a Carousel" and doesn't flinch from the chill observation of her adulthood that "all you can count on is the raindrops/that fall on Little Girl Blue." She's as understanding of the desperation in "Ten Cents a Dance" as she is of the pleasures of "Mountain Greenery."

She reaches even greater heights on the overwhelming five-volume set devoted to the Gershwins. Nelson Riddle did some of his finest work in that set. Duke Ellington, on the other hand, took it easy, arriving at his self-homage with little music other than a suite in honor of the singer. Somehow the alchemists worked magic, combining vocals and instrumentals, and producing a high-water mark for them both. Of recently excavated performances integrated into these discs, the most rewarding is a ten-minute rehearsal of Billy Strayhorn's "Chelsea Bridge," a fly-on-the-wall revelation of how Ellington manipulated his men. The other pantheon composers are Berlin, Harold Arlen, Jerome Kern, and Johnny Mercer, who is the subject of a high-intensity swing session with exuberant writing by Riddle.

Time and again in these and other exemplary performances, Ella Fitzgerald does something so reflexively inventive or poignant, so casually insightful, that you want to stop the disc and marvel in silence. Elsewhere, the ebulliance takes over and you can hardly believe your luck—to live in the world of Ella. It is to laugh out loud.

23 ❖ Artie Shaw
(Cinderella's Last Stand)

Few reissues in the '90s proved more satisfying or revealing than Artie Shaw's *The Last Recordings*, released in January of 1992, followed a year later by *More Last Recordings*. It did not much matter that the packaging is a bit misguided. In addition to the title, the cover of the double-CD box barks "Rare & Unreleased" and "Collector's Edition." All three phrases miss the point. The recordings are *among* Shaw's last, not all—as the second volume demonstated. As best I can tell (the liner information is obscure), only three of twenty pieces, including alternate takes, were previously unreleased, though the entire set is so rare that the point is hardly worth contesting. I don't know what "Collector's Edition" means, but the appeal to aficionados or completists is disheartening. For these are among the finest performances by one of the eminent clarinetists of the century, and among the most enchanting small band recordings in jazz history, virtually unrivaled in defining the nexus between swing and bop. That they were new to almost everyone heightened their wonder.

Shaw, born in 1910, stopped playing in 1954 after recording at his own expense the last editions of his Gramercy Five (really a sextet if you include Shaw) at a series of late night or early morning sessions (beginning after the band finished at the Embers about 4 A.M. and continuing until noon). He had walked away from his career, his music, his celebrity on a few occasions in the years since 1938, when his hit version of "Begin the Beguine" threatened to transform him from an introspective, adventurous, irreverent musician into a celebrity on autopilot—little better, in his unforgiving view, than a trained seal. But in 1954, he put down his clarinet for good, and it has been impossible to discuss his art without arguing his sullen individuality. Other musicians have quit performing while continuing to record (Glenn Gould) or managed to sustain a following while producing abstruse suites and tone poems (Duke Ellington). What is most paradoxical about Shaw, as quickly revealed in conversation with him, is his resentment of celebrity obligations and his desire to sustain a celebrity-sized following. Best take him at his word when he insists that he was temperamentally unsuited to the whole star-making apparatus.

Still, the mystery gnaws at those of us who haven't the holy gift: If you do something better than almost anyone else alive, how do you walk away from it? Shaw has been asked the question so many times that he's exasperated at having to go over old ground, yet the fact that he invariably comes up with different anecdotal ammunition to explain his decision helps keep the mystery alive. Visiting Shaw in 1990, I was given a couple of reasons for his abdication that I hadn't heard before. In 1949, the worst year in history to assemble a large orchestra (Ellington was scuffling, Herman and Basie gave it up), Shaw organized his most ambitious pure-blooded jazz orchestra: arrangers included Tadd Dameron, George Russell, Johnny Mandel, and Gene Roland; players included Al Cohn, Zoot Sims, Danny Bank, and Jimmy Raney. (Musicmasters, which issued *The Last Recordings*, has collected the marvelous proof in *1949*.) Here's one recollection of the moment he decided to walk:

> If that band had kept going, it probably would have been *the* band, but I had to break it up in three weeks, there was no point. Then I went out and put together what they wanted, a 1938 band and, this is a true story, it was highly successful. And I thought to myself, 'Well, if they hated the best band I've got and they like a band I finished with eleven years ago, which is a generation in jazz, let's see what happens—my own private joke—with the worst band that ever was.' So I put together a stock arrangement band. We played the top ten tunes on *Billboard*'s chart, one to ten—'If I Knew You Were Coming I'd Have Baked a Cake,' 'Blue Tango,' 'Hoop-Dee-Doo,' whatever they were. They *loved* that band. The last night I ever had a big band, we played in Pennsylvania, Allentown or Reading—a dance at a little American Legion joint. And after it was over, the last night—you couldn't make this up, it's like [Jimmy] Swaggert and his whore going, of all places, to Babylon—I finished the gig and a guy came up to me and said, 'Mr. Shaw, I heard you were a tough guy to get along with, but I want to tell you something. It's the best night we've had since Blue Barron.''

So help me God. I said "Thanks," and I was through with the music business. When the guy said, 'Blue Barron,' when those words came out, I knew it was over. The next time I ever played again, I had the small group.

The small group was formed for an engagement in New York at the Embers in 1953, and in a sense it represented compensation for every compromise Shaw had ever made. Though his clarinet was prominently featured in his big band recordings, he felt he had never fully tested himself as an improvising jazz clarinetist. The Gramercy Five itself originated in 1940 and was designed to let him shine at greater length than was generally possible in an orchestral setting. The first release, "Summit Ridge Drive," a blues, was an enormous hit, but later records didn't do as well. The group recorded only eight sides, the originals far outclassing the popular songs, and the performances are intermittently successful. Characteristically, Shaw had pianist Johnny Guarnieri play harpsichord, a novel sound that became predictable, as did the split-choruses and bright tempos. Billy Butterfield was confined to muted grousing (not his forte) and guitarist Al Hendrickson was no Charlie Christian. Though he never gives himself more than sixteen bars, Shaw is easily the outstanding player—highlights include his keening voicings for clarinet, guitar, and trumpet and his ebullient, unexpected klezmer turn at the close of "Dr. Livingstone, I Presume?"

In 1945, Shaw reconvened the Gramercy Five, this time with much stronger personnel that stood at the very bounding line between the heights of swing and the promise of bop. Shaw was among equals with Roy Eldridge, Barney Kessel, and Dodo Marmarosa sharing the terse arrangements. This time only six numbers were made and they failed to attract much attention. The audience wanted the Shaw of the radio hits, and in fact, he would never have another big record that wasn't primarily a vocal with instrumental accompaniment. Shaw's account of how Marmarosa left the 1949 band is a familiar indication of his frustration:

> We had to play "Frenesi," it was a rent-payer, something we had to play. I didn't like it very much by then. I mean it was perfectly all right in its day, but it was over. So we're playing in Minneapolis and we played 'Frenesi' and I had to give the guys a lecture on the tune. I said, 'You guys are great musicians, you can make that arrangement sound good, come on.' They used to play it with contempt. So Dodo Marmarosa, who was a very weird little guy but a marvelous player, said, 'I can dig it, I can dig it!' Then the men started to play it well, but it got to be a bit much. So this one night we started the gig at eight and by nine we had to play it. About ten, a guy calls, 'Frenesi.' I pleaded, 'We just played it!'—but we had to, it would have been fraudulent not to. By eleven, Dodo said, 'If we're going to play that thing once more I'm leaving.' Sure enough, a guy asked for it. I played it once more and Dodo left. I never saw him again. He went back to Pittsburgh.

The Gramercy Five recorded a few radio transcriptions, but its return to the studio (for Decca) was disastrous—trimmed down to a genuine quintet (no trumpet), it now served as support for vocalists. By that time, Shaw had been fighting the tide for fifteen years. After an apprenticeship of Harlem jam sessions and steady sideman work, he was initially invited to organize his own band for a 1935 swing concert. He showed up with a string quartet. His performance so impressed booking agent Tommy Rockwell, who was looking for a bandleader to rival Benny Goodman, that he goaded Shaw into starting a full-sized and full-time orchestra. Within a year, Shaw debuted at the Lexington Hotel, replacing Bob Crosby's neo-Dixieland with a surprisingly poised combination of reeds, brasses, and strings, arranged for the most part by his pianist Joe Lippman (who later orchestrated strings for Charlie Parker and Sarah Vaughan). The public snoozed.

In July 1938, however, at a single session inaugurating a new band (sans strings) and a new contract with RCA Bluebird, he hit three out of the park. "Back Bay Special" confirmed Shaw's credentials as a swinging player at the helm of a swinging band. "Any Old Time" was considered an instant classic by musicians, especially for the alluring vocal chorus by Billie Holiday—the only record she made with him, yet categorical evidence that she might have become one of the great big band singers. Shaw fought racial and generic restrictions at every turn, commissioning new works by William Grant Still and hiring Holiday, Leo Watson, Hot Lips Page, and Roy Eldridge at a time when they could not enter the front doors of the hotels they worked. The third piece, Jerry Gray's four/four arrangement of Cole Porter's exotic long-form song "Begin the Beguine," changed Shaw's life. It reached number one on the *Hit Parade* in the fall and, excepting the 1940 "Frenesi," remained his most successful disc. The producer did not want him to record it at all, arguing the tune was too complicated. But Gray opened it with a percussive intro, establishing a firm rhythm that is sustained throughout the performance by the drumming of Cliff Leeman (Shaw always used top drummers) and first-beat orchestral accents. Shaw's playing has a joyous constraint that builds with unself-conscious drama until the finish, which is marked by his piping high notes and glissando.

The Shaw style was unmistakable: evocative, sensuous, seductively serious. The critic Max Harrison described his vision as that of "a tutelary spirit combining Prospero and Ariel in one" and remarked on his "intense, almost harrowing, attenuation in upper registers." Hugely successful, he flinched at every cheer, complaining that comedy was pushing out the music on his Old Gold radio show, rankling at intrusions in his private life, resisting the obligations of hits, of which he enjoyed or suffered a great many. After collapsing onstage or walking off the bandstand on several occasions, he quit entirely—for about six months. After a long stay in Mexico, he reorganized. The public hardly had time to register his disappearance when it began buying "Frenesi" by the millions. He quit again, reformed again. Perhaps the quintessential Shaw big band recording is the 1941 "Star Dust," voted the greatest record of all time in a disc-jockey poll sponsored by *Billboard*. Now the strings were back, employed to underscore the unfailingly firm beat of the rhythm. Billy Butterfield, who had left Bob Crosby to go with Shaw, made his reputation with the first chorus. Shaw, demonstrating those "almost harrowing" high notes, shares the second chorus with trombonist Jack Jenny, whose fabled reputation (he died a few years later at thirty-five) is based almost entirely on his scintillating eight-bar episode. A year later, Shaw enlisted in the navy. By the time he returned to civilian action, the thrill and the swing era were gone.

So in 1953, for what amounted to his last stand, Shaw wasn't about to be diverted from first principles. After booking the Embers engagement, he organized a band with Hank Jones, Tal Farlow, Tommy Potter, and Irv Kluger. Because of his admiration for the George Shearing sound, he added Shearing's former vibraharpist Joe Roland. The recordings, with their after-hours feline grace and relaxed ambience (most selections are five to eight minutes and none of the charts were written) represent a state of grace for all involved, especially Shaw and Jones. For a final session in June, Joe Puma replaced Farlow on guitar, and Shaw's twisty ballad playing—intoxicatingly long phrases that sound like circular breathing and are produced in a timbre as light and inviolate as falling snow—is even more dazzling than before.

A selection of those recordings was briefly leased to Clef and Verve, but the albums quickly went out of catalogue and became expensive collector's items. In 1970, John Hammond played a few tracks for me in his office, exclaiming that they were possibly the best jazz clarinet records ever made and mourning the fact that Columbia refused Shaw's offer to put them out. In the '80s, the Book of the Month Club put out a collection of Shaw playing the classical repertory as well as performances from the 1954 sessions that had not been released on Verve. The Musicmasters compilation consists almost exclusively of material that had not been heard since the Verve releases of 1954 (with only two repeats from BOMC); "Mysterioso" was unreleased and "I Can't Get Started" and "Bewitched, Bothered, and Bewildered" are represented by alternate takes according to the notes (I'm unable to find evidence of the last having been issued in any version). The music is romantic, daring, and exquisitely played—it doesn't sound like that of any other small band of that era. Perhaps only Red Norvo's trio with Farlow and Charles Mingus comes close to suggesting comparable equanimity in crossing the rhythmic and harmonic Rubicons between prewar and postwar jazz.

Nowhere does one sense the slightest tension between players or styles. Jones has never sounded more liltingly attentive; Farlow is fleet and witting; Roland is percussively sure; and Potter is an oak. But, make no mistake, these sides represent a personal triumph for Shaw as clarinetist, perhaps the pinnacle of his work on the instrument. The first thing that grabs you is his sound, which is almost ethereal; the next thing is his breath control. His phrases aren't merely long, but cannily long— always pressing for one more detail, one more turn, rarely content to fold into the eight-bar phrases of the songs themselves. Indeed, Shaw seems to have a particular penchant for the ten-bar phrase, and often one phrase glides into the next so fluidly that you barely register the break. For all that, the performances are natural, self-possessed. The arrangements, apparently worked out on the bandstand, retain the formal charge of the original Gramercy Five but with far greater spontaneity.

For the first time in Shaw's career, at the very moment it ended, we hear him disporting himself in expansive play. Even his quotations have an air of inspiration. The most dazzling comes at the end of "Bewitched, Bothered and Bewildered," taken at a hazardously slow tempo. Jones capers through a diaphanous half-chorus, his tripping notes veiling the ambling beat, before Shaw returns with a release parsed into three witting phrases. In the last eight bars, he excerpts "The Song Is You" and sustains it for four measures, then flows seamlessly back into the intended song. At the end of the first chorus of "S'posin'," he bows no less fluidly to Charlie Parker. The selections include several Shaw originals, among them Gramercy Five standbys "Mysterioso" and "When the Quail Come Back to San Quentin." One of the most clever is "Pied Piper Theme," from his children's operetta, *The Pied Piper of Hamelin*. Following Jones's solo, the choruses split into four-bar chases between Shaw and Roland. After Shaw and Farlow get their own choruses (Shaw slips "Love in Bloom" into the bridge), the ensemble chases bass and drums, and attains a big finish, capped by a priceless Farlow glissando.

All the ballads are stunning. You may wonder how he can surpass the opening selection, "Imagination," but "Yesterdays" wins pride of place, a flowing hypnotic rendering in which Shaw rarely stops for breath and sustains an airily delicate tone that barely allows the notes to flutter; they ascend into the higher register with an intimacy that imparts high drama. When Hank Jones succeeds him, simulating a similarly understated timbre on piano, you may wonder how jazz did without these recordings, without this "Yesterdays," for so long. Over the past forty-five years, Shaw developed postmusical careers as a writer and conversationalist: his vital memoir, *The Trouble with Cinderella*, is in print from Da Capo; his wicked roman à clef, *I Love You, I Hate You, Drop Dead*, merits republication; his short stories (including "Snow White in

Harlem, 1930," an account of his first meeting with Willie "The Lion" Smith, Shaw's mentor) were collected in 1989 as *The Best of Intentions* by John Daniel and Company in Santa Barbara. He is in 1998 completing a massive manuscript called *Sideman*, which he describes as a jazz musician's *Jean Christophe*.

Shaw told me yet another reason for quitting clarinet; it began with a recollection of hearing Heifetz play the Bach Chaconne during the period when Shaw himself was mostly touring with symphonies and chamber groups. Shaw found the performance astounding, but when he congratulated Heifetz, the violinist said, "Really? I thought I was a little off tonight." Shaw then said:

> I realized, he's aiming at a hundred. He hits ninety-four regularly, so he hit a ninety-three that night. Nobody hits ninety-five regularly. There's not much difference, but he can hear it, and it's the same with clarinet. We had one night off a week at the Embers, and I'd come in the next day and I wasn't happy until about halfway through the evening. If you play really honestly, if you're cursed with that, even with one day off you can't hit the ninety-four. That's why I quit, it's too tough. There comes a point at which you say, Holy Christ, that's all you can do on this instrument. "Yesterdays" was the last time I ever played. There was no point after that.

24 ❖ Budd Johnson
(Chameleon)

Budd Johnson is one of the most benign and omnipresent figures in jazz history, and one of the least recognized. Despite a career in which he made formidable contributions to nearly every jazz generation from the late '20s to the mid-'80s, the adjective "underrated" clings to his name like ivy on a wall. Yet he was by no means underappreciated by those who knew his work. Many of jazz's titans—Armstrong, Hines, Webster, Gillespie, Eckstine, Gil Evans—were indebted fans. Critics came to admire his imperturbable dignity as much as his manifold talent (though historians have tended to overlook his contributions to big band music—not until recently did it become chic to honor arrangers). Audiences always responded to his forthright, sometimes impassioned tenor saxophone when they encountered it at jam-session-type concerts. But he made few records as a leader and none of them sold. When the accomplishments of his peers were recounted, Johnson's were often forgotten.

At the time of his death, at seventy-four, in 1984 (while playing a concert in Kansas City), Johnson had been a professional musician for sixty years, having initially gone on the road as a boy drummer. Born in Dallas, the younger brother of trombonist Keg Johnson, he learned some piano and cornet from his father and studied music with Portia Pittman, the daughter of Booker T. Washington. After two years working as a drummer, he switched to tenor and became a familiar face in the territory bands that traveled the Southwest. During a stop in Amarillo, he met Ben Webster, who was playing piano, and taught him the rudiments of the saxophone. With George E. Lee's band, he reached Kansas City and a recording studio in 1929. But the records that first document Johnson's developing style were made four years later in Chicago with Louis Armstrong ("Some Sweet Day" and "Mahogany Hall Stomp"). Johnson showed prescience in blending the linear fluency of Lester Young, whose music he knew long before Young recorded, with the sanguine attack of Coleman Hawkins, overlaying the result with the expressive hollars and moans indigenous to southwestern saxophonists.

His stylistic flexibility was impressive. Johnson could capture Young's sound, for example, without overt imitation but with evident satisfaction in the act of paying homage. His command of timbre was singularly resourceful, especially in the modern era, when he might play it cool for one chorus and turn on the heat in the next. But the idea of jazz repertory was unheard of then, and Johnson's protean flexibility worked against his solidifying a reputation with the public. A tireless sponsor of bebop in its early days, he didn't have to alter his approach to switch from "Blue Lou" to "Woody'n You." Rock and roll didn't fluster him either, as witness his choruses on numerous rock sessions (he was a musical director for Atlantic Records). Johnson's recordings in the late '50s and early '60s include mainstream, modern, and postmodern jazz sessions as well as rock and roll. Like Joe Turner, he fit in anywhere, fashion be damned.

Before he freelanced as a saxophonist, he had put his mark on the swing era. Johnson first worked with Earl Hines as early as 1933, but it wasn't until Cecil Irwin's death in 1935 that be became a regular member of the pianist's Grand Terrace Orchestra. His most successful arrangements for Hines include "Grand Terrace Shuffle" (which epitomizes his talent for setting up his own solos with dramatic orchestral figures), "Tantalizing a Cuban," "Number 19," and a lighthearted concerto for his boss, "Piano Man." Two of his finest solos with Hines were heard on Bingie Madison's ably arranged "In Swamplands," which demonstrates the yearning quality at the core of his cool, rounded tone as well as his penchant for blistering tremolos, and Buster Harding's "Windy City Five," in which he roasts some of Lester Young's ideas over his own impenitent fire.

It was Johnson who induced Hines to hire musicians from the pool of Young Turks congregating in New York in the late '30s and early '40s, including Dizzy Gillespie and Charlie Parker, who eventually took Johnson's seat in the reed section. He then went on to serve as musical director for Billy Eckstine and wrote arrangements for other forward-looking bands, including those of Woody Herman and Boyd Raeburn. He campaigned to get Gillespie's music a hearing on Fifty-second Street in 1944 and played with the band when it finally opened at the Onyx Club. In the same month, he instigated the seminal session that put bop on records: the magical Coleman Hawkins date featuring Gillespie and debuting "Woody'n You."

During the next decade, Johnson was associated with the big bands of Buddy Rich, Sy Oliver, Machito, Benny Goodman, Quincy Jones, Count Basie, Gerald Wilson, and others and turned up on occasional but almost unfailingly significant record dates. He accompanied Sarah Vaughan (alongside Miles Davis) on her famous "Mean to Me" session, nearly stole *Ben Webster and Associates* from Hawkins and Eldridge with his solos on "De-Dar" and "In a Mellow Tone," and joined with Gil Evans for *Pacific Standard Time* and *Out of the Cool*, producing an unforgettable solo on "La Nevada" that with little fanfare put him once again at the center of a new modernism. Yet his own discography in that period is minuscule: two albums in the '50s, five in the '60s, all quickly deleted from catalogue. Things didn't pick up much in his last fifteen years either, despite his formation of the critically acclaimed JPJ Quartet (with Oliver Jackson, Dill Jones, and Bill Pemberton), which successfully toured Europe, and vital performances on Roy Eldridge's *The Nifty Cat*, Buck Clayton's *Jam Session Volume 2*, *Newport in New York '72, Volume 3*, and a widely noted reunion with Hines. For a while he concentrated on soprano and baritone saxes, but he always returned to the tenor. He crafted an affecting rendition of "Yesterdays," a defining example of his emotional generosity, but though he played it frequently, it does not appear to have been recorded.

Much of his achievement is lost to us. Two examples come to mind from my own brief but formative experience working with him. For a Kool Festival tribute to Roy Eldridge that Ira Gitler and I organized, I mentioned to Budd that Roy's 1953 "The Man I Love" solo was a favorite of mine and might lend itself to orchestration. A few days later he brought in an arrangement for trumpet quartet (no rhythm) of his transcription of that solo, an endearing venture into the then largely alien turf of jazz repertory. At a subsequent retrospective of Gil Evans's music, he fortified himself for a recreation of "La Nevada" and embarked on an expansive fantasia (entirely different from the one on record) that brought down the house.

Within a year of his death, three masterful Budd Johnson albums appeared, beginning with the Riverside recording *Budd Johnson and the Four Brass Giants*, produced by Cannonball Adderley in 1960, a long unavailable session that helps explain how Johnson came up with that Roy Eldridge brass quartet so quickly. From the opening notes and diligent pulse, you know you're in rarefied territory. The brasses—Harry Edison, Ray Nance, Clark Terry, Nat Adderley—are scored to accentuate the swinging nature of the charts and the distinguishing traits of each stylist. Johnson glistens as he twists through the changes with a slight yodeling tremor. The key pieces are originals: a thirteen-minute "Memories of Lester Young" ("I am always thinking about Lester," he said), which combines a Lestorian blues section with a thirty-two-bar riff tune; a shorter but no less evocative feature for Ray Nance's violin, "Driftwood," in which Johnson's clarinet is voiced in unison with the brasses for an effect suitably redolent of Ellington; and an extended blues, "Trinity River Bottom," notable for its brass salvos after the bass solo and a typically wily riff-chorus by Edison. The standard material is prepared with no less care, especially an unlikely and flawlessly executed treatment of Al Jolson's schmaltzfest "All My Love" that rocks with acute deliberation, and a romantic reading of "Don't Blame Me," featuring Nance's violin and Johnson's '50s-cool sonority on tenor.

The International Jazz Group was organized by bassist Arvell Shaw and originally issued on French Columbia under the name of pianist Andre Persiany. Recorded in 1956, it is a curiously succesful set of the type that usually gets lost in the mainstream shuffle. A deft and powerful rhythmic undercurrent, courtesy Shaw and drummer Gus Johnson, enhances elegant solos by the crafty trombonist Vic Dickenson, trumpeter Taft Jordan, and Johnson, who also did much of the writing. "If It Weren't for You" recalls "What a Difference a Day Made" and shows off Johnson's casually ornamental way with a ballad. "Concerto du Blues" is a handsome minor blues. Most intriguing is "Budd's Idea," based on a riff introduced by Hawkins in his 1944 solo on "Woody'n You."

The Ole Dude & the Fundance Kid (Uptown) was recorded in Johnson's last year and affirms the exceptional energy he brought to his playing in his seventies. Indeed, he displays more grit and stamina here than on the earlier sessions. Phil Woods, the reveling altoist who frequently jammed with Johnson on the jazz party circuit, is also inspired by the company and carefree setting. Johnson blankets "More Than You Know" in boudoir vibrato and desentimentalizes "Street of Dreams" with surgical authority. His tour de force is an original called "Confusion," a contrapuntal blues in six and a prototypical Johnson performance shaded with the yearning, striving quality that animates his best playing. He charges in on the tail of Woods's last phrase with double-time figures and phrases in four over triple meter in the solo that follows.

All three albums have one thing in common beyond Johnson: Edgar Sampson's song "Blue Lou," which conveniently traces Johnson's chameleonic disposition. In the 1956 version, he is goodness and light; in 1960, he sets up an earthier solo with brisk brass punctuations and borrows the "Martha" lick Illinois Jacquet brought to the jazz lexicon; in 1984, the tempo is way up as he and Woods go two choruses together without the rhythm—an exhilarating exercise of the sort you usually get only at jazz parties, where musicians will do anything to rouse the audience, but in this instance is no less enlivening on record. Budd Johnson reminds us that individuality in art isn't always monolithic, that it can sometimes be gauged in the clarity, spirit, and invention brought to discrete projects in discrete methods. He reminds us as well that jazz is far richer than the achievements of its acknowledged titans.

25 ❖ Bobby Hackett
(Muzak Man)

Bobby Hackett was known primarily by two fringe audiences that otherwise barely recognized each other's existence: one actively pursued Dixieland, the other passively approved elevator music. Such was the absolute individuality of his approach to the cornet that you could immediately recognize his playing in either context. Several times in the '60s, in a supermarket or doctor's office, I found myself pulled short by the emergence of his horn and silently, gratefully registered his name. In those days, you were more likely to hear Hackett's muzak (Muzak, like Kleenex, is a brand name, but I use it as a generic label for the formula mood music of the '50s and '60s) than his jazz, and if you were hungry for his elusive, silvery sound, you basked in it wherever you could find it. Besides, Dixieland had become almost as regimented as the more vendible stuff, and Hackett never considered it much of a home; like Pee Wee Russell, Red Allen, Jack Teagarden, and other mavericks, he was always welcome there, but it had become restrictive and routine.

Hackett's involvement with commercial or generic musics did nothing to undermine his reputation with other musicians, especially trumpeters. Among his admirers of record were Louis Armstrong, Dizzy Gillespie, and Miles Davis. He was also a favorite of singers, having appeared on records with Billie Holiday, Frank Sinatra, Lee Wiley, and especially Tony Bennett, who took him on a European tour. The recordings that established him as a classic swing soloist in 1938 and 1939 were the same ones beloved by the first generation of bop. Gillespie singled him out as a favorite in his 1947 Blindfold Test. Years later Benny Harris explained what attracted him and Gillespie: "We jumped on a record like Bobby Hackett's 'Embraceable You' because it was full of beautiful extended harmonies and unusual changes. Bobby was a guitarist and knew his chords, just as Dizzy and Kenny Clarke knew keyboard harmony." Hackett recorded that haunting version of "Embraceable You" with an Eddie Condon group in 1938 (Commodore) and a year later with his own ill-fated big band (Vocalion). His phrases unfold with lyrical and logical sublimity inseparable from his impeccable, deeply personal trumpet tone.

For most listeners in the late '30s, Hackett boded nothing for the future. On the contrary, he promised to be a comforting reminder of the fabled past. Although he'd been playing guitar, banjo, and uke since dropping out of school at fourteen (in 1929) and had made a name for himself in Boston as early as 1933, playing in a trio with Pee Wee Russell, he was virtually unknown in New York until Benny Goodman's 1938 Carnegie Hall concert. He was present for one reason, to play Bix Beiderbecke's solo on "I'm Coming Virginia" as part of Goodman's twenty-year history-of-jazz medley. Hackett was immediately tagged the new Bix, an honorific he did nothing to dispel by recording "Clarinet Marmalade" and "Singin' the Blues" in 1940, though the latter especially is a notably subjective interpretation. Yet the comparison drove him nuts, and he kept his distance from Bix for the rest of his life. Louis Armstrong was his man, period. "Nobody's going to come along and play like Louis Armstrong. It can only happen once," he told Max Jones. "Such a special guy. Asked for a song, he'd play the song, which is so hard to do right. It's a little like being a writer—you edit as you get older, don't waste words."

An experienced listener can, with effort, hear Armstrong's influence in Hackett's phrasing, his modulated vibrato, and, of course, his rapturous way of limning melody (though he was far more prolix than Armstrong), all of which may suggest a deeper affinity than his tone-color resemblance to Beiderbecke, but any listener, experienced or not, can hear that Hackett doesn't really sound like either of them. He was his own man, not as idiosyncratic as Pee Wee Russell or Red Allen, but every bit as individual and original. Dan Morgenstern has argued that Hackett "never played a meretricious or unmusical note," a provocative comment to make about a musician who spent much of his life playing what seemed to be a hopelessly meretricious music. Although Hackett's muzak was generally ignored by jazz lovers, who fulminated at the waste of his talent, much of his best work can be found on those recordings, and it's time they were exhumed.

My introduction to Bobby Hackett's music in the mid '60s was typical of quite a few men in that era and in the decade before, when he first recorded with strings—I can blame it on a girl. For me it was a high school girlfriend who told me she, too, liked jazz, especially Bobby Hackett. Never heard of him. When she put on *The Most Beautiful Horn in the World* and *Night Love*, it was only my determined affection for her that kept my contempt in check. All those strings and the pipe organ and those lush, dilatory tempos: Where did she get the idea this was jazz? Yet on a subsequent occasion, when I wasn't paying attention (pay attention to what?), some rippling figure or perhaps one of his patented densely calculated cadenzas struck home.

During the next couple of years, we went in search of the real Bobby Hackett, finding ten-inch editions of his Vocalions in a cutout bin and delighting at every exceedingly rare example of his jazz playing, like that ninety-second "I'm Coming Virginia" from the Goodman concert or Armstrong's Town Hall triumph, at which he offered scintillatingly discreet obbligato to the great man on "Rockin' Chair." ("It's like playing in front of God," he later recalled.) When we learned from an album jacket (*Hello Louis!*, with a band that included Steve Lacy and Harvey Phillips) that he owned a hi-fi store on Northern Boulevard, we drove all over Queens looking for it. It had long since gone out of business.

But Hackett the jazz musician was steadily coming back into view. In the mid-60s, Epic, which took over from Columbia in issuing his mood music as well as *Hello Louis!* and *Jazz Impressions of Oliver*, collected most of his Vocalion recordings from the '30s, and a 1967 album on Verve, *Creole Cookin'*, featured him with a big band arranged by Bob Wilber. A few of the Capitols could still be found, including two with Teagarden, *Jazz Ultimate* and *Coast to Coast*, that are among the finest traditionalist recordings of the '50s. He recorded a lovely album with Gillespie and

Mary Lou Williams in 1971 for Perception that wasn't much heard. Best of all, he organized a quintet with Vic Dickenson, which debuted rather demurely on Project 3, the Enoch Light label that succeeded Epic in recording his mood music. The band got a better, multivolume hearing more than a year later when Hank O'Neal recorded it at the Roosevelt Grill in 1970 for his fledgling label, Chiaroscuro.

Before then, we had finally gotten to see him in an all-star ensemble at a hotel. Short and dapper at five-foot-four, wearing his hair slicked back and sporting a prewar trimmed mustache, he spoke with a slightly hoarse bark and played every number asked of him. In the years before he died in 1976, at sixty-one, I spent time with him at the Gibson Colorado Jazz Party and at the Carnegie Deli in New York and heard other musicians jive him about his inability to speak ill of anyone, with the possible exception of Jackie Gleason. It was Gleason who put him in the muzak business, paying him double scale and no royalties on records that enjoyed blockbuster sales for a decade. That relationship went back to the period 1941 to 1942, in which Hackett played with the Glenn Miller band, an association that can in turn be traced to his failed attempt to launch an orchestra of his own in 1939.

Miller took him on in part to help him pay off his remaining debt, an offer that was especially generous because Hackett had just undergone major dental work and was in no condition to play trumpet. Miller brought him in as a guitarist; Hackett recalled that a mike was always positioned before his instrument, but it was closed—no one could hear a note he played. When he finally returned to the trumpet, he performed the two most celebrated solos on Miller's recordings: the ingenious twelve-bar improvisation on "String of Pearls" that was later scripted into the arrangement and the introductory episode on *Rhapsody in Blue*. While filming *Orchestra Wives* with Miller, he met a young actor who told Hackett someday he was going to record him with a roomful of strings. Gleason's Capitol albums, recorded in the wake of his TV success, are iconographic landmarks of the '50s—seduction props with such titles as *Music for Lovers Only*; *Music, Martinis, and Memories*; and the immortal *Music To Change Her Mind*. Although the banal arrangements vary a bit, the basic routine was a chorus of strings followed by a chorus of Hackett (identified in small print on the back sleeve) superimposing embellishments against the strings, followed by a cadenza—the pièce de résistance, a rush of ideas squeezed into a few closing measures. But isolate almost any performance from the dulling sameness of the albums and you will find stunning trumpet playing: for example, a "Body and Soul" in which every note is urgently caressed in an unearthly and evocative timbre, almost a whisper, and an "I Can't Get Started" that takes up where Bunny Berigan left off. Inevitably, Capitol gave him his own outing with strings, *Soft Lights and Bobby Hackett*.

The best of the muzak records, though, are the three he made for Columbia between 1960 and 1962. Before I rediscovered them, I had remembered *Dream Awhile* and *The Most Beautiful Horn in the World* as having strings, but, in fact, the ensemble is very small, just a four-man rhythm section (including drummer Jake Hanna and pianist Dave Mc-Kenna, who, unlike Hackett, is forced to play way beneath himself, providing stilted transition passages), plus the Wurlitzer pipe organ, manned—according to the sleeve copy—by veteran big band arranger Glenn Osser and either Johnny Seng ("a demonstrator for the Wurlitzer company") or Fred Mendelsohn. In a 1991 letter, Seng recounted the circumstances of those sessions:

> In the late summer of 1960, Bobby Hackett signed with Columbia Records who intended to continue his successful Muzak format. There was only one hitch. His Capitol contract stated that for a stipulated period after leaving the label, he would not be permitted to record with strings. A Columbia A&R [artists and repertoire] man with the unlikely name of Tony Piano had been put in charge of Hackett projects and was familiar with a solo pipe organ album I rendered for United Artists a year earlier on what was to become the Wurlitzer designate. He phoned me in Chicago and asked if I would be interested in supplying orchestra backgrounds for a Bobby Hackett album. At age eighteen, my answer was a resounding *yes*.
>
> The next step was to sell the idea to Hackett; and, like any good musician then or now, he was not exactly thrilled with the concept. Remember that in this pre-synthesizer era the organ was the easiest keyboard instrument to play badly and therefore served almost as a magnet for incompetent performers. The upshot was that Columbia flew me to New York to play for Hackett. After fifteen minutes of listening to the "possibilities" of the instrument played in non-hackneyed fashion, he became quite enthused and the recording date was set for November of 1960.
>
> The album was recorded in three days, four songs per day. In addition to the sidemen you mention, guitarist Barney Kessel was flown in from Los Angeles. The cover credits me solely while the liner notes mention Osser. Subject to Osser's and Hackett's approval, I made and played the organ arrangements, which I still have. Osser did the rest. Since there was no time for the musicians to settle in, EVERY note [except Hackett's] was written out. Why Dave

McKenna was forced to play the organ's ghastly Kimball upright piano remains a mystery since there was a decent seven-foot Baldwin grand in an adjoining room. *Dream Awhile* was a tremendous success. Very few reviewers caught on to the organ bit, which I consider a feather in my cap. One cut from the album was used as theme music on the *Today Show* for some twelve years.

In a sense, the organ has a role similar to that of a string synthesizer today, providing wall-to-wall sound. Yet the fact that it's a solitary instrument may have inspired Hackett in his lapidary variations. The arrangements don't curtail him. He is featured throughout every track, and you get the feeling that he has said exactly what he intended on each song. He imbues "Star Dust" with a restive drama, suggested in the opening phrases and sustained through the coda. The squeezed and repeated pitches of his close on "Lazy Afternoon" recall Armstrong, as does the plush melody recitation on "Love Letters." But the most rewarding and individual moments are unique to Hackett: the exquisite passing notes and chords as he negotiates familiar passages, burnishing them with color; the tripping grace notes; his sumptuous sound.

Hackett made the cornet sing, and these records suggest the bel canto approach of faithful recitation followed by modest embellishments. That's especially true of *Night Love*, the one album with strings, arranged by Hackett himself. The material here consists of pop themes from the classics, and the presentation isn't quite as successful as its predecessors. But Hackett remains himself, and the charts give him space to work fleeting miracles, as when the strings sustain chords, from which he spins a succession of webs. His craftsmanship has rarely been more persuasive than in his reading of a theme from Brahms's Third Symphony—at this level of musicianship, he doesn't have to improvise to personalize the piece. These albums, with their '60s cover art of vacant, white models with a lot of eye makeup and fashionable melodies ("Chances Are," "Misty"), were popular with their target audience—romantically inclined teenage girls—but ignored by Hackett's jazz admirers.

The subsequent Epic albums combined jazz and muzak in salutes to trumpeters (*Trumpets' Greatest Hits*), Tony Bennett, Glenn Miller, Henry Mancini, and Bert Kaempfert. They are uneven to say the least, but an anthology of the best tracks would make an impressive case for Hackett's playing in infelicitous settings. The Kaempfort, surprisingly enough, is especially pleasing, with Hackett's unexpectedly intimate recasting of "Danke Schoen"; his very modern modal improvisation on "Afrikaan Beat"; and his sixteen-bar blues chorus on "Take Me." But they can't compete with the three Columbias; they are background music that lets you in for a second look, because for all the superficial appeal to an easy, even mindless, listening experience, Hackett gives you something unexpectedly rich. Like any good singer, he is unfazed by the setting and emotes from the heart.

26 ❖ Frank Sinatra
(The Ultimate in Theater)

That Frank Sinatra was a towering figure in the music of his century few would care to dispute. He overhauled the interpretation of popular song, revising its rhythms and instrumentation, burnishing its lyrics, establishing the postwar code in phrasing. As a radio and television entertainer, movie actor, and concert artist of matchless grace (and occasional distemper), he enjoyed a momentous career—even a dangerous career. Perhaps no one since François Villon played the troubadour with more bravado. Though he may have been, at his much documented worst, a foul-mouthed misogynist, unthinking lout, violent drunk, friend to criminals, sore loser, and political hypocrite, he was first and last The Voice. When he recovered from a professional crisis that left him for dead, he remade himself so completely that he remade his generation in the process. This most fastidious of singers was never exclusively a performing artist. He was also a *presence*.

The first time I saw him, in 1956, was on the cover of *Songs for Swingin' Lovers*, one of several albums my father brought home to inaugurate our first hi-fi. Something about the contours of his broadbrimmed hat, casually loosened tie, and watchful grin as he hovered over an innocuous couple about to smooch, suggested the quintessence of adulthood, an altered state I deeply coveted. The effect was underscored by the record itself, the coolly unabashed music brimming with confidence and far too rich for my preadolescent blood. Five years later, I glimpsed him in person in a Las Vegas casino where Sinatra had part ownership and an exclusive contract. It was August 1961, the height of the Rat Pack madness; he was just visiting. I watched him from a distance, less transfixed by his wide smile and loose-limbed manner than by the admiring light in my dad's eye as he took Sinatra's measure. I had only to consider their respective snap-brims and tailored suits and cigarettes to recognize a generational uniform and the perfection with which Sinatra served as its model.

Sinatra's myth has outstripped—as myths will—the details of its making. The wiry little guy who once introduced himself as "the Hoboken hoodlum" was that rare figure in American cultural life, high or low, who mirrored an entire generation, a performer who so perfectly embodied the experiences and outlook of a time and place as to become a vessel for dreams and predictor of the future. In Sinatra's case, it was the generation that fought the war and listened to Der Bingle; bought the first TVs to watch boxing and Milton Berle in drag; wore fedoras, wide ties, and cotton handkerchiefs that peaked from breast pockets like crests; smoked feverishly and without guilt; drank holdover concoctions from the days of Prohibition (usually made with rye); laughed at Bob Hope; ogled Betty Grable's sculpted legs; thought movie musicals would be produced forever; gambled in Vegas *because* of the mob; put their kids through colleges they never dreamed of attending; and placed more trust in God than cholesterol.

Most artists of Sinatra's stature would have been allowed to fade into retirement and beyond without a chorus of smirks. But Dr. S (honorary degree, Stevens Institute, 1985) eternally undermined his undoubted genius with an edgy kitsch that verged on self-parody and promoted skepticism. Perhaps the bad jokes he was subjected to at an age when his footfalls should have been graced with rose petals indicated he was finally no longer anyone to fear. For, puzzling as the fact may be to future generations, Sinatra was one entertainer who instilled a sense of fear in paying customers as well as paid attendants. It was not a fear of physical violence per se—though, yes, there were a few such victims—but of a more general sort, a fear of not qualifying for the vicarious ratpackery of the affluent society's Peter Pan-on-testosterone club for middle-aged rakes, of which Sinatra was Chairman of the Board, not to mention boss of bosses.

You can hear that fear stick in the throat before erupting in overeager guffaws during an *amazing* twelve-minute monologue on *Sinatra at the Sands*, a deeply embarrassing attempt at humor, replete with bad-natured cracks, including Amos-and-Andyisms in which Sammy Davis, Jr., is dismissed as a custodian (after seeing him on TV, Sinatra says, "I sent him a wire, 'No you can't!' "), Dean Martin is lampooned as a drunk, audience members are heckled, his father is belittled, and so on. One suspects Sinatra paid good money for the jokes ("I was so skinny, my eyes were single file") and was determined to make them work. But one of Sinatra's peculiar characteristics as an entertainer is that he could do anything—sing, act, dance—but be funny. In *Tony Rome*, he asks a pet owner, "You got a pussy that smiles?" and you squirm like a worm on a hook. Maybe he's just too self-conscious. If you want to be funny, it's usually a good idea to let the audience laugh at you before it is asked to laugh with you. Sinatra, however much he protested to the contrary, didn't want to be laughed at. Les Paul told a story of the first time Sinatra sang with Bing Crosby on radio; the younger man missed a low note that Crosby instantly collared, interpolating "Is this what you were looking for, son?" The king of swooners was not amused.

But there is another side of Sinatra, where parody doesn't intrude, where he is, in fact, emblematic of sage maturity, where his interpretations of lyrics of varying quality are evened out by a semblance of experience that promises and often delivers rapport, understanding, perhaps wisdom—the Frank Sinatra of our dreams. In song, the voice is honed with craftsmanship so knowing it doesn't have to call attention to itself. Many people give no thought to his technical virtuosity until they sing along with a record and find themselves gasping for air as Sinatra casually plots a sixteen-bar phrase with one exhalation, too subtly manipulated for you to notice anything but the absolute dramatic rightness of his decision. This Sinatra is above all else a great storyteller: in Ellington's memorable phrase, "the ultimate in theater." In the spell of his artistry, we forget the moral ambiguity associated with a Gambino poster boy; and we know—even if he doesn't—that the stalwart liberal of "The House I Live In" is the true Frank, not the disappointed favor-seeker who abandoned progressive politics for the Palm Springs militia.

Sinatra's street-tough persona is irresistibly softened by an artistic control that is innovative, physical, and hard won. The voice is transformed, its extraordinary clarity and directness sharpened for expressive purpose, so that even the residual Hoboken inflections achieve eloquence. The vocal styles of most pop and jazz baritones (Crosby, late Armstrong, Cole, Eckstine, Astaire) follow readily from their speech patterns and timbres; not so with Sinatra. The cynical diction of his Jilly's-barfly mode contravened the beauty of his timbre. Yet when he steps into a song, the manners of a punk are instantly abandoned for those of an overpowering troubador—almost as if the offstage Frank were chagrined by a perceived unmanliness regarding his profession. His pronunciations differ: he sings a short, English *a*, but he speaks a flat, nasal one. Just as Gene Kelly made movie dancing seem athletically heterosexual, Sinatra made singing a manly art, but a complicated one—sexual, aggressive, physical, vulnerable, sadistic, masochistic, disturbing. It's always difficult to reconcile the man who sings "Night and Day" on *Sinatra & Strings*, to choose one of a thousand examples, with the concert performer who demeaned women reporters as whores of the press, to choose one of dozens.

Sinatra was a fine actor. He brought to '50s cinema a restless kind of naturalism that is most credible when he plays small men, loners: Maggio, an assassin, a junkie, a cop. Teamed up with another man or a woman, he loses stature. He was infinitely more authentic as Nathan than Brando was as Sky Masterson in *Guys and Dolls*, but as the prole in *High Society*, he was outclassed by Crosby (who, significantly, considered his duet with Sinatra, "Well, Did You Evah," his favorite movie scene). Sinatra's real ability as an actor, however, had little to do with the movies and was defined by the character he created in concert, on records and record jackets, and on TV. To look at early photographs of the scrawny crooner who finagled his way out of Tommy Dorsey's band and lay siege at the Paramount is to be astounded at how little he had to work with, beyond The Voice. Skinny to the point of gaunt, he had a homely, lined face, wide mouth, and small obsidian eyes. His greased and wavy hair underscored his youthful aspirations. Sinatra's handlers could hire women to swoon as he crooned, but they couldn't convince anyone he was Gable. So the original image sold to the fan mags and eventually Hollywood was of an innocent, more often than not in a sailor suit, in need of a mother.

What counted was that seemingly unaffected voice—intimate, earnest, pretty, romantic. It ached, but stoically. It swung, but reflectively. It caressed, but gently. Even the male factor, the pure baritone edge that shaped his every phrase, was equivocal. In the '40s, with men overseas and their women unattended, Sinatra allowed himself a measure of musical androgyny that underscored his identification with the women. The swooning may have been a press agent's stunt, but it astutely pegged Sinatra as a singer whose effect on women stopped one step short of carnal: What can you do in a faint? No one would have thought to hire swooners for Bing Crosby, for example. Like the Beatles, who revived the practice on their first jaunt to the United States, Sinatra wasn't peddling sexual bait, but sexual safety. He was Frankie as much as he was Frank.

The androgyny was subtly unmistakable and became more pronounced as the war ended. Sinatra, still a bow-tied beanpole with a face as defined and quizzical as a marionette's, continued to croon ballads, but with operatic design and drama. "I Fall in Love Too Easily," one of several Sinatra classics by Jule Styne and Sammy Cahn, exemplifies his ability to combine genders even as he brings bel canto to pop. Cahn's lyric is characteristically simple:

> I fall in love too easily.
> I fall in love too fast.

> I fall in love too terribly hard
> for love to ever last.

How is one to approach the title phrase? Is it rueful, knowing, complaining, ironic, diffident? Sinatra sings it like a bird with a broken wing, remorseful and doomed. He *makes* the lyric deep, an expression of the singer's dramatic plight. We're in act three, scene two. Queen Ava, having thrown the Prince's young daughter (actually his wife in disguise) from a castle turret, has stolen his magic dice and fled to the barbarian king. Alone in his chamber, Prince Frank learns the terrible news and turns to his loyal jester, Dinoletto. "E strano," he sighs, and sings his aria, "I fall in love. . . ." The first two phrases are small-voiced and quiet, but in an early example of Sinatra's skillful technique, the third is an expression of unwavering, plaintive authority, gliding upward along one unbroken breath, followed by a rest that renews the poignance of the final five words.

What women surely identified in this oddly gentle baritone was a degree of tenderness, sympathy, and hurt rare in the daily opera of radio. When he sang "Try a Little Tenderness," was Sinatra merely a wise young man advising the world's husbands to do better? Was he not perhaps also one with the women, someone who knew about brutishness? Crosby, from the beginning, was a model of virility and nice in the bargain. Sinatra, in the beginning, was vaguely feminine and consequently a bit subversive. The records preserve the heights of his invention in those years. The cinema cheapened him, marketing him as the slightly goofy sailor boy. By 1946, the sexual confusion bordering on camp found its unrivaled emblem in the climax of the absurd movie *Till the Clouds Roll By*, as the camera arcs skyward to catch a rigid, no-longer-boyish Frank, standing atop a column and missing only a ribbon in his hair to qualify him as a Ziegfeld adornment, singing "Old Man River."

He was about to tumble. It is of interest to recall here that Sinatra was born in 1915, the same year as Billie Holiday, whose influence he often acknowledged. Yet Holiday, who began recording at eighteen, is largely associated with the '30s, while Sinatra, who didn't record until he joined with Harry James in 1939 (the epochal "All or Nothing at All"), is a figure of the war years. Most of the male stars of that period were either older favorites, beyond the draft, or younger and sometimes suspiciously undrafted men who in effect filled in for performers who went overseas. Sinatra was the first singer in a decade to challenge Crosby's hegemony, but even he was vulnerable to the postwar reaction against a generation of makeshift stars. Returning soldiers were none too sure they wanted their wives swooning to anyone, and as late as 1949, Sinatra was still trying to get by with moonlit ballads, bow ties, and a sheepish grin. Soon he was begging for work, selling cutlery on television and playing dumb and dumber in movies with Jane Russell (an actress mainly known for her bra size) and on records with a TV celebrity named Dagmar (who was known exclusively for her bra size). On top of all that, Sinatra was said to be a comsymp, which didn't play as well in the early '50s as it did a few years earlier or later.

And that's when Sinatra created the role of the century. In the mid-50's, he thoroughly reinvented himself: parted his hair, put on weight, changed his musical attack. *From Here to Eternity* certainly helped, re-establishing him as a serious talent and restoring a touch of vulnerability—toughs reportedly threatened Ernest Borgnine for knifing him in the movie. But Frank couldn't sustain a career as a likable Italian American wiseass who gets killed every time out. So in *Suddenly*, he took the Borgnine role, playing an assassin, and in *Young at Heart*, he took his turn as John Garfield. As a singer, he had to remake himself into a killer as well, a transition presumably facilitated by an agonizing marriage to Ava Gardner. The voice soon shook with sorrow and self-pity and resolve.

He began to swing; indeed, he invented a new style of swing, an optimistic four-beat volley that in its way was as removed from the fussier rhythms of the '30s as the contemporaneous developments in r & b. With Nelson Riddle and Billy May writing arrangements, he was supported by basic big band instrumentation dressed in the finery of flutes, strings, and a harp. His detractors dismissed his swing as a "businessman's bounce," but the more assured Sinatra became, the wickeder the bounce. Rhythmic integrity is one reason his recordings of the '50s and '60s have survived as classics.

The transformation could not have been more complete. During his years with Columbia Records, Sinatra had been virtually enjoined from swinging. Except for "Saturday Night," he didn't get a single rhythm number until the 1946 "Two Hearts Are Better Than One," three years into his contract. Only as the Columbia sojourn came to an end and he was coerced to bark like a dog for Dagmar did he began to proclaim the fruits of a new maturity in riveting numbers like "The Birth of the Blues" and "Azure-Te." Neither the company nor the public noticed. During the war, Sinatra had been obsessed with Crosby, covering many of his songs, but from the opposite direction—if Bing did them fast, Frank did them slow, and vice versa. Now, squiring his new muse, Sinatra would emerge not as a rival, but as a genuine successor, so much so that by 1956 Crosby was importuned to make a Sinatra-style album—along with everyone else. Unlike Crosby, a stellar jazz singer when he felt the calling, Sinatra was *of* jazz without quite being *in* jazz. Yet his renewal required a profound openness to jazz influence. Billie Holiday had taught him to delve deeper into lyrics; the jet-age rattling of big bands opened him up to rhythm and impulse.

He had everything in place but a personal style. No problem: The ideal attitude and outfit were close at hand in the person of his friend Jimmy Van Heusen, the gifted songwriter, who, until late in life, was a bachelor with the most envied little black book in town. He was beloved of Hollywood madams, one of the most prominent of whom is said to have bought him an airplane (he was a licensed pilot) as a token of appreciation. Van Heusen was the kind of guy who kept an icebox on his porch, empty except for rows of martini glasses and a pitcher to fill them. He was tall and immensely charming, not especially handsome, but catnip to women and effortlessly stylish. Born Chester Babcock (Bob Hope adopted the name for movie roles), he took his nom de plume from the famous shirt manufacturer. He favored fedoras with wide bands and liked to sling his jacket or trenchcoat over his left shoulder.

If Van Heusen hadn't lived, Sinatra would have had to invent him. On stage and on album jackets, he played the part to perfection. The new Sinatra of the affluent generation was dynamic and sure, the embodiment of good times, the keeper of old songs that somehow no longer seemed quaint or sentimental when he sang them (consider the provenance of "It Happened in Monterey"—in his hands a rigorous swinger, but previously a waltz warbled by the Brox Sisters, one of whom, coincidentally, would rob Jimmy Van Heusen of his bachelorhood). Above all, he was adult. He sang to adults. He had turned himself into the embodiment of those returning servicemen who were defining American society and business. He was *their* troubadour, as Elvis was that of their children. He said to them: This is what we look like, this is how we sing, this is how we treat our women and are treated by them, this is how we relax, and this is how we age. Sinatra's changeover was complete: he was handsome, suave, spellbinding.

By 1956 and the release of *Songs for Swingin' Lovers*, he had the accomplishment and bearing of an old master. His Oscared performance in *From Here to Eternity* reestablished him as a force in Hollywood, but it was the diversity of his roles (a drug addict in *The Man with the Golden Arm*, a journalist in *High Society*, a cowboy in *Johnny Concho*, a singing heel in *Pal Joey*, a soldier in *The Manchurian Candidate*) that erased short-term memories of the Hoboken hoodlum. The new Sinatra was larger than the parameters of showbiz. Women didn't want to mother him. Men didn't want to mock him. But everyone wanted a piece of him, and happily there were more than enough pieces to go around—a flood of records, television specials, one or two movies a year.

Yet Sinatra still had to endure a gap between the weight he wanted to throw around and the weight at his disposal. He would complain for more than thirty years at having to accept Nathan Detroit while Brando ("Mumbles," he called him) got the better role in *Guys and Dolls*. In fact, Sinatra stole the film—the only thing Brando had that Sinatra should have had was "Luck Be a Lady," and the producer could have given it to him with nary an adjustment in the script. It wasn't just a song that irked him. He wanted to be the handsome lead, not the shnook. He wanted to be the one who takes the gorgeous doll down to Havana and gets her drunk, before undergoing a sea change and trying a little tenderness. That he brought an unexpected tenderness and depth to Nathan, enriching the role not just in the picture but for subsequent revivals, escaped him. Still, if he couldn't be Sky on the lot, he could be A-number one in real life. Not for Sinatra the oldest established permanent floating crap game in New York. He fixed his gaze on the desert.

The turnaround was already complete, from Swoonatra to has-been to Representational Man. All the emperor of ice-scream required was an empire. He found one in western sands settled by eastern mobsters. With its flamboyant architecture, think-pink decor, legal gambling, legal prostitution, suspended time, and unlimited funds to purchase unlimited entertainment, Las Vegas was a metaphor for the prosperous, convenient, and infinitely air conditioned '50s. To that playland, Sinatra lured new playmates. The invitation was unequivocal, and through his album titles he extended it to the world: *Come Fly With Me, Come Dance With Me!, Come Swing With Me*. At a time when every child in the country dreamed of visiting the recently launched Disneyland, Sinatra's Vegas was a grown-up version. Small wonder the Rat Pack escapade was assiduously reported and is remembered still, even though it lasted merely five years.

The Rat Pack had its positives and negatives. Among the former was a determined expression of ethnic tolerance, the cornerstone of '50s liberalism. The youthful Sinatra won an Oscar for "The House I Live In," but the older Sinatra delivered on the song's sentiment by populating his house with an African American (Sammy Davis, Jr.), a Jew (Joey Bishop), a WASP (Peter Lawford), a fellow Italian (Dean Martin), and— the acme of tolerance—a woman (Shirley MacLaine), known in the parlance of the '50s as a "broad." The other side of the ledger was a cheap vulgarity that turned into ethnic disdain as the self-conscious race jokes and Davis's devotion to the emperor curdled over time. The clan fell apart because the friendships could not withstand the leader's demands and temper. Other reasons were the kidnapping of his son and the assassination of President Kennedy.

Not until the mid-'60s, when he was in his early fifties, did Sinatra attempt to elicit the good opinion of his audience's kids, with two arguable exceptions: recording "High Hopes" from Capra's film *A Hole in the Head*, an attempt to reach toddlers, just as Crosby had with "Swinging on a Star," and having Elvis make his first postarmy appearance with him on TV, a patronizing if savvy bow to the Nielsens. Teenagers in the '50s were resentful of as well as bored by Sinatra, and as adults would be surprised to realize that his peak years coincided precisely with those of Presley. But he wasn't singing to the young. He sang of supreme assurance, and teenagers are confident of little. He celebrated love the second time around when most teenagers are lucky to have gotten there once. He idealized the comforts of booze. He sang about sex in the voice of someone who had been there—a lot.

In the course of redefining adult pastimes, Sinatra frequently made himself a candidate for derision, along with those dopey adults who followed him to Vegas, actually wanting to be part of the clan that gave us *Ocean's 11*. He compensated for his hair-trigger temper with exaggerated hilarity. Occasionally, the grand performance was shaky, the meta-adult apparently unmoored. The smart Sinatra of the songs became unglued by the aroma of real political power. If he pimped for JFK, he gave better than he got. He was more himself in "the house I live in" than the Oval Office he allegedly shtupped in. The beautiful fantasy of the affluent generation ended in ratpack insipidity two years before Dealey Plaza. Francis Albert Sinatra's contributions to the American language: "Sheesh!" "Ring-a-ding-ding!" "Clyde."

Forget his pop hits of the '60s. His image was no longer tenable. He seemed somehow to deserve a daughter who sang like Nancy Sinatra. In 1971, it didn't mean all that much when he walked away to retirement at fifty-six. But a few years later, he was back, preceded by a press campaign that saluted him as "Ol' Blue Eyes," a sobriquet not earned with affection but purchased from a publicity firm. At first, the comeback didn't promise much. He was ensnared in his usual press feuds and was out of voice and overweight when he hit the Uris Theater (with Ella Fitzgerald and Count Basie), looking sullen and sounding defensive. The children of the '50s took their shots. The fool jazz critic in the *Village Voice* wrote, "I have never found his interpretations of popular songs more substantial than those of most pop singers, who are usually content to hit the right notes and enunciate the lyrics, however moronic. . . . Sinatra's records are more catalytic than absorbing. For Sinatra is a great craftsman but not an artist."

But Sinatra's audience was changing, and so consequently was his standing. As his original audience pushed sixty, he was at long last discovered by its children, who, no longer acne-scarred or bell-bottomed, finally understood what those songs were about. Lost love, one for the road?—hey, let me get this round. Now his champions were younger than Frank, Jr., and they didn't treat him with the casual admiration/ contempt due a contemporary, but with the awe reserved for a living . . . well, legend. His movie days were finished, and for a while nobody wanted to record him, and Gary Trudeau reminded everyone who needed reminding what a scumbag he could be. But the album *Trilogy* was a huge success, and so were his concerts, which drew bigenerational crowds. He embodied a major life lesson: Never dismiss an artist just because he plays golf with Spiro Agnew. And, yes, an artist he was, not a craftsman. He loomed over the cultural life of a tumultuous half century, defying analysis, because every generation had to figure him out from scratch.

And where to begin? The list changes with the weather. But you wouldn't want to miss his aching lament, "I'm a Fool To Want You" or "Time After Time" or "I Fall in Love Too Easily"; or the ecstatic duet with Louis Armstrong on "Birth of the Blues" (*The Edsel Show*, 1957); or the Metronome All-Stars' trim "Sweet Lorraine." Or the two studio albums with Basie, especially the first with his ingeniously embellished "Pennies from Heaven" (an inevitable riposte to those who insist Sinatra has no feeling for jazz). Or the prolonged inspiration of *Songs for Young Lovers, Swing Easy, Songs for Swingin' Lovers, Come Dance With Me!, Close to You, Come Fly with Me, Come Swing with Me, I Remember Tommy*, with its improbably fast "I'll Be Seeing You," *Moonlight Sinatra, Sinatra & Strings*, and *All Alone*. Or "Let's Fall in Love," "South of the Border," "I Have Dreamed," "I Wish I Were in Love Again," and "I Had the Craziest Dream." Or "Thanks for the Memory" from *She Shot Me Down*, his last great album. Or the neglected and deliciously dilatory *Francis A. and Edward K.*, with Ellington.

Did I miss some of your favorites? Mine, too: I forgot the Dorseys and *Only the Lonely* and *A Swingin' Affair*, and a dozen others. It's a vast legacy. The Sinatra achievement is not least a guide to modern orchestration, a how-to concerning the adaptation of old pop to a postbop consciousness. And Sinatra, no less than his great arrangers—Riddle, May, Johnny Mandel, Sy Oliver, Don Costa, Neal Hefti, Quincy Jones, Gordon Jenkins, Axel Stordahl, and the rest—knew all about reclamation projects. A peerless interpreter of our best lyricists, Sinatra was expected to demonstrate unexpected depths in the work of Larry Hart, Ira Gershwin, Johnny Burke, Cole Porter, Johnny Mercer, and Irving Berlin. But the real test of his transformative powers were those songs beyond redemption, an area in which his ability was at one with Armstrong, Crosby, Holiday, and very few others. Who else would tackle "The Curse of an Aching Heart," previously a subject of burlesques by Fats Waller and Laurel and Hardy (*Blotto*), but in Sinatra's hands a joyous, straight-faced romp? Sinatra's imperviousness to the song's clumsiness is symptomatic. Once, as a lark, he recorded a serious treatment of a nonsense song written for a Crosby radio routine, "There's a Flaw in My Flue," and damned if he didn't almost get away with it. The generosity he wasn't always able to summon in life is the very marrow of his gift to music.

PART FOUR

❖

A Modern Music

27 ❖ Duke Ellington
(Part 2: The Enlightenment)

In March 1940, Duke Ellington signed an exclusive contract with RCA and entered a state of grace: with few exceptions, his every recording session in the early '40s produced an Ellington classic, if not two or three. He was a success commercially as well as critically. According to *Metronome*, his records outsold those of other bands in 1939, 1940, and 1941, and the unprecedented critical and popular acceptance he enjoyed in and out of jazz may have hastened the completion of *Black, Brown and Beige*, the expansive tone poem on African American history that crowned his unexcelled miniatures of 1940–42. As always, obstacles had to be hurdled: a union strike forbade him from performing any of his own music on radio; he could not finance a Broadway presentation of his beloved revue, *Jump for Joy*; he lost one of his essential soloists to a rival band and lost the heartbeat of his rhythm section to tuberculosis; *Black, Brown and Beige* was trashed by the critics. Other than that, he was on top of the world, his genius unfettered and soaring.

Ellington's achievement was in large part a consequence of the personalities in his band as of 1941, sixteen in addition to the leader, most of whose poker-playing habits he had long since analyzed. With one exception, the reed section consisted entirely of veterans. The exception made all the difference: Ben Webster was the first featured tenor saxophonist Ellington ever hired. He had worked with the band briefly in 1935 and 1936, but didn't become a regular member until 1940. Having developed "a yen for Ben," Ellington elected not to hire a tenor until Webster—whose hugely aspirate sound could be gruff (he was known as "The Brute"), smoky, or candidly tender—was available. All three trombonists were old hands. Of the three trumpeters, only Rex Stewart, who joined in 1934 and would remain until 1945, had been with Ellington for any length of time. Wallace Jones replaced the ailing Arthur Whetsol in 1938, assuming the duties of lead trumpet. The only new addition to the band in 1941 was Ray Nance, the replacement for the enormously popular Cootie Williams, who had been lured away by Benny Goodman.

Ellington helped Williams to clinch the deal with Goodman, thinking he'd be back in a year. As it turned out, Williams did return, but not until 1962. The band easily survived his departure because within weeks Ellington discovered a remarkable surrogate. After a few years in the bands of Earl Hines and Horace Henderson, Ray Nance had tired of the road and taken a job at Joe's De Luxe, a club in his hometown, Chicago. Several members of the Ellington band heard him and urged their boss to drop by. He did, and in November Nance was hired. In addition to playing the trumpet (later cornet) and violin, Nance sang, danced, and mugged.

The chairman of the band's rhythm section was Sonny Greer, who had been with Ellington since Washington in 1920. Except for Elmer Snowden, who played briefly with and was momentarily the leader of the original Washingtonians, Ellington employed only one guitarist, Fred Guy; when Guy left in 1949, Ellington kept the rhythm section at three members. The bassist, however was a recent find, a teenager whom Ellington discovered in a St. Louis ballroom in 1939, the ingenious and revolutionary Jimmy Blanton, the most influential bassist in jazz history. Ellington himself completed the rhythm section, of course, though by this time he occasionally deputized Billy Strayhorn to take his place. Hired in 1939 as a lyricist, Strayhorn didn't really show how valuable he could be until 1941 when a dispute between ASCAP (American Society of Composers, Authors, and Publishers) and radio broadcasters prevented the music of ASCAP members from getting played. Ellington was a member, but Strayhorn and Ellington's twenty-one-year-old son, Mercer, were not, so Duke turned to them for desperately needed material. Strayhorn, whose childhood enthusiasm for the European tradition was suspended when he discovered Ellington's music, displayed an innate ability to write in the Ellington style.

Mercer Ellington grew especially close to Strayhorn, and they spent hours together studying Ellington's scores. With the advent of the ASCAP struggle, Ellington had an additional reason to encourage his son. During its stay in Los Angeles, the band played at the Casa Mañana, and while Ellington went to work, he assigned his only child homework. As Mercer explained:

> He would leave me problems to solve by the time he got back, and I would work at the piano while he was out. He never put a note down, but he scratched out what was in poor taste. "Moon Mist" was a number he wrote almost by omission. . . . He'd present a harmony and tell me to write a melody against it, making certain that I never used any note in the harmony as part of the melody.

Other works were born in a similar manner, including "Jumpin' Punkins," "John Hardy's Wife," and the exquisite "Blue Serge." In later years, after a period when he led his own bands, Mercer managed the Ellington orchestra and played section trumpet. He kept the orchestra going after Ellington's death in 1974 until his own death in 1996. He also completed his father's final work, the suite "Three Black Kings"; published a candid memoir; conducted the orchestra for the hit Broadway revue, *Sophisticated Ladies*; released many hours of Ellington's privately recorded music; and deposited Ellington's scores with the Smithsonian.

Another reason for Ellington's ascension in the early '40s—beyond personality and beyond the most important consideration of all, the cumulative experience of twenty years leading and composing for an orchestra—was the laissez-faire recording contract with RCA. Ellington could do as he pleased, and fortunately for everyone, his commercial instincts in those years were as sound as his musical ones. With his many expenses and his newly launched publishing firm, Tempo Music, he was as inclined to score occasional hits as any record biz executive. He was also partial to continuing his custom of producing small band sessions, and these, too—recorded under the nominal leadership of Johnny Hodges, Barney Bigard, and Rex Stewart—produced exceptional results.

Although Ellington's vendible records were made for RCA, others of equal interest were not. A young fan named Jack Towers, who later became a master audio engineer, tested his equipment with Ellington's blessings at a 1940 appearance in Fargo, North Dakota, providing posterity with the fantastic gift of a live two-and-a-half-hour performance of the band at its mythic peak. Of equal or greater interest is a pedestrian recording of the complete and never commercially documented *Black, Brown and Beige*, along with the 1943 Carnegie Hall concert at which it premiered. In addition, in 1941 Ellington made a series of sixteen-inch discs for the Standard Transcription (ST) company in Hollywood, exclusively for radio play. Performers were encouraged to record new tunes for transcription, and Ellington did, but he also used the ST discs to audition several untested pieces, and they are revealing on two counts: they show us how a few of his classics developed and provide an invaluable glimpse into the workings of the Ellington rhythm section, which was favored by the ST microphone placement.

The most revealing of the ST recordings is "Take the A Train." Strayhorn's piece, as recorded for RCA in 1941, was an immediate hit and soon became the band's theme and inevitable set opener. Along with "Flamingo," it made Tempo Music a going concern. The title and Strayhorn's original lyric, which was wisely omitted from the first recording, were intended as travel instructions—people were taking the new D-train to Harlem, not realizing it went only as far as 145th Street before turning off into the Bronx. The thirty-two-measure AABA melody is impressively spare: the first four measures have only six pitches and two are held beyond a full measure. This provides space for the orchestral interjections at which the band excelled and reflects Strayhorn's ambition to write a piece in the manner of Fletcher Henderson, with the three horn sections arranged in call-and-response fashion. Although the chord progression is standard (it's based on "Exactly Like You"), the melody—which includes two flatted fifths and an augmented fifth in the first eight bars—suggests more ambitious harmonies. The ST and RCA versions are alike but for details, yet those details define the difference between a first draft and a masterpiece. Everything about the RCA became famous and widely imitated: the piano vamp, the trumpet solo, the crescendo of discrete voicings in the third chorus. Yet a month earlier, at the ST session, those elements were still vague.

The first twenty-four measures of the first chorus in both versions are similar, with distinct roles for the trumpets, trombones, and reeds (the trombones are omitted from the release). But the last eight measures of the chorus were altered for the RCA session so that the two brass sections are voiced in unison, increasing the dramatic impact. Neither Ray Nance's trumpet improvisation nor the responses by the reeds were in focus for the ST. Nance, still unsure of the piece, hugged the melody and even miscalculated his first four-measure exchange in the third chorus, playing a phrase one bar too short for his allotted space. By contrast, his RCA solo is superbly assured and witty, yet delicate and immensely personal—note, for example, his wily hesitation in measure fifteen of the third chorus. It was the kind of solo that—like Webster's on "Cottontail" or Blanton's on "Jack the Bear"—soon became as renowned as the written material, and it established Nance as an Ellington star. His variation became so much a part of the performance that when Williams, for whom the solo was initially intended, returned to the Ellington fold, he inherited it verbatim, though adapting it with his own unique articulation. (Even though the solo is in every way characteristic of Nance, especially in the very human sound he got from the trumpet, part of it is often miscredited to Rex Stewart. The confusion probably stems from the fact that Nance uses a mute in his second chorus—the part ascribed to Stewart—but not in his third, the four-bar transition and three bars of delayed entry providing him with ample time to remove it.)

Another impressive alteration in the RCA occurs in the two measures that conclude the release of the third chorus. In the ST, Nance and the orchestra play the release all the way through, but the RCA has a marvelous two-measure crescendo of instrumental voices that suspends the time and greatly increases the excitement of the performance. In effect, it's the climax, precipitating three readings of the initial theme, in which the reeds call the melody while the brasses respond, first with open horns to conclude the third chorus and then with mutes for the final sixteen bars. Ellington's piano plays a more significant role in the RCA (for example, the three chords with which he provides a breather at the end of the first chorus), as does Blanton's bass (walking firmly as Nance finishes the second chorus); but, then, everyone plays beautifully, as usual for the Ellington musicians of 1941.

The band's biggest hits came from outside the orchestra and established Herb Jeffries as the first of Ellington's male ballad crooners. Jeffries had starred in a series of cheaply produced black westerns, and one of them, *The Bronze Buckeroo*, happened to play the Apollo opposite the band. Ellington was impressed. He offered him a theaterical tour as the band's vocalist. In his memoirs, Ellington recalls that Jeffries was at first "inclined to the falsetto." But "between shows, while everybody else was playing poker, Herb would be ad-libbing and doing imitations all over the place. . . . One day he was doing his imitation of Bing Crosby, when Strayhorn and I both said in unison, 'That's it! Don't go any further. Just stay on Bing.' " Jeffries fills in the story:

> Duke thought Bing was one of the greatest baritones of all time. When I first went with Duke's band, I was sort of a tenor, up in that range. But Ellington used to talk so much about the mellow, rich, baritone voice of Crosby, and I began to lower my range. Then I started listening to his records and he became sort of my guru. One day Ellington heard me doing an impersonation on "Where the Blue of the Night," and he said, "That's the voice I want you to record with!"

The result, "Flamingo," arranged by Strayhorn and recorded during Christmas week of 1940, but not released until the following summer, proved a huge and enduring hit with estimated sales to date of fourteen million. Yet if "Flamingo," a ballad by Ted Grouya and Edmund Anderson, paid the band's bills and boosted the singer's career, other records featuring Jeffries are of greater musical significance.

Jeffries was never more effective than in his appearance—two minutes into the recording—on "I Don't Know What Kind of Blues I've Got," an ingenious mini-epic on the subject of the twelve-bar form. Ellington employs his tonal resources in simple but matchlessly effective combinations, as the canny melody is passed among reeds and brass for the first three choruses. Following a four-measure intro of dissonant piano chords, Barney Bigard essays the theme in the clarinet's low register as trombonist Lawrence Brown provides a delicate counterpoint. The timbres are reversed in the second chorus: muted brass instruments play a variation on the theme, while Ben Webster offers a gallantly restrained improvisation, heightening the tension. The third chorus repeats the clarinet-trombone instrumentation, but this time the clarinet carols in the upper register and Brown joins him there. (Who is the clarinetist this time? The discographies say Bigard, but the rich tone suggests Harry Carney, whose baritone sax is not discernible in this or the previous chorus.) After this peak, a two-measure interlude sets up the second theme, which is sung.

Although Ellington fancied himself something of a wordsmith, his lyrics were often precious. Yet the blues inspired him. Here he avoids the usual couplet-with-repeated-line structure, aiming for another kind of poetic repetition with the word "two" and the parallelism in the third and fourth lines:

> There's two kind of woman, there's two kind of man.
> There's two kind of romance since time began.
> There's a real true love and that good old jive.
> One tries to kill you, one helps to keep you alive.
> N' I don't know what kind of blues I've got.

During the last two measures of the chorus, the ensemble enters with an exciting, double-time riff that extends into the first six measures of the fifth chorus, the call-and-response between the reeds and the brass echoing the earlier relationship between clarinet and trombone. Jeffries concludes the chorus with an additional lyric and the orchestra adds a two-measure coda. Ellington's thoroughly modern setting in no way undermines the traditional attributes of the blues, as his sonorities trace the progress of jazz from New Orleans (Bigard) to Kansas City swing (the riffing), with a hip ballad crooner absorbed along the way. Yet nothing sounds forced or contrived or dated.

Just how much Mercer contributed to the four masterful and frequently neglected works associated with him has been debated, as he never came close to duplicating their excellence in later years. But the melodies have a non-Dukish quality, and there is no reason to question his authorship of the basic material. Who was "John Hardy's Wife," and why did Mercer serenade her? His own explanation was that the title refers to a "threatening woman," which hardly suggests a connection to the "pretty little wife" who cries, "Johnny, I been true to you," as John Hardy—the outlaw sung about in a traditional ballad recorded by Leadbelly in 1939—is about to be hanged. Yet the piece's charm stems not least from its unmistakable folklike elements—the A part has a touch of "I've Been Working on the Railroad" and the release, a hint of "John Hardy."

The most obvious development from the ST version to the RCA is the addition of a chorus that expands Rex Stewart's contribution from eight to thirty-two measures, but of no less significance is the modification in tempo and the far greater precision in execution. Blanton served as a kind of guardian angel, entrusted with sustaining and at times even setting the right tempos, but he and the band sound stiff on the ST, while the RCA exemplifies the orchestra's panache at a medium-up tempo. The question of precision is most relevant to Carney's dialogue with the trombone. In the last half of the ST's first chorus, Carney phrases with the brass (measures nineteen, twenty-two, twenty-seven) before essaying his breaks; the division of labor is immaculate on the RCA, as Carney enters punctiliously on the second beat of measures twenty, twenty-three and twenty-eight.

The lightly nostalgic melody is countered by a keening quality traceable to two facets of the arrangement: four-bar transitions between choruses (the last two bars always anticipate the next soloist or, in the last instance, the reeds) plus an abrupt two-measure coda; and a phrasing motif that leads the soloists or sections to play one beat over the expected duration of a phrase (even the coda is nine beats). The result is a kind of spillover momentum, especially on the ST, where Carney's phrasing is freer and Stewart nearly careens into the orchestra. A more interesting aspect of the arrangement (highly characteristic of Ellington) is its symmetry between sections and soloists. The fabulous Ellington sonorities result from his ability to use every instrument fully and equally, as well as to arrange them in creative combinations. In "John Hardy's Wife," responsibilities are meted out to each section, and each section produces one soloist. In the first chorus, the AABC composition is introduced with sixteen bars of piano and rhythm, followed by sixteen of Carney and the trombones. The piano returns in the first and third transition passages, and a trombonist (Brown) concludes the last chorus. In the second chorus, Carney continues to duet with the brasses for sixteen bars, followed by sixteen bars of the reed section. The reeds reappear to play the first sixteen bars of the fourth chorus. Note the parallelism between Carney and the reeds: each plays BC before AA. The third chorus is given entirely to Rex Stewart's acerbic, punchy, wry plunger solo, accompanied in the first half by the reeds and in the second by the trombones. The orchestra is united at the precipitous coda.

"Jumpin' Punkins" is something of a sequel or at least a companion to "John Hardy's Wife." Once again the tempo is medium, the rhythm section is generously deployed, Ellington introduces the theme, Carney converses with the trombones, and tone colors are carefully balanced. In this enchanting AABA romp, Mercer's compositional talent is best represented by the attractive release. The Fletcher Henderson tradition is expertly advanced in the last eight bars of the third chorus, where the three wind sections are efficiently contrasted, suggesting the helpful hand of Strayhorn. This time the rhythm section really steps out. The "reluctant" Sonny Greer, as Ellington called him, is featured in the six-bar intro and the coda and dominates half of the secondary theme, exchanging two-bar figures with the band for eight bars and following with a four-bar break. But as exuberant as his sashaying confidence is, it's the astounding Blanton who paces the performance, most prominently toward the end. He escorts the band in the third chorus and leads the pianist in the secondary theme, which begins with Ellington and the orchestra introducing a written variation on A, building tension that is resolved when Ellington heeds the walking bass. Another splendid touch is the hot four-bar transition after the second chorus; its materials are recycled in the ensuing exchanges with Greer.

Aside from the rhythm players, the only soloist is the noble Carney. (Bigard joins with the rhythm players for the restatement of A in the first chorus, anticipating the reeds in the release, but he doesn't solo by jazz standards). Carney's chorus doesn't have the give-and-take of his work on "John Hardy's Wife," as the trombones are confined to two-measure figures plus a couple of supporting riffs. In the interest of rhythmic symmetry, those riffs accent the third beat of the measures in which they appear; orchestral punctuations in the last eight measures of the chorus also begin on the third beat—the more closely you look at these recordings, the more fastidious they seem. The ST (recorded eight months *after* the RCA) is a treat. The arrangement is the same and so, in most respects, is Carney's solo. But the rhythm section is better displayed, and not only because of the recording setup. Rarely is Blanton heard to such powerful effect as in this transcription, particularly in the first chorus: his double-time runs in bars fifteen to sixteen; his first-beat accents in measures seventeen, nineteen, and twenty-one; and—the chief rhythmic surprise of the performance—his entirely unexpected syncopation in measure twenty-five. The pianist also plays a more aggressive role this time around.

Although Mercer is credited with the exquisitely sensuous melody of "Blue Serge," the opulence and mystery with which it unfolds can safely be attributed to Ellington's fascinating orchestration. In a work such as this, the theme and arrangement are all but inseparable. "Blue Serge" is evidence that Ellington belongs as much to the tradition of painterly composers—Berlioz, Ravel, Delius—as he does to jazz, even (*especially*) if he evolved his methods intuitively. Unlike Strayhorn, Ellington's earliest influences were American—Will Marion Cook, Will Vodery, Don Redman, the stride-styled pianist composers; he didn't begin investigating Europe until critics alerted him to similarities with his own work.

But there was little precedent on either continent for the colors he created and balanced with such dazzling precision or for the structural designs with which he enhanced the musical elements (blues, swing rhythms, eccentric tonalities, big band instrumentation) indigenous to jazz.

The pure music of "Blue Serge" is so straightforward in its expressive beauty that one is surprised to discover on closer inspection the subtle manipulation of form, melody, and harmony. In fact, the piece is never quite what it seems. It appears to be an eight-bar blues with Ellington's usual transition passages of two and four bars. Yet the choruses and transitions work together in ways to suggest a superimposed structure with real or implied phrases of two, four, six, eight, ten, twelve, and fourteen bars. At first look, the structure is clear: a four-measure intro followed by a two-measure vamp, two choruses, a two-measure transition, and two choruses. But look closer. Ellington might well have extended the clarinet-and-brass introduction, which telescopes the theme, into the first chorus, but instead he breaks it off for two measures of muted trombones and cymbal. This passage serves at least three purposes: it sets the mood, increases melodic and rhythmic interest, and establishes unexpected transitions as a motif.

The first chorus, movingly played by Stewart, is the purest recitation of the theme in the performance. Martin Williams described the second chorus as a "thematic variation scored for reeds and muted brass, a thing of marvelous color and one of the hundreds of examples in Ellington where only the closest listening will reveal what combinations of what instruments with what mutes are playing what, to produce this shifting sonority." The following two-bar transition works much as its predecessor did while extending the chorus to ten bars. For the third chorus, Joe Nanton's plunger-muted trombone plays a variation on the theme over shadowy muted chords and, in the last three measures, an echoing clarinet. The fourth chorus begins as a logical extension of the third, with a riffing variation played by muted brass and "answered" by the reeds. But again Ellington doesn't do what you expect. You expect the riffing to last through the chorus, at which point another transition is due to appear. Instead, the orchestra is preempted in measures seven and eight by what amounts to a two-bar piano break, which leads seamlessly into the fifth chorus, a piano rendition of the theme.

We now expect a secondary theme, or at least a bolder variation. A four-bar transition introduces Webster, rhapsodizing over relatively static chords intoned by the trombones. But this passage expands directly into the next chorus, turning a four-plus-eight episode into the illusion of a twelve-bar chorus, even though it doesn't follow the modulations of a twelve-bar blues. The last chorus is, in Williams's words, "a beautifully orchestrated variation, just barely thematic but strong enough to leave the performance with a feeling of resolution and with no lingering need for recapitulation." A diagram (where I = intro, X = transition, and A = chorus) illustrates the basic eight-bar blues framework and the superimposed forms its contents imply:

$$\overset{\lceil 6 \rceil}{I_4\ X_2}\ \overset{\lceil 10 \rceil}{A_8\ A_8\ X_2\ A_8}\ \overset{\lceil 14 \rceil}{A_8\ (or\ 6\ +\ 2)}\ \overset{\lceil 10 \rceil}{A_8}\ \overset{\lceil 12 \rceil}{X_4\ A_8\ A_8}$$

The performance is so seamlessly rendered—with irreproachable passages by Stewart, Nanton, Ellington, Webster, and Blanton, whose intonation and choice of notes, even when embedded firmly in the background, always suggest deep feelings—that the mathematic deliberations in no way intrude on the listener's pleasure. But they are there all the same, submerged in the work's overall enchantment.

"Moon Mist" is the piece Mercer said his father wrote by omission and with such practical advice as, "When you write, write something that *sounds* good." Even by the usual standards of range favored by Ellington and Strayhorn, where octave leaps are commonplace ("I Got It Bad," "Day Dream"), the span covered here is imposing: two-and-a-half octaves upward from G-flat below middle C. But the music is evocative and coherent, and the romantic ardor—Tchaikovsky could have written the third bar—never gets out of hand. The bluesy release, with its rhythmic adjustment, provides just the right contrast. The work as a whole is a fine setting for Nance's cagey violin. The ST is something of a blueprint for the RCA. The only significant changes are not in the arrangement but in the instrumentation of the soloists. On the ST, Nance plays his first solo on trumpet; for the RCA, he's heard on violin throughout. On the ST, the last half-chorus is given to the violinist; for the RCA, he relinquishes the final eight bars to Lawrence Brown. An interesting facet of the record, which is only a chorus and a half plus intro (Ellington with a touch of stride) and coda (Nance), is that the theme is divided into exchanges between soloists and ensemble. Hodges, Nance, and Brown deserve much credit for keeping the performance sober. A touch more hedonism on anyone's part would have engulfed it in sentimentality. Hodges plays down the large intervals, not—as the most cursory study of his recordings will attest—because he couldn't negotiate them with swelling glissandi, but for reasons of good taste that are the hallmark of his work in the orchestra. Similarly, Nance, who loved to rhapsodize on the violin, finesses his role.

Although "Take the A Train" represented Strayhorn's main commercial contribution to the Ellington band (he would pull another hit out of his hat a decade later with "Satin Doll"), he quickly revealed his forte to be dreamily impressionistic pieces, of which "Chelsea Bridge" is outstanding. Strayhorn titled his score under a providential misapprehension. He thought the James Whistler painting that inspired him, *Nocturne in Blue and Silver: Old Battersea Bridge* depicted a bridge in Chelsea. Like Whistler, whose stimulus is evident in the blurry orchestration, Strayhorn turned for instruction to French impressionists—in his case, musicians rather than painters, of course, and specifically Maurice Ravel. It's one of the most intriguing of all thirty-two-measure AABA songs, with sixths, ninths, elevenths, and thirteenths often used as melody notes; a key change from D-flat in the A section to E-natural in the release; and a seven-note chromatic pickup phrase. So evocative and consistent is the mood, from first note to last, that melody and orchestration once again seem indivisible.

Ellington recorded it three times in 1941: a Standard Transcription, a rejected studio version on September 29, and the RCA classic. Modifications were made each time, though not in the essential structure. Ellington plays piano on the ST only, and his four-measure intro is livelier but less fittingly harmonized than those played by Strayhorn on the RCAs. The first chorus is substantially the same in the ST and the RCA: the first sixteen bars combine hazily muted trumpets and reeds, with the former playing the melody notes and the latter, the chords. Ben Webster plays the release accompanied by the reeds (in 1954, he memorably recorded the entire piece with a Strayhorn arrangement for strings). The final eight bars of the chorus are ingeniously plotted, with the trombones playing melody and Harry Carney leading the saxophones in off-beat punctuations. One difference between the two is that on the RCA Strayhorn's piano plays a prominent role in the backdrop. (On the rejected RCA version, Juan Tizol plays the first sixteen bars and the phrasing of the trombones is syrupy.)

Strayhorn's expanded role in the final version is more evident in the second chorus, and it reflects the tragic loss of Jimmy Blanton. In September, the bassist, who roomed with Strayhorn, discovered he had tuberculosis. He played a few more engagements with the band, but by November Ellington placed him in the first of several institutions in California, where he died the following July, at twenty-four. (Within a year, Oscar Pettiford was expanding on Blanton's legacy, which was further amplified three years later by Ray Brown. Bebop could not have developed as it did without Blanton's example and the way Ellington featured him.) At the outset of the second chorus of the ST, Blanton initiates a bold dialogue with the saxophones, who play a written variation on the theme. On the rejected RCA, Blanton is still the primary soloist, but the variation leaves less room for him to maneuver and he evinces less energy. On the issued RCA, with Blanton gone, the action is between Strayhorn and the reeds. The new bassist, Junior Raglin, is decidedly low key. In all three, Tizol plays the final release with muted accompaniment, but the concluding measures are different each time: in the ST, they are played by Tizol and the reeds; in the rejected RCA, they are played by Strayhorn; in the final RCA, they are orchestrated in a lush and subtle counterpoint between reeds and brass. Some critics have argued unconvincingly that "Chelsea Bridge" isn't jazz—in the '40s, "effete" was the invective of choice. Whatever else it isn't, it is undeniably and marvelously Ellington-Strayhorn music.

One more example will suffice in suggesting their collaborative power and versatility. "Just A-Settin' and A-Rockin' " is *perfect*: perfect tempo (aptly described in the title), perfect solos, perfect presentation—not a hair out of place. The four-bar introduction is divided between Ellington and Blanton, who establishes the rhythmic gait. Webster states the theme, although the division of labor between Webster and the orchestra is even—each exchanging one-bar phrases in an Ellingtonian demonstration of figure-and-ground. In the final eight bars of the chorus, after Nance plays the release in his yearningly personal style, the figure-and-ground is reversed. Webster has the second chorus to himself, and he sounds suitably comfortable, as though he were fanning himself on the front porch. At the bridge, the band prods him with stop-time accents. Joe Nanton gets to purr for the first half of the third chorus, in which figure-and-ground is reversed again: he leads the ensemble in the first eight and follows it in the next. Bigard whirls into the release over stop-time pumping to complete the chorus. The punctilious coda allots two bars to Ellington, one to Blanton, and one to the orchestra. Perfect.

These few numbers barely scratch the surface of what Ellington achieved in the early '40s and exclude most of the better known works, which have been subject to numerous musicological studies. "Concerto for Cootie" is a contender for the most extensively analyzed jazz recording ever made; "Ko Ko" is likely a close second—those and three more selections from the period are the subjects of an illuminating book by Ken Rattenbury, *Duke Ellington Jazz Composer*. Other celebrated titles from the era are "In a Mellotone," in which the unison ensemble figures during the solos by Johnny Hodges and Cootie Williams are as swinging and seemingly spontaneous as the improvisations; "Cottontail," which did for Ben Webster what "Body and Soul" did for Coleman Hawkins and "Lady Be Good" for Lester Young (Webster also wrote the widely imitated chorus for the reeds); two evocative Ellington portraits, "Bojangles (A Portrait of Bill Robinson)" and "A Portrait of Bert Williams";

two advanced up-tempo concoctions by Strayhorn that found favor with the '60s avant-garde, "Johnny Come Lately" and "My Little Brown Book"; a flashy concerto for Barney Bigard, "Are You Sticking?"; a candidate for the fastest big band record ever made, the stirring "Giddybug Gallop" ($\downarrow$ = 368); two of Ellington's most gorgeous nocturnes, "Warm Valley" and "All Too Soon"; the bass concerto "Jack the Bear," in which Blanton demonstrated that pizzicato bass, played with impeccable intonation, could be a far more adaptable and involved instrument—harmonically, rhythmically, melodically—than the four-to-the-bar plodder it had become; and more than six dozen others, including the small-group sessions and three imperishable songs employed in Ellington's 1941 musical revue.

One of Ellington's biggest disappointments was his failure to bring off a hit on Broadway. Although he was involved in a few Broadway ventures (*Beggar's Holiday*, written with lyricist John LaTouche and starring Alfred Drake, lasted fourteen weeks in 1946 and produced no memorable songs), the closest he came to a success was *Jump for Joy*, which never got east of Los Angeles, where it had a three-month run. It was while working on the revue that he recorded the Standard Transcription discs and all the RCA classics made that year. Though virtually unknown until 1988, when J. R. Taylor and Margaret Robinson produced a simulated cast album (scrupulously annotated by Patricia Willard) for the Smithsonian Collection, *Jump for Joy* was a milestone in Ellington's career and a benchmark in American theater. It was the first all-black musical to avoid, in the words of librettist and lyricist Sid Kuller, "black humor performed by blacks for white audiences from a white point of view. Our material was from the point of view of black people looking at whites." For his finest score, Ellington produced no less than eight lasting numbers, of which the most enduringly popular are "I Got It Bad (and That Ain't Good)," "Rocks in My Bed," and "Jump for Joy."

Yet the show is legendary principally for the usual bad reason that little is known about it. Five of Ellington's songs that were widely acclaimed at the time (as was the entire show) have been wiped from human memory, except for their titles. Original programs, scores, and publicity materials have also vanished. Two-hundred feet of silent eight-millimeter movie footage exists, but the villains in possession (in alleged violation of the agreement by which they obtained it) refuse to let it be shown. James Lincoln Collier's execrable biography of Ellington dismisses the venture in half a page, and even Ellington's recollection in his scrapbook memoir, *Music Is My Mistress*, is spotty, if intense. He neglects to note such relevant trivia as the origin of the term "zoot suit" in one of Kuller's sketches for the show or that Charlie Chaplin asked to direct and then reneged. He does report that on the basis of seeing one performance Orson Welles dictated stage directions to revamp the show from top to bottom—"the most impressive display of mental power I've ever experienced," Ellington recalled.

Jump for Joy was from the beginning a rallying point for the Hollywood left, though even the staunchest of its boosters were taken aback by the show's irreverence. John Garfield, who helped back it and attended every rehearsal, suggested that singer Herb Jeffries blacken up to disguise his blue eyes—an idea nixed by the composer. According to Ellington, "the original script had Uncle Tom on his death bed [with] a Hollywood producer on one side of the bed and a Broadway producer on the other side, and both were trying to keep him alive by injecting adrenalin into his arms!" That was cut before opening night. After several performances accompanied by threats of violence from the KKK, they also agreed to cut "I've Got a Passport from Georgia," which concluded with this verse:

> Give me that northern royalty
> Where Goldberg marries Casey
> Where the only Duke is Ellington
> And the only Count is Basie
> I've got a passport from Georgia
> And I'm sailin' for the U.S.A.

Another sketch also shook up the establishment, tame as it sounds today. Wonderful Smith was a carhop until he achieved fleeting celebrity in *Jump for Joy* for his telephone routine satirizing the New Deal and war preparation. He stopped the show every night and was hired to perform a slightly bowdlerized version in a B-comedy called *Top Sergeant Mulligan*. Republicans reveled in it, though a horrified Red Skelton told him, "The communists will love you."

Still, the show was a hit, a highpoint in the careers of virtually everyone involved and a shock of recognition to those who saw it. The critics were uniformly in its corner; one wrote several reviews, documenting the various changes during the first month of performances. It boosted the careers of Maria Bryant and Dorothy Dandridge and solidified the reputation of Joe Turner, who left a gig at New York's Cafe Society to join the production and brought the house down with "Rocks in My Bed" and his own blues. It inspired some of Paul Francis Webster's finest lyrics, which inspired Ellington, who was never a better songsmith than when he had a great lyricist at his side. And it provided Ivie Anderson, the most gifted and frequently recorded of Ellington's singers, with perhaps the most incandescent moment in her career, singing "Chocolate Shake" and the dejected "I Got It Bad." She was thirty-six and had only eight years left to live, but her success in the show enabled her to open a club in Los Angeles.

The idea behind the Smithsonian series of reconstructed musicals is to use recordings made by original cast members in the period they were appearing onstage. For its 1988 edition of *Jump for Joy*, the selections include the relevant 1941 RCA classics, alongside records made for Soundies (jukebox videos) and Standard Transcriptions, which employed singers from the show instead of Ellington regulars and boast two previously unknown dance numbers ("Stomp Caprice" and "Bugle Breaks"); Joe Turner's record of "Rocks in My Bed"; and the filmtrack of Wonderful Smith's monologue, "Hello, Mr. President." Hearing this material in a context designed to approximate the revue is to hear it anew (the set was remastered by Jack Towers, forty-seven years after he recorded the Fargo concert). *Jump for Joy* is a period piece, never likely to get the revival its creators long coveted, but it's a richly entertaining and high-minded chapter in the history of theatrical nose thumbing and a monument to Ellington's pluck.

Two years later, he offered a still more ambitious and significant work to the East Coast and didn't fare as well. He had continued on a roll until the summer of 1942, when the American Federation of Musicians instigated its two-year recording ban. In the period before he began work on *Jump for Joy*, Ellington made plans for an opera to be called *Boola*, about the travails of an immortal African who is brought over in chains and survives to witness three hundred years of African American history. Dissatisfied with the work, he abandoned it in favor of an instrumental scheme that would tell the same story in a pioneering format he felt better able to handle; he called it "a tone parallel to the history of the American Negro." In the decades following its premiere, it became a work of impervious mystery, known only through excerpts (including the great hymn, "Come Sunday") and, like *Jump for Joy*, esteemed in its absence. When New York's governor, Hugh Carey, declared April 29, 1976 (the seventy-seventh anniversary of the composer's birth), Duke Ellington Day, he singled it out in his proclamation. Many critics declared it his greatest extended work. How did they know? Ellington never recorded *Black, Brown and Beige* in its entirety, and even today, though readily available thanks to the belated release of the Carnegie Hall recording, it is rarely performed.

Ellington had been promising a long concert piece on African American history for several years when the unveiling was scheduled for January 23, 1943. He was riding high on the wave of his greatest artistic successes and reeling from losses in the band's ranks—Bigard and Ivie Anderson departed shortly after Blanton's death. Wartime sentimentality contributed to an easing of tension between representatives of lofty art and pop culture, and Ellington, who was creating internationally acclaimed art in what was natively considered a folk milieu, was the ideal symbol for what turned out to be the false promise of oneness in American music. As it happened, the January concert was both a benefit for Russian War Relief and the anniversary of Ellington's twentieth year as a bandleader in New York. He was presented that evening with a plaque signed by thirty-two prominent members of the musical world, among them Leopold Stokowski, Walter Damrosch, William Grant Still, Earl Hines, Arthur Rodzinski, Roy Harris, Count Basie, Fritz Reiner, Kurt Weill, Paul Robeson, Aaron Copland, Benny Goodman, Jerome Kern, and Marian Anderson. He had prepared a bountiful program appropriate to the event.

Black, Brown and Beige was placed right before intermission. Ellington has said it ran fifty-seven minutes, but he must have been including the spoken introductions. His biographer, Barry Ulanov, clocked it at forty-five, which is more consistent with the tape and subsequent re-creations. The hall was sold out, as was the repeat performance at Boston's Symphony Hall the following night, and Ellington was acutely aware that the magnitude of what he was attempting—a concert work by a "jazz" musician—might obscure the actual accomplishment. This was a time when everyone pretended to know what jazz was except the people who created it.

Older jazz critics, of the Rudi Blesh–Rex Harris ilk, considered *Black, Brown and Beige* empty; they expected Ellington to stick with hot jazz circa 1927. The classical critics, except long-time Ellington admirer Irving Kolodin, were dubious about its structure, agreeing with the usually astute Marxist classical/jazz critic Sidney Finkelstein, who lauded the parts but not the sum. Others attacked Ellington for being pretentious, a charge that in this context was unfathomable but predictable. In any case, after recording excerpts in 1944, about eighteen minutes' worth, Ellington abandoned *Black, Brown and Beige* until the late '50s. On the other hand, the concert was successful enough to ensure his annual return to Carnegie Hall with a new work throughout the decade.

Black, Brown and Beige is frequently characterized as a suite, a string of unrelated miniatures, but it is no such thing. The "Black" segment alone is a twenty-one-minute tone poem composed of two central themes, "Work Song" and "Come Sunday," which develop and intertwine, emerging simultaneously in the final section of "Black," called

"Light," and are then reprised in the "Beige" finale. There are also two ingeniously crafted subordinate themes: a heavily rhythmic ensemble counterpoint to the seven-note "Work Song" phrase and a keening introduction to Johnny Hodges's celebrated exposition of "Sunday," plucked and bowed by Ray Nance on violin. "Black" is overlong, however; trombonist Joe Nanton fails to justify the generous space allotted him, and some of the transitional segues are ill-considered and obvious.

"Brown," the most episodic section, is the most nearly perfect. Acknowledging "the black contribution in blood," it is compassionate, witty, patriotic, and acidic. It includes the raucous "West Indian Dance"; the immensely effective "Emancipation Celebration," where the jubilance of the young free blacks—expressed by Rex Stewart—is set in relief by the fearful commiseration of the older folks, represented in mournful duets; and "The Blues," a recitation sung by Betty Roche, which, naturally, is not a blues. This last part, dealing with the blues as a state of despondency rather than the cyclical form with which Ellington frequently dispelled blue feelings, is curiously un-Ellingtonian. In fact, the passage indicates Ellington's interest, beginning in the mid-30s, in composers and orchestrators tangential to his own tradition, including Gershwin, Delius, and Debussy. The line "sighing . . . crying . . ." is rooted in Gershwin's "They Pass By Singing," a fragment Gershwin may have speared from Debussy's *Nuages*. Ellington's eclecticism was the conscious manifestation of his best instincts, though, and "The Blues" is more effective than one might have expected.

A more ironic eclecticism is reflected in the "Sugar Hill" section of "Beige," which depicts Harlem's crème de la crème (the piece is also known as "Creamy Brown"). The suitably nostalgic "Sugar Hill Penthouse" builds to a voicing of clarinet above the saxophones—the trademark sound of Glenn Miller. It may be, as Gunther Schuller has pointed out, that Ellington himself invented that sound with the 1938 "Lost in Meditation," but in 1943 the technique was a signpost of white dance music, and therefore appropriate to a concluding passage wherein the assimilated Negro has gone from black to brown to beige. It is followed by the reprise of Hodges playing "Come Sunday," Ellington's magnificent spiritual. "Beige" is a continuing movement, but again the seams show. At the conclusion, "Come Sunday" is taken at a dance band tempo, in prophecy of "David Danced," his '60s feature for tap dancer Bunny Briggs. Percussive motives, patriotic airs, and a constant, shifting antiphony give the work added cohesion, but the most important unifying factor is the programmatic content. Much of Ellington's finest music was conceived with programmatic specificity; *Black, Brown and Beige* anticipates the masterly thematic suites (*Such Sweet Thunder, Far East Suite*), the extended impressionistic orchestrations (*The Tattooed Bride, Ad Lib on Nippon*), the luminous rhapsody *Harlem*, and the pioneering television revue *A Drum Is a Woman*.

In 1958, Ellington collaborated with Mahalia Jackson for the Columbia album *Black, Brown and Beige*. It consists of five extended movements based on "Work Song" and "Come Sunday," plus a spontaneous setting for the Twenty-third Psalm. Ellington's lyric for "Come Sunday," introduced here, is the best he ever wrote. But why was this excellent session so misleadingly titled? Had he decided that these themes were all that were worth preserving from the original? If so, he soon changed his mind. Five years later, he reorchestrated "Come Sunday," adding the "David Danced" variation, "Light" (retitled "Montage"), and "The Blues" to the revue *My People*, presented at the Century of Negro Progress Exposition in Chicago; "Come Sunday" was interpreted three times in the 1965 *Concert of Sacred Music*.

During that same hectic year, Ellington revised "Beige" as "Beige No. 2," retitling one episode as "Cy Runs Rock Waltz" (released posthumously), and performed "Black" as his offering at the White House Festival of the Arts. The event elicited Dwight Macdonald's unwitting manifestation of jazz's ambiguous station: Macdonald protested that "no composers of any note were present," then observed parenthetically that the "best thing at the festival" and "the only happy-looking people, in fact, were Duke Ellington and his bandsmen." (Macdonald's confusion was affirmed by the Pulitzer Prize board, which rejected the unanimous recommendation of its jury to recognize Ellington for his overall achievement. Aaron Copland remarked, "He's deserved it for so long." Ellington said, "Fate is being kind to me. Fate doesn't want me to be too famous too young.") In 1971, Ellington paid one last visit to *Black, Brown and Beige*, privately recording a languorous interpretation of "Sugar Hill Penthouse," retitled "Symphonette" and issued posthumously.

Meanwhile, in 1972 the English arranger, composer, and saxophonist Alan Cohen recorded a performance, having assembled with Brian Priestly a complete arrangement from the tape and the score, with fifteen minutes "surmised." Cohen's version is distinguished by fine section work, but the rhythms are sluggish and the solos disappointing—"Come Sunday" is played on soprano saxophone with ornamentation that Hodges would have found intolerable. Still, his landmark achievement brought *Black, Brown and Beige* into the light. In 1976, two years after Ellington's death, Dick Hyman conducted Cohen's transcription, slightly altered, at the Newport Jazz Festival at Carnegie Hall. Months later, Maurice Peress brought the Kansas City Philharmonic to Carnegie and conducted his own symphonic amplification, made at Ellington's request. Peress inexplicably called his adaptation *Black, Brown and Beige Suite*, though it is based entirely on the first episode. The truism that Ellington wrote for specific individuals implies a concomitant truth—that the instrumental techniques of those individuals must be replicated in repertory performances of his music. The Kansas City Philharmonic's alto saxophonist was intent on matching Johnny Hodges gliss for gliss, but lacking Hodges's precision and taste, he verged on parody. The violinist was no better at essaying Ray Nance's part, and the brasses missed the shaded deliberation that makes a plunger solo convincing.

A year after the Peress concert, Prestige released, at long last, *The Duke Ellington Carnegie Hall Concerts—January 1943*, giving the debut performance a public airing that had conflicting results: it spurred a positive reassessment of the music, but intimidated conductors from trying to compete with the Ellington orchestra's execution. Not until 1989, on the occasion of Ellington's ninetieth birthday, was another complete revival attempted, this time by the American Jazz Orchestra, conducted by Peress, who had left Kansas City for New York. In that performance, Ellington's narrative (read by Bobby Short) was woven into the tapestry for the first time. More significantly, Peress made alterations, especially in "Beige," based on his discussions with Ellington, giving the conclusion added definition through a recapitulation of themes from the first movement. In 1992, conducting the Louie Bellson Orchestra, Peress recorded his version, which (notwithstanding the arguable decision to assign an alto saxophone solo to Clark Terry's trumpet) is the most accurate presentation available other than the 1943 recording; it conveys the luster of Ellington's melodic fabric and the diversity of his rhythms and orchestrating techniques. Yet it falls short in failing to match the expressiveness of Ellington's musicians, especially in solos, and in coming up with a comparably individual articulation.

Ellington is made for repertory and will doubtless be heard more frequently in the concert hall, sometimes in liberal adaptations that ought not to be dismissed out of hand—Luther Henderson has revised a delightful version of *Night Creatures*, for example. But unless a conductor has as intransigent a vision as Ellington's, the music ought to be treated in the Ellington style, for that's where his deepest meanings lie. Yet his recordings ought to liberate interpreters from rank imitation. A growl solo is generic: it doesn't have to played in the manner of Cootie Williams to be legitimate, any more than Williams had to play Ray Nance's variations on "Take the A Train" in the manner of Ray Nance. As more orchestras interpret Ellington, we will be better able to evaluate their virtues and vices without worrying about obeisance to the original records. Conductors should be no more intimidated by Ellington's recordings than by Stravinsky's or Copland's, though they can't ignore his stylistic quiddities.

When the two-year recording strike ended in 1944, two new musics suddenly flowered, each having mutated in relative privacy as enforced by the ban: in jazz, the byword was bebop, and Charlie Parker was its avatar; in pop, the coming fashion was rhythm and blues, with which Louis Jordan attracted capacity audiences. Ellington had a few wilderness years during which he wrote light pieces (including a wizardly bop-inflected "Perdido") in both genres, along with the extended works annually presented at Carnegie. He survived the big bust up of the bands, and though he suffered the near fatal defections of Johnny Hodges and Lawrence Brown in the early '50s, they returned in time for the spectacular appearance at Newport in 1956 when "Diminuendo and Crescendo in Blue" put Ellington back on top, where he stayed his remaining eighteen years. By then he had found his ideal format, the suite—a large structure consisting of short structures. Many triumphs followed, among them *Such Sweet Thunder, The Queen's Suite, The Nutcracker Suite, Far East Suite, And His Mother Called Him Bill, Latin American Suite, The Afro-Eurasian Eclipse,* and the sacred music. In the mid-'60s, he had perhaps the finest band of his career, an exemplary blend of soloists, leads, and section players (the orchestra never sounded more regal than on *The Popular Duke Ellington*). Yet he never surpassed his towering legacy of the war years. Nor has anyone else.

28 ❖ Billy Strayhorn (Passion Flower)

Billy Strayhorn died on May 31, 1967, at age fifty-one. In a sense, his rebirth began that day—since then, popular interest has brought him out from the immense shadow cast by Duke Ellington and into a light he seemed determined in life to abjure. Today his name is familiar enough, his music the subject of homage and discussion, and his life recounted in a biography, *Lush Life*, by David Hadju. He is often cited as second only to Ellington among jazz composers and orchestrators—as he invariably was by the critics in jazz polls conducted by *Esquire* in the '40s. His songs are performed all the time, his body of work increasingly recognized for values that set it apart from the music of the man to whom he devoted his entire career.

At the time of his passing, however, Strayhorn was an enigmatic man, famous enough to warrant election to the *Down Beat* Hall of Fame (by the magazine's readers, not critics), yet obscure in the specifics of his contribution, even among buffs. Although he shared the composer credits on hundreds of Ellington titles, recorded occasionally under his own name, and was identified with a handful of art songs, of which only one, "Lush Life," had no Ellingtonian associations, Strayhorn shunned attention beyond the inner circle. Much loved by those who knew and worked with him, he had little desire to take bows, his reticence reportedly induced in part by his homosexuality, which he refused to deny. He worked at Ellington's pleasure on a lifetime handshake contract, secure and apparently content in the mythic realm of an ideal and idealized collaboration.

Ellington called Strayhorn "Swee' Pea" (for his resemblance to Popeye's baby) and offered a characteristic response to those who called him his alter ego: "Let's not go overboard. Pea is only my right arm, left foot, eyes, stomach, ears, and soul, not my ego." Truly, Ellington's ego required no assistance, and both men appeared to revel in the supernatural aspects of a musical partnership so exclusive that Strayhorn's contribution could only be surmised, never quantified. The myth reaches full proportion in Gordon Parks's description of the two at work: At 1:30 in the morning, after watching a terrible horror movie, Ellington switches off the TV and hands some manuscript paper to Strayhorn: "Gather up the genius, Swee' Pea. The maestro is limp at the heels," he says, then turns to Parks, and, before falling into a deep sleep, advises him, "You are about to witness a remote and covetous collaboration between flower and beast."

Strayhorn works about ninety minutes and then wakes Ellington, whom he called Monster. "Wake up, Monster. I stopped on C minor. Take it from there." Parks, writing in *Esquire*, describes Ellington rising, yawning, tottering over to the manuscript, mumbling about the plebeian nature of C minor, as Strayhorn takes his place on the couch. Two hours later, Ellington wakes Strayhorn. The work is completed by dawn. "Four hours later the big band was rocking the studio with their arrangement," Parks writes. "And no one knew where the Monster started or Swee' Pea left off. Only one big fine sound, one grand, remote and covetous collaboration."

The idea of an impenetrable alliance is appealing, with its suggestion of perfect friendship, especially among two such very different individuals: Ellington the tall, handsome, glib showboater; Strayhorn the short, cherubic, modest loner. Yet the very obscurity of Strayhorn's contribution was certain to encourage curiosity over time. Ellington himself did his part in emphasizing Strayhorn's importance to the organization. He never failed to play his theme without introducing it as "Billy Strayhorn's 'Take the A Train,' " and in one instance, *The Nutcracker Suite* (Columbia), shared the album cover with him: the bespectacled protege posed behind the maestro's left shoulder, looking down, demure, while Ellington stares into the camera. Tchaikovsky's music underscored the not uncommon assumption that Strayhorn's influence was primarily a reflection of his "classical" background, when, in fact, Strayhorn's background was primarily in the music of Ellington, which is what made him such an extraordinary find.

Ellington delegated most of the orchestra's adaptations to Strayhorn, including witty and sometimes sardonic (consider the jungly subversion of innocence in "I Want To Hold Your Hand") versions of pop songs and swing-band anthems. On a more serious note, Strayhorn was invariably credited though not pictured on the majority of extended works, from *The Perfume Suite* in 1945 through the *Far East Suite* two decades later. He served as deputy pianist, conductor, and lyricist, as well as arranger, composer, and songwriter. He saved the band's hash on at least two occasions: first, in the early '40s, by supplying "Take the A Train" and several other preeminent numbers in the Ellington catalogue during the ASCAP strike that prohibited Ellington from transcribing his own music for radio; and second, a decade later, by contributing "Satin Doll," the royalties for which helped finance the orchestra for years. Ellington's own reservoir of pop melodies had dried up by the middle '40s, and "Satin Doll" was the band's last bona fide hit, just in time to subsidize his increasingly diverse store of suites and tone poems.

Strayhorn was a force in most of the longer works—usually we can detect his input even when we aren't absolutely certain of its extent. In *The Perfume Suite*, "Strange Feeling" is as unmistakably Strayhorn as "Dancers in Love" is unmistakably Ellington. In the fluid precincts of full-bore collaborations such as *Such Sweet Thunder, A Drum Is a Woman,* and *Far East Suite*, we can sense the prevelance of one against the other. On rare occasions, Strayhorn could be persuaded to record under his own name, but the results are invariably unfulfilled, excessively moody or too casually swinging. He needed the Ellington orchestra to realize his music beyond the sad and lovely poignance of his piano—so gentle (he called his most personal album *The Peaceful Side* [Capitol]) where Ellington's is so heartily percussive. Even when placed in charge, he did his best work in the shadows, as on *Blue Rose* (Columbia), the Ellington–Rosemary Clooney pairing, or *The Big Sound* (Verve), Strayhorn's most buoyant setting for Johnny Hodges.

The Nutcracker exemplifies how finely blended their work could be.

Strayhorn is said to have been the instigator in planning the movements, and Ellington the editor who finalized them. Or maybe not. Who can tell? If the project was natural to Strayhorn and originated with him, no one but Ellington could have made it happen. By the late '50s, jazz adaptations from classical repertory were generally limited to "jazzing the classics," a swing era fashion that amounted to little more than riffing on Chopin instead of Gershwin, and discrete interpolations, from Louis Armstrong quoting "Ridi, Pagliaccio" in "Tiger Rag" to Woody Herman prefacing "Let It Snow" with a glance at *Petrushka*. Ellington himself riffed on Liszt in the 1934 movie, *Murder at the Vanities*, after which disgruntled "legit" musicians mow down his entire band with machine guns.

Ellington and Strayhorn had little precedent in electing to reorchestrate an extended piece. The choice of material was cautious and smart—*The Nutcracker* is a bauble unwrapped every Christmas for children, with melodies everyone has had a whack at, from Disney to Spike Jones, before George Balanchine virtually took over the franchise with his ballet. The familiarity of the canvas could only underscore the ingenuity of the adapters, whose faith in the project was thoroughly justified. The two men employed all the Ellington trademarks, faithfully refashioning Tchaikovsky in a language largely of their own invention, rich in buoyant swing, intricate voicings, plunger-muted brasses, lilting clarinets, baritone-led reeds, a swirling tenor saxophone. From the loping introductory bass to the plaintive trombone adieu, Ellington and Strayhorn infuse Russian song with a cool glow of urban elegance, recasting ballet as a demotic dance for anyone who cares to step lively.

Ellington himself was most responsible for triggering the posthumous inquiry into Strayhorn's art. They had been a fabled team for twenty-eight years, and Ellington wasted no time in preparing a memorial tribute that turned out to be one of the most sublime recording projects of his own last decade. *And His Mother Called Him Bill* (RCA) was a triumph, masterfully executed (Johnny Hodges, for one, never played better) and programmed—it made the most dramatic case possible for reassessment. The closing selection in the original sequencing (despoiled on CD) is a wrenching, unplanned performance of "Lotus Blossom" by Ellington alone at the piano, the intensity of his reading reducing the musicians who had started packing up to stunned silence. But the high point (vying with a definitive reading of "Day Dream") is the official debut of Strayhorn's great swan song "Blood Count," perhaps the finest of the several concertos he wrote for Hodges.

Several years after Ellington's death, the genesis of that haunting melody was revealed with the release of *The Greatest Jazz Concert in the World* (Pablo), an album culled from a succession of concerts in early 1967, including one in March at Carnegie Hall, where the piece debuted. Near death, Strayhorn wrote it in the hospital and had it delivered to Ellington shortly before the band went on stage. (He submitted an early version weeks before that had been tried out during the band's just completed European tour.) Not surprisingly, the premiere is a mere foreshadowing of the insuperable rendition to follow, lacking the hushed poise, the glimmering cymbals, and marchlike snare taps of the studio recording. In concert, the orchestration is less well balanced and spacious, the closing brass figure not fully realized. But Hodges's relaxed reading, flooded with grace notes, builds to a bravura climax before the final section and is moving in its own right. In later years, Stan Getz would adapt the piece as one of his most candidly expressive vehicles.

Ellington constantly invoked Strayhorn's name. He pointedly recalled Strayhorn's four articles of moral freedom for the benefit of the morally challenged Richard Nixon at the White House in 1969 on the occasion of Ellington's seventieth birthday. A film made of the occasion shows Nixon withering under the steady glare of Ellington's recitation: "freedom from hate, unconditionally; freedom from all self-pity; freedom from fear of possibly doing something that might help another more than it might help himself; and freedom from the kind of pride that could make a man feel he was better than his brother or neighbor."

As Strayhorn compositions appeared more frequently on jazz recordings of the '70s and '80s, the wheel turned and some argued that he was the real force behind Ellington, a preposterous claim Ellington may have anticipated, for he was never more productive than in the seven years that separated Strayhorn's death from his own. Yet the myth of a seamless collaboration was somewhat punctured by persistent attempts to liberate the shy genius from his master. Indeed, the evidence of scores confirmed conjectures of Strayhorn's contributions. But the fact remains that however distinct Strayhorn's musical disposition (dreamy, reserved, at times florid), the prevailing qualities in his music are rooted in the lessons of that same master. The introductory octave leap found in such Strayhorn songs as "Day Dream" is also heard in Ellington's "I Got It Bad"; the chromatic melodies of "A Flower Is a Lovesome Thing" and "Chelsea Bridge" hark back to chromatic voicings in "Mood Indigo." The virtuoso muted brass effects found throughout Strayhorn's writing recall such antecedents as "Braggin' in Brass." The tricky riffs and large intervals of "Johnny Come Lately," "Raincheck," and "U.M.M.G." and even the stately rhapsodies conceived for Johnny Hodges, extend principles well established by Ellington. Yet only Strayhorn could have written those gemlike miniatures, as well as "Something to Live For" (which Ella Fitzgerald once called her favorite song), "Grievin'," "Passion Flower," "My Little Brown Book," or "Lotus Blossom" (aka "Charlotte Russe").

The Strayhorn legacy is invaluable on at least three levels: First, the songbook, available to any singer with the ability and imagination to tackle songs of uncommon harmonic and melodic sophistication. Despite sumptuous assessments by Ella Fitzgerald and Sarah Vaughan, they are overdue for the overblown operatic treatment that will accurately pinpoint his every devious interval and extended phrases against a world of strings. Second, the instrumental pieces, a portfolio of charming, fanciful, swinging, often ingenious orchestrations that complement but in no way get lost in the larger portfolio of Ellington. Finally and most important are the collaborations—the geographical suites, the dances and portraits, the parodies and homages. Ultimately, only pedants can care where one pen left off and the other began. In giving Strayhorn his due, it isn't necessary to shatter the image of a "remote and covetous collaboration." We need simply render unto the Flower his due, confident the Beast is in full accord.

29 ❖ *Spike Jones* # *(Chasin' the Birdaphone)*

From genuine satire to submoronic silliness, comedy records have been around as long as any other kind, and probably longer—the Victor Company recorded Bert Williams before it got around to Caruso. Al Jolson was considered a singing comedian in the teens, as was Eddie Cantor when he supplanted him in the '30s, and jazz records of the era were replete with inside and frequently off-color jokes. The age of comedy music *ensembles* really took off in the '30s with country bands such as the Hoosier Hot Shots, polka bands such as Freddie Fisher and the Schnickelfritz Band, and jazz bands such as Fats Waller and His Rhythm. Yet they all respected the conventions of their idioms and kept a lid on their ids.

Spike Jones was different. A free-ranging parodist who took no prisoners, he avoided specific genres in favor of a comprehensive assault on musical decorum. Jones offended everyone and, in the process, found a much larger audience than his genre-bound predecessors. Yet burlesque was only the beginning. Jones did something more than poke fun at easy targets. Though he patterned his first bands after Red Nichols and his '20s jazz groups and made his living as a studio drummer backing Bing Crosby and other radio stars, Jones recognized that rhythm walks a tightrope. Play it right, and it's hip and powerful, subordinating all stray impulses to hilarity in its cool drive; but push it over the edge, and it plummets into lunatic hysteria. Spike went over the edge, where most of the mainstream audience was waiting for him. A link between Carl Stallings's arrangements for Warner Brothers cartoons in the '30s and Jerry Lewis's spastic dancing of the '50s, he understood that most people's internal rhythms are artless and not a little embarrassing. He made his meticulous art out of seeming chaos and embarrassed us plenty.

From the time he organized his City Slickers, Jones began substituting the usual sounds of trap drums with a battery of percussive proxies, including gunshots, cowbells, auto horns, and whistles. But his second line of offense really pushed the envelope: vocal sounds. For these he raided the entire panoply of bodily functions. We're talking burping, belching, spitting, coughing, gurgling, gulping, hiccuping, sneezing; we're talking backfires, breezers, raspberry tarts. Like no other musician before or since, Spike had the upper and lower digestive tracks covered.

Yet he might not have sustained his arsenal but for that great Wagnerian, Adolf Hitler. In 1942, Jones got an advance look at "Der Fuehrer's Face," a song that was to debut in a Disney cartoon originally called "Donald Duck in Axis Land." The lyric required a sound effect for which Jones introduced the "birdaphone." According to Jordan R. Young's comprehensive *Spike Jones Off the Record* (Past Times), the powers at RCA insisted he record an alternate take with trombone before reluctantly agreeing to release the unfettered version, complete with repeated blats on the birdaphone. To their surprise, the record shot to the top of the charts, establishing the City Slickers as a going concern, complete with a Hollywood debut in the flag-waving *Thank Your Lucky Stars*. The Disney people should have been deja vu-ing, for who anticipated Spike more than they, with the early Mickey Mouse cartoons that routinely employed weird and rhythmic sounds. In "Steamboat Bill" (1928), the original irksome Mickey drums on a cow's teeth, strums a chicken's neck, and plucks a pig's tits. Mickey was Spike with an attitude.

Almost everyone who has written about Spike Jones begins by recalling the First Encounter, which would seem to rank Spike up there with the loss of virginity as a formative experience. They seem genuinely awed that one of the flakiest cultural figures of our youth should return— somewhat apotheosized—in our confounding adulthood. Part of the astonishment surely reflects the unforgettable visual component, as conserved on video compilations of Jones's '50s television series—not the knockabout vaudeville, funny costumes, and dopey expressions of his sideman, but Spike himself, a strange-looking dude. His face was a perfect square, very nearly the shape of a TV screen; his thick hair rose in a never ending, wavy pompadour; if his eyes had been any farther apart, they would have been off his head; and his mouth was a slit almost as wide. He accentuated his small size by wearing a preposterous suit with huge checks and padded shoulders. But the oddest thing was the way he carried himself, chewing gum and looking glazed as he conducted or beat the cowbells or fired his gun, all with the apparent indifference of any slightly harried professional.

By the time he died in 1965 at fifty-three, Jones had long since ceased to be a commercial entity and had become for many a different kind of embarrassment, an adolescent indulgence it was time to purge. At four or five, under the anarchic influence of *Ding Dong School*'s Miss Frances, who instructed preschool viewers to make ashtrays out of unwanted 78s by submerging them in boiling water, I vainly soaked "All I Want for Christmas (Is My Two Front Teeth)" for hours, not for want of an ashtray but to rid myself forever of that hideous, cloying child's voice. That voice, I now learn, belonged to trumpeter George Rock, whose talents, along with those of the other City Slickers, we are implored by Jones revivalists to venerate. That record notwithstanding, I'm inclined to agree. Rhino's two-disc *The Spike Jones Anthology* and BMG/Catalyst's *Spiked!*, with only five duplications between them, are revelatory and very funny, and also very musical.

Spiked! takes itself more seriously, boasting crafty liner notes by Thomas Pynchon and terrific cover art by Art Spiegelman and a selection too fastidious to be truly illustrative. Except for the belch that ends "Pal-Yat-Chee," there's nothing to irritate my Aunt Sally, but much to keep her in stitches. The set does have an admirably broad historical reach, stretching from a relatively subdued rendition of the traditional New Orleans warhorse "Red Wing" (the Klaxon horn, cowbells, guns, and whistles fall short of the full measure of terrorism) to two exuberant selections from an unfinished 1961 project: the inimitable Raymond Scott's "Powerhouse," with every clanging tone perfectly captured, and "Frantic Freeway," which reconfigures the old "La Conga" rhythm from *Strike Up the Band* as traffic noise. The collection closes with the entire twenty-minute *Nutcracker Suite*, which has its moments, but is too often indistinguishable from the era's many serious childrens' oratorios.

The inevitable hits include "Holiday for Strings," in which the harp arpeggio goes on just long enough to induce giggling and the climactic chorus is sung by a chicken-imitator, and the incomparable "Hotcha Cornia," in which the sound effects get incrementally weirder, always scrupulously applied and never failing to surprise. The rarer highlights are "Minka," George Rock's devastating parody of Harry James and muted brass effects (à la Ellington), most of which is played straight, as if Spike wanted to prove he could lead an authentic swing band (he probably couldn't—the end cries out for the birdaphone); "I Dream of Brownie with the Light Blue Jeans," which takes on Rudy Vallee and Dover Boys glee clubs; and "Our Hour," with a "woof-woof" lyric that falls midway between Stuff Smith's "Ise a-Muggin' " and Frank Sinatra's "Mama Will Bark." The 1952 "Deep Purple" features impressionist Paul Frees's parody of the Billy Eckstine bass-baritone ballad style: the singer snoozes while the band sets off alarms to keep him up, and the over-the-top rhythm never wavers.

Jones was not averse to sending up black artists: the Rhino set includes "You Always Hurt the One You Love," where he pillories the Ink Spots on a Mills Brothers classic, hitting two stones with one bird. Pynchon worries about ethnic offense, but that's hardly an issue when everyone gets a drubbing. On Rhino, Jones takes apart Jessica Dragonette and other airwave divas on "The Glow Worm," Hawaiian music on "Hawaiian War Chant" (the obbligato goes, "Hubba hubba hubba—zoot!"), Jean Sablon on "Morpheus" ("what ze Hildegarde, Cherie?"), grand opera in "Ill Barkio" (reprising an old vaud stunt executed definitively a few years earlier by Joan Davis and Eddie Cantor in *Show Business*) and "William Tell" (which devolves into a Doodles Weaver racing routine). Jones's rudenesses are well displayed throughout Rhino's compilation, never more deliriously than in his biggest hit ever, the ingeniously orchestrated "Cocktails for Two," in which every lyric is given an obbligato sound effect. Spike's deconstruction of the odious "Chloe" should be heard back-to-back with Ellington's idiomatic transformation and his "Dance of the Hours" compared with Disney's dancing elephants.

Three of the funniest records are "My Old Flame," which follows a straight chorus with a second one of traffic noises and a third by Peter Lorre (Paul Frees's finest moment); "None But the Lonely Heart" (a soap opera narrated by Jones's wife Helen Grayco); and "Rhapsody from Hunger(y)," which begins with a voice fearfully cowering in response to every musical phrase. In each of these performances, one is struck over and over by the paradox of how apparent chaos is created by an obsessive regard for timing, timbre, and contrast. Rarely does the laughter overwhelm the pleasure we get from the band's diligence. Jones was every bit as fastidious as the radio propriety he lampooned.

But he unleashed a comic tempest. Mickey Katz, his one rival at mixing parody and musical distinction, spent eighteen months as a City

Slicker; Red Ingle, who went on to subvert the usually impeccable Jo Stafford on "Tim-Tay-Shun," was one of Jones's key singers. In turn, Stafford and Paul Weston went on to create off-key alter egos in Jonathan and Darlene Edwards. Even veteran comics were inspired to greater musical ventures in the '40s, including Groucho Marx (whose "Dr. Hackenbush" is the finest unfilmed musical extravaganza on record) and Jimmy Durante (whose Club Durant spoofs are the truest indication of his wit). Beboppers attacked jazz traditionalists in Chubby Jackson's "Moldy Fig Stomp" and polka enthusiasts attacked beboppers in Freddie Fisher's "Schnickelbop," among countless examples of '40s musical anarchy. Slim Gaillard undermined them all, while Anna Russell and later Peter Schickele, a Spike loyalist, took on the highbrows. Stand-up comics of the '50s made music part of their shtick, none more resourcefully than the Old Philosopher, Eddie Lawrence, who wove his one-liners into a 1956 Top 40 record. Fittingly, the '90s Spike revival was accompanied by other less noted resurrections. After decades of silence, Lawrence returned with a delightful album, *The Jazzy Old Philosopher* (Red Dragon), and Gaillard finally received his due with a dreamily farcical compilation, *Laughing in Rhythm* (Verve). Not a moment too soon. If the '40s deserved to be Spiked, what manner of mayhem befits the fin de siècle? Let the old clowns spur the new.

30 ❖ Charlie Parker
(Flying Home)

In 1945, just twenty years after Louis Armstrong jolted and essentially redefined jazz with his initial recordings as a bandleader, Charlie Parker made his recording debut as a leader and redefined jazz once again. A virtuoso alto saxophonist, Parker was the only musician after Armstrong to influence all of jazz and almost every aspect of American music—its instrumentalists and singers, composers and arrangers. By 1955, his innovations could be heard everywhere: in jazz, of course, but also in rock and roll, country music, film and television scores, and symphonic works. Parker altered the rhythmic and harmonic currents of music, and he produced a body of melodies—or more to the point, a way of melodic thinking—that became closely identified with the idea of jazz as a personal and intellectual modern music.

The new jazz was popularly known as "bebop," a term of dubious origin often cited as the onomatopoeic equivalent of the two-note phrases (frequently the interval of a flatted fifth) that capped many of the melodic figures improvised by the modernists. The term may seem somewhat regrettable today, especially when a newspaper reviewer glibly pigeon-holes a musician as "a bebopper," but, like the terms ragtime, jazz, and swing before it, bebop does indicate a fresh rhythmic quality. And it was the music's rhythmic quality that most distinguished it for the public. By the late '40s, the press and many musicians had established bebop, or bop, as a kind of cult, as though it were less a music than a lifestyle, complete with flashy clothing, dark glasses, berets, beards, secret hand-shakes, and an extensive lingo of jive talk.

Yet bop, as initially presented, was surely the most demanding vir-tuoso music ever to take root in the American vernacular, much as rock and roll, as initially presented, was very likely the most elemental. Both were soon compromised, for predictably opposite reasons. What was naive, direct, and simple in rock and roll gave way to worldly ambition: increased technique, expanded instrumentation, modern chords, self-conscious lyrics. What was rigorous, absolute, and unyielding in bop was toned down by impatience and exhaustion: fewer chords, steadier tem-pos, a firmer backbeat, blues that felt like blues. Bop revolutionized mu-sic, but by pop statistics, which measure revolutions by their impact on mass taste, it was a clique, albeit a large and extensively influential one. Jazz and pop, no matter how symbiotic the relationship, never lodge at the same inn for long, and by the mid-'50s, they waved at each other across a widening distance. The simultaneous arrival of bop and rhythm and blues indicated the polarities to come.

Parker, a devout blues player who found the excesses of r & b honking laughably coarse yet prized communication above all other musical vir-tues, had little use for the bop cult. It implied that his music was too esoteric for outsiders to comprehend. "It's just music," he said. "It's play-ing clean and looking for the pretty notes." Still, unlike Armstrong, Par-ker created his music against a background of more than twenty years of impressive, documented jazz history, and he had to confront not only neglect and the disparagement of a frequently hostile public, but some-times the contempt of a jazz community reluctant to change its ways of doing or hearing things. Although the musical style he helped found soon supplanted the swing era with the bop era, Parker was celebrated chiefly by fellow musicians and a coterie of modern jazz enthusiasts. At the time of his death in 1955 at thirty-four, Parker was arguably the most influential musician in the United States, but he never achieved the pop-ular adulation enjoyed by Armstrong, Ellington, Basie, and other titans of the '30s and '40s.

❖ ❖ ❖

Charlie Parker was born in Kansas City, Kansas, on August 29, 1920. His father, a former vaudeville hoofer, left home before Charlie turned ten, and a few years later his mother leased a house on the other side of the Kaw River, in Kansas City, Missouri. The large house on Olive Street was a short walk from the dance halls and nightclubs that made that city a mecca for jazz during the Depression. Parker's own immersion in music was hesitant at first. After hearing Rudy Vallee play alto sax on the radio, he asked his mother to buy him an alto, but he soon tired of the instrument and lent it to a friend. In high school, he played alto horn and then baritone horn in the school band. Encouraged by the school's bandmaster, Alonzo Lewis, he retrieved his alto sax and began to concentrate on music seriously.

By the time he was sixteen, Parker was playing in Kansas City dance halls, usually with pianist Lawrence Keys, who put together a band called the Deans of Swing, consisting mostly of former students of Alonzo Lewis. Parker dropped out of school and married—and he also began experimenting with the narcotics that were to plague his career and hasten his death. At first, he showed little inclination of having exceptional talent. On at least one occasion, he was hooted off the bandstand by other young musicians for playing in the wrong key. He took such humiliations stoically and resolved to master all the keys and ultimately win over his detractors.

Although he was not old enough to join the musicians' union, he found plenty of work in Kansas City and surrounding areas. For several months, he worked in the Ozarks with a group led by George E. Lee, for which he wrote numerous arrangements. When pianist Jay McShann heard him one night in 1937, he told Parker he sounded different from everyone else in Kansas City, and Parker explained that he had been "woodshedding" in the Ozarks, developing his style. Parker's unique approach reflected the influence of many of the musicians he heard in Kansas City and on records. Some were local favorites and some were on tour with the big bands of Duke Ellington, Cab Calloway, Count Basie, and others. He is said to have learned how to double-time (phrasing at twice the stated tempo) and prepare saxophone reeds to get a hard, edgy sound from Buster "Prof" Smith, an altoist who took Parker under his wing and found him work. He was also enamored of the leading tenor saxophonists of the day, especially Lester Young and Chu Berry.

By 1938, the city fathers had begun to clamp down on crime and corruption in Kansas City, and as a side effect of this, many of the nightclubs closed. Parker found difficulty in getting work, and after an altercation with a cab driver that resulted in his arrest, he decided to leave town. He jumped a freight train to Chicago that fall, and the morning he arrived, Billy Eckstine, Budd Johnson, and a few other musicians heard him at a place called the 65 Club. Parker borrowed an alto from a musician working at the club and, in the words of Eckstine, "I'm telling you he blew the hell off that thing!" Within a week he took a bus to New York, where he worked for three months washing dishes at a Harlem hangout called Jimmy's Chicken Shack so that he could hear the pianist appearing there, Art Tatum.

During his first visit to New York in 1939, Parker became friendly with guitarist Bill "Biddy" Fleet, who instructed him in passing chords and harmonic theory. "We used to sit in the back room at Dan Wall's chili joint . . . and Biddy would run new chords," he recalled. "For instance, we'd find that you could play a relative major, using the right inversions, against a seventh chord, and we played around with flatted fifths." Together they would improvise on songs with challenging chord progressions—"Cherokee," "Get Happy," "All God's Chillun Got Rhythm"—and focus on the higher intervals of chords. Until that time, ninths, elevenths, and thirteenths were generally ignored in jazz improvisation. They were considered dissonant and obscure; the higher you played in the scale, the more likely you were to confuse the listener or, if you were improvising on a popular song, obscure the melody.

Parker also wanted, when improvising, to play through all of a tune's chord changes, as Coleman Hawkins did, but as Lester Young did not. Often Parker and Fleet would practice before going to Monroe's Uptown House, where they participated in late night jam sessions. During one of those practice hours, Parker experienced the revelation that became the basis of his music. He described it this way:

> I remember one night before Monroe's I was jamming in a chili house on Seventh Avenue between 139th and 140th. It was December 1939. Now I'd been getting bored with the stereotyped changes that were being used all the time at the time, and I kept thinking there's bound to be something else. I could hear it sometimes but I couldn't play it.
>
> Well, that night I was working over "Cherokee" and, as I did, I found that by using the higher intervals of a chord as a melody line and backing them with appropriately related changes, I could play the thing I'd been hearing. I came alive.

Shortly afterward, Parker received a telegram notifying him of his father's death, and he returned home to Kansas City. With renewed confidence, he began playing in the local big bands. He briefly toured with

Harlan Leonard and His Rockets, until he was fired for habitual lateness. During that engagement, Parker met the band's pianist and arranger, Tadd Dameron, who shared many of his ideas about harmony and was to become a key figure in the bop movement. Duke Ellington, whose band passed through town, offered Parker a job, but he demurred, preferring to go on the road with his old friend Jay McShann.

It was about this time that Parker acquired his nickname "Yardbird" or "Bird." According to McShann, the band was en route to a concert at the University of Nebraska when one of the cars hit a chicken. Parker jumped out, cradled it in his arms, and took it to their destination, where he had it cooked for dinner. Parker remained with McShann on and off for the next two and a half years and made his first recordings with the band. These include some privately made transcriptions from a Wichita radio session that were first released in 1974, offering significant illumination of Parker's emerging style. Of particular interest are "Body and Soul" (Parker cites an eight-bar episode from Hawkins's celebrated solo on that piece); "Lady Be Good" (he pays tribute to Young); a blues (later titled "Wichita Blues") for which he scored a background from an old religious song he later used as "The Hymn"; and especially "Honeysuckle Rose," in which, finally, we hear Parker's alto erupt in a fluent, melodic reverie that prefigures his maturity.

He also recorded with McShann for Decca Records, and those few sides had a powerful effect on several younger musicians around the country. On "Hootie Blues" (Hootie was McShann's nickname), in addition to demonstrating his ease with the blues, he showed off his wit as an arranger by interpolating a phrase from "Donkey Serenade" as a background riff. On "The Jumpin' Blues," his chorus begins with a characteristic phrase that was later expanded into the famous bop theme, "Ornithology":

Because of the two-year ban on recordings initiated by the American Federation of Musicians, Parker was not to record again in a studio until 1945. In the interim, he had left the McShann band and joined first the Earl Hines Orchestra, for which he played tenor saxophone, and then the Billy Eckstine Orchestra. In the Hines band, he associated with several young musicians who shared his interest in adventurous harmony and a new, more challenging form of jazz. Chief among them was Dizzy Gillespie, whom Parker later referred to as the other half of his heartbeat.

They had first met in Kansas City when Gillespie passed through with Cab Calloway's band, but it was during the period with Hines that they really began to trade and develop ideas.

Private recordings made in a Chicago hotel room in 1943, first released in 1986, capture Parker, on tenor, and Gillespie (accompanied by bassist Oscar Pettiford) exchanging solos on an extended version of "Sweet Georgia Brown," and suggest that Gillespie was more at ease (on that occasion at least) with the new style than Parker, who depends on allusions to the saxophonists who influenced him. Gillespie, however, insists it was Parker who showed "how to get from one note to the next." He argues that because of Parker's innate ability to play blues, he was able to transcend experiments in harmony to produce a finished and convincing new way of playing. Duke Ellington's trumpet soloist Cootie Williams once observed that "every instrument in the band tried to copy Charlie Parker, and in the history of jazz there had never been one man who influenced all the instruments." A similar claim can be made for Armstrong (Williams's own major influence), but for no one else.

By the time Parker had left the Eckstine band and returned to New York, where he appeared on Fifty-second Street with Gillespie, musicians of every stripe were paying close attention to him. Drummers Kenny Clarke and Max Roach shifted rhythmic accents from the skins to the cymbals, replacing the bass drum's thud-thud-thud with the lighter sound of the snare drum and the sibilant pulse of the ride cymbal. Oscar Pettiford, picking up where Ellington's bassist Jimmy Blanton left off, showed how the bass could provide more than the usual cycle of tonic notes. Bud Powell exemplified the new role of the pianist, paring down his accompaniment to a brisk, jagged series of chords and soloing with the linearity of a wind instrument. Sarah Vaughan, who worked with Parker in the Hines and Eckstine bands, developed a progressive vocal style. Almost all of the best young wind players—including such influential men as trumpeters Fats Navarro and Miles Davis, tenor saxophonists Dexter Gordon and Stan Getz, trombonist J. J. Johnson, and clarinetist Buddy De Franco—emulated Parker's almost vibratoless, unmannered tonal production, his rhythmic and harmonic values, and his emphatically emotional melodic ideas, which transcended ground rhythms and chords and attempted to bring the listener into a more attentive and a deeper communion with the music.

In the '40s, the years immediately following Kansas City's decline as a creative center for jazz, no community offered nearly as prestigious and challenging a home for the music than the strip of brownstones on New

York's Fifty-second Street between Fifth and Sixth Avenues. "The Street," as it was known, was a banquet of small clubs, bars, and restaurants snuggled one against the other and spilling over with entertainment. The clubs dated back to Prohibition days and had always welcomed music.

Budd Johnson, a tireless activist for venturesome jazz, helped to get some of the modernists employed there. In 1944, with the recording ban over, he organized the Coleman Hawkins session that featured Gillespie, Pettiford, and Roach and debuted Gillespie's landmark piece, "Woody'n You." When those recordings were made, Parker was back in Kansas City, having returned home after leaving the Eckstine band. A year later, however, Gillespie finally got his opportunity on The Street at the Three Deuces, and Parker was his co-leader; the rhythm section consisted of pianist Al Haig, bassist Curly Russell, and drummer Stan Levey.

With a seating capacity of about 125, the Deuces was usually packed, though many listeners admitted they did not understand the new music, with its often fast, barbed ensemble themes and flaring solos. Still, they found it different and compelling, and they returned for more. The responsiveness between Parker and Gillespie was unlike anything in jazz since the early '20s when King Oliver and Louis Armstrong crossed trumpets at Chicago's Lincoln Gardens. The way they enunciated theme statements was subtle and sure, and the "chase" choruses, which usually consisted of four- or eight-bar exchanges by the horns and sometimes the drums, were delivered at tremendous velocity and were a kind of dazzling musical conversion.

An exceptional example of the Parker-Gillespie unison sound can be heard on "Shaw 'Nuff," one of several stunning pieces recorded at a 1945 Gillespie session. The group included four out of five members of the Three Deuces band—the fifth member, Stan Levey, was replaced by Big Sid Catlett, a brilliant swing era drummer whose style adapted readily. The theme has three parts: an eight-bar rhythmic vamp, a sixteen-bar introductory theme, and the thirty-two-bar main theme, which is loosely based on the harmonies of "I Got Rhythm" with the addition of numerous passing chords. Despite the velocity and rhythmic complexity of the theme, the trumpet and alto sax seem to breathe as one, especially on the slurred notes of the tune's roller-coaster bridge.

The performance is relatively straightforward. After the written material, Parker, Gillespie, and pianist Al Haig each improvise a full chorus. The record ends with the tripartite theme played in reverse order, from theme to vamp, providing a clever symmetrical touch. Parker's solo is mature and authoritative, though his reliance on a series of scales during the bridge is more characteristic of his early playing than that which followed. (Incidentally, the Shaw of the piece's title was Billy Shaw, the booker-manager who helped Gillespie and Parker get work when few other showed faith in them; the female Billie of Parker's blues, "Billie's Bounce," was Shaw's wife.)

During 1945, Parker appeared on several record sessions as a sideman with musicians who were associated with earlier styles, including Tiny Grimes, Clyde Hart, Sir Charles Thompson, and Red Norvo. Parker's playing is always commanding, but the general impression of the music suggests a transitional stage from swing to bop. Finally, on November 26, Parker was offered his own date by Savoy Records. Though strangely bedeviled from beginning to end, the recording session turned out to be a revelation.

Parker had been contracted to record two original blues and two variants on standard songs "Cherokee" and "I Got Rhythm." He hired a quintet that included Bud Powell and Miles Davis. When Powell could not make it, he recruited Argonne Thronton (a.k.a Sadik Hakim), who was then too young to have a union card, and Gillespie, who doubled on piano and trumpet. (Davis found some of the music unfamiliar and difficult.) Parker composed most of the themes that morning, but when he started playing, he was beset with technical problems and spent part of the session searching for new saxophone reeds. Still, he managed to record two classic F major blues, "Billie's Bounce" and "Now's the Time"; extemporized memorably on the chords of "Embraceable You" (retitled "Meandering"); on the chords of "I Got Rhythm" for "Thriving on a Riff" (the piece was later called "Anthropology") and "Warming Up a Riff," and completed the session with the masterpiece, "Koko," based on "Cherokee."

Down Beat's reviewer called the recordings "the sort of stuff that has thrown innumerable impressionable young musicians out of stride, that has harmed many of them irreparably." Such comments, by no means unusual, underscored modern jazz's reputation as a revolutionary and even destructive music. It is not difficult to understand the original effect of "Koko." Even now, decades later, unprepared listeners often respond to it as an explosion of sound, a mad deluge of notes—as listeners did in 1945. On repeated hearings, however, the logic and coherence of Parker's solo is revealed. "Koko" became the point of departure for jazz in the postwar era, having an effect that paralleled Armstrong's "West End Blues" in 1928. Armstrong's record begins with a clarion cadenza and "Koko" begins with an equivalent bang: an eight-bar unison theme of daunting authority, coupled with eight-bar arabesques improvised by Parker and Gillespie. Parker followed with two choruses of extraordinary originality:

♩ = 310

63 B♭   Cmin   F7   B♭

67 Fmin   B♭7   E♭

70   A♭7

73 B♭   C7

76   Cmin   G7(♯9)   Cmin

80 F7   B♭   Fmin

84 B♭7   E♭

87 A♭7   B♭

91 C7   Cmin   F7

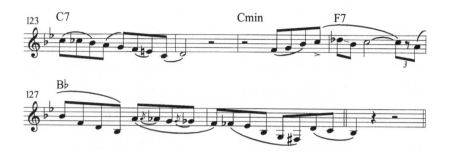

The tempo is brutally fast ($\downarrow$ = 300–310), but despite the speed and the general impression of volatility, Parker colors his solo with ingenious conceits, such as the clanging riff in measures five to eight; the dramatic, arpeggiated figure in bars thirty-three to thirty-four, slightly modulated in bars thirty-seven to thirty-eight; the casual reference to the piccolo obbligato from ''High Society'' and its development at the outset of the second chorus (bars sixty-five to seventy); the falling, chromatic arpeggios in the second bridge (bars ninety-seven to one hundred) and the related follow-up triplets (bars one hundred five to one hundred six); and the ebullient, breathless figure that ties the bridge to the final episode of the solo (bars one hundred ten to one hundred fifteen).

Note, too, the extended rests, the unexpected places where phrases begin and end, and the range of the solo, which climbs to high G (bar nine of the first chorus) and dips down to an E-flat below middle C (bar thirteen of the second chorus [bar seventy-seven in the transcription]). Parker's sound is fat and sensuous yet jagged and hard, utterly unlike the cultivated approach of his great predecessors on alto, Johnny Hodges and Benny Carter.

Within weeks of the ''Koko'' session, Parker and Gillespie made their first trip to Los Angeles to play at Billy Berg's club on Sunset Strip. Many local musicians and radio jockeys dismissed their music as inscrutable, but they were soon converted and an audience for the new jazz grew quickly, turning Central Avenue, the city's black nightclub area, into a stomping ground for modern jazz. During that trip, Parker began recording for Ross Russell's Dial Records, an association that accounted for six important studio sessions between February 1946 and December 1947 in which we can trace his rise, fall, and resurrection during a troubled yet inspired period. In the first session, Parker produced four instant and enduring classics with a septet that included Miles Davis and tenor saxophonist Lucky Thompson: ''Moose the Mooche,'' a characteristic theme; ''Yardbird Suite,'' perhaps Parker's most lyrical composition, and one for which he also wrote a lyric (he called the vocal version ''What Price Love?''; ''Ornithology,'' elaborated by trumpeter Benny Harris from the figure Parker had improvised on McShann's ''The Jumpin'

Blues"; and Gillespie's "A Night in Tunisia," with Parker's dazzling four-bar saxophone break—a jumping-off point for his solo:

This break, played in one breath, utterly confused the rhythm section at the recording date. The musicians had trouble counting the four bars and could not coordinate their reentry. After a couple of cues were missed, Miles Davis, who played trumpet on the session, agreed to count the bars and conduct. The break remains one of jazz's great virtuoso feats. It seems to burst against the bar lines. The highly original alto saxophonist Lee Konitz once expressed amazement that Parker could have invented anything so complex yet perfectly timed.

Perhaps Parker's most influential solo of the period was one recorded at a public concert in the Jazz at the Philharmonic series in March 1946, during a performance of "Lady Be Good." Entering after a theme-statement solo by pianist Arnold Ross, Parker plays two choruses that instantly change the character of the piece, altering a familiar Gershwin ballad into what sounds very much like the blues, as shown in the first sixteen bars, which begin with four notes of Gershwin's melody, then change course with the D:

At the second Dial session, in July, Parker had a mental breakdown triggered by his abuse of inferior-quality narcotics and perhaps the tensions caused by public attacks on his music. The crisis was cruelly captured by the microphones as Parker attempted to play "Lover Man" while reeling around the studio. He considered the release of that record humiliating and a personal betrayal by producer Ross Russell. Yet we dare not dismiss this most controversial of all jazz recordings. Opinions have finally settled on *Free Jazz* and *Ascension*, but "Lover Man" can still get an argument going—does it appeal only to the voyeur in us, or is it musically valid? Why did so many musicians memorize the solo down to the last painful misstep? Undoubtedly, Parker commands attention, even in this state, climaxing faltering phrases with an emotionally devastating arpeggio at measure twenty-four. Frazzled and irrational, he was committed to the California State Hospital in Camarillo, where he was incarcerated for the next six months. He celebrated his release at another Dial session with an intricate, jaunty blues, "Relaxin' at Camarillo," before returning to New York in apparent good health.

Parker's records during the next few years are remarkably consistent, and they exerted incalculable influence. The press tended to harp on bebop's jargon and getups, which became emblematic of what was later tagged "the beat generation," many of whose leading poets, novelists, and painters apotheosized Parker. But musical life in postwar America had also changed radically, and Parker's imprint, though not his name, was ubiquitous. Big bands gave way to small groups, usually quintets and sextets, despite attempts by Gillespie, Woody Herman, and others to integrate bop into their orchestras. Modern jazz was associated less with dancing than intense listening. Rhythm sections grew leaner (rhythm guitar had all but disappeared) and "light" instruments, notably the clarinet, fell out of favor. Improvisors continued to focus on a song's chords rather than its melody, but now they were far more likely to superimpose their own themes in place of the original tunes. More significantly, the harmonies were increasingly broad. Chromaticism was standard; the use of bitonality, whole-tone and diminished scales, and even modality (introduced by George Russell in a piece for the Gillespie orchestra "Cubana Be/Cubana Bop") became common practice. Tempos grew extreme, very fast or very slow. The pulse of the music centered on sixteenth or eighth notes rather than swing's eighth and quarter notes.

Two of Parker's greatest recordings exemplify his genius for enriching the standard material on which most jazz is based, pop songs and blues. At a 1947 Dial session, he recorded two thoroughly different takes on "Embraceable You." The second take, though mesmerizing in its patterns of tension and release, is the more orthodox and its relationship to the original Gershwin theme is obvious. The supremely beautiful first take is also a variation on the theme, but this time Parker barely touches base with Gershwin:

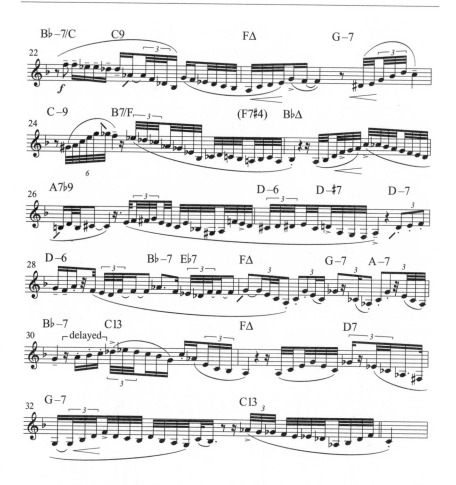

Like his "Bird of Paradise" (based on Jerome Kern's "All the Things You Are" and recorded the same day), "Embraceable You" is so unmistakably a work of Parker's imagination that he might well have given the performance a title of his own. Had he done so, the source material, unlike that of "Bird of Paradise," might not have been recognizable to the average listener.

Parker's earlier "Meandering" and his several subsequent improvisations on "Embraceable You" (including the superb up-tempo "Quasimado") show he was at ease with the song's harmonies. But the other performances have nothing to match the way he develops the Dial solo out of its opening six-note motif. The source of that unforgettable phrase, strangely enough, is a relatively banal pop song called "A Table in the Corner" by Sam Coslow, best known for his scores to a few of Bing Crosby's earliest films. The song was recorded by several bandleaders in 1939, including Artie Shaw, whom Parker admired. Parker imposes the ditty's initial phrase and the first modulation as a melodic template on the Gershwin harmonies, ignoring Gershwin's melody entirely and turning the almost ridiculous into the absolutely sublime. (The importance of Duke Jordan's piano introduction and accompaniment to the overall success of the recording can hardly be overstated.) Parker plays the opening motif five times in all, and variants on it appear throughout the solo. This is one of the slowest performances in jazz (less than $\downarrow$ = 56), and it is laced with thirty-second notes. When he develops the six-note motif into a two-measure phrase (bars six to seven), imposing a triplet over an already rapid-fire figure, he runs out of breath. But not again; for the rest, his phrasing is so supple and relaxed and songful that when he winds down with a legato two-measure configuration (bars twenty-seven to twenty-eight), only the listener is left breathless.

The second example of Parker's ability to bring new life to overworked material is from a 1948 Savoy session and is one of his finest blues performances, "Parker's Mood." Once again, there are two entirely different takes; both begin with a heraldic two-bar phrase that constitutes the only written material in the performance:

(Intro, mm. 1–2)

The earlier take has a marvelous eccentric quality, as Parker slowly pokes his way through the most familiar of jazz terrains, a B-flat blues. Note the two sudden thirty-second note arpeggios followed by a series of modulating triplets in bars eight to eleven of his first chorus:

By contrast, the later take, the one originally issued, has a relatively glossy perfection, as Parker brings together a lexicon of blues phrases, new and old, for a penetrating performance. He presses ahead with charismatic authority, as though he had no doubt about the direction in which the solo was going:

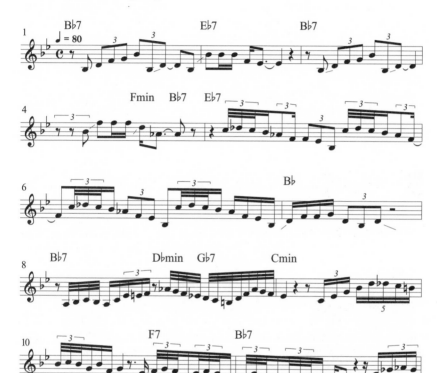

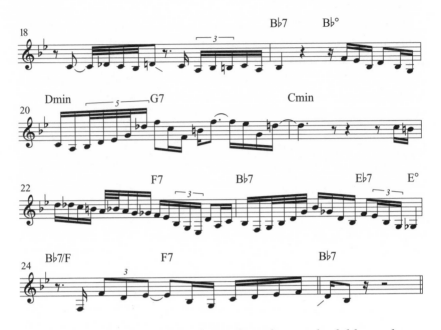

He begins with four bars of tantalizingly standard blues phrases, though his slightly acrid tone and emphasis lends them startling immediacy. In the fifth measure, Parker introduces a series of repeated arpeggios, each leading with a C above middle C, in an insistent manner that is strongly reminiscent of Louis Armstrong in, for example, his climactic chorus on "West End Blues." There is a ruminative quality to the solo as Parker moves from the upper register (note the little ascending figure at the beginning of the second chorus) to the lower register (the downward slurs in bars five and six of the second chorus). After a spare and worthy interlude by pianist John Lewis, Parker returns for a final chorus, which he closes on a major second, before repeating the heraldic phrase with which the performance began.

Parker made so many notable recordings, it is difficult to choose among them. "Chasin' the Bird" and "Ah-Leu-Cha" stand out as the only pieces in which he wrote contrapuntal themes. "Kim" is an exceptional variation on "I Got Rhythm," and "Buzzy," "Cheryl," "Bluebird," and "Barbados," are a few of his approaches to the blues. His solos on "Bird Gets the Worm," "Crazeology," "Little Benny," "Klact-oveeseds-tene," and "Klaunstance" are unrivaled examples of emotionally vital yet overwhelmingly bright inventions that take their structure but not their character from the harmonic contours of popular songs.

By the time most of these recordings were made, however, Parker's professional life, and that of most musicians, was changing. In New York, for example, the clubs along The Street welcomed Gillespie's 1946–47 big band, and welcomed Charlie Parker's 1947 quintet with Miles Davis. But within five years The Street was in trouble as a haven for jazz of any style; the audiences weren't there any more. New clubs sprang up over on Broadway to accommodate the modernists: The Royal Roost (which failed), Bop City (which failed), and finally Birdland, named in honor of Parker, which succeeded and lasted for a decade or so. But in midtown Manhattan, one club invariably replaced several. And Parker, because of his increasingly erratic conduct—years of addiction and riotous living were taking their toll—was banned from Birdland before his death.

Still, by 1949, Parker's acceptance by the best and brightest musical artists of his generation was complete. One could hardly ask for a better example than the thrilling concert, unearthed after more than forty years and released as *Charlie Parker and the Stars of Modern Jazz at Carnegie Hall, Christmas 1949* (Jass). On this relaxed yet inspired evening, key members of the first and second divisions of modern jazz offer a near-perfect statement of what distinguishes their music from the swing jazz that preceded it and the hard and cool variations that followed. What impresses is not the velocity of the music, but the level of invention and daring—and the sensational ease and clarity with which the players handle it.

Bill Minor, who assembled the material from various collectors (the show was recorded backstage and excerpted for Voice of America broadcasts), points out that the concert was not widely noted at the time. Not a single New York daily or jazz magazine reviewed the evening, which was produced by a formidable trio of advocates, Leonard Feather, Monte Kay, and Symphony Sid. Yet the lineup, in addition to Parker, included Bud Powell, Miles Davis, Max Roach, Serge Chaloff, Sonny Stitt, Stan Getz, Kai Winding, Sarah Vaughan, Lee Konitz, Red Rodney, Al Haig, Roy Haynes, and Lennie Tristano, who at thirty was the oldest in the bunch. Not the least enticing pleasure afforded by its discovery is the chance to compare live performances with famous recordings of the same pieces, most of them waxed within a year of the concert.

"Move" is particularly fascinating when compared with the Miles Davis Nonet version—it's a head-solos-head performance, without ensemble riffs or arranging of any kind. Though Davis had long since displayed the rudiments of his spare lyrical style on records, he shows here he was still in thrall to Gillespie as he rifles through the chords with lightning prolixity. "Hot House" indicates he was listening closely to Fats Navarro, too. His performance was anything but cool that night. Bud Powell's gambits, especially in his third chorus of "Move," are astonishing, and on "Hot House," he too borrows a page from Gillespie.

You'd have to turn the metronome up to burnout to approximate the tempos on the opening pieces. The problem bop presented to many jazz fans was a matter of relativity: they couldn't hear fast enough to recognize the abundance of melody. But they recognized, as musicians did, that the blowing format was a dead end, no matter how overwhelming the blowers. On each piece, the soloists proceed in the same order, like a batting lineup.

Parker's twenty-five-minute set is one of the most treasurable of his concert performances, preserving the best playing on record by his quintet with Red Rodney. By 1949, Parker's inventions on "Koko," "Ornithology," and "Now's the Time" had been thoroughly assimilated into the diction of jazz improvisation, yet his every phrase in these versions is fresh and vigorous, with barely a nod to the recordings. His performance of "Cheryl" is superior to the Savoy version and is renowned for his wicked paraphrase of Louis Armstrong's "West End Blues" cadenza. "Bird of Paradise" makes no more reference to the Jerome Kern source material than the Dial recording and weaves into its balladic spell such incongruous asides as "I'm Popeye the Sailor Man."

More impressive are his celebrational renditions of masterworks from the "Koko" session, a mere four years to the month earlier. The head of "Now's the Time" is partly refashioned, and the first chorus is as spellbinding (and undoubtedly would have been as widely imitated) as the original. But this time we are allowed to hear him play additional choruses, hitting a dozen trademark licks in what amounts to an autobiographical blues. "Koko," as expected, pushes the metronome into red alert and in some ways outpaces the original. Parker plays variations on his benchmark 1945 solo, paced here by Al Haig, who runs "Cherokee" changes at him as though he, Haig, were an old retainer nervous about losing his impetuous ward. The drum solo is gone, replaced by a startling third chorus from Parker, extending instead of quoting the "High Society" lick. It builds to a series of fierce permutations in the bridge that made the Carnegie Hall audience cheer. What did people think when they filed out that Christmas night? Did their feet ever touch the ground? Did they think it would go on like that forever?

For the twenty-nine-year-old Parker, the end came soon enough. His decline was marked by a determined effort to achieve public acceptance and a contrary desire to push further into uncharted territory. He recorded and toured with a string ensemble that earned him a modest hit, the radiant "Just Friends." But the arrangements were poor, and in the early '50s he commissioned stronger charts from Jimmy Mundy, Gerry Mulligan, and George Russell, though they were never recorded except informally at clubs and in concert. At the same time, intrigued by modern composition and frustrated by his limited scoring skills, he asked Edgard Varese to take him as a student. He died shortly afterward, in 1955, grieving over the death of his youngest child, prematurely aged by drugs and booze, and apparently dislocated from his own genius. "Bird lives!" the hipsters crowed. In death, he had been transfigured into the biggest jazz cult of all—an irony he would not have enjoyed.*

31 ❖ Dizzy Gillespie (The Coup and After)

The romantic disposition we reserve for geniuses who live fast, die young, and usually leave ravaged corpses must be something of a trial for those who persevere. Between 1945 and 1950, two gods dominated American music: Bird and Diz. Every young jazz musician and compos- er, regardless of instrument, emulated them. Pop arrangers and film composers and conservatory students entertained themselves by appro- priating the hip chords, cool dissonances, and inwit of bop. As the his- tory of the movement became elaborated and mythologized, genesis was located at two Harlem after-hours clubs, Monroe's and Minton's, where Bird and Diz merrily intimidated the second-rate or out-of-date, often in collusion with drummer Kenny Clarke (credited with coining the term "bebop") and pianist Thelonious Monk.

Of the four, only Dizzy Gillespie was an instant celebrity. He enter- tained; he mocked the seriousness of the venture; he insisted that jazz was evolving and not rebelling. It was actually doing both: as late as 1956, Hugues Panassie assured readers of his *Guide to Jazz* that Gillespie "abandoned jazz and launched out into bop . . . with hardly any swing left, and in slow tempo, a sad, declamatory manner which has none of the 'singing' tone of jazz musicians." (It is customary for reactionary critics to dismiss visionaries for the heretical crime of having "aban- doned jazz"—compare the attacks on Cecil Taylor.) Clarke, who might have attained the most secure position of all, forsook a safe haven in the Modern Jazz Quartet and settled in Europe. Monk, disparaged for years,

---

*I am indebted to Thomas Owens, a leading Parker scholar (and the author of *Bebop: The Music and the Players*, 1995), for the use of musical transcriptions from his thesis, *Charlie Parker: Techniques of Improvisation* (1974).

made the cover of *Time* in 1964, but spent the last years of his life co-cooned in silence. Parker ruptured, an old man of thirty-four.

As the legend of Bird flourished, Gillespie was relegated to a supporting role in the drama he helped create. He was, after all, a working musician, appearing nightly, ruddy-cheeked and irrepressible, not the stuff of which legends are made. He often credited Lorraine, his wife of fifty-two years, as the shield who kept him from the epidemic of drugs that took Parker and so many of their colleagues. Or he'd laugh and say, "I was always scared of needles." In the studio icebox of his Englewood home, he kept a supply of nonalcoholic beer; occasionally he smoked pot. Once an old friend in Florida gave him some, which he smoked on returning to New Jersey. "It made me feel like this," he said, pushing himself up on his toes and miming the action of a flutist, "so I sent him a flute." No note, just the flute. Gillespie let nothing interfere with his concentration on music, however. Coasting was not in his nature.

He was my introduction to modern jazz; I saw him on a triple bill at the Village Gate in Greenwich Village, in the mid-'60s: the Gerry Mulligan Quartet (with, if memory serves, Jim Hall on guitar), comedian Dick Gregory, and the Dizzy Gillespie Quintet. I soon came to revere Mulligan's music, but my initial impression of his coolly glazed sound was of trying to climb a glass wall, and neither the European classics, Dixieland, nor rock and roll—my musical education to date—had prepared me for getting a toehold. Gregory was funny, but I recall only one line of his routine, something about his parents instructing him not to eat in the bathroom, and his rejoinder that the family toothbrushes resided there all day long. The Gillespie band riveted me, and my recollection of his performance is strangely vivid after nearly thirty-five years. With his first number, the temperature of the room went way up. Yet I didn't really "get it" any more than I did Mulligan. What brought me into the fold were the comic routines that ensued. Dizzy announced he would introduce the members of the band, then introduced them to each other. The joke wasn't nearly as funny as the context in which it was so expertly delivered. I had assumed that modern jazz was a fairly arcane discipline, coherent if you knew the language, but essentially serious. Gillespie's comedy, not unlike Peter Schickele's (P.D.Q. Bach), was unabashed, abundant in absurd postures, double takes, and caustic asides, and because of them, the music was unintimidating.

Gillespie is an American paradox in the manner of Louis Armstrong or of Constance Rourke's "Negro minstrel"—a quintessentially critical and innovative artist who plays, often superbly, the clown. Of musicians of his stature, only Armstrong and Fats Waller were his equal at walking the tightrope from jazz complexity to inspired silliness and back. Yet

Armstrong and Waller played a relatively accessible music. Gillespie was a fearsome modernist—the man who helped invent jazz modernism in part to repudiate the very entertainment values that were thought to have dimmed the music's power during the commercially extravagant swing era. He proffered a physical trait, like Armstrong's teeth and Waller's girth, to emphasize the humor: beachball cheeks (he wore out the restraining muscles, a condition now known to medical science as "Gillespie's Pouches"). And he had a strange-looking instrument—a personally designed trumpet with an upturned bell that, he insisted, let him hear himself better. Like all comedians, he was forgiven a degree of irreverence: at the White House he addressed the Carters as "your majesties" and importuned the president to join him and Max Roach in chanting "Salt Peanuts."

But the humor, the professional bemusement, were at least in part a pretense and a defense. His extraordinary fame did not extend to his art. Gillespie never had a hit record, and though he succeeded in packing nightclubs, he was never a prominent concert draw. Despite occasional attempts at broader commercial acceptance (novelties for Dee Gee in the early '50s; rock rhythms in the late '60s; the overproduced GRP glitz of the '80s), his muse was unforgiving. He could not simplify an art that found beauty in disciplined complexity, though his scarifying flights of improvisational fancy were often thrillingly accessible.

Gillespie was from the small southern town of Cheraw, South Carolina, where blacks grew up to be sharecroppers and whites grew up to abuse them. With a borderline education and a musical talent sufficiently acute to win him a big city conservatory scholarship, he put his trumpet in a brown paper bag and went north, where first he made himself a pesty presence of the swing era and soon thereafter one of the figures most closely associated with the word "modern." How did this happen? What wellspring produced the intricately subdivided rhythms that altered the conception of swing from a suave and dependable four beat to the rustling winds of modern jazz, tabulated in the mind because the foot can't keep up? Gillespie once said he might have gotten the idea for "Groovin' High" from a childhood matinee serial (starring Yakima Canutt, he thought) that had "Whispering" as the theme song—a poetic and perhaps calculated juxtaposition of eras and cultures that agreeably disguises the scope of his sorcery.

Not that Gillespie was shy about acknowledging specific musical influences. On the contrary, his sometimes embarrassingly candid interviews are usually marked by a rare and loving display of gratitude—toward Roy Eldridge, "the messiah of our generation," or Monk, whose sixth chords he delineated so animatedly you'd think he himself was a mere bystander to the reharmonization of jazz in the '40s. He revered

Louis Armstrong, with whom he played an unforgettable "Umbrella Man" on TV, and Mary Lou Williams, whose career he tried to revive at the 1957 Newport Jazz Festival, and admired Bobby Hackett, his neighbor and jamming partner for several years in Queens. But about no one was he more expansive than Charlie Parker. They were different, and they had differences between them, but Gillespie's loyalty to Parker was constant. "He showed us how to get from note to note," he once said. On another occasion, "We used to kiss each other on the mouth." People tried to put them at odds—Gillespie was blamed for leaving Los Angeles when Bird was hospitalized at Camarillo and resented for his fame. Indeed, the sight of his obituary on the covers of all four New York dailies brought to mind the fact that only one printed any notice at all of Parker's death.

Gillespie never seemed as mystifying as Parker because, like John Coltrane (who apprenticed in Gillespie's 1952 sextet, playing a grim solo on "We Love To Boogie"), he developed his style in full view. His absolute command of the trumpet was apparent on Lionel Hampton's 1939 "Hot Mallets," recorded with many of the elders—Charlie Christian, Coleman Hawkins, Benny Carter, Milt Hinton—who would play major roles in his career. After three years in Cab Calloway's band, during which he developed as a composer and arranger, he brought the after-hours workshop sounds into daylight for the first time on an obscure Les Hite recording of "Jersey Bounce." For the next two years, his activities were obscured by a recording ban instigated by the musicians' union. By 1944, the Hite recording had been forgotten, so when he debuted "Woody'n You" on a Hawkins date it was hailed by some as the first recorded example of modern jazz. For others it was primarily a very good Hawkins performance, and Dizzy's solo a personal coup rather than a preview of the new world order. The neglected "Jersey Bounce" merits a closer look.

Except for Gillespie's work, it is a negligible effort, but that's one of the reasons it's so instructive. The song "Jersey Bounce" was introduced by Tiny Bradshaw and recorded by Earl Hines in 1941, turned into a number-one hit by Benny Goodman in March 1942, and covered by several other bands, including those of Jimmy Dorsey, Shep Fields, Red Norvo, and Jan Savitt. Hite's 1942 version undoubtedly had the lowest sales of any, but it has the surest place in history because of the trumpet solo. Hite's version consists of three choruses infused with uneventful solos in the idiom of the day on tenor sax, piano, and guitar. After the second chorus, a four-measure transition sets the stage for Gillespie's improvisation, which is one of those defining musical moments when it seems as though a window has opened onto the future. Earlier examples include the triumphant élan of Armstrong's performance on Oliver's "Chimes Blues" or Bix Beiderbecke's cooling eight-bar episode on Whiteman's leaden "Love Nest." The distinction between Gillespie's sixteen bars and the playing that precedes and follows it can suffice as a primitive but emphatic example of what modern jazz offered in pyrotechnical expressiveness and thoroughgoing originality.

Gillespie's solo begins with a spare melodic figure of which the first two notes are separated from the rest by a dramatic pause (bars one and two); his second phrase (bars three and four) expands that initial idea with triplets, breaching the orchestra's plodding four/four time while suggesting a nearly aloof authority. His next figure is a dazzling, frenetic arpeggio that begins with high notes and continues uninterrupted for four measures (through bar eight), ending precisely on the first beat of the ninth measure. The second half of his solo is a more stately version of the first half, conveying something of Gillespie's penchant for symmetrical form. This is Gillespie in embryo; the full force of his trumpet playing and his mature conception would be revealed in the mid-'40s in dozens of performances that constitute the most innovative body of trumpet playing since Armstrong. But it's a crucial step in his progress— and in the progress of jazz itself—during the seven years between his Eldridge-inspired solo on "Hot Mallets" and his first recordings as a leader.

At the "Woody'n You" session, Gillespie brought along another tune, "Salt Peanuts," that Hawkins recorded months later without Gillespie's participation (he was away touring as music director and soloist with the Billy Eckstine Orchestra). At his first session as a leader, in January 1945, Gillespie offered his own version of the tune, in the company mostly of advanced swing players. Musicians must have wondered what kind of reformation *that* was supposed to manifest. Was "Salt Peanuts" a jive tune, a "rhythm changes" spin-off with a funny interval, a novelty vocal? On May 11, four days after Germany surrendered, Gillespie recorded it again, this time with Parker and Al Haig and an Ellingtonian scheme of intricate transitional passages. If the subsequent release, in early 1946, of Parker's "Koko" let everyone know it was time to circle the wagons, "Salt Peanuts" sent mixed signals: it challenged jazz conventions, but with prankish burlesque that diverted attention from the complexities "Koko" underscored. Those early records by Gillespie and Parker heralded the postwar era. Thad Jones, one of countless young musicians awakened by the Gillespie-Parker assault, heard a side from the May 11 date over the radio in a tent on Guam, and along with the other soldiers waiting for transport home, fell out laughing in affinity: "They spoke our minds," he recalled forty years later.

❖ ❖ ❖

In 1946, Gillespie signed with RCA and organized a full orchestra. He recorded "Manteca," one of the most important records ever made in the United States, at the band's third session. With justifiable immodesty, Gillespie told an interviewer for a PBS documentary series, *Routes to Rhythm*, "It was similar to a nuclear weapon when it burst on the scene. They'd never seen a marriage of Cuban music and American music like that before." If "Manteca" had done nothing but demonstrate that such a marriage was possible, its impact on Latin music and jazz would be incalculable. In a sense, the salsa movement of the '70s can be traced back to that performance, recorded on December 22, 1947. The oddest thing about "Manteca" is how little of Gillespie's trumpet is featured. Yet in two eight-bar statements, he offers a comprehensive foundation for modern jazz, while auguring a direction in jazz improvisation—the use of modes instead of chords—that wouldn't be popularly assimilated for more than a decade, when Miles Davis began using modes on such recordings as *Milestones* and *Kind of Blue*.

Practically every moment in "Manteca," which is a breath longer than three minutes, rewards scrutiny. But before we look too closely, perhaps the obvious should be noted: the key virtue of the recording, which assured its reputation as an instant classic and warrants lasting admiration, lies less in details than in the work's overall luster. Few of the progressive elements in the performance were genuinely new in 1947—bass vamps, modes, multiple rhythms, tritones, and other aspects predate jazz history. Gillespie himself had made earlier attempts at fusing Afro-Cuban rhythms and jazz, including his most famous composition, "A Night in Tunisia" (which is relatively conventional in its approach to rhythm and harmony), and "Cubana Be"/"Cubana Bop," his collaboration with composer-theorist George Russell and Cuban drummer Chano Pozo, a two-part composition recorded eight days before "Manteca" that is considerably more advanced in its use of the same elements. "Manteca," however, had the requisite emotional and intellectual allure to successfully effect a Cuban American fusion.

The origin of "Manteca" is well known. Gillespie became interested in Cuban music in 1939, shortly after the veteran Cuban-born trumpeter Mario Bauza encouraged Cab Calloway to hire him. When Gillespie started his own big band, he asked Bauza to recommend a Cuban percussionist. Bauza introduced him to Chano Pozo, a thirty-one-year-old immigrant already famous in Havana as an entertainer, composer, and brawler. Pozo spoke little English, but he had no trouble communicating musically with Gillespie, who was extremely receptive to his ideas. While touring California, Pozo came to him with a suggestion for a new piece. It would open with three layered rhythms, introduced one at a time. First, a B-flat-7 bass vamp—not a customary four-beat bass walk, but a singular melodic-rhythmic figure:

Then (at measure seven of the 1947 recording) the saxophones enter with another vamp, a simple B-flat octave stretch:

Finally (at measure thirteen), the trombones enter with a third B-flat-7 melodic-rhythmic figure:

As Gillespie tells the story, he wrote out the three riff figures and realized he didn't have a finished piece of music. Missing was a bold harmonic interlude that would play off the rhythms and give the piece variety. He devised a sixteen-bar bridge, a harmonic oasis that dramatizes Pozo's vamps by providing contrast and furnishing a compelling basis for improvisation. Gillespie gave the various parts to his staff arranger Gil Fuller, who fleshed out the big band orchestration. "Manteca" had its premiere at Carnegie Hall on September 29, 1947, and was an immediate success. Since the birth of jazz nearly half a century before, musicians had attempted to fuse it with Latin rhythms and forms. Jelly Roll Morton asserted the importance of "seasoning" music with "tinges of Spanish," Louis Armstrong recorded "The Peanut Vendor," and numerous bandleaders from north and south of the Gulf of Mexico, including such popular entertainers as Paul Whiteman and Xavier Cugat, attempted to blend the musical cultures. One reason "Manteca" was so successful is that it doesn't disguise or vitiate its dual patrimony. The jazz and Cuban aspects—plush harmonies, passionate rhythms—exist side by side with equal integrity.

As heard on the 1947 recording, the performance unfolds as follows. The introduction consists of the three vamps (measures one through fourteen) and an eight-measure Gillespie improvisation in the same mixolydian mode as the rhythmic figures—played in the key of B-flat-7 in concert, but written:

In these eight measures, which connect Pozo's vamps to the interlude that sets up the actual melody, Gillespie provides a dazzling if seemingly offhanded display of virtuosity. His earlier piece, "A Night in Tunisia," included a stunning four-bar break (in which the entire ensemble except for the soloist drops out) between written theme and improvisation. Gillespie's first appearance on "Manteca" isn't a break; the ensemble continues to simmer while he plays so that the soloist and ensemble carom into the interlude together. Yet it functions similarly to a break, providing transition while raising to a fevered pitch the excitement generated by the vamps (and further heightened by the vocal shout, "Manteca! Manteca!"). One quality that distinguishes Gillespie from great trumpeters who preceded him is his ability to think coherently at breakneck tempos. These eight measures last only ten seconds, sustaining from first note to last the headlong rush required to cap the intro and set up the next episode. Yet the statement glows with a relaxed logic and wit.

Gillespie's first two notes are enticing. By beginning on the first beat of the measure with a quarter note, G, he underscores the rhythmic feeling of the performance (the saxophones and trombones also enter with first-beat quarter notes); the leap to E provides a rather colloquial two-note setup for the following chromatic run that descends, via a characteristic triplet, to the E one octave below before dropping to a B-flat in a tritone, or flat fifth—the infamous interval that provided one of bebop's lines of harmonic demarcation (Eddie Condon famously wisecracked, "The boppers flat their fifths, we drink ours") before it became accepted as a blue note scarcely more alarming than a minor third. The long rest is a masterstroke of symmetrical balance, and a lull before the torrent of quadruplets and quintuplets that advance unabated until he hits the sustained high A (the sixth of the C-7 scale and another favored Gillespie interval). The bluesy finish ends with the shrewd clang of a flat ninth, befitting the clashing return of the ensemble.

After a six-measure interlude (two measures by the winds, four by
the rhythm section), we hear the theme proper. Now the piece becomes
a fairly orthodox jazz performance, notwithstanding the marvelous rumbling of Chano Pozo's conga drums. The stout rhythms of the melody
represent a perfect rapprochement between the Cuban influence and jazz
riffs, but they are molded into the standard thirty-two-bar AABA pop
song format, except that the bridge (the B section) is sixteen measures
instead of the usual eight. The A parts employ commonplace "rhythm"
changes (so named because of their codification in the song, "I Got
Rhythm"), while the bridge is an original pattern by Gillespie built on a
progression of dominant seventh chords. In this chorus, the reeds play
the first half of the bridge and Gillespie plays the second. The gorgeous,
entreating quality of his sound might cause a modern listener to wonder
at the accusations of "thin tone" that plagued Gillespie for much of his
career. His volatile style demanded a relatively sleek sound, and though
some of Gillespie's disciples developed fatter or more personalized approaches to timbre (Fats Navarro or Miles Davis, respectively), Gillespie's timbre was unfailingly vigorous and evocative, if never grand or
indulgent.

After another rhythmic interlude, this one of ten measures, the second
and last chorus of the theme is played, beginning with a sixteen-bar tenor
saxophone solo by Big Nick Nicholas. Though robust and generally effective, this solo contains, for me, the record's one flaw. Nicholas begins
its second half by paraphrasing Rodgers and Hart's "Blue Moon." The
practice of quoting other songs in the course of improvisation has a long
honorable history in jazz; Gillespie's youthful "Hot Mallets" solo begins
with an effective reference to Irving Berlin's "Cheek to Cheek." Yet perhaps because everything else in "Manteca" bubbles with creativity, the
"Blue Moon" quotation seems conspicuously retrograde. Perhaps, too,
the familiarity of the harmonies in this section warrants an especially
inventive response. The return of Gillespie's bridge is thus all the more
welcome. This time, the first half is played by the brasses, and Gillespie's
half is a canny variation on the written material:

He begins on F, pushing it an octave to high F. The fact that F in the key of B-flat-7 is a major fifth may remind the listener that the introduction also began with a major fifth (G in the key of C-7). What follows is a headier version of the written material, made increasingly dynamic by three well-placed triplets, the first of which (measure eleven) comes on the heels of a rapid B-flat/G turn. He paces himself with beautifully articulated eighth notes (measures thirteen through fifteen), leading up to the highlight of the passage—the crucial last measure. Measure sixteen displays, in summary form, the harmonic changes bebop brought to jazz. It's also pure Dizzy Gillespie, exemplifying the kind of ideas that have inspired generations of trumpeters. The indicated chord is G-7, but Gillespie plays a tritone substitution, suggesting a D-flat-7 chord instead. The centerpiece of the measure is the D-flat, which he anticipates with a flat ninth, A-flat, and resolves with his final notes, B and C. Today, that conceit serves as an appealing touch of spice; in the '40s, it epitomized a way of playing that was vilified as bombastic, divisive, and worse. In this measure, we stand at the door through which Gillespie, Parker, Thelonious Monk, Miles Davis, George Russell, Gil Evans, and others brought modern harmonic ideas to jazz. Beyond that, "Manteca" allows us to glimpse the coming affinity with world rhythms and scalar improvisation.

The Gillespie recordings and documented concerts by his '40s orchestra are incomparable, though he fronted several equally great big bands in later years—by all rights, his 1957 Newport performance of "Cool Breeze" should have done as much for him as "Diminuendo and Crescendo in Blue" had done for Ellington the previous summer. The number of important musicians he introduced and nurtured is legion, and includes Chano Pozo, George Russell, John Lewis, Milt Jackson, Ray Brown, James Moody, Jimmy Heath, John Coltrane, Slide Hampton, Lee Morgan, Leo Wright, Lalo Schifrin, Kenny Barron, Jon Faddis, Danilo Perez, and David Sanchez. Yet for all that he accomplished in so many areas of modern music, nothing surpasses the casual precision and diverse colors of his trumpet playing: from the flaming splendor of "Night in Tunisia" in the '40s to the serpentine shine of "My Heart Belongs to Daddy" (as fine a straight mute trumpet solo as exists on records) to the muzzy, sometimes brittle, and often scalar inventions of the duets with Max Roach in the '80s. He was invariably game when an ambitious canvas was prepared for him, and at least on one occasion, the concerto was worthy of its ingenious soloist.

Gillespiana Suite, the five-movement concerto grosso Lalo Schifrin wrote for him in 1960, elicited an inspired performance that his disciple Jon Faddis has described as a culmination of his work in the middle and late '50s, when his timbre grew mellow and he developed a delayed affinity for the blues. Yet as that period was often ignored or patronized as a popularizing aftermath to his revolutionary work in the previous decade, *Gillespiana* was long lost to critical discussion until Faddis's Carnegie Hall Jazz Band, which Schifrin conducted, gave it a fresh airing in 1995.

Gillespiana was highly regarded at the time of its release and often cited by people who were drawn to jazz because of it. Indeed, 1960 was a good year for Gillespie. In late fall, Verve announced a yearlong promotion by offering free copies of his *A Portrait of Duke Ellington* to the first 5000 who wrote in for it, but queries ran many times that, and in the end everyone got it for a buck. Two weeks later, combining Gillespie's quintet and an ensemble of brasses and rhythm, Schifrin, who played piano in the quintet, supervised the recording of *Gillespiana*. The results encouraged the label to seek a date at Carnegie for a formal debut. No prime-time bookings were available, so the March 4, 1961, concert was called "Genius at Midnight," with a bronze head of Gillespie prominently displayed. Auxiliary highlights included premieres of Gillespie's "Kush" and Schifrin's variations on "A Night in Tunisia" ("Tunisian Fantasy").

Gillespie also made news that year when Tulane University canceled a contract with his quintet because he wouldn't replace Schifrin with a black pianist—his manager, Joe Glaser, and the union backed him up in refusing to refund Tulane's deposit. He broke the house records at San Francisco's Jazz Workshop in the summer and returned for an unprecedented eight-week booking. The fan-driven competition between Gillespie and Miles Davis, who unseated him in the *Down Beat* critics' poll in 1958 and 1959, was briefly decided in Gillespie's favor: they tied in 1960, and Gillespie won in 1961 by one vote. But the victory was illusory, as was the success of *Gillespiana*, which triggered a second work by Schifrin, *The New Continent*, that (with Benny Carter conducting) debuted at Monterey in 1962 and was recorded a few weeks later—it wasn't released for three years. Again the reviews were enthusiastic, but by 1965, jazz was rent on one side by rock and on the other by the avant-garde, and Gillespie was no longer at the center of anything. Even Davis's sales began to flag.

The neglect isn't hard to understand. Few recordings in jazz history or in the LP era had the romantic provenance of the collaborations between Davis and Gil Evans. Everyone wanted to follow in their steps and many tried, even Louis Armstrong and most especially Gillespie and Schifrin. (At least they had the satisfaction of beating Davis and Evans to Carnegie by more than two months.) Gillespie first encountered Schifrin in 1956, on a tour of Buenos Aires—a lucky break for Schifrin, who was living in Paris at the time and only visiting South America—and offered him a job. Schifrin, who had won arranging and piano prizes in Argentina in his teens, took him up in 1960 and spent three years in the quintet. Despite of or because of his diverse education and background (his father was concertmaster of the Buenos Aires Philharmonic and his teachers included Messaian and a student of Schoenberg's), he was no more able to match Evans's indigenous voicings than Gillespie could match Davis's dark moody drama.

The Davis-Evans records helped define the period. In contrast, *Gillespiana* was a tribute to Gillespie, a summing up rather than a manifesto, a concerto that derives its power from provoking the soloist while suggesting the range or his historical achievement in big bands, cutting-edge harmonies, Afro-Cuban rhythms, and more. Yet it successfully avoids pastiche, sustaining genuine excitement in the dialogue of ensemble and soloists (how promising saxophonist and flutist Leo Wright was in those years, before he relocated to Europe). Nor does he fail to create memorable tableaux that, absent Evans's cloudlike chords, have an arresting quality of their own—for example, the flute and trombones and cannily altered changes of "Blues" or the elephant shrieks of "Africana." In the latter, Gillespie begins his solo in what is for him the lower register and plots an insightful, responsive muted statement over a dramatic landscape of conga and timbale rhythms and brass tuttis, while reacting to a contrary theme played by the ensemble. His imagination never falters.

Gillespie's postrevolutionary years are packed with stellar recordings, but the irony of his career is that, as his fame increased, the critical regard for his current work declined—not because of a falling-off in his music, but because of the first law of cultural revolutions: The radical who doesn't continue to fan the flames of revolt will soon be consigned to the limbo of "living legend." At the age of thirty, Gillespie had changed jazz and was confronted with the prospect of earning a living. Had he burned himself out in his prime like Charlie Parker, he would have joined the ranks of the jazz saints. Instead, he endured. As audiences grew more enamored of younger players who, building on his foundation, pushed the music to new frontiers, Gillespie took on an ambassadorial role, doing talk shows and good-will tours. He never lost the respect of serious listeners, but he didn't always have their full attention, not even for the dazzling take-no-prisoners jam sessions, *Sonny Side Up* and *For Musicians Only*, or the crooning warmth and brassy bark of his trumpet on *On the French Riviera* (the sexy "No More Blues") and *Something Old, Something New* or the bottomless bag of expressive tricks (many of them premodern enough to fully justify his claim to being an evolutionist) brought to bear in album-length collaborations with Benny Carter, Roy Eldridge, Oscar Peterson, and Count Basie.

In his final years, often with the help of Faddis, Gillespie organized unexpectedly aggressive bands, big and small (including one with saxophonist Sam Rivers). Yet no performance in the last act of his life is quite as startling as the Paris concert with drummer Max Roach, *Max + Dizzy: Paris 1989*. The sheer physical effort of sustaining a ninety-minute recital of duets is unprecedented for a jazz brass player of his age. But that is nothing as compared with the ingenuity he displays. At moments, Roach seems bent on tripping him up, but Gillespie responds with un-failing assurance—this at a time when his customary nightclub perform-ances found him playing one prominent solo early on, then featuring the other musicians as he stored up sufficient energy for another extended solo toward the end of the set. In Paris, he enjoyed a state of grace.

One of the most beguiling selections is "Salt Peanuts," not least be-cause that redoubtable warhorse had been traversed by him on hundreds of occasions since the 1945 recordings. If the basic chorus structure is routine, the piece is made more interesting by Gillespie's use of inter-ludes and transitions. On the original recording with Parker there are transitions composed of two-, four-, six-, and eight-bar units. The most effective is a ten-bar episode, consisting of a six-measure written passage played by the ensemble and a four-measure break improvised by Gilles-pie, leading directly into his thirty-two-bar solo. This device has the effect of a springboard and, as such, recalls the break with which Arm-strong launched his own solo on the 1928 recording "Muggles." Gilles-pie's solo is based entirely on the chord changes, as would be expected.

The 1989 version is entirely different. Gillespie's tone has now suffered the decay of age, and one doesn't expect to hear the old radiance. Yet he compensates with a looseness and ingenuity that ought to have en-deared him to leading lights of the avant-garde; the lessons of modality, as sampled in "Manteca," have not been lost on him. After the intro-duction by Roach and a theme chorus with the two-bar vocal riff "salt PEA-nuts, salt PEA-nuts," he plays the written six-measure interlude and the four-bar break, leading into his solo of two choruses. The transcrip-tion (written in G but played in concert F) begins with the break, which occurs ninety-seven seconds into the performance.

The tempo is formidable—Gillespie and Roach play sixty-four bars in about forty-six seconds. As the interplay between trumpet and drums is unfettered by the presence of harmonic instruments such as bass or pi-ano, neither musician is obliged to count a resolute four beats per mea-sure. Roach sustains the quarter-note beat, but his responses to Gilles-pie's two- and four-measure phrases are fluid. If the outline of the chorus is evident, the time is indefinite. At this speed (every second represents about five-and-a-half beats), it would almost have to be. As a result, the music sustains an avid, unpredictable quality as they race over the ter-rain. And yet how fantastically relaxed Gillespie is in ordering his ideas. A constant pleasure of his solo is the way he staggers the rhythm, using triplets to suggest the imposition of a slower meter in measures five through seven (as though he were thinking in half-time); or adamantly accenting the F-sharps in measures twenty-one through twenty-four (implying a three-against-two rhythm and calling to mind a kind of phrasing associated with avant-garde trumpet player Don Cherry) or riding the series of ten Gs (in measures fifty-eight through sixty) before shooting up to a high F-sharp:

Harmonically, the piece is far more advanced than the 1945 recording, yet it's also more elemental. On the progressive side, though Gillespie plays on the chords in the bridge sections, he develops most of his ideas in the A sections by playing in G and ignoring the changes. In measures nine through twelve, for example, he fastens on two notes, B-flat and C, that are related to the G scale but not to the chords. In the twelfth measure, the only other note (D-flat) is our old friend, the once forbidding flat fifth. Because of that D-flat, and Gillespie's phrasing, the twelfth bar is perhaps the bluesiest in the chorus. Another savory moment is the series of ascending fourths and thirds in measures forty-one through forty-four. Yet the scalar approach also encourages a more basic limning of blues tonality, embodied in the solo's constant motif—the varied grouping of three notes: tonic, minor third, and fourth (G, B-flat, C). As Gillespie became more adept at playing the blues in the '50s, his penchant for fourths became more apparent; he used this gambit to open his "After Hours" solo on the 1957 *Sonny Side Up* album. On the 1989 "Salt Peanuts," he plays the motif four times between measures nine and fourteen and at the end of the second chorus.

What I most admire about this solo, this concert recording, this man, is the self-assured authority with which he braves the turf. We are endlessly familiar with artists in every field of music, serious or popular, who are saddled with hits or encores they are expected to play at virtually every appearance. How rare to find a mature artist surveying one of the benchmarks of his youth and turning it into a startling test of his skills. At the time he turned sixty, Gillespie said he had once thought that playing the trumpet would get easier over time, but that it got harder—not because his lip was showing wear, but because he had exhausted so many ideas he used to explore. He could spell himself with comedy and other diversions, but in the heat of improvisation, he was served only by the truth. At the close of *Mr. Sammler's Planet*, Saul Bellow's eponymous hero gazes at the body of his deceased nephew and benefactor and silently delivers a benediction: "He was aware that he must meet, and he did meet—through all the confusion and degraded clowning of this life through which we are speeding—he did meet the terms of his contract." And so did John Birks Gillespie, who died on the morning of January 6, 1993, at seventy-five. As Mr. Sammler observes, "A few may comprehend that it is the strength to do one's duty daily and promptly that makes saints and heroes."*

32 ❖ Sarah Vaughan (Divine)

Sarah Vaughan is the ageless voice of modern jazz—of giddy postwar virtuosity, biting wit, and fearless caprice. Take it as symbolically significant, at least, that Charlie Parker and Dizzy Gillespie recorded as her sidemen before they recorded as bandleaders. Though she was not one of the musical experimenters who invented the new jazz in after-hours Harlem laboratories, Vaughan was in sync from the beginning, in the bop-breeding orchestras of Earl Hines and Billy Eckstine. Her harmonic acumen, to say nothing of her impeccable time, stupendous technique, and absolutely drop-dead gorgeous timbre, was as advanced as that of anybody in the bebop boys' club. Indeed, she validated the boys: it was the Divine One and not they who triggered the assimilation of their music into the mainstream. For forty-five years, from timid, toothy teen to sleek, sultry Circe to stout maternal diva, she enchanted audiences who didn't know bop from chop suey—making them swallow every raised fourth and like it. They didn't call her "Sassy" for nothing.

In 1950, Columbia Records set about making her a star, interring her in huge studio orchestras, usually upholstered with strings, but only once—once in five years—featuring her with a small modern jazz ensemble. At that historic outing, backed by Miles Davis and Budd Johnson, she recorded "Mean to Me," "East of the Sun," "Come Rain or Come Shine," and other consummate masterworks of twentieth-century vocal gymnastics that are invariably offered as examples of her extraordinary intelligence and radiant power. Naturally the company didn't want *that* to happen again. No matter; it wasn't the presence of a jazz band that made Vaughan a jazz singer. Consider two other rec-

*The transcriptions used here are by the composer and trumpet player Jon Schapiro, whose insights into jazz musicology helped me make sense of the stories they tell.

ords she made in more routine circumstances, but look closely—in her music, the details are everything.

"Thinking of You" is a 1927 ballad that was revived in 1950 when its writers, Kalmar and Ruby, were the subject of an MGM musical, *Three Little Words*. Three versions made the charts in less than two months: those by Don Cherry and Eddie Fisher sold best, but only Sarah Vaughan's has been selling ever since. Accompanied by a studio band playing a Norman Leyden arrangement that has the virtue of staying out of her way (those occasionally jutting piano runs are by Bud Powell), she begins with a wordless two-bar cadenza that swells dynamically before gliding without a rest into time and the first word, "Why," which she sings as two pitches (a motif). Her sustained notes repose easily over the methodical tempo, sensuous yet pulsing. She completes the eight bars by expanding the last word in the title phrase, "you," into a two-bar wordless croon leading directly into the next eight.

Vaughan is so musical she is often underestimated as an interpreter of lyrics. Note how during the next sixteen bars she accents words for meaning, imparting a sexy current while heightening the rhythm and varying the phrasing. She peels off the *b* in "bliss" (prefiguring Marilyn Monroe). She mines the title phrase in the lower part of her midrange, making it coy and husky. She lightens up on "night" and the second syllable of "tiptoe" ("When I fall asleep at night it seems/You just tiptoe into all my dreams"), making them exceedingly seductive. Other words are held forth like great sunsets: "seems" ranges over three notes and is sustained eight beats; "I" spans six beats and floats into the next phrase without pause. After singing the first chorus, she essays an embellished repeat of the bridge, this time over an unexpected four-bar stop-time rhythm (accenting the first two beats of each measure), now stressing "fall" and "asleep" in the course of varying the line. In the last eight bars, she makes the first two words, "So I," two pitches each and detours into a Billy Eckstine-style coda that leads into the last, sustained note. Word by word and note by note, it is an enthralling performance, exuding a voluptuous virtuosity quite without precedence in the music of, say, Billie Holiday or Ella Fitzgerald.

A few weeks later, she recorded "Perdido," the Ellington standard, written by his trombonist Juan Tizol in 1942 and fitted with lyrics by Ervin Drake. Leyden's arrangement swings enough to serve as a springboard for Vaughan, who goes for broke on the two bridges. In the first one, she goes high on "high," a hint of what's to come. The first half of the second chorus consists of two-bar exchanges between orchestra and singer, and climaxes as she flings the word "sombrero" into the release and twirls the passage ("High was the moon when we first came close/

Low was the moon when we said adios"), fanning "high" over nine notes and finishing with a brassily tossed-off "adios," all accomplished in an instrumental manner with harmonic and melodic impetuousness that other singers may have envisioned but that only Vaughan could actually bring off. The rest is relatively anticlimactic. She outriffs the band, altering "perdido" to "perdidio" at one point for rhythmic effect and landing on cat feet after a scat break.

The "sombrero" episode, so characteristic of her, is the kind of thing that shook up mezzo-soprano Jan DeGaetani the first time she heard Vaughan in concert in the '70s. "She'll wire out her voice if she keeps doing that," she remarked to a companion, who astonished her with the information that she had been doing precisely that for thirty-something years. One of her celebrated set pieces at the time was an arrangement of "My Funny Valentine" (happily documented on *Live in Japan*, 1973), where she turns the bridge into an escalator-arpeggio, her voice beginning as a cello and ending as a flute. Seeing her in those years—the commanding concert performer alternating strenuous arias with self-deprecating jokes, bebop gallops, and sensuous ballads—was a revelation. And so was the audience, which behaved like the gallery in a Baptist church, cheering and whooping every spellbinding conceit. Vaughan enjoyed that, but she did not court or accept mindless acclaim, and she could not abide people clapping in time, a practice she found incomprehensible, vaguely insulting, and intrusive—they drowned out the rhythm section and interfered with her concentration. Her way of dealing with it was to subtly modulate to a different rhythm until the clappers realized to their chagrin that they could no longer find the two and four and, after the last of them desisted, slip back into the original rhythm.

Sarah Vaughan was born in 1924, in Newark, New Jersey, and she sang in the Mt. Zion Baptist Church, where her mother played organ. She had begun studying piano at six and by twelve was subbing for her mother at the organ. Like Carmen McRae and Dinah Washington, Sarah was a capable pianist who sometimes accompanied herself in performance, but her true forte at the keyboard was something she kept to herself—a talent for exploring the altered chords that ultimately informed the liberties she took singing. As a shy and awkward eighteen-year-old, she sang "Body and Soul" on Amateur Night at the Apollo, winning the contest and a job. In the audience that night was Earl Hines, and though he wasn't impressed by her demeanor, he was delighted with her voice; she was delighted when he came backstage and offered her a spot in his orchestra. Within weeks, she was playing second piano to Hines and sharing the vocals with Billy Eckstine in a band (unrecorded because of the AFM ban) that also included Parker and Gillespie. In 1944, she recorded one of the first bop sessions (produced by Leonard Feather, who wrote that Bird and Diz had been "hailing her voice as a new development in jazz"). Two years later Sarah headlined at Cafe Society. By the time she was twenty-five, Vaughan developed a masterful stage presence and enough assurance to allow her contagious humor to blossom forth.

She also began taking greater musical chances. Her 1945 recording of "Mean to Me" is impressive, but the version introduced at the Christmas 1949 Charlie Parker Carnegie Hall concert, with its soaring second chorus, was something else entirely. Her voice had wings: luscious and tensile, disciplined and nuanced, it was thick as cognac yet soared off the beaten path like an instrumental solo, delivering on ideas other singers don't permit themselves to contemplate because even if they can pull off the improvisational gambits that were her trademark, the risks would be too great and the cost of failure humiliation. That her voice was a four-octave muscle of infinite flexibility made her disarming shtick all the more ironic. In her concert years, she would introduce herself, for the benefit of those who happened to come in out of the rain, as Della Reese, Carmen McRae, or June Carter. Several songs into the set, mopping perspiration from her brow, she would lament, "I come up here looking like Lena Horne and walk off looking like Sarah Vaughan."

Those of us who discovered her at that stage in her career were surprised to learn that her role as concert diva was fairly new, in part an expression of her frustration with the recording industry, which had been stifling her for years. All her life, Vaughan was poised between two careers: indomitable jazz creator, exquisite pop star. She sang "Lover Man" with Dizzy, made the charts with "Tenderly." After an apprenticeship at Continental and Musicraft, Columbia put the glam on her, as well as the occasional novelty ("De Gas Pipe She's Leaking, Joe")—why should she be different from everyone else on the roster? She did laudable work for Columbia, sometimes under trying circumstances, and ended up a high-priced supper club act. But they couldn't turn her into much of a hit maker—she cracked the Top 40 a dozen times, but never the Top 10 (the closest she came was with the flip side of "Thinking of You," "I Love the Guy"). She simply didn't sound persuasive singing idiotic songs such as "If Someone Had Told Me."

She switched to Mercury in 1954, an affiliation that lasted more than a decade, notwithstanding a brief sojourn in the early '60s with Roulette. This label honored her proven appeal to both audiences, and it seemed to work; that is, she made several unspeakably bad records at the same sessions that produced many of her greatest artistic triumphs, and the former made a great deal of money. In the first year she signed, she had a major chartbuster with "Make Yourself Comfortable," a shovelful of syrup from Bob Merrill, the demon who one year earlier provided Mercury and Patti Page with "(How Much Is) That Doggie in the Window." With her voice locked in an echo chamber, Vaughan is reduced to hackwork. Columbia had never been that bad, or that successful. But within a few months, she had Clifford Brown by her side for *Sarah Vaughan*, recording the exhilarating "It's Crazy." And so it went: at one session, she made the dreadful "Oh Yeah" and the intoxicating "I'm in the Mood for Love"; at another, the ghastly "How Important Can It Be?" and the inspired "The Touch of Your Lips." Meanwhile, she was appearing live with one of the great piano trios: Jimmy Jones, Richard Davis, and Roy Haynes, whose work throughout her entrancing 1957 *Swingin' Easy* (on the line about off-key singing in "They Can't Take That Away from Me," she scores a bull's-eye dissonance) is a lesson in empathic drumming.

For a while, the good albums were issued with the company's jazz logo, Emarcy, while the rest came out under the parent name. But the distinction was fudged by the high-class pop records she also made for Mercury, like the incomparable *Great Songs from Hit Shows*. Bad songs might disengage her, but sugary arrangements of good songs did no harm. Sometimes, they perversely inspired her to go an extra step, as in her immensely poignant "Little Girl Blue," where she mimics and mocks the strings with a suitably wordless croon. She was ever alert, and given room to maneuver, she did, especially with her trio, turning the phrase "and when your fortune's falling" into an ascending glide on "Pennies from Heaven" or reacting to Roy Haynes's bump on the line "I felt a bump" in "Polka Dots and Moonbeams." She had her biggest hit with the ineffable "Broken-Hearted Melody" (1959), a song that might have suited Connie Francis or Annette Funicello, but not the thirty-five-year-old artist who once sent Miles Davis into a paroxysm of admiration: "Sarah sounding like Bird and Diz," he enthused, "and them two playing everything!" The record paid a lot of bills, but she refused to subject paying customers to it. On the other hand, she recorded Erroll Garner's "Misty" in the same period and brought down the house with it for thirty years.

As long as she could have it both ways, everything was fine. But by the early '60s the label sought only middle-of-the-road hits. A new generation of producers and song pluggers was less than enchanted by her spontaneity, rapier reflexes, and invention. Vaughan complained that her producers were handing her lead sheets for new songs in the studio on the day they were to be recorded, depriving her of rehearsal time on the assumption that unfamiliarity would breed obeisance to the written score. They underestimated her resourcefulness—she could deconstruct a chord as quickly as any instrumentalist—and her pride. By 1966, she had had enough of songs like "Dominique's Discotheque" and attempts to market her as a middlebrow pop star. When her Mercury contract was up the following year, she turned her back on the industry and refused to record for four years. She signed with Mainstream in the early '70s, reuniting with producer Bob Shad, who had piloted most of the Emarcy dates, but he now submerged her in studio orchestras and dubious material. The records, however, no longer mattered: she was onto something else. Refusing offers from supper clubs, she began nurturing a new following in concert halls. The next sixteen years were in many ways the most triumphant of her career. She bonded with audiences. Records were almost irrelevant.

The best evidence of her altered standing was the evolution of her longest-running encore, "Send in the Clowns." She first recorded Stephen Sondheim's song shortly after it was introduced in *A Little Night Music*, but her record went nowhere. Then she worked the song into a closing routine: She'd coyly solicit requests, nod her head in patient solicitude as they were shouted back at her by the dozens, then announce, "I don't know how to tell you this, but I'm not gonna do any of those." Her pianist would limn a waltz, she'd intone the words, "Isn't it rich?" and the clock stopped for the next several minutes. As she built to the final cadenza—a characteristic antic that followed the phrase "losing my timing this year," demanding flawless timing and breath control—audiences roared. Within a couple of years, word was out and people started responding to her invitation for requests by calling out, "Send in the Clowns." By the mid-'80s, the whole audience was shouting it. The "I'm not going to do any of those" bit didn't work any more. To exploit the unusual if not unique phenomenon of a concert hit without a corresponding record, her current label recorded a new version accompanied by Count Basie's orchestra. Yet after all those hundreds of renderings with her trio, Vaughan passed away without leaving a representative recording of what had become her signature tune.

Vaughan's true comeback on records took place in 1978, when Norman Granz signed her to Pablo (inadvertently adding to the insecurities of Ella Fitzgerald, whose personal manager he was). Her bumpy five-year association with Pablo began with the compelling if flawed *How Long Has This Been Going On?*—Vaughan's first jazz album since an uneven session arranged by Jimmy Rowles four years earlier, and her most effective since *Live in Japan*. Coming after so long a drought, the record, with its ten familiar songs and accompaniment by a stellar foursome—

Oscar Peterson, Joe Pass, Ray Brown, and Louie Bellson—received a strangely varied response. Those who came to admire La Vaughan as an opera singer without an opera were disappointed, but those who treasured the albums she made in the company of her musical peers were elated. Once again she was swinging hard, and she was in outstanding voice, rejecting the archness that sometimes undermined her recordings in favor of blues locutions, audacious variations, and riffs. It's one of the earthiest records she ever made.

Despite her apprenticeship in the Mt. Zion Church, gospel orthodoxies do not often crop up in Vaughan's singing. Aside from her prized 1947 recordings of "The Lord's Prayer" and "Motherless Child," she avoided spirituals. But the rudiments of soul singing do peek through here. They are apparent in the three-note melisma she attaches to the word "life" at the end of the first chorus of "I've Got the World on a String," and to the word "see" in the second chorus, and in the way she growls "anytime" in the third. They are unmistakable in the way she has rewritten "Teach Me Tonight," in the way she handles the second half of the bridge on "How Long," in numerous blues phrases, and several riffing out-choruses. The high note right before the tag ending on "Teach Me Tonight" recalls Jackie Wilson—it is not standard Vaughan procedure, although the range itself is nothing out of the ordinary for her.

How Long Has This Been Going On? was recorded in one day and sometimes sounds it. A not especially inspired "Easy Living" deserved a retake if for no other reason than that she botched the lyric; her pacing and pronunciation on the first eight bars of "Midnight Sun" are faultless, but the song finally gets away from her and she compensates with overindulged vibrato. Still, there are at least six stirring performances, more than on most people's records. Start with the first cut, "I've Got the World on a String," and then proceed directly to the second half, where she does only one number with the quartet, and one number with each member. It's hardly necessary to note how difficult it is to sing a ballad creatively with just piano or guitar or bass, or to effectively trade two-measure breaks with drums. Vaughan makes it seem effortless and natural. Peterson introduces "More Than You Know" with a few notes from the Adagio from Rodrigo's *Concerto De Aranjuez*, and Vaughan sings the verse (note the way she puts the affected emphasis on "true" in perspective with the soulfully phrased "remain") before setting up the chorus in her mightiest trombone intonation. This is a masterly, emotive Vaughan performance: she picks up the first release with the same breath as the preceding phrase; the second release is patterned with descending parallel arpeggios; and the protracted ending has her repeating the title line four times, returning to the tonic only on the very last note. "My

Old Flame," accompanied by Pass, is just as good. She makes the crawling tempo swing (especially on the release), and she resolves a treacherous ending so cleanly it seems planned, though I'm sure it wasn't.

The 1978 version of "Body and Soul" is her third, and it relegates the recordings of 1946 and 1954 (as good as those are) to apprentice work. Accompanied only by Ray Brown's bass, she begins with the release at a medium up-tempo. The practice of starting a song in the middle is pretty unusual, although it's an obvious way of creating immediate tension and surprise. In his 1961 recording of "Let's Fall in Love," Frank Sinatra began with the release, moved backward to the verse, and then, after a dramatic pause, forward into the chorus. "Body and Soul," with its strenuous key change, lends itself better to such tinkering, and Vaughan heightens the drama by halving the tempo as she begins the chorus fresh. She keeps you alert to every measure's nuance, and a couple of gambits are outstanding: the paraphrase melody she introduces on the line, "I spend my days in longing," and the single, bulleting arpeggio she makes of two sentences fragments, ". . . you're making. You know I'm yours. . . ."

Excepting his splendid work on "More Than You Know," Peterson's solos are superficially bluesy, but he's attentive, and there are moments when Vaughan works closely with him, as when she scats his segue chords coming out of the release on "I've Got the World on a String." Pass's best work is his counterpoint on "Teach Me Tonight"; Brown and Bellson play well together, as usual. Vaughan never required much more from a rhythm section than reliable, observant backing, and when she sang as well as she did here, she inspired it to keep pace.

The most disappointing of her Pablo projects—because it was so promising—was the two-volume *Duke Ellington Songbook*, made in 1980. Like every artist, Vaughan had doubts, and they came out in mannerisms that she leaned on in the absence of inspiration. Yet in retrospect, the successes of the Ellington project outweigh the failures. Granz didn't give her much in the way of orchestral support (especially in comparison to Ella Fitzgerald's Ellington songbook, a collaboration with the maestro himself): a few uneven Billy Byers arrangements; and for the rest, a four-piece rhythm section and one or two soloists. For once, the chief failing is the kind of liberties Vaughan takes—the very liberties that elsewhere are the key to her genius. Not that Ellington's songs are sacred texts (though it would be a tonic to hear someone record them as written, every far-flung interval hit with precise articulation): the problem is that her playfulness occasionally minimizes the material, at times suggesting a lack of conviction.

The outstanding ballad selection, "In a Sentimental Mood," is the exception—brilliant Vaughan that dwarfs everything else on the record. She works the arpeggios with scrupulous care, her luscious voice swelling and decaying with total control, her low notes booming sonorously. Byers's arrangement is, for once, rich and supportive; after the strings interlude, Vaughan returns not at the release but five bars early. Her "Solitude," however, sacrifices Ellington's poignancy and clarity with coy variations and a brassy second release in which she whoops it up with trombonist J.J. Johnson. "Day Dream" is a spare and elegant song in which every note is essential, and Vaughan's ornaments aren't improvements: the three notes she applies to the word "glow" obscure the gracefulness of the original line, as do the three notes she adds to "came" in "Sophisticated Lady" and the two she uses for "heart" and "part" on "All Too Soon." And while the half-note/dotted-quarter/eighth-note rhythms of the "Day Dream" release can seem facile, her dotted-half/two-eighths substitution is no improvement. She scats most of "I Didn't Know About You," with results that are no more than pleasantly glib.

Elsewhere, the Vaughan imprint is so beguiling that one revels, as usual, in her willfulness, for ultimately this is a personal testament. She never goes near the original melody of "I'm Just a Lucky So and So," turning it into a febrile blues with falsetto and stop-time episodes. It isn't preferable to the original, but it's pure Vaughan in a histrionic mood, and she seems to be having fun. She also toys with "I Let a Song Go Out of My Heart," displacing rhythms in the first release, then swinging the out-chorus, concluding with a trumpetlike high note and glissando. She makes the flame in an otherwise perfunctory "Sophisticated Lady" really flicker, and she's so authoritative on the release of "All Too Soon" that you wonder why the rest of the interpretation is so pale. This "Lush Life" hasn't the rich certainty of her 1956 version (a comparison of the two is particularly damning to Byers's arrangement and the sound mix), but her huskier voice, subtle parlando, and diminished tempo are earmarks of the mature and tougher Vaughan. Although the band arrangement on "In a Mellow Tone" is nondescript, this is one piece that she's made her own through frequent performances. On the combo selections, Jimmy Rowles is the most helpful accompanist; obbligati are provided by Frank Foster, Frank Wess, Zoot Sims, J. J. Johnson, and Waymon Reed—never more than two men to a selection.

If Vaughan was proud of being a jazz singer, she was—like Ellington—impatient with those who wanted to limit her. Not all the mainstream projects amounted to much (a disastrous collection of Beatles songs; an album of lyrics by Pope John Paul II; an album she never completed with Quincy Jones). But she reveled in diverse challenges, and some of those projects—her 1957 duets with Eckstine on Irving Berlin tunes, her *Gershwin Songbook* of the same year, the 1977 *I Love Brazil*, and her last major album, the 1982 *Gershwin Live!* (featuring her thrill-ride version of "Fascinatin' Rhythm")—are momentous. Yet there were moments when her nerve failed her. Her good friend Leontyne Price tried to convince Vaughan to tour Europe with her, performing together on stage as they had done informally. Sarah agreed at first, but ultimately reneged. The prospect intimidated her, she said. It's hard to imagine Vaughan intimidated by anyone, though outside of music her life had its rocky places. Four marriages failed. She worked off her nervous energy by fast driving, developed a taste for coke, and for many years smoked too much—lung cancer took her life in 1990, at sixty-six.

On stage, she could be caustic if her requisite chair and glass of water weren't awaiting her, but talent always stimulated her. When reunited with the class of 1945—Gillespie, Eckstine (whose bass baritone she liked to mimic)—she positively glowed. For the three-concert Vaughan festival George Wein produced in her honor in 1979, she requested he hire the undervalued Eddie Jefferson and Betty Carter, allotting each a full set, and additionally boosting them by singing the girl's part on Jefferson's "Moody's Mood for Love" and instigating fours with both. She tried more than most to accommodate contemporary songwriters and inevitably made poor choices—Michel Legrand, the Beatles, Barry Manilow, "Feelings"—almost always giving more than she got. But by 1980, she was choosing her songs on merit only, and the lame material disappeared altogether from her concerts.

"The Island" was a new song she made her own. She introduced it on the album that ended her Pablo deal—significantly, the only one she produced herself, *Crazy and Mixed Up* (1982). As good as the record is, that song became more and more seductive as she explored it in concert—to the point where she would sometimes laugh. Vaughan's approach to lyrics, long underappreciated, was usually governed by a mischievous wit. It's true she often sacrificed verbal import to improvisational brio—the big arpeggio in "My Funny Valentine" has nothing to do with the song's meaning—but given a line like "climb the highest peak" in "Cheek to Cheek" (*No Count Sarah*, 1958), she could be depended on to scale Everest. "Goodnight, Sweetheart," from the thoroughly engaging 1962 Roulette album, *Sarah + 2*, is an erotic benchmark, a lullaby in which every vowel winks.

She ought to have recorded more; she ought to have had the kind of label support Pablo provided Fitzgerald, Concord Jazz provided Rosemary Clooney, and Verve provided Betty Carter and Abbey Lincoln. She might at least have rerecorded the two '40s classics she reintroduced in concert, "The Lord's Prayer" and Tadd Dameron's "If You Could See Me Now." But she died before the revival of interest in postwar singers took hold. One person who knew what the world was losing was Frank Sinatra, who, much to her surprise, remained in daily contact with her during her final weeks.

Vaughan's playful irreverence and dauntless musicality made unmistakably clear her assumption that Tin Pan Alley is at best a starting gate and never a shrine. Yet she was as fine an interpreter of the standard pop-song repertory as we have had and almost certainly the most self-possessed. Her control of timbre, articulation, and dynamics was matched by infallible pitch; the rare ability to improvise harmonically, melodically, and rhythmically; and an unfettered imagination that made it all count for something. She was a full partner in the germination of modern jazz. But no matter how closely we dissect the particulars of her talent, marveling at her range and energy and intelligence, transcribing and analyzing her performances, tracing her development over time, we must inevitably end up contemplating in silent awe the most phenomenal of her attributes, the one she was handed at birth: a voice that happens once in a lifetime, perhaps once in several lifetimes.

33 ❖ *Thelonious Monk*
(Rhythm-a-ning)

I used to have a phobia about pictures or anything on a wall hanging just a little bit crooked. Thelonious cured me. He nailed a clock to the wall at a very slight angle, just enough to make me furious. We argued about it for two hours, but he wouldn't let me change it. Finally, I got used to it. Now anything can hang at any angle, and it doesn't bother me at all.

Nellie Monk (in *The Jazz Life* by Nat Hentoff)

When Nathan Zuckerman fishes for approbation in Philip Roth's *The Ghost Writer*, the great Lonoff tells him he has "the most compelling voice I've encountered in years, certainly for somebody starting out. I don't mean style. I mean voice: something that begins at around the back of the knees and reaches well above the head." Voices like that are rare in any art, but when one turns up in the jazz world it often has an unusually comprehensive and immediate effect. I'm referring to the kind of musician with a voice so startling, a grasp so sure, that the whole music seems to stop in its tracks to confront the interloper and emerges enhanced and fortified. This was certainly the case with Armstrong, Young, Parker, and Coleman. But not with Thelonious Monk, who conducted his first record session at thirty, organized his first working band at forty, and dropped from sight at about fifty-five. Although a small coterie of musicians (notably Coleman Hawkins, Mary Lou Williams, Dizzy Gillespie, Charlie Parker, and Bud Powell) esteemed him from the beginning, he labored in solitude for much of his most creative period. His records were ignored, his compositions pilfered, his instrumental technique patronized, his personal style ridiculed. Yet no voice in American music was more autonomous and secure than Monk's, and no voice in jazz relied more exclusively on jazz itself for its grammar and vision.

The controversy about Monk must be difficult for younger listeners to comprehend. One can readily appreciate why Schoenberg and his disciples or the jazz avant-garde of the '60s caused dissension. Those musics were conceived as attacks and practically demanded rejoinders. Monk's music is more accurately compared to Stravinsky's early ballets, which, though new and daring for the time, proved accessible to the general public long before intransigent critics saw the light. Monk isn't merely accessible; he's almost gregarious in his desire to entertain, as long as the listener is willing to be entertained on Monk's terms. By this, I don't mean to suggest that Monk's music is light-headed or lighthearted, though on occasion it can be both, but that everything he did was designed to heighten the listener's response to melody, rhythm, and harmony. His tools were traditional, his craftsmanship impeccable. Monk relished swing and the blues and the freedom to do with them as he pleased (his motto was "Jazz is freedom"); he pursued his muse with dauntless concentration, impressive faith, and an almost childlike glee. This, after all, was the musician who more than anyone else transformed the minor second from mistake to resource.

Immersing oneself in Monk's art is both an exhilarating and dispiritng experience—the former because his music is eternally fresh, the latter because so much else seems tame and trite by comparison. Rummaging through *The Complete Blue Note Recordings of Thelonious Monk*, I find that even the most familiar pieces unveil new mysteries and reveal new charms. One obvious reason is that this treasure box, comprising the six sessions he conducted for the label between 1947 and 1952, plus a middling 1957 session under the leadership of Sonny Rollins, includes no less than fourteen previously unreleased performances. Eleven are alternate takes, but don't for a moment think that they are merely flawed warm-ups with slightly different embellishments or changes in tempi. In almost every instance, they afford us the chance to hold familiar gems to the light and discover new refractions of Monk's genius; his work on some of the alternates—including "Nice Work If You Can Get It" and "Skippy"—is actually superior to that on the master versions. The remaining discoveries (all from 1952) are a mildly amusing reading of an obscure Fred Ahlert melody, "I'll Follow You", and two takes of a previously unknown Monk original, "Sixteen," that reharmonizes "Ja-Da" much in the way "In Walked Bud" reharmonizes "Blue Skies." Although Monk never officially recorded the tune, he recycled a key lick from his tumbling, all-in-one-breath first-take solo five months later for his improvisation on "Little Rootie Tootie." Some years later, Sonny Rollins employed similar changes for "Doxy," and one can't help but wonder if they were a lesson from the master.

The Blue Note years capture Monk in the throes of youthful assertion, training musicians of varying abilities in the exigencies of a music unlike but indebted to the hopped-up modernism of the age. They remind us, as indeed all of Monk's work does, that he was the quintessential New York jazzman. A proudly chauvinistic resident of West Sixty-third Street—where a circle is now named in his honor—for most of his life (his family moved there from North Carolina when he was six), Monk lived and breathed the sounds of the city as surely as Louis Armstrong was nurtured by New Orleans. It's there in everything he wrote and played: the clangor and ambition; the nostalgia and irreverence; the influences of the church, big bands, Tin Pan Alley, Harlem stride, modernism. He embraced it all. On the other hand, despite a teenaged sojourn at Julliard, Monk knew less of the European tradition than most of his contemporaries, particularly Parker and Gillespie. Quincy Jones once credited this combination of self-absorption and willful ignorance with Monk's ability to avoid "contrived" experiments. Monk's modernism may once have seemed difficult to comprehend and remains difficult to play, but it was never self-conscious. An appreciation of complex Monkian neologisms should in no way vitiate one's ability to listen ingenuously, too. Monk delights the brain, but he also animates the heart and viscera.

His first masterpiece, appropriately called "Thelonious," was recorded at the close of his first session and was greeted by *Billboard* as "a controversial jazz disking worked out on a one note riff." Though only a prelude to the more accomplished work to come, it merits close inspection. I don't know a better example of the way a musician can draw extensively on the jazz past and come up with something indigenous and wonderful. A first listening tells us nothing if not that the composition and execution are pure Monk, and something new in jazz in 1947.

Yet the materials continuously summon ghosts from the past. For starters, there is the rhythmic/melodic concept that governs the entire piece—a hammering, repeated theme that appears to be confined to one note, though it is really built on three. The antecedent I'm reminded of is the first of Louis Armstrong's two choruses on "Muggles" (1928). Armstrong constructed the entire episode by ping-ponging two notes, A and C, and then climatically springing up an octave to high C. Monk works just as exclusively with F and B-flat, increasing tension with B-flat octaves, only he sustains this motif for the entire performance. Monk announces his rhythmic intentions with an introduction by piano and drums. The theme is voiced on piano while the winds (in their sole contribution to the piece) play descending arpeggios—not functionally unlike the vamp for reeds at the beginning of Ellington's "East St. Louis Toodle-oo" (1927). Ellington is more explicitly suggested in the theme's unusual structure: AABA with a ten-bar release, plus a two-bar interlude between choruses. The unchanging interlude also suggests the kind of blues fillips Jimmy Yancey often employed as transitions between choruses (for example the 1939 "How Long Blues"). The eight bars of B-flats that end the first improvised chorus recall not only Armstrong, but the king of the one-note ride, Lester Young, especially since the sequence begins a measure ahead of time (a favorite Lestorian ploy). The second chorus, however, opens with stride piano out of James P. Johnson (albeit with Monkian minor seconds) and concludes with an au courant rhythmic lick that contemporaries called "Salt Peanuts" (after Gillespie's record) but that older fans may have remembered from Armstrong's "I'm a Ding Dong Daddy." And the final chorus climaxes with a series of triplets à la Count Basie. So here, in three minutes, we can reasonably infer echoes of Armstrong, Ellington, Yancey, Young, Johnson, Gillespie, and Basie in a performance that any fool knows is 100 percent Monk. I don't believe that Monk was much interested in sprinkling his music with homages or clues; the lesson here is that Monk found in jazz all he needed to elaborate his own devious fantasies. By contrast, a good many deliberate glorifications of the jazz tradition sound fabricated and coy.

Monkian revelations proliferate in these recordings. How did he think of so many odd notions that sound so unalterably right in performance—such as the single measure of boogie woogie bass in the bridge of his gorgeous ballad, "Ruby, My Dear" or the introduction to "In Walked Bud," which is nothing more than a cascading arpeggio that caroms into the oddly accented theme with algebraic precision (Art Blakey's press rolls in this piece have the same effect) or the two measures of whole-tone phrases right before the first improvised turnback on "Off Minor"? Blakey, of course, requires more than parenthetical mention as one of

Monk's finest collaborators. You can almost hear him hearing the pianist, so deftly and emphatically does he shift dynamics, bearing down when appropriate, floating the rhythm with unfaltering exactness. The other major voice here belongs to Milt Jackson, whose unperturbed grace inspired Monk to some of his most outlandish ideas, such as the erupting sevenths on "Misterioso" that might have been turned into a new tune, in the manner of "Evidence." There are memorable turns by other players as well, but it's Monk who consistently steals the show, whether he's doubling the bass line behind the trumpet solo on "Suburban Eyes" or closing an eight-bar solo on "All the Things You Are" with blues licks or clipping chords (raising all his fingers but one) and pounding minor seconds on "Introspection" or playing havoc with four/four by displacing the melody accents of "Criss Cross" or making his sole comment on the cool school with the melodious "Let's Cool One" or voicing ripe alto sax on only the third and eleventh bars of " 'Round Midnight" or orchestrating tritones on "Skippy" or playing with waltz meter on "Carolina Moon." This is music that pleases first time out, but I wonder if it ever gives up all its secrets. Consider the alternate take to "Well You Needn't." Apparently Monk hadn't absolutely determined the way the piece should be played when he arrived at the studio; after he recorded the master, he tried a version with a slight change in the thematic accents—the result is practically a new piece.

Michael Cuscuna points out in his notes to *The Complete Blue Note Recordings* that the label capitalized on Monk's rumored eccentricities for promotional purposes. In addition to brandishing phrases like "the High Priest of Bebop," it issued a press release that referred to him as "the genius behind the whole movement [modern jazz] . . . an unusual and mysterious character . . . a strange person whose pianistics continue to baffle all who hear him." Monk's oddest behavioral trait, by all reports, was his reticence: he didn't talk a lot and saw no need to promote himself through the usual channels. Although his few interviews show him to have been articulate and candid, he usually chose to let the music speak for itself. Very weird. Granted, Monk did nothing to discourage his growing reputation for being odd. He became famous and finally notorious for his hats, his bamboo-frame sunglasses, his dancing on stage, and his faith in tenor saxophonist Charlie Rouse and in a small body of compositions that he played nightly. By 1969, Columbia could get away with (and win a prize for) displaying him amid armaments, Nazi paraphernalia, and a slogan of the French resistance on the album *Underground*. His detractors attacked him first because he was too far out and later because he wasn't far out enough. Monk kept his own counsel.

Still, the phrase from Blue Note's press release that had the widest currency was "genius." In 1951, the label issued his 78s as LPs entitled *Genius of Modern Music*, and when they were collected anew in 1976, the title was *The Complete Genius*. The only other American performer I can think of who was publicized so hyperbolically was Ray Charles. But in Charles's case there was a large record-buying public pulling the band-wagon. Blue Note's enthusiasm was generally regarded as hype of a peculiarly desperate sort. It was as if you had to be a genius yourself to join the club and understand his angular music. This misconception might have been quickly righted if Monk had been on view. But the same year that greeted his first album also found him convicted on a trumped-up drug charge. LaGuardia's medieval cabaret laws were never exploited more flagrantly than in the early '50s, and Monk lost his cab-aret card for six years; from the age of thirty-four until he was forty, he couldn't work in any room in New York that sold alcohol.

So Monk continued to work in a kind of solitude, except that he was surrounded by many of the best young musicians in the country. Genius shrivels up if it isn't shared, and Monk responded to his misfortune with an astonishing increase in energy—not only as composer and pianist but as teacher. Monk's pedagogical role goes back to the early '40s, when he proved a constant source of ideas for Parker, Gillespie, Powell, and other more immediately accessible modernists. In the '50s, he had an equally great impact on several of the musicians who would dominate the music during the following decade, including Sonny Rollins, who credited his command of thematic improvisation to Monk, and John Coltrane, who said he learned how to play chords on the saxophone from him. There are numerous stories of young players rehearsing with him and being forced to play above what they deemed their own capacities. "But this is impossible," the novice protests. "You a musician? You got a union card? Then play it," Monk insists, and somehow it gets played. Though not always. At the *Brilliant Corners* session in 1956, they had to splice together a master version of the title tune, so daunting were the tempo changes and intervallic leaps. Even when Monk had no audience of his own, his genius was seeping into the mainstream. In a sense, his disciples prepared the way for him. By the time he began to sustain his own following (after making one crucial compromise with the audience: a couple of sometimes pallid albums of standards and Ellington themes), he was still regarded as eccentric, but no one doubted his competence.

If Monk's first acceptance came as a teacher, his second came as a composer. A familiar refrain of the '50s was the line that he wrote won-derful tunes, but wasn't much of a pianist. By then Monk's writing was impossible to ignore. "Hackensack" and "Epistrophy" were bop classics,

" 'Round Midnight" was a hit, "Straight No Chaser" and "Blue Monk" were fast becoming postbop standards. Strangely enough, he never recorded (and hardly ever played) his most famous melody after " 'Round Midnight," "52nd Street Theme," yet this piece was as close as Swing Street ever came to an anthem. Monk has been called the greatest jazz composer after Ellington, yet his output was relatively small. By my count, there are seventy pieces, including the posthumously discovered lead sheet for "A Merrier Christmas" (debuted by Sphere, the 1980s quartet with Charlie Rouse and pianist Kenny Barron). Other unpublished tunes may come to light, but it's doubtful they'll add greatly to Monk's reputation. In this number are a couple of contested items, like "Eronel" (the late Sadik Hakim claimed partial credit) and "Rhythm-a-ning" (which combines a lick from Ellington's "Ducky Wucky" with an episode from Mary Lou Williams's "Walkin' and Swingin' "), but not items that Monk is believed to have written but received no credit for (like "Dizzy Atmosphere").

It's a modest number, though much larger than that of Varèse or Webern and with no more fat. " 'Round Midnight" is the only Monk ballad that has won wide acceptance from singers as well as instrumentalists, but it's only one of several beautiful compositions and by no means the best; of the others, "Reflections," "Ruby My Dear," and "Ask Me Now" are highly singable, while "Crepuscule with Nellie" and "Coming on the Hudson" are more exclusively instrumental. No tally of Monk's writing is complete without mention of the many standards he adapted and transformed into original works for the piano. His various recordings of "April in Paris," "All Alone," "Sweet and Lovely," and "I Surrender Dear" are ultimately as indigenous as many of his blues and riff compositions. His 1957 recording of "I Should Care" is a no less original and startling invention than some of the configurations he built on familiar changes, like "Evidence" ("Just You, Just Me") or "Bright Mississippi" ("Sweet Georgia Brown"), and at least two classical recitalists have performed a transcription of it. Nor can Monk's work as a composer be separated from the way he organized his groups, not merely as regards the orchestrations, but also the improvised piano accompaniments and architectonic designs for the rhythm section.

It's often assumed that Monk's greatest flowering as a composer took place during the '40s, but I would argue that the '50s were just as fruitful and even more ambitious. He introduced twenty-three originals at the Blue Note sessions (including the posthumously discovered "Sixteen"), but between the final months of 1952, when he first recorded for Prestige, and 1961, when he concluded his sojourn with Riverside, he introduced thirty-three pieces. These include "Little Rootie Tootie," "Trinkle Tinkle," "Reflections," "Bemsha Swing," "Monk's Dream," "Friday the 13th," "Let's Call This," "Think of One," "Wee See," "Nutty," "Work," "Gallop's Gallop," "Brilliant Corners," "Crepuscule with Nellie," "Coming on the Hudson," "Jackie-ing," and "Light Blue"—a selection that would itself constitute one of the most impressive bodies of melodies and springboards for improvisation in American music. This same period also accounts for many of his most ingenious blues, ranging from the exceedingly personal tour de force "Functional" to the irresistible "Blue Monk." In the early '60s, Monk's output as a composer fell off sharply—some thirteen pieces in more than a decade, the best of them blues. But his ability to pump energy into his quartets abides: Charlie Rouse, notwithstanding his fondness for his own lexicon of licks, became an increasingly incisive interpreter—not even Coltrane's tenor blended as evenly with Monk's piano. Monk himself often played more ebulliently, and at long last he achieved widespread recognition in the third realm of his genius, as a piano player. Paul Bacon's 1948 observation that the technique of Horowitz might not be up to Monk's needs as a pianist finally became a commonplace.

Monk's keyboard attack remained more consistent than the public's response, which has mutated from incomprehension to contempt to begrudging admiration to utter enchantment to boredom to unquestioning acceptance, bringing us full circle if you agree that received wisdom is only marginally more illuminating than ignorance. Still, his piano playing underwent more than one transformation: he began partly in the shadows of Teddy Wilson, trotting conventional arpeggios over his always unconventional harmonies; developed a stimulating gift for rhythmic displacement and an aggressive, percussive touch (almost completely deflating the arches of his fingers); entered into a period of protracted lacunae, rubato, and crushed chords; and ultimately settled on a fluid middle ground that makes up in brio what it lacks in drama. Compare his two best solo recitals—the brilliantly idiosyncratic 1957 *Thelonious Himself* and the accessibly eccentric 1964 *Solo Monk*—to gauge the final stages. Monk's influence on pianists is sometimes primarily compositional and harmonic (as it is on Tommy Flanagan or Barry Harris), but is more frequently declamatory (percussive touch, concentrated dissonances, bold rests), as can be heard in the playing of Randy Weston, Herbie Nichols, Andrew Hill, Mal Waldron, Abdullah Ibrahim, and most profoundly, Bud Powell and Cecil Taylor, among a great many others. Like the crookedly hung picture frames that forced his wife Nellie to accommodate visual distortion, Monk's hammered minor seconds and odd rhythmic accents have forced all jazz to accommodate new musical slants.

❖   ❖   ❖

Monk's albums, especially in the Riverside period, have a unity and integrity that has often been sacrificed to subsequent compilations. The 1957 *Monk's Music*, for example, should be heard as intended, with the wind arrangement of the hymn "Abide with Me" as the opener and the lovely hymnlike "Crepuscule with Nellie" as the corresponding closer. The latter, incidentally, was never used by Monk as a basis for extended improvisation. In each of his recorded versions, he plays it alone on piano and arranges the final half-chorus for the ensemble. Coltrane, who because of a contractual skirmish is not mentioned on a cover that boasts Hawkins, Blakey, and Gigi Gryce, plays with respectful emotional fervor, that is, he expands on the emotional content established by Monk. Coleman Hawkins, robust and curious, provides stimulating contrast, especially as he swallows whole the changes to the release on "Epistrophy." Monk's solo here is only one chorus, and it's a miracle of compression and mathematical rectitude. For the first eight bars, he paraphrases the tune, accenting raised fifths and minor seconds; the next eight alternate chromatic runs with repeated sevenths; the release consists of a single phrase prodded, tailored, and lengthened (it's like a miniature version of "Straight No Chaser"); the sensational last eight reduce the theme to clusters, the last two of which arrive where you least expect them, on the downbeat of the penultimate measure.

The transitional Prestige recordings of 1952–54, connecting the low-profile productivity of the Blue Note years with the ascension to public acceptance at Riverside, are often neglected, but they delightfully capture his vital if peculiar virtuosity. "These Foolish Things" is brazenly reconceived in his own dissonant and wildly swinging image; "Trinkle Tinkle" (later the subject of his most rewarding collaboration with Coltrane) has a surprisingly melodic release and a plethora of clanging accents; "Bemsha Swing" and "Bye-Ya" exemplify his ability to reconfigure the piano as tuned drums; "Friday the 13th" is one of his most naggingly memorable melodies and "Reflections," one of his prettiest.

The controversial period at Columbia started extremely well with *Monk's Dream* and the riveting *Criss Cross*, sustained fairly high standards with live recordings and *Solo Monk*, but crashed in an ungainly big band album (*Blue Monk*) arranged by the miscast Oliver Nelson, for which Monk was importuned to play two pathetic pieces by his producer. Some of his best work for the label was not released until long after his death in 1982, notably *Live at the It Club*, with its rare performance of the aptly titled "Gallop's Gallop," and *Live at the Jazz Workshop*, with its striking Monk solo on "Well You Needn't": he begins his second chorus with conjoined and telescoped references to a spiritual ("Happy Am I with

My Religion"), a nineteenth-century cavalry song familiar from John Ford movies ("The Girl I Left Behind Me"), and the West Indian theme Charlie Parker recorded as "Sly Mongoose."

Columbia has also posthumously released unedited editions of albums formerly issued with excised or abridged solos. (They have done the same for Miles Davis and Charlie Mingus LPs, and in each instance, complete is better than abbreviated.) The CD version of *Straight No Chaser* is more involving than the original, not least because Rouse's restored solos now make sense (he was in top form at that session). The most rewarding restoration is *Big Band and Quartet in Concert*, the 1963 Philharmonic Hall collaboration with Hall Overton, whose arrangements recapitulate Monk's pianistic voicings and accompaniments ("Four in One" is exceptional in this regard and in its execution). Considering the limitations of space, the deletions were sensible, but it is a boon to now have two additional Overton charts, two quartet numbers (including a fine rendition, despite Rouse's initial pitch problem, of the alluring "Misterioso"), and Frank Dunlop's full-bore drum solo, a familiar part of every Monk set—"Four in One" shows how deeply Dunlop, like Rouse, was in Monk's groove. Monk's first concert with Overton, at Town Hall in 1959, was recorded for Riverside and includes a remarkable orchestration of his 1952 train song, "Little Rootie Tootie."

A third big band Monk concert was not recorded, nor was it anticipated. By 1974, Monk had begun to curtail his activities and within two years would stop performing altogether, vanishing into a seclusion few if any could penetrate. So when the New York Jazz Repertory Company announced a program of Monk orchestrations in April of that year, he was not expected to participate. The music was rehearsed with Barry Harris on piano. As the musicians began to take the stage, Harris among them, Monk, slightly ashen but resplendent in a red blazer, brushed past them with deliberate short steps—he played two full sets. The charts were adapted from the Overton models by Paul Jeffrey, the last saxophonist to appear in Monk's quartet, and were augmented by a string section with a second bassist (Dave Holland). The violins played breezy introductions on "Monk's Mood" and "Blue Monk," contrasting with the geometrical precision of Monk's themes— the composer's eyes flashed from the concert master to the conductor, awaiting his cue. The soloists included Rouse, Budd Johnson, Cecil Payne, Charles Sullivan, and most memorably, altoist Charles McPherson, whose glib bop phrasing on "I Mean You" was shredded by Monk's rocky obstacles. McPherson hesitated a moment, listening to the crazy quilt of dense piano chords, then began to work in tandem *with* Monk, finding himself in the master's implacable sense of form and leaving the stage a changed man. Monk performed in concert again in 1976, his last performance before the six-year silence that preceded his death. It was as if he had said everything he had to say, and had nothing to add but a long, long rest.

34 ❖ Bud Powell
(Strictly Confidential)

In the absence of medical records, which have never been released by the Powell estate, some doubt now exists as to whether Bud Powell recorded his apocalyptic first session for Clef in May 1949, shortly after he was discharged from Creedmore Hospital, as all discographers believe. Recent research in Verve's files suggests that those six titles may have been recorded in January or February, a conclusion that jibes with Allan Morrison's notable *Ebony* profile of August 1953. According to Morrison, Powell was incarcerated in November 1947, released at the end of 1948, and rehospitalized only ten weeks later, after a breakdown that came hard on the heels of the Clef session; he specifically mentions "Celia" as having been recorded in the interim. We're sure he was released again in April, so if the revisionist theory is accurate, Powell's next session was the equally historic Blue Note date in August, when Bud Powell's Modernists made their one and only appearance.

Why do I care when Powell was hospitalized or how his stay meshes with his performing and recording schedule? Not because of a morbid obsession with the apparently unknowable nature of his pathology, which I don't find all that meaningful in itself. My fascination is inseparable from my interest in his art, and the mystery of how it wilted and blossomed, blossomed and wilted, for twenty years, never entirely disappearing, yet always averting the sustained brilliance that would have represented a complete fulfillment of its original promise. With Powell we are always listening beneath the surface for premonitions, disclosures, revelations, the deepest and most profane secrets. His disposition and technique obviously derive from different parts of his brain. Sometimes the technique fails him, but the ideas and emotions are vividly specific; at other times, the fingers do his bidding precisely, but the bidding is mechanical and remote.

What's remarkable about the Clef sessions is that they capture him at his pinnacle in both realms. When all six titles were assumed to come from one day in May, you could make the case that they constituted one of the most impressive recording sessions in jazz piano history. Verve researcher Ben Young believes that the first three titles ("Tempus Fugit," "Celia," and "I'll Keep Loving You") were recorded in the beginning of the year and the next three ("Cherokee," "Strictly Confidential," and "All God's Chillun Got Rhythm") at another session—as early as February or as late as May. However they break down, those performances were accomplished in close proximity to hospitalizations in which he is reputed to have been subjected to electroshock, among other tortures visited on the mentally unstable. Yet here is some of the most mentally and technically stable music in the canon. I have little use for the van Gogh theory that genius and mental illness are inextricably linked. But the irony can't be ignored.

Much of Powell's unique approach is decisively expressed in those pieces; much of modern piano, as it has evolved over the past forty-five years, stems from them. Here, lurking within the disarming surface of virtuoso acrobatics—bop rhythms, bubbling triplets, dazzlingly even sixteenth-note runs, unpredictable harmonic refractions, phrase repetitions and permutations, and filled octave chords—is a confluence of feelings ranging from lacerating rage to the kind of benign elegance more often associated with, say, Fred Astaire or Teddy Wilson. Each selection is masterful in a different way and testifies to Powell's originality as composer and pianist.

In its economy and hurtling power, as well as its impeccable articulation, the 155-second "Tempus Fugit" (also known as "Tempus Fugue-it") represents a point of demarcation for jazz piano and for jazz itself. The Bachian counterpoint and crashing Lisztian chords in which the relatively conventional melody is swaddled, the close harmonies of the release, the thrilling riff configurations of the solo, and the wonderfully smashed arpeggio just before the out-chorus are fused with enormous intensity. No less spectacular are "All God's Chillun" and especially "Cherokee" (a definitive performance, equaled only by Charlie Parker's versions)—knuckle-breaking ruminations played with fantastic precision, arranged with shifting tiers of chords, an original approach that fleshes out every facet of the song's harmonies in the course of stating the melody. For a man judged to be mentally incompetent (as Powell was) or, indeed, for a man judged to be exceedingly competent, the equilibrium is exceptional: as with Parker and Gillespie, it isn't that he plays so fast, but that he thinks coherently and imaginatively at such forbidding tempos.

And then we have the "ballads," an imprecise way of describing Powell at relative ease, for it is often in slow and medium tempos that he takes his most jarring risks. In its laid-back canter and rolling triplets, "Celia" may be the prototypical bebop ballad, its silken rendering as exacting and masterly as anything he recorded. Yet the composition is an introspective variation on "I Got Rhythm," with two distinct eight-bar transitions, a trademark fourth-bar hesitation, a captivating two-bar break, and a preponderance of first-beat accents that incline the listener to identify instantly with Powell's muse. "I'll Keep Loving You" is based with equally canny independence on Richard Rodgers's "You Are Too Beautiful," and the purity of its expression and resolve opens a window on a kind of romantic piano playing that would inspire disciples as diverse as Hank Jones, Lennie Tristano, George Shearing, Erroll Garner, Bill Evans, Tommy Flanagan, Barry Harris, and McCoy Tyner.

But then what modern pianist who came up in the postwar era wasn't directly influenced by Powell? When Cecil Taylor released his breakthrough album *Unit Structures*, shortly after Powell's death on August 1, 1966 (he was seven weeks shy of forty-two), he ended his liner notes with a cry: "Where are you, Bud? . . . Lightning . . . now a lone rain falling thru doors empty of room-jazz Naked Fire Gesture Dancing protoplasm Absorbs." (Powell's 1956 recording of Dizzy Gillespie's "Be-Bop" makes his connection to Taylor almost palpable.) But Powell's music isn't all dark corridors and stormy nights—far from it. In every phase of his career, he radiates the light of pleasure, of ribald swing and antic charm. The final selection among the early Clefs, "Strictly Confidential," serves as a warning against facile characterization. The introduction is pensive enough, but the head, voiced in block chords (he had that covered, too) is a romp: I have a semifacetious theory that Dave Brubeck's every solo is an attempt to play that head. Although George Shearing became the key exponent of the locked-hands, block-chords style originated by Milt Buckner, the style remained an important part of Powell's arsenal as well, in such enticing works as "Buttercup" and his irresistible arrangement of Harry Warren's "There Will Never Be Another You."

The cliché about Powell is that he translated the modern style of Charlie Parker and Dizzy Gillespie to piano. This is partly true—Powell was the ideal bop pianist. But not only is it unfair to his mentor Thelonious Monk and his contemporary Al Haig, it diminishes the originality of Powell himself. It carries the suggestion that Powell did little more than adapt Parker's phrases to the keyboard. Fredric A. Harris, a pianist and medical researcher who wrote one of the finest studies of Powell, the as yet unpublished *Blues in the Closet*, observed that he believed the cliché until he began to transcribe and study Powell's solos. He then realized:

> The only thing Powell *may have* borrowed from Parker and Gillespie was the "syntax" of bebop—that is, the temporal distribution

or *timing* of notes and rhythmic accents within the measure. . . . In any case, the *melodic content* of those phrases or sequences of notes that Powell played were distinctly his own, as were certain characteristic rhythmic variations upon (or embellishments of) the basic eighth-note pattern. I've studied transcriptions of solos played by each of the three men, but never have come across phrases lifted from either of the horn players and incorporated (or even paraphrased) in Bud's lines. [The emphases are Harris's.]

Perhaps more than any other pianist, Powell codified the now standard trio configuration of piano, bass, and drums. The most significant of his predecessors substituted guitar for drums, like Art Tatum and Nat Cole, or worked solo or in larger ensembles—Monk, for example, made his recording debut with a sextet. In Bill Evans's conception, the piano trio would cede parity to bassists, but Powell had already worked out a heightened level of interaction with drummers. He worked only with the best: Max Roach, Kenny Clarke, Roy Haynes, Art Blakey, Art Taylor, Osie Johnson—percussionists who complemented his dynamics, speed, and shifting rhythms. He also worked with the best bassists: Ray Brown, George Duvivier, Charles Mingus, Curly Russell, Percy Heath—and they faced the same challenges. In the headlong torrent of a Powell recording, however, a bass solo would have been a distraction. The drums seemed to extend his palette, most conspicuously on the tantalizing "Un Poco Loco," where the effect of Roach's clanging cowbell and cymbals is as bracing today as in 1951. As Blue Note has never reissued "Un Poco Loco" without the two alternates that preceded the master take, it has become a kind of de facto triptych in which the trio wrestles with and finally subdues the beast.

Surely his most prized Blue Note session is the one that produced the quintet known as Bud Powell's Modernists, the only time he led a five-piece ensemble and, notwithstanding the frequently euphoric 1946 Bebop Boys octet (on Savoy), the best evidence of what he was capable of as a bandleader and orchestrator. In this context, his succinct solos, stirring as they are, take a backseat to his work as organizer, composer, and accompanist. With Fats Navarro and nineteen-year-old Sonny Rollins in the front line and Tommy Potter and Roy Haynes in the rhythm section, Powell crafted four indelible pieces, including the heraldic "Bouncing with Bud," another of his unforgettable "I Got Rhythm" derivations, and the enigmatic "Dance of the Infidels," for which he adapted a Navy bugle call (dropped from his 1955 trio version) as prelude to a winding melody with characteristically seductive rests on the third and fourth beats of alternate measures.

"Wail," with its stupendous piano intro and a precipitous Powell riff built into the head, is all high spirits, a relay of contagious cheer among the four soloists (including the drummer), the leader most buoyant of all. Powell was loyal to Thelonious Monk all his life (he introduced " 'Round Midnight" to Cootie Williams, who first popularized it; recorded "Off Minor" ten months before Monk had the chance; and in later years regularly played half a dozen Monk pieces), and he closed the Modernists session with his friend's "52nd Street Theme." He transforms The Street into a carnival, echoing the theme with brilliantly impetuous piano fills, milking the release, and having Navarro extend the theme's final riff well into Rollins's solo. The beginning of his own solo sounds like a match igniting. In short, a perfect afternoon, and additional evidence of Powell's originality; by no means does this session echo the numerous quintet dates of Parker and Gillespie, not even those in which Powell participated.

Christopher Finch once published a short memoir, "Growing Up With Bud," about the impact Powell's records had on him and his school chums living off the coast of Normandy: "Parker was a god. Dizzy was a crowd-pleaser. Bud's style was more intimate. His gift was essentially human. You had only to hear a single chorus of 'Sometimes I'm Happy' to know he was vulnerable, and that made him easy to identify with." It's certainly true that Powell inspires a measure of empathy equaled by few artists in any field, and that must be part of the reason we can't get over the nightmare of his malady. In 1945, at twenty-one, he was brutally beaten by cops—the scars are still evident in photographs from his later years. A handful of broadcast recordings from 1944, with Cootie Williams and Ella Fitzgerald, preserve the glow of his youth as well as his perfect pianistic articulation. But the assumption that his skills steadily deteriorated from the moment he was brutalized is contradicted by the radical ups and downs of his career, including those epochal 1949 sessions. Say rather that his life was a battle against demons that may or may not have been unleashed by the beating—a battle exacerbated by the substance abuse and physical neglect that were the proximate cause of his death. Besides, some of Powell's fumbling fingerwork is a direct result of his insistence on taking enormous risks with his technique, pushing his fingers beyond what he knew they could do. That was one of his most admirable traits.

Dr. Harris suggests Powell might have developed epilepsy as a result of the beating and cites witnesses who observed the appearance of grand mal seizures. Misdiagnosed and mistreated, the condition undoubtedly would have worsened. But Powell's playing did not consistently decline.

The enduring mystery about Powell is how magnificently he could summon forth his powers right up to the end. Even the 1964 engagement at Birdland elicited testimony by those who reported he was incandescent on one night and incoherent the next. Ample proof of extreme inconsistency exists in his later recordings. And yet he appeared to maintain a will toward innovation, which is quite different from originality. Powell was always changing—the great Roulettes of 1947 are more approachable, lighter, than the whirlwind performances of 1949, and the latter hardly prepare us for the staggering lustiness of the 1950 "Tea for Two" session (especially the often neglected take ten) or the compelling restraint of "The Glass Enclosure" in 1953. The sound of surprise never left him.

In 1955, he paid enchanting homage to Tatum, his worthiest rival, in "Someone to Watch Over Me." The next year, for RCA, he introduced the reharmonization of "There Will Never Be Another You" and adapted the emphatic style of slow-tempo playing, which made his haunting "Glass Enclosure" so potent, to standard songs. Those increasingly laid-back and deliberate inventions—in which he appeared to stalk the melody, contemplating each chord before accepting its inevitability, pouncing on dissonances with Monkian resolve while wringing a forlorn beauty that was strictly Bud—found particular resonance in his several versions of "I Remember Clifford." Yet at the same time, his original "John's Abbey" could almost always be counted on to restore the old mischievously stalwart Powell. In 1958, after two disappointing Blue Note albums, he offered a stunning recoup in *The Scene Changes*, his decisive discourse on the minor key. In France and Copenhagen in the early '60s, he appeared to have made peace with the whole synthesis of straggling ballads, bop, Monk, and blitz offensives in the albums *Bouncing with Bud* (Delmark), *A Portrait of Thelonious* (Columbia), and *'Round About Midnight at the Blue Note* (Dreyfus).

One of the most heartening documents from that period is *Bud in Paris* (Xanadu), including an especially forceful "John's Abbey" (from June 1960), playful renewals of three bop classics (notably "Confirmation"), an idiosyncratic and argumentative, yet well-played (!) "Crossing the Channel," and two blistering duets with speed-demon saxophonist Johnny Griffin. Francis Paudras, whose 1986 Powell biography and memoir, *La Danse Des Infidèles* inspired the dopey movie *'Round Midnight*, released ten albums on Mystic Sound, including broadcasts and private tapes. The sound is rough and so is much of the playing, but many passages are indispensable, increasing our understanding of Powell. Most rewarding are *Early Years of a Genius, '44–'48* (which opens with a short "West End Blues" duet by Cootie Williams and Powell, who provides expert rolling tremolos), *Burning in U.S.A.*, '53–'55, *Cookin' at Saint-Germain*, '57–'59, *Return to Birdland*, '64, and *Holidays in Edenville* '64 (with Johnny Griffin and including a Chopin prelude).

The reason we read more deeply into Powell than into many of his contempories may be quite simple: no other pianist, and precious few musicians in any age, speak to us with such electrifying urgency. One paradox of Powell's career is that he influenced virtually every pianist who followed him, yet none fully captures his immediacy, emotional power, and vulnerability. He was our Schubert and Liszt rolled into one, perhaps the only jazz musician who could impart the stately melancholy of the former's Sonata in B flat and the demoniacal exhilaration of the latter's Sonata in B Minor. For me, he remains the central figure in the holy hexagram of jazz piano—Hines, Wilson, Tatum, Powell, Monk, Taylor—but I can also imagine a day when a great interpreter will program transcriptions of Powell's masterpieces alongside those of the ninteenth-century icons, at which time Powell will be recognized as one of the most formidable creators of piano music in any time or idiom.

35 ❖ *Chico O'Farrill*
(North of the Border)

The arranger Chico O'Farrill is one of those anomalous figures who drop into American music from time to time, securing a perch here and a footnote there, without staying long enough to earn the spotlight—until a defining event focuses renewed attention, and we suddenly realize we missed him without knowing it. In this instance, the event was double-tiered: the 1995 release of *Pure Emotion* (Milestone) and a corresponding concert for Lincoln Center's jazz program, encompassing the album and more. At seventy-four, he had encouraged a reconsideration of his jazz writing over fifty years.

With a name like his, it was perhaps inevitable that O'Farrill would find himself straddling cultural categories. Born in Havana to an Irish father and Cuban mother of the privileged class, he became a Jelly Roll Morton-type pariah when he announced his decision to work in jazz—a possibility that first presented itself when he was sent to an American military school to get him away from his j.d. friends in Cuba. By 1948, he was ensconced in New York, writing canny if conventional bop-inflected arrangements for several big bands (he is represented in the Smithsonian's *Big Band Renaissance* by Benny Goodman's "Undercurrent Blues") and studying how to accommodate jazz orchestration to Cuban rhythms. He once told Helen Dance, "I truly believe jazz ended up influencing Cuban music more than Cuban music influenced jazz," which may seem obvious today but suggests the distinction between prewar Amero-Cuban pop and postwar Afro-Cuban jazz. The former was mostly polite rhumbas and congas, toned down by Xavier Cugat and Desi Arnaz; the latter was not only rhythmically explosive but a safe harbor for the avant-garde from bop to modalism.

Several Cuban bandleaders and musicians in America had been pushing toward a fusion that would restore the clave rhythm to full strength while drawing on modern harmonies and improvisational skills, most significantly bandleader Machito and his brother-in-law Mario Bauza, who formed the Afro-Cubans in 1940. Throughout the war years, Latin music became increasingly popular and popularized, a consequence of both the ASCAP-BMI squabble and the good-neighbor policy. Walt Disney's *Saludas Amigos* and *The Three Caballeros* introduced half a dozen popular South American songs that were widely covered by North American entertainers, including "Tico Tico" and "Bahia." (They were so successful that even Charlie Parker recorded the first, and Stan Getz resurrected the second at the outset of the bossa nova.) With the end of the war, movies and music became harder-edged and good-neighborism less patronizing. In 1947, when Machito shared a bill with Stan Kenton (who had already recorded his tribute, "Machito") and Dizzy Gillespie held his explosive "Manteca" concert at Carnegie Hall, the Cubop movement was born.

O'Farrill was the right man at the right time. He idolized jazz musicians, and brought rhythmic and formal authenticity, as well as a successful apprenticeship as a big band craftsman and as a student of modern classical music (his teachers included Stephan Wolpe and Hall Overton), to the new music. His major achievement was 1950's *The Afro-Cuban Jazz Suite*, performed by an augmented version of Machito's orchestra, with soloists Charlie Parker, Flip Phillips, and Buddy Rich. Its haunting melodies and contrasting dance rhythms stand up beautifully, and it introduces a five-or-six-note phrase that recurs and permutes in his later work. Think of it is as the "Cancion" melody since that's the name of the movement where it first appears—it also resembles the title phrase from the '30s pop song, "There's a Lull in My Life." O'Farrill recorded prolifically for Clef and Norgran, the labels that later became Verve, accenting the orchestra rather than soloists, and in 1954 culminated his association with Cubop and New York with "Manteca Suite," written for Dizzy Gillespie's orchestra—an inventive deconstruction of the pivotal theme into four melodic or rhythmic components.

O'Farrill lived in Cuba and Mexico for the next decade and had relatively little impact when he wrote for several bands during his return in the mid-'60s. In 1975, he reunited with Gillespie and Machito for *Afro-Cuban Jazz Moods* (Pablo), consisting of two extended works that cheerfully survive the synthesizer effects that seemed to date the recording more then than they do now—and Gillespie's playing is superb. Then another twenty year respite, during which he wrote symphonic works and commercial jingles. Significantly, he played no roll in the salsa movement of the last thirty years—the composer of one of the few undoubted classics of the Afro-Cuban era remains unknown to the Monday-night Latin-music enthusiasts. He is, after all, an arranger, not a bandleader.

So it was an unexpected pleasure in 1995 to find him conducting essentially the same orchestra as on *Pure Emotion* at Alice Tully Hall. In addition to substituting welcome endings for a couple of board fades, the concert diverged from the album in adding his prototypical bebop theme, "Undercurrent Blues"; a bright and efficient "Chicago," written for Basie; and the entire *Afro-Cuban Jazz Suite*. Newer compositions included "Carnegie One Hundred," written in memory of Mario Bauza and offering a driving flute cadenza, an episode for the five-man rhythm section, and a much awaited interlude by the incomparable congas showman, Candido Camera. The evening's premiere, "Trumpet Fantasy," restated the "Cancion" melody and presented Wynton Marsalis in call-and-response dialog with the ensemble as well as a handsomely played variation. Unhappily, he remained on stage for the third movement of *Three Afro-Cuban Jazz Moods*, with which he was uncomfortable—no amount of buzzes and growls could compensate for a corny solo.

The rest of the concert luminously reiterated the contents of the album, one of the year's most pleasant surprises. "Igor's Dream" is a gem, deriving most of its melodic charm from two three-note phrases, one up, the other down, fixed over the mirthful rhythms. "Pianitis" is a brief concerto for piano as played by the composer's son, Arturo O'Farrill, Jr., and again restates the "Cancion" theme. Written for the recently deceased Lenny Hambro, once the yeoman leader of Machito's reed section, "Pura Emocion" is an Ellingtonian ballad with modern harmonic touches; "En La Obscuridad" is a bolero for Mario Rivera, one of the strongmen of Latin reed sections; and "El Loco Blues" is a mambo concerto for orchestra, with riveting, limber section work and succinct improvisations. Orchestrated over an undulating vamp, "Campina" is a siren song, a guajira—and since I don't know a guaguanco from a guaracha,

I'd better quote John Storm Roberts: "The guajira is similar to the slow son montuno but is more delicate and less driving. Its lyrics frequently deal with rural nostalgia." This one would fit a Sam Peckinpah western.

The benchmark of the album is the twelve-minute "Variations on a Well-Known Theme"—"La Cucaracha." The Mexican folk song has been pummeled into insensibility, or at least chronic silliness, over the past half century, but unexpectedly it emerges from O'Farrill's often whimsical, eclectic mutations as a song worth taking liberties with. In slowing it down, speeding it up, reharmonizing its melody, altering its rhythms, O'Farrill discovers that it turns into other songs, from the ballad "Comes Love" to the novelty "The Woody Woodpecker Song." Some passages are irreverent teases, but others recall the pure mid-'60s voicings of Henry Mancini (for example Mancini's " 'Round Midnight" on *Big Band Renaissance*) and the Basie brass section—complete with tightly muted trumpets and stutter-phrasing trombones.

With "Variations," "Campina," "Igor's Dream," and other selections in the new album, O'Farrill brings a measure of compositional skill to the characteristic salsa orchestra that is as removed from the present-day idiom as his *Afro-Cuban Suite* was from the arrangements of his predecessors in Machito's band. He is not precisely of salsa, nor is he precisely of jazz. Maybe a bit of the thrill he imparts with *Pure Emotion* is a recollection of the Cubop days, before everyone grew up. It has that quality of Edenic delight—but with the greybeard wisdom of someone who has seen the story end and so knows what was best about its beginning.

36 ❖ *Stan Kenton* *(Big)*

Among the peculiarities of jazz, considering its central role in American culture, high and low, over the course of a century, is the relative dearth of kitsch. There are numberless bad, inept, meretricious, vulgar, and fatuous performances, but the kind of campy awfulness that is so readily found in every other aspect of the culture is curiously lacking. Where is the jazz equivalent of Jeff Koons sculptures, Norman Mailer novels, and Edward D. Wood, Jr., movies? Candidates can be found, from the vocals of Putney Dandridge or Chick Bullock to the riper conceits of Paul Whiteman and Jimmie Lunceford to the disco phase of Miles Davis, but in practically every case the kitschy elements are tangential to jazz—we listen to the records in spite of them, not because of them. Other possibilities, for example Cab Calloway's Yiddish flavorings and Harry the Hipster's carryings-on, belong to the realm of hokum. True kitsch must be exquisitely, deliciously, and conceitedly bad; we must be drawn to it as a guilty pleasure, confident that the artist produced precisely the effect desired.

A vast oasis of jazz kitsch exists, however, and the place to find it is in the New Directions in Neophonic, Mellophonic, Supersonic, Progressive, Innovative Artistry of Stan Kenton. Pardon the tongue in my cheek, but there is something about Kenton and his music that wedges it in there. Perhaps the malady is traceable to music professors and band instructors who clutched *New Concepts of Artistry in Rhythm* or *Stan Kenton's West Side Story* to their bosoms, speaking glassy-eyed of his "progressive" music, placing an LP reverently on the turntable and growing misty at the bombardment of shrieking brasses and Latin percussion. They were the sort of classical pedagogues who wouldn't know Ellington from Hal Kemp, but believed fiercely in a college of musical knowledge that embraced Kenton's version of "Maria," which begins with a piano solo they could play by ear and feel darned progressive doing so.

Kenton's music is a subject that eludes but never completely alienates me. The pomposity, of course, is staggering in a deeply kitschlike way. Not for him an album of standards or blues, but rather *Adventures in Standards* and *Adventures in Blues*. Like Berlioz, he believed that more was more; build a bigger stage, and he would build a bigger orchestra. His response to every fashion in jazz or pop was "Mine is bigger than yours." Everything he did was hyped as newly broken ground. The reality was shrieking brasses and Latin percussion. His kitsch masterpieces are *Kenton/Wagner* (the Valkyries ride to the pounding of . . . bongos) and *Stan Kenton! Tex Ritter!* The punch line of the former is not the amalgamation of apparent opposites, but similarities between the two; they're a perfect match, a sort of sturm and real slow drang. The album is ghastly only in the sense that the Ed Wood Jr. film *Glen or Glenda?* is ghastly. In each case, the outlandishness is real, sincere, exquisitely and deliberately awful. The collaboration with Tex Ritter, which includes new directions in "Take Me Back to My Boots and Saddle," promoted itself as "a completely new vocal-instrumental concept," assuring us that "neither one of these fine artists makes any concession to the style of the other." All true! Madness has its own logic.

Kenton had a mystique, not to mention an audience that listened to little else. When he left Capitol in 1968, he started the most successful musician-owned independent jazz label ever, Creative World. A class operation in every respect, the company believed in its product. Spurred by its professionalism, I tried to measure up, poring over every new release, as well as reissues of albums leased from Capitol, and catching Kenton whenever he appeared in town. To be sure, his catalogue included many enduring performances, ingenious arrangements by Bill Holman, Gerry Mulligan, Pete Rugolo, Johnny Richards, and others, with solos by saxophonists Lee Konitz, Art Pepper, Zoot Sims, Bill Perkins (whose tenor solo on Johnny Richards's arrangement of "Out of This World" is worth discovering), and Lennie Niehaus (for all the heavy-handed brasses, the reeds had the best soloists), and brassmen Carl Fontana, Frank Rosolino, and the Candoli brothers. For a while, drummer Mel Lewis, who gave the band much of its heart, and bassist Max Bennett made a vital rhythm team.

Kenton's name is above the title of one of the indisputably great orchestra albums of the '50s, *Contemporary Concepts*, but Bill Holman was behind that one and there are stories to the effect that Kenton didn't much like it—swung too hard. *Cuban Fire!*, written by Johnny Richards, is another hotpoint of orchestral jazz in that era. Kenton's entirely admirable willingness to indulge eccentric writers also led to recordings of two suites by Bob Graettinger, notably *City of Glass*, which is indispensable in its singularity, as Kentonesque pyrotechnics are taken to the brink of hysteria. But none of these works seem characteristic of the Kenton sound, that kitschy fullness of texture combined with dramatic retards and California goofiness, the latter embodied in the weirdly sexy innocence of the vocalists, not only the gifted singles, Anita O'Day and June Christy (and their numerous less talented imitators), but in murderously well-behaved groups—the Pastels, the Modern Men, the Four Freshmen. Like the Republican Party, Kentonism is a big tent. Somewhere between the vocal choirs and the mellophone contingent, I lose my place and begin to notice that many of his musicians have names that read like anagrams: Ed Leddy, Bart Varsalona, Archie LaCoque.

Capitol released in 1992 a telling four-CD compilation, *Stan Kenton Retrospective*, tracing his twenty-five years with the label, beginning in 1943. Liner notes by Ted Daryll, notwithstanding an occasional New Age gloss ("Stanley Newcombe Kenton's tenure on the planet began, inauspiciously.... His spirit left its sixty-seven-year frame on August 25, 1979"), offer a first-class primer to the ins and outs of his career, without quite explaining Kenton's special allure. Almost every aspect of his music in that period is represented, including one movement from *City of Glass* and the Prelude to Act III of *Lohengrin* (but nothing with Tex Ritter. If I read Daryll correctly, Kentonites are chagrined by that entire episode). The box opens with "Artistry in Rhythm," a defining selection that sounds today like nothing more or less than music for a '40s *noir* movie, complete with a drum break for Elisha Cook, Jr., and, as the band kicks into tempo, a loopy piano interlude, overwrought and undernourished, for Clifton Webb. Some of the early vocal hits, each the quintessence of '40s kitsch, follow, including "Tampico," the biggest record Kenton ever had—a song so big in its day, 1944, that an about-to-be-released Edward G. Robinson flick was retitled *Tampico* to capitalize on its popularity, even though the movie hasn't a thing to do with Tampico, the place or the record.

You might do better to search out complete editions of *Contemporary Concepts* and *Cuban Fire!* than settle for excerpts; even so, the montage of good and garish performances as collected makes for an impressively rangy whole. On the one hand, there is Mulligan's evocative "Young Blood" or Holman's glistening "Stomping at the Savoy" (two benchmark recordings in their time). On the other hand, there is the riotously serious Marty Paich version of "My Old Flame," salvaged by a Bill Perkins tenor solo and complete with one of those corny unison trumpet shakes that compares poorly with the kind Basie was perfecting at the same time. The album closer, "How Are Things in Glocca Morra?" opens with a parody of outmoded styles before going into a Dee Barton arrangement that is now every bit as outmoded itself. Some songs that one would expect to find are missing: Kenton found his original inspiration in the spit-and-polish music of Jimmie Lunceford, and his openly derivative "Intermission Riff" is one of the more surprising omissions from this set. After the war, he took on the full panoply of bop and cool modernism, producing an unmistakably original and loud synthesis of his own. *Retrospective* is a reminder that his bands—excuse me, orchestras—reflected not only sundry approaches to music, but the pretentiousness that goaded jazz when schoolmasters still thought it needed refinement. I'm delighted to learn from the notes that Kenton balked at recording new directions in *Hair*. We all draw the line somewhere.

37 ❖ *Dexter Gordon*
(Resurgence)

The King of Quoters, Dexter Gordon, was himself eminently quotable. In a day not unlike our own, when purists issue fiats about what is or isn't valid in jazz, Gordon declared flatly, "jazz is an octopus"—it will assimilate anything it can use. Drawing closer to home, he spoke of his musical lineage: Coleman Hawkins "was going out farther on the chords, but Lester [Young] leaned to the pretty notes. He had a way of telling a story with everything he played." Young's story was sure, intrepid, daring, erotic, cryptic. A generation of saxophonists found itself in his music, as an earlier generation had found itself in Hawkins's rococo virtuosity. Young was also the first piper whose song was heard differently by blacks and whites, and this amused Gordon. "We used to jam together," he once recalled, "Zoot [Sims], Al Cohn, Allen Eager. Zoot and I worked in a club in Hollywood for Norman Granz. He was playing Lester and I was playing Lester, but there was always a difference." Of Young's children, Gordon had the deepest and most lasting influence.

The racial implications in Young's music became increasingly pronounced in the '50s. Black tenors modified his legato phrasing with a heavier forthright attack, accenting the muscularity of his style, even to the extreme of rhythm and blues honking. White tenors focused on his airy lyricism, even to the extreme of a limpid preciosity that vitiated what was generally called West Coast jazz. In the end, though, the key tenors blended both sides of Lester along with the lessons of Hawkins and the third member of the prewar tenor trinity, Ben Webster, producing a new troika of modern tenors in Sonny Rollins, Stan Getz, and John Coltrane. Gordon greased the transition.

He combined Young's laconic melodies with the progressive harmonies and asymmetrical rhythms of Charlie Parker, and he made the results lucid, persuasive, mesmerizing. After flirting with Young's timbre, he developed a sound entirely his own. If Rollins found his way independently (marrying Hawkins to Parker), Stan Getz offered an outright Gordon impersonation on his 1946 debut ("Opus De Bop"), and Coltrane switched from alto to tenor to better emulate Gordon's seductive tone. More recently, David Murray composed a perceptive homage to him, and Joshua Redman won the Thelonious Monk Saxophone Competition playing "Second Balcony Jump," which he had learned from Gordon's *Go!*

Gordon's appeal was to be found not only in his Promethean sound and nonstop invention, his impregnable authority combined with a steady and knowing wit, but also in a spirit born in the crucible of jam sessions. He was the most formidable of battlers, undefeated in numerous contests, and never more engaging than in his kindred flare-ups with the princely Wardell Gray, a perfect Lestorian foil, gently lyrical but no less swinging and sure. And yet he was lost to us for most of the '50s, busted for drugs in 1952, paroled in 1955 (when he recorded two minor albums), rearrested in 1956, paroled in 1960, at which time Cannonball Adderley produced the Jazzland album, *The Resurgence of Dexter Gordon.*

That led to a commission to score the West Coast production of Jack Gelber's *The Connection* and a contract with Blue Note. By then the public had forgotten him, though musicians and critics had not. Asked in an interview just prior to Gordon's resurgence to name the outstanding tenor of the day, Coltrane said Rollins, then quickly added "in formative days, Dexter Gordon."

Gordon was born in Los Angeles in 1923; he started on clarinet at thirteen, switched to alto two years later and to tenor two years after that. He has described L.A. as being isolated in the '30s. "It was almost like living in Europe. Only the biggest bands came out, like Dorsey, Hines, Duke, Louis, but there were some good locals, like Hampton and Marshal Royal. All my lunch money went to used 78s." In 1939, he heard the Basie band with Young. "Pres! He had that special thing that floored me. I tried to play like him. He was the first to play color tones, like sixths and ninths." Gordon was very much under the Young influence when he joined Lionel Hampton's band, where his fellow tenor was Illinois Jacquet. "We were both listening to the same thing, but he leaned more to Herschel [Evans, also of the Basie band] and I leaned more to Pres. At that time Hawkins was the dominant figure with purists—Lester, with the light sound, wasn't considered in the same class. But he had such spirit and joie de vivre."

In 1941, Hampton's orchestra appeared in a battle of the bands at the Savoy opposite Jay McShann. "I dug his alto player, he had a lot of Lester in his playing, and also Jimmy Dorsey." Jimmy Dorsey? "He was a master saxophonist, Bird knew that." The altoist was Charlie Parker, of course; he provided the third major ingredient in Dexter's evolving style. "He was playing so much saxophone, new tunes, new harmonic conceptions, he extended the chords, altering them fluidly. Pres stayed around ninths—he must have listened to Ravel and Debussy—but Bird went all the way up the scale." Gordon became a part of the new movement. "We used to go by Dizzy's house and he'd be playing piano and changes; it was like a little school 'cause cats went up there all the time. I didn't like Monk at first because he wasn't an impressive pianist like Bud Powell; later on, of course . . ." He met the other tenors who had come up the same way, listening to Pres and then Bird, like Wardell Gray and Gene Ammons. "Ammons was playing like Ben [Webster] when he first joined the Billy Eckstine band. After I joined, the mutha changed his style in a minute."

Before Eckstine, however, there was a stay with Louis Armstrong's big band. Louis had walked up to him in a club in Los Angeles and said, "Hey, gates, I like your tone, kid, you got a nice tone." The next night,

Teddy McRae, the band's straw boss, hired him. Dexter was unhappy with the '30s arrangements Armstrong used, and the spiritlessness he perceived among the band members, but he loved Armstrong.

By the late '40s, Gordon had become involved in a series of immensely popular tenor battles. It began with Eckstine singing, "Blow, Mr. Gene, blow Mr. Dexter, too." In addition to Ammons, he took on Teddy Edwards, Budd Johnson, baritone saxophonist Leo Parker, and, most rewardingly, Wardell Gray. At the same time, he composed an impressive number of riff tunes for recording sessions on Savoy and Dial. Jimmy Heath has described Gordon as the central influence on the second wave of modernist tenors, because even Young seemed dated to them by 1949. One of the musicians most profoundly touched by Gordon's music, particularly his harmonic inventiveness, was Coltrane, three years Gordon's junior. By 1960, Coltrane would build a new lexicon on Dexter's foundation, using Indian and pentatonic scales, chord patterns within chords, and phrase permutations, which Gordon, like Hawkins learning from Parker, would incorporate into his own playing.

The Dexter Gordon Blue Notes, seven albums recorded over four years (May 1961–May 1965), represent the apogee of his art. (Two additional albums, rejected as subpar by the canny producer Alfred Lion, were issued many years later.) Gordon enjoyed numerous triumphs before (the '40s Dials and Savoys, and the recorded concerts) and after (*The Panther* on Prestige, *More Than You Know* and *Biting the Apple* on SteepleChase), but on Blue Note he achieved transcendence—in Joyce's phrase, "ear-piercing dulcitude." Splendidly conceived and recorded, they are insuperable examples of the streamlined elegance of which jazz quartets and quintets are capable.

Unlike the quartets of Rollins, Getz, and Coltrane, Gordon did not record with a working band. He and Lion chose players they hoped would be alert and empathic, leaving a great deal to chance. They effected a miracle in the course of three days in August 1962: two complete albums—*Go!* and *A Swingin' Affair*—with pianist Sonny Clark, bassist Butch Warren, and drummer Billy Higgins that incarnated Gordon's unpretentious majesty as never before. On the indispensable *Dexter Gordon: The Complete Blue Note Sixties Sessions*, a six-CD set, those albums are brought together on a single disc, blessedly unencumbered by rejected takes. Hardly a measure fails to stir the blood. His playing is unfailingly direct and entertaining, at times quite beautiful.

Clark, who died at thirty-one and is remembered chiefly for his work with Gordon as well as his own sessions, was a pensive but limpid pianist who took Bud Powell's dazzling rhythms but not his sturm und drang; his light-fingered solos are crafty and deliberated, economical and measured, frequently surprising, often underpinned by minor-key melancholy, even when played in a major key—"You Stepped Out of a Dream" is a sterling example. Higgins is no less stunning, his ride cymbal a polite ocean roar, never rushing, never intruding, but always there. Everyone had to be alert because Gordon's uses of tempo and variation were unpredictable. Aren't "Smile" and "Love for Sale" thumb suckers, perhaps a touch maudlin? Not here. No musician had a better sense of where sentiment and sentimentality part company.

Each of the seven original albums is savory. *Doin' Alright* (an important showcase for the young trumpet whiz, Freddie Hubbard) set the stage for a comeback of major proportions, beginning with the rigorous transformation of the Gershwin title tune, followed by a shining example of what was soon recognized as Gordon's distinctive approach to ballads, "You've Changed." *Dexter Calling* is still more accomplished, a loomingly smart quartet session that loses little in a comparison with the Clark albums. *Our Man in Paris* is a vital time capsule, one of the last great and authentic bop sessions, with Bud Powell and Kenny Clarke. Playing with a suitably lighter tone, Gordon bounds into action, fleet and festive, ripping "A Night in Tunisia," caressing "Stairway to the Stars," and apparently restoring the troubled Powell in the process. *One Flight Up*, which seemed prescient in the '60s in its extended modalism, wears less well, though attention paid is attention rewarded. The underrated *Gettin' Around* is a bright and happy romp, irradiated by Bobby Hutcherson's vibes.

I have but one quibble about the Blue Note compilation: the sequencing—an art in itself—has been pointlessly disfigured to represent the order in which the tunes were completed. Only in jazz does this sort of thing pass for logic. If a chamber group had to redo the adagio after completing the last movement of a string quartet, would any label reissue the music in the order it was recorded? Listeners will want to program their CD machines at least once to experience the albums as originally offered: *Doin' Alright* (disc one) tracks 1, 3, 7, 4, 6; *Go!* (disc three) tracks 4, 5, 2, 6, 3, 1; *A Swingin' Affair* (disc three) tracks 9, 12, 11, 8, 10, 7; *Our Man in Jazz* (disc four) tracks 6, 5, 2, 3, 4; and *Gettin' Around* (disc six) tracks 2, 7, 8, 6, 4, 1. *Dexter Calling* and *One Flight Up* are each spread to two discs. *Landslide* (a compilation drawn from three sessions) and *Clubhouse* (which Lion never sequenced) weren't released until 1979 and 1980, to capitalize on Gordon's return from Europe.

Gordon was an honest and genuinely original artist of deep and abiding humor and of tremendous personal charm. He imparted his personal characteristics to his music—size, radiance, kindness, a genius for discontinuous logic. Consider his trademark musical quotations—snippets from other songs woven into the songs he is playing. Some, surely, were calculated. But not all and probably not many, for they are too subtle and too supple. They fold into his solos like spectral glimpses of an alternative universe in which all of Tin Pan Alley is one infinite song. That so many of the quotations seem verbally relevant I attribute to Gordon's reflexive stream-of-consciousness and prodigious memory for lyrics. I cannot imagine him *planning* apposite quotations.

Instead, I hear a whirl of melodies, some of which burst forth unbidden, like memories. One example (among dozens, maybe hundreds on Blue Note): in measures twenty-five and twenty-six of the opening theme of "Three O'Clock in the Morning," he inserts six notes from "My Melancholy Baby" that are absolutely germane to the song at hand. The reference is so natural and fitting it defies calculation: it's an inspired melodic fillip, the right phrase at the right time. Which is precisely what jazz improvisation is about. Gordon's stream-of-consciousness, which in a different context won him a deserved best-actor Oscar nomination for his work in an unworthy film, *'Round Midnight*, also informed his compositions. The long-unreleased "Landslide" is a thirty-two-bar song he wrote in 1961 in recognition of the undervalued tenor saxophonist Harold Land, but the key melodic phrase stems from a 1952 blues he recorded with Wardell Gray called "The Rubaiyiat." Perfect: who in 1961 had more Wardell in him than Harold Land? Another example of the octopus at work is "Soul Sister," written for *The Connection*. The four/four extrapolation is pure Dexter, wonderfully resourceful, but the waltz-time head is a thinly disguised rewrite of the New Orleans second-line anthem "Junko Partner." Synergy never wore a broader smile.

Gordon continued to perform and record in Europe, occasionally passing through the United States. Not until 1975, when the last and most glorious of his resurgences (notwithstanding several disappointing recordings) was brought to pass by Bruce Lundvall, then presiding over Columbia Records, did Gordon meet with widespread acceptance—from the entire jazz community and, after the movie, beyond. By 1985, he was strained by illness and his playing was in decline—ironically, the film represents him more accurately as an actor than as a musician. Yet shortly before his death in 1989, he summoned his strength for a stalwart and profoundly moving concert at a stadium in Perugia, Italy. As was his custom, he finished by holding his saxophone horizontally aloft, like an offering to the audience, which stood cheering for several minutes.

❖

PART FIVE

A Mainstream Music

38 ❖ Miles Davis
(Kinds of Blues)

The rumor, abroad for three or four weeks, that Miles Davis was in intensive care in Santa Monica and fading fast did nothing to alleviate the immense sadness that attended the confirmation of his death on September 28, 1991. After the news broke, I had an overwhelming need to hear "He Loved Him Madly," Davis's threnody for Duke Ellington, which I hadn't heard in well over a decade but had played to distraction when it was first released on his 1975 *Get Up with It* album. Unlike dozens of conventional tributes to Ellington, that piece captured the holy calm and fear suitable to a great man's passing. A thirty-minute dirge based on an organ drone in which little happens, it advances and sustains an inscrutable mood suggesting echoes in a medieval cathedral. Most powerful when most inert, "He Loved Him Madly" falters during the flute solo—a solo of any kind would be too decorous for the occasion's deep solemnity. And it's too long, a reflection of the maximalist trance-music omnipresent in the mid-'70s. Yet somehow, in ways I can't explain, it incarnates the ennobling ache of the instrument most conspicuous by its absence, Davis's trumpet.

Listening now to the entire album, which was recorded over four years, I remain especially puzzled by the lamentation's intangible form, but am certain that the jury is still out on the diverse and complicated "directions" Davis attempted to forge in that controversial period. Evidence that Davis's fusion records were constructed in the editing room, sometimes by a producer without Davis's input, was taken as proof that they represented a cynical concession to Mammon. That bias is hardly borne out by a thirty-minute dirge or by the thirty-two-minute "Calypso Frelimo," with its mockingly elliptical calypso strain, or the crushing keyboards-sitar-rhythm novelty, "Rated X." But there is filler, too: the electrified Ellingtonian jungle of "Mtume," which does sound like a razor job, and the empty-headed "Red China Blues." Miles never made it easy.

In 1947, at twenty-one, Davis recorded as a leader for the first time, for Savoy Records. He had been on The Street two years, had played on Charlie Parker's first official session at nineteen, though not on the pivotal number, "Koko," for the crucial reason that he did not have the requisite chops to play the furious eight-bar exchanges Dizzy Gillespie was asked to supply. But on "Billie's Bounce" and especially "Now's the Time," Davis showed he had his own way, even though he might be confined to the middle register and incapable of nudging every passing chord implied in the harmonic sweep of bebop. He brought something pressing to the new music. His timbre, influenced by Freddie Webster, was individual, if not yet achingly individual, and he could fashion melodic variations by skimming chords for the most persuasive notes. So in 1947, with his mentor Charlie Parker serving humbly as a sideman on tenor sax, the Juilliard dropout and his doctorate-seeking friend John Lewis were inclined to show off. Miles brought out "Sippin' at Bells," a twelve-measure blues with an inverted melody and a flurry of chords that all but camouflages blues harmony. As a gift to Davis, Lewis presented him with "Milestones," a line with so many harmonic bottlenecks that Parker insisted he'd play just the bridge because the tune was too hard for a country boy like him. That gave Davis and Lewis something to ponder, but not enough to deter them from a taste for cool intellectualism.

In 1949, Davis demonstrated for the first time his powers as a visionary and persistent organizer. He assembled some of the finest writers and players in New York to put into practice the ideas they'd been discussing and that Gil Evans—at thirty-seven, the senior conspirator—had been developing in his arrangements for Claude Thornhill's dance band. They met at Gil's pad, a cellar room on West Fifty-fifth Street, to consider new methods of instrumentation, improvisation, and orchestration that would offset the steeplechase rigors of bebop. Evans, a phenomenal autodidact whom Thornhill discovered writing charts for Skinnay Ennis on Bob Hope's radio show, venerated Armstrong, Ellington, and Parker and found inspiration everywhere. Combining swing, bop, and classical techniques, he was known for cloudlike chords in which the harmonies slipped seamlessly one to the next and breathlessly long phrases. The prolific Gerry Mulligan did most of the writing, but Miles was in charge. He formulated the nine-piece combination (heavy on brass), secured an isolated gig (two weeks in a club, the only time the group performed for an audience), and contracted for three record dates, producing twelve sides eventually collected as *Birth of the Cool*.

John Lewis and Max Roach from the Parker quintet participated, along with Lee Konitz, Mulligan, J. J. Johnson, Kai Winding, and bassist Al McKibbon, plus four guys (including Gunther Schuller and Bill Barber) alternating on French horn and tuba. A perfectly integrated ensemble, racially and musically, it configured improvisers and writers, soloists and ensemble, hot and cool. As the public was indifferent, the nonet went straight from cult to classic, and the celebrated sides—"Boplicity," "Israel," "Godchild," "Moon Dreams," "Move," "Rocker," "Jeru," "Rouge"—

endure as an indelible achievement, uncontaminated by the musty imitations that came to be associated with West Coast jazz. Its musicians redesigned jazz in the '50s, calming bop's fevers, soothing its brow, bringing wreaths to the entombment. Counterpoint and polyphony reappeared, tempos slowed, timbre lightened. In 1952, John Lewis organized the Modern Jazz Quartet, renovating the blues with counterpoint. That same year, Mulligan created the pianoless quartet with Chet Baker, unleashing "cool" as a popular movement. Roach created the last classic bop band in collaboration with Clifford Brown, then embraced an encompassing postmodernism with political and historical implications. Schuller coined the phrase "third-stream" to formalize the merging of jazz and classical traditions. Johnson and Winding organized a quintet that employed counterpoint while stimulating a vogue for trombonists. Konitz abided as a maverick soloist, one step ahead of the sheriff and beyond category.

And Davis? Having formulated cool, he found it chilly and dull. He would develop a series of the most aggressive quintets and sextets in jazz. He would collaborate with Evans on three albums that redefined the concerto form in jazz, exemplifying improvisational angst while doubling—strange, but true—as make-out albums of international application. He would focus with singular emphasis on the blues, mining fine gradations between earthy and mellow. But before any of that, he helped spur and codify the counterreformation known as "hard bop" with his 1954 blues "Walkin'," a stirring accomplishment on at least three counts: First, the twenty-bar head with its baronial eight-bar preamble is executed with rare drama: like Monk's "Brilliant Corners" or Ellington's "Such Sweet Thunder," "Walkin' " has the strutting grandeur of a jazz march. Second, the rhythm section is a unit of glowing, erotic beauty: between the years when Jo Jones tattooed the hi-hat for Basie and Tony Williams shivered the ride cymbal for Davis, nobody made concave plates resound with more colorful, emphatic hues than did Kenny Clarke on this record, in meticulous accord with Percy Heath's stalwart bass and Horace Silver's hungrily inspired piano. Third, it offers spellbinding improvisations that unfurl without recourse to pyrotechnics, working their magic with the penetrating logic of impeccable fables impeccably told.

Thus the warring subcultures, West Coast jazz (cool) and East Coast jazz (hard bop), had the same midwestern parent: one Miles Dewey Davis of Alton, Illinois. And though Davis rejected cool jazz, he came to personify jazz cool. Miles looked cool, dressed cool, and talked cool—in a guttural, foul-mouthed sort of way. His posture was cool as he approached the mike or turned away from it. His notes were cool: fat voicelike plums sustained in a siege of meditation or serrated arpeggios ripped into infinity. Cool, too, were his rests, those stirring oases enacted with flashing eyes and shrugged shoulders. Miles was an ongoing musical drama. In the world of Marlon Brando and John Osborne, he was the angry young trumpeter: handsome, unpredictable, and smart, driving fast cars and squiring beautiful women. Miles was the first subject of a *Playboy* interview. Miles didn't need a last name. Miles was an idiom unto himself.

Davis did not become a bona fide jazz star until 1956, after he cold turkeyed heroin and healed from a throat operation that left his voice little more than a menacing rasp (which fueled the Prince of Darkness legend after his producers included snippets of it on his albums). He knew the only way he could cross beyond a coterie audience was to sign with the best network label, CBS's Columbia Records, where the canny head of A&R was George Avakian. Davis had met Avakian in 1947 at the Three Deuces, where Dizzy was playing—the three men posed for a photograph. Davis later told George that he decided that night he was going to maneuver his way to Columbia. He asked Avakian to sign him up in 1954, but with three years remaining on his Prestige contract, they decided to wait. After Miles triumphed at the 1955 Newport Jazz Festival as the added guest to an all-star quintet (Gerry Mulligan, Zoot Sims, Thelonious Monk, Percy Heath, Connie Kay), Avakian realized he'd better not wait any longer. Davis wanted an advance on signing of $4000, which was considered a fortune, especially for someone who had been a junkie and might prove unreliable. But the executives at Columbia were impressed by the unrelenting perseverance of Avakian, who told them, "He may be as big as Dizzy." The only problem was the intransigence of Prestige.

The first Miles Davis Quintet proves, as the Hot Fives and Sevens did before it, that tenure and prolificacy are no indications of a band's quality, influence, and durability. The quintet existed on and off for little more than two years and was widely regarded as the finest small jazz ensemble of its day—one critic thought it the most accomplished since the Hot Five. Its impact was immediate and lasting, leading directly to the sextet and the recordings with Gil Evans and bringing Davis and jazz itself to a high ground. Between 1956 and 1960, Davis exerted an inescapable hold on the imagination of the jazz world. So it is startling to realize how little music we have by the band that not only established him as an artist with formidable commercial power, but launched John Coltrane, Red Garland, Paul Chambers, and Philly Joe Jones and popularized nearly a dozen songs that became standards in the modern jazz repertory. We would have even less if Columbia hadn't stepped on Prestige's toes.

In the fall of 1955, as his new band developed its style at Greenwich Village's Cafe Bohemia, Davis still owed Prestige one year and four albums. A deal was made: Davis would record the albums in the coming year, and Columbia would refrain from releasing its first Davis album until 1957. All Columbia apparently got out of the bargain was the right to record him immediately, though it had secretly jumped the gun with an October 1955 session before the agreement was struck. Prestige received a windfall: on a roll, Davis recorded enough material for five albums instead of four, enabling the company to release "new" Davis albums annually through 1961, while partaking in the publicity that only an industry giant like Columbia could generate. The importance of Prestige's catalog increased when Avakian elected to produce only one album by the quintet, having decided to feature Davis in orchestrated concertos. Alas, neither company thought to record the band live—only bootleggers and the Armed Forces Radio Service had the foresight for that.

Davis completed his 1955 obligations with a November date, recording six selections released as *Miles*. To cancel the remaining debt, he agreed to two marathon sessions in May and October of 1956, recording twenty-three full-scale selections (quintets and quartets), two set closers, and a trio number in two days. A marathon date differs from the usual recording setup for the obvious reason that quantity is emphasized. But something else happens in the pressure-cooker ambience of single takes and no backward glances (no after-the-fact edits): an enforced faith in the spontaneity that governs a nightclub set. To sustain that mood, Davis chose each number just as the band was about to play it, as he would in a club. He combined pieces in the current book with adaptations by Red Garland (a storehouse of unlikely show tunes), numbers from his previous recordings, and pieces newly devised in the studio.

The most efficient studio marathon recordings are those Art Tatum made for Verve between 1953 and 1955—124 numbers in four days. In their own sweet way, Davis's final two days at Prestige are no less impressive since the music they produced wasn't the work of a single musician but of a band that was discovering its power as the tapes rolled. They required extraordinary concentration and stamina, and a willingness—often vaunted by Davis as a cardinal virtue—to allow mistakes a good and candid airing. (At the close of a Bing Crosby recording date, the composer of one of the songs was present when Crosby muffed a phrase on it. The horrified composer, too timid to approach the singer, pleaded with a musician to request a retake. "That's alright," Crosby told the go-between, "let them see that I'm human.") The major difference between the Prestige and Columbia recordings becomes apparent in perusing a discography. In contrast to the Prestige one-shots, the Columbias were often edited from two or three partial takes, a composite approach that reflects more detailed arrangements and seeks perfection beyond that of an honest "live" performance. If Davis was letting them see he was human at Prestige, he was also burnishing the legend. For his uniquely poignant mistakes were admired as the introspective slip-ups of an artist responding to a higher calling.

Except for a Steve Allen broadcast from Basin Street and the covert Columbia session, the November 1955 Prestige album *Miles* represented Davis's initial recorded work with John Coltrane and the new quintet. Years later (in his autobiography), Davis would observe, "The music that we were playing together was just unbelievable. It was so bad that it used to send chills through me at night, and it did the same thing to the audiences, too." Yet the first album was a tease of what was to come— Coltrane struggles for authority, and the rhythm section is relatively tentative. Also, the recording (Rudy Van Gelder was still working out his method) lacks the presence of the suppressed Columbia sessions. Garland is occasionally overmiked, and ambience is favored at the expense of a tight, unison radiance.

Yet the album offers much to admire. It's startling to hear Coltrane work through licks in "How Am I To Know?" that in time would be recognized as his patented phrases, licks that were at first misperceived as the exertions of a derivative hard bopper. "Just Squeeze Me," which Duke Ellington fashioned from an instrumental piece ("Subtle Slough") into a jokey vocal feature for Ray Nance, is the first of several unlikely vehicles to display Davis's particular form of alchemy. Another worthy if less successful transformation is "S'posin'," despite a stiff Coltrane performance; note how Davis worries one motif in the second sixteen-bar stretch of his second solo and how the rhythm section hews to the song's (presumably unfamiliar) harmonies—the result is a chance to hear the coolest band in town working in a curiously traditional mode. Davis often expressed his admiration for Frank Sinatra, so, though it may be sheer coincidence, it's impossible not to note that Sinatra's 1960 recording of "S'posin'" echoes Davis's tempo and temperament. Benny Golson's "Stablemates," the one piece with a polished ensemble head, is as close as the quintet came to emulating Art Blakey's Jazz Messengers.

Of the first of the two marathons, Davis noted, "I remember this session well because it was long, and the playing was great. We did no second takes. We just recorded like we were playing a nightclub set." But that stimulating day's work was a prelude to the far more accomplished second marathon, recorded shortly after another Columbia date and during a week the band was in residence at Cafe Bohemia. With a total of twenty-six performances at its disposal, Prestige chose to begin its release program with the quintet at its height: it collected the *last* five numbers of the second marathon. This decision would have a baleful short-term result: as the incrementally weaker albums were issued, the illusion was created of a band running out of steam, when, in fact, it had progressed every step of the way. According to Ira Gitler's liner notes, Davis himself titled the first album *Cookin'*, and it was released after the band temporarily broke up in the spring of 1957.

Cookin' is a landmark recording. It offers Davis's first go at "My Funny Valentine," an emblematic performance and a sultry start for an album otherwise given over to heady tempos. (Columbia's *'Round About Midnight* employed a similar strategy.) Coltrane lays out on "Valentine," but Garland sets the scene with a firm vamp-arrangement, augmented by Paul Chambers's two-note bass figure, ushering in Davis's muted meditations. The trumpeter's chops were shining that day: gorgeous sustained notes, surprise arpeggiated detours that uncover pining melodies. The oddly elastic rhythm section, speeding and retarding the tempo with reflexive dispatch, suggests the unity of a chamber group—every note apparently preordained and every phrase wasteless. The performance closes with a reprise of the vamp, girded by Chambers's bowing.

"Blues by Five" boasts an ingeniously songful eight-chorus improvisation by Davis, borrowing a few licks from Gene Ammons's "Red Top" solo. His third choruses consists of three phrases that perfectly mirror the AAB structure of a traditional blues vocal. Philly Joe, when he isn't briskly ching-ching-a-chinging, pushes and anticipates Davis in a manner that prefigures Elvin Jones's relationship to Coltrane. Coltrane himself enters with a characteristic left-field figure. For a powerhouse take on Sonny Rollins's "Airegin," Davis surfs rhythmic waves and Coltrane exhibits confidence and daring. A medley, apparently born of impatience to move on, tags Davis's "Tune Up" with Benny Carter's "When Lights Are Low." The former, commenced with cool counterpoint that complements the brazenly contrapuntal version of "Ah Leu Cha" on Davis's Columbia debut, explodes with a skyrocketing trumpet solo, almost matched in intensity by Coltrane, before the leader parachutes into Carter's pleasing melody at a medium clip.

Relaxin' followed the release of Columbia's *'Round About Midnight* and combined four selections from the second marathon with two from the first, giving more of a platform to the ballads that were clearly becoming Davis's trademark. Studio chatter precedes Garland's memorable adaptation of Frank Loesser's "If I Were a Bell," from *Guys and Dolls*, which subsequently became a recurring number in the jazz repertory. Solos are relayed from Davis to Coltrane (a bit shaky) to Garland via breaks, a device as old as Armstrong's "Hotter Than That" and employed no less effectively. After chatter and a breakdown, "You're My Everything" offers an early instance of Coltrane's nascent ballad style, albeit with more rests than would soon be customary. Paul Chambers intensifies "I Could Write a Book" with mounting, responsive accompaniments to each soloist.

Workin' and *Steamin'* are, excepting one selection on each album, taken from the first marathon and are less consistent and aggressive albums, yet they give much pleasure. The former opens with a quaintly alluring and rehearsed arrangement of "It Never Entered My Mind" (sans Coltrane), played over a wonderfully incongruous piano figure, all stately pomp, and a two-note bass vamp that rings the first beat of each measure. Some find this performance a bit ripe, an overbaked reflection of Davis's fascination with Ahmad Jamal (Garland sounds at times as though he were playing the lobby of a cheesy hotel), but what's life without a bit of Camembert? Also included: remakes of "Four" and "Half Nelson," from Davis's 1946 date with Charlie Parker; all three versions of "The Theme," two set endings (the second closing with a riveting Philly Joe extension), plus a sustained variation with a closing interpolation of Parker's "The Hymn," retitled "Trane's Blues"; and a poised and practiced version of Dave Brubeck's charming, "In Your Own Sweet Way." A trio version of an Ahmad Jamal blues emphasizes Davis's high regard for Jamal's innovations in dynamics and organization.

Steamin' puts its best foot forward with a highly plausible version of "Surrey with the Fringe on Top," from *Oklahoma!* For all its elegance, however, it isn't as fully realized a conversion as, say, "Bye Bye Blackbird" (on *'Round About Midnight*), which is so thoroughly transformed that you don't pause to think of the incongruity of the material. But "Surrey" has Coltrane's most forceful statement from the first marathon (untypically, he interjects a reference to "Fascinatin' Rhythm"). An even more unusual selection is "Diane," a '20s waltz revived the previous year by, ahem, Mantovani, again made savory by a Coltrane solo that, despite a cold reed (unintended shriek), stands as one of his most buoyant solos to that time. An agitated version of "Salt Peanuts" is shanghaied by a long, invigorating drum solo, and Monk's "Well You Needn't" compensates for a careless head with high energy and wicked arco bass. Two dilatory ballads offer little beyond demure and muted trumpet solos. Davis sounds tired, and who can blame him?

The most distinctive selection on the Columbia album is an interpretation of Thelonious Monk's " 'Round Midnight" (for some reason, the song's publisher insisted on the insertion of "About" in the album title, though it was never used again). Avakian brought in Gil Evans to craft the arrangement. Gil and Davis had not worked together since 1950, but this reunion reaffirmed their friendship and Davis's regard for his skills. Evans made the quintet seem fuller and more cohesive than on the other selections, and his organization of the song's components, complete with a dramatic change in tempo, became standardized. During Davis's long engagement at Cafe Bohemia, he began to meet with Avakian and Evans to plan an expansion of the nonet. In mapping out the instrumentation one night at Lindy's, they came up with a nineteen-piece ensemble. Evans wanted to compose links between the selections, something never done before. Because of the complexity of the arrangements, Davis's determination in getting the solos right, and the limited time for rehearsal and recording, they also explored the options of splicing and dubbing. *Miles Ahead* was unprecedented in every respect.

From the dynamic swing of "Springsville," one of the most audacious attention grabbers ever, to the thirsting lyricism of "I Don't Wanna Be Kissed," a daring close, *Miles Ahead* is peerlessly seductive. Not since Ellington had any arranger extended the cross-harmonization between orchestral sections as rigorously as Evans, who for the first time was granted complete freedom. And not since Ellington had any composer adapted the concerto to jazz as ingeniously as Evans, who recognized in Davis the ideal partner. The singularity and expressiveness of Davis's voice encouraged Evans to try for the most intrepidly burnished settings he could devise. Evans realized that the cornerstone of Davis's eloquence is his strength. Imbalance is not an issue. The ensemble motivates the soloist and is parried by him—the melancholy veracity of Davis's timbre matches the plush brassy brilliance of Evans's voicings. Together they refashion Delibes's "The Maids of Cadiz," Kurt Weill's "My Ship," and Jamal's "New Rhumba" as though they were original compositions. And so they are.

The only drawback was the cover—a sailboat against a blue sky, intended to express the idea of Miles forging ahead, with a blonde model on the boat. Davis protested, "Why'd you put that white bitch on there?" But the company wasn't about to burn the 50,000 jackets already printed. *Miles Ahead* was a commercial and critical landmark in the music of the '50s. Possibly no other album in that era, outside of a few by Ellington, did as much to awaken the affluent society, in and out of the academy, to the range of progressive (a regressive term) jazz. Brubeck, who was represented on the album by his composition "The Duke," sold more records and had a clamorous following on the campuses, but Miles's albums and Miles's ascension delineated a new and dangerous sexiness that would have a far more durable impact here and abroad.

❖ ❖ ❖

At thirty-one, he was the representative black artist. People wanted to hear what he had to say. He was featured in fashion magazines. People who didn't buy jazz records, except maybe Ella singing Cole Porter, bought Miles. He defined the era's stance and tone, its beat irreverence, high life, wounded introversion, and causeless belligerence. When Armstrong attacked Eisenhower and segregation in 1957, he was harassed by a columnist who demanded a boycott as well as scrutiny from the FBI. When Davis stood up to the cops who bloodied him in front of Birdland a few years later, he was a symbol of the Civil Rights era. He now had the clout to kill the offensive *Miles Ahead* cover. He used his wife as the cover model for *Someday My Prince Will Come*, a milestone of a different sort, in 1961.

One of the arrangements that didn't make the final cut of *Miles Ahead* was a particular favorite of Gil's, "Summertime." From that seed, however, grew the second and most enthralling of the three key Davis-Evans collaborations, *Porgy and Bess*. Never before had Davis's emotional range, from the chillingly stark laments to the unexpected closing splash of big band euphoria, been so compellingly displayed. Yet for many people, the third album, *Sketches of Spain*, struck a deeper chord. Here the arrangements were scaled down to minimal scrims, drunk with color. Davis's improvisations stand naked before the ensemble, the jazzman as confessional poet, working out a timbre that had never been heard on trumpet, that suggested the obverse not only of conventional jazz intonation but of the robust Spanish style the album celebrated. Though marred by inadequate rehearsal, the power of the spectacle overwhelmed reservations. If the general effect is less opulent, less persuasive than *Porgy*, the unparalleled "Saeta" remains a taunting cry from the heart, a sequestered peering into the dark before the expressionistic deluge of New Things and electronics run amuck.

Sketches of Spain was originally intended to represent a more capacious response to Third World music, an exploration of sounds coming from Asia and Africa. Avakian had been collecting records from Columbia's international division, which he headed, and had turned many of them over to Evans, who became obsessed with Spain. By the time Evans and Davis were ready to record the project, Avakian had left the company. One of the rejected tunes from the original concept was Cyril Scott's fin de siècle "Lotus Land," which continued to haunt Avakian and Evans— the former produced "Lotus Land" for the Calvin Jackson Quartet and Evans arranged it for Kenny Burrell's *Guitar Forms*. Davis's mind had been turning elsewhere. In between *Porgy* and *Sketches*, he scheduled a far less fatiguing two-session sextet album that exerted an incalculable impact on generations of young musicians.

The serenely Zenlike *Kind of Blue*, with its one-take meditations and heightened consciousness (Davis kept the music from the musicians until the recording session so that no one could bring a glib or practiced set of responses to it), involved a logical blending of modal improvisation with familiar song forms. Davis had been working in this direction for some time, encouraged by Evans's harmonic schemes—his 1958 *Milestones* was the first indication. *Kind of Blue*, with Coltrane, Bill Evans, and Cannonball Adderley, represented a culmination of the turnaround he had made over the past dozen years, from the tyro of 1946 who piled on harmonic changes so as to disguise a blues-based structure to the mature improviser who was too concerned with melody and feeling to be distracted by harmonic obligations. On *Milestones*, the title piece was not the old John Lewis bebop obstacle course, but a genuine original in which multiple changes were reduced to a few scales. The new approach, especially on *Kind of Blue*, underscored all his strengths and none of his weaknesses. The scalar arrangements and modified tempos suited his predilection for the middle range, his measured lyricism, his hot-ice disposition.

The dark flowing introspection of *Kind of Blue*—one thinks of Joyce's "pure yawn lay low"—is so accessible few people recognized the album as the insurrection it was. He remodeled the blues in "Freddie Freeloader" and "All Blues," introduced modulating tempos in "Blue and Green," supplanted chords with modes while retaining the AABA song format in "So What," and improvised form itself in "Flamenco Sketches." Due to its immense impact in popularizing modality, "So What" long seemed the most prophetic selection—a thirty-two-bar song based on the Dorian mode with a second scale for the release. Davis, holding firm to the D-minor scale, found it melodically liberating and not harmonically constricting; his variations, like those on the 1954 "Walkin'," are lucid and songful and moving. By the late '70s, "Flamenco Sketches" appeared more relevant, in challenging the soloists to play five scales, the duration of each to be determined by the improviser. For the most part, Davis and his musicians play it safe, modulating every four or eight bars and telegraphing every modulation for the benefit of the rhythm section. It's a warm-up for the extrapolations he achieved with his next great quintet.

Kind of Blue attained a plateau, but it was also a transition. Freed of harmonic obligations, unapologetic about fluffs that in his playing indicated truth rather than inadequacy—vice turned to virtue—Davis became a more ambitious trumpet player. He began to forage in the upper register at precipitous tempos, ideas spilling from his horn like autumn leaves, his new spiraling confidence matched by a quest for new forms (the influence here of Wayne Shorter can hardly be overstated), resulting over time in such fervent performances as "Country Son," "Petit Machins," and "Right Off." But the change did not come easily. After the back-to-back triumphs of *Kind of Blue* and *Sketches of Spain*, Davis endured a brief slump of uncertainty. Exciting live recordings with Hank Mobley and Gil Evans and a one-shot reunion with John Coltrane obscured his difficulty in putting together a stimulating band. Wayne Shorter, who had appeared on a strange 1962 Davis session with singer Bob Dorough, refused his original bid, preferring to stay with Art Blakey. After trying many other tenors, including Jimmy Heath and Sam Rivers, Davis settled on George Coleman, whom he introduced along with Herbie Hancock, Ron Carter, and seventeen-year-old Tony Williams on his 1963 bicoastal ballad album, *Seven Steps to Heaven*. Then the storm broke.

Nothing could have been less like *Seven Steps to Heaven* than *In Europe*, a tenacious assault (much edited, we now know) on his preferred repertoire, recorded in Antibes in 1963. Here on a sixty-two-minute LP was a band of young musicians and mercurial versions of pieces originally conceived at slow and medium tempos, including a stunningly high-powered "Milestones" with opening notes fired at a clip and an "Autumn Leaves" floated by Hancock's block chords and routed by the authoritative (and much maligned) Coleman. The big news about the record, beyond Davis's explosive energy, was the rhythmic brushfire ignited by Carter and Williams, who provides the album's emotional apogee with his stampeding solo on "Walkin'."

A year later, Davis and his new quintet reclaimed "My Funny Valentine," the 1937 Rodgers and Hart ballad he had triumphantly adapted at the Prestige marathon session. The new version, nearly fifteen-minutes long, was recorded at one of two concerts to benefit voter registration in Mississippi and Louisiana at Philharmonic Hall on February 12, 1964. For some reason, after the triumph at Antibes Davis declined to do a follow-up in the studio. His next two albums were drawn from these concerts: *My Funny Valentine*, a program of ballads, and *Four & More*, a collection of some of his speediest presentations. The programming of the albums was mad (the bruising "Walkin' " and the ponderous "All of You" would have complemented each other on record, as they had in concert), but they were widely celebrated for two reasons. They revealed Davis at his most poignant and defiant, traversing the fiercely honed edge of romance, and they captured close-up the marvelous interchange in a rhythm section that redefined itself every measure.

"My Funny Valentine" is taken mostly at a snail's pace, with metric shifts that range from rubato to swinging long meter. So much time is opened between beats that the rhythm players at times resemble a council of kibitzers, filling in the spaces with everything but the obvious—for example, a backbeat. Davis is out front for nearly half the performance, sculpting three exceedingly personal choruses at the outset and returning at the bridge of Hancock's provident improvisation. Even Coleman, often derided for his smooth surfaces, cries a little—his last chorus restates the melody, stretching his tone into a Milesian plea. Still, Hancock and Coleman are premier filler; Miles is beyond words. His first phrase ends on a decayed note, shorn of vibrato—an antiromantic gesture. His second phrase is exactly parallel. But his third, despite a notorious clam right at its center, grabs you where it hurts. It's an arpeggio that descends, surprisingly, before arching into the clouds and then, after a rest as dramatic as death, landing on two perfectly composed pitches. From that point on, excepting the first bridge, which serves to prove he really is playing "My Funny Valentine," Davis waves at Rodgers and Hart from a far and distant shore.

Later that year, Shorter finally accepted Davis's offer and left Blakey, with whom he had earned an impressive reputation as a composer and tenor saxophonist. Relying on pieces written by members of the band, chiefly Shorter, Davis struggled to make a separate peace amid jazz orthodoxy, modalism, the avant-garde, and the rock hegemony led by musicians older than a couple of his sidemen. Just how much that band achieved was clarified in 1995 when Columbia brought out *The Complete Live at the Plugged Nickel 1965*, a project that derives singular interest from its pioneering comprehensiveness. It contains, unedited, each of the seven sets that Davis's quintet played in a Chicago club on December 22 and 23. We hear how the band interacts over the course of a weekend and how it navigates repertory during a long night. Moreover, we get an intimate, illuminating view of an artist in transition.

To fully appreciate the value of the *Plugged Nickel* disks, consider Davis's output back then. After the three live recordings in France and New York, the revised quintet went into the studio in January 1965 and produced a surprisingly tame effort, *E.S.P.* The next studio recording—the far more confident *Miles Smiles*—took place twenty-one months later, in October 1966, and once again consists of pieces by members of the quintet, plus two selections by Jimmy Heath and Eddie Harris. Almost exactly equidistant between them came the Plugged Nickel engagement, which is significant not least in documenting Davis's adieu to his standard repertoire. It is not true, as is often surmised, that Davis ceased playing jazz and pop classics after Chicago. In fact, his book remained little changed in 1966 and 1967, the primary alteration being the addition of Heath's "Gingerbread Boy." Even as new pieces—soon to be established on the *In a Silent Way/Bitches Brew/Jack Johnson* trilogy—became increasingly familiar, he continued to play standards through late 1969, including "I Fall in Love Too Easily" at Fillmore East in the summer of 1970. But he never *recorded* another standard until the '80s. The Plugged Nickel is our only extended experience of how Davis's last great quintet responded to the challenge of songs written for movies and stage shows.

Much of the music on these eight disks (the long second set required two discs) had been part of Davis's portfolio since the '50s, though the interpretations are quite radical. Altogether, there are thirty-nine performances (including "The Theme," which caps every set) and twenty songs. Only two numbers are played more than twice, "I Fall in Love Too Easily" and "Stella by Starlight." Only one, "Agitation," originated with the second quintet. For the rest, he plays the ballads ("My Funny Valentine," "Autumn Leaves") and jazz classics ("Walkin'," "All Blues") that a well-heeled audience—and maybe the label—expected of him.

Standards often require collusion with the audience. When Davis introduced his arrangement of "If I Were a Bell," everyone recognized its origin in *Guys and Dolls* and responded as much to the metamorphosis as to his solo. If you didn't know the song, you missed part of the point, the wit with which he claimed it as a suitable vehicle. Perhaps Davis abandoned "I Fall in Love Too Easily" on the Fillmore stage because he knew it no longer registered with his targeted audience. Four elaborate performances at the Plugged Nickel of the Jule Styne melody written for Frank Sinatra already betray some doubts. In his 1963 studio recording, he played the head straight with the gorgeously intimate, mournful timbre that was his trademark.

At the Plugged Nickel, the song has other meanings. Given his mid-'60s embouchure problems and knowing his well-rehearsed penchant for acceleration, you don't expect to hear his ripened timbre, but you do expect him to mine a ballad for its bounty. Otherwise why bother? Davis himself seems to wonder. On all four outings he begins with a meditative theme statement, then faithfully picks away at the changes until the rhythm section succeeds in pushing him farther afield, at which time he lets loose the ripping arpeggios and bellowing tremolos that had become his new patented attack. You wonder at his motive as you wouldn't have in 1963. Yet these versions are in many ways more arresting than the original. What they lack is emotional consistency. A telling clue is an odd change that Davis introduces in the melody. In measure eleven (where Sinatra sang "too terribly hard"), the five notes are in a minor key, which is how Davis played it in 1963. Now he substitutes a bright whole tone figure. He plays it every time out. By the end of the gig, Shorter is mimicking it.

Davis begins each night with the same tunes, same order, though mood and attack differ greatly—the first set of the second night (disc four) is irresistible and would have made an enchanting album at the time. He takes increasing risks as the evenings progress, and on the closing sets brings out songs that had not previously been heard in the engagement. Of these, the most appealing is the antic "Yesterdays," which is restored in this release (previously, the tenor and piano solos were cut). It's Saturday night, late, the audience is nodding, and the band has been at it for four hours. Davis is audibly exhausted though yeomanly, but Shorter is getting signals from another world. His intonation drifting in and out of his grasp, he parlays a series of drowsy phrases, trills, puppy shouts, and other vocal feats into a laughably engrossing solo.

None of the members of the quintet went on to the kind of careers expected of them by the Miles Davis fans of 1965, but all were successful, some achieving pop stardom. Before Weather Report, Shorter was the most promising player on his instrument. Notwithstanding his work for Blue Note and with Blakey and Davis, the Plugged Nickel performance significantly increases what we know of him, and there may be no better example of his uncanny reflexiveness and his derring-do. His keening timbre is beautifully captured as he fixes on an idea and quickly discards it—he apparently thinks a riff is a figure you play once because on the second pass it'll be a cliché. On "All Blues" and elsewhere, he enters with one eye open, as if waking, but eight bars later the spinach has hit and Bluto better watch his ass. His playing on Davis's studio albums was never as vivid as this.

Hancock is undermiked; you hear the notes fine, but not the resonance. His solos are uneven—much strolling to make a point, though the point is usually worth waiting for. He overdoes the blues locutions and rarely creates emotionally generous moments. Yet almost every time he's allowed a solo, he comes up with a conceit that makes you shake your head in wonder. Ron Carter is the stoic servant who quietly controls the action because he's the only one who knows where everything is, including the slippery beat. Although Tony Williams is never especially loud, there are times when his drums totally take over. He keeps time one moment, then instigates menacing levels of aggression the next. He's fate knocking on the door.

Of course, the key luminary here isn't an individual, but a rhythm section of surpassing excellence, unprecedented at the time and unequaled since. The best thing about these recordings is the chance to hear the rhythm players at length in a club, responding to hecklers as well as soloists. Hancock, Carter, and Williams unite and divide like cells; they respond to the leader and then they usurp his power. "My Funny Valentine" (disc two), introduced by Hancock with a handful of notes that lets you know the harmony is wide open, is one of the few performances where Davis consistently inserts long rests, yet the rhythm team can't agree on how to make the most of them until it's half over, at which point they go to town. On "Agitation," they are happy as conventioneers. Davis is in a Don Cherry bag on one version (disc two) and resplendently his old self on the other (disc five—who else combines lyricism with fast tremolos?), but in both cases the piano fillips and lockstep rhythm formations are unfailing.

Davis was one of four musicians in the '60s who achieved an oddly suspenseful relationship with his followers. Transformations of Bob Dylan from folkie to rocker, the Beatles from rockers to art rockers, John Coltrane from hard bopper to New Thing prophet, and Miles from bopper to jazz-rocker were played out inch by inch on records. And each alteration irradiated the culture itself. Of the four, Davis had the longest span of influence and demonstrated by far the largest capacity for change. Yet he was surely the least attended. His records sold miserably and were chided for being too far out or not far out enough. From the time Shorter joined the band, every Miles album wrestled with conventional form. Davis accelerated, deconstructed, and finally jettisoned standard songs, reducing new pieces to serial repetition or fragmented riffs. He added electric keyboards and, on one track, guitarist George Benson. The trip from *Nefertiti* to *Miles in the Sky* to *Filles de Kilimanjaro* (an unannounced collaboration with Gil Evans) to *In a Silent Way* generated debates, arguments, recriminations, doubts, celebrations. When he busted through the rock barrier in 1969 with the sometimes impenetrable *Bitches Brew*, debate no longer counted for much. The beast had come slouching toward Bethlehem, and its name was "fusion." The blitz was so disconcerting that many people overlooked the superior *Jack Johnson* issued in its shadows.

Then came the onslaught of double albums and that tangled period in the mid-'70s between *Get Up with It* and *Agharta*, in which the best selections offer the promise, if only sporadically the fulfillment, of an open-ended form that defies harmonic conventions and regulation eight- and twelve-bar phrases in favor of a flexible but contained form, music's most elusive grail. Despite the contempt they provoked, those works are accruing esteem and will continue to be reexamined for what they convey about the potential for blending acoustic and electronic instrumentation, free form and song form, jazz improvisation and multiple rhythms. The drawback with many of those sessions is that Miles himself sounds so raw, his timbre mottled by electronic attachments. The '80s

Miles, restored after a six-year hiatus, is more satisfying even though the rhythms cloy and the bands are less radical. At that time, he effected a rapprochement between the old Miles, wailing recognizable blues and ballads on acoustic trumpet, and an electronic ensemble that sometimes postured more than it played. In his exasperating but indispensable autobiography, Davis makes it clear that the bands of the '40s, '50s, and '60s continued to hold for him more glory than what followed. But the later works are hardly negligible, especially *We Want Miles*, *Star People*, and the radiant *Aura*—his last outstanding achievement, a suite written for him by the Danish composer Palle Mickelborg.

Aura was recorded in 1985 and suppressed by Columbia for four years, giving Davis an impetus to leave the label and indicating that he knew his best work even if his packagers didn't. He affirmed that understanding with his last public performance. Through all the years when he pointedly refused to play with the musicians he came up with, Davis kept alive the possibility of working again with Gil Evans. In interviews and at press conferences, he would insist that he wanted to work with Gil but that Gil was too busy, which didn't make much sense but left the door open. For a time, they discussed adapting themes from *Tosca*. But in 1988, Evans died. Three years later, in the summer before his own passing, Miles appeared with the remains of the Gil Evans orchestra at Montreux, a union instigated by Quincy Jones. It suggests a closed circle only if you make the mistake of reducing Davis's legacy to a single period, even one as gloried as 1956–61. Miles contained multitudes.

39 ❖ *Gerry Mulligan*
(Beyond Cool)

Jazz is filled with autodidacts, and in that respect and others Gerry Mulligan was firmly in the tradition of Ellington and Benny Carter. The house he shared with his wife and manager, Franca Rota, is filled with books and magazines and recordings, reflecting wide-ranging interests about which he discoursed with contagious enthusiasm and a twenty-megabyte memory. He could become equally animated while enthusing over Gil Evans's arrangements for Claude Thornhill's singers or summarizing papal plots or recalling American trains, which he knew down to the whistles. He was, for all his ties to modernism, a profoundly nostalgic man. Who else would bring an orchestra into Carnegie Hall and sing "I'd Rather Lead a Band," which he borrowed from Fred Astaire in *Follow the Fleet*? Although he made his reputation as a small-group innovator, big bands were his first love.

Mulligan was one of the quintessential jazz musicians of his generation. As much as the silhouette of Dizzy and his upturned trumpet, the image of bone-thin Mulligan, tall enough to dominate the baritone, his hair country-boy red (before it turned great-prophet white) had an iconic familiarity. The harmony of body and instrument and the intense davening motion as he played were constants. No musician in the postbop era was more adept at crossing boundaries. Though a confirmed modernist credited with spreading the amorphous notion of cool jazz, he achieved some of his finest work in collaborations with his swing era idols Ben Webster and Johnny Hodges; he displayed a photograph of Jack Teagarden in his studio. He was specially proud of appearing in the Billie Holiday segment in *The Sound of Jazz*—typically, the only modernist, the only white musician, the only improviser to play a double-time solo. The trumpet player Rex Stewart, who also appeared on that telecast, once compared the first time he heard Mulligan with the first time he heard Armstrong: "I felt a kinship with him right away. If a man doesn't feel him, he must he dead."

Mulligan fashioned a music in which all aspects of jazz commingle, from Dixieland two-beats and polyphony to foxtrot swing to modern harmonies, yet he remained something of an outsider, set apart by his devotion to certain not always fashionable musical principles, including lyricism and civility. By lyricism, I mean an allegiance to melody that, in his case, was as natural as walking. In the late '60s, when lyricism and understatement were in short supply, he turned his back on new music and recorded pop covers. It seemed doubtful he would make another significant contribution to jazz. But then he toured with Dave Brubeck; recorded *The Age of Steam*; and made a winning appearance at a 1972 Charles Mingus Town Hall concert, limning one melodic idea after another. Better was yet to come.

By civility, I mean his compositional focus on texture. Mulligan was chiefly celebrated as a baritone saxophonist, for good reason. He is the only musician in history to win a popular following on that instrument, the only one to successfully extend the timbre of Harry Carney and develop an improvisational style in the horn's upper range. He initially studied piano, clarinet, and tenor, but the baritone best expressed his warmth, humor, and unerring ear for sensuous fabrics of sounds. Yet he insisted he was less interested in playing solos than an ensemble music—

even in the context of his quartet. He was, as he proved from the beginning of his career, a master of blending instruments.

Born to a peripatetic Irish Catholic family in 1927, Gerry left home at seventeen and signed a short contract to tour as arranger with Tommy Tucker, a Mickey Mouse operation. As Mulligan told the story, he spent his off-hours listening to the hippest bands like those of Hines and Eckstine and then interpolated what he heard into his writing for Tucker— who consequently fired him with a promise to stake him in any venture he might want to pursue as long as it wasn't in music. At twenty, Mulligan wrote "Disc Jockey Jump" for Gene Krupa, one of the first dance band pieces to incorporate a bebop melody and chord progression. Krupa reluctantly fired him when Mulligan accused the ensemble of shoddy playing. Krupa agreed, but Gerry's mistake was to make the complaint in a public place. He became more politic, but no more tolerant of imperfection. When the American Jazz Orchestra played his arrangements, he drove in from Connecticut to supervise rehearsal, but not for the concert itself.

It was around 1945, while broadcasting with Elliot Lawrence's band, that Mulligan first encountered Charlie Parker, who insisted he jam one night at a club in Philadelphia. Later Parker commissioned him to write two pieces for his string ensemble, including "Rocker." Gil Evans brought him into Claude Thornhill's band, which led to his association with Miles Davis and the *Birth of the Cool*—Gerry wrote seven of the album's twelve pieces (including the definitive version of "Rocker" and the equally memorable "Jeru"), an achievement he felt was underappreciated. In 1950 he hitchhiked to Los Angeles and took a job with Stan Kenton, whose overgrown and frequently turgid orchestra was the antithesis of all that Mulligan valued about big bands.

After initial resistance from Kenton, Mulligan made himself heard and with just a handful of arrangements exerted a profound influence on the West Coast style. "Young Blood," a masterwork of the era, incorporates a reverse of the changes Parker used for "Scrapple from the Apple" (Mulligan's A section is loosely based on "I Got Rhythm," his bridge on "Honeysuckle Rose") and is an exercise in counterpoint, asymmetrical phrasing, and superimposed meters—techniques that would later inform his quartets and sextets. His impact ("Limelight," "Swinghouse," "Walking Shoes") was enormous. Bill Holman told Ted Gioia that Gerry provided him with the "glimmer of light" about what could be done with Kenton's band. He also formed his own ten-piece ensemble and elaborated on the instrumentation used in the Davis nonet. He was obliged to use a smaller combo, however, when he secured a weekly Monday night job at the Haig, a kitschy little restaurant with a white picket fence that stood across the street from the Coconut Grove. He assembled a quartet: Chet Baker on trumpet, Bob Whitlock or Carson Smith on bass, and Chico Hamilton on drums. In no time he attracted a faithful following (a story in *Time* didn't hurt) for a balmy and breezily swinging music that forever identified Mulligan with a coast he spent little time on, a temperature (cool) unequal to the fevers of his improvisational purpose, and an instrumentation (no piano) he rarely used.

He was an overnight phenomenon, a star. "Line for Lyons," "My Funny Valentine," "Festive Minor," and "Bernie's Tune," among several others, were hugely popular records. As cool jazz became increasingly associated with the West Coast, Mulligan was often the standard by which West Coast jazz was defined. The idea that a movement had taken root was largely a fabrication of the press and entrepreneurs eager to cash in on the first sign of a salable musical commodity. The exacting development of a style that took place at Minton's at the dawn of bop or at Gil Evans's flat in planning the Miles Davis Nonet simply didn't occur in this instance. Yet the sudden flurry of activity in a community that had been off the musical map for several years (Los Angeles was notoriously inhospitable to bop until Kenton boosted it with pop and pomp) could hardly escape notice.

In New York, the cool stylings of Davis or the Modern Jazz Quartet represented one fashion among many. But in California, cool jazz—laid back, vibratoless, contrapuntal, understated, melodic—seemed positively emblematic. College kids soon swarmed to hear Dave Brubeck, who pounded away in a manner that was anything but cool, but whose quartet featured Paul Desmond, an ingeniously ethereal melodist who typified the West Coast inclination to lighten up. Desmond made the alto sound almost like a flute; Jimmy Giuffre made the tenor sound almost like an alto; and Gerry Mulligan made the baritone sound almost like a tenor. If they didn't constitute a movement, they surely had the right sound for the right time and place, not unlike the Beach Boys a decade later. The rolling of the Pacific Ocean was faintly heard in their rolling rhythms—but since it was jazz, it wasn't all sunshine and surf. When Hollywood came calling, Mulligan's playing was used to symbolize a low life of hookers, junkies, and killers in *I Want To Live* or as background for the disturbed but extremely well-heeled and stylish beats in *The Subterraneans* and *All the Fine Young Cannibals*—in which Robert Wagner plays a character inspired by Chet Baker, or at least by Chet's haircut.

Everything about the short-lived Gerry Mulligan Quartet of 1952 suggested extramusical drama. Audiences flocked to hear the dreamily supple themes and variations, but also to check out the unlikely musicians playing them. Mulligan, sporting a carrot-hued crewcut, manipulated the huge baritone as though it were an instrument renowned for wistful romance, which in his hands and no one else's it became. Baker, with his neatly boxed pompadour and baby-face handsomeness, was short, introverted, and intense; he was a natural, creative in any key, exceptional ears, liked to play with the mike against the bell of his trumpet, which he occasionally put aside to croon a song in a girlishly attenuated voice. That Hamilton, the curly-haired drummer with big eyes and a penchant for beating complicated rhythms with his mallets, was black added to the mystique—integrated bands were not yet the norm. Only the bassists lacked charisma. Meanwhile, the critics licked their pencils and pondered the affair of the missing piano. This was one of jazz's pointless controversies. No one called Benny Goodman's trio "bassless" or Art Tatum's trio "drumless." But conventions in instrumentation had congealed by the early '50s, and the absence of a piano was considered adventurous. The Mulligan group became universally known as the "pianoless quartet."

"Line for Lyons" is a good example of how the unit worked, and why a piano was unnecessary. The first chorus of the recording states the seductive thirty-two-bar melody, an exemplary cool tune that has stymied many would-be lyricists (Mulligan enjoyed quoting the more improbable submissions): trumpet states the theme, backed by the baritone's chords and counterpoint. In the second chorus, Mulligan and Baker each improvise sixteen measures, the latter again shadowed by Mulligan's chords. The third begins as a canon (with Baker echoing Mulligan's riff-like phrases), becomes a round in the bridge, and restates the melody in the final eight bars. (The canonical angle was more fully explored in the irresistible "Festive Minor.") When Ornette Coleman organized his pianoless quartet at the end of the '50s, he was rejecting what he felt to be the constraining harmonies of a keyboard instrument. Mulligan, a pianist himself, *liked* chordal harmony and furnished it as best he could on baritone. In later years, he made a point of searching out gifted young pianists (notably Bill Charlap and Ted Rosenthal) for his quartets. Yet if his pianoless group was a happenstance rather than a manifesto, it caught on in a big way, even inducing wind players like Sonny Rollins to perform with just bass and drums. Surprisingly, given its impact, the first Gerry Mulligan Quartet lasted one year.

Mulligan's subsequent pianoless quartets with Jon Eardley (*California Concerts*, 1954), Bob Brookmeyer (*At Storyville*, 1956), or Art Farmer (*What Is There To Say?* 1959), and the highly textured sextet with Zoot Sims (*Presenting the Gerry Mulligan Sextet, Mainstream, A Profile of Gerry Mul-*

ligan, 1955–56) improved on the original format and cemented Mulligan's importance as a player, composer, leader, and increasingly bright and charming personality. Generous with his talent and hungry to play, he frequently turned up at jam sessions and recorded with numerous peers of all generations, from Jack Teagarden and Pete Johnson to Duke Ellington and Teddy Wilson to Paul Desmond and Stan Getz to Dizzy Gillespie and Thelonious Monk. He was a celebrity and his longtime romance with actress Judy Holliday put him in the columns and got him a funny bit in the film *Bells Are Ringing*. But no matter what he did, he was constantly importuned to reunite with Chet, which sometimes he did (*Reunion*, 1959; *Carnegie Hall Concert*, 1974), with a driving intensity that served notice he had no intention of catering to anyone's sentimental memories; of course, that verve had the paradoxical effect of justifying those who hankered after more of the same. But it infuriated him to be stereotyped by the music he made at twenty-five. What he really wanted to do was lead a big band.

Big bands were so closely associated with dancing during the swing era that their revival in the '50s—by which time bop had produced a more meditative jazz listener and rock and roll parted dancers not only from swing rhythms but from each other—required something new in the way of justification, for example, music qua music. The days of famous smiling baton-wielding bandleaders who didn't read music were long gone. The desire for orchestras was now generated by arrangers bored with studio work and by musicians bred in bop but ardent in their belief that big is better. The transitional period was exquisitely symbolized by the firing of Count Basie from the Camel Rock and Roll Party because, in Alan Freed's immortal words, "musically [Count] has the greatest band in the country, but it isn't a dance band."

Of the few bands that survived the swing era, Kenton ignored dancers whenever possible; Herman openly disdained them, but knew where his bread was buttered; Basie maintained a single book for concert halls and ballrooms; and Ellington rarely performed his extended concert works on the road. As a rule, dancers who clung to each other in the face of twists and frugs could still find safe haven in their plush ensembles. Ellington, of course, had been writing listener-intensive music all along, and by 1940 his fans were disinclined to dance even to his dance music for fear of missing something. Two decades later, the difference between his dance and concert music was often illusory: I attended a performance at a 4-H Club in Iowa at which he played almost the same set for the concert half as for the dance half—the primary difference was that they removed the chairs for the latter. Prerock pop singers continued to rely on expanded dance band instrumentation, as arranged by Nelson Riddle, Billy May, Benny Carter, Van Alexander, Sy Oliver, and Ralph Burns, among others; in that setting, big bands were so much the norm they were almost invisible.

A purely musical big band—no dancers, no singers, no hits, no nostalgia—was a risky proposition, despite a large and growing number of innovative jazz composers, among them Gil Evans, George Russell, Thad Jones, Bill Holman, Chico O'Farrill, Ernie Wilkins, Frank Foster, Manny Albam, Bob Brookmeyer, Neal Hefti, Johnny Mandel, Gerald Wilson, Oliver Nelson, Gary McFarland, and Mulligan himself. If anyone could make a go of organizing such an orchestra, Mulligan was the man. A bona fide jazz star steeped in big bands since his teens, he had the autocratic temperament to enforce discipline in the ranks and the easygoing charm to allay suspicion in the audience. He also had, at least in the beginning, the financial backing of Norman Granz and Verve Records. In case anyone doubted his intentions, Mulligan called his ensemble the Concert Jazz Band. It debuted to critical acclaim in 1960 and lasted long enough to issue five recordings and spur a big band restoration.

A concert band's first order of business is a reevaluation of the basics. In the absence of dancers, such fundamentals as swing, duration, and melody are open to revision. The constant foxtrot-four had become excruciatingly dull, making tempo changes, contrary meters, and rubato cadenzas increasingly attractive. New voicings, abetted by a wider span of instruments (one legacy of the Miles Davis Nonet), promised bolder colors, cluster harmonies, headier brews of every kind. Longer melody lines mirrored the linearity of improvised solos. Three-minute miniatures, suitable for 78 r.p.m. records, were no longer demanded or desired. Composition was its own reward. Ellington, having made his own way in the music world, had been doing all these things for thirty-five years. But most staff arrangers with other orchestras could do little more than pay homage to his genius and covet his independence. Mulligan gave them oxygen. He hired the best musicians in town and turned them over to the best writers in the country.

Mulligan did not use the CJB as a showcase for his own arrangements, in part because the administrative duties of running the organization demanded most of his time. Indeed, he wrote only one new arrangement, but he found something of an alter ego in the valve trombonist and pianist who had worked in his quartet, Bob Brookmeyer, whom the composer-writer Bill Kirchner astutely describes as "a totally personal mixture of the gutbucket and the cerebral." Brookmeyer became a prominent arranger through his work with the CJB, his contributions including the cantering clarity of "You Took Advantage of Me," with its now-you-see-it-now-you-don't ensemble backing and an exuberant chorus by the reeds; the close harmonies of "Manoir de Mes Reves"; and the cool esprit of "Big City Blues," with its piano/clarinet opening, and magical solos by Jim Hall and Clark Terry.

The CJB didn't have a pianist per se—Mulligan and Brookmeyer took turns when necessary—but it had a staunch rhythm section in bassist Bill Crow and the gently propulsive drummer Mel Lewis, a master of the idiom. Not the least significant upshot of the band was Lewis's decision to relocate from Los Angeles to New York. Within three years of the Concert Jazz Band's 1963 demise, Lewis and Thad Jones took Mulligan's gambit another step and created the Monday night orchestra at the Village Vanguard, which in their absence celebrated its thirty-second Vanguard anniversary in 1998. Brookmeyer, who was the band's music director after Jones left, was in the original lineup and demonstrated at the outset how far his music had developed since the CJB with his serial "ABC Blues" and "Willow Tree." In the same period, he formed a sterling quintet with Clark Terry, who in turn would organize an orchestra (Clark Terry's Big B-A-D Band) in the '70s.

Other composers, old and new, gloried in the CJB's rigorous attack and in the opportunity to set off Mulligan's infinitely supple baritone sax, which could assume almost as many colors as the ensemble. At Mulligan's suggestion, Al Cohn added a rousing ensemble chorus—in homage to Ellington and Ben Webster—to his "Lady Chatterly's Mother" and expanded "Blueport" from Mulligan's quartet version, opening it up for spirited exchanges between Mulligan and Terry. In adapting his own "Israel," written for the Miles Davis Nonet, John Carisi transcribed Davis's solo for the trumpet section. Johnny Mandel, an alumni (like Mulligan) of Elliot Lawrence's band and of Basie's and Herman's, was establishing himself as a film composer and offered a darkly beautiful adaptation of the triple-meter "Barbara's Theme" from his score for *I Want To Live*.

Perhaps the most celebrated CJB performance is George Russell's update of "All About Rosie," originally something of a concerto for Bill Evans, but in Mulligan's performance a newly burnished play of light and dark, satin and steel, with glowing precision in all the sections, especially the reeds. Gary McFarland was unknown at twenty-eight when he turned up at a 1961 rehearsal with two pieces, "Weep" and "Chuggin'," profoundly influenced by Ellington and Strayhorn. When he died tragically ten years later, his reputation had been sullied by several commercial projects. But the McFarland that Mulligan sent on his way was an impressive writer (he soon fulfilled his promise with *The Jazz Version of How To Succeed in Business, Point of Departure*, and *The October Suite*), with an ear for melody and the ability to layer rhythms in the wind sections. Like Bob Brookmeyer and Thad Jones, McFarland extended Ellington's harmonic density, employing what the arranger and educator Rayburn Wright called "grinds"—major and minor seconds woven into the voicings.

By the late '70s, Mulligan had a strangely distant relationship to the music business. He dreaded leaving his home in Darien for New York and resented requests from clubs and record labels to bring back the quartet. He organized a new, highly disciplined orchestra, wrote several pieces for it, and wanted nothing more than to work exclusively in that context. He was a big enough name to get work for the band, but much of it was abroad, where his stature soared during the last fifteen years of his life. In New York, his stature in the business was depressingly summed up by an incident involving a record label with which he had been profitably associated in the '50s. Invited to an executive's office, he was effusively flattered, then told that the label had uncovered previously unreleased music from his early years. The company had no interest in him or his current orchestra, only in marketing him as a living legend. Mulligan said he felt already dead sitting in that office, listening to a eulogy. He did manage to record his orchestra in a prize-winning but poorly distributed album, *Wade in the Water*, that captured the souffle lightness and crisp edges of the ensemble, but was—despite its high musicality ("Song for Strayhorn" and "For an Unfinished Woman" exemplify his gilded lyricism)—mild to a fault.

He appeared as the guest soloist with several symphony orchestras and wrote at least four works that feature him alone or with his rhythm section in a symphonic context; Zubin Mehta and the New York Philharmonic successfully performed his Entente for Baritone Sax and Orchestra. But these are hardly major achievements. He worked on film scores abroad and in numerous collaborations with jazz musicians, including Jay McShann, Lionel Hampton, Astor Piazzolla, Brubeck and Desmond, Mel Tormé, Chet Baker, and others—he made an especially fine album with Scott Hamilton, *Soft Lights and Sweet Music*. He spent more time at home writing songs, lyrics as well as melodies. One project that fully engaged him was *Re-Birth of the Cool*, a fascinating restatement of the twelve nonet pieces, with John Lewis and Bill Barber from the original sessions, Wallace Roney playing the trumpet solos, and Phil Woods bringing startling fire to the alto solos (Lee Konitz was tied up with other commitments). The idea took shape when he decided to recreate several of the arrangements for Gil Evans's memorial service; after discussing the idea with Miles, he moved forward and recorded the album in 1992. It captures the sensuousness of the music while avoiding slavishness, underscoring the indigenous qualities with an unforced contemporaneity. The notes are the same, but the articulation is refurbished.

In concert, Mulligan amplified the ensemble by adding a second trumpet and tenor saxophone, making the polyphonic weave even more elaborate, especially on Evans's sumptuous "Moon Dreams": a perfect unison statement for eight bars, followed by counterpoint in the second eight as the theme is shaded and interpreted by the full complement, and a marvelous poetic finish with arco bass subtly bonding brasses and reeds. Konitz reclaimed the alto chair, and one of the most memorable unrecorded performances of Mulligan's later years was their duet on "Alone Together," an essay in contrast between the altoist's tensile asymmetrical figures and the baritonist's sagacious melodicism.

When he died in January 1996 after a long illness, Mulligan was remembered, predictably, for his work in the '50s, a decade that in the mirror of his music remains abundant in optimism and pleasure. In the end, his music changed far less than the world, and some found its stubborn sanguinity trite or insufficiently responsive to the calamities of the day. In any case, when a jazz artist is reduced to the simplistic formulae of pop-cult synopses, he is invariably honored for his role in the zeitgeist and not for the development of his art. Still . . . Mulligan was playing at the top of his game in his last decade, and his writing assumed a warmth and immediacy—for example, "Noblesse" and "Lonesome Boulevard"—that reflected his heightened mastery.

Two of his finest albums are *Lonesome Boulevard* (1990) and *Dragonfly* (1995). In the former he is the last romantic, buoyed by a rhythm section that gives him plush, wall-to-wall harmony, in a program of new pieces that typify his affecting themes and ever-confident rhythmic gait, among them the title piece, with its oddly rural ingenuousness, and "The Flying Scottsman," his last buoyant train song. *Dragonfly* covers more territory, from mournful ecstasy to airy cool and from outstanding brass-choir arrangements on "Brother Blues" and "Art of Trumpet" to three-way improvisations by Mulligan, Warren Vaché, and John Scofield, who confide in each other with inspired candor.

The best of Mulligan's songs is "I Never Was a Young Man" (from *Little Big Horn*, 1983), the autobiographical lament of a man who spent too much of his life striving for success and now desires only to be "a really, really old man"—perhaps the only ambition Mulligan didn't fulfill. When he sang it at one of his last concerts, the amplification died, though he still managed to fill the hall. After the applause, he observed, "I'm probably the only singer on Broadway who's not miked," a funny line to those who recall the pre-1970 acoustic New York theater, one in keeping with Mulligan's hardly uncommon conviction that many things of value disappeared along with his youth. Maddeningly, one thing that didn't vanish was the indelible association of Jeru and something called "cool jazz."

40 ❖ *Art Blakey*
(Jazz Messenger)

Art Blakey's death from lung cancer on October 16, 1990, at seventy-one, robbed the world of music and the city of New York of a kind and faithful sorcerer. His legacy was threefold, as drummer, bandleader, and teacher. I'm not at all sure in what order of importance those gifts ought to be gauged. During his last thirty-five years, he led an ensemble that not only ranked among the most rewarding in jazz, but remained absolutely trustworthy as an indicator of the music's future. This despite the relatively immutable style of his Jazz Messengers. The fact is, no one in any style of American music apprenticed more musicians who went on to bigger, if not always better, things. He was an advocate for musicians and a prosyletizer to the general public. His devotion to jazz, his sermonlike effusions on its behalf, characterized the man as surely as his ability to drum audiences into a state of unembarrassed elation.

As he grew older and his hair grayed, Blakey affected the mannerisms of a country boy, simple and earthy. He'd wear overalls and a stetson and sing. He was squat but muscular, and vain about his fitness. He had one of those matchless faces that are both homely and charismatic, and the image of his head thrown back while he comps a soloist, his mouth open to reveal parallel fences of perfect gleaming teeth, is as iconographic as Dizzy's cheeks and Lester's hat. The earthiness was more than affectation. He came out of the Pittsburgh steel mills, where he briefly worked as a kid, doubling at night as a pianist in clubs. At seventeen, he was leading a fourteen-piece band though he couldn't read music; he liked to tell how he took up drums one night after another local kid who couldn't read—Erroll Garner—showed him up at the piano. The owner of the place insisted Art switch to drums, and since he carried a .350 magnum, Blakey consented. In 1942, he joined Mary Lou Williams's band at Kelly's Stable, the first in a long line of New York clubs he made his own, followed by a lengthy tour with Fletcher Henderson. Chick Webb and Sid Catlett were his models, but he was on to something else.

What that was became clear when Dizzy Gillespie recruited him for the Billy Eckstine Orchestra.

With that gig, which lasted nearly three years, he affirmed his stature (along with Max Roach and Kenny Clarke) as one of the premier drummers of the new music, modern jazz, bebop. You can see the eminent jaw in old clips of the Eckstine band, presiding over the ensemble as he executes a fiery break or spurs soloists with deft explosions. Blakey was an emphatic drummer, instinctive and always musical. Great drummers are not always great listeners, as countless disgruntled soloists will tell you, but Blakey was. With his impeccable sense of dynamics and drama, he'd stay out of the way when a solo was hot, though he'd counter with ingenious fills. When a solo flagged, his sticks became the baton of an impatient conductor. Blakey employed musicians who could eventually assimilate his muscular rhythms and conception. You couldn't survive in the Jazz Messengers without that sturdiness. If you faltered, you were steamrolled. His solos, which sometimes were of marathon length, were as impassioned as tent revivals and often ended with him tossing his sticks away, as if no other resolution were possible. His ten-minute incantation on "A Night in Tunisia" from the 1971 *Giants of Jazz* album is typical.

David Letterman once told a musicians' joke on TV about a circus drummer who excelled in "cutting" an act—that is, following a performer's every move with precisely the right cymbal whack or pressroll. In the joke, the drummer is accompanying a high-wire acrobat who misses a trapeze and begins the 200-foot plunge to his death; the punchline: the drummer cuts him all the way down. Blakey was that kind of drummer. In the parlance of Roy Eldridge, he'd swing you into bad health and back again. The best known of his techniques was a pressroll so individual in style it became known as the Blakey Pressroll: a rumbling on the snare, usually employed at turnbacks, which had the effect of lifting the soloist, the band, and the listener into the air for a few seconds and then gently depositing everyone in the next chorus. He also had a wholly personal way of keeping time on the hi-hat, producing a choked sound so dry that the beat is as coercive as if he were keeping it on the bass drum. His time was resolute, his reflexes expeditious—the classic example is his alliance with Thelonious Monk, especially the 1957 album on Atlantic, though Blakey was present on Monk's very first and very last sessions as well.

Between selections on the 1954 *Night at Birdland* records, Blakey said of his sidemen (including Clifford Brown, Horace Silver, and Lou Donaldson), "Yessir, I'm going to stay with the youngsters—it keeps the mind active." And that's the way it was for him. A year later, with Silver,

Hank Mobley, and Kenny Dorham, he organized the Jazz Messengers as a cooperative. He'd led bands with that name as early as 1947, but it was in 1955 that he codified the five- and six-piece units that came to epitomize hard bop, a brash fusion of bop and funk that would test the moxie of dozens of young players over the next four decades, and which is now enjoying an unprecedented revival—thanks to bands led by Blakey alums. Someone could and probably will write a book about the bands that were offshoots of the Blakey message, including Ray Charles's septet in the '50s. Throughout thirty-five years of gimmicks and trends, not to mention the valid expansions of the music, he managed to sound fresh and vital.

Blakey was not an ordinary teacher. For one thing, he paid his students. Here is a partial list of musicians who served and in many instances learned the jazz message on his watch: Horace Silver, Clifford Brown, Kenny Dorham, Hank Mobley, Donald Byrd, Walter Bishop, Bill Hardman, Jackie McLean, Sabu Martinez, Johnny Griffin, Lee Morgan, Benny Golson, Bobby Timmons, Barney Wilen, Wayne Shorter, Walter Davis, Curtis Fuller, Freddie Hubbard, Cedar Walton, Reggie Workman, John Hicks, Victor Sproles, Gary Bartz, Keith Jarrett, Chuck Mangione, Billy Harper, JoAnne Brackeen, Woody Shaw, Carter Jefferson, Mickey Bass, Dave Schnitter, Bobby Watson, Valerie Ponomarev, Dennis Irwin, James Williams, Ray Mantilla, Wynton Marsalis, Bill Pierce, Lonnie Plaxico, Branford Marsalis, Terence Blanchard, Donald Harrison, Mulgrew Miller, Jean Toussaint, Charles Fambrough, Philip Harper, Robin Eubanks, Javon Jackson, Bennie Green, and Peter Washington. On his last record, *Chippin' In*, he introduced yet another accomplished band including Brian Lynch, Frank Lacy, and Geoff Keezer. One reason Blakey's repertoire never faded is that he encouraged his players to write; since he enlisted several of the major composers of the postwar era, he was assured of an important body of work. It was in Blakey's band that the world first heard classics by Silver, Golson, Shorter, and Timmons, among others.

Timmons's "Moanin' " gave Blakey a major hit, and there were others, notably *Drum Suite*, one of several sessions in which he combined jazz and Afro-Cuban drummers. He worked on a couple of film scores, of which *Les Liaisons Dangereuses* was the most successful. Toward the end, on a blues-driven workout with Dr. John and David Newman, *Bluesiana Triangle*, he croaked a vocal on "For All We Know," accompanying himself on piano, that probably shouldn't be as moving as it is. Blakey is said to have recorded 100 albums, at least 60 with the Jazz Messengers, and many of the titles are illustrative: *A Night at Birdland, At the Cafe Bohemia, Moanin', Buhania's Delight, Holiday for Skins, The Freedom Rider,*

Mosaic, The Big Beat, Indestructible (all on Blue Note); *The Jazz Messengers, Hard Bop, Drum Suite* (on Columbia); *Caravan, Ugetsu, Kyoto* (on Riverside). In 1981, Timeless issued the combatively titled, *Album of the Year*; other jaunty records followed, including *Straight Ahead, Keynote 3, New York Scene, Live at Kimball's* (on Concord Jazz); *In My Prime I* and *II, Reflections in Blue, Oh—By the Way, The Jazz Messengers Big Band* (on Timeless); *In Sweden* (Amigo); and *Not Yet* (Soul Note).

Yet Blakey was preeminently a concert musician, which is to say a nightclub musician. As much as anyone else, he defined the kind of music that best suited the postwar, no-dancing-allowed jazz clubs of the '50s and '60s. And because he was tireless and never had to beg for an audience, he played more regularly than almost anyone else—downtown at Sweet Basil one week, uptown at Mikell's the next. Virtually every set ended with a plea for more understanding and respect for music, for his music, for everybody's music. He was so faithful a propagandist that he became the subject of an apocryphal tale. This is the way Bill Crow tells it in his book, *Jazz Anecdotes*:

> Art was driving to an out-of-town job and passed through a village where traffic was completely tied up because of a funeral procession. Since he couldn't get past the cemetery until the service was over, he got out and listened to the eulogy. The minister spoke at length about the virtues of the deceased, and then asked if anyone had anything else to add. After a silence during which nobody spoke up, Art said, "If nobody has anything to say about the departed, I'd like to say a few words about jazz!"

41 ❖ *Billie Holiday (Lady of Pain)*

Lady Day is unquestionably the most important influence on American popular singing in the last twenty years.
                                                        Frank Sinatra, 1958

And yet the matter of influence seems almost academic today. Sinatra was speaking a few months before Billie Holiday died, at forty-four, when countless singers considered themselves directly in her debt, and when her gutted voice, drawled phrasing, and wayworn features were widely construed as evidence of a self-immolating decline. Now the verdict is less dependent on what we know of her story and more on what we perceive in her music. Now it's obvious that, like Lester Young, whose career paralleled hers, Holiday achieved two discrete musical styles in a short, calamitous life. That their later styles were forged in response to outrageous fortune is a fact that continues to offend naive listeners who look to art as an expression of innocence and youth. Holiday's later recordings are all the proof we need of her ability to transfigure hurt and confusion into theme and variation. Had she been able to sing "What a Little Moonlight Can Do" at the end of her life as she did at twenty, she wouldn't have counted for much—she'd have been what Young contemptuously called a "repeater pencil."

Holiday's influence can be calibrated in the language of musical technique: in her use of legato phrasing, ornamentation, melodic variation, chromaticism. But musicology cannot do justice to the primary impact of her singing, which is emotional. Even in her apprentice years as the golden girl in a man's world, taking no more than the single chorus allotted each instrumentalist and transcending the material no less completely, her technique was limited by any standard, blues or bel canto. Paul Bowles wrote in 1946 that "one of the chief charms in Miss Holiday's art is that she makes absolutely no attempt to approach any of the elements of art singing, at the same time cannily making the most of all the differences that exist between that and her own quite personal style." Despite a thin voice and a range of about fifteen notes, she seduced listeners with her multilayered nuances. She embellished melodies, tailoring them to her own needs and limitations; lagged behind the beat, imparting suspense; harmonized well above the range of the composition, projecting a bright authority; and inflected words in a way that made even banal lyrics bracing.

Bessie Smith and Louis Armstrong refurbished pop songs with blues and improvisational devices, and Bing Crosby intoned lyrics as though they meant everything even when they meant nothing (he could elicit tears with doggerel like "The Sweetheart of Sigma Chi"). Holiday combined those achievements, pushing song into the realm of unmitigated intimacy. Hers was the art of reflection and not of melodrama. In that respect and others, she was a beacon for her exact contemporary, Sinatra, who scaled down her example even further, redefining the good singer as one who subordinates instrument and technique to the art of interpretation (of course, unlike Holiday, he usually got flustered when attempting to embellish a melodic phrase). But the paradigms she offered applied no less stringently to singers who could match her improvisational skills. No singer was more stubbornly verbal than Carmen McRae, who inflected words as though she were giving them a tongue-lashing. McRae was famously outspoken and her songs had a similarly tart appeal. You didn't necessarily turn to her for profane insight into the songwriter's art, but you occasionally got it anyway. This is especially true of the numerous Holiday tunes she covered. If Holiday made the word *love* shimmer with unrequited longing, McRae cast it in caustic languor. Consider her 1965 live recording of "No More": Holiday sang the line, "you ain't gonna bother me no more no how," as if trying to key up her resolve; McRae phrased those words as if she had a gun in her purse.

The Columbia recordings on which Holiday's legend primarily rests were produced by John Hammond and directed by Teddy Wilson, a brilliant pianist with an instantly recognizable bell tone attack and melodic, caroling style. Hammond recruited the finest musicians of the era from whatever big bands happened to be in town. The idea was to make quick and relatively inexpensive sides for the jukebox trade, particulary in the South; the Holiday-Wilson discs proved so successful that RCA hired Lionel Hampton to do the same. (Hampton's sessions were not distinguished by the singing, often by Hampton himself, but were instrumental milestones that documented the best of the swing stylists and the shift—with offerings from Charlie Christian, Dizzy Gillespie, and Nat King Cole—toward the modernism of the '40s.) Hammond, out on the town with Red Norvo, had originally heard Holiday in Harlem and added her to a couple of Benny Goodman numbers in 1933. Nothing much happened, although Duke Ellington used her anonymously for his 1934 Paramount film short, *Symphony in Black*. Norvo, in whose home Wilson first performed with Benny Goodman, may have suggested the match with Holiday. In any case, when she finally resumed recording after two long years, at the first Wilson session in the summer of 1935, she was an undoubted original whose time had come.

Oddly, she did not especially impress Wilson, or so he insisted in his later years. His preferred vocal style, he told the Smithsonian Oral History project, ran more to the school of Ella Fitzgerald, who began recording that same summer. Holiday was a novelty, he thought—a girl who sang like Louis Armstrong, though she was immediately identifiable and that was a good thing, he conceded. If the implied criticism is difficult to fathom, his perception in linking her to a musician whose recordings she had studied for years, was not. For Armstrong helped teach Holiday to swing. Beyond that, he taught her how to recompose a tune to suit her range, while improving the melodic line and projecting the emotional candor of an instrumentalist. The other singer she named as an inspiration was Bessie Smith, whose blues tonality was formative, even though Holiday rarely sang the blues per se. She didn't speak of

Ethel Waters, but Waters's influence is also unmistakable, in Holiday's diction and shading and vibrato.

The first Wilson-Holiday session was a benchmark. The band included Goodman, Roy Eldridge, and Ben Webster, and three of the four songs became Holiday classics: "I Wished on the Moon" (recorded two months *before* Bing Crosby introduced it in *The Big Broadcast of 1936* and forever identified with her despite Crosby's unmatched fame), "What a Little Moonlight Can Do," and "Miss Brown to You." Wilson and Holiday were back in the studio four weeks later and, then, on an almost monthly basis. After a year, Holiday was given the first of her own sessions (with Joe Bushkin on piano and Artie Shaw and Bunny Berigan as soloists). At a Wilson date in January 1937, he, Holiday, and Goodman were the ringers in an ensemble that included five members of the Count Basie band—its rhythm section; Buck Clayton, who would become her lover; and Lester Young, who would become her instrumental doppelgänger. At their first encounter, Holiday's voice and Young's tenor entwined like ivy around the trellises of "This Year's Kisses" and "I Must Have That Man."

In song after song, Holiday adapted written melodies with a taste and economy worthy of Armstrong. "A Sailboat in the Moonlight" is a characteristic and sensational example of the way she worked. The song, written by Carmen Lombardo, was the number one hit in the country for Guy Lombardo and His Royal Canadians in the summer of 1937; Holiday's version enjoyed an exceedingly modest success. Today, Lombardo's recording is unlistenable chiefly because the song's cadences are so sentimentally feeble that they underscore the banality of the lyric. In Holiday's version, supported by Young and an expert Wilson-imitator (Jimmy Sherman), the melody is charmingly suggestive and the lyric is unreasonably touching. How did she do it? The transformation begins with the first three notes, as she eschews a corny ascending figure in favor or a single repeated pitch, each note ("a/sail/boat") shaded for maximum rhythmic effect, not unlike the beginning of many Young solos. From that point, she alters a note here, a note there, stretching one at the expense of another—never for a moment obscuring the sweetness of the Lombardo song (which has the saving grace of pretty chord changes), yet demonstrating that the heavenly dream of sailing away with her lover to a remote place of their own is profoundly, deeply, urgently important.

Before long, her recordings lost much of their impulsive, huddling spontaneity. The singer became the star, not just one of the gang singing one chorus among many, but the performer around whom the entire recording was built. The switch was inevitable, and Holiday's craftsmanship rarely failed her. But life did, and latter-day Holiday is formed in part by those failings. Some of her last records, recorded when the instrument was worn to the nerve endings, are painful, yet the overwhelming body of work from her last fifteen years is as rewarding as jazz singing gets. The early records wear a golden-age sheen of sunny rhythms and instrumental bravura; later records are built entirely around the singer. The tempo is slower, the mood more conversational. The alterations remain provocative and full of surprise. The enunciation is, if anything, more compelling—the emotions more urgent. The differences between early Holiday (the Columbias, 1933–42) and late Holiday (the Verves 1952–59) is emphatic in the different moods they evoke, and a listener could no more confuse their respective values than those of, say, Beethoven's early G major and late A minor string quartets. The artist has undergone a sea change, no matter whether the cause involved heroin addiction or deafness, and while the parallel withers at this point—Beethoven did not lose his technique—the fascination with later Holiday stems from her ability to mine her compromised technique for expressive value. We don't attend her pain out of pity, but out of recognition. Her voice retained its enchantment, a lapsed beauty, a thin, pure, noble siren gleam.

The change in Holiday took place during the decade between those two major label affiliations and began in 1942. That was the year she apparently began using hard drugs to alleviate difficulties with her first husband, an addict she had married the previous year. It was also in 1942 that she worked two months at Billy Berg's Trouville Club in West Hollywood with Lee and Lester Young, during which she met Jimmy Rowles, the band's pianist and sole white member (Lester had to assure her "this cat can blow"), and the young producer of the club's jam sessions, Norman Granz. She recorded "Travelin' Light" with Paul Whiteman, a hit, though she received no royalties, and a few months later, in Chicago, had her first encounter with the police. That was the pattern for the rest of her life: triumph alternating with catastrophe.

She recorded for Milt Gabler, first at Commodore with written band arrangements, then at Decca, where she became the first jazz singer to record with strings—a gamble that paid off handsomely with such milestone performances as "Lover Man," "I Loves You Porgy," "Good Morning Heartache," "Don't Explain," "No More," "Ain't Nobody's Business If I Do," and "God Bless the Child." Underpaid and underappreciated (she never won a *Down Beat* poll), Holiday may have felt that the complement of strings was a compliment to her showbiz stature. These are transitional recordings—her voice, still in flower, meets the challenge of the imposing repertoire, but the staid settings dilute the expressive content of her singing.

The addiction began to take over; her marriage broke up and she canceled engagements. Yet she remained unbowed. At the same time she seemed to be retreating from life, she asserted herself in ever bolder directions: embarking on her first solo concerts in 1946 (the second of which was recorded as part of Granz's Jazz at the Philharmonic package), undertaking an acting role in the odious 1947 movie *New Orleans* as a maid (she walked out in the middle of filming), and hooking up with an expert accompanist, Bobby Tucker. In 1947, she took a voluntary cure for addiction, but shortly after she was discharged, she resumed her habit and was arrested in Philadelphia and sentenced to a year and a day at the Alderson Reformatory in West Virginia. She served nine and a half months.

Upon release, she returned to New York for a glorious concert at Carnegie Hall. Newspapers that previously ignored her singing now sensationalized her troubles. A few radio stations blacklisted her. Worst of all, the City of New York refused her a cabaret card (La Guardia's cabaret law was in effect until 1967), which meant she would never again sing in a New York room that served liquor; it meant that the only work she could get was on the road or in theaters. More arrests followed, though none of them stuck, and the bad publicity tripled, then quadrupled, her salary. In 1950 a *Down Beat* hack referred to her as "Lady Yesterday." She continued to cast dangerous playmates in the role of Lover Man, resulting in betrayals and beatings—her second husband, the unmourned John Levy, framed her on a drug rap, which she beat at the cost of permanent insolvency. After Decca dropped her in 1951, she recorded one session for Aladdin and drifted until Norman Granz signed her to his Mercury label (the parent company of Clef and Verve) a year later. Except for one Columbia album, he supervised her records for the remaining seven years of her life.

The jazz art is ever at the mercy of the record companies that own its recorded legacy. In the '80s and '90s, Verve did an excellent job in collecting all of Holiday's work for that label, while Columbia did a terrible job, reversing their track record in the '60s and '70s. For the first time, the later work achieved more prominence than the youthfully dazzling masterworks of the '30s. The work is extremely uneven, including some of her best as well as unlistenable recordings made when she could barely find energy to enunciate or keep in tune. The lapses, poses, and clichés—at least two dozen songs end with her most overworked tic, the interval of a ninth or major second down to the tonic—are trounced by

numerous glories that neither demand nor require a morbid or sentimental response. The musical elation she affords is often inseparable
from the pleasurable tension of hearing a great artist wrestle with and
frequently surmount technical and personal cumbrances. Billie Holiday
never stopped wrestling.

Consider two performances: the 1952 "These Foolish Things" (which
André Hodier singled out for praise) and the 1956 "All or Nothing at
All" (which John Chilton singled out as "the nadir"). In the earlier recording, her voice is strong and the inspiration of the opening paraphrase is sustained throughout the chorus; in the later one, she's hoarse
and her variations are occasionally tremulous. Yet in both instances the
overriding impression is of a singer intent on making variations, of an
artist refusing to accede to what Holiday called "close-order drill." She's
feeling her way through both songs, refurbishing melodies and lifting
rhythms, and if her artistic control is surer in "These Foolish Things,"
as it surely is, "All or Nothing at All" is compelling—and frequently
risky, as in the extremely legato swing of the release.

For all but one of the Verve albums, Holiday returned to a setting
that superficially resembled her Columbia recordings. Once again she
was surrounded by an intimate coterie of superb improvisers. But the
resemblance stops there. The tempos have stalled to a medium nod-time,
fit for ruminating, often sensuous. The singing is economical and so are
the arrangements, which were mostly ad lib. Instead of a couple of winds
escorting her through the changes, as on many of the Teddy Wilson
classics, she is usually heard in dialogue with one soloist. (Harry Edison's obbligati throughout are ingeniously alert.) Holiday is at the musical and emotional center of nearly every performance; when she is radiant, the musicians are correspondingly radiant. When she falters, the
entire session is as a rainy day (come back tomorrow, fellas, we'll get it
right then). The instrumentalists now take their cues from her. The spectacle of Young and Holiday jogging shoulder to shoulder could never be
duplicated. She is no longer the girl singer, a member of the band, one
of the boys. She is a diva surrounded by gentlemen in waiting. The
rehearsal banter, much of which has been preserved, may suggest otherwise, but the music doesn't lie: the obbligato is respectful, which is to
say unequal.

Holiday draws you into these songs as if they were translucent baubles to be held to the light and languidly examined. And whereas once
she transcended silly lyrics with the intensity of her rhythmic and melodic skills, now she makes them work for her. What a gorgeous irony
that the dog tunes she got stuck with in the '30s became so immutably
associated with her that twenty years later people requested them of her

as though they were Holiday's greatest hits. Every stanza seems auto-biographical. When she was twenty, she made "What a Little Moonlight Can Do" a boisterous jaunt, precocious and exhilarating; twenty-two years later, worn down by numberless ills, she makes a valiant and winning effort to sing it for the crowd at Newport. For the first time you hear the words, and suddenly what was trite—"You only stutter cause your poor tongue/Just will not utter the words/I love you"—is made jarring.

Holiday had lost nothing of her technique when she first signed with Verve, as witness her 1946 appearance at a JATP concert in Los Angeles. She is scintillating and robust. Her alterations on "The Man I Love" are as ingenious as those on the Columbia version, although this time Lester Young's contribution is confined to obbligati in the second chorus; listen to the way she glides over "seems absurd" or rushes "someday, one day" or drapes "my" over two notes. The 1952 and 1954 studio sessions are ornamented with masterly work by Charlie Shavers and Flip Phillips, though Oscar Peterson is heavy-handed and oblivious. It hardly matters; nothing could bring Holiday down when she was singing so well. (By contrast, at a 1954 German concert, a direct if rather wan Holiday skims the surface of Carl Drinkard's hyperventilating piano.) In 1955, she was feted by a more orderly Tony Scott unit (with Shavers at his peak) and consistently worthy material: she freely reharmonizes key phrases in "Always" and "Ain't Misbehavin'," italicizes the fine lyric of "Everything Happens To Me" (hear the inflection on "measles" and the percussive push on "thought you could break this jinx for me"), adds the verse to her classic "I Wished on the Moon," and debuts the first of her two acutely personal versions of "Do Nothin Till You Hear From Me," on which Budd Johnson echoes her mood.

Perhaps the best sessions are those with Jimmy Rowles, Harry Edison, and either Benny Carter (his "What's New" solo is a song in its own right) or Ben Webster (wailing on the second and superior "Do Nothin' "). In a rehearsal conversation Verve recovered from the public domain—and expanded by thirty minutes for its ten-disc *The Complete Billie Holiday on Verve 1945–1959*—Holiday says to Rowles, "It's a pleasure working with you again. Jesus Christ! I've been with some pretty big shots and they don't dig me no kinda way." Rowles trails her like a bloodhound, his footing as light and sure as hers—for example, "Day In, Day Out" and "I Didn't Know What Time It Was" (with verse). Edison is startling, booting her final chorus on "I Get a Kick Out of You," feeding her shots on "One for My Baby," and answering her every phrase on "Do Nothin'." Holiday occasionally sounds exhausted, but she regularly comes up with fresh twists, such as the curtailed rest at the opening of a shyly romantic "Isn't This a Lovely Day." A 1956 session with Tony Scott and Wynton Kelly is sluggish, and the big band album with Ray Ellis, recorded four months before her death in July 1959, is a matter of taste. The voice is haggard, but its soulful cry remains penetrating and I find several of these performances heartrending.

If a turnabout is in the making, with people saying they *prefer* the Verves to the Columbias (I don't mean to disparage the great Commodores or the less consistent Deccas and Aladdins, but they are transitional recordings between the polarities of early and late Holiday), that will be redressed as Columbia goes back to its vaults and remasters its cache. But the change in heart is not entirely novel. Several of the original Verve albums, especially *Body and Soul* and *Solitude*, were rarely out of print and were favored by her public and musicians. A musical adjunct to postwar noir, they spoke to audiences directly, without explanations or apologies. The best of the earlier Columbias are beyond praise: intrepid explosions of youthful genius, the work not merely of an inspirational singer but of an entire generation of princely musicians who burnished her vigilant joy with a glowing, compassionate optimism. Holiday is the lynchpin, but the results outshine any one participant, even her. The later recordings incarnate her indictment of the world as well as the spirit and dignity she sustained through all its blows.

42 ❖ *Modern Jazz Quartet (The First Forty Years)*

"In creating, the only hard thing is to begin," wrote James Russell Lowell. For the Modern Jazz Quartet, the world's most venerable chamber group in or out of jazz, the beginning was a three-year trial. Few people in the early '50s would have entertained the idea that a small jazz band could flourish over four decades, bridging generations and styles. Big bands had proved durable in part because, like symphony orchestras, they could withstand changes in personnel, and because they counted on dancers to sustain their appeal. No jazz chamber group had ever lasted more than a few seasons.

When the MJQ first convened, American music was in one of its many transitional phases. The public's taste changed with frightening alacrity. A decade earlier, the country was jitterbugging to swing. After the war, bop ruled jazz, while big bands struggled for survival and pop songs grew increasingly bland. In 1952, there was talk of a cool school in jazz, while younger listeners were drawn to rhythm and blues. A couple of years down the road, there would be hard bop, soul, and rock and roll. Then the deluge: third stream, free jazz, neoromanticism, acid rock, new music, fusion, neoclassicism, disco, original instruments, hip hop, grunge, and more.

Yet through it all, the Modern Jazz Quartet persisted and prospered. We do well to remember that the fortieth anniversary of the MJQ in 1992 was only the seventy-fifth anniversary of jazz on records, if we honor as genesis the sensationally successful 1917 Victor release of the Original Dixieland Jazz Band's "Livery Stable Blues" b/w "Dixie Jazz Band One-Step." Thirty-five years later, on December 22, 1952, John Lewis, Milt Jackson, Percy Heath, and Kenny Clarke met at a Manhattan recording studio leased by Prestige Records and recorded two standards ("All the Things You Are" and "Rose of the Rio Grande") and two Lewis originals with exotic names: "La Ronde," which had its origins in a piece recorded by the Dizzy Gillespie orchestra, and "Vendome," which prefigured the merging of jazz and fugal counterpoint that became an abiding trademark of the MJQ. The records were widely noted, but less widely embraced. With Lewis spending most of his time working toward a master's degree at the Manhattan School of Music, the first session was—notwithstanding a gig in an obscure Greenwich Village bistro called the Chantilly—an isolated foray.

The world was a different place that chilly day. At the very moment the quartet cut those records, President-elect Eisenhower was at the Commodore Hotel a few blocks away, meeting with a group of Negro clergymen to whom he expressed "amazement" that discrimination was widely practiced; he promised to appoint a commission to study the matter, adding that he was determined to abide by the law even if every Negro in America voted against him. Also in the news: the Soviets accused the U.S. of murdering eighty-two North Korean and Chinese POWs; allied fighter-bombers strafed Korean supply depots; more than seven hundred protesters staged a rally for the Rosenbergs at Sing Sing; Sugar Ray Robinson announced his retirement from the ring. *The New York Times*'s music pages noted a concert by George Szell and Guiomar Novaes and two debuts by Stravinsky, but, as was customary, expended not a word on jazz or popular music, and devoted twice the space to radio listings as to television.

In jazz, 1952 is best remembered for the formation of the MJQ, but it was also the year Count Basie (a profound influence on Lewis) returned to big band music after leading an octet for two years; Gerry Mulligan started his pathbreaking quartet; and Eddie Sauter fused with Bill Finegan. Norman Granz took Jazz at the Philharmonic to Europe, where Dizzy Gillespie's sextet was also on tour. Fletcher Henderson died, and trombonist George Lewis was born. Clifford Brown went on the road with an r & b band, while John Coltrane played section tenor for Earl Bostic and Cecil Taylor matriculated at the New England Conservatory. Louis Armstrong had two hit records, "Kiss of Fire" and a remake of "Sleepy Time Down South"; George Shearing introduced his "Lullaby of Birdland"; Thelonious Monk recorded with a trio for the first time in five years. Charlie Parker didn't record in a studio, but he kept busy, performing "Hot House" with Gillespie on TV, leading his strings at the Rockland Palace and Carnegie Hall, and working Birdland with four musicians who, one month later, would make their recorded debut as the Modern Jazz Quartet.

If it is relatively clear when the MJQ first called itself by that name, the prelude to that moment is as elusive as most historical events, though all the participants trace the beginning to the Gillespie orchestra of 1947. To reach that point, we have to go back further still. In the words of Thomas Mann, "The unresearchable plays a kind of mocking game with our researching ardor." So let's arbitrarily start in 1944, when Kenny Clarke of Pittsburgh was stationed at an army base in Rouen, France, and encountered John Lewis of Albuquerque.

Clarke (1914–85) had played drums with various bands in the East and Midwest, including those of Roy Eldridge, Louis Armstrong, Benny Carter, and Teddy Hill. During the stint with Hill, in 1939, he met Gillespie, and the two developed a close association. As house drummer at Minton's Playhouse in Harlem, Clarke was a key innovator of the new jazz later known as bebop. Lewis, born in 1920, had been playing piano and arranging for several years; he led his own dance band ("dance band or jazz band, it was all the same then") at the University of New Mexico, where he studied music and anthropology. His education was interrupted in his senior year when Pearl Harbor was bombed. A month later, he was in the army for a four-year stint. He recalls, "You didn't think much about what you were going to do afterward, because you weren't sure you'd come back. But I played in the Special Services band and met Kenny Clarke in an entertainment unit. Kenny was an original. He had a completely different way of playing drums, unlike anything before or since."

Clarke spurred Lewis's ambitions, and together they created a large ensemble. But the younger man was already thinking of jazz as something that went beyond the confines of a dance band. "I knew that jazz had ceased to be primarily a dance music in 1939 when I heard Ellington play at a dance. His music was too exciting to dance to." When Clarke was posted to Heidelberg, he told Lewis that he had connections in New York and to call him when he got out of the army. After his discharge in 1945, Lewis planned to finish his education in New Mexico, but a teacher in Albuquerque encouraged him to return to New York. With aid provided by John Hammond, he enrolled at the Manhattan School of Music.

By that time, Lewis had heard live broadcasts of Parker, Gillespie, Milt Jackson, and others and was infatuated with their music. As soon as he hit Fifty-second Street, he began sitting in whenever circumstances permitted. In June 1946, he contacted Clarke, who invited him to a rehearsal of Gillespie's big band and suggested he bring one of the arrangements John had written for the army band, "Bright Lights." Dizzy agreed to listen to the piece and, before the band finished playing it, offered Lewis a post as arranger. "Bright Lights," retitled "Two Bass Hit," became a defining work of the era. When the band's pianist, Thelonious Monk, left a month later, Lewis took over that role as well. Gillespie's rhythm section now consisted of Lewis, Clarke, bassist Ray Brown, and vibraphone virtuoso Milt Jackson.

Jackson, born in Detroit in 1923, studied piano and guitar, but made his professional debut as a singer in a gospel quartet. When he realized that by slowing the vibrato on the vibraphone (an instrument that had been almost exclusively the province of Lionel Hampton, Red Norvo, and Adrian Rollini), he could simulate the sound he produced with his voice, he put everything else aside. Jackson was additionally encouraged by Gillespie's enthusiasm for the instrument and for Jackson's stunning, blues-driven legato way of playing it. A year after accompanying Gillespie in Detroit and traveling to New York at his request, he was a charter member of bebop's premiere big band. With Lewis on piano, Gillespie realized he had an ensemble within the ensemble. Ever since Benny Goodman introduced his trio in 1935, bandleaders had contrived to give their musicians and arrangers a rest by introducing smaller units to spell them. Goodman, Duke Ellington, Woody Herman, Artie Shaw, and others even recorded those combos, securing acceptance for what was often characterized as chamber jazz.

Thus the MJQ began life as a kind of entr'acte. As Jackson recalls, "From the first time we performed in that band as a quartet, we became prominent and a part of the band. We would play fifteen to twenty minutes, two or three tunes, and everybody loved it, including Dizzy and the band." The pieces were standards, and they weren't arranged. "It was just tunes that everybody knew," Lewis notes, "and, anyhow, it was just a temporary thing, not planned or anything. There wasn't enough musical advancement." But much was learned in the Gillespie band, playing an arduous regimen of one-nighters, including a tour of the South, where those who came to dance were put off by the music's complexity. Among other things, Lewis absorbed Gillespie's example of showing up on time, and the importance he placed on a presentation that respected the audience. Lewis also had the opportunity to perform his first extended work, Toccata for Trumpet and Orchestra, which he now dismisses with a grimace as "juvenilia."

The possibilities of fugal jazz had intrigued Lewis as far back as his studies in New Mexico. A few weeks before Gillespie hired him, he attended Ellington's annual Christmas concert at Carnegie Hall and was most impressed by a new piece, "Fugue-a-ditty," that demonstrated one way of using counterpoint in jazz. "It's a very formal piece and for years I tried to tell people about it, but Duke never recorded it. Then, a few year ago, they released the tapes of the concert. Of course, others also used fugues in jazz—Alec Templeton, Benny Goodman, Artie Shaw." Lewis abandoned his original toccata to history, but he adapted three selections from the Gillespie book as MJQ staples: "Confirmation," " 'Round Midnight," and "A Night in Tunisia." In addition, he retained reworked versions of "Two Bass Hit" and Gillespie's "Woody'n You," which Lewis had co-orchestrated for the big band.

When the Gillespie orchestra broke up, the rhythm section considered continuing as a quartet, playing under Jackson's name. But for the next three years its members went in different directions. Jackson joined Woody Herman's band for nearly a year and then Gillespie's sextet. He collaborated with Thelonious Monk on some of the most admired records of the period. Lewis and Clarke settled in Paris for a while. On returning, Clarke reunited with Jackson in a Tadd Dameron band and with Lewis in the Miles Davis Nonet. Lewis's association with Davis had begun when Davis introduced him to Charlie Parker, with whom he recorded such classics as "Parker's Mood." (Lewis wrote "Milestones" for Davis as an expression of gratitude for introducing them.) For the "Birth of the Cool" project, he arranged "Move" and "Budo" and composed "Rouge," which would reappear in the MJQ book as "Delaunay's Dilemma." Davis subsequently recommended him to Illinois Jacquet, with whom Lewis toured for several months before returning to New York, where he pursued his education and worked on and off with Lester Young. Meanwhile, Ray Brown had married Ella Fitzgerald and was working almost exclusively with her.

Finally, on August 18, 1951, Gillespie brought his erstwhile rhythm section into the studio to record as the Milt Jackson Quartet for his new label, Dee Gee. The arrangements showed little of the polish to come, yet each of the four selections would resurface in MJQ duds a few years later. Lewis's "D and E" is one of the longest-lived pieces in the MJQ repertoire. Jackson and Brown's "Milt Meets Sid" was refashioned as the MJQ's mid-'50s theme, "Baden-Baden," which appeared along with the session's two standards, Jerome Kern's "Yesterdays" and Harold Arlen's "Between the Devil and the Deep Blue Sea," on *The Modern Jazz Quartet*, also known as "the album-without-a-title" because the traffic-stopping cover depicts four musicians sporting matching three-piece suits and much facial hair but has no writing of any kind. Yet if the Dee Gee session held much promise, an immediate hurdle presented itself: Brown was working full-time in support of his wife. They needed a replacement for jazz's leading bassist. Percy Heath was the obvious choice, despite his relative inexperience.

Born in North Carolina in 1923 and raised in Philadelphia, Percy is the oldest of three distinguished musician brothers. But unlike saxophonist-composer Jimmy Heath and drummer Albert Heath, who performed professionally when still in their teens, Percy didn't commit himself to music until he was discharged from the air force, having trained as a fighter pilot for more than two years. He had played a little violin as a kid, but only after returning to civilian life did he switch to bass, inspired by a Coleman Hawkins record featuring bassist John Simmons. Within six months, he was playing gigs. Howard McGhee, who helped many young musicians in the '40s, brought him to New York in 1947. A year later, Heath performed in concert with Lewis and Clarke in Paris at the First International Jazz Festival—all three then accompanied Coleman Hawkins at a matinee. In 1950, Heath joined Dizzy's sextet, which included Jackson, as well as Jimmy Heath and an unassuming section player named John Coltrane. When the Milt Jackson Quartet recorded for Hi-Lo in the spring of 1952, the personnel of the MJQ was in place. Among the four selections recorded were two that became MJQ standards: Jackson's "True Blues" and Sigmund Romberg's "Softly, As in a Morning Sunrise."

Now came the moment of decision. "Those records attracted some attention, and we decided to stay together," says Lewis. "Since all four had reputations—Kenny was the most famous—no one could afford to pay the other three, so we had to make the band a cooperative." In Jackson's words, "The quartet became a unit because John was not going to be a sideman for me and I was not going to be a sideman for him. A collaboration had to come about." Here were two powerful personalities, one an adventurous idea-man and accomplished composer, the other a renowned soloist. Did either of them sense or admit the possibility that they might replicate the kind of association symbolized in American music by Ellington and Johnny Hodges? Today they insist they had no such thoughts, but the comparison has been drawn repeatedly by others.

In Clarke, who was universally admired, and Heath, who had quickly become one of the hottest bassists in New York, they had the makings of a historic team. All four men were indispensable to jazz in the transitional early '50s. You can sense how critical they were simply by perusing Miles Davis's work in that period: Lewis and Heath appeared together on Davis's first Prestige session and individually on several that followed; Heath and Clarke attained much of their finest work together on four 1954 sessions with Davis, including one with Jackson that produced an incomparable version of "Bags' Groove." Yet Lewis conjured up a different kind of life and music.

As Heath recalls, the key discussion took place in Jackson's old Cadillac:

> John had this idea to write some different music for the instruments that were in the quartet, and wrote "Vendome" and a few other very orchestrated pieces. He wasn't interested in writing for Milt Jackson's quartet, so we became a partnership, a corporation—the Modern Jazz Quartet was the performing entity. John's vision for the group was to change the music from just a jam session, or rhythm section and soloist idea, to something more. We were all equal members, and the dress, the wearing of tuxedos, and trying to perform in concert rather than always in nightclubs, was part of what he envisioned to change the whole attitude about the music.

Jackson agrees: "Everything was methodical, a system. We practiced walking on stage, the appropriate attire. We set a precedent in doing that. We wanted to bring back a level of dignity that we all remembered from watching all those great big bands in the swing era. That was a very important part of jazz that I think we lost somewhere along the way." Similarly, Lewis says of the tailored suits, "That's the Ellington-Lunceford tradition." Although Lewis wasn't tempted to add a wind instrument, he did not consider the instrumentation of vibes, piano, bass, and drums ideal. But he knew he had the right musicians and was determined to do everything necessary to keep them together.

Because of Heath's relative inexperience, Lewis was forced to do more notation than he originally planned. Indeed, Lewis argues that he did not at first conceive of the MJQ as a highly "composed" group.

> It just turned out that way. Percy hadn't started playing until 1947, the rest of us started playing in the '30s, so a lot of things had to be written for him, chords or whatever, and that was the beginning.

We couldn't do what we had been doing before, all the tunes we'd put together with Ray Brown. But that didn't matter because that's the way the other two members, Milt and Kenny, wanted it to be. So the composing evolved by itself, by necessity.

Asked about the notated bass parts, Heath laughs and asks:

Did you think "Vendome" was improvised? John still writes a lot of bass parts, and not only bass but drums. Certain things are written all the way through, but in other compositions there is space in there for me to play. There are other things in the repertoire, holdovers from bebop days, where I'm completely on my own. When we started in '52, I'd been playing about four-and-a-half years, and John told me, "Percy, you don't know enough about what we're going to do, so you better get yourself lessons." So I went to [Charles] Mingus for a few lessons, but his whole political thing got in the way. I had to correct my intonation and read some more kinds of music. Most of what I'd been doing was just getting chord changes to songs and playing a bass line. John's music was a challenge and I appreciated it.

For Jackson and Clarke, John's musical control was more problematic. "There is no leader in the Modern Jazz Quartet," Jackson is quick to underscore, "but John is the music director, and his personality dominates the music, just as mine does when I'm the music director of a group. My playing is much different in the quartet than in my own groups. Sometimes, I get tired of playing the same arrangements, but as a dedicated artist you go along with whatever is necessary." Jackson would assert his creativity by contributing many originals, blues and ballads, to the MJQ book while sustaining an incredibly voluminous recording career outside the quartet. Clarke, on the other hand, could not make peace with the new chamber style, despite the large following it soon attracted.

Still, in December 1952, when the four men first recorded for Prestige, the only skepticism came from the label, which was none too sure about putting out a record without a famous name above the title. Three or four cooperative names had been considered before Modern Jazz Quartet was chosen, but Prestige's producer and owner, Bob Weinstock, insisted on putting out the initial ten-inch LP as Milt Jackson and the Modern Jazz Quartet. A year later, when the MJQ played Birdland, management once again used Jackson's name in the billing. Heath contends, "The people in the business had to be programmed because there was no such thing as a no-name group." The audience had to be programmed as well, although it would have few chances to see the MJQ during the next two years. With Lewis studying to complete his master's degree, the MJQ existed primarily as a recording group.

The MJQ's second session for Prestige took place on June 25, 1953, and once again produced two dramatically stylized standards ("Autumn in New York," "But Not for Me") and two Lewis originals ("Delaunay's Dilemma," "The Queen's Fancy"). In October, the MJQ accompanied Sonny Rollins at a Prestige session and, a few weeks later, commenced its first major booking, at Birdland. Heath remembers:

> We had a hard time getting people to quiet down and listen. At that time in nightclubs, people were talking about hanging out. In order to break that down, instead of trying to play over the conversation, we'd use reverse psychology and play softer. Suddenly, they knew we were up there and realized the conversation was louder than the music. Of course, if it got too loud, we'd come off— just stop playing and walk off. It didn't take long for them to realize they were wasting their time because we weren't going to entertain them in that sense. We didn't have funny acts, we didn't have any costumes. We were conservatively dressed, we played conservative music, and if you didn't listen you didn't get it. We were four instruments going along horizontally, contrapuntally. There was no backup and soloist, the concept was changing.

After the Birdland gig, there were engagements in Boston, San Francisco, Los Angeles, Philadelphia, and Carnegie Hall, but the MJQ didn't record again for more than a year. Two sessions ensued on December 23, 1954, and on January 5, 1955, producing one standard, "I'll Remember April," Gillespie's "One Bass Hit," and John's expanded version of "La Ronde," now a four-part suite. The new selections were Lewis's "Milano" and a tribute to Django Reinhardt that became an instant jazz classic, solidifying international interest in Lewis and the quartet.

With his master's degree in hand, Lewis was now planning the group's assault on the musical community. He already had the attention of fellow musicians: reviewing the MJQ's debut appearance at Birdland, Nat Hentoff wrote, "If the success of the Modern Jazz Quartet depended only on the support of jazz musicians, this could be the most in-demand unit in the country." Lewis was ready for the general public, for the world. He was determined to undo popular misconceptions about jazz. Contrary to what several skeptics wrote, he wasn't concerned with the kind of prestige conferred by academic respectability—a subject that provokes his most acerbic comments, especially if he suspects any kind of compromise is involved—but with the fundamental consideration accorded every art worthy of the name.

But first the quartet had to deal with a momentous change in personnel. Two weeks after the "La Ronde" session, the group returned to Birdland, and Kenny, who chafed at the direction of the MJQ and expressed interest in returning to Europe, announced his decision to quit. In 1968, he told Les Tompkins that he did so "not because I felt restricted, but because I couldn't accept the overall conception. It should have leaned more towards folklore than to classical music." He had no regrets, he insisted, adding, "Probably, if I'd stayed they wouldn't have been a success!" "He was trying to find himself," says Lewis. "There *was* a change in the music, but it was early when Kenny left so it was easy to handle and adjust to. If we had to make the change later, it would have been a disaster. We had to give up a lot of pieces we played when Kenny left." Heath affirms, "It had to change, because there is no other Kenny Clarke. Kenny didn't want to have such orchestrated music because he was an innovator and didn't want his part dictated." Jackson emphasizes the idea that Clarke left too early to derail them: "The three years Kenny was in the group was an experimental stage. We were still looking for a direction."

Clarke gave notice on the last night at Birdland. Monte Kay, the jazz producer who helped create the music policies at the Royal Roost and Birdland, was now the group's manager, a fifth member of the cooperative until his death in 1988. He immediately recommended Connie Kay (no relation) as a replacement. "Early the next morning, after they closed at Birdland, Monte called me," Kay recalled:

> and asked if I wanted to make the gig. I said yeah, and then he told me the quartet had a one-nighter that very night and two weeks at Storyville in Boston. I had heard the records and liked the music they were playing, so it wasn't a problem. It was written, but the only thing that was kind of different was "Django"; the drum part on "Vendome" was straight ahead. So it wasn't as difficult as it got. The first piece I had to really concentrate and learn fast was "Fontessa." When I first joined the quartet, we would rehearse every day. I had to find a way to be able to play things that I wanted to play and not overshadow what they were doing.

Kay, born in 1927 in Tuckahoe, New York, began playing professionally at seventeen at Minton's with Sir Charles Thompson and Miles Davis. In 1949, he toured with a rhythm and blues show and began a long association with Lester Young, two jobs that defined his career in the years before he joined the MJQ. Though most of his live appearances were with jazz bands (often on tour with Jazz at the Philharmonic), he earned a parallel reputation in r & b that brought him countless early rock and roll record dates at Atlantic. In time, Kay emerged as an adept colorist and an assured rhythm player, seated behind an array of drums, chimes, triangles, and cymbals, sustaining a subtly invincible pulse. In time, the quartet followed him to Atlantic. But first there was another session for Prestige, which now used Rudy Van Gelder's studio in Hackensack. On July 2, 1955, the MJQ recorded several standards, including its first ballad medley and the fugal version of "Softly, As in a Morning Sunrise," as well as Jackson's "Ralph's New Blues" and Lewis's second major fugue, "Concorde."

The MJQ found ways to handle most of the problems in taking a band on the road. Monte Kay's attentiveness, advice, and influence helped to break down doors, and the quartet divvied up responsibilities: Lewis was in charge of the music; Jackson assumed the duties of public relations; Heath oversaw finances; and Kay attended to accommodations and transportation. The one thing they needed was the nurturing support of a strong record label. The new year brought them a contract with a young but successful company determined to switch from singles to LPs.

Before 1955, Atlantic was primarily involved with r & b; its stunning string of hits included records by Big Joe Turner, Ruth Brown, the Clovers, and the Drifters, most of them produced by Ahmet Ertegun, often with Connie Kay on drums. Atlantic also recorded a few jazz sides as early as 1949, but didn't make a commitment to jazz until Ahmet's older brother, Nesuhi, joined the enterprise to create a line of LPs. Nesuhi had the distinction of teaching the first accredited jazz course at a university (UCLA), but his interests were primarily focused on prewar jazz. At Atlantic, however, he began to concentrate on modern sounds, and his first signings were Lennie Tristano, Lee Konitz, and the Modern Jazz Quartet.

To Jackson, Nesuhi Ertegun was "the most gifted of record producers, the most compassionate and sympathetic when it came to jazz. The sessions with Prestige were just jobs, a way of getting exposed, but with Nesuhi it was always a collaboration between him and John, or between him and myself when I recorded. It was never a question of him saying, "Now, look, this is what I want you to do." "It made a big difference," said Kay. "In Hackensack, we hardly practiced anything, it was more like a business. With Atlantic, we signed a contract so we couldn't get robbed and we had a place to develop." Heath points out that the change in labels complemented the change in the group:

Nobody ever told John what to do. He brought in the music and that's what we recorded, at Prestige or Atlantic. But after we started working more regularly, it became a really systematic thing. We played the songs on the job, so when we came into the studio it was like playing a set. A lot of things were one take, with another take just for security. Tommy Dowd, the engineer, and Nesuhi would be in the control room, and the tape would just roll, and we'd play as though we were on the job. It wasn't like other record dates where you go in and the guy scratches out some chords and hands it to you at the date, like a lot of the Miles recordings. Everything was not only rehearsed, it was *refined* before we got to the studio.

A key to the MJQ's success is the unruffled blend of European finery with the traditions of jazz, which may help to explain why the band was lauded in Europe first. Lewis knew that the European audience was discerning and influential, and he had no intention of taking the group there "until we were ready. And when we did go to Europe, we *were* ready and everyone knew it." First, they joined a Birdland All-Star tour in 1956 with Bud Powell, Miles Davis, and Lester Young, then played a major engagement at the St.-Germain-des-Prés in Paris. The big breakthrough came in 1957, when they returned to Europe on their own. Heath recalls, "All the American critics were talking about Dave Brubeck and that kind of West Coast cool sound, and we came along with a sound that was also cool. But it wasn't until we made an impression on the European critics—they voted for the MJQ as the group of the year—that American critics jumped on the bandwagon." They toured Germany, France, and the British Isles—eighty-eight concerts in four months. That same year, Lewis completed his first film score, *Sait-on Jamais* (briefly released here as *No Sun in Venice*, the source of some of the MJQ's most durable music) and headed the jazz faculty at the Music Inn summer school launched in the Berkshires. The MJQ had become an institution.

Without sacrificing its ideals, the quartet performed in halls previously inimicable to jazz (including the Mozarteum in Salzburg) and enjoyed the favor of music lovers who didn't think they would like or understand it. Detractors criticized the MJQ for being "academic" or "effete," though its roots in bop and the blues were everywhere apparent. To those who complained of his juxtaposition of the blues and the baroque, Lewis was quick to point out that jazz itself developed along baroque lines, specifically the "linearity of Charlie Parker's music or the call-and-response writing in the big bands." The MJQ is nothing if not a model for creating inventive variations on the most time-honored elements of jazz. Indeed, no contemporary band was more devoted to or as enterprising in exploring and sustaining the worldly elegance of the blues.

In Jackson, the quartet had one of the most passionate blues improvisers in jazz history, a soloist whose every pealing variation is as informed by his background in gospel as by his perfect pitch. For his part, Lewis remains as steadfast an admirer of the paradigms of Ellington and Basie as when he first heard them long ago in the Southwest. As musical director of the American Jazz Orchestra from 1985 to 1992, he interpreted their actual scores; but with the Modern Jazz Quartet, he maintained their precepts in the contemporary arena on his terms. André Francis has called the MJQ Lewis's finest creation: "From four musicians, he made a sensitive instrument which vibrates in the same universe of sound, achieving at the same time a communion unique in the world of jazz." Martin Williams described the quartet as "perhaps the best small ensemble in jazz history, an important contribution to the synthesis that modern jazz achieved in its second decade." Leonard Feather acclaimed its devotion to "affirmative values of order and reason—melodic invention, harmonic beauty, subtlety of rhythmic pulse—within which limits all the participants have the option to do as they please." Whitney Balliett described the MJQ as "tintinabulous. It shimmers, it sings, it hums. It is airy and clean. Like any great mechanism, its parts are as notable as their sum."

But no one has captured the intent and achievement of the MJQ more plainly than the visionary who created it. John Lewis told *Metronome* in 1955:

> My ideals stem from what led to and became Count Basie's band of the '30s and '40s. This group produced an integration of ensemble playing which projected—and sounded like—the spontaneous playing of ideas which were the personal expression of each member of the band rather than the arrangers or composers. This band had some of the greatest jazz soloists exchanging and improvising ideas with and counter to the ensemble and the rhythm section, the whole permeated with the folk-blues element developed to a most exciting degree. I don't think it is possible to plan or make that kind of thing happen. It is a natural product and all we can do is reach and strive for it. Most groups these days do not or cannot stay together long enough to reach a real understanding and project it.

Lewis had other things to say of equal interest throughout the '50s and '60s: "I think that the audience for jazz can be widened if we strengthen our work with structure." "The music will have to swing, but remember that all music must do this, must have a meaningful rhythmic sense." "The most important thing we're doing, the bulk of what we play is improvisation. The rest is to give us a framework. And even those frames get moved or bent to fit what we're trying to project." "All of what we do is relative, and can be different at different minutes in different sets in different nights." "If everybody was like us it would be dull. It could be monotonous if everybody decided to play inventions and stuff. Or if we played only funky kind of music. We are exploring *some* of the possibilities."

In a taped discussion with Nesuhi Ertegun in 1956, Lewis was asked if his training in European art music influenced the music of the MJQ, and he responded, "No, it's only one of the means to an end. I'm only conscious of finding a means to some variety. You get sick of the same thing, the challenge runs out. We use an invention form. I use my own imagination to find things, to find a correct way to manipulate tones. Since we are using a harmonic system that comes from Europe, we have to learn to use it." Asked about his preference for clubs or concerts, he said, "We'd almost always rather play concerts than clubs. Clubs are backbreaking, so they make you strong. But if we play three concerts, it's so good it's amazing to me. You can't do that for hours in a club every night. It's good training, but now we have the training."

The rest is music. Here are some highlights:

"Vendome" (1952) In a 1959 interview, John Lewis told the Italian magazine *Jazz de Oggi e Ieri*, "Some of the music we've played, 'Vendome' for instance, was very unnatural when we started playing. On the record it is not natural at all. Now it has become natural, but it has taken a long time." Max Harrison, an astute commentator on Lewis's use of contrapuntal devices, agreed, finding it "dangerously near to being a Bach pastiche." Widely noted and discussed in its day, this is the first piece to reveal the MJQ's interest in the art of fugue and its unwavering determination to bind it to the art of blues. The canonical melody, introduced first by vibes and bass, then taken up by piano and drums, may curb the improvisers, but it's comely quality prefigures the more accomplished writing that would follow and is hard to shake out of your head.

"Delaunay's Dilemma" (1953) In this admirable recasting of "Rouge," the key melodic phrase is simplified to abate the overt boppishness of the source material. Percy Heath has a notable part, playing the eighth-measure breaks and the two-measure bass break in the release. But the centerpiece of the performance is the playing of Milt Jackson, which André Hodier singled out as "the most significant" indication of his progress up to that time. No less notable is Lewis's solo, especially the wash of notes with which he gets out of the bridge and into the riff that carries him through the chorus. Kenny Clarke's incomparable sound is well captured.

"MILANO" (1954) A bass note augurs the stately beauty of Lewis's minor-key ballad; the bells in the percussion part prefigure the colors that would soon become a routine part of the MJQ palette; the use of stop-time (a vintage jazz tradition and one of Lewis's favorite compositional ploys) exhibits the MJQ's ability to enliven a straightforward melody with formal change-ups. The tune has stronger ties to conventional songs and bop harmonies than Lewis's more mature work, but remains an evocative recording, primarily because of Jackson's flawless interpretation, at once emotional and reserved.

"LA RONDE" SUITE (1955) This elaborate piece marks the end of the MJQ's first developmental stage—its association with Clarke. The quartet had been a unit for little more than two years, but "La Ronde" had evolved over a decade, from the wartime big band number "Bright Lights" to a feature for Clarke at the first MJQ session, as "La Ronde." In the four-part suite version, the melodic line is effectively deconstructed—it turns up as foreground and background, often rent by stop-time, in a variety of voicings and variations that are at least as fascinating as the leading roles assigned each member of the quartet.

"SOFTLY, AS IN A MORNING SUNRISE" (1955) Sigmund Romberg and Oscar Hammerstein II introduced it in their 1928 show, *The New Moon*, which also introduced "Lover Come Back to Me." Despite Artie Shaw's famous recording, the song was generally ignored in jazz until the MJQ took it up. Today it is a jazz standard, famously interpreted by Sonny Rollins, Abbey Lincoln, John Coltrane, and many others. The first MJQ version goes back to the days when that acronym stood for Milt Jackson Quartet; but at the 1955 session—which brought Connie Kay into the ranks—Lewis added a delightful eight-bar introductory fugue, adapted from Bach's *The Musical Offering*. The counterpoint of that episode is elaborated in Lewis's accompaniment to Jackson's theme statement. Each of them improvises three choruses. The vibist builds much tension through the use of double time, while the pianist exemplifies the truth of a comment he made to Nesuhi Ertegun: "I think of playing and composing as essentially the same activity." Note the guitar-like sound Lewis produces at the outset of his second chorus.

"BLUESOLOGY" (1956) "I guess you could say it's a study of the blues,"

Jackson says of a piece that appeared on the quartet's first Atlantic album, *Fontessa*. Ralph J. Gleason noted, "It has all the earthy swing and
solidarity of Basie." Jackson introduces it with a concentrated eight-bar
cadenza before the theme is played twice. The first time, Kay uses sticks
and cymbal; the second, brushes and snare drum. Jackson's seven-chorus
solo is as good an example as you could ask of his endlessly creative
way with the blues. It also exemplifies Lewis's alert style of accompaniment.

Lewis never felt that the quartet needed a wind instrument, and he
knew that, in time, the group would be able to collaborate with guests—
individual soloists and entire orchestras. The MJQ had already performed in support of Charlie Parker and Sonny Rollins. The first formal
alliance with an invited guest, however, was with clarinetist Jimmy Giuffre. The venue was Music Inn, a resort near Lennox, Massachusetts; the
proprietors, Phillip and Stephanie Barber, presented summer colloquia
on jazz, organized by writer and curator Marshall Stearns. In 1956, the
MJQ was invited as the inn's first resident ensemble, a step that greatly
increased the aspirations of Music Inn and led directly to the establishment of a school. Soon jazz musicians of all periods were involved. In
his notes to the first MJQ album recorded in that setting, John S. Wilson
wrote, "As the discussions moved along, the barriers which had isolated
jazzmen since World War II . . . melted away. The older men were soon
being drawn out on intimate details of early jazz history." Giuffre, a
member of the faculty, wrote in the *The Jazz Review*, "All elements seem
to come together to inspire players and to involve listeners." Lewis was
appointed director of the school.

"A FUGUE FOR MUSIC INN" (1965) Although Lewis's piece is an ostensibly free improvisation built around a four-bar motive, the solos generally fall into twelve-bar blues configurations, never more so than when
Jackson has the spotlight. The adventurous Giuffre offers a pure sound
and legato phrasing that complement his penchant for unusual melody
notes. He also performed on David Raksin's "Serenade," which is not a
jazz piece (Lewis told Wilson that he programmed it because "I refuse
to be restricted by any formulas") and his own "Fun," which has the
feeling of a sharp-witted conversation.

"THREE WINDOWS" (1957) The first and most popular of the themes
that constitue this triple fugue is "The Golden Striker," named for the
lifelike figure that strikes the hour on the clock tower near St. Mark's
Cathedral in Venice. It's the central work from Lewis's score for Roger
Vadim's *No Sun in Venice*. Lewis tackled the assignment without having
seen the film. He worked only with a script and timings. If the film is
no great shakes (Lewis, who eventually caught up with it in Greenwich

Village, says, "It isn't good, but it's very beautiful, the photography is great"), his music remains an enduring benchmark in the MJQ's repertory, its chiming ebullience smartly capturing the gorgeous, gilded museum-city.

"FESTIVAL SKETCH" (1958) The quartet recorded its second album at Music Inn with the participation of Sonny Rollins on two numbers. Rollins did not play on "Festival Sketch," which may be why this gem from that album is so often overlooked. It covers a lot of ground in a short amount of time: the theme, with its staggered accents, seems to promise a shrewd invention with much interplay, but though the performance delivers on interplay—Max Harrison marveled at the "sheer diversity in configuration of Jackson's and Lewis's simultaneous phrases"—it is primarily a swinging gambol. Lewis's solo opens with tricky rhythmic shifts, but in no time he and Kay and Heath are burning rubber. Note that from the bridge of his second chorus, Lewis is backed by Jackson—a rare occasion.

"BAGS' GROOVE" (1958) Along with "Django," Jackson's blues is the MJQ's best known anthem. Of the countless versions, the one with Rollins is surely the most intrepidly witty. Gunther Schuller described the musical drama between Rollins and Lewis: after three choruses, during which Lewis "prods him soberly with beautiful sustained chords," he "realizes that Rollins will not be swayed, and 'joins in' with little discordant semi-tone 'bleeps,' which later he develops into a relentlessly building, insinuating rhythmic figure, which Sonny finally can no longer resist. He almost becomes serious for a few choruses, only to return eventually to the prevailing punning mood." When Rollins *is* serious, the quartet knows exactly what to do—all five men bond in blissfully intense accord.

"ROMAINE" (1959) The MJQ recorded Jim Hall's haunting ballad at Music Inn in 1959, a couple of months after the composer recorded his own celebrated duet version with Bill Evans. With the virtually simultaneous release of the two performances—the MJQ's appeared on *Pyramid*—the theme seemed likely to become a modern jazz standard. It isn't played much anymore, but its appeal has not withered in the intervening decades, no more than Lewis's alluring arrangement.

"ODDS AGAINST TOMORROW" (1959) Robert Wise's psychosocial crime thriller provided Lewis with his best opportunity as a film composer, and the result was one of the most successful uses of jazz ever in a Hollywood film. Lewis credits Wise with showing him the right way to compose for movies, which is to work with a "click track" while viewing the scenes that are being scored. Two versions of the score were released: one by the MJQ, another by the twenty-three-piece ensemble (Bill Evans on piano) heard on the soundtrack. Among the highlights are "No Happiness for Slater," a sixteen-bar blues with a properly ominous theme that showcases the quartet's decisive teamwork; the poignant title selection, a shimmeringly intimate mood piece (especially when Jackson "bends" notes over Lewis's repeated vamp), and the radiantly lyrical "Skating in Central Park."

In its first forty years, the MJQ performed with nearly forty major orchestras from around the world. In 1960, the still timorous inclination to combine the quartet with other ensembles was given a boost by the vogue for third-stream music, a briefly fashionable movement in which Lewis emerged as a major figure. The phrase was coined by Gunther Schuller in an attempt to describe a merger of techniques from the streams of jazz and classical music. Several recordings were issued and concerts staged, employing the talents of such composers as George Russell, Jimmy Giuffre, John Benson Brooks, Charles Mingus, Milton Babbitt, Ornette Coleman, David Amram, and others. Yet jazz itself was a third stream drawing on Europe and Africa, and jazz and the academy had always flirted with each other, forming alliances of various degrees of success. In any case, the trend was short-lived and left hardly a ripple as the tides of free jazz and new music inundated the decade. Yet a few durable works abide.

"EXPOSURE" (1960) Adapted from music Lewis composed for a United Nations-sponsored documentary film about the world's refugees, "Exposure" was performed by the MJQ and a chamber sextet. Highly characteristic of Lewis is the clarity of line, the carefully individualized role of each instrument, and the graceful permutations in rhythm.

"ENGLAND'S CAROL" (1960) A few months after the release of *Third Stream Music*, Lewis invited Schuller, André Hodier, and Werner Heider to compose music for a more ambitious venture that would combine the MJQ and a symphony orchestra. For his contribution, Lewis chose and renamed a traditional piece he had previously arranged for the quartet, "God Rest Ye Merry, Gentlemen." The impromptu orchestra assembled in Stuttgart for the recording may have found Lewis's phrasing somewhat alien, but it produced rich sonority as well as third-stream's only hit. "I like the melodic line," Lewis had said of the carol. "It has a lift." Audiences agreed, and he later devised other settings for it. The dashing violins and contending cellos of the opening passage hardly prepare you for Jackson's exuberant entrance, a splash of wintry cheer.

"EUROPEAN CONCERT" (1960) Asked individually to name their favorite MJQ albums, each member said *European Concert* or *Last Concert* or both. Among the reasons given were the retrospective nature of the albums, the inspired interplay, the presence of enthusiastic audiences.

European Concert, recorded in Stockholm, Guttenberg, and Copenhagen, was the culmination of nearly a decade's work. As Kay described it, "The music sounds juiced to me, like everyone is flying, it swings a lot, and it gives an example of almost everything we played." Some people didn't see how the quartet could continue after attaining what to all appearances passed for perfection. Martin Williams suggested that the concert "might almost stand as a summary of some of the highest achievements of ten years of working together."

"THE COMEDY" (1960) Before the year was out, all the talk of perfection gave way to controversy as Lewis presented his most expansive quartet work to that point. The suite in seven movements embodied the realization of ideas he had worked on as far back as the 1956 "Fontessa," his initial attempt to depict characters from the commedia dell'arte in jazz. Fontessa, unlike Columbine or Harlequin, was a figure of Lewis's own invention. "The main thing about the commedia dell'arte was that the things they did were principally improvised until Carlo Goldoni started to write them down," Lewis says. "It reminded me very much of the way jazz developed from small groups of musicians traveling place to place and having to make sure they satisfied the local audience." The critical response ranged from "frequently ponderous," with Jackson asked to execute "some fairly mechanical ideas" (Martin Williams), to "the Modern Jazz Quartet's greatest single achievement, the peak to which all their preceding work together leads" with "some of the most astonishing passages" Jackson ever recorded (Max Harrison). Fifteen months before the rest of *The Comedy* was recorded, Lewis recruited Diahann Carroll for a movement called "La Cantatrice" (the singer), the spry complaint of an understudy longing for her chance.

"LONELY WOMAN" (1962) The very day on which the MJQ completed *The Comedy,* it began work on a more conventional album, though it included a luminous rendition of Ornette Coleman's title ballad (the MJQ virtually established "Lonely Woman" as a standard) and reductions of the music Lewis wrote for his ballet, *Original Sin.* Among the latter was "New York 19," one of Lewis's most fetching melodies. In its suggestion of songs from the early years of the century, Lewis shows how deeply imbued he is with the American ballad tradition. Jackson sounds positively regal as the others chaperone his every elegant step.

"BACHIANAS BRASILEIRAS" AND "CONCORDE" (1963) Recorded on successive days for successive albums, these pieces complement each other as successive ways of looking at Bach. The first is Lewis's arrangement of a piece by Heitor Villa-Lobos, who shared with Lewis a concern for musical education and a desire to affirm the popular music of his country. Also like Lewis, he made many painstaking transcriptions from Bach and was convinced of an affinity between Bach's compositions and pop-ular melodies of his own day. Villa-Lobos wrote nine Bachianas Brasi-leiras. The one Lewis adapted was performed in a quintet version with guitarist Laurindo Almeida at the Monterey Jazz Festival, where Lewis served as music director for twenty-five years. The quartet version was conceived first, however, and is emblematic of the group's matchless accord. "Concorde" was the MJQ's second fugue, universally regarded as a giant leap beyond "Vendome." Lewis revised it extensively for the 1963 version. The instruments enter in characteristic sequence, and the performance and blending of elements is nothing if not natural. As Rob-ert Schumann wrote (though not about the MJQ), "The best fugue is the one the public takes for a Strauss waltz; in other words a fugue where the structural underpinnings are no more visible than the roots that nourish the flower."

"RALPH'S NEW BLUES" (1965) The following year brought another an-imated collaboration, this time with an all-star big band. The MJQ had become so associated with chamber groups and symphonies—that is, strings—that *Jazz Dialogue* provided a long overdue opportunity for the quartet to return to its womb, as the rhythm section of a seventeen-piece band. One of the highlights of that album was written in 1955 by Jackson and named for critic Ralph J. Gleason, who gave the MJQ a major boost with an article he wrote in the *San Francisco Chronicle* at a time, Jackson says, "when we were getting more attention in Europe than here." The new element of the title is the modal quality of the main phrase. Notable among the solos are those by Heath and Lewis, who is comped by muted brass of his own devising.

"THE CYLINDER" (1966) One of Jackson's most frequently performed and singular pieces, "The Cylinder" was composed early on, when he was still struggling to master the principles of writing, so he asked Ken-ny Dorham to transcribe the melody for him. The tune is a perennial favorite in Lewis's setting, which is animated by the conceit that this blues "has the rickety feeling of an old car." From the canonical theme statement to the humorous close, piloted by Kay, the performance is a model of interplay. One of the best and rarest performances was record-ed at a 1966 concert in Japan and released here on the anniversary com-pilation, *MJQ40*. In his laconic solo, Lewis suggests the stride piano tra-dition in his use of time and early Basie in the defining purity of his chords.

"MIDSOMMER" AND "WINTER'S TALE" (1966) "Midsommer" was orig-inally recorded in 1955 by Lewis and a nine-piece ensemble called the Modern Jazz Society (including Stan Getz and J. J. Johnson). Lewis later enlarged it for symphony orchestra and reduced it for the quartet. In the latter configuration, it received a model performance in Japan (as heard on *MJQ40*), as the interaction between Jackson and Lewis weaves a miraculous spell. "Winter's Tale," another important Lewis composition, is an irresistible example of his use of tzigane style—it brims with Gypsy weltschmerz, underscored by Heath's arco bass and Kay's chimes. Perhaps the most moving performance is the one recorded by the John Lewis Sextet in the '70s, but the quartet version performed in Japan is exemplary, with just enough self-awareness to banish sorrow and a climax of whirling frenzy.

"BLUES AT CARNEGIE HALL" (1966) A month after the concert in Japan, the MJQ was in Carnegie Hall with a program that devoted an entire set to the blues, including such imaginative gems as "Monterey Mist" and "Blues Milanese." Jackson wrote the first, a second cousin to "Bags' Groove," which debuted on one of his big band albums as "Extraordinary Blues." Notable for its apparent simplicity and contrasting textures, it offers a twice-played theme and four-bar transition to set up Jackson's sparkling six choruses, closely shadowed by Lewis, who, though never intrusive, tracks him with unmistakable determination. By the fifth chorus, you can hardly tell them apart. Lewis plays his own six choruses on a spare, stop-time stage. His "Blues Milanese" uses altered harmonies to construct a thirty-two-bar song out of discrete eight-bar blues episodes—note Jackson's two stunning choruses, Lewis's unaccompanied rubato interlude, Kay's dynamics, and Heath's pensive opening and closing statements.

"NOVAMO" (1967) Jackson says the title has no significance, "it just seemed like a unique title for the Barcelona thing." This sensational performance was recorded at The Lighthouse in Hermosa Beach and doesn't suggest much in the way of Spanish intentions. The musicians' roles are discretely patterned, the release swings fiercely, and the solos are knockouts, especially Jackson's three bebopping choruses, inflected with triplets, doubled-up phrases, riffs, and even a tremolo turnback. As usual, Lewis has revved up his solo long before Jackson has finished his, but when the spotlight is on him, the texture changes radically—he uses breaks to impart a blues-drenched enchantment.

The news of a change for the Modern Jazz Quartet didn't make the papers until the summer of 1968, six months after recording its initial session for a new label in England—The Beatles' shortlived company, Apple—ending the group's twelve-year association with Atlantic. The times they were a-changin', and there were those who feared the staid and stoic MJQ was tilling dangerously close to the fields of rock. In fact, this was nothing new; Atlantic had been a pop label looking to expand when it signed the MJQ. But history did not repeat itself. As Lewis, who handled the production, recalls, "Monte Kay was a friend of the president of the Beatles' company, and he felt we weren't getting the attention we should have, so we went there and had two good records." The music on *The Jasmine Tree* and *Space* was entirely in character, but the graphics and liner blurbs were embarrassingly au courant.

"VISITOR FROM VENUS" AND "VISITOR FROM MARS" (1968) These were the two Lewis originals on *Space*, the former notable for its tingling opening crescendo (the kind of thing synthesizers would take care of a few years later) and the latter, an infectious swinger that, as the title portends, builds to warlike ferocity.

"WALKIN' STOMP" (1971) Three years passed before the MJQ was back in the studio, once again for Atlantic. Those three years were among the most difficult jazz has ever known; the death of John Coltrane seemed to sap the music of its spirit, and the death of Louis Armstrong robbed it of its North Star, its Big Dipper. Rock was pandemic, jazz clubs were on the ropes, and band uniforms were definitely passé unless they were tie-dyed. The new MJQ album was a product of its time: adorning the cover of *Plastic Dreams* was a psychedelic drawing of a woman with balloon breasts. Magazine ads vowed the MJQ was "swinging like hell within the structures of a form." On a few selections (including updated versions of "England's Carol" and "Piazza Novona," from *The Comedy*), a brass quintet was added. "Walkin' Stomp," the most infectious piece, ended with what is truly an anomaly for one of the most fastidious composers of our time—a fadeout. Yet it's a savory number, beginning with an exotic rhythm that becomes increasingly foursquare as the performance develops. The head, set against a bass vamp, is forty-eight bars, though the improvised choruses are based on a forty-bar reduction. The bridge represents the closest John Lewis has come to writing or playing rock and roll. Kay sounds right at home. Other selections from the session were justifiably suppressed, among them one forbiddingly called, "The Trip."

It may be difficult for contemporary listeners to believe that in the early '70s just about every jazz pianist other than Monk and Basie tried to elicit a personal sound from electric keyboards—even Bill Evans, even John Lewis. Those were trying times: the MJQ was now in its twentieth year, and there were signs of exhaustion. Jackson began griping about the regimen of constant touring and rehearsing. Yet Lewis had a couple of tricks in his hat, and he produced them in November of 1973. With the MJQ, his greatest achievement, on the rocks and talk of a farewell tour making its way through the grapevine, it's no surprise that he was thinking about death. He wrote "In Memoriam" for Walter Keller, the man who had taught him piano in New Mexico, but there was a somber quality to all the music he created that November.

"In Memoriam" (1973) For this album, which required the participation of a symphony orchestra directed by Maurice Peress, Lewis reconceived two earlier pieces. "Jazz Ostinato" dated back to the third-stream era and derived its title from the presence of three ostinato figures: the first accompanies the vibes in the initial passage, the second the piano, and the third was originally conceived as backing "for an Ornette Coleman–Eric Dolphy approach." Lewis went on to say, "There is in the piece homage to Arnold Schoenberg and Igor Stravinsky so this work also plays a part in the memorium." Yet the exceptional solos by Lewis and Jackson suggest less a homage than a defiant celebration of self. The quartet had previously recorded the Adagio from Joaquin Rodrigo's *Concerto de Aranjuez* with guitarist Laurindo Almeida in 1964 and later in the decade on its own (on *Space*). With *In Memoriam*, it found an especially eloquent interpretation in the warming climate of a full orchestra that emphasized, by contrast, the powerful cadenzas by the principals.

"Blues on Bach" (1973) Three weeks later, the MJQ recorded its inevitable if long-deferred homage to Johann Sebastian. The album closed with one of the most movingly mournful performances the MJQ ever recorded, "Tears from the Children," Lewis's adaptation of Prelude no. 8 in E-flat Minor from *The Well-Tempered Clavier*. A decade later, Lewis would recast the piece in one of his most ambitious projects, a profoundly personal investigation of all twenty-four of Bach's preludes and fugues. This initial version, however, with Lewis playing harpsichord and Jackson assigned the melody, couldn't help but suggest tears for the end of an era.

Yet when the MJQ appeared in Avery Fisher Hall exactly one year later for the official farewell concert, there were no tears and no accusations that the quartet was tired or mechanical. *Last Concert* was an exhilarating return to form, an incisive and consistently brilliant retrospective that temporarily banished all sorrow. When the records were released (with, incidentally, the first MJQ jacket in seven years to offer liner notes), the magic of the moment was confirmed. Lewis told Nat Hentoff, "After all, we knew this was *it*. The end. Either play now, or forget it!" And Heath says today, "I think that's the best we'll *ever* do, because that was a live performance of what we had gotten to in twenty-two years. It was a very emotional night—we played three hours that night and the audience wouldn't let us stop. The music was very inspirational and said everything we had to say."

"Last Concert" (1974) You couldn't ask for better evidence of the inspiration achieved that evening than the definitive readings of MJQ classics, pieces played almost nightly over many years, now made new again. Listen to Heath during (it seems inappropriate and wrong to say behind) Jackson's solo on Lewis's most alluring waltz, "Skating in Central Park," from *Odds Against Tomorrow,* and you cannot fail to hear the mastery that took twenty-two years to secure. In this scintillating performance, every note has purpose and resolve. Jackson's "The Legendary Profile" is a carnival of traditional jazz and blues effects, imbued with barrelhouse soul and garbed in stop-time, Basie-style climaxes, even a boogie-woogie bass. "The Jasmine Tree," part of Lewis's documentary film score set in Morocco, is a thriller that peaks in some of the most electrifying ensemble passages the MJQ has recorded to date.

"DJANGO"—above all, Lewis's good-luck charm, the piece that made him and the MJQ world famous; the piece that led directly to the commission for his first film score; the piece most associated with the heightened level of jazz composition in the '50s—was played at the "last concert" in a decisive version. "Django" is a memorial homage, a cortege for the great Gypsy guitarist Django Reinhardt, whom Lewis first heard during the war on a weekend pass.

> I was tremendously impressed. Then I heard some records he made with members of the Teddy Hill band, including a duet with Bill Coleman that was unbelievable. I definitely got to know his music when he came to this country in 1947 to play with Duke Ellington. He came down to a club where we were working on Fifty-second Street, and we played overtime to make a good impression. It was wonderful to watch the change that took place in his playing, from things that were made in 1937 to things he was doing at the time he died. He kept changing. And I was so sorry when he died. I would have liked to spend more time with him.

The MJQ received the Prix du Disque for its 1954 recording of "Django" at the American Embassy in Paris; in 1992 Heath observed, "The original version with Kenny is of sentimental value, but the one in *Last Concert* is my favorite." Here all the elements of Lewis's skill and the MJQ's interpretive power are as one: the evocative Gypsy feeling in the main theme, recalling the Adagio of Mendelssohn's Octet; the eloquently stout bass motif; the congruence of delicacy and force, discipline and spontaneity, tragedy and joy.

Today Lewis calls the temporary dissolution of the MJQ "a vacation that we took after twenty-two years. It wasn't a retirement, it just wasn't time to retire. We had regularly taken vacations of three months, or a season, but now the music business and other things had changed so much, and we took the longer vacation that we deserved." For the rest of the '70s, Connie Kay played constantly at Jimmy Ryan's and other New York clubs; Percy Heath joined forces with his siblings to create a highly successful band, The Heath Brothers, when he wasn't fishing on eastern Long Island; Milt Jackson recorded and performed as prolifically as ever and even attempted to sing again; John Lewis performed in various piano clubs (he called it "paid practice"), initiated several recording projects (many of them in Europe, where he lives part of the year), taught at City College and the Manhattan School of Music. All got to spend more time with their families. The breakup of the MJQ was endlessly lamented, as the "last concert" turned out to be one in a series of farewell concerts.

Then, in 1981, the MJQ regrouped for a tour of Japan. A few months later, the announcement went out: the MJQ was back, under management of erstwhile teammate, Ray Brown. This time, Lewis said, things would be different—"We're not doing the constant traveling anymore, and the pay is better." Inevitably, Monte Kay returned to manage the quartet, and the touring resumed at full pace. Indeed, Lewis and Jackson seemed to be working harder than ever. On those few nights when the MJQ wasn't appearing in concert, Jackson was leading a quintet in a jazz club. Lewis, working closely with his wife, Mirjana, commenced a series of recordings of Bach for Japan's Nippon Phonogram and signed on, pro bono, as music director of the American Jazz Orchestra.

"THAT SLAVIC SMILE" AND "SACHA'S MARCH" (1984) After ten years, the MJQ was back in the recording studios: *Echoes* was the first of four albums for Pablo. Among the most memorable selections were Lewis compositions inspired by his wife ("That Slavic Smile," a song ironically rooted in American balladry) and son ("Sacha's March," a whimsical number he originally introduced on a piano anthology in the '70s). The reformed MJQ also adapted pieces that had surfaced during the long vacation: Jackson's lush interpretation of "Nature Boy" and Heath's comic "The Watergate Blues."

"A DAY IN DUBROVNIK" (1987) The MJQ returned to Atlantic in 1987 and brought Nesuhi Ertegun back to the fold. The first album, *Three Windows*, continued the policy of recomposing early works, notably the title piece and "Django" (a rendition inspired in part by the arrangement Gil Evans wrote of it for his 1959 album, *New Bottle, Old Wine*), this time to accommodate arrangements that employed the New York Chamber Symphony. But the centerpiece was a wholescale reevaluation of the suite, "A Day in Dubrovnik," a magnificent work commissioned by the Yugoslav musician Bosko Petrovik and heard in its original form as "Na Dubrovacki Nacin" on Lewis's album *Misterij Bluesa*. A difficult work to play, it was performed repeatedly by the MJQ after 1983, often nightly at the quartet's annual engagements at New York's Cafe Carlyle and with increased fervor since the devastation of that city, which John and Mirjana Lewis knew well and loved. Lewis tried to capture the feeling of Vivaldi and Giuseppe Tartini, the eighteenth-century composer who was born up the coast from Dubrovnik. The second movement Adagio is one of the most sumptuously romantic passages he has written.

"FOR ELLINGTON" (1988) A year later, the quartet released one of its most admired works: the only full-scale homage the MJQ has paid any composer other than Bach. Oddly, Lewis did not greatly venerate Ellington when he was young until he saw the band play a dance in New Mexico in 1939, and watched Ellington put together his arrangement of "Chloe." For Lewis, the Ellington pieces of the early '40s "were all masterpieces." Adapting them to the MJQ meant a comprehensive investigation of original scores, many of which he had interpreted in their original form as musical director of the American Jazz Orchestra. The most remarkable thing about *For Ellington* is the degree to which he was able to retain so many of the original melodic and rhythmic ideas in context of a quartet. The title composition, an original, is a waltz that moves into four for the solos. "Rockin' in Rhythm," a particular favorite with audiences, dates back to 1930, though Ellington updated it as assiduously as Lewis has "Django," adding an increasingly important ad-lib section at the top. Following the lesson of the master, Lewis similarly begins his version with improvisation, building to a climax at which the delayed melody is finally stated.

In 1992, the year of its fortieth anniversary, the MJQ was often regarded as the finest small band in jazz and worked more than ever, notably in long stints at the Cafe Carlyle, where the acoustics approximate the intimacy of a living room. It was a very different world than in 1952. President Bush was amazed to discover enough discrimination to warrant a civil rights bill to guarantee fair employment practices and promised to veto one even if every African American voted against him. Korea was in conflict with itself; allied fighter bombers geared up to destroy Iraq's capacity to make war; the guilt of the Rosenbergs was still debated, though protests against the death penalty were now routine; George Foreman announced his retirement from the ring, but changed his mind. The *Times* devoted more space to TV than radio and now provided jazz coverage, but conflated it with pop and segregated both from the "Arts and Leisure" music page.

In jazz, young bands customarily performed in concert and at festivals, often in tailored suits. Composition was as widely vaunted for small ensembles as improvisation, and flawless intonation was considered vital. Such traditional jazz devices as polyphony, riffs, breaks, boogie bass, mutes, and fugal counterpoint, as well as a repertory that ranges over the entire history of the music, were everywhere apparent. You could say that the Modern Jazz quartet now resided in a world at least partially of its own making. Indeed, so sure was its standing that the death of Connie Kay in December 1994, which many feared would be fatal to the quartet itself, seemed only to spur the survivers to a greater intensity of purpose. Within a year, they were back on the road with Albert Heath on drums, and though its days were clearly numbered, anyone who had the fortune to hear the MJQ in concert during that tour could be forgiven for hearing intimations of an ever deeper sagacity.

43 ❖ Nat King Cole
(The Comeback King)

The resurrection in 1991 of Nat King Cole, clinched but by no means precipitated by a ghostly appearance on his daughter's recording of "Unforgettable" (released on Elektra!) twenty-six years after Cole's death, forty years after he first recorded the song and fifty-five years after he debuted on records, had little precedence in popular music. Every comeback of comparable amplitude conveys exclusive mysteries. Jolson was around and fit to capitalize on the movie that revived him; Sinatra and Judy Garland revived themselves. The closest antecedent to the Cole phenomenon is, not surprisingly, far more recent: Louis Armstrong's posthumous (by seventeen years) hit with "What a Wonderful World." Yet commercial considerations aside, Armstrong continued to be acknowledged as the foundation for America's serious vernacular music; his return to the Top 40 was pleasantly titillating, but his esteem was hardly in need of salvaging. When Nat Cole's records turned up in Hollywood movies ("A Blossom Fell" in *Badlands*, "Smile" in *Smile*), the point was either nostalgia or irony. Though several Cole albums endured as perennial sellers, most of his work was forgotten by the general public or fetishized by jazz lovers who were surprised to find that the throaty crooner was a distinguished pianist.

American pop music can be divided into three exceptionally discrete periods: the post–Civil War era, when the songwriting profession first went into overdrive to furnish minstrelsy with new material and ragtime, blues, spirituals, and jazz signaled the intensifying dominance of the

African American underground; the nearly fifty-year golden era, from Jerome Kern to Frank Loesser, when theater, radio, and movies created a far more capacious appetite for fresh songs and when the unprecedented range and virtuosity of interpretive performers (instrumentalists no less than singers) helped boost and sustain high standards of melodic, harmonic, and verbal ingenuity; and the rock and roll, rock, and postrock era, in which songs are almost always generated by or for performers, as opposed to theatrical enterprises, and technology replaces song per se as the primary musical currency.

At the peak of the songwriting boom of the late '30s and '40s, people hungered for the simpler ditties of the preceding period, a hunger that was requited as performers and producers realized the economic utility of those seemingly more demotic songs no longer protected by copyright. Sinatra can sing "I Fall in Love Too Easily," but you can't; by contrast, Stephen Foster's "Beautiful Dreamer" could soothe any savage breast, even that of Mighty Joe Young. It's easy to foresee an avalanche of musicals, films, and recordings in the early years of the next century combining clever new librettos with the glorious melodies that will have slipped into the public domain, free for the exploiting. The Nat Cole boom is in part a harbinger. Some pop critics decry the phenomenon as conservative backpeddling, and clearly Cole's sudden ubiquity does satisfy a hunger for that which is perceived absent in contemporary pop: melody, simplicity, clarity, romance, even a kind of vocal individuality that subsumes technology and recapitulates the mirage of demotic song.

Of course, an irony at the heart of Natalie Cole's triumph and its spur in restoring interest in her father is the song she chose for her technological miracle. Whatever else it is, "Unforgettable" is not a standard. Excepting Dinah Washington, other performers ignored it—not because Nat's modest 1951 hit was too closely associated with him (on the contrary, signature hits usually ensure covers), but because the song itself isn't much. Cole, in true 'tain't-what-you-do fashion, enriched the tune with his unique timbre and phrasing, as he did numerous mediocre songs—"Nature Boy," "Too Young," "Pretend," "Darling, Je Vous Aime Beaucoup," "Ramblin' Rose"—throughout his career. Yet if "Unforgettable" isn't a classic song, I suspect it answers the need for the idea of classic songs in an era when performance-oriented material has all but canceled the notion of evergreens. More than that, it helps put the trove of standard songs in commercial perspective, underscoring their validity for mainstream performers caught between rock and a hard place.

The Cole juggernaut was actually a long time coming. He was completely out of fashion in the late '60s and much of the '70s, at least in this country. Yet reissues of his jazz records did well in Europe and Japan, and as imports began to proliferate, they activated a new perception of Cole. The reissue of his 1956 masterpiece, *After Midnight*, became something of a rallying point for revisionist evaluations, further buoyed by releases of Cole's recordings with the Sunset All-Stars, Jazz at the Philharmonic, the trio with Lester Young, the quintet with Dexter Gordon, and his own trio recordings, which had been unavailable for so long they seemed little short of revelatory. Now Cole, whom one remembered from childhood as a gushy balladeer, seemed like a fount for everything from bop to r & b. Dizzy Gillespie called him one of his favorite pianists and credited him with introducing the unofficial bop anthem, "How High the Moon." Tiny Grimes and John Collins have attested to his influence on Art Tatum, whom Collins recalls taking a front-row seat whenever Cole performed. Ray Charles's trio recordings show that Cole's impact on him was, at that stage of his career, every bit as strong as on Charles Brown.

A few aspects of Cole's musicianship are immediately evident: the astonishing independence of voice and piano, for one—he rarely settles for mere pacing chords, preferring octaves and chromatic bass lines and subtly configured harmonies that complement and deepen the vocal interpretation. Then there is his wit and speed, lightning reflexes that hardly ever call attention to his technique but constantly spice his solos, interludes, intros, and codas. Then there is his lucidity and swing: on practically every one of those relatively rare occasions in which he performed with major jazz soloists, he stole the limelight. His solos are melodically sure, often sounding through-composed. His famous quote-heavy version of "Body and Soul," of which there are several versions, is a spectacle of compression and relaxation.

Cole is always in control, never more than when he is flat-out rocking, as on the trio performance "Jumpin' at Capitol" when he breaks the headlong rush of his solo with a sexy hesitation in the fourteenth measure. He had an individual sound on the piano, and a rare ability to shade that sound to the setting. For the *After Midnight* sessions, he uses a far more dynamic approach on the pieces with violinist Stuff Smith than those with trumpeter Harry Edison. (The piano-violin exchanges on "I Know That You Know" contain some of the fastest improvisational thinking you can find anywhere.) His orchestral keyboard sound is more cocktailish on *Penthouse Serenade*, another key instrumental album from the '50s, appropriately plush and open as suggested by the before-midnight theme. On one of his first TV shows, he played a chordal solo on "I'll See You in C-U-B-A" that successfully mimicked the sound of steel drums.

No other performer in history had two such profoundly different public personalities as Cole: the hip and jivey leader of a black jazz combo and the eminent crooner whose predominantly white following was so large an attempt was made to secure him a network TV show. (*The Nat King Cole Show* failed chiefly because of commercial anxieties about the South. A Revlon executive withdrew support, commenting that a Negro could not sell cosmetics; "Madison Avenue is afraid of the dark," Cole tersely replied.) Yet the split between his jazz and pop selves is probably overstated. The thing about Cole's singing that becomes heightened after you detour through the instrumental work is how infused with jazz it is, even when the material is dire. Comparisons have been drawn between Cole's vocal timbre and phrasing and that of tenor saxophonist Lester Young, the casual swing and cool intonation. The connection is obvious in masterful jazz performances such as "Gee Baby, Ain't I Good to You," recorded with the trio, or "You Stepped Out of a Dream," recorded with a large orchestra, but it's also apparent in quasi-country pieces. On some ineffable level, "Ramblin' Rose" is a jazz record; the soulful dynamics of the chorus, the subtle syncopations, the openness of the phrasing, the unfettered calm all suggest a close link to the Cole of "Sweet Lorraine" (which is far from a blues, after all, never mind its Earl Hines ancestry) or "Route 66."

During his life, Cole was constantly criticized for being facile. The buzz word is often "genteel." Much as "facility" was once the pejorative of choice when musicians were supposed to sweat for their dissonances, gentility is now considered the converse of authentic soul. In truth, Cole could be facile and genteel, perhaps more on uptempo pieces than on ballads—consider *Big Band Cole* or the weird version of "A Cottage for Sale" (on the otherwise superb album *Just One of Those Things*), which is taken so inappropriately fast the lyrics are rendered senseless. Cole, like Crosby and Sinatra, recorded too much and too often and was no less than they importuned by song pluggers pushing shabby goods. Yet facility implies glibness and gloss, while gentility often suggests affectation as well as urbanity. Cole's admirers know that his credibility keeps him current, as does his attention to detail, unmistakable rhythmic elan, and nonstop inventiveness. Those strengths are found in his singing and his piano, most especially in the trio recordings, which have a life and integrity apart from his other work.

After decades of famine, the Cole trio became the subject of more feasting than most people thought possible, in the early '90s. The banquet included a one-volume sampler of studio selections, *Jumpin' at Capitol* (Rhino); a five-volume collection of MacGregor radio transcriptions, *The Trio*

Recordings (Laser Light); a four-volume collection of the first radio transcriptions, when the trio sang en masse and Cole hadn't yet figured a winning formula, *The Complete Early Transcriptions* (VJC); a one-volume collection of 1947–48 radio guest appearances, *The King Cole Trio: Live* (VJC); and, overwhelmingly, the eighteen-volume *Complete Capitol Recordings of the Nat King Cole Trio* (Mosaic). That's twenty-eight CDs of unduplicated material, some thirty hours of the Nat Cole Trio, not including the Deccas, JATPs, and other instrumental performances from Cole's primary jazz period.

The *Complete Capitol Recordings* is clearly the most important. On the basis of the Capitols, Cole's reputation as pianist, innovator, bandleader, and singer was definitively and comprehensively established. The reputations of other musicians are also enfolded here, including three important guitarists: Oscar Moore, Irving Ashby, and John Collins (who had the alternately enriching and frustrating experience of spending fourteen years with Cole, making the switch from Tatum's trio to Cole's at the very moment when Capitol was doing everything it could to restrain Cole from the piano and the trio from doing anything but keep time while banks of strings and winds carpeted every vocal; occasionally threatening to quit and constantly cajoling Cole to play more, Collins finally got his licks on *After Midnight*).

The box is easy to evaluate, but given its size, harder to recommend. The production is first-rate—an ever enlarging tour through Cole's evolution, every step of it monitored by Will Friedwald's argumentative, original, often persuasive notes, which effectively muse on Cole's use of vernacular lyrics and his attention to the trio's polyphony and key changes. Many sessions are included in which the trio is buried beneath an orchestra or choir, and they help to fill out the picture and vary the menu. "Nature Boy" is here, but so is "You Stepped Out of a Dream" and so, of course, are *After Midnight* (arranged by session for the first time and perhaps gaining something for the revision) and *Penthouse Serenade*.

Having listened to each of the eighteen discs at least once, and some several times, I can say that little seems to me negligible: a few of the alternate takes are tedious, and there are tunes ("Pigtails and Freckles") beyond the resuscitation powers of Cole or anyone else. On balance, the sheer variety of the material is mesmerizing: novelties, kids' songs, jazzing the classics, ballads, instrumentals, pop tunes, jazz riffs, blues. You could break it down thematically and come up with half a dozen angles to program this amazingly prolific decade-plus in the career of a man who had to be convinced to sing but knew he was one hell of a pianist and combo arranger. It will never again be possible to make glib judgments about Cole's bipolar career. Indeed, the bulk of his trio work, now that it is finally available, may put to rest the eternal complaints about his selling out. We can now say with near certainty that he found time to record all the piano he knew. Thank heavens he found time to croon "Star Dust" and "Autumn Leaves," too.

44 ❖ *Stan Getz*
(Seasons)

If it hadn't been "Early Autumn," it would have been another record, but since that was the setting for the breezy interlude that put Stan Getz at the foot of the summit, it may be worth recalling that the piece itself had origins as chimerical as Getz's sound. In 1946, Ralph Burns presented Woody Herman with a three-part suite called "Summer Sequence," which Herman recorded in the fall, when the band's chief saxophone soloist was Flip Phillips. Columbia sat on it for a year, finally insisting that a fourth movement be added in order to release the entire work on two 78s. During Christmas week 1947, a new edition of the band with a sax section that boasted Getz, Zoot Sims, Herbie Steward, and Serge Chaloff recorded "Summer Sequence (Part IV)," complete with an ethereal eight-bar Getz solo and a closing melody that promised more than was realized in that arrangement. Almost exactly one year later, the band was back in the studio, this time for Capitol, playing a new piece by Ralph Burns built entirely on that elusive closing melody, called "Early Autumn." Once again, Getz was delegated an eight-bar solo (plus a pickup bar). That was enough.

One of the pleasures of 78s and, later, of 45s, was how they focused the attention of musician and listener alike. Confronted with the three-minute limit, the former was pressed to undertake perfection—lapses permissible in a novel are less tolerable in a short story. In jazz, this meant training yourself, if you were an arranger, to make certain something colorful occurred in every measure. It forced soloists to maximize the few bars—eight or sixteen, rarely more than thirty-two—they were assigned. Listeners, in turn, savored every detail. Today it is inconceivable that a musician could make his or her name with an eight-bar variation, not because the gift for brevity in jazz has all but disappeared, but because we are no longer as discriminating as listeners. The CD encourages us to wallow in bulk, not particulars.

When "Early Autumn" was released in 1949, a new generation of tenor saxophonists had demonstrated that Lester Young and not Coleman Hawkins was the path to modernist enlightenment. The most compelling of them, Dexter Gordon, showed how to combine Young's airborne melodies, smooth timbre, and advanced harmonies with the dictates of Charlie Parker. Getz himself was caught in Gordon's spell, as demonstrated on his 1946 recording debut, when he was nineteen. His "Opus De Bop" was as beholden to Gordon as Gordon's 1943 debut was to Young. (Three decades later, when Getz was the most famous saxophonist in the world and Gordon was making a heralded comeback, the two encountered each other on tour, and Getz, showing a side of himself he rarely allowed anyone to see, pressed Gordon to assure him that he, Getz, was really playing well. The last time I saw Gordon perform was on a 1987 bill with Getz in a stadium in Perugia, Italy. Gordon, his health suffering, pulled himself together for a devastatingly authoritative set. Getz, obviously inspired, performed in kind.) By "Early Autumn," Getz had discarded the Gordon influence, finding his own way of interpreting Young in the age of bop, with a light, beaming timbre, almost completely lacking in vibrato. He sounded like a cool, burbling spring, disarmed—almost feminine—yet sure. More than that, for white musicians he took the lead in suggesting a kind of racial honesty in broaching the new music.

The thing that distinguished Getz even more than his undeniable lyricism, which was unfailing even at breakneck tempos, was his sound, a paradoxical blend of light and heavy. With his rigid embouchure and slightly aspirate sonority, he produced a breezy tone backed by heroic force. Beholden to Young for his phrasing and his phrases, which he freely borrowed in his early years, as well as his energy and swing, Getz avoided Young's parched sound, that wounded echo of autumn leaves that characterized the older man's playing in his last years. Getz's emotional disposition, at once sensitive and aloof, seemed somehow emblematic of the white middle-class coming to grips with '50s America, much as the music of Gordon, Wardell Gray, or Gene Ammons seemed to evince the confidence of postwar blacks. The touchiness of the subject was evident in the clumsy semantics it inspired, but everyone knew that code phrases like West Coast/East Coast or cool/soul meant white style and black style, no matter how many exceptions (and they were legion) fudged the issue. Getz's sound incarnated springtime and romance—it had the inspired zing Young brought from Kansas City in 1936. The first time Young heard him play, he walked over to the bandstand and pronounced a benediction of five words that Getz forever treasured: "Nice eyes, Pres. Carry on."

Still, no one could miss the irony and the sadness in the fact that Getz achieved a popular renown that was denied Young—for that matter, denied just about everyone. Many critics and musicians resented his success: when an idiot writing in *Life* in the early '70s called him the greatest tenor saxophonist in jazz, it became commonplace for frustrated enthusiasts to deride Getz for the excesses of an overwrought scribe. In the same period, one often heard Getz's bossa nova albums faulted as inauthentic, though it is partly their inauthenticity—that is, the superimposition of progressive harmonies on Brazilian melodies—that makes them great. Getz's audience never wavered.

How he sustained his enormous following despite fifteen-round battles with drugs and alcohol, expatriation, and a reputation for surliness and worse is a mystery, until you go back to his discography. The consistent level of his playing matched by the resolution with which he persistently tackled new projects is startling. Getz was on or near the vanguard of several movements, but he didn't rely on any of them, not even the bossa nova, which made him a rich man and a household name. He is remembered less as an innovator than as one of the uncompromised stylists of his time: the tenor saxophonist who, regardless of the setting (including flirtations with fusion), suggested the fervor of well-being, candlelight intimacy, and flaming youth, all strengthened by a capacity to peer into the void. His best solos are often giddily discursive nightmares of melodic fragments; his ballads resound with frustration and longing.

In the late '80s, when Getz and Mel Lewis were both fighting cancer, Getz told the drummer, "I'm too evil to die." For a while, it looked like he might be right. Four months before his death, he made a remarkable recovery and stopped in New York to record with Abbey Lincoln en route to Denmark (where his playing awed the press) to prepare his last recordings, the glistening duets with Kenny Barron. "There are only three pianists left," he said at the time, "Hank [Jones], Tommy [Flanagan], and Kenny." By that time he had adapted Billy Strayhorn's swan song as his signature theme, playing it almost nightly.

"Blood Count" was the "Early Autumn" of his last years, the composition that best embodied the maturity of his playing, which was still romantic but girded with an emotional gravity that his younger self would not have recognized. "Blood Count" was hardly an unlikely vehicle for him: it was composed by one romantic for another (Johnny Hodges). Getz initially recorded it on the 1983 Concord Jazz album, *Pure Getz*, the jewel in a session that represented a reaffirmation for him, after several joyless attempts to make an au courant hit. Getz's deeply personal performance comes to some of the same conclusions about the piece as Hodges's, though there is no direct influence. Getz had not heard the Ellington account when he made his version—his pianist Jim McNeely brought the piece to him, and he recorded it in one take, working from a lead sheet. (Charlie Haden, who appeared with Getz on the Abbey Lincoln album, *You Gotta Pay the Band*, has said that Getz played all the pieces from lead sheets, without rehearsal or hesitation or error.) Up to that point, the song had an elusive history. Strayhorn wrote it in the hospital, submitting the final version in time for a Carnegie Hall concert in late March, where Ellington introduced it as "Manuscript." Strayhorn died in May, and Ellington recorded his final work in August on *And His Mother Called Him Bill*. Neither Ellington nor Hodges ever played it again. Possibly because their recording is decisive in emotional resonance as well as execution, the song was laid to rest. It didn't reappear until the '80s, when Jimmy Rowles created an ingenious piano reduction on his 1981 Ellington/Strayhorn album, followed by *Pure Getz*.

Considering the penchant Getz and Hodges share for extreme dynamics, it comes as no surprise to find Getz balancing his phrases with meticulous attention to intonation and volume. The most poignant episode is his forte-piano treatment of the release, which, unlike Hodges, Getz plays only once. It's a sublime exercise in equilibrium, an evenly calculated montage of roaring cries and quiescent moans. The phrases (each only two or three notes) couldn't be more economical as he alternates them loud and soft, concluding with a two-note figure that, repeated three times, makes for a seamless transition into the next episode. Interestingly, Hodges opted for a forte-piano treatment of the release for the Carnegie Hall performance (which is marred by a slightly rushed tempo and insensitive drumming), but rejected it for the more expansive studio recording. Hodges's decision was right for him, as it increased the songfulness of his interpretation. And Getz's was right for him, as it underscores the turmoil that animates his introspection. The other changes are also relevant. In the Ellington arrangement, "Blood Count" was fifty-six measures (AABABAC); Getz excised the second AB. Hodges consigned his intimations of the blues to subtle glissandi, whereas Getz uses vivid blues cadences as well as a two-note stutter phrase near the close.

With "Blood Count," Getz joined the relatively small group of jazz stylists who could lay personal claim to material by sole virtue of their interpretive integrity. Like Hodges, Ben Webster, Pee Wee Russell, Art Tatum, Miles Davis, and a handful of others, he didn't have to improvise variations to make his point. He demonstrated this capacity to look at a song from the inside out as early as "Early Autumn" but that was a fragment of a solo, and the ballad performances for which Getz was acclaimed in later years were as notable for the facility of his variations as the sensuousness of his sound.

When his liver gave out in June 1991, Getz, sixty-four, was mourned as one of the paramount stylists on the tenor saxophone, which he undoubtedly was. Yet a year later, when memorial tributes were mounted, it became clear that the sound he brought to jazz, once so influential and widely admired that European saxophonists were known to imitate his mistakes, had pretty much departed with him. A heavier timbre had returned to fashion. Not only was it hard to find young tenors who played in the "four brothers" manner that Getz helped create in Woody Herman's band, it was hard to *imagine* a young tenor of the '90s advancing that luminous timbre. Without Getz himself carrying the torch, the graciousness of his approach seemed beautifully atavistic. All the same, he remains popular. His records continue to sell, and he left a great many of them.

Getz's masterful variations on "Old Black Magic," which he called "Diaper Pin" to commemorate the birth of his son, defined melodic improvisation in the late '40s, along with the harmonic trickery of his blues, "Prezervation," and his rich live recordings, including club remotes where he works through the Young influence in fascinating increments. In the '50s, despite demons and a much publicized arrest, he could do little wrong when the mike was on. The Storyville recordings with Jimmy Raney and Tiny Kahn and the quartets with Al Haig or Horace Silver produced an unforgettable stream of gazelle-like numbers such as "Hershey Bar," "Tootsie Roll," "The Song Is You," "Parker 51," "Rubberneck," and the blistering "Mosquito Knees." When in 1952, he launched his two-decade association with Norman Granz's labels, he put his stamp on some of the most familiar ballads of the era (*Stan Getz Plays*), including "Lover Come Back to Me," "Body and Soul," "These Foolish Things," and his incomparable "The Way You Look Tonight." He organized a short-lived but memorable quintet with Bob Brookmeyer (*At the Shrine*) and stood his ground in a fierce display of bebop pyrotechnics with Dizzy Gillespie and Sonny Stitt (*For Musicians Only*). There were forceful collaborations with Oscar Peterson (the drummerless context spurred him rhythmically), J. J. Johnson (their Opera House concert converted a great many listeners who had previously dismissed Getz), Harry Edison, Lionel Hampton, and, in a weird and only partly successful joust for which they exchanged instruments, Gerry Mulligan. On the cover of *Stan Getz in Stockholm*, he waves from an airliner like the pope; the change in scenery didn't hurt, and when he settled down in Copenhagen at the end of the decade, he briefly found some peace.

The '60s were a period of rejuvenation. He made more jazz history with *Focus,* an Eddie Sauter chamber suite to which Getz appended un-fettered improvisations (in something of a sequel, he roared over the Sauter melodies composed for the movie *Mickey One*). Then he made pop history with *Jazz Samba* and *Getz/Gilberto,* releasing singles ("Desa-finado" and "The Girl from Ipanema") that climbed the charts and trig-gered the vogue for bossa nova. What is perhaps most rewarding about those recordings, beyond his affecting interpretations of handsome mel-odies like "Bahia," is his abiding economy, almost aphoristic in its pre-cision, evident in his one-chorus solos, his charging eight-bar exchanges with Charlie Byrd, his muscular accompaniment to João and Astrud Gil-berto. For all the popularity of those records, he never banked on them, displeasing customers who hoped to hear nothing else. After a relatively unproductive three years, he surprised everyone by demonstrating that while everyone else was basking in his bossa nova, he had absorbed the latest developments in the music of Sonny Rollins, Wayne Shorter, and others. His 1967 *Sweet Rain,* on which he introduced Chick Corea, em-bodied a final flirtation with bossa nova in the context of cryptic themes (especially two by Corea), fraught with edgy chords and stop-and-go tempo changes. Getz was as fastidious as ever, but in a mode as chal-lenging as *Jazz Samba* was comforting.

In the '70s, he purified himself of fusion temptations in the company of Jimmy Rowles on *The Peacocks,* strengthened his resolve with *The Dol-phin* and *Pure Getz,* consummated his association with Albert Dailey in *Poetry,* and embarked with Kenny Barron on *Voyage.* His sound gained weight, and his ballads occasionally took on a heaving urgency. In con-cert halls, he would demand the amplification be shut off, and his ten-or—swooping, imploring—would penetrate the air with its full panoply of colors. He attempted a dire commercial project with Herb Alpert, but he kept his head, and when he made his much acclaimed tour of Co-penhagen in 1987 with a quartet including Kenny Barron, Rufus Reid, and Victor Lewis, he was playing at peak force, producing some of the most riveting performances of his career in recitals released as *Anniver-sary* and *Serenity.* Even more lustrous are the final duets with Barron, *People Time,* recorded at the Club Monmartre in Copenhagen in March 1991. With siren shouts bursting forth in the first eight bars of "East of the Sun," Getz announces himself fully adrenalized and ready to soar. He is provocative, moving, and focused, and Barron marks him every step of the way, making the piano thunder with a romanticism of his own. Indeed, what makes this late winter colloquy indispensable is the attentiveness between them—empathic and quite often uncanny.

45 ❖ Sonny Rollins
(The Muse Is Heard)

Sonny Rollins turned sixty-seven in the fall of 1997, and beyond a whitened beard, exhibited no signs of attenuation in his physical or mental powers. Perhaps hidden in his attic is a magical reel of tape, aging into a lump of flaking iron oxide, while he defies time's gravity in life as in music. The old saw about the elder statesman who now does it better than ever understates the supremacy of his position at century's end. One of the last immortals to come of age in the mid-'40s, Rollins looms as an invincible presence after fifty years: one of the most cunning, surprising, and original of jazz visionaries and one of the very few musicians whose (infrequent) concert appearances and recordings generate intense expectations and heated postmortems.

But Rollins is also jazz's most provocatively enigmatic man. In the first place, his performing life is as partitioned as the opposing outlets of a lake. Headed upstream is the concert star, dressed in stylishly dramatic finery for magnetic performances in which he invokes tempests of sustained exhilaration that have not often been heard in jazz since the glory days of Louis Armstrong. Where Armstrong hammered perfect pieces of eight, Rollins upturns whole chests of treasure, a piratical excess of euphoric benevolence. Headed downstream, though, is the recording artist, whose far too methodical studio efforts strive to contain the euphoria, revealing an inconsistency that—accentuated by rhythm sections of variable empathy—can't be ignored as easily as in concert.

More troubling than the disparity between performance and recording is the specter of competition that has stalked him from the beginning. Coleman Hawkins once expressed incomprehension as to why every tenor saxophonist felt obliged to try and cut him. Rollins has been seriously challenged by only two saxophonists: John Coltrane briefly and himself eternally. The problem isn't that Rollins, like most artists, is his own toughest critic, but that other critics persist in comparing everything he did after 1960 with his historic achievement in the preceding five years. The analogy with Armstrong is unavoidable. Armstrong's arrival coincided with the introduction of electrical recording; his Hot Fives and Sevens codified the elements for an improvisational art. Rollins's apprenticeship paralleled the introduction of tape and the long-playing record, which transformed the art by generating extended solos; his quartets and trios made a compelling case for long improvisations. Armstrong's trumpet embodied the exuberant call of the new jazzman. Rollins's saxophone exerted a far more modest claim, but was endlessly imitated all the same. His breakthrough recordings were greeted with a daunting consensus of high praise.

Rollins's apprenticeship was brief but intense, the jazz equivalent of a conservatory education. Raised in Harlem with such young musicians as Jackie McLean and Art Taylor, he began on piano, took up alto saxophone at eleven, and though enamored of the two altoists who created a stir uptown in the mid-'40s, Charlie Parker and Louis Jordan (the swing band veteran, who in reinventing himself conjured rhythm and blues), switched to the tenor at sixteen. He sought out Coleman Hawkins, rehearsed with Thelonious Monk, and jammed wherever possible, utterly obsessed with music. Within a year, he was playing professionally; within three, he was hired for recording sessions by Babs Gonzalez, Bud Powell, and J. J. Johnson. For the next six years, from the time he was nineteen, Rollins recorded as a sideman, usually with Miles Davis (who teamed him with Charlie Parker at a 1953 date) or as a leader of studio units—quintets with a name player added to beef up the billing.

In 1955, Rollins made his first twelve-inch LP, *Work Time*, at the helm of a quartet. He begins the proceedings with a distinct countdown before sweeping in with, of all things, "There's No Business Like Show Business," and he finishes with an impeccably dilatory "There Are Such Things," capped by a stately cadenza. No finer coming-out exists in jazz recordings of the LP era. But that's not the album that parted the critical waters. Within four months, he recorded as nominal leader of the Clifford Brown-Max Roach Quintet (*Sonny Rollins Plus Four*), demonstrating greater agility and speed, a leathery resolve, and a continued interest in unlikely pop songs (for example, Irving Berlin's "Count Your Blessings" from *White Christmas*). Weeks later, he invited the little known John Coltrane to do battle on *Tenor Madness*. Those records didn't secure his standing either.

But a few months after that, he convened another quartet for *Saxophone Colossus*, which not only sustained the unimpeachable level of playing he had already achieved, but elicited a widely read review by Gunther Schuller that dangled the phrase "thematic improvisation" around Rollins's neck and assured the album's status as an untouchable classic. From that point on, Rollins—who was already regarded, at the very least, as the most significant tenor since Dexter Gordon and Stan Getz and, in the opinion of a growing coterie, the most influential since Coleman Hawkins and Lester Young—was a critic's darling. Everyone understands theme and variations, and the clarity of Rollins's thought obviated the need for a road map. Recorded in 1956, *Saxophone Colossus* remains his *Citizen Kane*, that is, his most universally celebrated but by no means best work. It introduced the first in a long series of calypsos, "St. Thomas," and a diligent minor blues, "Blue 7," that Schuller singled out as emblematic of Rollins's variational rigor. In a music that increasingly encouraged soloists to run changes, a musician who elaborated on a composition's melody as well as its predetermined harmonies (he absorbed Monk better than most) was refreshing, to say the least.

At a time when Lester Young's disciples dominated the tenor saxophone, Rollins was frequently characterized as guttural and even angry, especially after the early '50s recordings with Miles Davis where his low notes practically bark from the grooves. And yet he is among the least angry of players. Rollins's music is almost always magnanimous, imparting a generosity of spirit and discerning wit, qualities that inform his choice of material and the way he organizes that material. Those qualities are most evident in his authoritative and gracious yet changeable timbre.

All five selections on *Saxophone Colossus* are worthy, but three are worthiest. "Blue 7" is notable for Rollins's methodical deployment of the quartet and for his own meticulous solos, which are built on a sequence of minor blues motifs. Yet (pace Schuller) it is diminished by emotional restraint and retarded dynamics, unlike the more pointed performances of "St. Thomas" and "Strode Rode." The first chorus of Rollins's improvisation on the former is based entirely on a two-note figure with subtly and frequently altered intervals. Max Roach, whose playing is irreproachable throughout, follows with a thematic solo of his own (this at a time when drummers tended to be more concerned with technique and speed) and is no less impressive fanning the beat behind Tommy Flanagan's piano. Rollins returns in jazz time (not calypso time) with yawning slurred notes, reintroducing ideas from his earlier solo. "Strode Rode," a rhythmically cunning piece, begins with a staccato figure that obscures the beat, but is basically a twelve-bar blues with a four-bar bridge. In Rollins's and Flanagan's solos, that translates to a pattern of twelve/twelve/sixteen. Each plays an admirable two-chorus solo; Rollins's is accompanied only by bass, a practice he had explored on *Work Time*.

Though thematic improvisation is only one of several gambits employed on *Saxophone Colossus*, the phrase was fused to Rollins, who suddenly became a case study, a bellwether for the future of jazz. He was promptly lured *Way Out West*, as a soul-of-the-East emissary (cheerfully sporting six-guns and a Stetson on the album cover), and shook up the City of Angels by going pianoless while tackling a buckaroo repertory with focused ingenuity. Later that year, he recorded again with a trio at a charged engagement at New York's Village Vanguard. He employed still another trio early in 1958, for his skillful "Freedom Suite," a fastidious multipart work that Rollins annotated with a brief jacket statement (opening the door for jazz recordings of conscience), yet juxtaposed with such typically wry fare as Noel Coward's "Someday I'll Find You." He was not yet thirty in 1959 when the pressure to constantly outdo himself became oppressive, and like Artie Shaw before him, he opted for a long and much publicized furlough—more than two years, during which time he meditated, exercised, and practiced late at night on the Williamsburg Bridge. In 1995, Rollins told David Yaffe, "When I went to the bridge, I wanted to learn how to arrange and improve my musicianship. . . . That kind of self-initiative was very important to me."

He exhibited a more rugged, direct timbre when he returned, with a lucrative RCA contract and *The Bridge*. (In the '50s, he had recorded exclusively for small independent labels, including Prestige, Contemporary, Blue Note, MGM, and Riverside.) Rollins sloughed off comparisons to his earlier work and upset critical preconceptions by constantly tinkering with his sound, while sampling in his uniquely jocular (many said sardonic) way the avant-garde and the new Latin wave. Some people were offended by his humor, some by his implacable authority. Others presumed a rivalry between Rollins and Coltrane that must have been galling to both men. Of the six controversial albums that emerged from his association with RCA, *The Bridge* was initially the most widely admired, probably because it was the most conventional—the most like his '50s LPs. Although the album presents his quartet, with Jim Hall on guitar, Rollins's solos are usually backed by bass and drums, so there is a connection to the trio albums. Yet the jazz world had changed in his absence: the new music surfaced and Rollins was intrigued.

Despite his edgier sound, never gruff but rounded and nutlike, he displays a curiously succinct approach to ballads, content to paraphrase or ornament the written melodies. "Where Are You" is an almost inert example, in which Rollins's modestly embellished theme statement makes Hall's inspired half-chorus that much more welcome. "God Bless the Child" is a different story: Rollins delivers a slow, respectful, and quite beautiful recitation of the theme and, after Hall's solo, returns for a lyrical improvisation of great warmth and poise. "You Do Something to Me," the best of the ballads, begins with a cadenza and vamp before Rollins exemplifies his ability to put a completely individual stamp on a well-known song while sticking to the melody; even his subsequent solo consistently makes use of Cole Porter's tune. "Without a Song" is a swinging (and thematic) performance that ends with a protracted rubato coda. The remaining selections bode what was to come. "The Bridge" is a novel piece with time changes (four/four and six/eight) in the head and improvisations. Rollins's solo is stunning: bebop turned furious, full of scorching riffs that threaten to but never quite abandon the chord changes. More adventurous is "John S.," which is built on an intricate rhythmic pattern reminiscent of "Strode Rode" and a thirty-four-bar chorus. Rollins begins with a riff and propels himself into a solo that contrasts short and long phrases, suggesting ambiguous harmonies and profound vexation with the dialectics of bop.

The groundbreaking *Our Man in Jazz* was recorded only five months after *The Bridge*. In that time, he disbanded the much ballyhooed quartet with Hall, retaining only bassist Bob Cranshaw (his sidekick for much of the next thirty-five years); expanded his calypso book under the rubric of bossa nova (*What's New?*); and paid close attention to the music of Ornette Coleman. His rather ingenuous response to Coleman was ultimately the same as John Coltrane's—to borrow his band outright. But while Coltrane's collaboration with Coleman's partner, trumpeter Don Cherry, took place in the studio and was supressed for several years, Rollins hired Cherry, Billy Higgins (Coleman's drummer), and Cranshaw for a gig at the Village Gate and promptly released the results as part of RCA's *Our Man in* . . . series. With only three selections, one of twenty-five minutes duration, the album dismayed many. Yet it remains one of the most entertaining benchmarks of the entire free jazz movement.

Rollins is at the top of his form, and the rhythm section lines up behind him like students in a fire drill. Serendipity rules. The response of most listeners tends to hinge on feelings generated by Cherry, whose sound is thin and unstudied compared with the opulent timbres of bop trumpet. Yet Cherry is an almost infallibly lyrical player, and he works closely with Rollins. The long version of "Oleo" consists chiefly of extended solos based on harmonic changes. Even Cherry, who begins with tremolos before developing a series of freely melodic riffs, invents long, knotty phrases that indicate the underlying chords. The real spontaneity comes in transitional passages and rhythmic change-ups, including the gratifying slow blues toward the end, in which the band colludes as a solid phalanx. "Oleo," the best known of Rollins's rhythmically wily originals, tends to incite his capricious nature (the 1954 Miles Davis debut is no exception). In this version, the melody is never definingly stated—the musicians begin free, setting up a spectacular Rollins improvisation: fast, hard, exhilarating. Cranshaw provides a loping rhythmic gait in support, and Higgins alternates a loose four with a decisive backbeat. The melody is skirted, never confronted.

"Doxy" is more orthodox, though antithematic. Rollins's solo is rife with ideas, but few relate to the sixteen-bar blues head. A highlight is the call-and-response chorus between Rollins and Cherry, followed by a protracted tag ending that suggests their reluctance to stop playing. An undoubted highlight of the album is the third piece, the only standard and relatively short at eight minutes: "Dearly Beloved" is a rousing display of free-ranging wit that, despite the allegiance to Jerome Kern's tune, is a particularly fine example of the way the four men could improvise as a unit. The tune is stated in a stop-and-go manner by Rollins and Cherry. Rollins milks it in a swinging solo. Cherry introduces a transitional figure, answered by Rollins, and then embarks on his own improvisation. After a bass solo, Rollins restates the tune as a march, which Higgins instantly picks up as the quartet steps into formation. They toss fragments of the tune like a football. Rollins restates the melody and the march, closing with a cadenza that puts the performance back in the lap of Jerome Kern. It's a number that makes people laugh with pleasure.

RCA showed some courage in releasing *Our Man in Jazz*. The album didn't sell, and the whole association between artist and label was considered a corporate disappointment, though each of the six issued albums is fascinating. Rollins continued to experiment with free jazz in the '60s, notably with the acerbic *Sonny Meets Hawk* and the desultory *East Broadway Run Down*, before taking his third and longest sabbatical. When he returned in 1972, he once again had a new sound (it would mutate many times over the next twenty years) and agenda. But no matter the context—hard bop or free jazz or jazz rock—and however much he adjusted his timbre, he never abandoned a few enduring principles: a style of improvisation that combines thematic development with melodic paraphrase; a large and ever-changing book of standard songs complemented by distinctive originals; and a dedication to stout rhythms verging on dance.

Certainly, an unevenness in his work became more pronounced. Though some of his best albums were recorded live (*Live at the Vanguard*, *Our Man in Jazz*), an audience's enthusiasm was not a reliable antidote to his shyness around recording paraphernalia. Every visit to the studio became a trial to him. Perhaps the representative post-*Bridge* album is the 1965 *Sonny Rollins on Impulse!*, in that it begins with a colorless "On Green Dolphin Street," improves by incremental leaps with each successive selection, and closes with the emblematic masterpiece, "Three Little Words," taken at a brutal tempo that never topples Rollins's balance and completed with a succinct and spellbinding cadenza—arguably his best on records until the 1978 "Autumn Nocturne."

Today Rollins's RCA and Impulse records of the '60s are much admired, but at the time they seemed to evince the eccentricities of a performer who chronically altered his look, style, band—everything but his bass player, Bob Cranshaw. Sonny Rollins was the musician who sported a mohawk; who began his Vanguard sets in the kitchen, strolling to the stage while playing; who composed at least half a dozen of the most creative and widely performed jazz themes of the '50s and '60s, yet fetishized songs from such dubious sources as Al Jolson and Edward MacDowell. After Coltrane died in 1967, Rollins refused to record for five years. And then dawned the Milestone era, in which we presently live. His return to action was announced with the whimsically entitled *Sonny Rollins' Next Album* and an exuberant week at the Vanguard, where he was in sterling form. Yet soon enough the compulsion to redefine his music set in, and he spent the better part of the '70s assimilating jazz, pop, and calypso, attempting to forge a stylish music that would distill his high spirits without leveling them, often with grim results.

Rollins recorded twelve albums between 1972 and 1982, and the product was extremely mixed, plummeting to a nadir with *Horn Culture*, a confused jumble that should never have been released, and *The Way I Feel*, an egregious if candid attempt to cross over to the pop market. Yet overlooked in those indifferent productions were many notable performances: "Skylark" and "The Everywhere Calypso" on *Sonny Rollins's Next Album*, "To a Wild Rose" on *The Cutting Edge*, "Harlem Boys" and "My Ideal" on *Don't Ask*. What was one to make of *Don't Stop the Carnival*, a two-record set that included two of the most astonishing virtuoso rants ever recorded, "Autumn Nocturne" and "Silver City," amid selections of numbing mediocrity, among them an unsteady "President Hayes" that little resembles the masterful versions of the piece Rollins performed in concert the following year? In 1996, he confessed to Gene Santoro, "I hate recording." Commenting on his uneasiness with virtual reality, he said, "Playing live is like having sex live, as opposed to recording, which is like having cybersex."

Like Sarah Vaughan, he established a loyal concert following apart from the record-buying public. On stage, his inspiration or the lack of it was transparent, a corollary to his restless and remorseless honesty. When the muse was with him, he was transcendent. When abandoned, he lacked whatever is required—cynicism? professionalism?—to fake it. The polarization between recordings and concerts increased, as Rollins grew disillusioned with the awkward confines of the modern studio, with its multitrack editing and dubbing and overall artificiality. Even when he recorded successfully, critics carped more in sorrow than in anger that canned versions of, say, "If Ever I Would Leave You" or

"Long Ago and Far Away" could not compare with those heard in live performance. The concert hall offered no guarantees: the same complaint was made of "To a Wild Rose," taped at a jazz festival, and I can recall an evening at the Vanguard in the '60s, when he belabored the head of "Take the A Train" for forty-five-minutes, yet in his next set brimmed with fiery imagination. At a recording session nearly a decade later, he poked continuously at "Stella By Starlight" like a needle stuck in one groove. At a 1995 concert, he played the "St. Thomas" theme for twenty minutes with unabated energy, holding to its shell, though his guests, Jackie McLean and Wallace Roney, tried to crack it open—it was an obstinate, claustrophobic performance fixed tight in an unbridgeable rut. Yet even when he is stuck, Rollins coasts with more energy than others muster in the throes of creation. To his concert audience, infrequent disappointments mean less than the promise of sated expectations. After all, in an age of technological immortality, the musican who saves his best for the concert hall is as rare as the actor who prefers stage to screen.

Yet posterity has its claims, and in that dominion, technology rules. In the early '80s, Rollins took control of his recordings, producing them in tandem with his wife, Lucille. A sea change was almost immediately apparent. The temptations of fusion began to disappear, though he maintained his fancy for electric bass (he prefers the attack, the faster decay), and he appeared to relax more, as evidenced on "Mava Mava," "Tell Me You Love Me," and other selections on the delightful *Sunny Days, Starry Nights*. In 1987, the exhilarating Rollins of the concert stage was captured in the extended title selection on *G-Man*, his ultimate statement on the middle ground he sought between traditional contraints and free jazz—a disciplined howl of joy that seemed to steady him for the inevitable task of building a postfusion repertory.

Jimmy Heath suggested in a conversation in the '70s that a growing problem with jazz was the reluctance of young musicians to play tunes they hadn't written. Coming from one of the most resourceful tunesmiths to emerge in the '50s, a composer whose catalog had been recorded by Miles Davis, Milt Jackson, and many others, only to become nearly dormant, the complaint was as personal as it was warranted. The question of repertory—of standard material versus new material, of classic pop versus contemporary pop—is ongoing and complicated. Most improvisers require blueprints for their variations, and listeners are attracted by blueprints they recognize. Some musicians excavate forgotten pop songs in order to evade the usual chestnuts; others, taking Heath's cue, mine the growing body of classic tunes by other jazz musicians. In every instance, however, the artist must convince us that he or she has something vital to add.

Rollins has written several jazz standards: "Airegin," "Oleo," "Doxy," "Pent-Up House," "Valse Hot" (the first successful bop waltz), "Sonnymoon for Two," "Tenor Madness," "Alfie's Theme" (from his film score), and his adaptation of "St. Thomas" for starters. But he has also done as much for and with standard material as any musician of the past forty years. Like Monk, he not only took seriously the dictum that a theme ought to have consequences, but found his themes in unlikely places, from Russ Columbo and Patti Page to Lehar and the Caribbean islands. Rollins has given us a broad range of full-dress ballads since the incomparable 1955 "There Are Such Things," and he has offered provocative fragments, as on the 1964 *The Standard Sonny Rollins*, where he provides little more than an idea of how to individuate each piece. His stubborn honesty makes him a frequent captive to songs, at which times rather than resorting to the stable bebop grammar he mastered while still in his teens, he meanders around in the tune looking for a way out. Even so, his repertory choices rarely seem arbitrary.

In his sixties, Rollins appeared more in thrall than ever to the verities of songs that underscored his romantic disposition. The inclination had always been discernible, but it became especially pronounced in the series of albums beginning with the 1988 *Dancing in the Dark*. On the title selection, Rollins's action on the saxophone keys was recorded, conferring a shadowlike castanet effect during his performance. He begins with a cadenza and continues with a deconstruction of the elegant, ever climbing Arthur Schwartz melody, poking around without milking it, ultimately establishing a peace between the song and his own energizing riffs, doubling the time, before an anticlimactic fade. On "I'll String Along with You," which offered as much promise as a vehicle, he is fatally roped to a contrived dance-beat vamp, and, though Rollins opens his solo with a singing riff, he soon collapses back into the melody, never finding one of his own.

In three originals, however, he suggests a renewal of his compositional talent. "O.T.Y.O.G." is a jubilant number parsed in sixteen-bar passages, with a change in rhythm between the first and second eight-bar units, so that at first Rollins retards the beat and then leaps on top of it. "Duke of Iron" is an enormously appealing calypso with a six-chorus Rollins solo, at once lucid and boisterous—a sustained yawp of contentment. "Allison" is a fifty-two-bar construction in which two eight-bar segments are followed by one of ten bars. Rollins improvises a neat countermelody and exchanges fours with drummer Marvin Smith for a chorus. As usual, these selections became increasingly bold as he played them live. One of the enduring ironies of jazz recordings is that musicians record new pieces to publicize live performances at which those pieces are belatedly mastered, but not necessarily rerecorded.

If *G-Man* was an invocation to the gods, *Dancing in the Dark* and its follow-up, *Here's to the People* (with fine performances of "Someone to Watch Over Me" and "Lucky Day," but elsewhere marred by Steve Jordan's garrulous drumming), are the equivalent of a gentleman caller's bouquet of roses—exercises in controlled lyricism. Still, the less successful selections reveal a cloying melodicism, the reverse side of Rollins's euphoric thrust, that inhibits his improvisation. Gone with the sardonic probing of his earlier playing is the introspection that allowed him to breach a ballad, taking from it what appealed to him and then fleshing it out with his own variations or fleeing for parts unknown. Strong melodies now exerted a too powerful gravity that he could dispel only with pyrotechnics that were likely to defuse the song's appeal. In that regard, his albums of the mid-'90s—*Old Flames* and *+3*—represented a major advance.

A Rollins album that isn't a little eccentric would not be worthy of the man, and *Old Flames* doesn't disappoint. On the surface, it's a straightforward evocation of romantic, in some instances sentimental, ballads from the interlocked idioms of jazz, pop, and operetta. The title is indicative and so is the cover design (by Phil Carroll and Jamie Putnam)—an incandescent rose among lifeless autumn leaves. For a change, Rollins put together a faultless studio quintet, at least theoretically: trombonist Clifton Anderson is along mostly for counterpoint (he deftly handles his one solo) and Tommy Flanagan, Bob Cranshaw, and Jack DeJohnette are as attentive and provident as expected. The garden is marred only by Rollins's insistence that Cranshaw play electric bass on several selections, a particular problem on "Where or When," where the bass buzz tends to disconnect rather than unite piano and drums. On two numbers, the band is augmented by a brass quintet arranged and conducted by Jimmy Heath in a style reminiscent of his long neglected Riverside albums (notably *Swamp Seed*), which were also heavy on brass though never with this instrumentation (two flugelhorns, French horn, tuba, trombone).

Rollins wears his heart on his sleeve to the extent that the song titles alone suggest the dreamy amorousness of the project: "Darn That Dream," "Where or When," "My Old Flame," "I See Your Face Before Me," "Prelude to a Kiss," and even *The Merry Widow*'s "Vilja, O Vilja" (listed as "Delia," a title Rollins clings to for sentimental reasons—that's how he recalls it from childhood). The ringer is an original blues with a bridge with the distinctly unromantic title, "Times Slimes" (his response to a New York journalist who knowingly misrepresented him), and it's a knockout. Oddities? For one thing, Rollins explores his upper register almost to the exclusion of the barreling low notes that are his patent. His sound at times takes on a keening wail greatly underscored by tempos that are in several instances almost languorous. His playing is so laid back that the rhythm section assumes a role of prickly watchfulness—the consort pecks away at time as the leader edges his way through melody, retarding this phrase, baroquely enhancing that one. His solo choruses are embellishments of the themes, emphasizing his considera-tion in choosing them and his determination to get to where they live.

It doesn't always work. "My Old Flame" disappoints except for Flan-agan's wittily elliptical solo. Rollins takes it too slow and never gets a sure grip, asserting himself only in his last eight bars. "Darn That Dream" and "Prelude to a Kiss," each with the brass choir, are de-lights—yearning, pliant variations that spin melodies within melodies. The former is two and a half choruses long, including eight-bar inter-ludes for the brasses and Flanagan, and capped with a characteristically lucent and flamboyant minute-long Rollins cadenza. In both selections, Heath's arrangements back the leader throughout his solos as well as during the heads. "Where or When" is taken unaccountably fast (actually medium, but by comparison with the other selections, it feels fast); An-derson counterpunches the theme, and Rollins and Flanagan fillet the chords. Flanagan plays an especially pretty improvisation on "I See Your Face Before Me," an obscure Dietz and Schwartz song from 1938. It's almost as slumberous as "My Old Flame," but the melody is so attractive and underserved that the deliberation is justified.

The album's most unlikely material provides two highlights. "Times Slimes" is an exemplary blues, with a hooky riff that winds from the fifth bar through the twelfth, and produces Rollins's most liberating and least pensive solo. "Vilja" is as aptly quaint as "To a Wild Rose." Rollins addresses the melody in a champagne duet with Flanagan, the clicking of saxophone keys audible as he wrestles his way through that passage and (rhythm section, please) into the famous Lehar melody. Rollins may be playing high, but he is no soprano, so after trombone and piano have their turns, he vigorously swings his way through the tune's contours before setting up two choruses of exchanges with DeJohnette. This pas-sage is the album's flashpoint, a telling colloquy in fours in which Rol-lins's phrases invariably exceed a literal four bars. The closing vamp is ambiguous: is it an evasion of the beauty he tentatively seeks or a logical retreat?

The quartet date *+3* is the most consistently effective disc Rollins has made for Milestone, an entertaining survey of overlooked songs that is a triumph of thematic embellishment over thematic improvisation. The record was instantly dismissed by intransigent reviewers who cannot hear beyond the pulsing shield of electric bass. Admittedly, that sound is at first blush distracting—it is not the sound of jazz, or at least not the sound associated with a musician of Rollins's mettle and age. But if one listens to his superlative work in spite of the electric bass, one may discover in time that Cranshaw's attack is more complementary than we are predisposed to concede. The mix centers the bass, which animates the action around it and buttresses Rollins with a reliable and liberating harmonic platform. Given the amplification, Cranshaw's unwavering support is oddly unassuming. Flanagan is back, spelled on two selections by Stephen Scott, and so is DeJohnette, though the equally adept Al Foster does most of the drumming.

Two originals, "Biji" and "H.S.," suggest a continuation of Rollins's compositional powers, but the most impressive aspect of this album is his intensified ability to invent freely within the melodic constraints of such familiar songs as "What a Differerence a Day Made" and "They Say It's Wonderful," such unlikely ones as "I've Never Been in Love Before," and the album's masterpiece, "Cabin in the Sky," one of the most unusual and accomplished performances Rollins has recorded. Embracing that song for all the nostalgic power he likely associates with Ethel Waters's renditions, Rollins ornaments it with inspired effulgence, as though the song were a trellis and he the latticework, and caps it with another brilliant cadenza. Measure for measure, he combines everything he has learned over the long haul about the suppleness of timbre and the chimerical distinction between free and orderly improvisation. As "G-Man" represents the development of ideas merely hinted at in "John S" and *Our Man in Jazz*, +3 suggests an interpretive confidence that makes the sacred "Blue 7" seem experimental and studied by comparison. Rollins's music encompasses one of the most generous dispositions in modern music. It glistens with oversized and contagious energy and bespeaks the character to sustain a course of singular purpose, despite the blandishments of the hip and the enticements of the powerful, with imagination and grace.

46 ❖ Dinah Washington
(The Queen)

"I sure miss Dinah." Johnny Hartman's voice, leveled by awe and directed at no one in particular, penetrated the sudden silence at a rehearsal for a concert of jazz singing at Lincoln Center in 1981. The commotion of musicians and stagehands had subsided a few minutes earlier for the first time all afternoon, when a clip of Dinah Washington, from *Jazz on a Summer's Day*, a film of the 1958 Newport Jazz Festival, was projected on stage. Wailing "All of Me," accompanied by a Terry Gibbs Quintet, she wears a short, sleeveless, white blouson dress fitted just below the hips with a huge bow that bumps flirtatiously in time, and her face, under closely cropped hair, is a radiant pond of brown and red hues. During the vibes solo she grabs Gibbs's spare mallets and with the unrivaled sass that made her a tigress in and out of music, she invades his territory, not playing much, but taking contagious pleasure in hammering away. After Urbie Green's trombone solo, she resumes singing, the cadences glancing upward trumpetlike.

Few performers have taken a stage or stormed off one with quite the noblesse oblige of the Queen, who died at thirty-nine, in 1963. Over the next quarter century, her stature was in serious disrepair. One reason is that all her recordings except for a couple of sessions in her early years and eight albums made in her last year were done for one company, Mercury, which—much to its surprise, though not to Washington's—achieved a Top 10 crossover hit with her version of "What a Difference a Day Made" in 1959. The result was a siege of commercial records that remained steady sellers, while the jazz and blues performances that established her standing in the pantheon of singers were reissued fleetingly or not at all. Her vibrant career as a jukebox star in the late '40s and early '50s was largely forgotten or, worse, patronized: at the height of her fame, Mercury issued a compilation called *The Good Old Days*, picturing only a straw hat on the cover. As a result, it was considerably more difficult to get a handle on her twenty years in the studios than to get one on the careers of her very few peers—Smith, Holiday, Fitzgerald, and Vaughan.

In 1988 that changed when, under the guidance of Kiyoshi Koyama, PolyGram and Nippon conspired to release her complete work for Mercury, a project completed over two years with the release of twenty-one compact discs parsed into seven boxes—additional evidence, if any were needed, of how dependent musical artists are on the alertness of the corporations that own their art. The first two boxes forced a reconsideration of the overlooked years in which she forged her style. Washington, as befits a performer who insisted on her right to sing without generic restrictions, was many things: the finest blues singer in the generations after Bessie Smith; an entrancingly original interpreter of ballads; a bold and graceful embellisher of melody and the jazz singer who most closely assimilated the brassy euphoria of Louis Armstrong's climactic flourishes; a pop star. *The Complete Dinah Washington on Mercury, Vol. 1 1946–1949* and *Vol. 2 1950–1952*, documents the formation of her career, the choices she made, and those made for her.

The figures alone bear daunting witness to the neglect of Washington's work. Of the 119 selections, 56 are new to LP, let alone CD. Of those, 12 are alternate takes; 33, among them a few hits, were out only as singles; 11 weren't issued at all. Here's the rub: although some material in these collections is simply abominable ("My Heart Cries for You," "That's Why a Woman Loves a Heel"), little of it is found in the rediscovered material, which offers many savory blues and ballad performances. The era under consideration is from Washington's apprenticeship, when the label had her tackling every fad and fancy of the day. She was obliged to cover songs made famous by the Andrews Sisters, Kay Starr, Billy Eckstine, Rosemary Clooney, the Four Aces, Bullmoose Jackson, Hank Williams, and many others. Some of those arrangements are stodgy, tasteless, inert, and tactless. During and after the recording ban of 1948, she was choked by dreary vocal choirs.

In a way, this period mirrors the end of her career, when smoother but no less suffocating choirs and dubious songs became the norm. A difference is that in the beginning Mercury strove to enlarge her appeal among blacks; in the end the company conceded what the singer had long insisted, that she could reach the white mainstream as well. But just as Dinah persisted in singing dynamic jazz and earthy blues when they were out of fashion, she steadfastly insisted on first-rate songs throughout her initial "singles" period. Virtually every tediously arranged session is alternated with one that is lean and efficient. Whether the date was promising or meretricious, Washington remained assertively and saltily her own woman. No singer ever approached song with a greater reserve of pluck. Even in dire circumstances, her powerful wit, shining from deep inside, mitigates the obstacles.

In prime surroundings, another quality peeks through: a candid and teasing sexuality. Alberta Hunter, who once said, "They don't have blues singers now like they had then, except maybe Dinah Washington," considered Bessie Smith to be the greatest of all because even when she was "raucous and loud, she had a sort of a tear—no, not a tear, but there was a *misery* in what she did." Dinah, who came to resent the constant comparisons with Bessie, had a sort of laugh, a simmering ebullience, even when she sang self-pitying laments. Where Smith was sorrowful and Holiday disaffected, where Fitzgerald was girlish and Vaughan operatic, Dinah was gloriously carnal. She never got high-toned, unless it was with the kind of humor that lets you in on the joke. Her very cosmopolitanism was streetwise. At the height of her powers, from 1954 on, Washington's virtuosity was so completely at the service of her personality that its raiment all but disappeared. By then she had developed and perfected her most characteristic mannerism. It was a unique appoggiatura, an effect seemingly as natural to her as her stinging timbre—an upward glide pinned to or squeezed out of a note, usually at the end of a phrase. Like so many attributes of her style, this one suggests a trumpet: a brief gliss pressed with an extra dollop of vibrato (she was the ultimate mistress of vibrato, swelling and decaying neighboring syllables to maximize the expressive values of every word); an echo of the pitched note that sometimes states and sometimes merely suggests an overtone of a fifth or an octave.

By the mid-'50s, when she recorded a peerless series of vocal jazz albums (*Dinah Jams, After Hours with Miss D, Dinah!, In the Land of Hi-Fi, The Swinging Miss D, Dinah Sings Fats Waller*) all the components of her style were in place, and she could successfully dare to outclimb the high-note trumpeters on "Lover, Come Back to Me" or out-roister Waller on "Christopher Columbus." Yet listening to the earlier work, you realize how long it took her to consummate the ideal blend of technique and personality. Her timbre was enticing from the beginning, but full recognition of all that her voice could do, beyond the relatively obvious areas of range and dynamics, took time.

Consider the matter of that appoggiatura. You hear only its implications from time to time in the records of 1946 and 1947. Not until the thirty-eighth track, "Record Ban Blues," probably recorded on the last day of 1947 and not released for twelve years (perhaps for fear of offending union boss James Petrillo, who demanded the ban and is named in the lyric), does it come fully into view. The high point of a good session with Cootie Williams's band, the song is simply the standard blues—complete with stop-time chorus—that Washington sang and recorded countless times. Maybe the daring lyric inspired her or the apocalyptic fever of the coming ban (she would record only seven sides during the next twelve months). In any case, she is loose and invigorating. The soon-to-be trademark gliss is heard on the words "boss" in the first chorus and "late" in the second. She does it once on the next song, "Resolution Blues," too, but you hardly hear it again until April 1951 on the ballad "I Won't Cry Anymore."

If Dinah's sound wasn't fully matured at twenty-two, she was already a starkly distinctive performer. Indeed, if one considers all the singers who sounded like her or reflected her influence after she came to prominence—a list that includes Esther Phillips, Ruth Brown, Nancy Wilson, Etta Jones, Dodo Green, Dionne Warwick, and Diana Ross—one is all the more conscious of how original her approach was. Washington always named Billie Holiday as her favorite singer, but aside from the shared inclination to phrase behind the beat, albeit to rather different effect, the influence is faint. A more fruitful search could undoubtedly be made in the vineyards of gospel. If Dinah was the Queen of the Blues (a title she held like an escutcheon), she was a product of the church.

She was born Ruth Jones in Alabama in 1924 and raised in Chicago, where her mother played piano at St. Luke's Baptist Church. After performing piano duets with her mom for the congregation, she became known as a local prodigy, and at fifteen won a talent contest at the Regal Theater, singing "I Can't Face the Music." (Two versions of that song appear in the Mercury collection, each with an interpolation of Benny Carter's "Blues in My Heart"; the first was never issued, the second was released only as a single.) Neither the prize nor her growing infatuation with Billie Holiday pleased her devout parent.

The Jazz Singer is repeatedly filmed as a Jewish story, but it's really a black one. Few of the immigrant Jews who dominated songwriting in the Golden Age experienced religious versus secular pressures anywhere near as profound as those facing not one but several generations of black musicians. (Artists as disparate as Ethel Waters, Hampton Hawes, Ray Charles, and David Murray have described those pressures). To be sure, Ruth Jones was torn between the sacred and the profane—she sang secretly in nightclubs under adopted names, but finally took flight as the sixteen-year-old piano accompanist for a legendary gospel singer, Sallie Martin. For two years she traveled the gospel circuit, working with the Reverend C. L. Franklin (Aretha's father), Mahalia Jackson, and Roberta Martin, who greatly inspired her. Dinah was a charter member of the first all-women group, the Sallie Martin Colored Ladies Quartet. Then she briefly married the first of her many husbands (the best estimate is nine, though no one seems to know for sure) and returned to the Chicago clubs.

An indication of the ease with which she returned to secular music can be gleaned from a story Anthony Heilbut tells in *The Gospel Sound*:

many years later, the highly successful Dinah mischievously suggested to an old friend, the then struggling gospel singer Deloris Barrett, that she moonlight in the more lucrative blues field. Heilbut quotes Sallie Martin on Dinah's willfulness. "She could really sing," Martin said, "but, shoot, she'd catch the eye of some man and she'd be out the church before the minister finished off the doxology." Washington's experience on the gospel trail surely helped her to formulate an expressive use of melisma and scatlike humming, though Louis Armstrong, too, undoubtedly served as a prototype for those elements in her work. James Haskins cites another source of her style in his biography, *Queen of the Blues*: Bette Davis movies. Like Ethel Waters before her, Dinah was obsessed with proper diction and the possibilities of inflection. Her articulation, the luxuriant correctness of her vowels, the parlando with which she emphasizes meaning, are among the fundamental joys of her art. Her ability to lend credibility, sometimes underscored with sarcasm, to foolish lyrics is another bond she has with Holiday.

Yet her jazz career languished for a while. She remained in the twilight zone for years, despite the triumph at the Regal; the enthusiasm of clubowner Joe Sherman and manager Joe Glaser, who landed her a job with Lionel Hampton (all three boasted of having changed Ruth Jones to Dinah Washington, though none could remember why); and the acceptance of audiences and critics. Decca actually refused to let Hampton spotlight her on records, and he was careful not to let her overshadow his band in concert. The critic Leonard Feather changed all that by convincing the small Keynote label to record her with members of the Hampton band in a program of his own blues. Hampton was so impressed with her at the session that he sat in for two numbers and permitted his name to be used on the label. When "Salty Papa Blues" became a hit, Decca sued and Hampton's name was removed from the label. The bandleader now featured her on another Feather blues, the wacky "Blow Top." It was a hit, but she remained in recording limbo. A 1945 date for Apollo with a then nonstar band (Lucky Thompson, Milt Jackson, Charles Mingus) produced a dozen titles, mostly blues, but it wasn't until 1946, three years after the Keynote session, that she signed with Mercury and showed what she could do with a broader range of material.

Dinah began her Mercury contract with "Embraceable You" and "I Can't Get Started" and in the following years took a poke at every type of song making the rounds. In those days, a straight blues like "Baby Get Lost" (another Feather lyric) or "Long John Blues" (a fashionably double-entendre Washington original about a dentist with a soothing drill) could make the top of the rhythm and blues charts. So she recorded dozens of blues—most of them with the same melody and stop-time climaxes, many in the key of C, though with varied tempo. She would remain a nonpareil blues singer until she died (her 1962 "The Blues Ain't Nothin' but a Woman Cryin' for Her Man," recorded for Roulette a year before her death, is a candidate for her best-ever work in the idiom). Strangely, the only awkwardness to be found in her blues recordings is on the album she made of Bessie Smith songs, probably a consequence of the hokey arrangements, which condescend to the material, and the pressures of the tribute. To trace her progress along the familiar twelve-bar route is to confirm steady advancements in wit, nuance, and bravura. On two magnificent sessions in 1952, she fulfilled all her early promise and intimated how much more would come with the exquisite "Trouble in Mind" (supported by her husband, drummer Jimmy Cobb, and saxophonist Ben Webster) and "Mad About the Boy," in which she locates the soul within the whimsy of Noel Coward.

The pleasures she took in her reign as Queen can be adduced from two stories told by James Haskins. Once she inadvertently boarded a bus chartered for mentally retarded people and threw off the head count. The driver began to question the passengers. When he asked Washington who she was, she looked him in the eye and said, "I'm the Queen of the Blues." "Yes, you definitely belong here," he replied. During her tour of England, Dinah was cautioned not to say anything about the recently crowned queen. The first time she walked on stage, to a standing ovation, she announced, "Ladies and gentlemen, I'm happy to be here, but just remember, there's one heaven, one earth, and one queen, and your Elizabeth is an impostor."

By that time, the press was covering her private and public behavior in lurid detail—all the marriages, the attempt on her life by a jealous woman, her temper tantrums on stage, her packing and firing a pistol, her outspoken and often hilarious comments to the press (Dinah's acerbic "blindfold tests" in *Down Beat* are classic), her principled refusal to appear on TV if she had to lip-synch. Then, at thirty-five, she convinced Mercury to go whole hog in the production and promotion of "What a Difference a Day Made," which lyric she changed to the present tense. Floated by the arrangement's even triplets, she soared onto the pop charts. The label expected her to stay there, providing her with new motives for rebellion. Four years later, fighting a lifelong weight problem, she took too many diet pills while drinking and it was all over. Neither the blues nor jazz has found a worthy heir.

47 ❖ *Rahsaan Roland Kirk* *(One-Man Band)*

Roland Kirk could have achieved renown had he done nothing else but play tenor saxophone—for example, "Memories of You" and "Evidence" on *The Jaki Byard Experience*. Good thing he didn't have to. Kirk was a piece of work on which Rabelais and Barnum might have collaborated. His dream life alone was apparently more invigorating than the waking lives of most mortals. In dreams came the names of his band, the Vibration Society, and his person, Rahsaan; in dreams came the shape of programmatic albums, for example, *The Inflated Tear* and *The Case of the 3-Sided Dream in Audio Color*. Most important, a dream gave him the idea of playing three saxophones simultaneously. Dreams, he said, "led me to see music even more clearly as a way of setting off vibrations within a person so that he can more deeply feel and recognize his identity and his potential." Whatever. He bounded onto the scene like Gargantua, who entered the world through an ear drum, shouting "Drink!" Kirk's shout was an invitation to partake of jazz in all its miscellaneous splendor, and some people found that intimidating.

No one who experienced him in performance can forget the sight: a stocky blind man swaying precariously back and forth on the lip of a bandstand, dressed in a yellow jump suit, his face implacable behind black wraparounds, blowing dissonant counterpoint on three saxophones of varying lengths, while other instruments, some of his own invention, dangled from his shoulders, neck, ears, and, on occasion, his nose. Talk about one-man bands. In later years, he also sang—a hardly dreamlike exertion that seemed to progress naturally from the preceding decade when his vocalisms were confined to bellows and grunts, often in tandem with his flute playing. He didn't take singing lightly: Kirk put words to Mingus's "Goodbye, Pork Pie Hat" and commissioned a lyric for Coltrane's "Giant Steps." The whole trajectory of his career suggested a willful increase in size and presence, from blues-rooted musician to virtuoso marvel to mystic philosopher and political gadfly. Kirk coined the peace-generation greeting, "Bright moments," and created the Jazz and People's Movement, which in the early '70s burst onto several TV talk shows demanding more turf for jazz. The one memorable result was Kirk's own surreal appearance on the Ed Sullivan show.

Someone—it may have been LeRoi Jones, who took umbrage when Kirk performed while twirling a bass atop his head in the early '60s—must have accused him of gimmick mongering because by the time I became aware of Kirk in the mid-'60s his admiring critics were in high dudgeon on the issue: No gimmicks here, they emphasized. Yet to say of an artist who played Dvořák and Les Brown concurrently because it hadn't been done before, sustained a solo for two hours in the hope of getting an entry in Guinness, conducted sing- and whistle-alongs, attempted to replicate the sound of bagpipes, recorded a three-sided LP, and considered the central "miracle" of his achievement an ability to employ circular breathing while playing contrapuntal melodies on two saxophones, even if the outcome suggested a Polish wedding march (for example "One Breath Beyond" on *Prepare Thyself To Deal With a Miracle*)—to say of such an artist that he had no ear for the gimmick is like saying that Art Tatum never played florid runs and John Coltrane never squealed. What counts is what they did with the gimmicks, the runs, the squeals.

Kirk's persona, musical and otherwise, came into focus during four highly creative years, 1961–65, when he was signed to Mercury Records. The story is traceable on a ten-CD cube, *Rahsaan: The Complete Mercury Recordings of Roland Kirk*, complete with a sorry denouement in which his flair for showmanship encourages the label to lead him down the garden path of commercial excess. In 1961, Kirk was a twenty-five-year-old phenomenon who appeared to have too much fun playing at a time when solemnity was big. The new music was taking off with a roar and a clatter, and Kirk—like pianist Jaki Byard—had a penchant for playing at and around it without quite declaring himself a believer. Like many virtuosi, the only school he chose to belong to was the one framed by his imagination and technique. He spent four months that year with Charles Mingus's Jazz Workshop (*Oh Yeah!*, *Tonight at Noon*), but Kirk's mercuric individuality, buoyed by his crucial irreverence, guaranteed him a place on the outside.

Which was ironic because Kirk was nothing if not a jazz patriot. A list of his compositions reads like a register of jazz saints and includes tributes to Lester Young, Clifford Brown, Sidney Bechet, Don Byas, Fats Waller, Charles Mingus, Dizzy Gillespie, Johnny Griffin, Harry Carney, and Barney Bigard. He even appropriated signature musical phrases from predecessors and contemporaries in pieces of his own, a practice that in the music of a man less effusively generous than Kirk might cause consternation: his "My Delight," "A Breath in the Wind," and the intro to "We Free Kings" borrow from Tadd Dameron, Benny Golson, and Miles Davis, respectively. He was a familiar face in jazz clubs as a member of the audience, especially during those many occasions in the '70s when someone was making a comeback. In interviews and on panels, as well as in his music, he tried to reconcile the avant-garde with the mainstream.

Born in 1936 in Ohio, Kirk was fundamentally a bebopper. Educated at the Ohio State School for the Blind, he was playing professionally at fifteen. Five years later, he made his first recording for King, a characteristic brew of blues and ballads on tenor sax only. Albums for Argo (with Ira Sullivan) and Prestige (with Jack McDuff) followed and, incidentally, suggest some confusion about the early attempts to pigeonhole him: bluesman, modernist, funkmeister? By now, Kirk had his basic arsenal. In addition to tenor, he played an obsolete cousin to the soprano sax that he called a manzello, a straightened alto with modified keys that he called a stritch, a siren, a whistle, and, a conventional flute. He found the manzello and stritch in the basement of an old instrument store and taught himself to finger two saxophones while using the third as a drone. In this way, he could play a variety of reed-section voicings and accompany his own solos with stop-time chords. Kirk's thorough grasp of the saxophone served him well when he suffered a paralyzing stroke in 1975, two years before his death: he invented an attachment that enabled him to play all the keys with his one good hand.

His first Mercury album, *We Free Kings*, remains a classic of the era and is, for me, one of his two most satisfying albums, along with *Rip, Rig and Panic*, recorded for Mercury in 1965. His flute playing represented the first persuasive new approach on that instrument after Eric Dolphy. His stop-time blues, expansive melodies, and voluptuous swinging on all the saxophones were compelling. What made the record overpowering, however, was the alleged gimmick: the ecstatic sound of the unison reeds, riffing like a big band, soaring before and after the improvisations, which were themselves heightened by unpredictable shifts between tenor, stritch, manzello, and flute. It was a genuinely unique album. Kirk rejected the total immersion in protracted improvisation preached in Ornette Coleman's *Free Jazz* and John Coltrane's "Chasin' the Trane," but he did embody a prophetic refusal to relinquish the lusty pleasures of big bands (albeit a one-man version), swing, lilting waltzes, and nostalgic ballads, all of which he made aggressively new. A particularly worthy find among the previously unissued material in the Mercury cube is a ridiculously greased and tortuous trip through "Spring Will Be a Little Late This Year." Maybe it was too much for the label back then.

Kirk's success on Mercury continued with the release of *Domino, Reeds & Deeds* and *The Roland Kirk Quartet Meets the Benny Golson Orchestra*, each suggesting his growth as a composer and his determination to personalize his albums beyond the norm, to surmount the decorous manners of traditional recording by putting more of himself on vinyl in the form of gruff vocal asides. For another long-deleted gem, he played second fiddle to the English tenor saxophonist and vibes player Tubby Hayes; *Tubby's Back in Town* also included James Moody, who was having an off day, but Hayes ("Alone Together" is one of his best ballad performances) and Kirk complement each other in a surprisingly civilized match. Most of the previously unreleased tracks come from Kirk's 1963 recordings at Denmark's Cafe Montmartre. Placing two versions of "Narrow Bolero" back to back is bad programming, and the piano is so out of tune you wonder how a record company could even consider releasing an album recorded under such circumstances. Yet three new ballads and an alternative of a blues with guest Sonny Boy Williamson are revealing. The released version of "Mood Indigo" begins with adroit harmonies but is derailed by trite quotations; an alternate take shows the triteness was practiced.

In 1964, Kirk recorded an underrated album that represented a leap forward in his ambition to assert himself comprehensively on records. He wanted his voice out there, and beyond that, his laughter and vision and mystic wisdom—the man himself. *I Talk with the Spirits* was his most intimate recording; the fact that he focused exclusively on flute assured a quieter tableau, and he took advantage of the wider spaces and lower decibels to spin what sounds like a spontaneous montage of melodies, verbal quips, and musical jokes. Among the best of the latter are the inclusion of a cuckoo clock in the theme of "Serenade to a Cuckoo" and the twelve-bar "Bye Bye Blackbird" exchanges between Kirk, who pops the keys of the flute without blowing into it, and drummer Walter Perkins, who applies his mallet to a hand-held cymbal on "A Quote from Clifford Brown." Perkins was an inventive musician who had a personal way of keeping time on the snare instead of the ride cymbal and Kirk obviously enjoyed working with him. Among the more serious numbers are passionately individual readings of "My Ship," "Django" (Horace Parlan plays celeste), and, unbelievably, "Trees"—*that* "Trees," here magically alchemized into a rigorous waltz.

Kirk's next session was a milestone, a near perfect album that didn't change anything, but captured four musicians on a day of mutual inspiration: *Rip, Rig and Panic* put Kirk in front of a kinetic rhythm section—Byard, Richard Davis, and Elvin Jones. He revived a great neglected ballad, "Once in a While," which his idol Don Byas had memorably recorded in 1945, and wrote six new pieces, among his finest ever. "From Bechet, Fats, and Byas" employs stride piano not as a novelty, but as an integral part of the composition. "Black Diamond" was his most luscious ballad since "The Haunting Melody." "No Tonic Pres" employs a very modern whole-tone riff that Kirk said he heard Lester Young play. The title piece appears to start as a rare journey into concrete music, but all those presumably prepared electronic sounds were actually played by the foursome on their all-purpose acoustic instruments. The subsequent theme is a jolly riff that in this context can stand as a definition of Kirk's nervy wit.

What happened next was insane. Having now released the album of a lifetime, Kirk was importuned to do a follow-up for Mammon. The very first note of *Slightly Latin* (the adverb is the operative word) is vulgar, and the cha-cha rhythm that follows, overlaid with Kirk's shouts (suddenly he's an intemperate Bob Wills), is maddening. On other tracks, a vocal choir intrudes and won't go away. Wade through and you'll find two marginal moments, the outer space writing on "Ebrauqs" and a blues called "Nothing But the Truth." "Raouf" is a temptation to hurl the disc out the window (you can't—*Rip, Rig and Panic* is on it), though it boasts startling if utterly empty tenor pyrotechnics. This was Kirk's last album for the label, though he also participated in a grim Quincy Jones project that did not merit rerelease.

Within two years, he resurfaced at Atlantic and embarked on a long series of thematic, sometimes blustery, always vigorously titled albums, notably *Here Comes the Whistleman, The Inflated Tear, Volunteered Slavery, The Case of the 3-Sided Dream in Audio Color,* and the 1970 declaration of his new name, *Rahsaan Rahsaan*. A peculiarly inspired album, *A Meeting of the Times,* paired him with the bass-baritone Al Hibbler, who had sung with Ellington and enjoyed a few hits in the '50s. Hibbler was blind, idiosyncratic, and unstoppably mannered, his wry twisting of vowels frequently leading him into faux-cockney pronunciations. In Kirk's parlance, the teaming is dreamlike. With *Bright Moments* in 1973, Kirk had a quasi-hit, not through corporate manipulation, but in a full airing of the Rahsaan-id, complete with poetic evocations. Kirk had by now so fully succeeded in putting himself on records that the music was the main attraction in his overarching self-dramatization. Yet his playing was unfailingly dynamic, including one of his most disarming ploys, a four-minute medley of "Satin Doll" and "Für Elise" played in one breath.

During the next few years, however, as his self-invention grew, his music lost shading and depth—the "miracles" began to outstrip the substance. He rarely allowed a blues or ballad or jump tune to unfold on its own terms without recourse to trickery. The overproduced albums shifted from thematic continuity to grab-bag variety. Shortly after his death, in 1977 at forty-one, Warners released the often disheartening

Boogie-Woogie String Along for Real, Kirk's last record and the only one made in the interim since his disabling stroke. His weakness and determination to swagger a bit in spite of it is heartbreaking—solos begin well and peter out, he can barely articulate a couple of Gershwin themes.

And yet . . . a six-minute treatment of Ellington's "In a Mellow Tone" is genuinely affecting. Shadowed by fine swing era rhythm players (including Art Tatum's guitarist Tiny Grimes and Louis Armstrong's bassist Arvell Shaw), Kirk maneuvers his way through an eloquent legato theme statement and into variations laden with breathless phrases (a ten-measure tremolo) and fragrantly melodic riffs. He is always on point—none of the razzle-dazzle triple-tonguing and circular breathing he uses elsewhere to compensate for the loss of his right arm. This understated invention really is a miracle, a modest capstone to a short and prodigious life.

PART SIX

❖

An Alternative Music

48 ❖ Art Tatum
(Sui Generis)

Toward the close of *Art Tatum 20th Century Piano Genius* (Verve), one of the most significant vault restorations since the advent of the CD, something unprecedented almost occurs. Tatum has embarked on "After You've Gone," conjoined in medley fashion with "Would You Like To Take a Walk?" At bar seven, he suspends gravity for a characteristic two-bar arpeggio, a whooshing turnback that you expect to end on the down beat of bar nine. But just as it begins to touch ground, another spins away with furious élan, and then another, and then another, like fireworks—as one pinwheel fades, another explodes in its place. When he lands, eight bars later, at the outset of the bridge, he offers the least Tatumesque of devices, a rest, a momentary but unmistakable silence, and you think: He's lost! Maybe, contrary to Fats Waller's declaration, he isn't God, merely the son of God. (That at least would explain his death at forty-seven in 1956.) But listen again, and count: he may be flummoxed as to what to play next, but he is in on a dime, the tempo and harmonic gauges exactly met. Definitely God.

If the perversely thrilling notion of Tatum executing an imperfect run is never to be borne out in fact, this chimerical near miss betokens the risk taking in all his best performances, and never more so than in the 20th Century recordings—so called because most of them were originally released on the 20th Century Fox label as *Discoveries*. In later years, additional titles from the same sessions showed up on a Smithsonian anthology and an Emarcy compendium that purported to be "complete and unedited" but wasn't close. This Verve release offers thirty-nine selections, twelve previously unissued, and "the most accurate and comprehensive song sequence," itself no small revelation. The music was recorded during two gatherings in the home of the acclaimed (eighteen Oscar nominations, three wins) Warner Brothers music director, Ray Heindorf, in 1950 and 1955. Playing for an audience that could appreciate the subtlety of a G to F-sharp key change and in full knowledge that he was being taped, Tatum was inspired on both evenings.

Along with Horowitz, Tatum is the most storied pianist of the age, the one about whom other pianists most enjoy regaling each other with hyperbole and apocrypha, as well as with facts. Many of the tales concern Horowitz himself, a musician Tatum esteemed and one who shared his penchant for low-arched hands. Yet the stories are indistinct. Horowitz's love of jazz is known, and evenings he spent listening to Louis

Armstrong or Joe Bushkin are documented. The same cannot be said
regarding Tatum. All we know is that he went to hear Tatum, probably
in Chicago, and complimented him (moving Tatum deeply). The fact that
Horowitz entertained friends with an arrangement of "Tea for Two,"
employing showy double thirds, suggests but doesn't prove Tatum's inspiration. Horowitz's biographer, Glenn Placksin, mentions Horowitz's
admiration for Tatum, without sourcing. Tatum's biographer, James Lester, reports on rumored connections. Years ago, when I put the question
to Horowitz's office, an ambiguous one-liner was the response: "Mr. Horowitz says he didn't really know Mr. Tatum, but had great respect for
him." The apocryphal story that boasts of a private cutting contest is
more fun, but there is no need to borrow prestige or inflate facts—the
truth is head spinning enough.

The son of amateur musicians, Tatum was born in Toledo in 1909 with
cataracts on both eyes. Whatever gains he made through operations were
undone when he was mugged as a teenager and lost all use of his left
eye, retaining a sliver of light in the right. He began picking out melodies
at three, attended the Cousino School for the Blind and the Toledo School
of Music, studied violin and guitar as well as piano, led his own bands
at local clubs at seventeen, and received his first two-year radio contract
two years later. His reputation spread. When Duke Ellington passed
through Ohio, he made a point of seeking him out, encouraging him to
head for New York, where the competition would raise his sights and
sharpen his wits. The singer Adelaide Hall provided him with his ticket
in 1932. The New York wizards faded instantly, a capitulation made
easier by Tatum's unassuming friendliness and generosity. George
Gershwin threw a party at his Seventy-second Street apartment to introduce him to the classical elite, an evening Oscar Levant recounted in *A
Smattering of Ignorance*:

> Among George's invited guests was Leopold Godowski, who lis-
> tened with amazement for twenty minutes to Tatum's remarkable
> runs, embroideries, counter-figures and passage playing. The suc-
> ceeding hour and a half of the same thing bored him, however.
> Some time after he arrived in California Gershwin discovered that
> Tatum was playing at a local night club, and we went together to
> hear him. It was a small, dingy, badly lighted room—an intimate
> version of the too-intimate Onyx Club. We joined the group of en-
> thusiasts clustered around the piano where the blind virtuoso was
> in full swing. To George's great joy, Tatum played virtually the

equivalent of Beethoven's thirty-two variations on his tune "Liza."
Then George asked for more.

Levant describes all-too-familiar polar responses: Godowski, who is
ultimately blinded by Tatum's extravagance, and Gershwin, who can't
get enough. Much of the wonder Tatum generated had less to do with
his technique than its provenance. No one had played quite like that,
applying a level of pyrotechnics that wowed even Rachmaninoff (who
is said to have remarked how great Tatum might have been had he
pursued "serious" music) to pop songs, blues, improvisation, and swing.
Tatum credited Fats Waller and Lee Sims (a midwestern radio pianist
and composer known for his intricate harmonic patterns) as influences,
along with the piano rolls he taught himself to imitate. He undoubtedly
listened to Earl Hines as well, and Ellington thought he recognized a
smidgen of Willie "The Lion" Smith. Yet if Tatum was a product of jazz,
he was by no means a conventional jazz pianist and disdained the tag.
He was too prolix to be an effective accompanist, and he was diminished
rather than emboldened by collaboration. Although best known to the
public for his piano-guitar-bass trio, which was modeled after Nat King
Cole and inclined toward unison riffs and jokey juxtapositions, he was—
like Chopin or Scriabin—a creator of sui generis piano music.

Tatum has always mystified jazz fans. In a poll of 101 musicians conducted by Leonard Feather in 1956, 68 of them named Tatum as the
greatest jazz pianist of all time—only two others, Bud Powell (21) and
Teddy Wilson (10), scored double digits. But in various readers' polls
that same year, he invariably lost to Oscar Peterson or Dave Brubeck or
both. It isn't that Tatum is difficult to listen to, but that he requires concentration. Too many jazz lovers are seduced by and dependent on the
beat, which Tatum withholds and reshapes. What is most astonishing in
his music is not the digital control, but the shifting harmonies and
rhythms that he modulates and controls as no other musician has. His
unequaled knowledge of chords profoundly influenced Coleman Hawkins, Charlie Parker, and Charles Mingus, among others, but he used it
as only a pianist can: in contrary patterns that demand parity for both
hands, in rapid key substitutions, in entering and exiting chords at
oblique angles. Oscar Peterson has speed, but his arpeggios are harmonically dim and therefore predictable. Tatum is as a rainbow, his music
glimmers and cascades.

Heard with half an ear, it may sound like little more than virtuoso em-
broidery. Critical complaints are always the same: he has a weak melodic
sense, questionable taste in material, and is excessively ornate. To the first,

I would say that he has virtually no melodic sense at all, beyond the trust he puts in the songs he chooses to play, and that he raises embellishment to a plateau as high as anyone else has ever achieved by melodic improvisation. The second quibble is repudiated by a cursory examination of his repertory. Though he maintained sentimental fondness for a few childhood themes, Tatum recorded more than 300 pieces, and they are a glossary of the songwriter's art, revealing an especially astute appreciation for inventive chord progressions. The third is the nub, underscoring the problem of how to listen to Tatum. Those magnificent arpeggios, runs, and flurries, those supersonic turnbacks and contrary figures and thumb-driven bass walks *aren't ornamental*: they are the nerve center of his art, the jewels in his treasure box—an embarrassment of rewards. One has only to compare the many versions of his favorite songs to see how varied they are, even within his rigidly preset arrangements.

It is often said of Tatum, in spite of ample evidence to the contrary, that he was unduly restrained in the recording studio and the concert hall and reserved his best work for after-hours clubs attended by the cognoscenti. One document does, in fact, show a side of Tatum the public did not get to see. In the early '40s, Jerry Newman, a Columbia University student, privately recorded his favorite musicians on a disc cutter, at first in his living room, and then in after-hours Harlem nighteries. When his Tatum discs were made public in 1973, as *God Is in the House* (Fats Waller, seeing Tatum enter a club he was working, ceased playing and announced, "I play piano, but God is in the house tonight!"), they created much excitement. The album confirms Tatum's reputation for making untuned pianos sound almost acceptable by ignoring the more damning keys and offers a few suprises, including his credible blues singing on an ode to pot called "Knockin' Myself Out" and a full-bore, seven-minute duet with the highly personal, yet neglected trumpeter, Frank Newton, on "Sweet Georgia Brown." In a duel of wits, Tatum breaks up the rhythm with staccato chord clusters that augur the angular blitz of Thelonious Monk and suspends time altogether for long sinuous figures that anticipate Bud Powell.

But that's the exception. On his other private recordings, which admittedly were not made in Harlem or in the wee hours, he is breathtakingly direct and brief, and consequently more potent than at the famous marathon studio sessions produced by Norman Granz in the '50s (great as they are), where he was encouraged to stretch out. A short list of his peak achievements would include the 1949 studio recordings made at Capitol and a concert that same year at the Shrine Auditorium. Even more impressive, however, than the after-hours, studio, and concert performances are a fourth category, those recorded privately in the homes of wealthy admirers with state-of-the-art equipment. The first of these took place in the late '40s when Tatum was invited to the home of Hollywood pianist Buddy Cole to break in a new invention: a tape recorder. Cole's employer, Bing Crosby, who financed and encouraged the development of tape, had made him a gift of a first-generation Ampex. The sound is excellent, as is the piano, and Tatum is in winning form, yet the selections are almost too immaculate. By contrast, the Heindorf tapes, despite a burbling crowd and the raking of Tatum's cufflinks on the keys, suggest a death-defying immediacy.

At the 1955 Heindorf party (which Verve programs before the one in 1950), Tatum plays "Someone To Watch Over Me" and "In a Sentimental Mood" back to back—two pentatonic melodies in which the same opening six-note phrase is altered harmonically and rhythmically by Gershwin and Ellington, respectively. Each song invariably reminded Tatum of Stephen Foster, either "My Old Kentucky Home," which he interpolated in the former, or "Old Folks at Home," which is configured into his arrangement of the latter. Given those set proclivities, the references are different in every recorded version. In this instance, he plays Gershwin with stormy bravado before settling into plush stride and ringing trills, and mines Ellington in a disarmingly sentimental mood, suggesting a shell game between the Foster and Ellington themes.

Staggering details proliferate in virtually every selection from 1955, not least a newly discovered ninety-second fast-and-furious fragment of "Makin' Whoopee." An ebullient "Begin the Beguine" is anchored to the vamp Horace Silver later made his own in pieces like "Song for My Father." Several selections begin with oblique Garneresque intros, obscure and funny, among them "Don't Blame Me" and a definitive "Sweet Lorraine," shorn of the many quotations he often ladled onto it (as he does in the 1950 version). Most selections are only two and a half choruses—Tatum prefigured r & r in cutting to the release for the last chorus—but feel whole and satisfying, often with dramatically telegraphed climaxes. "Love for Sale" is a lode of thrilling breaks; "Moon Song" offers a blinding permutation of phrase before the bridge; "Little Man, You've Had a Busy Day" (Tatum's only recording of a nostalgic tune by the forgotten Mabel Wayne) receives a leisurely meditation charged by a walloping second chorus. "Danny Boy" is by contrast an instance of Tatum's Haydnesque wit: a surprise sonata in which melodrama is persistently undermined by jarring dissonance—far more here than in the marathon version. Tatum was already visibly suffering from the uremia that killed him when he entertained the Hollywood crowd, but his art remained unsullied; in fact, he had yet to make the best of his conventional jazz albums, the quartet with Ben Webster.

In some respects, the 1950 session, most of it unknown before Verve's 1996 compilation, is of greater interest. Although Tatum reached his re-corded apogee in 1949 in such definitive Capitol performances as "Aunt Hagar's Blues," "Willow Weep for Me," "Blue Skies," and "Somebody Loves Me," he had been superceded in the public's affection by the mod-ernists. Except for a trio session, he did not record for the next four years until Norman Granz produced the marathon solo sessions of 1953 and 1955 (124 selections in four days, orginally on Verve, now on Pablo). Granz also recorded Tatum with his peers, among them Roy Eldridge, Benny Carter, Lionel Hampton, and most rewardingly, Ben Webster. Had he not come to the rescue, Tatum's discography would be scandal-ously thin.

So the 1950 evening at Heindorf's captures him at a zesty pinnacle, playing things he had never recorded before and never would have again if not for Granz. Two "new" songs—a dynamic rendering of Gershwin's "Mine" and the celebrated "Mr. Freddie's Blues" (nine sub-lime choruses with a stomp in the middle, its contrary harmonies at once progressive and rural)—exist in no other versions. In addition, there are two medleys unique in his discography. Among the previously unre-leased gems are his first recorded takes on "Love for Sale" and "Jitterbug Waltz"; a mercuric "Sweet Lorraine" (with references to "Frankie and Johnny," "Three Little Words," "Over There," and many others); and a superb "Yesterdays," with a top-speed vamp Eddie Heywood must have heard him play. The most renowned performance from that evening is the magical "Too Marvelous for Words," in which the first eight bars of the second chorus are sufficiently abstract as to suggest a transitional melody. The third chorus opens with a four-bar run and ends with Ta-tum slipping through chords like oysters down a gullet—after which, you may be speechless, or at least inclined toward a moment of silence.

49 ❖ Charles Mingus
(Bigger Than Death)

Charles Mingus's music came fully alive at the intersection where bop rebelled against itself and the avant-garde rebelled against the half-measures of rebellion. The first faction was a prisoner of influence, trying to expand and personalize a music that in its originators' hands was already perfect. Mingus, whose role in the genesis of bop was obscured by his isolation on the West Coast, reproached faction one with a song-title warning: "If Charlie Parker Was a Gunslinger, There'd Be a Whole Lot of Dead Copycats." The second faction honored the historical verities, but insisted on a clean slate. Mingus acknowledged faction two with a paternal caution: of Ornette Coleman, he said, "It's like not having anything to do with what's around you, and being right in your own world."

By 1959, the year Mingus's impact as a bandleader-composer was finally established as absolute and inexorable, Coleman and Cecil Taylor were still regarded as troubling new voices. One year later, Mingus himself provided Eric Dolphy with his first major platform; a year after that, John Coltrane dramatically broke with jazz doctrine. The following year, 1962, with jazz in flux and pop becalmed, Mingus endured the most humiliating event of his career: the disastrous Town Hall concert that eventually came to be reckoned as a defining moment, impenetrable yet decisive. We have always known—Mingus said so—that Town Hall led directly to the stunning recovery, three months later, of *The Black Saint and the Sinner Lady* (the only jazz album with liner notes by the artist's psychiatrist). What we did not know until 1989, when it was debuted in an edition edited and conducted by Gunther Schuller, is that the Town Hall music had been privately recycled into his magnum opus, *Epitaph*.

Those megalosaurs, in tandem with the equally emphatic 1971 recording *Let My Children Hear Music*, show how persistently, indeed quixotically, Mingus redefined tradition—his four points of light were gospel, Ellington, Tatum, Parker—in the face of anarchy by resurrecting that liveliest of fossils, the big band. The triumph of *Epitaph* and the cataloging of Mingus's scores inspired his widow, Sue Mingus, to go beyond the posthumous success of the first Mingus repertory band, Mingus Dynasty, which followed in the footsteps of his small groups, and start the highly successful Mingus Big Band. As a composer, Mingus was obsessed with size, might, and emotional extremes. Had he been formally trained in orchestration and not forced to farm out most of his arrangements, he might have made the orchestra speak with the personal urgency of his Jazz Workshop groups. Even so, he managed to put his mark on every measure of his music, so that no matter who did the transcribing or voicing or editing or organizing, each of his large-scale pieces is unmistakably his, each reflective of his Promethean energy.

He died January 5, 1979, of a heart attack, while in Mexico undergoing treatment for amytropic lateral sclerosis. Though confined to a wheelchair for most of the preceding year, he had completed two extended orchestral works, "Something Like a Bird" and "Three Worlds of Drums," and supervised their recordings. In his fifty-six years, most of which were consumed with music (he dated "The Chill of Death" to 1939, when he was seventeen), Mingus was a bassist, pianist, composer, arranger, bandleader, record producer, festival organizer, and autobiographer, and he achieved something of lasting importance in every area.

If Mingus didn't actually introduce fear and trembling into jazz, he was its most persistently apocalyptic voice. He could communicate joy as generously as any practitioner of what is generally considered a joyous music, but he often asked us to run the gauntlet with him before merging triumphantly on the mountaintop. The records affirm the diversity and courage of his music, its relentless honesty and prophetic impact, its masterpieces; and they show that no composer-bandleader-instrumentalist since Ellington encompassed more of jazz's accomplishment and promise. Mingus *was* the black-music experience in the United States—in its hybridization, its questing after form, its improvisation, competitiveness, impertinence, outrage, intellectualization, joy, emotionalism, bitterness, comedy, parody, and frustration.

He was one of the handful of jazz composers who developed the small ensemble, contributed durable works to its repertoire, and enlarged its potential. His presence was a beacon on any bandstand. Bass walks edged with iron prodded and halted, chastened and praised the members of his Jazz Workshop, and if his instrumental comments alone were insufficient, he would shout encouragement or criticism, on occasion firing and hiring a musician in the same set. Yet only a moment later he would look as impassive as Heifetz, his imposing figure hulking around the bass, listening, listening. And always those leathery fingers were in control.

The power and expressive tone of Mingus's bass was immediately recognizable. In the early '60s, he made the bass talk ("What Love," "Epitaph"), but those were merely extreme examples of a style that always suggested something of the human voice. His solo introduction to "Haitian Fight Song" is potent and pleading, and even the vamp with which it concludes, rising and lowering in dynamics, suggests a new tonal virtuosity, as does the invincible ostinato on "Prayer for Passive Resistance." Mingus avoided the purity of sound passed from Jimmy Blanton to Ray Brown, preferring to make each note reverberate as though the string had snapped against the wood. In this sense, there was a link between his peerless technique and the expressive slap-style bassists of Pops Foster's generation. Sometimes he enjoyed reviving Foster's style with affectionate parodies, and when he made the change from a two-beat to his own driving four/four, as he does on "Jelly Roll," the point was always the continuity of tradition and never modernistic put-down. Although his influence on contemporary bassists is widely acknowledged by jazz and classical players, Mingus frequently insisted that he was unable to develop fully as an instrumentalist because of the time devoted to composing for and training the various editions of the Jazz Workshop. Yet there are numerous bass solos of rare magnificence in his recorded work, for example, the five-chorus improvisation with which he climaxed Jimmy Owens's "Lo-Slo Bluze" at the 1972 Newport Jazz Festival—New York (released on the defunct Cobblestone label as *Newport in New York '72, Volumes 1 and 2*). It's a fantasy for bass and a microcosmic interweaving of several aspects of his compositional style: authentic rural blues licks, bebop, the Ellington influence (the third chorus is built on "Rocks in My Bed"), metrical ploys (double-timing and half-timing) handled with an emotional wallop that recalls Louis Armstrong's "Muggles," chromaticism, and swing era walking (fast and slow).

Mingus revered Duke Ellington, with whom he shared the knack for composing vivid musical portraits of musicians, friends, and places—they were, in fact, the most autobiographical of composers—and the detemination not to be limited by fads and categories. Only Mingus rivaled Ellington's compositional variety in the jazz tradition, and in the area of longer works, he was in some respects more successful. Ellington's reputation is in no way dependent on his extended compositions (I except the suites), as rewarding as they are, but Mingus's concert music—"Half-Mast Inhibition" (1946), *The Black Saint and The Sinner Lady* (1963), "Meditations on Integration" (1965), "The Shoes of the Fisherman's Wife Are Some Jive Ass Slippers" (1965), "Music for 'Todo Modo' " (1976)—is essential to any evaluation of his work. Moreover, Mingus pioneered extended compositions for small ensembles, replacing the string-of-solos method with elaborate, architectonic structures in such remarkable performances as "Pithecanthropus Erectus" (1956), "Los Mariachis" and "Ysabel's Table Dance" (1957), "Folk Forms" (1960), "So Long Eric" (1965), "Sue's Changes" (1975), and numerous others.

"Pithecanthropus Erectus" established Mingus's place in the jazz vanguard, signaling his rejection of clinical experimentalism in favor of the blues tradition itself. The thematic material is striking—a mysterious, modal melody propelled by a throbbing bass walk, climaxing with a three-beat rest, and resuming, with a sudden shift in dynamics, as a thirty-two-bar extension played with steadily increasing polyphony. Its most startling feature in 1956 was not the modality or the break or the uncommon structure, but the intensity that resulted from employing the extreme registers of the saxophone. Like the same album's "A Foggy

Day," which also employs cacophony, "Pithecanthropus" was conceived programmatically (it concerns the evolution and destruction of the first man), which may explain why the saxophone blasts and squeals sound a bit studied.

Mingus also shared with Ellington an ability to train musicians in the exigencies of his music, compelling them to avoid clichés, and ultimately drawing from them their finest work. The question of autonomy in the Jazz Workshop is a difficult one. It is often noted that Mingus not only encouraged but insisted on originality—his exhortation to "stop copying Bird" was familiar to musicians and audiences alike at one time—but some workshop graduates complained of chafing at Mingus's autocracy. Shafi Hadi said that he didn't feel free to express himself, and Ted Curson recalled Mingus ordering Eric Dolphy not to play the bass clarinet. (That Dolphy played it anyway was interpreted as evidence of Mingus's particular respect for him.) At least one broken jaw and one sprained ankle have been attributed to musical disagreements. Still, the evidence adds up in Mingus's favor—many journeyman musicians, including Jerome Richardson, Richard Williams, Dick Hafer, J.R. Montrose, Wade Legge, Bobby Jones, and Lonnie Hillyer, achieved their best playing with him. The reputation of trumpeter Clarence Shaw is dependent solely on his three albums with Mingus; equally impressive is the consistently high quality of Shafi Hadi's performances on several Mingus sessions. Then there are the workshop graduates who became major personalities themselves: Dolphy, Jackie McLean, Rahsaan Roland Kirk, Ted Curson, Jimmy Knepper, Booker Ervin, Roland Hanna, Jaki Byard, Charles McPherson, and Michael Brecker. The most loyal Mingus disciple was Dannie Richmond, a onetime rock-and-roll tenor saxophonist, who at Mingus's suggestion switched to drums for *The Clown* and became the heartbeat of his music, sensitized to its every nuance, much as Sonny Greer's intuitive approach to the drums was annealed to Ellington's music.

In the late '50s, Mingus loomed over jazz, personifying the period's modernism and confessionalism. "I am about me" was the theme of his numerous public statements. With so much emotion so freely conveyed, he was soon characterized as angry and unpredictable, and even his humorous works were interpreted with wrinkled brow, both the scathing caricature of "Fables of Faubus" and the dadaistic slapstick of "Passions of a Man." Mingus was angry and proud, but he knew how to gauge his own abilities and didn't take New York like a hurricane until he was ready—there had been a long apprenticeship with Louis Armstrong, Dinah Washington, Lionel Hampton (who recorded Mingus's first influential composition, "Mingus Fingers," in 1947), Red Norvo, and others. He recorded and composed throughout the '40s and early '50s, working briefly with his two idols, Ellington and Parker, and experimenting with cool jazz and what would later be termed third-stream directions before everything fell into place with the first Jazz Workshop sessions. His combativeness against the exploitation of black musicians also began long before he had a national reputation when he formed Debut records, the first of several musicians' attempts to operate independently of the recording industry.

He was always good with words, and by 1959 was known to berate noisy audiences with brutal contempt and chilling wit. Diane Dorr-Dorynek once transcribed a diatribe at the Five Spot:

> I listened to your millions of conversations, sometimes pulling them all up and putting them together and writing a symphony. But you never hear that symphony—that I might dedicate to the mother who brought along a neighbor and talked three sets and two intermissions about the old man across the hall making it with Mrs. Jones's son in the apartment below where the schoolteacher lives with Cadillac Bill. And how she's thinking of taking up teaching if Mary gets any more minks like that white one she just gave her sister Sal, who's in and out on weekdays and leaves town on weekends with her Rolls-Royce full of pretty teachers. And how it's difficult to keep the facts of life from her daughter Chi-Chi.

Recitations were employed in his music—there were collaborations with Lonnie Elder and Jean Shepherd—and rumors about a 1000-page autobiography called *Beneath the Underdog* were rampant throughout the '60s. Provocative excerpts appeared, but they didn't show up in the 365-page book that eventually appeared under that title in 1971. Mingus decided against a strict autobiographical approach or an exposé of the music business, producing instead a fearsome *bildungsroman* that depicts his initiation into sex, music, therapy, depression, and love in a singular style—mostly dialogue, party dialectic, sometimes parody. The evocations of Ellington and Fats Navarro have been widely admired, but there are equally accomplished passages about his father, other musicians, and women (the sixteenth chapter portrays one relationship in the style of the breakfast sequence in *Citizan Kane*). Edited by Nell King, it is harrowing and revealing, obfuscating and boastful.

The book's publication signaled Mingus's return to music after a mystifying hiatus of five years, when he was said to be semiretired. The comeback was formally marked by a triumphant concert at Philharmonic Hall early in 1972, with a twenty-piece orchestra and several guest soloists (Gene Ammons was most prominently featured). The music, eventually released on the album *Charles Mingus and Friends in Concert*, includes rousing performances of two nearly forgotten pieces from the early '50s, "Jump Monk" and "E.S.P.," and his euphoric Methodist hymn, "Ecclusiastics." "Mingus Blues," a dialogue with Ammons, demonstrates his profound respect for the elemental power of church music and the classic blues form, as does "E's Flat, Ah's Flat Too," a blues jam with a standout contribution by flutist James Moody. The high point is a new work, "Little Royal Suite," written for Roy Eldridge and played by eighteen-year-old Jon Faddis, whose reputation was made that night. It is characteristically varied in design, as serialism and Jelly Roll Morton meet on a stage of billowing ostinato figures and throbbing dissonances.

More impressive still was the release that year of *Let My Children Hear Music*, his first studio-recorded orchestral record since the 1960 *Pre-Bird Mingus* and his densest and most exhausting album. The weakest selection, "The Chill of Death," is a naive period piece from his confused teens, when he fell under the sway of Strauss's *Death and Transfiguration* and Yoga and attempted to will himself to death. A spoken parable describes death as a woman and hell as Mingus's fate; its inclusion served to emphasize his eclectic, "pre-Bird" interests and to illuminate his development as a composer. In the album's masterpiece, "The Shoes of the Fisherman's Wife," the early concerns—courage, fear, hesitation, acceptance—find a purely musical correlative. It's tempting to interpret its three major themes impressionistically, but then Mingus operated at an emotional, often rapturous level. It was in part the vividness of his romantic imagination (he rejected techniques that weren't "spiritual") that makes the longer works credible and absorbing. Recurring stylistic episodes—improvised dialectics by two or more horns, modal ethnicity, Ellingtonian Sugar Hill sophistication, Parker's extravagant virtuosity—are used as building blocks in Mingusian fantasies, where the lingering shadow of childhood is as alive as the intimacy of death.

The *Three or Four Shades of Blues* album (1977) represents an attempt to broaden his appeal by using electric guitars and young white musicians associated with pop-jazz fusion. The results are amiable and relaxed, particularly the title work, a witty casserole of acknowledged influences. Yet when Mingus first heard the tapes, he was contemptuous and sent a scathing telegram to his producer, accusing the label of making him look ridiculous. When the record outsold all his others, he changed his mind. But if Mingus controlled those collaborations while he was alive, they've gotten out of hand since his death.

Mingus is misinterpreted by those who take his example as license for facile eclecticism. He believed and rejoiced in the priorities of swing and the blues; he extended the emotional and technical scope of jazz within its essential idiomatic constraints. The *Pre-Bird Mingus* album was designed to show that Mingus was precocious, ambitious, and modern before he encountered Charlie Parker, but he was a pre-Bird musician in a more profound sense: in his love of pure emotion as exemplified in the blues, the church, and the polyphony of New Orleans; in his willingness to embrace the full panoply of jazz styles; in his absorption of the colors, styles, subtleties, and charms of Ellington and Tatum. He brought all of that into the modern era with individualty and magnanimity. He could swing as hard as any musician ever had (the last chorus of the remake of "Better Get Hit in Yo Soul" or "Hora Decubitis," for example), he wrote distinguished ballads ("Old Portrait," "Good-bye Pork Pie Hat," "I X Love," "Carolyn Keikki Mingus"), and he continuously drew on tradition, assimilating European techniques as well as those of African American music, rejecting only cant, slavishness, sentimentality, and dishonesty.

Persistent attempts to renew Mingus's music as a living art attest to its power, but underscore the tiresome inclination to translate it into something else. Posthumous Mingus is a textbook case for the ups and downs of jazz repertory. Shortly after his death, his songs were played at a memorial concert by a fusion band and his larger works treated by an orchestra laden with fusion soloists who sapped the music's drive and purpose. A collaboration between Mingus and Joni Mitchell, as completed by the singer, was tepid and unswinging. Mingus Dynasty, made up of Jazz Workshop alumni, suggested how vital a role his music could play in the jazz repertory, but it, too, foundered in the absence of Mingus's leadership. In the '90s, the polarities of interpretation were demonstrated by three far more ambitious projects, by turns pretentious, authentic, and creative.

The album *Hal Willner Presents Weird Nightmare: Meditations on Mingus* accentuates, as the title indicates, not the ebullient Mingus or the Jazz Workshop Mingus, not even the romantic rebel or angry Mingus, but rather an affected pomo Mingus of neurotic melancholy, midnight poetry, and spooky effects. In one of five often defensive liner essays, Frannie Thumm, who introduced percussion instruments built by Harry Partch into the project, defends it against objections from the "fanatical following[s]" of Partch and Mingus by quoting Stravinsky, "You 'respect,' but I love." Yet it is precisely respect bordering on fake reverence that makes this music so stupefying. I should think that loving Mingus means embracing his vitality. It might even mean honoring the context in which his music was produced.

The pitfall in divorcing notes from context and intent can be, as it is in this instance, the most stilted kind of homage. Many of the musicians assembled could not have passed muster in the Jazz Workshop, and they flatten the music to a level at which they feel comfortable. Even when Mingus's distinctive lyricism pokes through the alien bric-a-brac, arrangements that seem to pale before the threat of improvisation cloud that lyricism in smoke and mirrors—the smoke of Partch's glass instruments, the mirror of an overstressed regard for Mingus the trendy poet. Mingus's gift for language, displayed in his composition titles, recitations, memoirs, and interviews, was potent because he used it sparingly. Nearly half of *Weird Nightmare* is high-tech poetry and jazz, enforcing the suspicion that Willner's reverence is largely metaphorical: he likes the *idea* of Mingus.

If Mingus is a composer worthy of our attention, it must be because his melodies are one with his voicings and scaffolding. Set adrift among Harry Partch's globes and mallets, the melodies are reduced to a sequence of heads or samplings, robbing Mingus of the identity he fought so long to maintain. A decade of academic experiments divides the early Mingus (pre- and cum Bird) from the stage when he achieved his maturity as an artist. His genius flourished from the mid-'50s on, when he renewed himself as a jazz composer, as a jazz instrumentalist, as leader of the Jazz Workshop. It's a weird nightmare indeed that promotes Mingus as too grand for jazz, rather like arguing that Mozart is too grand for nineteenth-century musical practices and constricting his music to a sampler of favorite tunes.

Epitaph, on the other hand, is a reasonably authentic recreation of Mingus's largest work, a treasury of themes and movements, pictures at an exhibition—though it would be hard to argue that the sum is greater than or even equal to its parts, many of which are sumptuous. The piece is bulky and amorphous, a teeming excursion into Mingusiana (with transitions of dubious provenance) that is more effective in performance as an all-star endeavor than on the record, where the disparity between enthusiasm and rationale is magnified. Length is never an issue with the work Mingus himself presented. If he did indeed begin work on *Epitaph* shortly after the debacle at Town Hall, an evening of insufficiently rehearsed music (it was still being copied as the audience took its seats, a singular example of deadline blues) that nonetheless produced half a dozen recorded gems, we may wonder why he suppressed it and whether he would ever have released it in this form.

No matter. *Epitaph*, as we have it, is in the tradition of American music's white elephants: oversized, strangely fascinating, hard-to-reproduce oddities, lofty as Virgil Thomson's *Four Saints in Three Acts* or Ellington's *Black, Brown and Beige*, ludicrous as Bernstein's *Mass* or Marsalis's *Blood on the Fields*, usually in between, that are taken down from the top shelf at rare intervals, marveled at, then put back behind the hat boxes. The most important result of *Epitaph* and the subsequent cataloging of Mingus's scores is that it inspired his resourceful widow to build an orchestra devoted to Mingus's music in Mingus's manner. With Sam Burtis at the helm (Sue Mingus presented him with fifty pounds of music), the Mingus Big Band opened shop in September 1991 and with varying conductors has appeared weekly ever since at Time Cafe, recording every couple of years.

That an orchestra of changing personnel (it draws on a pool of more than a hundred of the best musicians in New York) and rotating leadership should sustain so high a level of energy and surprise must be accounted one of the great and mysterious victories of jazz repertory, given the absence of an oversized personality out front or on bass. Even on an off night, the vitality is astonishing, a contagious good cheer emanating from virtually every member of a band that encompasses several generations and wouldn't have it any other way. A hopelessly ragged performance of the first half of *The Black Saint and the Sinner Lady* got by not on the pleasures of overweening ambition but on the acceleration of riveting details: Vincent Herring's saxophone cadenza, interrupted by a thunderous ensemble crescendo; a transition from the heave-ho galley ship theme to Britt Woodman's plunger-mute trombone; several luminously funny Kenny Drew, Jr., transitions that sounded like cocktail piano on speed; a churning James Carter tenor saxophone solo that unshackled all restraints, yet remained in tune, landing nimbly in the right harmonic pockets and closing on a sustained two-note burr. And that was the band at its *worst*—overlong, raucous, blaring.

At its best, the band is a Mingusian carnival, each musician his own sideshow, each conductor his own barker, the ensemble a brightly shimmering canvas. Some arrangements are Mingus's (as old as the oddly timeless "Mingus Fingers"); others are by such longtime associates as Sy Johnson and Jack Walrath; still others were crafted by members of the orchestra. Several were worked up from small-band recordings, revised to allow for the modified instrumentation. The conductors include Steve Slagle, Craig Handy, and Ronnie Cuber, and they have found ways of shaping the pieces on the bandstand—configuring counterpoint, curtailing or expanding solos, setting background riffs—that recall Count Basie's spontaneous arrangements at the Reno Club. On some evenings, more musicians show up than the band can accommodate. One night a superfluity of trombones left Sam Burtis on the sideline, though he was introduced to conduct Sy Johnson's arrangement of *The Shoes of the Fish-*

erman's Wife are Some Jive Ass Slippers: a performance with flags flying, brimming with characteristic melodies that wed exultation and fear, and yield the promise of liberation.

On a 1993 album, *Nostalgia in Times Square* (Dreyfus), the Mingus Big Band revels in suitable reconsiderations, executed with brio and affection. Cuber's adaptation of the title selection accommodates a narration on his experience sitting in with Mingus for the first time. "Mingus Fingers" is treated at last with contemporary articulation, "Weird Nightmare" is emboldened by the absence of its distracting vocal, "Invisible Lady" is rescued from neglect. A revised arrangement of "Don't Be Afraid, the Clown's Afraid Too" cuts down on clutter and counterpoint while adding nothing to Mingus's recording, but a stirring version of "Ecclusiastics" makes the most of the gospel episode and its scripted glissando.

An earlier and no less revealing exploration of big band Mingus was made in 1988 by the imaginative trombonist Jimmy Knepper, who remained loyal to Mingus's music long after breaking with the man, who punched him in a fit of pique. In a concert released years after the fact as *Live at the Theatre Boulogne-Billancourt/Paris* (Soul Note), Knepper guides a blustery twenty-five-minute version of the first half of *Black Saint*, but is far more successful with three less complicated pieces that spotlight Mingus's steadfast mastery of the blues.

Knepper's adaptation of "My Jelly Roll Soul" mediates between Mingus's fine 1959 Atlantic record of that name and the parodistic "Jelly Roll" recorded three months later for Columbia. The former melody ascends and the latter descends, but both hew to the same strange fourteen-measure structure that was designed to get each soloist to improvise a traditional chorus followed by a modern one. Unfortunately, modernists in 1959 were still smarting from the bop wars and tended to patronize their forebears—only John Handy tried his hand at it (on the Columbia version), and he lapsed into unintentional mockery, a problem that also bedeviled the shtick-heavy tag chorus. In Paris, they got it right: Knepper opens with the ascending "Soul" and the ensemble follows with the descending "Roll." The real fun begins with the five-and-six chorus solos, which go through three steps, marked by Reggie Johnson's bass— from two-beat trad to four/four modern to double-time go-for-broke.

The overexposed "Good-bye Pork Pie Hat" is also made fresh in a performance for three reeds and rhythm that heeds Mingus's intention of wedding the ingenious twelve-bar major-key theme to a twenty-four-bar solo grid, the first half in a minor key and the second in a major/minor variation on the first. If any improvisation on a Mingus album is unusual and famous enough to warrant deference, it's Handy's 1959 tenor solo with its second-chorus flutter; yet playing alto with Knepper, he refrains from self-homage. The orchestra (a genuinely stellar cast: Jaki Byard, David Murray, Jon Faddis, Randy Brecker, Nick Brignola, Billy Hart) plays with disarming abandon on an endlessly entertaining version of "Boogie Stop Shuffle," though it does not abide by the composer's intention of sequential solos based on two-chorus structures that vary rhythmically from boogie to bop.

Neither did the original recording, as released on *Mingus-A-Um*. But in a two-step process, instigated by Columbia in 1979 and completed by Mosaic over a decade later, the performances on that album and *Mingus Dynasty* have been restored to previously unsuspected lengths. Nor were the heaviest abridgements the most egregious. Only eighty seconds were deleted from the 1959 release of "Boogie Stop Shuffle," hardly the same order of butchery as, say, Von Stroheim's *Greed*, but an instance of corporate folly all the same—though this time the footage was saved. And it shows that the composer's intention was betrayed: as Mingus actually recorded it, each of the soloists improvised sequentially on two discrete chorus grids, varying from boogie to bop. The edited version omits the second chorus improvisations and almost all of John Handy's solo.

Charles Mingus and his music gave the impression of howling assurance and terrifying emotions. His bass echoed like a giant's threat, to be soothed by his balmy melodies. More than any other jazz composer of his generation, he was willing—determined—to confront his fears and force his musicians to confront theirs. He was dogmatic, pensive, demagogic, irreverent, furious, nostalgic: a far cry from the cool and collected brainy music rife in jazz in the '50s, but nowhere near as anarchic as the orphaned dissidents of the shrieking '60s. He is the best example we have of disciplined turmoil.

50 ❖ *Cecil Taylor*
(Outer Curve)

What a glorious sixth decade Cecil Taylor enjoyed: major prizes and grants, cover stories on international jazz journals, the release of his first American label album in many years, as well as the unprecedented munificence of *Cecil Taylor in Berlin '88*. He appeared to be taking his success pretty well: on the cover of the American LP, *In Florescence*, he looks the camera in the eye, practically flirting with an audience he's usually addressed through a mask of dark glasses and knit hat. In 1990, he and I were guests on a radio show, and the enjoyment he took in his belated recognition as a national resource was unmistakable. "You've won," I told him. But everybody wins when a visionary achieves the valued appurtenances of a life in art without having to cede his vision. He could have made it easier on himself—and not by taking offers such as that proffered by the rock promoter who thought Taylor could earn a mint playing funk. There were other ways: shorter performances, familiar repertoire, a conventional concert style. But those were never really options.

Taylor is Taylor is Taylor. His celebration of self is bound up with a stubborn intransigence. You can no more separate them than you can Louis Armstrong's might from his timbre. Just as he was making his breakthrough in the '70s, he started chanting and dancing, encouraging even the converted to cavil. Personality itself is technique. Given Taylor's holy role as the eternal outer curve of the avant-garde, it isn't his function to make things easy. When we can listen to him with half an ear, he's lost.

For that reason, among others, it's hard to believe that he's been at it so long—more than forty years on records, notwithstanding a couple of layoffs (1963–65, 1968–72). On September 14, 1956, in Boston, with Dennis Charles, Buell Neidlinger, and on two selections, Steve Lacy, he made his first album, one of the most remarkable statements of the '50s. *Jazz Advance* consists of three originals, two romantic standards, and one piece each by Monk and Ellington. What makes it more fascinating today than at the time it was first issued is our awareness that Taylor was already employing many of the pianistic techniques and figures associated with his more mature period, especially evident in his boldest achievement, "Rick Kick Shaw." The album is dated only by his attempt to parse those figures over a steady beat and wed them to predetermined harmonies. It aroused sufficient interest to secure him a spot at the 1957 Newport Jazz Festival in a program devoted to "experimental" jazz and was followed by several records over the next five years, culminating in three arrangements released under Gil Evans's sponsorship as *Into the Hot*.

During the interim period, Taylor, who was born in New York in 1929, washed dishes and tended counter in a department store while lining up occasional gigs in Greenwich Village boites and concert halls. He practiced obsessively. Ted Curson has told of the time he and Bill Barron rehearsed with Taylor every day for a solid year in order to play one engagement. Critics and listeners didn't know what to make of him, though none could fail to recognize his stunning virtuosity. The album jacket adorning a 1959 album by the band with Curson and Barron (United Artists) depicts a man in a trench coat lighting a cigarette for a hooker leaning against a brick wall, arms akimbo and a provocative glint in her eye. The legend reads: "*Love for Sale* Cecil Taylor Trio and Quintet," and the liner notes describe the three Cole Porter readings as "impressionistic," demonstrating the degree to which Taylor befuddled even those who produced his records.

Taylor's audience grew slowly. For most people, it was love or hate at first blush, but often the hate turned to intrigue and then to love. Extreme responses were exacerbated after the winter of 1962, when he achieved a major stylistic breakthrough. Working at Copenhagen's Cafe Montmartre with alto saxophonist Jimmy Lyons and drummer Sunny Murray, he realized he did not have to suit his improvisational impulses to a set rhythm and chords; he could, to the contrary, create a kinetic center and force time and harmony to accommodate him. Murray undoubtedly helped to provoke this liberating insight: he was the first drummer to reach beyond countable time to a place where rhythm was as supple as Taylor's impulses. *Into the Hot*, their first recording together, was too much a showcase for Taylor's compositional skills to permit the unison improvisation achieved at the Cafe Montmartre a year later. Taylor's epiphany, captured on the pivotal "D Trad That's What," was not unlike the shock of recognition that hit Charlie Parker while jamming in the chili parlor. Parker was trying to push beyond the confines of conventional harmony. Taylor—like John Coltrane, Ornette Coleman, and Albert Ayler—was pushing farther.

Not surprisingly, classical musicians often responded more sympathetically than jazz players; outsiders, less threatened by revolutionaries than members of the club, are more inclined to accept innovation as long at doesn't threaten their own ways of doing things. But then Taylor has never sued for a place in any particular club. Jazz proved commodious enough to provide a forum to debate and finally encourage and honor his work, but one can't help but suspect that if Taylor were white he'd have played different venues, enraged a different forum, and attracted different champions. Not that his place in jazz history is anything less than categorical. Yet despite the constant presence in his music of such unmistakable jazz-inspired facets as trap drums and improvisation (not the same thing as indeterminacy), Taylor is an autonomous marvel, and people tend to hear in his music echoes of what they already know. Some find traces of Ellington, Powell, Monk, Silver, or Brubeck; for others, it's Brahms, Stravinsky, Cowell, Messiaen, or Boulez; for still others, it's Africa, the pentatonic scale, and microtones. Some years ago, Taylor shared a concert bill with Oscar Peterson: one jazz titan stormed out, calling it an insult to an art he'd spent a lifetime developing; another shrugged off Peterson's lapidary technique and said Taylor gives you hope for the future.

The question that continues to haunt his art is: What precisely is he doing and why must he do it with such intensity and at such length? In *Comes Through in the Call Hold*, the poet Clark Coolidge refers to Taylor's "amphetamine of dares" and admits, "I too would rather than listen not listen." Taylor is a threat, a heretic in the cathedral of music, who questions such fundamental issues as harmonic improvisation, swing, and endurance—his and the audience's. At the time of his debut on records, jazz was mired in harmonic labyrinths. Taylor was one of the few musicians who saw no reason that chord progressions could not be replaced by spontaneous invention within the confines of composed music. In questioning the cyclical blues and song structures on which jazz improvisation was based, he inevitably had to wonder why rhythm sections were cast primarily as timekeepers and not as equal participants in an ensemble's inventions. He never implied that the conclusions he reached would somehow counter or negate jazz tradition (he is, after all, a jazz fan, a lover of Erroll Garner and Bud Powell). He devised a way that worked for him, not necessarily for anybody else.

Yet if he never issued a broadside on the order of Ornette Coleman's *Change of the Century*, Taylor did show with his first albums and the afternoon appearance at Newport that jazz could never again be the *exclusive* province of finger-snapping hipsters who liked nonconformist art only when it conformed to standards they knew and loved. Over time he conjured an improvisational attack that articulated arcane longings and emotions very much at the heart of the most traditional jazz impulses. He invented keyboard parallels for brassy high-note climactic blasts, embodying jazz's profane luster; he reasserted the dialectics of call-and-response in his pianistic play between bass and treble; he raised dynamics to a level of subtlety and contrast surpassing that of any improvising pianist since Earl Hines; and, in his band music, he aligned reeds and brasses and strings and drums in combinations that suggest more of history and memory than can ever be notated.

Taylor's way is a natural extension of the man. Growing up on Long Island, he began piano at five (encouraged by his mother, whom he has described as an accomplished player) and studied percussion with a timpanist. From 1952, Taylor spent three years at the New England Conservatory in Boston, where he heard many of the jazz giants who lived in or visited the area. Although Taylor evades specific questions about his development as a musician, he obviously assimilated an astonishing variety of music. The frame of reference suggested by his composing and keyboard techniques is immense, yet his work is profoundly anti-eclectic; pastiche can not be found in it. In his use of tone clusters, Taylor may be historically indebted to Henry Cowell, but Taylor's peerless virtuosity allows him to do more with them than did Cowell or anyone else. Every note and method in a Taylor performance is instantly recognizable as uniquely his own.

The German critic Ekkehard Jost has written that Taylor developed "a kind of playing whose dynamic impetus arose not from off-beat phrasing, but from combining the parameters of time, intensity, and pitch, thereby creating a new musical quality, *energy*." He goes on to argue that Taylor uses energy as a replacement for conventional swing. Indeed, the velocity, the urgency, the almost intolerable tension Taylor creates on the piano and by extension with his ensemble define his rhythms, which are themselves constantly in motion, accelerating and decelerating. His sensibility is closely related to that of a drummer. The piano is a sounding board for his rhythms no less than for his melodies, which are often bewitchingly lovely and are always played with a digital precision that would be the envy of any pianist.

Many people who are awed by Taylor's dazzling technique are worn down by his tenacity and endurance. The problem of how to listen to his extended works (an hour-long piano solo is not unusual) is one each listener has to answer individually. No artist has given me more pleasure than Taylor, in part because I know that what I get from him I can get nowhere else. He recharges my batteries, alerts me to possibilities, and exonerates my mind for wandering—because anywhere it wanders is sanctified by the music that took it there. Familiarity with his work breeds familiarity, not boredom. Like any other worthy artist, Taylor rewards attention to the details, even if they appear subsumed in the velocity of his barrage. Consider a typical performance, a sixty-fifth birthday concert at Lincoln Center (financed by his MacArthur Foundation award) in 1994.

He begins with an expected but nonetheless startling, whimsical, theatrical opening: a blackout, the silence broken by a long thin guttural vocal sound; then a chanting of numbers ("one, two, one, one"), a poem of words and not-words, a silence (not a cough from the audience), and finally soft lights revealing Taylor, who is lying on his back, reading from a text. He sits up and turns to the house, still reading, and rises to reveal a flowing purple robe with white shawl and sleeves and red and turquoise ribbons falling from the shoulders. He sits at the piano and stirs the waters. The first and longest piece (just under an hour) is unusually deliberative, much of it played at middle velocity, which is to say that moments of candid lyricism and pealing streaks of lightning during the first section are ornamental. Taylor doesn't manipulate emotion in obvious ways—his most entrancing melodies can be ambiguous, and his fervent onslaughts, eagerly awaited and always satisfying (not unlike Tatum's arpeggios, once decried as ornamental, now appreciated as the marrow of his music), have, in the '90s, evolved to a point where you can't predict their duration or resolution. When, about twenty minutes into the piece, he initiates those cascades that sweep up notes in bunches, ringing them like great bells balanced on the beams of his bounding bass chords, Taylor fulfills the promise of his virtuosity and the hall glows.

Digression. In a 1982 lecture on Beethoven's concert recitals, Michael Tilson-Thomas pointed out that Beethoven's audience would have been disappointed had he merely played his published sonatas. His fans wanted him to deliver on his ability to command its emotions with powerful displays of brooding anguish and lilting variations in his uniquely flamboyant style. In other words, the public could *buy* the sonatas; they wanted to hear Beethoven improvise. Beethoven was himself an ambiguous melodist, using architectonic structures to disguise the limitations of the riff-like figures he amplified in the absence of ripe melody. The concert hall Beethoven is lost to us, though one can surmise him in the fury of his most prodigious piano music. Taylor is likely the closest we have to an improviser of such breadth and force, and his too infrequent recitals must be attended with a like-minded expectation of spontaneity fired in the cauldron of a matchless bravura.

The second piece at Taylor's birthday concert, half as long as the first, is more overtly dramatic and opens with a serene lyricism, the keys tenderly pressed, not struck. But just as you began to anticipate his direction, he pulls to a quick stop and resumes in an altogether different vein, sustaining a terrific high-velocity fusillade, then pulling back to an almost decorous passage of restrained meditation, building up a dialogue between the blinding speed of the right hand and the ominous weighing of the left. A culminating volley of chords seems to shake him up and, after a brief pause, he continues with a bass walk, croons the word "roses," and, establishes as his motif a figure that encompasses two octaves and extends methodically to a shapely, subdued close. For the rest, he plays five encores that range in duration from more than ten to under two minutes and in disposition from swinging fury (what Serenus Zeitblom did for Beethoven, a future explicator will have to do for Taylor) to a surprisingly relaxed diversion (as though he'd wrung out the fury, and could now indulge the pure pleasure of his ability). Each of the seven pieces brings the audience to its feet.

Taylor's recitals increasingly remind me of concerts by Earl Hines and

Art Tatum; all three addressed structural balance and engaged the keyboard top to bottom. Hines fancied precipitant dynamics and change-ups; Tatum favored swirling washes of color. But beyond any similarities, which will appear abstract to those who are predisposed not to see any continuity whatsoever, is the rhythm issue. Hines and Tatum are worshipped now, but neither enjoyed particularly successful careers in the concert arena. Hines defined jazz piano in the '20s, yet with the collapse of the big band era, struggled for several years and virtually disappeared between his tenure with the postwar Louis Armstrong All-Stars and his rediscovery in the '60s as an eternal modernist. Tatum, whose concert appearances were few and far between, was a musician's musician whose intimidating pyrotechnics placed him on the outskirts of jazz fashion. The chief difficulty they and Taylor pose is rhythmic: each insists on constantly reshaping rhythmic parameters with rubato episodes and breakneck shifts that make rote foot-tapping impossible.

Listening to them, one is reminded that swing is liberating only when it's an option; if someone tells you to swing or else, it's tyranny. After all the years of controversy, it's natural to presume the problem of Taylor's obscurity, though that, too, is a faded issue. I invited a friend from the rock world to a Taylor concert and belabored her with grim projections about how she might respond. She was utterly entranced, laughing in awe afterwards as she aptly described one passage after another. The next day my wife entered the room where I was listening to Taylor's just-released 1986 concert performance *Olu Iwa* (Soul Note) and asked, "Is that Cecil? I like that." All of which could not help but cue me to the fact that the pervasive influence Taylor has had on the way we hear goes way beyond the faithful. My friend was even knocked out by the opening routine, and why not?—those inured to pop theatrics are bound to respond a lot less prudishly than the organization men trying to maintain jazz as a preserve for mainstream finger-snappers.

My first encounter with Taylor's music came through television, strangely enough. I don't recall the program (it has yet to surface on videocassette), but I think it was in 1965; the host was Nat Hentoff, and Taylor engaged my curiosity not least by plucking the inner strings of the piano. His superb Blue Note albums, *Unit Structures* and *Conquistador!*, came out shortly afterward. I was hooked by those "mature" albums and soon discovered the earlier ones. John Coltrane dominated the '60s, but Taylor's music promised a different way of dealing with the perplexities of free music. Most of his work on records until that time was with his bands, the Cecil Taylor Units, and the relationship between his written and improvised passages suggested an alternative to the head/solos/

head format that even Coltrane and Ornette Coleman preferred. His ensemble has a textural bite unlike any other: the contrast between Jimmy Lyons's Parker-inspired alto sax and the Taylor-fashioned phrases Lyons transfigures is haunting, as is the high, whining pitch of Alan Silva's arco bass set against Henry Grimes's deep, savvy pizzicato bass, and the lucid voicings of reeds (including Ken McIntyre's oboe and bass clarinet) and trumpet, shadowed and enhanced by Taylor's burbling piano—Count Basie on mescaline. If the Blue Notes are arresting chiefly for their pioneering structures and sonorities, a performance like "Tales (8 Whisps)" affirms the prime marvel of Taylor's pianism.

The late '60s and early '70s were Taylor's years in academe. He taught at Antioch and the University of Wisconsin and brought his quartet—Lyons, Sam Rivers, Andrew Cyrille—to Grinnell College in Iowa for a four-day seminar that included a contentious discussion group and a Cyrille drum clinic in addition to a four-hour concert. (A classical violinist in residence, who much admired *Unit Structures*, held a faculty party in Taylor's honor after the concert, which had included a one-hour piano interlude that cleaned out the theater. At the party, the violinist and his wife heaped compliments on him, comparing him with Mozart and Ravel—the long solo recalled Ravel's *Sonantine*, the wife said. Taylor looked at them and asked, "Why don't you talk about Duke Ellington and Bud Powell?" A week later, the student government brought impeachment proceedings against the concerts chairman for wasting funds on an "elitist" and "charlatan.") Taylor was dismissed by Wisconsin for flunking too many students. That turned out to be a good thing. In the mid-'70s, he went beyond anything he had previously done. In rapid succession, *Indent*, *Spring of 2 Blue-J's* (half quartet, half scintillating piano invention), and *Silent Tongues* established his place at the pinnacle of contemporary recitalists. After Rivers left the band, Taylor's trio with Lyons and Cyrille epitomized musical interaction.

A series of projects, most of them triumphs, followed: the 1974 Carnegie Hall big band concert; intransigent but fascinating collaborations with Mary Lou Williams, Mikhail Baryshnikov, and Max Roach; the stunning performance at a 1976 White House jazz party (President Carter impulsively leaped up and followed Taylor as he retreated from the stage to a wooded area, perking the attention of the secret service. "Does Horowitz know about you?" the president asked him); and recordings. Two particularly fine albums were produced during four days of recording for New World Records in the summer of 1979. For *The Cecil Taylor Unit* and *3 Phasis*, he introduced a sextet with trumpet (Raphe Malik), violin (Ramsey Ameen), bass (Sirone), and drums (Ronald Shannon Jackson) in addition to Jimmy Lyons and himself. Not since the Blue

Note recordings had he crafted so effective an ensemble tableau. The instrumentation—three front line, three rhythm—is Dixieland in its simplicity, and the music heightens the role of each player, averting clutter amid melodic figures that, while customarily terse, are less angular and taut than in the '60s.

If Taylor is the nervous center of his music, Lyon's alto saxophone might well be considered its heart. His playing on the New World albums is relatively spare, but his elegance of phrasing and warmth of sound permeate the performances. Taylor's method in that period was to rehearse without allowing the musicians to see his scores. He would play each figure for Lyons, who would master them and pass them to the rest of the players; his interpretation of Taylor's melodies would govern the approach of the ensemble. *The Cecil Taylor Unit* clarifies the way Taylor relates to and centers the band. "Idut" is especially revealing in this regard: although he paces the piece with solo piano transitions, he takes a subordinate role in ensemble passages. The striking theme is introduced by violin and bass, augmented by trumpet and alto. Taylor responds to the ensemble, supporting and prodding it and filling out the body of sound—note how closely he trails Lyons, and the ringing overtones he produces at the extremes of the Bosendorfer piano. By contrast, he is the meditative center of "Serdab," as the winds and strings repeat his melodies—for example, an arpeggiated minor chord (tonic, minor third, fifth), about a minute into the performance, that Lyons takes up and relays to the others. Like "Enter, Evening" (*Unit Structures*), it displays an arranging style that requires relatively few notes of each participant yet produces ornate colors.

Taylor's musicians rarely equal his technical aplomb, but like Ellington, he manages to extract from them precisely what he needs; many of them (including Ameen and Malik, who acquit themselves well) have produced virtually nothing of interest outside his web. The most stirring of the new participants is the drummer, Ronald Shannon Jackson, who went on to create some of the most intriguing jazz-rock alloys of the '80s but was known then chiefly for his work with Ornette Coleman's Prime Time. Jackson's preference for a backbeat was certainly known to Taylor, who may have hoped for a rhythmic scrimmage, even though Jackson played with respectful restraint throughout the rehearsals and most of the recordings. Yet on "Idut," he asserts the beat where he can, and on the thirty-minute "Holiday en Masque" he sets off a thunderstorm in concert with Taylor and in a stomp episode with Malik. He really lets himself go, however, during the shuffle section in the second half of the magnificent hour-long *3 Phasis*.

An elastic suitelike assemblage of themes, *3 Phasis* was the most challenging work of the New World sessions, and the ensemble played it several times (once in less than fifteen minutes), before Taylor got the performance he desired (in the last hour on the last day, finishing within a minute of the allotted studio time.) At the midway point (section four on the CD), Taylor introduces an appealing melody that Lyons echoes and transmits to the ensemble. Suddenly, Sirone, who had been playing against the time, instigates a steady four-beat shuffle meter, and Jackson jumps on it, driving the band home with Taylor gamely enjoying the ride.

Other remarkable ensemble recordings followed. On a 1985 release, Taylor led an eleven-piece orchestra through a singularly merry caper called *Winged Serpent (Sliding Quadrants)* (Soul Note). Ever since the 1961 "Bulbs" (*Into the Hot*), Taylor has shown a tantalizing talent for voicing saxophones; all he's ever needed is two to get a firm, woodsy, consistent sonority that sounds like nothing else in or out of jazz. This despite constancy in one chair (Lyons) and constant change in the other: Archie Shepp on *Into the Hot*, Ken McIntyre on *Unit Structures*, Sam Rivers on *The Great Concert* (Prestige), and David S. Ware on *Dark to Themselves* (Enja). For *Winged Serpent*, Lyons was one of five reed players (Frank Wright on tenor saxophone, John Tchicai on tenor sax and bass clarinet, Gunter Hampel on baritone sax and bass clarinet, Karen Borca on bassoon), and the variants produced by that choir moor the work. To say that Taylor is in his element, threading his way through the reeds, two brasses, two drummers, and bass, romping polyrhythmically in and around every collective outburst and sigh, is to say nothing of the measured care with which he organized his unit structures.

On the mysteriously delayed *Olu Iwa* (recorded 1986, released 1994), he has a band unified primarily by its rhythm, suggesting at times an Africa-inspired percussion group or a Basie-inspired rhythm section interlude, depending on your frame of reference. Taylor interacts and blends with Thurman Barker on marimba and the ingeniously volatile Steve McCall on drums. Taylor's inherent understanding of jazz's ebullient power comes to the fore in the second half of "B Ee Ba Nganga Ban's Eee!" with a paint-peeling solo by Peter Brötzmann and the tailgate slide of Earl McIntyre. Brötzmann's appearance augured Taylor's most singular achievement, two years later in Berlin.

When Jimmy Lyons died in 1986, bringing to a close a partnership of twenty-five years, many worried that Taylor would be devastated. But like Ellington after the death of Billy Strayhorn, he compensated for the loss with increased activity, a schedule that culminated in 1988 with his triumphant stay in Berlin, documented on thirteen CDs, eleven of them sumptuously packaged by the German label FMP as *Cecil Taylor in Berlin '88*. Just as the Berlin Wall was about to make its way to the rock collection at Bloomingdale's, Taylor was the focus of a festival in the western zone that included recitals, duets with some of the leading figures in European jazz, big band concerts, workshops, and a master class. He also appeared twice in the eastern half for a recital and a duet with drummer Gunter Sommer, which FMP released separately as *In East Berlin*. Good-bye Checkpoint Charlie.

A project as comprehensive and costly as *Cecil Taylor in Berlin '88* and its smaller addendum was not designed for dilettantes or the merely curious. Nor was it destined for a long shelf life before being broken into its separate components. Even by the usual standards of holiday largesse, when record producers outdo themselves with immense boxed sets, crypts for the sainted dead, *Berlin* is amazing, not least because it honors the living. The big black box contains nine single CDs, a double-CD of a big band concert, a 120-page discography of the twenty-two principal players, separate annotations with each CD, and an exquisite album-sized volume of nearly two hundred pages, on glossy photographic stock, replete with pictures, essays (in German and English) by a dozen European writers and musicians, and a transcription and analysis of a performance by the Cecil Taylor Workshop Ensemble.

The comments, by no means entirely uncritical, address the phenomenon of Taylor and, specifically, his monthlong visitation in Berlin, in several ways, from elaborate critical exegesis to anecdotal recollection, with more than a touch of the feverish poesy Taylor often inspires. Of particular interest are Ekkehard Jost's "Instant Composing as Body Language," a demonstration of Taylor's developing pianistic technique as revealed in his albums of the '80s (a considerable advance on Jost's pioneering 1975 examination of Taylor in *Free Jazz*), and a complicated, sometimes incomprehensible, but intriguing deconstruction of "Legba Crossing" by Daniel Werts, who plays oboe in the performance—the closest measure by measure reading of Taylor's music to date.

I cannot think of a more impressive presentation of newly recorded music by an artist at the height of his powers. The only precedent is Louis Armstrong's mid-'50s autobiography, *Satchmo*, a mere four albums of historical reconstructions and a thin booklet. But Armstrong was exploring his past, and Taylor's Berlin adventure represents his finest achievement. The variety of the performances in length (from a seventy-three-minute duet with drummer Han Bennink to encores that average forty-five seconds) and instrumentation (from solo piano or voice to seventeen-piece orchestra) is exceeded only by the emotional dimension. Here are the glistening fusillades, blues locutions, sustained adagios, humorous asides, dark romances, and melodramas. But they are weighted, controlled, intensified, leavened by the accountability of collaboration.

Five of the recorded concerts are duets with percussionists, each fully distinct from the others. In every instance, Taylor's response to music and moment, to the idiosyncrasy of sound and attack, embodies a measure of concentration and generosity that, when considered cumulatively, becomes quite overwhelming. Range is suggested by Paul Lovens's tentative, almost microscopic attention to detail and Han Bennink's rigorous, marchlike vivacity; each coaxes from Taylor a responsiveness and energy that, while hardly new or unexpected, takes on added authority when heard one after the other. All the drummers—the others are Tony Oxley (who along with bassist William Parker appeared in Taylor's 1989 Feel Trio), Louis Moholo, and Gunter Sommer—embrace Taylor's approach while exalting their own varied commitments to the aesthetics of free jazz.

Every performance is illuminating: "The Hearth," an expansive trio by Taylor, cellist Tristan Honsinger, and (here in a long-awaited encounter) saxophonist Evan Parker, is a romantic effusion, occasionally discursive and consistently beguiling. The two duets by Taylor and guitarist Derek Bailey, including a dicey yet successful guitar-voice exchange, are rewarding instances of Taylor's nanosecond reflexes and mastery of extreme dynamics. The two solo performances are exemplary, particularly the East Berlin recital, "Reinforced Concrete," with its blazing block chord runs and ardent middle movement.

The two orchestral concerts are among the best executed examples of improvised big band music since the free jazz movement came to life. The sonorities are kaleidoscopic and the solos incisive. They are unique in the Taylor discography. "Legba Crossing" and "Alms/Tiergarten," reminiscent of Coltrane's *Ascension* in its moments of transcendent agitation though leavened by an irresistible cycle of duets, are light-years beyond Taylor's 1969 collaboration with Michael Mantler and the Jazz Composers Orchestra Association. Clarinetist Louis Sclavis burns through the ensemble and in a dialogue with trombonist Hannes Bauer; the better known players include Peter Brötzmann, Evan Parker, Tomasz Stanko, Enrico Rava, Gunter Hampel, and William Parker. This approach to orchestral music has been sustained chiefly in Europe by organizations like the Globe Unity Orchestra, but the amorous fervor, the lightning change-ups, the zealous assurance are pure Taylor.

Cecil Taylor in Berlin '88 is testimony not only to Taylor's centrality as a towering figure in the music of the age and to the increasing accessibility of his art, but to the continued vigor of free jazz in Europe, especially Germany. Though the big box has long since disappeared, it ought to be restored from time to time, uniting the discrete concerts and the exegeses. Taylor remains the grand magician, disguising his secrets in poetry and rhetoric, propelling himself by will and energy, collapsing whole eras and traditions into one rhapsodic accord. Still, idiom-bound casuists continue to praise Taylor with faint damns, accompanied by censurious warnings about his pedigree. "Mr. Taylor," writes a reviewer in the *New York Times*, "has over the years left jazz and formed his own distinct vocabulary for composition and improvisation, one that relies heavily on European classical music, one that has never quite been taken as an idiom." Taken by whom? In truth, more musicians in New York in the '90s routinely reflect the impact of Taylor's music than play in the "idiom" of, say, Dixieland or swing. And when exactly did he leave jazz? Was it after the Montmartre trio of 1962 or the Blue Note albums of 1966 or the tour with Sam Rivers in 1969 or *Spring of 2 Blue-Js* in 1973 or *Dark to Themselves* in 1976 or *3 Phasis* and the duets with Max Roach in 1979 or Berlin in 1988 or the septet with Charles Gayle in 1996? Cecil Taylor can't leave jazz—he *is* jazz. Not all of jazz, obviously, any more than jazz is all of him. Trying to extricate one from the other is a pedant's game, like trying to remove Beethoven from symphony because he, too, broke the bonds.

51 ❖ *Ornette Coleman (This Is Our Music)*

The Ornette Coleman Atlantics, which have been collected in their entirety as a six-disc cube called *Beauty Is a Rare Thing* (Rhino), are—like the Armstrong OKehs, the Wilson-Holiday Brunswicks, the Basie Columbias, the Ellington RCAs, the Parker Dials, the Rollins Prestiges—imperishable recordings. Each such series embodies a time, place, and attitude, a unique way of looking at music and life. Jazz lovers can't imagine the world without them and are confident that, when history has filtered out the meretricious and second-rate, these performances and a good many others will abide as vital as scores by the guys sculpted in marble at your local symphony hall. We could be wrong, of course. No, actually, we couldn't. If any of those artists faded from memory, someone else would have to resolve the issues he or she raised, most assuredly the apocalyptic ones raised by Coleman.

In my mind's ear, I hear Martin Williams, who wrote about Coleman with more feeling and understanding than anyone, reminding me not to get too solemn. The primary message of Coleman, he would insist, is the joy of inspired creation, and he would be right. Yet Coleman's music remains so singular that, forty years after his debut recordings, I still can't hear it without marveling anew at how his privileged ear resisted the laws of harmony, melody, rhythm, and pitch, all of which he ultimately revised in the abracadabra of harmolodic. Quickly then. . . . Harmony: If you can resolve any note in any chord, why not do away with the chords and allow harmony to proceed serendipitously from melody? Melody: What will it sound like if it follows its own course, free of harmonic premises? Rhythm: What is four/four but an artificial subset of one/one, and who says we have to submit to it? Pitch: Screw the tempered scale and the lute it rode in on.

The language may seem combative, given the gentleness, the diffidence, of this man Coleman. But remember that a gauntlet was, in fact, thrown. We can celebrate the rarity of beauty today, but the original rhetoric was far more confrontational. Contemporary Records issued his second album as *Tomorrow Is the Question! The New Music of Ornette Coleman!* And if that didn't put you on your guard, the Atlantics warned us the old order was rapidly changing with *The Shape of Jazz To Come* and *Change of the Century*. Get out of the way if you can't lend a hand, another radical sang, and at first Coleman could find only a few with hands to lend: lanky Don Cherry, his pocket trumpet looking like a battered toy; Charlie Haden, who learned bass in his family's hillbilly band; and Billy Higgins, who had to wean himself off the downbeats but smiled all the while. In 1960, Higgins was replaced by Ed Blackwell, which in effect focused the drums on the snare instead of the ride cymbal. That was the quartet that posed for Coleman's third Atlantic LP, wearing dark suits and looking like Malcolm's bodyguards. The title was the declamatory but more modest *This Is Our Music*, and Coleman wrote of it, "Learned technique is a law method. Natural technique is nature's method. And this is what makes music so beautiful to me. It has both, thank God."

Coleman's initial recordings were hardly greeted as natural or beautiful at the time. In retrospect, they seem synergetically appropriate to a period in American history that is often characterized by grizzled clichés about how we lost our innocence along with our most carnal president. After nearly half a millenium of genocide and slavery, how much innocence was at stake? But even if we define innocence as complicity with our national homilies, Coleman's Atlantics suggest a fragmentation of spirit, a dislocation, that tells us much more about Lee Harvey Oswald's America than, for instance, the Pulitzer Prize–winning novels, plays, and musical works of that era. Had they been recorded in December 1963 instead of three and four years earlier, Coleman's records might be regarded today as additional evidence of a crack in the firmament, disputing as they do much of what we once held dear and thought reliable in our aural universe.

Coleman's music remains bracing, even shocking to many. By the late '60s, an avant-garde musician could remark with bemusement that Coleman seemed so incredibly "outside" a few years ago, but was now "inside," easily accessible. Coleman was dancing in our heads—harsh yet jubilant, alienated yet benevolent. Today, he once again strikes me as outside, which is to say the music hits me in unprotected areas of the brain, areas that remain raw and impressionable, uncivilized in the Huck Finn sense of the word. In short, they continue to make terrible background music, thank God. They command full attention, and at that price are immensely pleasurable. Coleman's heirs have not begun to displace him. He helped launch a new movement and named it free jazz, but some of his most gifted followers are like junior anarchists by comparison. On the one hand, they don't venture as far as he did beyond conventional pitch; on the other, they lack his genius for rich and ribald melody. Learned technique and natural technique.

If the icy texture of Coleman's voicings, played on alto sax and pocket trumpet over trampoline rhythms, and his harmonically free-falling but melodically thematic solos suggest dislocation from the accepted order, they also incarnate an eternal innocence more profound than whatever died in Dallas. His notion of beauty and individuality bespeaks a naive generosity. One always felt, even if he hadn't said so himself, that Coleman honestly expected a broad reception, or at least the untutored ability of listeners to register his music's emotion. In 1959, an enthusiastic Shelly Manne described Coleman's sound as "like a person crying . . . or a person laughing." At least he was sure about the person part. Coleman himself emphasized the importance of a vocal projection: "You can always reach into the human sound of a voice on your horn if you are actually hearing and trying to express the warmth of a human voice." The trick, he said, was playing in the right pitch. But many people heard only the sound of their own anxiety and shunned his music as impenetrable, a fact that amazed his admirers. True, he challenged every preconception of Western music, including areas of pitch and serendipity that Schoenberg had left alone and Cage accessed mainly in theory, but that was secondary to his magnanimous spirit, his blinding unison of purpose.

"Unison" is a tricky word in the Coleman lexicon. "You can be in unison without being in unison," he once told me. Indeed, if the Coleman of 1959 seemed isolated, his band exemplified unity. By comparison, Louis Armstrong and his colleagues in the Hot Five were a god and his disciples, barely of the same species. In the Atlantic quartets, everyone is god *and* disciple. On learning that Coleman didn't count off tempos, an astonished George Russell inquired, "How did that work?" "Insight," Coleman said. In some selections, Cherry's improvisations prove more melodically creative than Coleman's. Where Coleman will pace himself with the familiar mannerism of a discordant cry, Cherry can find his way in a solo without a single predictable ploy, nothing but tunes and riffs. Haden confidently hops alongside them both as though he were following a score. It's a mystery that the bassist is always right and that Higgins and Blackwell always swing despite an evasive downbeat and a defunct upbeat. They engender toe tapping of the willy-nilly variety.

Here is a bigger mystery: Why do they blend so well together when Coleman is the only one mining the quarter-tone? One way to think of his formidable sound is as unalloyed blues. Blues notes exist only in relation to not-blues notes. A B-flat by itself has no religion; played against a C major seventh chord, it can make you shudder with delight. Coleman's music comes to life in the clash between the B-flat and the B-natural, between any two adjacent notes, and so acute is his ability to hear the continuity of alternate pitches that he stays in tune with himself even as he remains at odds with conventional tuning. But if Coleman personifies a raw backwoods sound, his melodic skills cover the waterfront. For one splendid if arrant example, listen to him about three minutes into "Congeniality," when in the space of seconds he makes his way from a sustained blues wail through allusions to two classics (including Tchaikovsky's first piano concerto), connected by a-shave-and-a-haircut. Coleman rarely quotes anyone. What makes his every performance satisfying is the specificity with which his improvisations elaborate his compositions.

And what compositions! Yet another mystery is Coleman's willingness, somewhat allayed in recent years, to abandon most of them after a single recorded performance. The few that have become standards—"Turnaround," "Ramblin'," "Una Muy Bonita," the incomparably poignant "Lonely Woman"—are but a handful of the radiant pieces meriting additional investigation by Coleman and others. "Congeniality" is a stop-and-go theme that begins as a swing riff and rolls off into a ballad, rights itself, then rolls over again. "R.P.D.D." is a savory folklike melody with a dissonant tail and a blues riff for a middle part. After the head, Coleman takes his cue from Blackwell's jaunty snares and Scott LaFaro's resonating plucked bass and works up a calypso rhythm. The solo eventually works through every facet of the theme, modifying colors and tempo and dynamics.

That selection is from my favorite of Coleman's Atlantics, the album called *Ornette!* Unusual for LaFaro's ingenious sense of contrapuntal order, it has four of Coleman's finest tunes and consistently inspired long-form improvisations by him and Cherry. "W.R.U." is a flat-out rocker, with LaFaro holding down the beat behind one of Cherry's most lucid improvisations (Eddie Jefferson could have put a lyric to it); toward the climax, LaFaro's timbre takes on a vocal quality, as though conversing with the trumpet. Blackwell is at his attentive best, pumping like pistons. He converts Coleman's entrance into an extended turnback, never losing the beat. From the same session (but unreleased until 1971), comes the Tex-Mex serenade "Check Up," in which Coleman, navigating a deeply affecting solo, turns the rhythm around as Blackwell finds precisely the right kick to complement his hoedown inspiration. At moments like that, and they are plentiful, you realize that within the sphere of this music, avant-gardism per se is the last thing on anyone's mind.

Coleman's association with Atlantic peaked in influence with the thirty-seven-minute double-quartet improvisation, *Free Jazz*, an illuminating fantasia that inspired the new music movement and has yet to be equalled by Coleman or anyone else. It eloquently confirms two truths: (1) Virtuosity is relative—Freddie Hubbard is technically a more accomplished trumpet player than Don Cherry, but has a far more difficult time in a setting devoid of projected harmony; and, (2) Freedom is relative—musical patterns will assert themselves no matter how unbridled the situation. Coleman's Atlantic contract ended after two years, with *Ornette On Tenor*, a lovely oddity despite substandard tunes (the session's best selection, "Harlem's Manhattan," wasn't released until 1970), given the narrative strength and rakish tenor burr of Coleman's solos, especially on "Eos." After that, he participated in two pieces by Gunther Schuller, "Abstraction," playing a stark cadenza, and the clever "Variants on a Theme of Thelonious Monk (Criss-Cross)," which also has exceptional work by Eric Dolphy and Eddie Costa.

Having played Einstein to Charlie Parker's Newton, Coleman disappeared. After the final Atlantic session, in March 1961, he did not return to a recording studio for more than four years, marking the first of many sabbaticals. His intermittent returns invariably signaled new departures. In the '60s alone, these involved an ensemble that bonded strings and an r & b rhythm section; a swarming film score that was recorded but not used; a dazzling trio with bassist David Izenson and drummer

Charles Moffett (neither of whom were known in jazz circles before Coleman introduced them); a quartet with tenor saxophonist Dewey Redman
and Coleman's nine-year-old son Denardo on drums (ditto); works for
woodwind quintet and string quartet; and Coleman's own solos on violin, trumpet, and musette, on all of which he produced individual if
hardly orthodox sounds. His strongest work in those years are two trio
albums recorded in a Stockholm nightclub and released as *At the Golden
Circle, 1* and *2* (Blue Note).

In 1971, he signed with Columbia, and after recording an erratic album with a band augmented by poet and Indian singer, he debuted his
most ambitious work to date, a symphonic extravaganza of twenty-one
movements. *Skies of America* was designed to overwhelm, and does.
Boasting some of the most original yet diffuse writing for strings to be
found in or out of jazz, it was recorded in London in nine hours, after
two rehearsals, earning him a standing ovation from the eighty-five
members of the London Symphony. To describe the work, Coleman
coined the locution "harmolodic," a contraction of harmony, movement,
and melodic. As applied to a post–free jazz school that often configures
elements of jazz, rock, and Third-World musics (represented most decisively by the Master Musicians of Joujouka, Morocco), its meaning is as
nebulous as free jazz, bop, or swing. But regarding the symphony, Coleman had a specific idea in mind.

The harmolodic theory would permit every member of the orchestra
to improvise range at will, that is, transpose notes to any octave or key
while retaining the composed intervallic relationships. This method
would allow the musician to have creative input even though each part
is notated. The idea was to vary the music with each performance, and
toward that end he offered additional liberties: any instrument or group
of instruments can be substituted in improvised passages (played exclusively at Columbia's insistence by Coleman on the album); the work may
begin with any movement and the parts played in any sequence. The
only way to gauge the success of the theory would be to compare various
interpretations of the work, but since, as another one of those musical
white elephants, it is rarely played, the issue is moot. Ever the realist,
Coleman adapted the method to a small ensemble, which he introduced
more than three years later as Prime Time.

Skies of America is worthy of serious consideration. Coleman's for-
mulations give the impression of a more complicated and radical music
than the ear actually hears; his achievement is readily approachable and
can be enjoyed without the footnotes. If Coleman's skies are often sullen
and overcast, with storms sluggishly brewing above earthly rumblings,
they are illuminated by the robust glare of his alto saxophone and by

the heady thrust of festive melodies. The movements, ranging in duration from thirty-one seconds to four-and-a-half minutes, include such representative themes as "Holiday for Heroes" and "The Good Life" and an oddly Coplandish "Sunday in America." The textures are thick and occasionally logy, but numerous episodes indicating sadness, beauty, and passion are lucid and compelling. The opening theme, built on two long descending tones followed by two long ascending ones, is a recurring motif. Several melodic fragments reappear in different contexts, lending unity to the sundry themes. The first half concludes with "The Artist in America," in which Coleman's alto jubilantly courses over the strings. He is heard again in "Foreigner in a Free Land" and throughout the second half, including an unaccompanied solo on "The Men Who Live in the White House."

Prime Time made a clamorous debut with the 1977 album *Dancing in Your Head* (Horizon), which is something of a sequel in that the principal numbers, two versions of "Theme from a Symphony," are based on "The Good Life," now elongated by repetition from a quasi-blues to a fervid chant, and improved by an earthy final cadence. Beyond the guitar intro, which establishes an r & b framework, Coleman is the only soloist. Supported by a lusty unit of two guitars, bass, and drums, Coleman streams over the backbeat with dynamic certitude, offering one rousing lick after another, almost any one of which would fit the most primitive rural blues setting, or so it seems when one is caught in Coleman's spell. He undoubtedly wrote the two phrases bassist Rudy MacDaniel rotates during the theme and periodically throughout Coleman's solo. Only Mc-Daniel references the theme, in apparent collusion with Ronald Shannon Jackson, whose choked cymbals trigger its reappearances. The relentless, tempestuous rhythms and gut-wrenching intensity may prod some to dance. Most listeners are invariably transfixed or offended, never neutral. Significantly, the album was embraced by members of the rock press and reviled or ignored by the jazz commentators who had hailed the Atlantic-era quartets.

Body Meta (Artists House), recorded at the same 1976 sessions that produced "Theme from a Symphony" and released in 1978, expands Coleman's restive struggle to stay ahead of his audience. It's not the sustained firecracker that the earlier release was, but the variety of settings—five very different pieces—provide greater insight into the workings of his electrified quintet. Coleman's original approach to harmony was revolutionary because he did away with superimposed chord progressions, yet the serendipitous harmonies that resulted were basically consonant since the musicians were attempting to complement each other's key changes. With Prime Time, Coleman attacks harmonic rules from another angle, by deliberately placing different keys in opposition to each other. A wall-of-sound illusion is effected, as the contrasting keys make every instrument seem equal, and the sonic space created by these clashing harmonies makes it possible for the listener to sing or play along in any key and sound right. You have to learn to listen to Coleman's music all over again—his solos haven't changed appreciably, but a new environment has to be traversed to hear them. The rhythmic evolution is subtler; a backbeat is implied, yet the rhythms remain unimpeded by bar lines or, for the most part, fixed patterns.

Perhaps the most revealing place to begin is "European Echoes" since Coleman's 1965 recording of that waltz was a particular triumph. The first version (on *At the Golden Circle, Volume 1*) had an A theme with three notes per measure and an accent on every second beat, and a longer B theme with two notes per measure on the first two beats. In the new version, the A theme is twice as long, with the accent on the first beat (it's the difference between da DEE da da DEE da and DEE da da DEE da da; to accentuate the nursery-song effect in the later version, he syncopates initial measures as DEE da-da da-da), and the B part is completely revised as a brief anarchic figure that breaks with the waltz meter. This performance is unusual both because the harmonies are fairly consonant during the theme recitations (they broaden like parting icebergs during Coleman's improvisation) and because Coleman's solo is rather tenuous, lacking the compelling lucidity of his earlier version. "Voice Poetry" and "Home Grown" are excellent Coleman performances. The first begins with an interlude by the two guitars, bass, and drums on Bo Diddly's signature rhythm figure; Coleman enters wailing the blues with long, crying tones and proceeds with short, fragmented melodies that bustle and build with charismatic invention. "Home Grown" is a surreal hoedown, a swinging refraction of r & b with giddy colors from the discretely voiced instruments. Coleman's solo ends with a sequence of sustained pitches and frenzied, circular licks that wind seamlessly into the theme.

Prime Time's first phase culminated in 1979 with *Of Human Feelings* (Antilles), one of the first digitalized recordings, and was followed by another silence of more than five years. In the mid-'80s, Coleman was finally taken up by his hometown of Fort Worth, and presented in concert and on records by a geodesic arts center called Caravan of Dreams. Though usually heard with Prime Time, he participated in reunion appearances with Cherry, Haden, and Higgins, producing a superior but poorly distributed 1987 album, *In All Languages* (reissued in 1997 by Harmolodic/Verve). By this point, approaching sixty, he was regarded by many as something of a sage and attracted several unlikely musicians and other sympathetic artists. Jerry Garcia of the Grateful Dead jammed with him on a few selections for *Virgin Beauty* (Portrait). A more productive partnership with Pat Metheny produced a memorable Town Hall concert and *Song X* (Geffen), which, despite its passages of free-for-all density, offers a cooler, saltier Coleman than the Prime Time records. A good example is "Mob Job," a lighthearted performance of a tune that sweated heavy funk when introduced on *Of Human Feelings*; here, the appealing alto-guitar blend establishes a nearly elegaic mood. "Song X" is a bender that finds its soul in Coleman's serrated responses to Metheny's firestorm guitar solo. Coleman humanizes the piece, as he does "Video Games," entering with a fierce meow. "Endangered Species" is thirteen-minutes of free jazz without the spaciousness of *Free Jazz*, but "Kathelin Gray" is a twisty seductive melody played in flawless alto-guitar unison.

At the San Francisco Jazz Festival in 1994, Coleman's band shared the stage with a body-piercing expert whose bloody ministrations had the audience fleeing in disgust. The day was saved by the debut of Coleman's new quartet with Geri Allen on piano. Coleman hadn't worked with a pianist since his early years in Los Angeles, when he played an engagement with Paul Bley and recorded with Walter Norris. The received wisdom had it that Coleman felt constrained by piano, or at least by those pianists who could not get past its customary harmonic configurations. Of course, Cecil Taylor presented an ideal alternative, and they did rehearse privately on at least one occasion, but nothing came of it. In Allen he found an empathic collaborator, and two years later the piano quartet made a stunning debut on records with the release of two albums consisting almost entirely of the same material, arranged variously enough to circumvent accusations that they presented nothing more than alternate takes.

Sound Museum: Three Women and *Sound Museum: Hidden Man* (Harmolodic/Verve), described by Coleman as "one song and thirteen instrumentals," represent a return to straight-up acoustic quartet music and are among the most rapturously cogent recordings he has made. Coleman takes an inspired flyer at "What a Friend We Have in Jesus," balanced by a more tenuous undertaking of hip hop; revisits a few of his earlier compositions, including "European Echoes"; and endeavors once again, albeit briefly, to make sense of trumpet and violin. The support of bassist Charnett Moffett (the son of his drummer in the '60s) and Denardo Coleman is focused and stimulating, fully engaged with Coleman's jaunty inventions. Geri Allen is a revelation, her reflexes perfectly attuned to Coleman, so that she shadows his every conceit while greatly enhancing the spectacle. This is immensely pleasing music, and one is reluctant to return from it to the tempered world.

Through all the varied settings he has employed, Coleman never compromised his miraculous human sound. His quarter-tone pitch remains as fixed as the North Star, directing the listener to a distinctive realm where tears and laughter amalgamate. It may be that all his innovations in free harmony, polyphonic keys, and jostling rhythms proceed from his uneering accuracy in pitching his notes into the cracks of the tempered scale. Coleman has changed the way we hear the past as well as the present: we can't help but detect his ragged blues effects in earlier traditions, yet we know that the bluesmen he sought to play with in his native Texas dismissed him as simply out of tune. By the mid-'60s, Coleman seemed downright melodious in light of such torrential recordings as John Coltrane's *Ascension* and Cecil Taylor's *Unit Structures*. But he never allowed his audience to grow complacent. He kept upping the ante and changing the rules. All that remains constant is the "warmth of a human voice," which never fails him.

52 ❖ *John Coltrane*
(Metamorphosis)

"Chasin' the Trane," recorded by John Coltrane on a November 1961 evening at the Village Vanguard, is one of those crucial performances in which we can hear the subversion of a sensibility and a yearning for new worlds. Unlike Cecil Taylor and Ornette Coleman, Coltrane did not come to jazz from a tangential realm, like New England classicism or southwestern r & b. Though a late bloomer, he was a practiced, died-in-the-wool jazz player who apprenticed with Dizzy Gillespie and Johnny Hodges before making his name with Miles Davis and Thelonious Monk. When he began to attract attention, at age thirty, he was not universally acclaimed. On the contrary, he was reproved for lacking originality (believe it or not), a sweet tone, and concision—never because he lacked authenticity. By the time he arrived at the Vanguard that fall, however, he was a true jazz celebrity, basking in the afterglow of a huge and improbable hit, "My Favorite Things," and buoyed by an auspicious contract with an unfledged record label called Impulse. A few weeks later, *Down Beat* caught up with him in Hollywood. Coltrane, it reported, had plunged into "musical nonsense" and "anti-jazz."

A chasm had opened between the Coltrane available on records and the one appearing down the street, and it never really closed during his few remaining years. When his latest foray hit the stores, Coltrane was already three orbits beyond it. The closely timed releases of his first Impulse LPs, *Africa/Brass* and *Live at the Village Vanguard*, put the issue on the turntable for all to hear, pitting those ardent in their devotion against those who were appalled, exasperated, shocked, and so forth, ad nauseum. Several of his former allies threw up their hands in frustration. Martin Williams considered the first album diffuse and monotonous— "in effect, an extended cadenza to a piece that never gets played." Ira Gitler, one of Coltrane's earliest champions, dismissed the second album's "Chasin' the Trane" as boring and monotonous—"one big airleak." Pete Welding, taking a more-in-sorrow-than-anger tack, cited that performance as "one of the noblest failures on record." A newer generation of pundits, delighted with the turn Coltrane's music took, defended him at equal pitch. The oratory threatened to drown out the music: Was he a misdirected zealot or (consult the '60s journal *Jazz & Pop* for the most lurid hyperbole) the son of God?

"Chasin' the Trane" couldn't fail to cause a furor. For one thing, it is sixteen minutes long and seemed even longer when it occupied the entire side of an LP. For another, it is a marathon tenor saxophone solo, accompanied by bass and drums, based on the blues. Five years earlier, the establishment popped its fingers in admiration when Ellington's Paul Gonsalves played a twenty-seven-chorus blues entr'acte at the Newport Jazz Festival. Coltrane wails for about eighty choruses. *Of course it's diffuse, boring, and monotonous!* At least, for those who didn't share the vision. For those who did, those adjectives are no more relevant than, say, "supple," "lyrical," and "cool." It was the cumulative power, the existential yawp, the go-cat-go! mien of the piece that knocked us for a loop. Williams wrote that Coleman Hawkins and Jimmie Noone accomplished similar ends in a mere chorus or two, as if brevity was the predominant virtue. Is Webern sharper than Mahler and Beckett shrewder than Joyce? The duration of "Chasin' the Trane"—art as imposition—is part of what makes it preeminent and indispensable. That imposition is validated by a sweat-soaked fury of resolute musical invention.

A two-chorus version is not possible. Even a ten-minute version would not have had the same impact, we now know, because in 1977 Impulse released a performance of that length recorded the previous evening. The piece itself is basically a compact phrase modulated through the changes of a twelve-bar blues. Coltrane claimed the performance was spontaneous, and it is probably true that the head was not thought through (it certainly had no title). Yet he does draw on a specific motive in each of three versions recorded during the Vanguard engagement. In the short one, he is backed by drummer Elvin Jones and bassist Reggie Workman and spelled by Eric Dolphy, on alto saxophone. The pianist McCoy Tyner lays out. Coltrane dives in for twenty-four laps, and though he occasionally tromps bar lines, pulping a few choruses, the integrity of the twelve-bar format is intractably protected by Workman's bass and Jones's turnback rolls and first-beat accents. Dolphy aggressively attempts to blur chorus structure and creates a firestorm midway in his solo, but his presence dilutes the obstinacy of Coltrane's lone-eagle drive.

The second version is in a similar vein though posthumously released as "Chasin' Another Trane"—presumably because no one was able to identify the blues head played twice at the top and because Coltrane reprises the "Chasin' the Trane" theme in his final choruses. It's in B-flat (the other two are in F) and Roy Haynes sits in for Jones on drums, but the outline is the same—Tyner out, Workman on bass, Dolphy on alto—and the chorus structure is plainly defined. This performance is virtually as long as the classic one, but it is the least effective. Coltrane opens with thirty-six repetitious choruses, mowing down changes, subdividing meter, and cranking up dissonances, but always returning to the tonic at chorus-end, as though the blues were a vise he could not escape. You find yourself rooting for him to break free, and he almost does—midway (choruses seventeen through nineteen) and at the end, girding himself (chorus twenty-nine) with guttural honks. Dolphy's rhythmic patterns are more conventional than Coltrane's, but he goes further out, only to be soundly trumped by Workman's forceful four-beat walk and Haynes's elegant, turnback-attentive drumming. Not to be outdone, Coltrane rather brazenly cuts him off as he returns for another seventeen choruses of stubborn push-and-pull. Ornette Coleman once said he knew he was on the right track when he realized he could make mistakes, an epiphany that may have occurred to Coltrane when he made his decision about which version to include on the album.

The classic "Chasin' the Trane" is not intent on inducing a trance (at least no more so than any other piece of music), but it is intent on provoking immediate interest (like every piece of music) and sustaining it through an imaginative force of will. Coltrane's desire to generate an extended blues rush is indicated in his excluding Tyner. Like Sonny Rollins, he had contemplated the innovations of Cecil Taylor, with whom he recorded in 1958, and Ornette Coleman, with whose sidemen he recorded in 1960, as well as the scalar approach explored with Davis. In pushing jazz orthodoxies to but not through the wall, Coltrane employs everything he has learned in order to challenge the validity of what he had already mastered. It isn't just his sensibility on the line, but that of jazz. As a jazz insider, his metamorphosis had uniquely populist implications.

"Chasin' the Trane" was the most vivid documentation of his struggle to date. Bassist Jimmy Garrison (who took over from Workman and remained Coltrane's bassist until the end) instantly establishes a firm blues grid at a breakneck tempo: a measure per second. Midway through the second chorus, Coltrane rails against the grid with a squawking dissonance, yet returns to the confines of the twelve-bar form. No matter how far afield he goes, he upholds the playful quality of the theme, recurrent and childlike, for the duration of the performance, suggesting a kind of cantillation new to jazz. The more Coltrane limits himself—in a manner that reflects his interest in Indian and African musics—the more he seeks. The blues is the lowest common denominator in jazz, however much harmonic finery may be employed to dress it up. Coltrane certifies its primeval state by stripping away all mitigating niceties. Gone are the piano, routine theme, harmonic substitutions, auxiliary soloist(s), call-and-response, and conventional duration. He attenuates the music still more by draining his virtuoso technique—sanding the shine off his sound, indulging a glossary of false notes, overtones, and vocalisms. He pushes himself and the blues to the limits of endurance, drawing light from dark, pleasure from pain, liberation from constraint.

In honing his virtuosity, Coltrane had spent countless hours obsessively practicing Nicolas Slonimsky's *Thesaurus of Scales and Melodic Patterns* (1947). Where Coleman Hawkins had perfected a method of rifling every chord in a harmonic sequence, Coltrane experimented with a rapid-fire attack in an attempt to play all the notes in every chord, unleashing what Ira Gitler described as "sheets of sound." "Chasin' the Trane" implies dissatisfaction with that method, a desire to pare down harmony and escape any form—chords, choruses, the tempered scale—that keeps him from an elusive grail of total expressiveness. Garrison and Jones follow him (with formidable concentration), giving him his head, but whenever he threatens to push beyond the blues, they bring him home. On at least two dozen occasions, especially toward the end of the piece, when Coltrane sets up a Delphic flurry, Jones telegraphs the coming chorus with a roll. At one point Garrison backs him with two choruses of double stops, inspiring Coltrane to a kind of overblown dialog with himself. Imagine if they had followed his lead, abandoning the structure, encouraging him to go further out into space, as Sonny Murray did Cecil Taylor. Years later Coltrane did make that leap (and called it *Ascension*). In the meantime, notice that "Chasin' the Trane" doesn't really end; it stops. Nor does it really begin; it just starts. The performance is all middle, an immense tide, a transition.

John William Coltrane was as doubtful a candidate for revolution as Malcolm X. He was born in North Carolina in 1926 and educated at music schools in Philadelphia, where he joined Jimmy Heath's legendary unrecorded big band. That association led to a job for both of them with Dizzy Gillespie in 1949, by which time Coltrane had worked in a variety of jazz and r & b bands, some well-known (Cleanhead Vinson, Earl Bostic), others hunkered in music's lower depths. He is said to have "walked the bar," a crude display of contortionist honking for tips. By the time he auditioned for Miles Davis in 1955, he had a distinctive if not fully formed style, and within six months, Sonny Rollins invited him to take part in "Tenor Madness," a singular tribute if you consider that Coltrane's first important sessions with Davis hadn't even been issued.

Coltrane's breakthrough year was 1957, when he took a leave from Davis and participated in more than twenty recording sessions, exhibiting the glow and urgency that became his trademarks. His key recordings that year included the haunting ballad, "Monk's Mood" and the dizzying "Trinkle Tinkle," with Monk; trio performances of "Trane's Slow Blues" and "Like Someone in Love"; collaborations with Mal Waldron, Sonny Clark, Johnny Griffin, and Art Blakey; Prestige all-star dates; and the princely Blue Note album *Blue Trane*, which brought to the fore his great skill as a composer ("Moment's Notice"). He was equally prolific in 1958. One reason he recorded so much was to support a narcotics habit that had long stymied his career, and even now threatened to keep him running in place as a musicians' musician. He was the same age as Davis, thirty-three, and still his sideman on the epochal *Kind of Blue*. Yet in the immediately preceding months, something happened: Coltrane underwent a religious conversion (described in the notes to his celebrational masterpiece, *A Love Supreme*), and he renounced drugs and alcohol. With surprising assurance, he finally took up the reins as bandleader.

Coltrane's conviction and acumen impressed everyone who worked with him. He knew what he wanted and how to get it, musically and professionally. His 1961 contract with Impulse guaranteed him complete control of his recordings, graphics as well as music, something few pop stars had in those days. The speed with which he transformed his music has been attributed to his recognition that the years of drugs and drink wounded him irrevocably, that he was living on borrowed time and in much pain. Slonimsky's *Lexicon of Musical Invective* reminds us that locating an artist's quiddity in his organs is old hat. The "incomprehensible wildness" of Beethoven's later works was attributed in 1837 to his deafness: "His imagination seems to have fed upon the ruins of his sensitive organs." Beethoven, in fact, offers a template for several gripes about Coltrane. "If [the *Eroica* Symphony] is not by some means abridged, it will soon fall into disuse." The Missa Solemnis is "an incomprehensible production [generating] absolute bewilderment." The "incomprehensible" Ninth Symphony found "the great man upon the ocean of harmony, without the compass which had so often guided him to the haven of success." Every infatuation may not be luminous in its own way, but uncomprehending criticism is always the same.

Coltrane's first major signing was with Atlantic Records, a brief interlude of relative tranquility before the blitz. The Atlantics are often undervalued for reasons that have nothing to do with musical quality. Falling between the '50s apprenticeship and the deliverance at Impulse, they bear the stigma of mutation, a delineation underscored by the laggardly way they were released. The Atlantic contract covered little more than two years, 1959-61, yet the eight major albums were released over seven years, the later ones competing with the more timely and sensational records made for Impulse. Still, the Atlantics produced Coltrane's signature theme ("My Favorite Things"), his best known compositions ("Giant Steps," "Naima," "Equinox," "Mr. P. C."), his first widely noted montuna ("Olé"), and the beginnings of his defining ensemble. Reassessment was spurred in 1995 when his work for the label was collected as *Heavyweight Champion* (Rhino).

Coltrane *was* mutating, of course, but when was he not? He had just left Davis and had not yet formed his great quartet, though as of October 1960 McCoy Tyner and Elvin Jones were on board and the generic combination of tenor saxophone and rhythm began to turn into an association of interchange and engagement. Throughout these albums we hear Coltrane resolving some problems and leaving others unfinished. One could hardly hope for a more dramatic vault into sunlight than the journey from his tempered work with Milt Jackson through an aborted attempt at *Giant Steps* to the radiant accomplishment of *Giant Steps* itself. Also revealing is the contrast between his weak debut on soprano saxophone on "The Blessing" (from *The Avant-Garde*, a 1960 session with Don Cherry that wasn't released until 1966) and the incomparable "My Favorite Things."

Harbingers are everywhere. Coltrane's duet with drummer Art Taylor on "Countdown" has new implications in light of his work with Rashied Ali on *Expression* and *Interstellar Space* recorded a few months before his death. "I'll Wait and Pray," an obscure (has anyone else recorded it?) thirty-two-bar ballad that tended to get lost on *Coltrane Jazz*, assumes more interest among his complete Atlantics. For one thing, both the master and alternate takes end with a carefully prepared split-tone, also worked into the head and improvisation of the same album's "Harmonique," perhaps his first recorded multiphonics caper and charming in its coy precision. For another, "I'll Wait and Pray" is a telling precursor to the aphoristic ballad style he would unveil three years later in Impulse's songful triad (*Ballads* and the albums with Duke Ellington and Johnny Hartman), where he didn't need even that extra half-chorus to lay total claim to a song. His sculpted sound, as every note is diligently intoned, is already apparent. How odd that so mediocre a tune should engender new expressiveness in his ballad playing along with the antic hay of split-tones.

Of the pianists who preceded McCoy Tyner, Tommy Flanagan is the most impressive, more willing to absorb Coltrane's rhythmic designs—he personifies confidence on "Mr. P. C."—than Wynton Kelly, who favors the practiced canter of bebop rhythms. Yet not until Tyner arrives does Coltrane find a true soul mate, with a dark, muffled sound, full-bodied chords, a predilection for vamps, a gift for economy, and a rhythmic charge inseparable from his dramatic purpose. On "Body and Soul," he is Teddy Wilson to Coltrane's Benny Goodman, establishing the routine with his intro and playing a much superior improvisation. Coltrane tries harder on the alternate take, but to little avail. He may be the only great tenor saxophonist born before 1940 who didn't leave a mark on that tune. Coltrane's preferred approach to extended slow-motion improvisations would become apparent in such Impulse landmarks as "I Want To Talk About You," "Alabama," and (from *A Love Supreme*) "Psalm."

Coltrane's Sound and *Olé Coltrane* were in some respects the most advanced of Coltrane's Atlantic albums, and the former—with its raging Latin arrangement of "The Night Has a Thousand Eyes" and the indelible blues "Equinox"—would have had a greater impact had it been released when it was current and not in 1964. The selection that really shakes with impatience for a new music is "Blues to You," from *Coltrane Plays the Blues*, now coupled with an alternate take—an unmistakable predecessor to "Chasin' the Trane." Elvin Jones is at his most empathic here in what is essentially a duet, as Coltrane employs multiphonics and other harmonic feints to transcend the melodic figure at its heart.

Which leaves the other Coltrane, mourned by so many in the mid-'60s who felt abandoned by his leatherstocking jaunt into inner space. The symbolic masterwork of Everyman's Coltrane is "My Favorite

Things," one of the most purely voluptuous records ever made. The album of the same name was released in the spring of 1961 and was instantly taken up by jazz radio, one of the few blockbusters between Dave Brubeck's "Take Five" and Stan Getz and Charlie Byrd's "Desafinado." It was still getting airplay two years later, impressive for a cut nearly fourteen minutes long. But everything about it is impressive. Tyner opens with a piano vamp that may be the most famous intro since Duke Jordan's preamble to Charlie Parker's "Bird of Paradise." Tyner's figure didn't become the universally imitated cliché Jordan's did because few musicians could find much value in the song itself: its lineage is strictly by John Coltrane out of Mary Martin. Another aspect of the performance *was* widely imitated: Coltrane's use of and the sound he produced on the soprano saxophone. Excepting Steve Lacy (only a cult figure in the late '50s), Johnny Hodges (who stopped playing it twenty years before), and Sidney Bechet (who died in 1959), the instrument was largely ignored in jazz. Coltrane's sound combined his usual robustness with an eastern wail, underscored by the repetitive nature of the song's melody and a triple-time vamp that was appealing, modern, and novel. Within a decade, countless tenor, alto, and baritone saxophonists, including a number of Coltrane's seniors, were doubling on soprano, trying to keep the damn thing in tune.

Though he posed with the soprano on album jackets, Coltrane continued to focus on the tenor. But "My Favorite Things" took on a life of its own as a yardstick of his growth, tracking his flight through and beyond "Chasin' the Trane": some forty-five versions are said to exist on tape, recorded between 1960 and 1967. While his interpretations grew increasingly brazen (the one on *Live at the Village Vanguard Again* is a wondrously punishing example), he maintained the basic arrangement of the minor-key waltz that he introduced on the hit record. "My Favorite Things" was his good luck charm—all he needed was two-bars of the opening tremolo to bring down the house. The Atlantic version, recorded when he was still finding his way (you can hear him test some of its ideas on tenor on "Village Blues" from the same session), is an enduring delight—almost erotic in its opulence, emotionally generous, technically flawless.

Small wonder, then, that fans who expected him to revel in his success recoiled at the changes he exhibited at the Vanguard in November 1961. In 1997, Impulse finally got around to assembling all the recordings that were made during four evenings of that engagement and released them as *The Complete 1961 Village Vanguard Recordings*. "Chasin' the Trane" is still the centerpiece, but now it has a context that makes it seem even stronger and harder won. Unlike the Miles Davis Plugged Nickel restoration, this isn't a comprehensive document; the tapes rolled only when Coltrane played the nine candidates for inclusion in the album, preserving between thirty-six and eighty-five minutes of music from each of four nights. In reconstructing those evenings for the first time (with new versions of "India," "Naima," and "Miles' Mode"), the complete Vanguard tapes reveal a variety that is almost as startling as the intensity for which the performances are famous. A dissimilarity in instrumentation and style is far more noticeable here than on the original albums. Also underscored is the feisty dynamism of Eric Dolphy, who seemed rather shy on the initial albums.

Consider, for example, the second-night transitions from the two blues yawps—especially "Chasin' the Trane," which gets conspicuously strong applause—to "India" or "Greensleeves" and the medleylike convergence of "India" and "Spiritual," boasting one of Dolphy's most invigorating solos. Because the twenty-two performances cover only nine pieces, the four discs unfold with a catchy circularity, heightened by recurring vamps and triple meters. One piece that evolves most powerfully is "Impressions," a bobbing AABA spinoff of Davis's "So What" (Coltrane uses that title when playing it the first time), with a release built on a phrase from Ravel's "Pavane pour une infante defunte." In the first version, Dolphy plays the ensemble riff from *Kind of Blue*; on subsequent versions, he lays out. Other selections include "Spiritual," an elaboration on a recollected spiritual, played rubato and in three; "Greensleeves," a triple-meter adaptation in the manner of "My Favorite Things"; "India," based on a ragalike drone, underscored by Ahmed Abdul-Malik's oud; and the 1928 Sigmund Romberg aria, "Softly, As in a Morning Sunrise," altered so confidently into an uptempo chant, with Tyner stating the melody and Coltrane essaying inspired variations, that it is often assumed to be a Coltrane original.

If the Vanguard represented a new path—to anti-jazz!—the recordings of late 1962 and early 1963 suggest an abrupt detour, if not a retreat. A quartet session with Duke Ellington, in which each man's rhythm players take turns, proves a surprisingly heady experience as Coltrane turns increasingly to scalar improvisation and Ellington matches him with elliptical substitutions. Yet their most successful selection is "In a Sentimental Mood," in which Ellington shapes an indelible vamp and Coltrane demonstrates how completely he could transfigure a melody: it remains the finest recording of Ellington's great 1935 ballad. The strength of Coltrane's personality would subsequently inform Ellington's *Far East Suite*. Ellington's impact on Coltrane was apparent almost immediately in *Ballads*, a recital of eight songs closely associated with Frank Sinatra, Bing Crosby, Nat Cole, and Dick Haymes, all utterly transformed with minimal improvisation by Coltrane and his exemplary rhythm team. Tyner, Garrison, and Jones display subtlety and rapport throughout. A comparison of the three selections recorded before the Ellington date ("It's Easy To Remember," "Nancy," and "What's New") with those that followed reveal an increased intensity and economy, especially on the Sinatra classics, "All or Nothing at All" and "Say It (Over and Over Again)." The subsequent collaboration with singer Johnny Hartman expands on that emotional candor, his tenor caressing Hartman's baritone with sensuous affinity.

Throughout 1963 and 1964, Coltrane attempted, not always successfully, to blend the clamor and the serenity that infused his music. The records were generally more conservative than his live appearances, one of which—Newport, July 1963—is indicative of his impasse. With Roy Haynes briefly back on drums, Coltrane plays three career milestones: "I Want To Talk About You," an important ballad from his Prestige years; "My Favorite Things"; and one of the breakthrough Vanguard numbers, "Impressions." (These selections and "Chasin' Another Trane" were collected on CD as *Newport '63*.) Like Miles Davis at the Plugged Nickel three years later, he was working his old book, but in a new way. "I Want To Talk About You" had recently become a routine part of his sets, and in the fall he would record the definitive version during an engagement at Birdland. The Newport version is irresistible. Though Coltrane locks onto the melody, he and Haynes renovate the rhythms, beginning leisurely and moving in unison into the knotty, swinging momentum of the second chorus. The drummer monitors the saxophonist's every gesture, provoking him at one point with something akin to a shuffle beat. Instead of playing a third chorus, though, Coltrane returns to the bridge and after sixteen bars embarks on a spellbinding cadenza.

The dynamic if overlong version of "My Favorite Things" is noteworthy for Haynes's aggressive, rousing patterns. Where Elvin Jones creates a landscape of cymbals vibrations, Haynes sticks closer to the skins; where Jones superimposes three over two, Haynes thinks two even when he's playing three, and he varies the triple-meter rhythm with unflagging energy. The piece is an incantatory waltz, sustained by a riveting Tyner solo (the only one he played all evening), after which Coltrane returns with a shout of joy, amplifying his patented tremolos until they reverberate like the ecstatic thundering of two saxophonists. More hair-raising is "Impressions," which, except for a two-minute opening exposition and a forty-five-second coda by the quartet, is a duet for tenor saxophone and drums. The bar lines are shaken, the chords willfully abandoned, and Haynes has no light to guide him beyond the sparks of the saxophonist, who is on a tear—building to an outsized hallelujah chorus.

In December 1964, Coltrane recorded his most personal statement, the autobiographical four-part suite and canticle *A Love Supreme*, a quintessential recording that underscored Coltrane's preeminence in the '60s. It was the first new Coltrane album in several years to receive almost universally enthusiastic reviews. The album's breakthrough aura was emphasized by the record label, which replaced its patented orange spine and color graphics with a spartan black and white design. Coltrane's enormous influence was at this point undeniable. An expanding coterie of musicians looked to him as a leader (he used his clout at Impulse to get several of them recorded, including Archie Shepp, Roswell Rudd, and Marion Brown), and a generation of listeners depended on him as a shepherd for a music that was hurtling into no-man's-land. *A Love Supreme* solemnizes the enduring vigor of Coltrane's devotional conversion and his liberation from addiction. It honors the members of his quartet and indicates a culmination, a blending of his work in various styles and the reintroduction of formal discipline. Each compact movement is carefully organized. The improvisations combine scales, free-form departures, and dashing swing passages, and Coltrane's affecting *cri de coeur* grabs the listener with his first heraldic phrases.

Coltrane's liner notes, accompanied by a charcoal portrait of him, allude to his religious experience of 1957 and include a psalm that became the basis of the fourth movement, a triumphant adaptation of the traditional canticle. The episode is improvised entirely from the syllabic content of the psalm, beginning with the title ("A Love Supreme") and frequently punctuated with an amen phrase, "Thank you God." He had tried a similar gambit in "Alabama," which was inspired by the vocal inflection of Martin Luther King's eulogy for the murdered children, but here every melodic phrase is specifically wedded to the psalm. While not uncommon in liturgical music (a congregation of Orthodox Jews may simultaneously improvise many melodies for a prayer), the practice has little precedent in jazz—perhaps only Ellington's 1958 recording, *Black, Brown and Beige*, for which Mahalia Jackson improvised a melody to the Twenty-third Psalm. *A Love Supreme* was heard by many as a refuge from the torrential marathon solos. It was actually a prestorm lullaby.

At the very moment critics were cheering *A Love Supreme*, Coltrane was in the studio with ten acolytes recording a piece that made "Chasin' the Trane," which was only three-and-a-half years old, sound as comforting as Dixieland by comparison. After nearly thirty-five years, it is still impossible to speak of *Ascension* without a word of caution. It is the single most vexatious work in jazz history. So, a word of caution: It can't hurt you. In fact, contrary to its reputation as the apogee in '60s free-jazz rants, the piece goes down as smooth as bourbon, at least after you've heard it a few times and can no longer be intimidated by its shock tactics. The nearly forty-minute work was performed twice at a single session in the summer of 1965 by a band of good soldiers (including a couple of uninvited guests): the John Coltrane Quartet, four saxophonists, two trumpet players, and a second bassist. Shortly after take one was released, the second take was issued in an almost identical jacket; the only difference, not visible to the potential consumer, was the corrected last paragraph of the liner notes (originally, the annotator, A. B. Spellman, had confused the obscure Dewey Johnson with Freddie Hubbard in the lineup of soloists—ironically, the correction was only valid for take one). You couldn't tell which performance you were buying unless you surreptitiously slit the shrinkwrap and peeked at the disc: on the vinyl of the later version was scratched the legend "Edition II."

Ascension is based on a minor triad and a couple of ground chords for the ensemble passages—that's it. The format consists of alternating solos and ensemble passages, the latter mandated to climax as crescendos in which the wind instruments freely bellow. At first blush, it might be described as a terrible din periodically interrupted so that a soloist can bellow in peace. The density of the work is far beyond Ornette Coleman's comparatively airy *Free Jazz*. Once again, the length of the work is integral to its intent. Coming to the end of the music's long night, you may blink at the silence in stunned relief and inscrutable rapture. Or you may not. In any case, return visits to *Ascension* reveal it as decreasingly monolithic. Fake notes—cackles and hollers and shrieks and squawks—are still notes, and fortuitous harmonies and melodies, forged in the cauldron of chance, will on repeated exposure seem as preordained as composed music.

The combined strength of the two takes mitigates some of the melodrama that clings to the single work. Intentionality becomes clearer, as do the choices each musician makes. The listener is more likely to trust *Ascension* as he or she comes to realize that some passages are more successful than others. The second take has a more expansive mood, and at the time it slipped into stores, Coltrane said he prefered it. But the edgier hysterics of Edition I are not to be denied, and the first version has more electrifying solos by Coltrane, Archie Shepp (granite talking), and John Tchicai (an oasis of lyricism), as well as a shining bass duet by Jimmy Garrison and Art Davis. Dewey Johnson is lamentable, but brief.

Hubbard runs out of ideas before his solo is up, but the first two-thirds of his invention go right to the heart of the matter, and he is consistently effective in the ensemble passages, which are maddening at first but reveal many nits on which to hang one's attention, not least the splashing of Elvin Jones's cymbals and the grinding of the two basses.

The two versions of *Ascension* were brought together on CD in a collection with the preposterous title, *The Major Works of John Coltrane*. The other selections—*Om*, "Selflessness," "Kulu Se Mama"—are not major achievements, but they serve the perverse purpose of underscoring the distinction between free music at its best and free music that implodes. *Om* (long rumored to have been recorded on LSD) may not be the worst record Coltrane ever made, but it's a contender, a gallimaufry of self-indulgence. The more compelling "Kulu Se Mama" is far less adroit than the shorter selections initially released with it, recorded the same month as *Ascension*: the tenor-drums duet "Vigil" and the rubato quartet "Welcome." The latter, described by one Coltrane specialist as "a yearning altissimo melody," will be recognized by most as the third phrase of "Happy Birthday".

For that matter, "Pop Goes the Weasel" plays a significant role in *Meditations*, the consumingly tough yet tremulous album that embodied changes sure to try the souls of the most faithful loyalists. Coltrane was now using two drummers, Rashied Ali along with Jones, who soon got fed up and left. (Weeks later, Tyner was replaced by Alice McLeod Coltrane, the saxophonist's wife, whose heavy touch couldn't hide her limitations as a soloist.) The most sensational aspect of *Meditations*, however, was the introduction of Pharoah Sanders, a twenty-five-year-old tenor saxophonist from Little Rock, and Coltrane's first frontline partner since Eric Dolphy. Sanders was a one-man *Ascension*, all hidden register squeals and overtones, and Coltrane encouraged him to take up where he left off. Those who had followed Coltrane to the edge of the galaxy now had the added challenge of a player who appeared to have little contact with earth. Nevertheless, the music has an encompassing, sweeping, deliberate radiance. The musicians seemed to know what they were doing even if no one else did.

With Tyner's departure after *Meditations*, Sanders and Garrison became Coltrane's supporting soloists—the former magnifying his already blinding intensity, the latter no less ardent but a lot less loud. Rashied Ali's metrically free approach owed much to the innovations of Sunny Murray and Milford Graves, but he had a firm pulse, and his ability to maintain a responsive equanimity inspired Coltrane to some of his more exhilarating performances. He continued to use familiar themes as touchstones: "My Favorite Things" (nightly), "Out of This World" (*Live in*

Seattle), a few standard ballads (apparently unrecorded). Yet apart from stating the melodies, those late performances cruise beyond recognizable harmonic and structural guideposts: It's a wonder the musicians can make transitions in unison and end at the same time. *Live at the Village Vanguard Again* (May 1966), with explosive readings of "Naima" and "My Favorite Things," is an unbridled souvenir of Coltrane's last band at its best: nothing mystical or arcane, no verbal chanting, very little scene setting—just two strenuously effective post-*Ascension* performances. Also exceptional are the duets with Ali: "Offering" is the highlight of *Expression*, the last album Coltrane approved for release and the only instance of his ponderous attempt to play flute. The six selections that make up the posthumous *Interstellar Space* represent the pinnacle of his work with Ali, as does a session that wasn't released until 1995 (*Stellar Regions*), especially the stormy tenor-drums episode on "Configuration," which is a kind of eight-year update on the Atlantic-era "Countdown."

Never as undisciplined or anarchic as he sounded, Coltrane worked over familiar scales and hymnlike themes until the end. We are left with the artifacts of a brilliant career, of a journey into music's darker realm, available to anyone willing to put aside most preconceptions about music and art. Coltrane is almost certainly the only figure in American music in whose name a church has been consecrated (still serving a congregation in San Francisco), but you don't have to chant "omani-padme-hum" or buy into his religious ardor to board his express. Very few have. He was followed because he excited the senses and kept his audience in a state of balmy apprehension. It helped that he never gave cause to doubt his motives or aspirations. Everything about Coltrane other than his music was conciliatory, even ingenuous. We awaited each transforming step with the pleasurable tingle of foreboding. We retrace each step with the solace of affirmation.

Coltrane altered the flavor of jazz. He didn't force a comprehensive retooling of the music, as Armstrong and Parker did, but he instigated a reimagining of possibilities and brought back a solemnity of purpose that shook up the old order. Even Armstrong made records ("Chim Chim Cheree" and "We Shall Overcome") that demonstrated Coltrane's prevailing influence in popularizing scales, pedal points, vamps. Saxophonists as varied as Dexter Gordon, Harold Land, Art Pepper, Stan Getz, and Frank Foster adjusted their styles to accommodate the changes he brought about in the instrument. His urgent attack struck a chord with rock musicians, who improvised extended scalar solos built on pedal points. Conservatory saxophonists began exploring the harmonics and overtones he perfected. Coltrane was slavishly imitated then diluted then parodied. But he opened up doors that remain open for anyone with the nerve to tresspass.

When Coltrane died in the summer of 1967, jazz died a bit, too. Where was he headed? What was the next frontier? For thousands of people around the world, Coltrane *was* the '60s, an ethical and cultural leader, an exemplary guide. In his absence, the music faltered for several years until another generation forged ahead by pulling back. Coltrane was planning a trip to Africa at the time of his death, and it is likely he would have continued his investigation of world musics, perhaps treading with Ellington through the Afro-Eurasian eclipse and coming home to a rapprochement with the traditions he mastered and abandoned. "The main thing a musician would like to do," Coltrane said, "is to give a picture to the listener of the many wonderful things he knows of and senses in the universe." When Miles asked him why he played so long, he answered, "It took that long to get it all in." In truth, he didn't play long enough, and we can't help but ponder what he would have played next.

53 ❖ Duke Ellington
(Part 3: At the Pulpit)

The cover photograph on the original 1975 album from Duke Ellington's third sacred concert, *The Majesty of God* (RCA), is uncommonly affecting. Standing before a microphone with his hands clasped before him, he has an unself-conscious, boyish smile on his face. His eyes are closed, whether in deference to the spotlight or a prayer isn't clear. He appears to be basking in the artificial light, and the choirboy attitude is enforced by the ruffled bow under his chin, the collar of a blue satin jacket dappled with white or silver specks. His hair, carefully groomed in front, trails anarchistically over his shoulders. The picture denies the illness ravaging his tired frame. Six months later he was dead, and there can be little doubt that he attached great significance to the last edition of what he considered his most important work, the sacred concerts.

The third sacred concert is revealing, moving, and on occasion inspired. Performed at Westminster Abbey after hasty rehearsals, it is illuminating in part for showing how Ellington coped with the insoluble problem of having outlived his band. Of the major Ellington interpreters, only Harry Carney and Russell Procope were present. Cootie Williams did not make the trip, and Paul Gonsalves, who did, was taken ill at the last minute; his solos were given to Harold Ashby, the last of the saxophonists called upon to retain the Ben Webster sound in the Ellington palette. The fine Swedish singer Alice Babs was recruited, however, and the maestro predictably focused the new work on her, Carney, and the piano. The orchestra, a shadow of its precedessors, was relegated to the background. Most of the music acquits itself admirably on its own terms.

The three sacred concerts differ in several ways, so an arc in the composer's attitude can be traced from the energetic, proudly secular *Concert of Sacred Music* (RCA), created in 1965, to the more ambitious and strenuously verbal *Second Sacred Concert* (Fantasy), in 1968, to the quietly effective last work of October 1973. "These concerts are not the traditional mass jazzed up," Ellington wrote. His familiar dictum, "Every man prays in his own language and there is no language that God does not understand," reminds the listener that he did not attempt to apply his genius to an established idiom, but rather to bring his own music intact to the church. The difference between playing for people, whether at the Cotton Club or Westminster Abbey, and creating for the greater glory of God was not lost on him. When Father Norman O'Connor commissioned a jazz mass (apparently never completed), Ellington observed, "One may be accustomed to speaking to people, but suddenly to attempt to speak, sing, and play directly to God—that puts one in an entirely new and different position." He prayed on his own musical terms and celebrated the talents of his collaborators accordingly. "All the members of the band played in character," he said of the first sacred concert. He did not abandon the Cotton Club; he brought the Cotton Club revue to the pulpit.

Although the sacred concerts (hereafter SC1, SC2, and SC3) are preserved on records, it's necessary to note a quality of the music lost on disc—its aural affinity for the cavernous architecture of great churches. I did not attend any of Ellington's church services, but I recall how impressive even recorded excerpts sounded echoing through St. John the Divine at Ellington's funeral. Considering the ingenuity with which he surmounted the limitations of recording studios in the late '20s (which is why Ellington records sound so vivid compared with contemporary sides by Fletcher Henderson), it seems likely that he conceived his instrumental and vocal orchestrations in terms of the church acoustics he knew so well.

SC1 is a patchwork of the new and the old. Of the new pieces, the most important is "In the Beginning God," which occupies a third of the album. Throughout the concerts, Ellington used different modulations and intervals, culminating in the larynx-twisting "T.G.T.T." (SC2) and "Is God a Three-Letter Word for Love?" (SC3), one of his last songs. This characteristic is evident in the first six notes of "In the Beginning God," corresponding to the first six words in the Bible, and sonorously stated by the baritone sax of Harry Carney, who also introduces SC2. When I first heard the Brock Peters vocal, I thought it mundane; I've come to admire its openness and lack of pretension. Ellington was ambitious, but rarely pretentious, and those works for which he wrote narratives and recitatives suffer more from sugar-coated cleverness than undue extravagance. The verities Ellington held most dear are commonplaces—love, omnipotence, glory, freedom—and he honored them simply and directly. "In the Beginning God" becomes a series of climaxes: Cat Anderson playing his high notes, Louis Bellson dazzling on drums, the choir reciting the books of the New Testament over Paul Gonsalves's cumulus clouds of tenor sax. Another new piece, a rocking, offhanded new setting for "The Lord's Prayer," sung by Esther Marrow, is undistinguished.

A couple of selections were recycled from Ellington's 1963 production *My People*, but the best of the older music originated in the '40s. *New World a-Coming* was composed for one of his postwar Carnegie Hall concerts, and in the late '60s, he rearranged it as a piano concerto for the Cincinnati Symphony. On SC1, it is a superbly played piano solo, its jaunty spirit and tricky bass figures colored by sensitive minor-key melancholy (much of the sacred concerts is in the minor key). Of equal significance is the revamped "Come Sunday," outfitted with a new introduction, definitively performed, and thoughtfully revised from the original version in *Black, Brown and Beige*. Jimmy Hamilton's clarinet beeps reminders of the Ray Nance pizzicato-violin introduction, and there is now an interlude for Cootie Williams's trumpet and sensuous reed writing before Johnny Hodges's miraculous chorus. "David Danced Before the Lord," with tap master Bunny Briggs, brings the record to an exciting conclusion; it was originally performed in *My People*, but the music is "Come Sunday" played fast.

A change of heart overtook the composer for SC2, which consists exclusively of new music. Not content with his musical message, he added long recitatives of varying success, full of outright proselytizing. Some of the choral sections are reminiscent of school pageants, and I suspect he may have had in mind just such an application. This was one of the last times the classic Ellington band of the '60s would record, and his obsession with the project is reflected in his producing and financing the tapes himself, and then selling them to Fantasy records. Some of the melodies are dim—"Something About Believing" could have been turned out by any number of Broadway tunesmiths—and Toney Watkins's gospel shouting is a good deal less invigorating than intended.

Yet there is great Ellington here. "Praise God," a perfect vehicle for Carney, is reprised in a thunderous finale, "Praise God and Dance," including shining performances by Alice Babs and Gonsalves. "The Shepherd" is a slow blues for Cootie Williams, with stop-time passages and shifting orchestral accompaniment. Several selections have an airy, ecumenical quality. The uneven "It's Freedom" boasts a jubilant passage based on a Willie "The Lion" Smith lick and an evocative song crafted from just the word "freedom." Babs is impressive in her duets with Hodges and Russell Procope.

The winning vocalist is at the heart of SC3, where the purity of her a cappella work on "Every Man Prays in His Own Language" displays an emotional serenity one associates with the singing of children. The memorable "Is God a Three-Letter Word?" brings to fruition several melodic suggestions in SC2, notably "Heaven" and "Almighty Heaven." Ellington conjures a new and poignant unaccompanied piano setting for "The Lord's Prayer" and on "Every Man" allows for a solo by Art Baron on the recorder, its natural, diaphanous sound echoing with quiet awe in this hushed presentation. The scrupulously crafted "The Majesty of God" is the conclusion and highlight of the concert. Ellington's spirited piano sets the stage—a reference to "Things Ain't What They Used To Be" wafts by—and the variations are lovingly spun by Carney and Babs until the full orchestra plots the resolution.

I am told that significant portions of SC3 were edited from the record, including the final section of "The Majesty of God." Clearly there was tampering with "Every Man" since the music fades up on the third syllable of the title. There are more serious problems: Toney Watkins's feature is his most palatable on record, but his recitation in the middle of "Three-Letter Word" is disconcerting to say the least; there is a trite advertisement for the United Nations called "The Brotherhood"; and Ellington is zealous in his declaration of faith—he has Watkins sing, "If you don't believe in God/Then brother you don't exist." Considering the evident problems with space, the inclusion of a ninety-second speech by the chairman of the United Nations association is puzzling and annoying; the deathless message could have been printed on the liner. But such quibbles should not deter anyone from seeking out Ellington's last testament. Despite much adversity, he was even in his final months a perceptive and unflinching artist. Indeed, the superior moments of *The Majesty of God* suggest that his art was still peaking, an indication confirmed by the flood of works released in the years following his death.

The posthumous works of no major contemporary artist have excited greater interest than Ellington's, except perhaps for Hemingway's. The critical estimation of his music was revised upward throughout the '70s and '80s as previously unknown pieces were discovered and old ones reevaluated. In an incredible rush, beginning with *The Majesty of God* and *This One's for Blanton* (piano-bass duets with Ray Brown), Ellington's catalog flourished beyond all expectations: *The Queen's Suite, Goutelas Suite, Uwis Suite, The Degas Suite, The River, Three Black Kings* (completed by Mercer Ellington); countless live performances from 1943 onward; numerous private recordings ranging from revisions of his well-known pieces to one-shot experiments, like an orchestration of a Thelonious Monk piece or an entire album designed to feature Paul Gonsalves. On top of that, repertory companies began exploring neglected works: Mercer presented *The Liberian Suite*; Gunther Schuller revived "Reminiscing in Tempo" and *Symphony in Black*; the American Jazz Orchestra explored *Harlem* and the 1950 concert expansion of "Mood Indigo," as well as the '40s material; and the Lincoln Center Jazz Orchestra made the case for *Anatomy of a Murder*; among many other examples. Dozens of jazz musicians, among them Tommy Flanagan, the Modern Jazz Quartet, Kenny Burrell, Don Byron, Muhal Richard Abrams, Jimmy Rowles, Sarah Vaughan, Dee Dee Bridgewater, and David Murray adapted and performed overlooked compositions.

Inevitably there was a backlash. Ellington was pilloried by one pundit for hiring alcoholics and junkies. Unfounded accusations that he lifted his music from Strayhorn and other associates were renewed, echoing aspersions lodged against Irving Berlin. Conservative Europhiles took umbrage that he was routinely compared with classical icons like Stravinsky and Copland—one went so far as to describe Ellington's reputation as a deception created by an Afrocentric cabal (this fellow badly needs to read Mark Tucker's indispensable *The Duke Ellington Reader*, 1993). At the center of the blitz was James Lincoln Collier's ill-mannered and ill-researched 1987 pathography, *Duke Ellington*, which concludes that, notwithstanding thousands of copyrighted works and recordings, Ellington was a dilettante who didn't formally study piano because he could get along "without having to learn anything properly," and "never worked harder than he did at his music [because] he saw music primarily as a way into the spirit of the new age—the high life, to put no fine point on it." Offended by Ellington's regal manner, Collier traces the defect to Ellington's parents, whom he describes with censorious bafflement. Of Mrs. Ellington he writes, "Why Daisy so doted on her children we cannot know."

Collier is typical of his generation in denigrating Ellington's extended works, but unusual in the clichéd frivolity of his contempt, which extends to virtually everything Ellington wrote after 1946. "Any one of a number of jazz composers" could have written *The Tattooed Bride*. (Curious that none did.) *Such Sweet Thunder* consists of "self-indulgent fragments." He likens *The Far East Suite* to "slides of somebody else's trip." *The Latin American Suite* is "derivative and somewhat uninspired." *Afro-Eurasian Eclipse* is undone by "a lack of purpose." His critical method is revealingly exposed in a discussion of the masterpiece, *A Tone Parallel to Harlem*, which he repeatedly refers to as *The Harlem Suite*, though it isn't remotely suitelike. For Collier, it is "chock-a-block with wonderful moments," yet "holds the attention only briefly," which would seem to be a neat trick for a work that plays less than fifteen minutes.

Commissioned by the NBC Orchestra during Toscanini's reign, *Harlem* is formally a cross between a concerto for orchestra (it has no piano part) and a rhapsody—not unlike Gershwin's *Rhapsody in Blue*, which it resembles in its opening cadenza (a descending trumpet rather than an ascending clarinet, though in Ellington's case the passage is a recurring motif); its variety of tempos and rhythms; and its introduction of a haunting melody that dominates the last third of the piece. In *Harlem*, that key melody is a hymn introduced on trombone, rivaling "Come Sunday" in its nobility and poise and serving as the basis for a series of lucid variations that bring the work to a cresting conclusion, complete with a shattering high-note trumpet part that few musicians could play then or now. Collier hears none of it. Evidently more familiar with Ellington's written description of the music than the music itself, he writes, "No fewer than eighteen unrelated snapshots are presented in the space of fourteen minutes. Here lies the problem: no sooner has Ellington unfolded a nice bit of musical material than he drops it and shows us something else. Nothing is ever developed."

Harlem does, however, raise a genuine point for debate: Is improvisation an essential component of a jazz work? Ellington's art is centered on the interplay between written and improvised music. In composing settings that accommodate the poker-playing habits of specific individuals, he created a music in which improvisational license is broad yet bridled by the stylistic attributes of those individuals; a solo assigned to Ray Nance will produce a result predictably distinct from one assigned to Clark Terry. In selecting a particular soloist, Ellington is making a choice as categorical as that of a director hiring a prominent actor or a painter choosing one color over another. The soloist, like the actor, supplies the shading within the limits of his imagination (for example, the Ray Nance solos on the two recordings of "Take the A Train," discussed in Part Four). In *Harlem*, however, Ellington wrote all the parts and supplied all the shading, controlling as many details as possible—there are no improvised passages. Is it jazz? Does it matter? Ellington was no more willing to accede to what fans and critics expected of him as a jazz composer than to what society expected of him as a Negro.

Just how deadly those expectations could be was dramatized with savage explicitness in a 1934 Hollywood film, featuring the Ellington orchestra, based on Earl Carroll's Broadway revue, *Murder at the Vanities*. Ellington's sequence is called, "The Rape of the Rhapsody." The first movement, "The Rhapsody," begins as a white pianist plays and sings a laughably fey adaptation of Liszt; the music is then taken up by a white string orchestra in nineteenth-century livery. In the second movement, "The Rape," black musicians who have been hiding behind the white ones disrupt the music by playing fierce passages in the Ellington jungle style. The conductor looks around for the intruders but can't see them— they are everywhere yet invisible. In a flash, Ellington himself emerges to vie with the white conductor: his musicians rout the Lisztians and play their own version of the piece, an Ellington orchestration called "Ebony Rhapsody," the music now rapturous and alive. In the third and final movement, "The Revenge," the white conductor returns with a machine gun and—encouraged by the audience's laughter and applause— murders the black musicians.

At century's end, Ellington's place is more secure than that of all but a handful of twentieth-century composers. He is by no means immune to knowledgeable criticism, but however variable the value of individual works and periods, he remains an essential looming presence, America's most comprehensive musical scribe. Beyond the sacred music, Ellington's continuing prescience in the last decade of his life, perhaps the most tumultuous era in jazz history, is neatly bracketed by two posthumously released albums: one a relatively informal celebration of a star soloist that revamps familiar material, the other a suite that manifests his awareness of intervening musical modes and augurs the advent of world music.

In 1985, Fantasy released *Featuring Paul Gonsalves*, a previously unknown bouquet the maestro had tossed his yeomanly, critically neglected tenor saxophone soloist in 1962—a time when that instrument enjoyed special prominence, thanks to such recordings as Sonny Rollins's *The Bridge*, Stan Getz's *Jazz Samba*, and John Coltrane's *Live at the Village Vanguard*. Three months later, Ellington would prepare an octet album for Coleman Hawkins and one month after that participate in a quartet session with Coltrane; but in May, he employed the whole orchestra to spotlight his own master practitioner. Ellington wrote of Paul Gonsalves that his refusal to make demands on himself evinced a purity of mind worthy of a good priest. "His punch line, of course, is 'Jack Daniels,' " Ellington continued, "but that is just a kind of facade."

The image of Father Gonsalves must have amused his many friends, but none could have failed to understand what Ellington was getting at. The primary tenor saxophonist of the Ellington band for twenty-four years (1950–74) went Jesus one better. He could walk on sour mash, an ability that may have been either a consequence or a cause of his unusual diffidence. Gonsalves, known to colleagues as "Mex" and to Ellington's audiences as "the hero of the Newport Jazz Festival" (or "Strolling Violins"—he was known to hop off the stand to serenade a pretty patron), abjured power in any guise, including self-promotion. That he had a reputation at all was due to his lavish talent, the boss's loyalty, and his devoted fans, to whom the name Gonsalves was synonymous with "underrated." Not even his conquest of Newport in 1956—when he galvanized the audience with a twenty-seven-chorus blues solo that put Ellington on the cover of *Time* and his orchestra back on top after five difficult years—secured him much individual attention.

He didn't appear to care in the least. He and the people close to him knew who he was and, besides, to sit in the Ellington band was all he ever wanted from life. By all accounts, Ellington was his greatest admirer, which helps to explain why he tolerated Gonsalves's unrigorous approach to discipline—unlike Basie, with whom Gonsalves had formerly worked. Yet until the delayed (by twenty-three years) release of *Featuring Paul Gonsalves*, the full measure of Ellington's regard was known only to the orchestra's inner circle. As was his habit, Ellington leased a few hours of studio time to record music for his private cache. But as he hadn't written any new material (according to the band's longtime chronicler, Stanley Dance) he announced on the spot an entirely novel course of action: an album that would feature Gonsalves and only Gonsalves. Except for a few measures of clarinet on "C-Jam Blues," no one else—including the leader—gets to solo.

Gonsalves's playing probably seemed too effortless for his own good. He didn't do knee bends or look pained while he played, and he could produce a marathon solo with a near-marathon cadenza at the drop of anybody's downbeat. Though his style had its obvious influences—chiefly Ben Webster and Webster's mentor, Johnny Hodges—he didn't sound like anyone else. Whereas Webster was elliptical and gruff, Gonsalves was all liquid rhapsody. The notes poured forth in cascades; somewhere in the mist, the melody invariably renewed itself. Half of *Featuring Paul Gonsalves* is blues and all the pieces are familiar, but all the treatments are new and the energy dazzles.

In fact, it may not be quite accurate to say that Ellington wrote no new music since most of the pieces are revised and some of the revisions are too intricate to be head arrangements. Consider the bebop figures the band plays behind Gonsalves toward the climax of "C-Jam Blues" or the locomotive harmonies on "Happy Go Lucky Local" or the waltzy transitional passage on "Take the A Train." Hodges was taking it easy that day, but Harry Carney's edgy baritone powers the reed section; Sam Woodyard and Aaron Bell make for a steadfast rhythm section; and Ellington, as always, commands from the piano. On "Caravan," he states the changes with single bass notes while Gonsalves works up a sandstorm, and then vamps a clever change in tempo.

Gonsalves's quicksilver improvisations resonate with passion and wit, and though he hesitates momentarily, he never loses his footing—a remarkable feat, considering that he probably didn't have a clue what would happen when he walked into the studio. The present version of the blues "Ready, Go" is just as dynamic as the one on 1959's *Ellington Jazz Party,* and I prefer its slightly breathless cadenza. The present version of "Paris Blues" easily outclasses all others. The theme from the 1961 movie for which Gonsalves dubbed Paul Newman's tenor sax started life as a piano theme, but was arranged for Hodges and Lawrence Brown on the disappointing soundtrack album; Gonsalves was given a chorus on subsequent versions. Here he takes it at a much faster tempo, lagging behind the beat in the first chorus, interpolating two transitions and expanding his embellishments through each of five choruses. "Just a-Settin' and a-Rockin'," which he inherited from Webster and made his own, has a passage for tenor and rhythm that illuminates his impact on David Murray, and "Take the A Train" is thoroughly refreshed with two tempo changes and a flag-waving climax. Dance writes that after playing it (presumably most if not all of these performances are first takes), Gonsalves "turned to Ray Nance, whose showcase it usually was and gave his familiar, self-deprecating Stan Laurel grin."

The question arises: Why wasn't this session issued earlier? Ellington's 1962 recordings consisted of small-group encounters with Hawkins, Coltrane, and Mingus and Roach, and a couple of relatively undistinguished orchestral projects, such as his salvaging of a forgettable and forgotten Strouse and Adams musical, *All American,* the highlight of which was Gonsalves's interpretation of "I've Just Seen Her." The tenor saxophonist was between contracts—a year later he signed with Impulse—and might have benefited greatly from its release. Although maybe not. One recalls the general level of Ellington criticism and can easily imagine the most likely responses: "Not a single Johnny Hodges solo!" "We've heard these pieces before!" "Another instance of Ellington's decline!" *Featuring Paul Gonsalves,* though, is a triumph—the definitive Gonsalves album, and evidence of yet another ace up Ellington's capacious sleeve.

The Afro-Eurasian Eclipse, released by Fantasy eight years earlier, in 1976, was recorded in 1971, and although it consists entirely of new music, only one movement was generally known to Ellington's concert-going public. (A slight mystery still clings to it: the album has eight sections, the list of copyrighted compositions in *Music Is My Mistress* suggests twelve.) For reasons known only to himself, he teased his audience about it. He regularly performed the first section, "Chinoiserie," preceded by an unchanging introduction that made several cross-cultural references and promised a longer work, while customarily keeping the other sections under wraps (recalling his maneuver in doling out *Black, Brown and Beige*). The spoken shadow play is part of the finished album, and it serves—for all the hocus-pocus—as a concise and revealing explanation of the travel suites in general:

> Last year about this time we premiered a new suite titled *Afro-Eurasian Eclipse*. And of course the title was inspired by a statement made by Mr. Marshall McLuhan of the University of Toronto. Mr. McLuhan says that the whole world is going oriental, and that no one will be able to retain his or her identity, not even the Orientals. And of course we travel around the world a lot, and in the last five or six years we, too, have noticed this thing to be true.... In this particular segment, ladies and gentlemen, we have adjusted our perspective to that of the kangaroo and the didjeridoo. This automatically throws us either down under and/or out back. And from that point of view it's most improbable that anyone will ever know exactly who is enjoying the shadow of whom.

Two points come to mind that were not likely to intrude in the years Ellington charmed and mystified audiences with that address. For most of the '60s, Ellington pursued two themes, sacred music and secular travelogues, and in the latter he enacted his recognition, before the term was coined, of what McLuhan called "the global village." Also, hardly anyone who attended his concerts understood his reference to the didjeridoo, which now seems predictive: a decade later that aboriginal wind instrument (hollowed out of a tree branch several feet long and indigenous to Australia) was no stranger to the alternative jazz and new music scenes, especially as played by trombonist Craig Harris. Ellington never attempted to reproduce the music of other cultures; his impressions were referential but utterly idiomatic (he didn't actually use a didjeridoo). While acknowledging McLuhan's observation that cultures are losing their identities, he demonstrates that his music is broad-based enough to sample the world's disparate melodies, rhythms, and harmonies, and that he can retain *his* identity in the bargain. As he remarked on his first visit to one alien culture, "After writing African music for thirty-five years, here I am at last in Africa!"

Just as *Latin American Suite* was melodic in motive, *The Afro-Eurasian Eclipse* is about rhythm, one-chord harmonies, and chants. This one-world music reflects the ongoing jazz tradition as well: r & b, rock and roll, Albert Ayler, and Cecil Taylor are all woven into the fabric. Not to suggest that Ellington consulted Taylor before sitting down at the piano for "Didjeridoo"—which is virtually a piano concerto built on the premise that the piano is a percussion instrument—but that Ellington's genius was heightened by his sensitivity to the music of his time. Borges demonstrated that Hawthorne became a prophetic writer in the post-Kafka world; in that sense, much that is indigenous to Ellington is differently perceived in a world so manifestly altered by him. Harold Ashby's tenor saxophone solo on "Chinoiserie" is surely avant-garde.

The *Eclipse* may be Ellington's only extended work bereft of a single brass solo. It's constructed around the reeds and the rhythm section. "Chinoiserie" is the most complex piece, alternating between eight-and ten-measure themes. It is plotted thus: A(10), A(10), B(8), C(8), A1(14), A2(10). The A-theme, strongly reminiscent of Horace Silver, is rhythmically constructed on a hesitation in the fourth beat of the second bar. The rhythmic equilibrium is deliberately tenuous: the A-theme picks up from the piano vamp—based on one note—a beat late, while the fourteen-measure variation on A begins a beat before expected. Following the sixty-measure theme is Ashby's greatest moment on records, a gallivanting, eupeptic solo using both the eight- and ten-measure patterns, aggressively supported by Ellington's piano and culminating in a wildly exciting stuttering, shimmying stomp over static rhythm.

"Acht O'Clock Rock" begins with two blues choruses by Ashby, followed by a thirty-two bar theme for piano, another two blues choruses, and thirty-two bars for the ensemble with Norris Turney out front. It combines openhearted r & b with ominous chord substitutions. Ellington makes the piano sound like a marimba, and I do believe I hear an organ in parts, though none is listed in the notes. "Hard Way" is a sixteen-bar blues for Turney, with a four-measure interlude sewn in. The inexplicably titled "True" is actually an old friend, "Tell Me the Truth," from SC1, but this time it's been refurbished with a bright, bustling arrangement that features Paul Gonsalves, who's in high spirits. The only disappointing movement is "Tang," a heady concoction that begins well enough with dissonant chords and an erupting piano figure, but proves to be an exercise in redundancy, with two themes—one, twelve bars; the other, eight—traded between Harry Carney and the ensemble, and a rhythm riff thrown in four times along the way. "Gong" is a blues for Ellington and Carney, with a delicious flute and clarinet chorus, and

"Afrique" is both a drum feature for Rufus Jones and an exercise in the percussion value of all the other instruments.

On the eve of Ellington's centennial, it can safely be said that he is held in higher esteem the world over than ever before and that his music has been absorbed into the very nervous system of American life. Jazz, of course, is unimaginable without him, however restricting he found the category. Ellington's music is Shakespearian in its reach, wisdom, and generosity, and we return to it because its mysteries are inexhaustible.

54 ❖ *Muhal Richard Abrams* *(Meet This Composer)*

It would be presumptuous retroactively to cast Muhal Richard Abrams as the eponymous Black Saint of Charles Mingus's famed suite or the Italian record company with which he was affiliated for some fifteen years, but a better candidate would be hard to find. In considering his long, puzzling, and often inspiring career, or while observing him conduct an orchestra, I am impressed as much by his elegant reserve in getting the job done as by the accomplishment itself. At a time when artists with exalted reputations devoted their energies to justifying the debasement of their art and selling out or dumbing down was fashionable, the persistence of this dexterous composer, pianist, and organizer, untempted by compromise yet readily willing to please, abided as a tonic and perhaps a caveat.

Why isn't his music, so diverse and accessible, so striking in its devotion to craftsmanship and the pleasure principle, better known? Is it his exotic first name, his association with an avant-garde movement that never accounted for more than a portion of his work, or his unyielding concentration that alarms people? At a major 1989 concert for eighteen-piece orchestra, Abrams dedicated "Textro 88" to Meet the Composer and the New York State Council of the Arts, not because they provided him with a commission, he said, but for helping to keep music alive. I, too, bow to organizations that make evenings like that possible, but the unhappily widespread assumption that Abrams's music requires grants because it flies over the heads of Uncle Charlie and Aunt Gladys really needs to be blown out of the water. Had that orchestra found a steady

Monday night niche, it would have waxed a sizable coterie soon enough. Instead, we have at best annual Abrams sunbursts, at which audience members whisper or shout encomiums or shake their heads in grateful acknowledgment, then leap to their feet for the final ovation, before wandering away, asking how it is that so few know about this man and this music.

Abrams's New York career started in midlife, which may account in part for its purposefulness. In Chicago, where he was born in 1930 and began his career in 1948, he made a reputation as arranger for a jump band led by saxophonist King Fleming and as pianist for the solid postbop unit, the MJT + 3 (1957), which he left early on (Harold Mabern took his place) to emerge four years later as the founder of the unrecorded Experimental Band and the support group that sprang from it in 1965, the Association for the Advancement of Creative Musicians (AACM). He was almost thirty-seven when he made his recorded debut as a leader, *Levels and Degrees of Light*, which documented his influence on a new and largely untested generation of musicians, including Anthony Braxton, Leroy Jenkins, Maurice McIntyre, and Thurman Barker. It was followed by *Young at Heart, Wise in Time*, which introduced Henry Threadgill and Leo Smith, but is also remembered for a half-hour piano fantasia, "Young at Heart," in which Abrams explores the array of styles he honed during the years he accompanied dozens of visiting musicians, from Ruth Brown to Woody Herman to Miles Davis. Those albums, recorded for Delmark, are the first evidence of a talent second to none for encouraging and helping to establish young musicians of substance, an achievement made the more remarkable because, unlike Art Blakey or Miles Davis, he has not had a regularly touring or recording ensemble. He has chosen with care the casts for each project and provided contexts that show his players off to best advantage.

AACM-related music is no longer as widely chronicled as it was in the late '70s. When Abrams relocated to New York in 1976, he hastened the internationalization of a music that had received little more than token support in the United States (outside of Chicago), despite having already scored high marks in Europe. The ensuing storm of recordings and concerts by musicians associated with the AACM (Abrams, Braxton, Jenkins, Threadgill, Smith, the Art Ensemble of Chicago, Roscoe Mitchell, Lester Bowie, Joseph Jarman, Amina Claudine Myers, Chico Freeman, George Lewis), and the simultaneous flanking of musicians from St. Louis (Julius Hemphill, Oliver Lake, Hamiet Bluiett, Baikida Carroll, Phillip Wilson), California (David Murray, Butch Morris, Arthur Blythe, James Newton, Mark Dresser), and diverse points, realized the promise of an ongoing, eclectic, experimental music that had strong ties to jazz without being haltered by it. No easy territory to blaze, even with the support of a cooperative and an occasional grant.

That generation of musicians, building on the achievements of post-bop apostates who questioned the rules and put their ids on the table, began with the assumption that playing free meant just that. It wasn't a matter of whether or not you used chords or swing rhythms or the tempered scale, or of how you measured improvisation against composition, but of having the options—of choosing to do with or without any of the tools of music in any given performance. One measure of the Great Black Music vaunted by the Art Ensemble was embodied in the freedom to be or not to be free, and followed from a fundamental idea: Jazz is a classical music with an established yet expanding canon of masterworks, wed to a language of rules and structures. In playing off the acknowledged classics, the shared postulates, the new jazz of the '60s kept the intrinsic aesthetic alive, demonstrating to the max that a worthy foundation can withstand every sort of experimentation, however adventitious or provocative it may seem. The jazz avant-garde, like the classical avant-garde, is empowered by the fact that true classicism is impervious to anything but prostration. Imitation, as Emerson pointed out, is suicide.

The pandemic success of the new music in the late '70s, as fueled in large part by the artists and ideas of the AACM, led inevitably to a conservative backlash, not only because the jazz audience is as enfeebled by fearful Cassandras (the agony of modern music and all that jazz) as any other, but because experimentalism itself can wear thin. Every shock makes the next shock harder to generate; eclecticism especially can become rote very quickly. Not least among the glories of Cecil Taylor and Ornette Coleman are their abilities to keep us bristling decade after decade, while refusing to veer from their original visions. Monk spoke of the independent artist waiting for the audience to catch up. But avant-gardists don't really want the audience to catch up, not entirely; less than a decade after the audience caught up with Monk and *Time* put him on its cover, Monk stopped performing.

Most of the musicians who assaulted conventions in the '70s eventually established ties with those conventions. In some instances, the decisive factor may have been commercial pressure—the need to work jazz clubs, to record—but, in fact, much of the retrenchment proved fruitful. Artists who've stepped outside and then turned homeward have a lot more to tell than artists who've never been outside. The World Saxophone Quartet matured into a triumph of rapprochement between the new and the old without compromising either. Solo recitals by wind players have all but disappeared (they'll be back), and loft-era rumbles that were content to shake up the present without bowing to the good will of posterity are a bracing memory. Yet a rough, edgy approach to improvisation survived and is a healthy alternative to that generation of journeymen who put their faith in the commandments of the conservatory. I am disinclined to side with one group against the other, as we need and have always had both. Still, at a time when jazz has survived the excesses of fusion only to be visited by entrepreneurs attempting to sell the dishwater improvisations of New Age as the latest "cutting edge" (remember that cliché?)—in short, at a time when jazz ought to be allowed some surcease of abuse—I am thankful to those who not only know better but howl in protest. The AACM sat proudly mounted in the advance ranks of true believers in disbelief.

Few musicians have expressed greater determination to elude expectations while pursuing discrete interests than Abrams. His work has no relationship whatever to the avant-garde of the '60s, if we mean that term to signify long scattershot solos. To the contrary, Abrams is punctilious in all things, crafting alluring settings that are models of clarity and proportion. The solos are short and pointed, but they have mettle. His music has the energy without which jazz would do what the naysayers have been predicting it would do for seventy years—run its course. Abrams's long and surprising series of Black Saint recordings range in instrumentation from solo piano to big band and in style from back-o'-town blues to rubato romance. As his albums invariably combine multiple approaches, they fail to satisfy those who want to hear him work exclusively in any one of them. A rounded and often brilliant pianist with large hands that allow him to explore odd intervals with unerring articulation, he is singularly responsive to his musicians. Even a cursory examination of his work reveals his gift for inspiring them, sometimes to levels of interaction and lucidity that rival his own.

Abrams records only original material (an AACM dictum), a source of frustration for those who know how persuasive an interpreter of standards he is. Indeed, he is most authoritative when addressing structures closest to jazz. But he made his unwillingness to closet himself in familiar structures clear from the very beginning, for example his 1978 Novus album, *Lifea Blinec* ("life line" plus a,b,c). When that record appeared, Abrams had become something of a New York chameleon, blending so deftly into varied duos, trios, and larger configurations that it was impossible to put a handle on him. *Lifea Blinec* accented his methods as a composer rather than his prowesses as a pianist and suggested some stylistic parameters. "Bud P.," for example, combines the moodiness of Bud Powell's ballads and the vertiginous rhythms of his fast improvisations without derivative references. The first of two themes, introduced on piano and repeated more dramatically on saxophone, is gracefully nostalgic; the second is a stiff-legged rhythmic figure played with increasingly precise unity as the piece progresses. Thurman Barker's crisply swinging drums emphasize by comparison the second theme's keening quality. After the ballad theme is repeated, the two saxophonists (Joseph Jarman and Douglas Ewart) simultaneously improvise on the thematic material. A two-piano tableau (Abrams and Amina Claudine Myers) segues into reprises of the two themes.

Not unlike Benny Carter or Thelonious Monk, Abrams has said that an improviser should work with the fixed material in a piece to avoid hackneyed phrases. "Bud P." is conscientious enough in that regard; certainly nothing in it could be confused with the merrily deranged "Lifea Blinec." Here diverse voices come into play: a zonked-out Myers asking for instructions and exclaiming "wow" and "like dig"; an effete Abrams ruminating, "My, my, such a beautiful posture"; and the others growling with indignation or waxing academic on "cosmological reality." One of the voices cannot decide whether you put your life on the line or your line on the life, while a version of T. S. Eliot's barkeep insists, "It's time to close," after which they all march off with staccato horn bleeps. The music that grounds the talk mutates from a dirge to ragged r & b to a stride march. As different as they are, "Bud P." and "Lifea Blinec" are group endeavors that reveal little of the individual players.

By contrast, Abrams's Black Saint album, *Colors in Thirty-Third*, released ten years later, strikes a perfect balance between composer and improvisers. The precise grounding of each piece encourages the soloists to spin terse and telling variations though tending to the rigors of the written music. The seven selections are played by duet, trio, quartet, quintet, and sextet, and each combination gives the impression of a practiced band. Saxophonist and bass clarinetist John Purcell gets an exemplary showcase, as do violinist John Blake, whose own discs had become increasingly slick, and the ever dependable Dave Holland, on cello as well as bass. Drummer Andrew Cyrille and bassist Fred Hopkins are up to their usual high standards. For all the variety, the accent is on swing rhythms and the structures are fit and trim.

"Drumman Cyrille" begins with four-bar exchanges between the ensemble and Cyrille, continues with a longer strain, followed by more four- and eight-bar exchanges, and settles into splendidly concentrated solos that spring from the fragmentary nature of the theme. Purcell ends in the tense pursuit of a repeated motif, as Abrams comes bounding in with a prelude to his own solo. I don't know a better example of Abrams's lyricism than "Miss Richards," a haunting ballad for bass clarinet, piano, and bass (plucked and bowed). Articulation is everything here; Purcell expertly pitches his notes in the high and low extremities, while Abrams's enfolding chords and Hopkins's careful arco work sustain mood and pace. "Munktmunk," a half-step march, recalls Eric Dolphy's tribute to Monk, "Hat and Beard," and is floated by Cyrille's cheerful backbeat. Purcell's light timbre suggests some of the unison phrases Monk worked out with Charlie Rouse; Abrams turns things around with a salon-and-candelabra meditation that is soon deconstructed with Monkian dissonances and a resumption of the prancing theme.

Compound writing for soprano and violin are at the heart of "Soprano Song," which in its swallowing-its-own-tail repetitions suggests the restive quality of some of Roscoe Mitchell's work, though when Abrams sidles in and the beat becomes pronounced, the effect is quite festive. The relay from Purcell's solo to Blake's is seamless, and Abrams begins his solo with a phrase from Gillespie's "Bebop." The album's title piece has a hocketing theme in which the pitches are divided among the front line. Of the concise solos, patterned over a loping canter of plucked bass and cello, Abrams's is most inventive. His surprising permutations on the stillwater chords and closing clusters are enunciated with a light and assured touch. His intro on "Introspection" suggests a fugal rhythm, and indeed the soprano sax and violin enter in contrapuntal style, followed by an effective unison passage, until the parts split off again and revolve in the winds of the piece like a mobile. Only "Piano-Cello Song" comes off as labored because the thematic material is comparatively weak.

Abrams's New York projects, many of them one-shots, have often been too memorable. His audience longs for repeats; maybe that's the problem—as soon as you think you know his music, he switches stations. I occasionally hear people talk about his past accomplishments with a nostalgia that belies his current productivity: remember the trio gig when he played standards or the quintet with Stanton Davis or the amazing blues he improvised with Leroy Jenkins or the time he shook up the Kool Jazz Festival with his Ellington orchestrations? At his 1989 Merkin Hall concert, dedicated to the late drummer Steve McCall (an immensely likable man whose work with Air was a benchmark of the '70s), Abrams evoked lush pastels, extending the conventional big band spectrum with Dierdre Murray's dulcet cello, Fred Hopkins's arco bass, Joel Brandon's between-the-teeth, pitch-perfect whistling, and Abrams's fuzzed-up synthesizer. The band's voicings listed to the higher intervals, with lots of flutes, soprano sax, clarinet, and piccolo, supported by muted brasses, but the general impression was one of sustained chords, lustrous and dreamy. Typically, not a single expansive solo was heard. Most of the improvisations were four- and eight-bar exchanges or dramatic cadenzas or parts in shifting combinations (a duet that became a trio that became a quartet). Each player's contribution was the more distinguished for being so neatly framed, recalling those perfect sixteen-bar solos that blazed from orchestras of the swing era.

The Merkin Hall concert introduced material that was used in two of Abrams's most creative albums: *The Hearinga Suite* (1989) and *Blu Blu Blu* (1990). On the basis of these thoroughly engaging works alone, he must be accounted a preeminent figure in the development of big band music in the period since the '60s, when Gerry Mulligan's Concert Jazz Band, the Thad Jones and Mel Lewis Orchestra, the freelance orchestrations of Oliver Nelson and Gary McFarland, and the renewed vigor of Ellington, Basie, and Herman proved that big bands were here to stay. Abrams announces the character of a piece in its first measures, and a few examples from *The Hearinga Suite* may suggest the variety of his impulses: the four-note synthesizer vamp that sets up "Aura of Thought-Things"; a Jack Walrath trumpet cadenza that recalls Armstrong's "West End Blues" at the top of "Oldfotalk"; each member of the band reading different newspaper stories over martial drums at the start of "Seesall."

One of his most effective gambits is one of the simplest: synthesizer shadowing flute, building to great Mingusian blasts on "Hearinga," which offers some of the old "new music" bravura in a whimsical vein, falling between "City of Glass" and "The Sorcerer's Apprentice." By contrast, "Finditnow," while referencing the whimsy, employs swinging jazz rhythms and four-measure exchanges (the best are between Abrams's piano and Warren Smith's vibes, which in concert have been extended to greater effect than on the record), a Bach-inspired cello interlude, and memorable voicings for xylophone and trombones. "Finditnow" is bound by two ballads: the evocative "Oldfotalk," which suggests a '50s style of voicing and melody before fading out on a bass-cello duet, and "Bermix," a sly melody introduced by baritone over bowed bass and restated by vibes over muted brasses (with contrapuntal sighing in yet another reminder of Mingus's hovering shadow), the texture darkly colored by the cello's undertow.

Abrams introduced "Bloodline" on *Rejoicing with the Light*, in 1983, but, doubled in length and prefaced with a cadenza by whistler Joel Brandon (who can impart deftly modulated glissandi and triple-tongue rhythmic figures), this irresistible tribute to pre-swing-era orchestras is the centerpiece of *Blu Blu Blu*. In its original version, Abrams dedicated it to Fletcher Henderson, Don Redman, and Benny Carter, but in its expanded form the work's most revealing quality is Abrams's love of stride rhythms, previously evident in piano solos that reflect his admiration for James P. Johnson. Ellington often adapted stride rhythms in his arrangements of the '20s, and Gary McFarland attempted to mimic bounding tenths in his big band writing in the '60s, but neither of them seized and ran with those rhythms more confidently than Abrams does in "Bloodline," an orchestration that plays two-beat figures off four and at times achieves a klezmerlike giddiness. The album's title number, dedicated to Muddy Waters, is a masterful production of a sort that only Abrams can pull off: a full-bore roistering big band blues. It forms an informal trilogy with "Blues Forever," from the 1981 Black Saint album of that name, and "Big T," a dedication to Thad Jones that Abrams conducted on a 1988 recording by the Finnish big band UMO, *UMO Plays the Music of Muhal Richard Abrams.*

In April of 1989, a jury convened in Denmark through the Danish Jazz Center and sponsored by the Scandinavian Tobacco Company voted Abrams the first annual Jazzpar, a major international jazz prize that carries a financial award of $30,000 and occasions concerts in Denmark and France. Five judges representing Denmark, England, Poland, and the United States selected five nominees in the first annual competition and unanimously chose Abrams as the first recipient. As one of the jurors, I was especially intrigued by the response of the Danish press when the decision was announced. Much puzzlement and some grumbling was expressed: Who was Abrams? many critics asked. The concert and tour that took place the following spring was so successful, however, that one of the protesting critics admitted he didn't see how the committee could have made a better choice. Late in 1990, I asked Abrams to conduct the American Jazz Orchestra in a concert of the music he presented in Denmark. Once again, I saw the wariness of mainstream enthusiasts—this time, musicians—disappear as they examined his meticulous scores and gave themselves up to his authoritative conducting.

His subsequent records have sustained his high standard as well as the unpredictability that makes them such varied entertainments. *Family Talk* (1993) begins with a dulcet synthesized meditation and, through repetitive structures that recall Miles Davis in his *Nefertiti* period, explores the family of music, or as one piece is called, "Sound Images of the Past, Present and Future." On "DizBirdMonkBudMax (A Tribute)," a savvy update of "Bud P." and a more sweeping salute to the bop era, Abrams mischievously opens with the loopy piano introduction Sadik Hakim played on several takes of Charlie Parker's "Thriving on a Riff," and fully captures the sound of an era (given Warren Smith's solo on vibes, "Bags" belonged in the title). The sextet on that album and the septet on *Think All, Focus One* (1994), which confidently combines exotic rhythms and modish voicings, showcase several of the little-known musicians whom Abrams has successfully featured, most notably tenor saxophonists Patience Higgins and Eugene Ghee, trumpeter Eddie Allen, and drummer Reggie Nicholson. Abrams's triumphant first album for New World, *One Line, Two Views* (1995) has a ten-piece ensemble that reunites him with Marty Ehrlich (who also recorded a rewarding concert of duets with Abrams) and adds harp, violin, and accordion to the mix, the latter most agreeably on a disarmingly buoyant "Tribute to Julius Hemphill and Don Pullen." Abrams is never more graceful or luminous than when paying tribute to other musicians. It is his particular gift to mine a copious tradition and push it farther out toward the horizon.

55 ❖ *Roscoe Mitchell/Marty Ehrlich (The Audience)*

The most neglected component of a successful concert is a good audience. Back in the '30s and '40s, when animated characters and then actors began speaking to movie audiences, it was said they were removing the fourth wall or reviving theatrical immediacy. Filmmakers in those days were already catering to the theatrical habits of their patrons, inserting dead spots and slow fades after big production numbers to allow for applause. But as people lost the habit of going out and performers secluded themselves behind tape or digitalization, with all their technological lies (to the point that disco fans came to prefer canned to live music and even Pavarotti capitulated to the laborsaving device of lip-synching) the audience lost its clout, beyond the commercial power of buying tickets.

Indeed, the audience devolved. I savor the legend of the esteemed '70s music critic who pulled the valet-sized box of Good 'n Plenty from the hands of a woman seated behind him—she had been working on the cellophane for the better part of a Mozart adagio—and smacked her hand with it. Whenever I've been moved to comment on audiences in the past, it has been to fulminate at clubgoers who yell, "Waiter!" at the climax of a solo or at concertgoers who stroll in midnumber, or at a species of both who find music a stimulus to conversation or clapping in time. Perhaps the last serious audience is at the opera, and I was relieved to hear Pavarotti concede that the fanatics in the uppermost tier who boo every failing are well within their rights.

Good audiences can be a blessing, even a defining element in a performance. You may not recall what songs the Beatles sang on Ed Sullivan, but everyone recalls the squealing audience. Consider Ellington's 1956 Newport triumph: Was it the amazing twenty-seven-chorus blues intermezzo by Paul Gonsalves that landed Ellington on the cover of *Time*, or was it the crowd's response to it? When the album was released, producer and annotator George Avakian seemed to have no doubt when he included one photo of the young woman whose spontaneous dancing started the cheering and another of Jo Jones, who used a rolled-up newspaper to incite the rhythm section. The album was designed to make you feel as though you were there; as good as the music is, the energy of the *event* pushed it over the top—and would have been unthinkable within the isolation of a recording studio. Audiences are often the excuse for excesses, yet the same magic can happen in jazz clubs, which is why so many definitive recordings were made live at the Village Vanguard.

My own detour into jazz was greased by the audience at a hotel ballroom in segregated New Orleans, 1963. Although anger still coursed through the city, this crowd was integrated, exuberant, erotic, and charged by the music. If in choosing an art early in life one chooses a surrogate family, than this was the family for me. Yet an equally stirring example of audience participation resulted when the customers were bored to the point of self-righteous anger at a Carnegie Hall concert tribute to Chicago jazz. The performers were Roscoe Mitchell and Hugh Ragin, who sustained circular near-unison pitches until the audience was divided into two camps: those booing, cursing, throwing things; and those booing the booers. I'm not sure Mitchell didn't deliberately plan a provocation. But when the piece was finished the ovation was thunderous, and I remember little else played that night.

No one plays with an audience more diabolically than Roscoe Mitchell, a man who apparently thrives on jeers, a proponent of circular breathing who plys the technique (inhaling through the nose and exhaling through the mouth simultaneously) to sustain the one pitch or repeat the one riff that will incite howls of execration—which he then turns to avid applause by stopping, as the audience recognizes its own complicity. In the final weeks of December 1994, he helped celebrate the opening of the new and improved Knitting Factory, a focal point for New York's new music scene, with a band called the Note Factory, which had recently released the album *This Dance Is for Steve McCall* (Soul Note), a program mostly of short conceptual pieces that barely hint at Mitchell's achievement in concert. Even the lovely serpentine arpeggios of Joseph Jarman's "Erica," a piece from the mid-'70s that he completely transfigured for the album, achieved greater delicacy in concert as Mitchell exaggerated the dynamics in the alto sax episode, and greater intensity in the finale, as he crested the ensemble with his patented Möbius riffs, suggesting bagpipes.

"Erica" remains a fine piece. But the longer concert selections don't work as well on disc, perhaps because crowds are braver than individuals. Mitchell acknowledges this tacitly in focusing on shorter and airier works for release, even when he records live, as on the 1987 *Live at the Knitting Factory* (Black Saint). Not unlike Sonny Rollins, he relishes the communal event that makes the audience part of the performance—a preference for theater over film. The Note Factory allows Mitchell, who always makes the most of his available instrumentation, to generate drum duets, bass duets, and various composites with the addition of pianist Matthew Shipp and himself. His options were increased by two guests, guitarist A. Spencer Barefield, from Mitchell's Sound Ensemble, and veteran conga player Big Black. The payoffs were those episodes that displayed the unit in full array. In those long woolly tableaux, the static circularity of Mitchell's saxophone and the nonlinear textures of the rhythms brought time to a stop. You found yourself drawn to details, colors, small gestures (the ravishing compass of bowed and plucked sounds William Parker cajoles from the bass), matching your powers of concentration against theirs. For dessert, Mitchell played a generic blue ballad on tenor in what might be called Chicago pitch—flat, flush, deep in the groove, the audience's reward for its trust.

A good example of how much Mitchell will dare on record is *The Flow of Things* (Black Saint), released in 1988. It consists of three versions of the title work, which originated as an encore selection at a concert series devoted to Coltrane themes, and an installment of his ongoing work, "Cards." In the decades since the John Coltrane–Rashied Ali duets, which tested the extremes of improvisational equilibrium in a harmony-free vacuum, Mitchell has been a primary mover in the direction of method and control. Here his method involves intractable virtuosity and guarded commotion. Each version of "The Flow of Things" begins differently, but they all carom into a furious thematic figure that through constant repetition becomes the aural equivalent of an Escher drawing in which perspective is skewed and looped. The key phrase is forever descending yet remains in the middle register, emitting prodigious overtones—Mitchell eventually sounds like a choir of saxophonists. No one else solos, but it would be a mistake to hear the work as a solitary exercise with rhythm accompaniment. Mitchell is borne aloft by oddly harmonized piano chords (Jodie Christian), capering bass (Malachi Favors), and a sensationally reflexive battery of drums (Steve McCall). "Cards for Quintet," by contrast, is a measured inquiry into space, a respite from the molten fury of Mitchell's obsessive attack and a palliative for the solitary listener communing with a stereo.

The audience assembled for "Interpretations," a program of chamber music by Marty Ehrlich's Emergency Peace Ensemble in the fall of 1993, was most surprising for its size. As Weill Recital Hall filled to near capacity, Ehrlich remarked that he would come uptown more often. Since the early '80s, he has quietly issued a series of lapidary albums while doubling as one of his generation's most dependable and diverse sidemen. A stellar technician on clarinet, saxophone, and flute, Ehrlich has a rare capacity for disappearing into the music he plays, even his own. That is, the glimmering sounds he makes acquire their force from settings devised for them, not from any musicianly vanity, which in his case seems practically nonexistent. He forces the audience to lean a little closer to get his meaning. Although five of the six pieces Ehrlich performed were from his 1991 album *Emergency Peace* (New World), they were hardly well enough known to encourage assumptions. Indeed, chamber music as delicate and winsome as this requires an absence of assumptions, which is why you never hear it in conventional jazz settings.

One satisfaction of Ehrlich's music is that it reminds you that swing is, as a matter of fact, high on the evolutionary scale and not merely the elemental force it was taken for in the teens and '20s, when Stravinsky equated drums with pagan rites and Ellington was said to lead a jungle band. Using his own reed instrument, cello (Erik Friedlander), and bass (Lindsay Horner) on "Emergency Peace" and adding French horn (Vincent Chancey) on "Underground Overground," Ehrlich opened with arhythmic, fixed themes and harmonies that eventually separated into ostinatos and riffs. Tracking the route from European modernism to jazz, he makes the audience crave the rhythmic swagger of American music.

On "Emergency Peace," Ehrlich played clarinet—the dark edginess of the low notes swelling in a cadenza until they bled with the vibrating authority of full-dress chords—before the strings backed him with a stop-time figure. For "Underground Overground," he switched to alto saxophone and wove thin, almost vibratoless pitches with lusty multiphonics—an exercise in texture until he introduced a swing riff in unison with French horn while plucked bass and bowed cello underscored the pulse, and you realized that withholding swing increases its value. "Tribute" began with sumptuous voicings and later suggested an old rural blues as the strings splintered off, cello scratching high like a fiddle, climaxing as the quartet took flight in a four-part improvisation. Muhal Richard Abrams added his piano on the two selections he had recorded on Ehrlich's New World album, the programmatic "Dusk," which lacked traction in concert, and his own "Charlie in the Parker," a fiendishly difficult piece introduced with diminished piano chords and finessed with observable pleasure by Ehrlich, whose alto articulated every note in barreling arpeggios.

If Mitchell riles his audience, Ehrlich becalms his. But if Ehrlich is reluctant to let go on his own, Anthony Braxton produced a setting that demanded nothing less. The quartet he introduced in late 1994, as the last musician to play the old Knitting Factory, prompted interest chiefly for presenting Braxton as a pianist for the first time. But it also revealed Marty Ehrlich's secret: He is a stalwart theme-and-variations improviser, equally impressive on alto and clarinet, with his huge bracing tone and long supple phrases and his rhythmic authority and profound understanding of the rights and limitations of chord changes. Neither his own chamber jazz nor his work with other persuasive composers (John Carter, Muhal Richard Abrams) unveiled the power and energy he brought to Braxton's treatment of familiar themes.

The quartet plays standards with intrepid wit and amplitude, buoyed by drummer Pheeroan Aklaff and bassist Joe Fonda and with Braxton at the center, pounding clusters and close chords and strangely choreographed sprinklings of notes that signal stages of deconstruction. On Bill Evans's "Waltz for Debby," he blocked out an intricate chordal variation, more Brubeck than Taylor, that parsed the melody in great slabs. A drawback was the quartet's tripartite approach to every piece: inside the changes, outside the changes, howls. Parts one and two were individuated, but the howls were too much alike and the audience didn't need a telescope to see them coming. Yet no one minded much. The concert audience is always more forbearing than the one at home.

56 ❖ *Henry Threadgill* *(The Big Top)*

At first blush, Henry Threadgill's '90s band protests too much. Circus would be a suggestive title, and Very Circus a more adamant one. But Very Very Circus hardly leaves room to breathe—you expect three rings, a menagerie, peanuts, and a dozen clowns pouring out of a tiny car. You expect more whimsy and frolic than is reasonable or healthy. What you get on the band's compelling and undoubtedly original 1991 album, *Spir-*

it of Nuff . . . Nuff (Black Saint), is the leader's alto saxophone (or flute) winding its way though a clamorous thicket of two tubas, two electric guitars, drums, and trombone (on tour, the trombone was replaced by French horn). The density, the nearly combustible activity, and the constant change-ups all impart a circuslike temperament, but the music's sobriety and complexity counters that, especially in concert, where the absence of a decent sound mix can muddy the ensemble into incoherence.

That was the problem when the band made its New York debut in June 1991 at Time Jazz. The ensemble had been booked at the last minute, following a seven-week, twenty-eight-city tour. You had every reason to expect blinding polish, and yet Very Very Circus advanced as a strange and only partly convincing array of Prime Time counterpunching, indistinct brass blare, and the whiplash bite of the leader's alto, which gave Circus most of its direction. When I heard the album a day later, though, the live performance made more sense. I recognized a couple of the pieces and realized how ruinous the unsympathetic mix was. Still, this is a music that takes perverse pleasure in undermining assumptions, setting you up for events that never quite come off or that exist in the blink of an eye, and sustaining little beyond the state of surprise.

Surprise is Threadgill's preferred turf, earned after a long apprenticeship that took him through several kinds of music. Born in Chicago in 1944, he played drums in marching bands before taking up baritone saxophone and clarinet in high school. He played with Roscoe Mitchell and Joseph Jarman, when they were first beginning to push the envelope on conventional improvisation, and through them joined Muhal Richard Abrams's Experimental Band and the Association for the Advancement of Creative Musicians. After touring with a gospel singer for two years, he enlisted in the army and played in an army rock band. Discharged, he held down a chair in the house band of a Chicago blues club, while earning a degree in composition at the American Conservatory of Music. In 1971, while working in a theatrical production that derived part of its score from Scott Joplin, he met bassist Fred Hopkins and drummer Steve McCall. The three formed a cooperative trio called Reflection, which played locally. Four years later they toured as Air.

In the fallow years of 1970 to 1975, the hunger for genuine jazz ensembles—as opposed to leaders with rhythm sections—was met largely by groups from Chicago: the Art Ensemble of Chicago (Roscoe Mitchell, Lester Bowie, Joseph Jarman, Malachi Favors, and Don Moye), the Revolutionary Ensemble (Leroy Jenkins, Sirone, and Jerome Cooper), and Air, the most accessible and elusive of the three. At first Air recorded for a poorly distributed Japanese label (Whynot) and was not widely heard. But in New York, where it made an instant splash, Air had an irresistible quality. Part of its appeal was its driving rhythm section, but, inevitably, the axis of the group was Threadgill, who played baritone, alto, tenor, flute, and a percussion instrument of his own invention called a hubkaphone (two tiers of hubcaps). His saxophone playing had a gritty edge that at times recalled Earl Bostic, and his compositions were at once smart and funny, elemental and sophisticated, direct and askew.

The first album, *Air Song* (1977), remains an impressive balancing act of design and caprice, of individual and ensemble, of blitz and lyricism. The title selection is sweetly tenuous, rotating among solo flute, harmonized flute and arco bass, and trio crescendos. Threadgill's talent for ripe tunes and sardonic titles is represented by "Great Body of the Riddle or Where Were the Dodge Boys When My Clay Started to Slide" and the more generic thirty-two-bar "Untitled Tango," on which his tenor has some of the clarity and willfulness of late-'50s Sonny Rollins. *Air Raid* was released later the same year and is notable for "Midnight Sun," one of Threadgill's melodious Rollins-inspired themes (the Rollins swagger transmuted by the jagged cry of Threadgill's alto); "Air Raid," a more complete portrait of his alto in that period, as he alternates cold, brittle feints with voracious flurries and recedes cunningly as Hopkins comes to the fore; "Release," the most extensive piece, with a subtly eventful rhythm-section episode; and "Through a Keyhole Darkly," a ballad for tenor that begins as arch melodrama before achieving genuine drama.

Those records, long unavailable and little acknowledged when they were in print, merit rediscovery, but Air's most remarkable achievement was its sixth album, *Air Lore* (Arista Novus, 1979), which occasioned a return to the group's roots: the Chicago play with music by Scott Joplin. A torrid and funny inquiry into ragtime and blues, *Air Lore* is Threadgill's key statement on the repertory mania and tradition-mongering that gripped jazz in the '70s and '80s and a forceful refutation of the academicism that too often sucks the life's blood out of classic jazz. Selections by Joplin and Jelly Roll Morton are dissected, scrutinized, and stitched back into open-air suits for the principals. Threadgill recomposed the music to permit adjustments in texture and tempo as well as variations, while retaining its original character.

"Weeping Willow Rag" (1903), one of the most warmly evocative of Joplin's rags, was conceived with rare thematic unity. Following a four-bar introduction, the format is AABBACCDD, with each letter representing a sixteen-bar strain. The first two strains are in the key of G and the last two are in C, but all four employ the same motivic interval of a fourth (D to G), which sets up the first and last strains and recurs in disguise elsewhere. The unifying rondo form common to ragtime is found only in the repeat of A before the trio, but the last four measures of C are identical to those of D, and the winsome melody unfolds with a gentle logic. Air begins its interpretation with a three-minute drum solo, attacks the themes at never less than a canter, interpolates stop-time and double-time where least applicable (in the lovely trio and the repeat of D, respectively), and it works. The continuity and feeling of the piece are retained even in the improvisations.

The drum solo starts with a four-bar martial figure, but the bulk of McCall's melodious drumming (beginning a little more than a minute into it) is a variation on the first strain. Threadgill and Hopkins enter playing AAB, and before the first sixteen bars are done, McCall has suddenly switched his accents from the downbeat to the offbeat. Threadgill, with his bright, pinched alto sound, improvises five choruses on B, loosely holding to the sixteen-bar pattern; his second chorus is eighteen bars and the riff-filled fifth twelve, yet despite his structural liberties (reminiscent of early bluesmen), he cleaves to the melodic material, beginning each chorus with the high note of the written theme. He reprises B, repeats A (buoyantly accompanied by Hopkins), and, slowing the tempo, introduces the trio over a variously accented, unison stop-time. Hopkins improvises four thematic choruses on C, extending the last with a four-bar transition into a repeat of C by Threadgill, who follows with three stirring choruses (he pays homage to Johnny Dodds with his low-register work.) He plays the D strain without frills, and, though McCall and Hopkins double the time behind the repeat, Threadgill retards the melody to shape the climax.

All of which sounds more complicated or cluttered than it is. The tempo changes and improvisations are complementary, the musicianship is expert, and the spirit suggests a naturalness at odds with the effort required. Threadgill's alterations work because they amplify Joplin's melodies, underscore the unity of the discreet strains, and are swung with artless gusto. "Weeping Willow Rag" is the highlight of an engaging album, but Joplin's more atypical "The Ragtime Dance" gets almost as startling a revision.

Joplin's publisher cobbled together the six strains of "The Ragtime Dance" in an attempt to recoup his losses, after they appeared in an unsuccessful ballet in 1902. The piece is in E-flat except for the first strain (in B-flat), and the themes are presented in a straightforward fashion (AABBCCDEF). Joplin added instructions on how best to effect the stop-time rhythms indicated in the last three strains: "NOTICE: To get the desired effect of 'Stop-Time,' the pianist will please *Stamp* the heel of one foot heavily upon the floor at the word 'Stamp.' Do not raise the toe from the floor while stamping." Air, which plays stop-time where it is not required (on "Weeping Willow Rag" and "King Porter Stomp"), ignores the instruction, though on D and F, McCall's dashing cymbals obviate the need, and on E, he imitates the cascading sixteenth-notes of the melody. Air also modifies the order of the strains: AA (Threadgill's solo), BB (Threadgill and Hopkins together), C (McCall's solo), EFD (Threadgill's solo), D. Given Air's tempo, D makes for a strong conclusion. Threadgill's biting sound is imbued with the blues, especially in the first part. The two-beat rhythm is shared by Hopkins and McCall, bass accenting the one and three and drums the two and four.

Morton's "King Porter Stomp" is more problematic. Morton claimed to have written it in 1902, and he is said to have shown it to Joplin, who approved. Like Eubie Blake's "Charleston Rag," it is a transitional piece, combining ragtime form and a prescient stomp section. Fletcher Henderson made the title famous in the '30s, when he issued three recorded versions and orchestrated it for Benny Goodman, but he employed only the four-bar interlude and concluding stomp riffs. The opening strain, with its tricky first-beat syncopation, did not lend itself to swing scoring, nor does it lend itself to Air's purposes. The performance comes to robust life when Threadgill and Hopkins improvise on the stomp, but the reading of the first strains trivializes Morton's piece with a paraphrase that sounds more old-fashioned than the composer's 1923 recording. Nor are Air's structural changes enhancing; a stop-time contrivance during the first four bars of A and B is vitiated by gangly paraphrases. The trio strain, however, reclaims the interpretation, setting off fiery, expansive solos by Threadgill and Hopkins. The saxophonist returns for some excited riffing but at the climax, instead of the expected blaze, there is an abrupt fade. After *Air Lore*, Threadgill focused almost exclusively on his own compositions.

For most of the '80s, he led the Henry Threadgill Sextet, which offered a numerological surprise: the band was made up of seven musicians, but two were drummers, and Threadgill felt they were playing a single part. At the same time, his music began to show a preoccupation with death, specifically a work about the death of a computer, beginning with "Soft Suicide at the Bath" on *What Was That?* (About Time) and continuing with "Cremation" on *Just the Facts and Pass the Bucket* (About Time), for which he returned to clarinet. Another piece, "A Man Called Trinity Deliverance," also suggests a funereal theme, while "Gateway" celebrates the St. Louis arch and "Black Blues" is a blues that repudiates standard blues form. The change-ups between bright and melancholy

passages conjure the deep dirges and second-line euphoria of New Orleans, though the music is not directly connected to the New Orleans
style beyond the implication of the clarinet. These records represent
Threadgill's first major attempt to create a music in which soloists never
depart for more than a few measures from the ensemble—a music that
aspires to collective tumult in which the composer's hand is always apparent.

The records chronicle Threadgill's progression as a writer. *What Was
That?* alters selections with the ensemble center stage and others with
the ensemble accompanying solos. The second album lacks its wonderfully tempestuous moments but heightens ensemble textures and the
contributions of each musician. Threadgill finds his own way into the
tradition, avoiding pastiche and superficial reference points. The music
is understated and oddly formal, the harmonies rich with fourths and
fifths and minor thirds. Yet many of his techniques are as old as jazz
itself: muted brasses, stop-time, jump riffs. *Just the Facts and Pass the
Bucket* integrates its selections through the use of opening and closing
statements by the drummers, motifs, and stark phrases varying from
revival-house hollering ("Black Blues") to canonical repetition ("Cremation").

By the late '80s, the sextet was a work of streamlined symmetry: two
drummers, two brasses, two strings, plus the leader's solitary reed instrument. The jacket of *Easily Slip Into Another World* (RCA Novus) depicts a small band shell, but Threadgill's approach to the brass band has
a blowzy quality for all the precision of his orchestrations: even a slap-
dash effect requires practice to get it right. The lessons of Morton and
Joplin resurface in radically altered ways throughout this album and its
1988 successor, *Rag, Bush and All* (RCA Novus), where unfolding structures suggest the plotting of complementary strains. Yet results are uneven. "Black Hands Bejewelled" (on *Easily Slip Into Another World*) is a
persuasive take on the Spanish tinge as a setting for trombonist Frank
Lacy and trumpeter Rasul Siddik to solo over fat open-palm chords, but
the tune is cloying and Siddik hasn't the technique to execute his ideas.

Then comes "Spotted Dick Is Pudding," a revealing, raucous workout,
conceived and played in a spurt of measured euphoria. The rhythm *almost* arches into a second-line strut as Lacy growls the finish of his solo,
but it's the gospel chords that inspire Threadgill to his best work, voiced
high and tight and building to a shameless rapture stressed with split
tones and shouts. The music swells with shifting rhythms, a patch of
double-time in the bass, and a parodic finish with a fierce beating of
drums and a great bleating chord to bring down the curtain. "My Rock,"
with vocalist Aisha Putli crossing octaves, is reminiscent of the uses to

which Mingus put singers. "Hall" opens with a rhythmic vamp by bowed strings and shifts with the brasses into a kaleidoscopic mode that suggests Muhal Richard Abrams, to whom it is dedicated, though the humor is all Threadgill's. His wit suffuses "Award the Squadtett," which begins with the drummers (Pheeroan Aklaff and Reggie Nicholson) matching rhythms and tones in tribal style and settles into a theme that sounds like something Meredith Willson might have written for a brass band after spending a year locked up in the AACM rehearsal hall. Threadgill's sax barks over and through his ensemble with the rude authority of a drill sergeant. Murray's cello solo is something of a keynote interlude, setting up a theme so suggestive of convention music you can almost see balloons falling from the rafters.

All of which seems, in retrospect, like a warmup for Very Very Circus. Again we find the symmetry in instrumentation, the odd juxtaposition of elements from varying musics, and the densely calculated ensemble. The tuba alone establishes certain expectations, since its jazz reign was pretty much confined to the early days, before the string bass became boss of the bottom range. But for Threadgill, the tuba brings to mind less the Hot Seven than the Weimar version of America's new music as epitomized in scores Kurt Weill wrote for Bertolt Brecht. The influence of Weill has been a constant source for jazz composers in the past thirty years (beginning with Carla Bley's orchestrations in the late '60s), yet rarely has it taken on such aggressive crunch as in the two pieces that map the parameters of *Spirit of Nuff . . . Nuff.*

"Hope A Hope A" starts with one of the album's many alluring drum rhythms, not unlike a second-line march beat, and continues with an episode of off-center guitar murmuring. Threadgill enters with a magically smoky, evocative theme that, played twice, suggests the submerged frenzy of Weill until, pushing free with a series of ascending figures, he launches gloriously brazen, if too brief variations. The leader is resolute about not featuring himself unduly in Very Very Circus, with an inevitable and uneven result: On the minus side, you want more; on the plus side, his entries always give you a lift. After another interlude of guitar, trombonist Curtis Fowlkes sustains the enchantment; his big sound also helps to focus the ensemble, a duty not as easily realized on French horn.

The dirgelike "Unrealistic Love" was the most persuasive of the pieces heard live, perhaps because the quieter voicings allowed the colors to emerge more distinctly. The subdued opening—by Mark Taylor's French horn at Time Jazz, by Fowlkes on the record—consists of laconic two-note phrases, gently supported by guitar. Again, the alto introduces a glimmer of Weill in a balladic theme played with a plaintive directness almost vocal in timbre. Later, after a unison transition by guitar and trombone and a guitar solo by Brandon Ross, the tubas (Marcus Rojas and Edwin Rodriguez) imply a Weimar choir as Threadgill returns with that authoritative brilliance that makes him one of the most powerful altoists we have. In performance, it was impossible to hear what the three brasses and two guitars were up to in various interludes in which no central voice was present. On the album, you hear the parts, but you wonder what principle is ordering them. I am reminded of little instruments popularized by the Art Ensemble of Chicago. Threadgill employs big instruments, but the accruing details have a similarly fortuitous quality—the details become their own reward.

Occasionally, Threadgill marshals his brasses to suggest the inevitable clumping of a marching band, but he does it with a canniness that once again dispels expectations; he isn't literal about it. On "Bee Dee Aff," he initiates a childlike round that can be counted: one-two, one-two, one-two-three-four. The piece itself disarms you by opening with a simple if wrenching guitar lick and closes with kaleidoscopic changes, as snorting alto or rippling tuba flash through the practiced disarray. On "In the Ring," he uses a conventional march figure that can be counted like this: one, one, one-two-three-four, where the initial beats have twice the time value as the next four. This piece begins with the only extended drum solo on the album, though Gene Lake's ratatat snares and quick reflexes are conspicuous throughout. The alto introduces another theme reminiscent of Weill, and the closing passage prepares you for a march that doesn't happen.

Similarly, the ending of "Exacto" sets you up for a harmonic resolution that doesn't emerge, ending instead with a big, open sustained chord. Threadgill appears to have given much attention to his endings. The canonical repetition and the elemental snare rhythm make for a satisfying finish for the sometimes unwieldy "Drivin' You Slow and Crazy." The communion of trombone, flute, and drums on "First Church of This" offers an unexpectedly effective cap to one of the Circus's most intriguing pieces. It begins with a rising cathedral of sound, voiced for guitars and flute, survives an undertow of brasses, and finds light in the album's sweetest melody, a three-note figure played by the ensemble. The guitarist Masujaa and Threadgill improvise against the phrase, underscoring its simple, repetitive appeal.

Spirit of Nuff . . . Nuff didn't sound like anything else and made many ten best lists that year, including my own. It made you wonder what else the band could have in store. Music that sounds this free is usually far more composed than that which encourages soloists to wail dozens of B-flat blues choruses. More than Air or the Henry Threadgill Sextet,

Very Very Circus seemed limited by the peculiarity of instrumentation and concept. So consider the elation when it fulfilled its promise with an electrifying third album (the second, *Live at Koncepts,* was a concert recording made a few weeks before the New York debut) in 1993. Boasting an inspired title, *Too Much Sugar for a Dime* (Axiom) slaked the thirst for a modern sound that married jazz's edginess with the ecstasy of earth-beat rhythms. You didn't have to understand it to be caught up in its energy—it overwhelmed you with color and form. Once again, the tour was more unruly than the record: dancing was encouraged when the band appeared at New York's S.O.B., but most people preferred to ring the stage, transfixed by the graphic roar.

One way of fighting sloth and despair is to swell the energy. In modern music that impulse has often meant electronics or free improvisation, but it is now more widely signified by effusive multiculturalism, ripe with polyphony, contrary rhythms, eclectic juxtapositions, usually electronics, and almost always animated by the spirit of dance. In its most elemental form, dance is the soul of irreverence, if not revolution. It impedes aging, mental as well as physical, and is a bulwark against the death rattle of nostalgia. Threadgill has always been able to embody raw energy with his saxophone and in his bands. Even when Air played Joplin and Morton, you were less likely to meditate on tradition than submit to the immediacy of its racy attack.

Too Much Sugar for a Dime has its energy under control, but not to the extent that you can understand it too easily or too quickly. The two tubas and two guitarists are largely scored, but the serpentine flow supersedes notation. In concert, the audio mix never seems right, the leader is chary with his solos, and Mark Taylor's French horn deliberations can be enervatingly long. But the record fascinates, primed with spartan melodies and dense rhythms and counterpoint. "Try Some Ammonia" is especially inviting, with a hooky theme so spare it suggests a playground song. The leader's alto wails through most of the piece, followed by pointed guitar and French horn solos. It waxes steadily for twelve minutes before fading.

"Better Wrapped/Better Unwrapped" has guests Leroy Jenkins and Jason Hwang playing twisty violins over a rhythm contingent beefed up by two percussionists from Venezuela, Johnny Rudas and Miguel Urvina, who interrupt the instrumental episodes with vocal sections. Singers are also heard on "In Touch," backed by an instrument that sounds like a zither. Threadgill's alto has a gregarious bite that has endeared him to listeners on both sides of the jazz-rock divide from the time he arrived in New York, and his sound—a curiously human touch amid the brasses and drums—binds Very Very Circus. He solos at length on "Little Pocket

Size Demons" and with marchlike fervor on "Paper Toilet," the intricate background urging him forward. Remember the last scene of *Black Orpheus*, the three children dancing on the hilltop to Orfeu's samba? At its best, Threadgill's music produces that kind of ecstatic dance intensity. Like his earlier benchmarks, from *Air Lore* to *Rag, Bush and All, Too Much Sugar for a Dime* is a one-of-a-kind album.

Like them, too, it represents something of a culmination. In the mid-'90s, with *Song Out Of My Trees* (Black Saint) and *Carry the Day* (Columbia), Threadgill revised his palette once again, replacing the hallucinatory congestion of Very Very Circus with a dreamy sextet kept closer to earth by the organ of Amina Claudine Myers or the searching acoustic piano of Myra Melford and seasoned by Wu Man, playing Chinese pipa, and Tony Cedrus, on accordion. The distinctive supple rhythms and candid emotions abide, as does the composer's piping, elliptical, fervently swinging saxophone.

57 ❖ Charles Gayle/David S. Ware/ Matthew Shipp (Sweet Agony)

Nearly everyone who has seen Charles Gayle's Knitting Factory appearances remarks on his opening note, or blast—a unanimity of response that implies a trademark effect at odds with his expressed determination to be as unpredictable as is humanly possible. As trademarks go, however, it's sensational: a multihued squall obviously unlike the customary sounds avowed by saxophone manuals, but also unlike the gut-wrenching, reed-biting effusions of the now middle-aged avant-garde, if for no other reason than that it *is* his first note. Even Cecil Taylor warms up a little before commencing his marathon. Gayle starts by peaking and goes on from there. By the last number of the hour, he proves he's mortal by using longer and more frequent rests. In effect, the momentum of his sets is entropic rather than cathartic.

That opening shout is a kind of call to arms, specific and functional, ending all conversations immediately and turning every head to the stage. It's a well-suited descendant of Louis Armstrong's "West End Blues" call, a once-in-a-lifetime alarm for the whole jazz . . . I almost said "establishment," but there wasn't one in 1928, which is why Armstrong's avant-garde assault on conventional polyphony succeeded so quickly.

Some have said that after Armstrong the only contrary direction left to jazz's avant-garde was a retreat from the accompanied soloist back to the improvising ensemble. Certainly a primary tenet of postbop radicalism is a reaffirmed equity between figure and ground. But individuality is still the gold standard in jazz. The dynamic of Gayle's music is a given, especially since Gayle, who had been playing unaccompanied on the streets of New York for more than twenty years before coming in from the cold, never rehearses. He commands attention at all times, even in repose, because his very brief departures from the mix of his ever-restless quartet are at once respite and delay: you're glad for the surcease and hungry for his return.

Like sinus-clearing spices or ice-cold showers, avant-garde art is, in part, a socially acceptable form of masochism. Need I remind the neocons that even for those of us who aren't neurotic, a little pain often opens the way to pleasure? (Or are neocons different?) At fifty-four, Gayle is a latecomer to the meager world of avant-garde professionalism (gigs, records, reviews, interviews, in addition to spare change in Times Square). But he is made to order to refurbish an inchoate Downtown soured on eclecticism and minimalism—a Downtown as predictable as Uptown. The power and beauty of avant-gardism is only as strong as the pain. Hard to digest and hard to produce, avant-garde art combines the thrill of novelty, the transcendence of custom, and the pride of the recondite. It refuses to be understood too easily.

If only because they reject the rudiments of professional security, most avant-gardists are romantic figures. In his personal life, Gayle fits the bill. In his music, Gayle is as anti-romantic as it is possible to be and still accept applause. He sometimes closes performances with richly intoned pitches in the extremes of the instrument that have a burning, lyric edge—a kind of prayerful reward for the audience that accepts the foregoing ruckus. Gayle is otherwise so tough and unsparing, you can come to him in complete assurance that he will deliver you from wherever you were to somewhere else. If his music begins as a (familiar) avant-garde jazz harangue, its very relentlessness purifies the air, and before long you are inside the cacophony, chiming along with the details: the blistering speed, the grinding timbre, the simultaneous polarity of opposing phrases (that's not a second saxophone, it's all Gayle), the virtuoso indulgence in texture (that's not an arco bass effect, it's all Gayle), the breathless sustain suggestive of bagpipes, the swing. *Swing*?! By all means: The constantly pitching momentum builds to the kind of heady locomotion associated with chanted nonunison prayer; it isn't your foot that's tapping, but your whole body.

Conservative rhetoricians who patrol the arts for agitators often revert to literalism as a kind of mockery. They hold a generic phrase to the light, find it wanting, and conclude, Q.E.D., that any art so designated must be wanting, too. "Free jazz" gets them blathering about discipline; "new music" about longevity; and "avant-garde" about military divisions. The most common and yet inexplicable insult of all is the idea that extreme forms come easy. No one believes that Gaddis and Rothko had it easier than Bellow and Wyeth, but in jazz the suspicion that Albert Ayler was somehow cheating, while no longer as rampant as it once was, is far from dead. Having passed the fortieth anniversary of Cecil Taylor's *Jazz Advance*, though, it ought to be clear that, metaphorically accurate or not, avant-gardists don't ride ahead of the mainstream legion; the two help keep each other honest.

One reason Gayle has made so many converts is that his technical skill is unassailable, if profoundly autodidactic. After a bass clarinet solo at the Knitting Factory, someone shouted, "How did you learn to play the bass clarinet so well?" His impulsive response was, "I didn't learn to play it." But his considered response, a few seconds later, was funnier: "At the Berklee School of Music." Gayle did study, of course. His well-regarded but difficult to find FMP album (with Rashied Ali and William Parker) is tellingly entitled *Touchin' on Trane*. And if he eschews Ayler's rhapsodic melodies, he displays a kindred pleasure in developing guileless variations of disarming nursery-rhyme simplicity in pieces like "Justified" (on his Black Saint CD, *Consecration*). The stunningly protracted "Sanctification," on the double CD *More Live* (Knitting Factory Works) is a kind of essay on the blues without being a blues; Gayle frames his notes over maddening bowed bass with deliberation and force.

The last two, challenging as they are, could serve as relatively accessible points of entry in engaging Gayle. But no such trepidations should keep anyone away from the frontier's other scouting tenor, David S. Ware. A decade younger, Ware has had a considerably more decorous career. For one thing, he really did attend Berklee. From the moment he appeared with Cecil Taylor's orchestra at Carnegie Hall in 1974, his standing was inseparable from the burnished texture of his sound. His is an art of splintered multiphonics and spacious echoes. The weight of his sound contributed immeasurably to the drama of Taylor's 1976 *Dark to Themselves*, but he was more persuasive as a soloist two years later as a member of Andrew Cyrille's Maono on pieces as varied as Kurt Weill's "My Ship" (*Metamusicians' Stomp*) and Ornette Coleman's "A Girl Named Rainbow" (*Special People*). A decade went by before Ware reappeared with one of the finest quartets in a generation, heightened by his collaboration with the ingenious young pianist Matthew Shipp.

Ware's quartet, with bassist William Parker and drummer Whit Dickey, is a marvel of interaction, and most marvelous of all is Shipp's ability to anticipate and respond to every textural and thematic gambit Ware throws at him. Though not the shock-tenor abstractionist Gayle is, Ware can radiate a rare confidence when completely unmoored from set harmonies. (It would be something to hear them play together.) But Ware also nurtures an affection for standards and has found a way to do something genuinely new with them. On his mid-'90s DIW albums, *Flight of i* and *Third Ear Recitation*, he cracks open four chestnuts and a Sonny Rollins riff as though they'd been written expressly for his group. The latter album has two versions of "Autumn Leaves," different from each other and from the versions he often played at the Knitting Factory, like the time he worried the key melodic phrase in an endless series of configurations, dismissing the harmonic runway altogether. The first recorded version opens with Shipp intoning the melody as though he were Roger Williams pitching a collection of piano favorites in a cable TV ad, except that all the time he's playing the tune, Ware is fulminating at it and the changes, blowing free and yet touching down on the harmonies just often enough to make it a true variation.

For all his explosiveness, Ware is ultimately a warm player; even at his most turbulent, that warmth is palpable in his darkly capacious sound and generous spirit. He can be wonderfully evocative, as in his recordings of "Sad Eyes" and Jerome Kern's "Yesterdays," the latter a dizzying shakedown of the harmonies. He plays the changes, but not the linear melody, preferring to replace conventional note patterns with cries and tremolos. It's an ear-opener: the cries seem literally to flee from the tune, as though it were a prison. He makes you feel the constraint of the song and at the same time allows you to enjoy its ingenuity. In a way, the performance recalls John Coltrane knocking the blues off its hinges in "Chasin' the Trane," but Coltrane's subsequent distillations of standards ("Out of This World," "My Favorite Things") often abandoned the forms of the originals. Ware sees them through. "Yesterdays"and "Sad Eyes" are two of six startling selections on *Flight of i*, which Columbia imported as part of a cherry-picking deal with DIW. The company's inexplicable failure to pick up Ware's ensuing and superior release, *Third Ear Recitation*, stalled a career that warranted acceleration.

Shipp, who is blessed with originality and technical skill as well as humor and lightning reflexes, shares Ware's capacity to follow Pound's dictum to make it new. If you think there's nothing to be done with Monk but play his tunes, listen to parts two and four of Shipp's 1990 *Circular Temple* (Infinite Zero), in which he adduces his own Monkian theme with percussive certainty. He suggests by example the lineage between the high priest's austerity and Cecilian copiousness while maintaining thematic continuity. Shipp considers the album a "prelude" to *Third Ear Recitation*. His duets with the highly original and seemingly omnipresent William Parker, *Zo* (Rise), form a suite, with a pensive reharmonized "Summertime" as the second of four movements, and Shipp's hammering single notes and his chordal harmonies in part three show how fastidiously he controls his materials while charting his own course. Shipp's comfort with the avant-garde lineage allows him, no less than Gayle and Ware, to dispense with the intrusive issues of jazz authenticity. He showed off his gumption beautifully at a 1997 duet at the Knitting Factory with the masterly, highly theatrical Dutch drummer Han Bennink.

Their duet was one of eight in which Bennink encountered eight different musicians over four nights. Prone to dadaistic ploys, from kicking his cymbals over to playing on his wooden clogs to shouting, Bennink is a musician constantly in motion, and the challenge to his partner is to hold his attention long enough to sustain a cogent statement without getting trampled. Shipp began with the kind of responsiveness he demonstrates with Ware and most everyone else (his encounter with Roscoe Mitchell on *Matthew Shipp Duo* is another sterling example). On this night, however, empathy wasn't on the menu, and what ensued was a kind of Brechtian drama, suggested not simply by his Weill-type melodies and eight/four cadences, but by his determination to stand up to the drummer, who seemed more determined than ever to command center stage. Bennink produced every rabbit he had, and Shipp came back with music-box melodies, the flight of a bumblebee, the plucking of strings, and a long, long, long recitation of "Tenderly," pounded out in the bass as though it were Rachmaninoff. There was so much going on—cymbal throwing, woodblock rattling, furniture moving, more and more "Tenderly"—that the duet mutated into a sporting event. Bennink, mighty damned tired of "Tenderly," did his best to kill it, whistling, howling, crashing his chair down on his cymbals. Shipp pummeled away, then, finally, squirreled off into his own indigenous and most welcome figures, leading to a kinetic unison rhythm as he mimicked Bennink's drum patterns. Then Bennink reprised his shtick; Shipp reprised "Tenderly"; they lockstepped rhythms again; and closed with a lullabye. Bennink is an old hand at this sort of thing, and it was ultimately his show. But Shipp affirmed his ability to keep new music new, even if it's old enough to be his grandfather, even if he had nothing more profound with which to battle chaos than "Tenderly."

PART SEVEN

❖

A Struggling Music

58 ❖ *Hannibal Peterson*
(Out of Africa)

The years 1967 to 1972 were among the most fallow in jazz history, partly a consequence of rock's hegemony and the confusion wrought by free jazz. Time seemed to stand still for a long wake at the bier of John Coltrane, whose sudden 1967 death induced a spiritual pall made manifest in material disorder. Coltrane's label (Impulse) soon lapsed into irrelevance, while others were swallowed by corporate sharks. A generation of giants passed from the scene, led by Armstrong and Ellington, and numerous musicians prominent in jazz through the mid-'60s went on sabbatical or flew to Europe or hid in studios and pit bands for much of that period, among them Sonny Rollins, Hank Jones, Charles Mingus, Ornette Coleman, Zoot Sims, Art Pepper, James Moody, Tommy Flanagan, Al Cohn, Johnny Griffin, and Dexter Gordon. Even Dizzy Gillespie kept a low profile. The famine ended around 1975 when the new wave of musicians from the Midwest and California renewed jazz's forward momentum, simultaneously creating an environment in which a magnanimous and novel respect for established styles could also flourish.

The wave of 1975 introduced musicians' collectives and fueled a loft scene to accommodate the talented players and composers who turned up week after week. Yet that flurry of activity also tended to drown out the work of a handful of isolated figures who had come to New York a few years earlier, at a time when jazz clubs had weakened along with the independent record labels. They incarnated the promise of something beyond the concessions of makeshift fusion with its endless and often out-of-tune soprano sax arpeggios, exotic percussion instruments, and banal lyrics (flying was a big theme). The best of them found refuge chiefly in three ensembles: Gil Evans's big band, the Thad Jones–Mel Lewis Jazz Orchestra, and the various ensembles of Charles Mingus. Those were years in which musicians and critics started thinking seriously about jazz repertory, its practice and implications. Many young players, sensitive to the prevailing eclecticism, struggled to sustain a music that kept faith with the principles of jazz improvisation but was broad enough to incorporate the lessons of the street and the academy.

One of the most assiduous and talented of them was Marvin Peterson of Smithville, Texas. After a couple of years of study at North Texas State, he came to New York in 1970 and divided his time between playing music and writing poetry. While performing at the Blue Coronet, a persistent fan told him his true name was Hannibal and that in time he would accept it as such. Ever sensitive to signs and magic, he adopted the name. It's easy to imagine why one of his admirers might be moved to conjure an image of the Carthiginian general who hurtled the Alps. Hannibal Peterson's trumpet has a bravura force that can stop you dead in your tracks—it's fierce and immutable, yet rigorous and often deeply moving.

His solos, played over the full range of the instrument, surge with energy, and his sound is fat and robust in every register. Concise phrases proliferate in a kind of controlled ecstasy, bolstered on the one hand by high-note glosses and on the other by lyrical transitions. The overall impression is of elation, a dynamism that feeds on itself. Two widely noted solos of that era were characteristic. In 1974, Cecil Taylor organized a huge band for a Carnegie Hall concert under the aegis of the lamentably short-lived New York Jazz Repertory Company—Peterson's fiery effusion provided a climax that brought all the ensemble parts into proper affinity. In contrast, his balladic treatment of "Zee-zee," on Gil Evans's album *Svengali* (Atlantic), showed how persuasively Peterson could restrain his exuberance when crossing a stream instead of ascending a mountain range. He also recorded with Richard Davis, Elvin Jones, Eric Kloss, and Roy Haynes, who hired him after hearing him sit in one night with Thad and Mel.

Gil Evans was the first to apprise me of Hannibal's talent as a composer, which he predicted would lead to great things. Evans had encouraged him to study at the library since he was reluctant to return to school. Hannibal's primary influences already included T-Bone Walker, with whom he had jammed in Texas, and Coltrane ("Trane had the element of madness and purity, like Poe or Van Gogh," Peterson told me at the time). Now he began studying scores by Kodály, Janacek, and others. "He's a very special, serious, schooled musician," Evans said. "When you hear how he writes for strings on *Children of the Fire*, you will realize that." *Children of the Fire* was the record Peterson produced and recorded on his own label in 1974 and released a year later. It was nothing if not ambitious: Conducted by David Amram and performed by Peterson's eighteen-piece Sunrise Orchestra, including six violins and violas, five percussionists, koto and sitar, and two vocalists, it was the most powerful political statement to emerge from jazz in the mid-'70s, and it clinched his reputation as a prodigious emotionalist.

I recently listened to *Children of the Fire* for the first time in years and was struck at how forceful it remains. Dedicated to "the children of Vietnam," it is anything but a scattershot broadside on the immensity of that folly. Peterson's take on political atrocities invariably focuses on the loss of innocence, the death of innocents. The piece, in five movements, is cannily frank: it opens with birdsong, the "forest sunrise," and proceeds with a hopeful rhyme sung by nine-year-old Waheeda Massey, before the implacable bombing. But the diversity of sounds—a string quartet voiced in fourths after Kodály, a violin solo (played by John Blake) patterned after B. B. King, the mix of Asian and African instruments, the trumpet-driven holocaust, the lyrical closing prayer (sung by Alpha Johnson)—compels interest, and the sincerity is wrenching for being guileless.

Peterson continued to tour with small bands (which included cellist Dierdre Murray and saxophonist George Adams), but life on the club circuit grew less satisfying to him, and he never really had a major breakthrough on the local jazz scene. He appeared to strike a chord in Germany, though; the few records he made were on MPS and Enja, and in the late '70s, the Hanover Symphony commissioned him to write *The Flames of South Africa* for symphony orchestra, jazz quartet, singer, and soloist (sax or cello). For the first time, he heard his work played by the full complement of strings. On the basis of a tape of the Hanover performance, I suspect it may be his most consistently persuasive work. Written in four movements ("The Spirit of Biko," "African Queen," "Rage," "Victory"), it opens with an attractive flute solo, features some of Peterson's most constrained and eloquent trumpet playing, and underscores his ability to write for strings—the cello parts are especially strong—and integrate them naturally into the music's buoyant rhythms. In 1981, Enja recorded *The Angels of Atlanta*, a work for Peterson's jazz quintet and the Boys Choir of Harlem in which he returned to the theme of violated innocence, provoked by the serial murders of young boys in Georgia.

For flamboyance and reach, however, those works pale before *African Portraits*, his most daring and widely performed tableau. On November 11, 1990, the American Composers Orchestra, conducted by Paul Lustig Dunkel, debuted this stunningly theatrical, omni-idiomatic symphony in a Carnegie Hall program that also featured works by David Lang and Lester Trimble. So expansive is the concept, it may sound preposterous in outline. In less than fifty minutes, Peterson traces three hundred fifty years of African American history, in two languages (Mandingo and English), with an ensemble of more than one hundred fifty performers, including the ACO, the Morgan State University Chorus, the five-man African Drumsong Society, the Hannibal Peterson Quintet (with Arthur Blythe on alto), and seven soloists (griot, blues singer, gospel singer, boy soprano, two baritones, and a tenor). The core themes of Peterson's work—the middle passage, slavery, and reconstruction—were not new to jazz. In addition to Ellington's *Black, Brown and Beige* in 1943, Max

Roach introduced his cri de couer *We Insist! Freedom Now Suite* in 1960. In 1994, four years after the premiere of *African Portraits*, Wynton Marsalis would debut his tumid oratorio *Blood on the Fields*. Yet in its wedding of broad pageantry, historical gravity, and musical economy, Peterson's work is unparalleled. The very sight of the assembled cast is intoxicating, a triumph in internationalism and a riot of color. As the resplendently attired African musicians—bearing drums, gourds, and kalimbas—take their places, audiences applaud the sheer audacity of the enterprise.

Like *Children of the Fire*, *African Portraits* begins with a peaceful setting: harvest season in seventeenth-century West Africa. The slave traders arrive, killing and kidnapping, and the first act ("The Drum and the Cross") ends with the appalling passage across the Atlantic. In the first scenes, Peterson deploys strings to replicate and amplify the tribal rhythms; the writing for the orchestra is spare and efficient, splitting into call-and-response between the cellos and violins. During the voyage sequence, members of the orchestra slide their bows vertically to suggest the straining of the ship amid battering winds. Nowhere is Peterson's humanism more apparent than in this episode, reducing unspeakable horror to two laments: an African boy trying to understand why the white men are so quick to kill his people, yet also bind the wounds and feed those who survive; and the captain, in a missive to his wife, inquiring about his children, celebrating the "great stock of slaves," and invoking the blessings of Jesus.

The second act ("The Land of Milk and Honey") begins at an auction mart in Charleston in 1833 ("March 5, 1:00 P.M."), where the shouting of the auctioneer is counterposed by the plaintive singing of a slave and the forebodings of the chorus. The piece then moves quickly from cotton fields in Elgin, Texas, in 1940 (the spiritual sung by Vanessa Bell Armstrong is an emotional highpoint, a melismatic renting of the soul with no trace of concert finery) to the Mississippi Delta (the blues, sung by Honeyboy Edwards) to the Three Deuces club on Fifty-second Street (Hannibal, Blythe, and rhythm in a raucous, decidedly postbop fever, replete with circular breathing calisthenics) to a big finish in Bensonhurst in 1989 (a wonderfully percussive episode marrying strings, drums, and the griot's shouts), concluded by the choir's contrapuntal "Redemption."

Through it all, the sight of Peterson himself, beaming with pleasure and miming every rhythm and emotion, all but mirrored the music. Dunkel was in control of the larger design, but the performance was imperfect. Peterson wanted an authentic blues singer, but Honeyboy Edwards, whose guitar was barely audible, had not mastered the lyric, and the drama began to wane with his segment; by contrast, the jazz episode that immediately follows was overblown—a theme more in keeping with the Fifty-second Street era might have tightened it, no matter how free the playing got.

Those quibbles became academic as the piece gathered steam in subsequent performances with numerous orchestras, performers, and conductors, notably Daniel Barenboim, who took a particular fancy to the work and shepherded it through its 1995 recording on Teldec. The record proved to be as successful as the concerts, affirming Peterson's decision to fix his attention on extended works. Nathan Carter conducts the Morgan State University Choir, Jevetta Steele soars in the gospel episode, and Honeyboy Edwards, now in command of the material, enjoys acoustic equity. The jazz episode remains incendiary, in true Hannibal fashion, but is now grown tauter. Peterson has done something fine in bringing pageantry and Americana and history to the symphony—integrating diverse musics into a coherent drama. He has created a fresh and emphatic context for an oft-told tale that can never be told often enough.

59 ❖ *Jimmy Rowles (The Late Hurrah)*

I was pleased to discover in an old file the yellow flyer handed out at Johnny Mercer's 1973 "Interludes" concert at Town Hall. It offers little in the way of information, except the day (January 10) and time (5:45), a partial list of songs he would *not* be singing that afternoon, and a Hollywood-style credit for his accompanist: "Jimmy Rowles California's greatest Jazz Pianist." At the time, Rowles was virtually unknown in New York, so the West Coast chauvinism was justifiable, if a bit thick; maybe the typesetter set a lower case *g* for balance. By the end of the '70s, the regionalism was entirely pointless. Rowles may or may not have been California's greatest (some might argue for Hampton Hawes or Oscar Peterson), but at fifty-five he was about to cease being a local secret and become a national one—national being a synonym for New York. No sooner did he move east than his name, which had not adorned the front of a record jacket since 1962, began appearing above the title on album after album, more than a dozen in quick succession.

The discovery of Rowles was a good lesson for a tyro jazz critic since it demonstrated that you had to be on the lookout not only for young trailblazers, but for mature talents hidden in the wilderness. André Hod-

ier, in a widely noted essay, once asked of jazz musicians, "Why Do
They Age So Badly?" The '70s proved repeatedly that they often don't;
with the arrival of every new teenage wizard, an older musician who'd
been patiently perfecting his skills or recovering from premature retirement (from Muhal Richard Abrams to Joe Venuti) made a bid for attention. Rowles had long been a musician's musician, a coveted accompanist
with a coveted résumé. Now he was taking his own bows. The summer
after the Mercer concert, he appeared on a piano tribute to Art Tatum
at the Newport–New York Jazz Festival and with a trio in a club. He
decided to relocate and quickly became a fixture at the Cookery, Bradley's, and other New York piano bars. A few things about Rowles stood
out from the start. He didn't *sound* like anyone else; he knew more tunes
than Sigmund Spaeth; and he was, on occasion, droll in the way that
only a grizzled hipster can be. For example, he wrote a honky tonk song
called, "The Ballad of Thelonious Monk"; for another, he sang several
numbers in a gig with Zoot Sims from an opera-in-progress about Carmen Lombardo—his lyrics, Bizet's music.

Though Rowles was known only to the cognoscenti at the start of his
New York stay, he did not spring out of nowhere (nowhere being a
synonym for California). Born in Spokane, Washington, in 1918, he settled in Los Angeles in 1940 and worked with Slim Gaillard and Lester
Young before going on the road with several big bands, including those
of Benny Goodman and Woody Herman. Four years on Bob Crosby's
radio show led to diverse studio assignments, but he remained active as
an accompanist for visiting and local eminences, such as Charlie Parker,
Benny Carter, Stan Getz, Zoot Sims. He wrote neat spacey arrangements
for Julie London, and when Nelson Riddle elected to record his Nat Cole
arrangements without singing, Rowles was chosen to play all the solos,
for the most part with one finger.

Somewhere along the way, he earned a reputation accompanying
singers as the Gerald Moore of jazz. He was favored by Billie Holiday,
Peggy Lee, Ella Fitzgerald, Sarah Vaughan, Carmen McRae, Kay Starr,
and Carol Sloane, with whom he developed a close working relationship
in the mid- and late '70s. His move to New York coincided with the
release of McRae's *The Great American Songbook*, which includes her de-
piction of Rowles as "the guy every girl singer in her right mind would
love to work with (check this statement with Sassy)." Sassy seconded
the motion a few months later, with *Sarah Vaughan & the Jimmy Rowles
Quintet*. The contemporaneous release of *Billie Holiday Songs & Conversations*, a 1955 rehearsal tape of interest because of Holiday's loquacious
chat with Rowles, served as a reminder of his most fruitful (her *Body and
Soul*, for example) and fabled collaboration with a singer.

Now ensconced in New York, Rowles established close relationships with the bassists he worked with, especially Buster Williams and George Mraz. His cryptic, patient way of developing a piano solo was mirrored by a pun that developed at Bradley's, during his first engagement with the Czechoslovakian-born Mraz, whom Rowles took to calling Bounce. A few days into the gig, Mraz asked him why he called him that. The deadpan reply was, "Cause you're a bad Czech." Rowles soon recorded with duos and trios for a variety of labels. Among the best albums were *Jimmy Rowles* (Halcyon), which introduced his much performed original, "The Peacocks," and was produced by Marian McPartland; *We Could Make Such Beautiful Music Together* (Xanadu), which includes such oddities as "How Do You Do Miss Josephine," a turn-of-the-century vaudeville tune, and "Stars and Stripes Forever"; and *Jimmy Rowles on Tour* (S.I.R.), from a Swedish venture that includes Delibes's "The Maids of Cadiz" and is the most outgoing of his trio records. For the most part, those are subtle and understated performances.

But in 1977, he appeared with tenor saxophonists on three far more accessible albums that remain among the most satisfying of the decade. *The Peacocks* (Columbia), produced by and costarring Stan Getz, had actually been in the can for a few years. It typifies Rowles's range of interests, combining a heightened realization of the title selection with pieces by Ellington, Strayhorn, and Wayne Shorter (three composers to whom he was devoted) and standards, some of which feature his own appealingly froglike voice—Jimmy Durante on Valium. *Heavy Love* (Xanadu) pairs Rowles with Al Cohn for a series of tour de force duets that, despite familiar material, persistently lift the spirits of both men. Best of all is the reunion with Zoot Sims, *If I'm Lucky* (Pablo), an inspired quartet session that triggered a long collaboration: a particular delight is the hot version of Cole Porter's "It's All Right with Me," played in a rampaging long meter that perfectly captures the give and take between stalwart tenor and daring piano. During Zoot's first improvised chorus, Rowles pumps him up with chords; in the second, he brings in crescendo tremolos that gather like storm warnings. His own two-chorus solo is of a sort no one else would attempt—a coherent montage of hammered single notes, offhanded dissonances, wandering arpeggios, abrupt bass walks, trebly rambles. When Sims returns, the pianist probes every open space, spurring him until you think they might burst out of orbit. They made at least six Pablo records together, of which *Passion Flower, I Wish I Were Twins,* and *Suddenly It's Spring* are outstanding. Rowles shines brightest when he also functions as a catalyst.

Rowles is not an aggressive or showy player; he leaves lots of space, uses dynamics sparingly, and swings softly and at an even gait. What makes him remarkable is his ear for detail (the fills that make his accompaniments so stylish are no less disarming when he uses them to decorate his own solos), his depth of feeling (he could play a melody straight and make it sound like improvisation), and his harmonic ingenuity (he rarely attacks a chord head-on, preferring dense substitutions or oblique angles). His repertory is immense and arcane: originals, standards, and oddities, along with his mastery of Shorter (not the Miles Davis pieces, but those from the Blakey period, like "The Chess Players," "Running Brook," and "Lester Left Town") and the Ellington-Strayhorn book. For years, he was virtually alone in resurrecting such neglected works as "Isfahan" (to which he added lyrics), "Blood Count," "Black Butterfly," "Lost in Meditation," and "Lotus Blossom," as well as recreating on the piano the Ellington band's orchestral sonorities and classic improvisations. This obsession resulted in his masterpiece, *Jimmy Rowles Plays Duke Ellington and Billy Strayhorn* (Columbia), in which he offers Ellingtonian melodies, harmonies, voicings, and solos. He can do Ben Webster on piano, or at least come closer than anyone should reasonably expect. The more you know about Ellington and Strayhorn, the more jokes you'll get, but it's no requirement. Just turn the volume up so you can hear the muffled chords and the overtones, and adjust yourself to Rowles's dilated tempos. "Take the A Train," "Isfahan," "Jumpin' Punkins," and the intro to "Mood Indigo" are amazing, the rest merely remarkable. The record was in and out of print in a flash; soon after (no cause and effect, he suffered severely from asthma), he returned to California.

Once, in the fall of 1984, he returned to New York for an evening at Merkin Hall, produced by a dentist who "really missed Jimmy's playing." It was the first time he'd had star billing in a New York concert hall. Rowles entered in a tuxedo; California was so hot, he said, that New York seemed like Alaska, and then played Shorter's "Running Brook." He dabbled at several tunes, medley-style, including "Laugh, Clown, Laugh," "Remember When," and "No More" ("Lady Day," he croaked by way of introduction). It was apparent that he wasn't up for expansive improvisation but that he could still cast a spell with a good tune: the bridge on "Skylark" was a souffle with the barest hint of a striding bass. With the addition of Major Holley and Charli Persip, he embarked on a driving version of "The Chess Players" and lightened up for a few ballads (including "The Peacocks," which was itself a kind of testimony to Rowles's deep appreciation of Strayhorn), a blues, and Carl Perkins's "Grooveyard." Holley and Persip played hard, but Rowles remained unfrazzled and etched his solos with deliberation.

Then Zoot Sims came out, and the tone changed entirely. Sims had been seriously ill, so his guest appearance had an additional emotional wallop (Rowles said, "he's like my brother"). He appeared surprisingly fit, and sounded like his old self, spinning fervid, quicksilver melodies, pushing the rhythms (Persip whipped himself into a frenzy keeping up), and luxuriating in that hard-earned sound of his that made peace between Lester Young and Ben Webster in order to yield its own classic sonority. The concert was unamplified, and Sims's sound flooded the hall with a robust beauty. He played "In the Middle of a Kiss" (from *Suddenly It's Spring*) and "Shadow Waltz" (*If I'm Lucky*), the latter an all-out assault that had Persip and Holley pumping hard and Rowles feeding in with thick, staccato chords. The second set featured Rowles's daughter Stacy, a twenty-nine-year-old flugelhornist and trumpet player, who compensated for a thin sound by focusing on the middle register and phrasing in an efficient conversational manner, though relying too much on a mute. She contributed to a moving version of "Lotus Blossom," the Strayhorn song that Ellington played while the musicians packed up at the end of *And His Mother Called Him Bill*. The set's peak was Rowles's charmingly hoarse vocal on "The Leopard," his lyricised version of "Isfahan."

And he was gone. Almost annually in the years before his 1996 death rumors would abound that he was due for a visit, a club booking or a spot at the summer festival. They came to nothing, reportedly because of his illness and the difficulties he had flying. He continued to record, yet the energy level had abated, and only intermittently could he find the animation to match his unmistakable touch and harmonic palette. But he completed a reflective final statement in 1994, *Lilac Time* (Kokapelli), when he was seventy-six, a recording of unexampled gentleness, produced once again by an admiring musician (Herbie Mann). On who else's album would you find "A Night in Tunisia" *and* "Jeannine, I Dream of Lilac Time" or a medley fusing "Chloe" and "Maids of Cadiz" or a selection that runs twenty-two seconds? All those seances in dark bars, where half the attentive audience consisted of other pianists, now seem aberrational, and Rowles himself a beneficent ghost. The moral: Keep an ear out for the ghosts, even California's greatest.

60 ❖ John Carter
(American Echoes)

Is there a precise antonym for "flamboyant?" If so, it might serve as a partial description of John Carter, the quietly brilliant clarinetist, alto saxophonist, composer, catalyst, and educator, who died March 31, 1991, of lung cancer. He was only sixty-one, yet his loss felt like that of an even younger man because we really didn't get to know him until he was in his mid forties. The profound change in his art and life coincided with his decision to quit the alto saxophone in favor of the clarinet. On the former, he was a species of Ornette Coleman; on the latter, an innovative stylist. For some reason, the switch in instruments prefigured an astonishing maturation in Carter's work as a composer. Again, the result was a shifting away from Coleman—the lineaments of his brittle melodicism—to a capacious vision of America's motley musical history, realized in the five suites that make up his ponderously titled *Roots and Folklore: Episodes in the Development of American Folk Music.*

It sometimes seems that every musician to come out of Fort Worth after Tex Beneke was associated with Coleman in the '40s, a myth that tends to contradict the larger myth of Coleman's enforced musical isolation. Carter knew him in school, along with a couple of other musicians who made impressive leaps onto the international stage in the '60s, Charles Moffett and Dewey Redman. Like Redman, he served an apprenticeship in academia, but unlike him he remained in education long after getting his master of arts degree, and not in the plush groves of academe either. Carter spent virtually all his adult life teaching public school—a dozen years in Fort Worth, more than twenty in Los Angeles. After he left the school system in 1982, he started the Wind College, an academy for improvisers whose tutors included James Newton, Red Callender, and Charles Owens.

Of course, he also had another life as a performer. In 1964, he formed the New Art Jazz Ensemble with trumpeter Bobby Bradford, an association that led to his first recording, *Flight for Four*, in 1969. The blend of Carter's alto and Bradford's trumpet had an affirmative, stately quality— they were a more conventional version of Coleman and Don Cherry. As they continued to work together, the improvisations became increasingly intimate and conversational. Peter Bull captured the intensity of their relationship in his 1980 film, *The New Music*, a spartan documentation of the way they answered and anticipated each other's note patterns and colorational nuances. By that time, Carter had long since opted for the clarinet (he made the change in 1974). After a silence of nearly six years as far as recording went, he announced what he saw as a musical rebirth with characteristic rectitude: the release of a privately pressed album, *Echoes from Rudolph's,* recorded in 1977 with his son Stanley on bass.

After hearing that album, I portentously proclaimed, "Carter is the first clarinetist to say something really new on the instrument since Pee Wee Russell died, and this record will prove seminal when word gets around." But things didn't work out that way. *Rudolph's* was essentially a vanity production, and though the album's one unaccompanied solo, "Angles," is one of the liveliest keepsakes of an era in which unaccompanied woodwind solos were stupefyingly fashionable, it was never widely heard. Yet word of Carter spread slowly, steadily, and within five years he had bridged the gap from West to East Coast and to Europe. Surrounded by such colleagues as Bradford, Newton, Callender, and Owens, while building an additional coterie that included Benny Powell, Andrew Cyrille, Marty Ehrlich, Terry Jenoure, and Don Preston, he began to introduce sumptuous, rangy ensembles that spanned tuba to flute, Third World percussion to southern gospel, reconstruction minstrelsy to rock-era synthesizer.

He recorded a series of albums for the German label, Moers Music, including an entire recital of solo clarinet with the prophetic title, *A Suite of Early American Folk Pieces for Solo Clarinet.* His breakthrough year was 1982. In February and March, he recorded *Dauwhe* in Los Angeles for Black Saint; inspired by the African influence on American music and complete in itself, it proved to be the first in the *Roots and Folklore* series. At the end of 1982, he introduced Clarinet Summit at the Public Theater. That quartet—Carter, Alvin Batiste, and Jimmy Hamilton on soprano clarinet, David Murray on bass clarinet—was a miracle of jazz inbreeding. Hamilton's presence alone was surprising since he'd been teaching in the Virgin Islands following the death of Duke Ellington. Indeed, all but Murray had been earning the best part of their livelihoods in the classroom. What made the concert (recorded by India Navigation) a formative event was the ease with which the much-rehearsed ensemble glided over a program that encompassed Hamilton's pithy arrangement of "Creole Love Call" and Carter's "Ballad for Four Clarinets," which begins as the extended swelling of a single pitch.

Carter will be chiefly remembered, however, for *Roots and Folklore.* After *Dauwhe,* he signed with Grammavision, the label that commendably saw the project through four increasingly riveting additions: *Castles of Ghana* in 1986, *Dance of the Love Ghosts* in 1987, *Fields* in 1988, and *Shadows On a Wall* in 1989. In the 1989 *Village Voice* jazz poll, thirty-three participating critics voted the series second place (after the World Saxophone Quartet's *Revue*) among the best records of the '80s. I am especially partial to the last two because they most successfully draw on the specific skills of each musician and integrate the vocals into the ensemble. Beyond that, they most effectively convey all the memories, learned and experienced, that Carter used to spice up his deeply personal music. Despite the presence of guests (like Jelly Roll Morton, Carter brought in supporting players for extra effects), he settled on an octet as his ideal ensemble: he isolated and paired its members—two reeds, two brasses, two strings, drums and keyboard—and pitted them against each other in the manner of big band sections. The result is heady with dramatic reverberations and allusions that emerge like flavors in an exquisitely seasoned meal. His is the best kind of program music because it works its magic through the power of suggestion.

Fields, especially, is a beautiful and disturbing record. Here, in part four, he contemplated pretechnocratic America for the first time. The fields of the title, metaphorical yet real, were inspired, Carter wrote in his notes, by the rural community in north central Texas where he summered as a boy with his grandparents and the uncle for whom he was named. He actually employs a taped conversation with Uncle John, aged ninety, in an uncommonly human application of musique concrete, to personalize the piece. Like all successful program music, however, *Fields* is less concerned with the particularity of person and place than with a state of mind—a sector of emotion.

What an introverted journey Carter himself had taken. Not for him the maverick sojourn of Ornette Coleman, but rather a life committed to the public school system, so that he was almost forty when the quartet he formed with Bobby Bradford debuted. Nearly another decade passed before *Echoes from Rudolph's* demonstrated that his virtuosity, which had never been in question, was fully complemented by an individual, innovative, and compassionate approach to improvisation. Compassion is the odd word here, of course, but it suggests the warmth and reflection with which he addressed his instrument, his talent, and his music. In hindsight, the word becomes almost unavoidable because his subsequent recordings with ensembles of various sizes showed him to be equally responsive to all the musicians and instruments that came under his wing. *Fields* suggests that the benignity of his music had its roots in powerful familial bonds. That's why he got away with using the voices of four grandchildren to balance the recollections of Uncle John; it's why he was able to make an analogous point by juxtaposing synthesizer and harmonica.

Carter looked backward and forward with deadpan confidence. If *Fields* is picturesque, in the nature of program music, it is also decisively mysterious. A voice emerges as though it were a wooden flute; synthesizer replicates banjo; vamps are ominous and undulating; instrumental cries are almost ritualized into riffs (in some ways, *Fields* is about the way riffs are created out of inchoate cries). You hear more than is actually there because much of what Carter encourages you to hear is in your own imagination. The picturesque references are real, but submerged in a stream of subconsciousness. The jazz references alone would provide a pleasant game for a musical deconstructionist: swing and bebop, hard bop and free jazz, Mingus and Coleman, and a closing twelve-bar backbeat blues that is even more poignant than it is surprising, and it is very surprising. All of it is transmuted by Carter, who balances the parts like a painter balances colors and keeps each of his eight primary players—almost all of whom appeared on the two preceding suites—afloat and distinct.

Not the least rewarding aspect of *Fields* is the certainty with which it counters the prevailing lack of ambition and fear of innovation that stifled so much recording during the '80s. By ambition, I refer to the simple fact that jazz composers rarely had the option of recording with large ensembles. Record companies, big and small, are disinclined to offer great soloists the backing of compatible orchestrators or composers the complement of musicians necessary to flesh out their visions. By innovation, I mean the desire to go somewhere new simply because it is new. There was a time when we cheered that very impulse; now tastemakers are often exhausted by and impatient with innovators. Carter solved the first problem by voicing his musicians in such a way as to suggest a larger group and the second by refusing to accept the idea that by virtue of recording he is in the business of producing marketable product.

Fields is long and woolly, but by no means somber or inaccessible. Rich in ironies, luminescent in details, it sings the songs of Carter's collaborators, each of whom is impressively showcased. "Ballad to Po' Ben" opens with the clarinet's undulant repeated phrase; the vocal motif is heard in the undertow, the timbres of the woodwinds and brasses isolated in time and space. The first soloist is violinist-singer Theresa Jenoure, whose voice has a prophetic edge reminiscent of Abbey Lincoln, but with studied intonation and feeling. She has splendid pitch control, allowing her to indulge a falsetto exclamation, and she gives a shuddery thrill when she relaxes her mask for sustained notes that hover on the border of moans. The keening trombone solo, in which a plunger mute acerbically shapes each note, is testimony to the versatility of Benny Powell. This movement especially is held together by the shivery momentum of drummer Andrew Cyrille and bassist Fred Hopkins; the concluding drum solo is based on a march rhythm but with shifting accents.

In its controlled tension, it may be said to continue where the famous Shadow Wilson break on Basie's "Queer Street" leaves off.

The second part, "Bootyreba at the Big House," proceeds from the first without pause. A pulsing, dancing figure for clarinet, cornet, and bass clarinet, provoked ceaselessly by Cyrille and Hopkins, it achieves ever dizzier heights of jubilation while minding the structural imperatives. Marty Ehrlich's bass clarinet solo is played with Eric Dolphyesque finesse, building conscientiously on a motif, as does Bobby Bradford's cool cornet solo, paced with filigree arpeggios (and backed by sportive ensemble riffs); Don Preston's keyboard solo, in which he appears to exult in the sheer pleasure of playing so well; Jenoure's fiddle solo (Hopkins is especially forceful here); and Carter's clarinet solo, which soars into the upper register without sacrificing the liquidity of his sound or his ability to organize timbres into a compelling mosaic.

Carter is equally impressive on the subsequent "Juba's Run," his ripe, perfectly controlled pitches occasionally suggesting speech and often entwined with Ehrlich's bass clarinet. (One way to follow the whole work is to note how Carter doubles the two woodwinds, brasses, and strings as though each were a discrete family within the larger ensemble.) By contrast, the rhythms of "Seasons" are languorous and sunny, a setting for a conversation between violin and keyboards. Don Preston is best known for his years with Frank Zappa, but his belltone touch and modest use of sliding pitches and colors is consistently fetching in his work with Carter.

The title piece is the longest and the richest of the album. Like "Ballad to Po' Ben," it begins with an ominous vamp, dark and beguiling, with a flute sighing two-note chords and diverse moans filling out into haughty riffs that are extensions of the human voice; the minstrel era is eluded to in the ironic contrast of the strummed fiddle and a metallic synthesizer effect that suggests a banjo—a tableau of homemade music from which Carter's fat-toned clarinet emerges like libation in the desert. Uncle John's voice meshes with the instruments, and when it returns at the end of the movement, Benny Powell's urgent riffing appears to make his speech patterns swing as hard as the rest of the ensemble. The brief tripartite "Children of the Fields" works almost like a scherzo—disarming, spare, sentimental—before the final episode.

"On a Country Road" is introduced by the clarinet, bubbling like a swallow. Uncle John is telling a story to his nephew, and the cadences of his voice as well as the appreciative laughter of the composer (not the substance of the tale) are what count. The clarinet figure becomes a bit more complicated: it's an apparently simple, lyrical riff, but it requires a panoply of techniques to play, including a smooth switching of registers, circular breathing, and two-note chords. Hopkins picks it up, extending it into a vamp, and Cyrille comes in rocking. Without warning, we are returned to the twentieth-century with—what else?—a twelve-bar blues, racked over a vigorous backbeat. Bobby Bradford growls through two choruses, and then a new voice enters, Frederick Phineas on harmonica, that always evocative instrument. When the piece ends, quite suddenly, on his solo, we are, paradoxically, back in the fields after all.

Programmatic music challenges the listener. The listener needs to be as nonspecific in interpreting the work as the work itself. I've probably overstepped the bounds of nonspecificity in trying to describe parts of *Fields*. But program music as clear-eyed as this doesn't merely dabble in allusions. It also embodies a point of view, a political bite. Big issues are involved: life, art, family, tradition, fear, joy. Music cannot be translated into words or pictures, but *Fields* practically dares you not to try.

Carter must have been a fine teacher. One trait he shares with the best player-composers is a selfless distribution of star turns. In a sense, his music eschews showcases for individuals; the writing is so dense and the requirements of each player so specific that even when a soloist has the terrain to him- or herself you tend to be less conscious of the particular musician than of the instrument. That is, the relationships between, say, flute, trombone, and violin have a textural and spatial integrity that practically overwhelms the identity of the players. At the same time, no one can doubt that Bobby Bradford, Benny Powell, Marty Ehrlich, Fred Hopkins, and Andrew Cyrille, not to mention Terry Jenoure and Don Preston (who are little known in jazz beyond these recordings), have done some of their best work here. Carter's own role as clarinetist is fascinating. Listen to him connect with Ehrlich on "Juba's Run" on *Fields* or establish his solo on "Sippi Strut" on *Shadows on a Wall*. Here he burbles in midregister, there he croaks and squeaks, now he sustains long silvery arpeggios, then he flutters into the upper register with a robustness that belies the loss in gravity. He has total control over the instrument and can meld overtones into a kind of shadowy echo.

Jazz fans are luckier than we often realize. We inherit all sorts of musicians who don't fit the musical, racial, or social rules that govern more restrictive genres. It is as patently silly to label Carter a jazz musician as it is to call every American of color black. Enthusiasts of jazz clarinet know perfectly well that that genre is embodied in the tradition of Johnny Dodds, Jimmie Noone, Pee Wee Russell, Benny Goodman, Artie Shaw, Edmond Hall, Lester Young, Buddy DeFranco, and a few others and are perfectly justified in finding Carter a very different proposition. He came out of jazz, but his vision was neither limited nor compromised by it. Traditionalist Jimmy Hamilton knew how good he was, but you probably have to love the instrument more than the idiom to fully appreciate what he could do with it. And you have to admire the nature of indulgent virtuosity to share Carter's enjoyment in his mastery. In an old R. Crumb strip, the artist depicts himself listening to Virgil Thomson's film score for *The Plough That Broke the Plains*, strings and banjo, and comments, "Yup, American music." Yup, that's what John Carter made.

61 ❖ Dee Dee Bridgewater (Back Home Again)

The quietest moment during Dee Dee Bridgewater's breathless homecoming week at the Village Vanguard in the fall of 1995 was a reading of "Polka Dots and Moonbeams," which she dedicated to and claimed to have cribbed from Sarah Vaughan, after commenting that Sarah had perfect pitch, whereas her own pitch was merely relative. The apology was unnecessary. No one present would have registered the subtlety. She opened a cappella for two exquisitely prolonged measures, then glided into time, occasionally imitating Vaughan's high embellishments and using Vaughan's style as a launch for exploring her own. It takes one to do one.

The noisiest moment was a quartet of Horace Silver songs, beginning with one she said she hadn't had the nerve to record on her then current all-Silver album, *Love and Peace* (Verve). As she recounted it, with actorly pacing and deft impressions, the Silver project was ready to go, except for the lyrics to "Mexican Hip Dance." In a panic, she called the auteur, catching him in the bathroom, and moments later he faxed her what she characterized as "the sickest, most disturbed lyrics ever written," apropos the revenge of Montezuma. "It's a cult thing," she decided, after reciting the lyric, as prelude to singing it with a Chiquita accent at a whomping tempo, waving her hands and flashing her eyes. The medley proceeded with "The Preacher," "Peace," and "The Gringo" ("that's a sick one, too"), and she finished with a faux contralto cadenza that sounded like nothing so much as davening. The last artist to get that kind of response at the Vanguard was Professor Irwin Corey.

Not the least impressive aspect of the two numbers was their back-to-back propinquity. That was the third set I caught, and I still didn't know what to expect—except, as they say, the unexpected. Not that she didn't repeat songs; she did, but the context changed, as did the patter. The whole week was like that juxtaposition: discursive, inventive, lunatic, radiant. A resident of France for a decade, Bridgewater flew in with her trio and husband the same day she opened, and never fully settled to earth (jet lag? her?). Every set had an improvisational impulsiveness, as well as an end-of-evening raspiness, totally appropriate to her will o' the wisp career and art. Bridgewater can do anything on a stage, her only problem is choosing which of many options suits her at the moment. If she can't find one, she can always do a five-minute riff, in an impeccable shanty Irish brogue, on Mother's need to get off the stage or do an impression of Tina Turner dancing. It all fits.

A nostalgic glow rose from the fire. She had not performed at the Vanguard in twenty-one years. Back in the '70s, some of us thought she was a sacred monster, the only promising vocalist of our generation. She was, too; she just failed to deliver on the promise, until maybe now. Raised in Michigan, Denise Garrett came to New York in 1970, where she married Cecil Bridgewater and was heard by Mel Lewis at a rehearsal. He told Thad Jones, and for more than three years, through 1974, Dee Dee Bridgewater was the unbilled singer at the Monday night gig, flooring audiences with industrial-strength scat vocals that rapped out riffs like a trumpet and ballads that combined the supper club gloss of Nancy Wilson with the harmonic smarts of Sarah Vaughan and the deeper wail of Carmen McRae.

Unhappily, we don't have a true record of that work. She was a singing Paladin—have voice, will travel—at the behest of her employers. Her only album appearance with Thad and Mel was her wordless improvisation on "The Great One" (*Suite for Pops*), recorded in 1972 but released nearly four years later. Her voice was also used instrumentally on tepid fusion albums by Norman Connors and Carlos Garnett. More ambitiously, she recorded a twenty-minute duet with Reggie Workman on Heiner Stadler's setting of Lenore Kandel's poem, "Love in the Middle of the Air." In 1974, she auditioned for the part of the good witch in *The Wiz* and got it: less than ten minutes on stage, with about five lines of dialogue and two songs. To the envious grumbles of colleagues on and offstage, this performance won her a Tony—it wasn't just Vanguard habitues who couldn't resist her. But the promise seemed to dissipate. Atlantic Records released a faceless, over-produced soup of hack tunes and au courant rhythms. Divorced, she was lured to Hollywood by trite parts. Then she changed her life and emigrated to Paris.

Bridgewater's work since that time won her an enthusiastic European coterie, but was little heard here. In 1989, Impulse released a 1986 concert as *Live in Paris*, with a photo of her glowering on the cover. It begins with her best recorded performance to that point, "All Blues" (a number that has become her signature), but descends into hysteria with a few over-the-top ballads. Then Verve signed her, rather quietly, and released a 1990 concert, *In Montreux*, her first really representative album, fifteen years after the Vanguard. The free-scat intro to "All of Me" (and inventive pickup from the bass solo), the Sarah-sensitive "How Insensitive," the understated "A Child Is Born," the heaving "Night in Tunisia," and the Horace Silver trilogy, including his finest song, "Señor Blues," ground down with an impressive archness, affirm her formidable musicality. The record is additionally boosted by the presence of the Dutch pianist Bert van Den Brink, whose every solo is a model of clarity and melodic imagination; even on "Strange Fruit," where Bridgewater can add nothing to Holiday, his arrangement is enlightening.

Yet Bridgewater's real breakthrough on records came a couple of years later with the studio session *Keeping Tradition*, an album that might have scored big numbers had she been here to promote it with live performances. Bridgewater is not a chops singer, but the Vaughan influence is unmistakable in a scaled-down arrangement of the flag-waver "Fascinating Rhythm" and in "The Island," which is possibly steamier in Bridgewater's rendition than in Vaughan's, as well as "Polka Dots and Moonbeams." She pays canny homage to Holiday and Sinatra, and invokes her relationship with Horace Silver in two tunes. This is one record that accurately reproduces her voice. The raspiness that shows up in every lengthy concert performance is held at bay, and the songs are diverse and apt; she performed most of them at the Vanguard. Even her longstanding trio—Thierry Eliez, piano; Hein Van De Geyn, bass; Andre Ceccarelli, drums—is attentive and understated, if rarely inspired.

The next album, *Love and Peace*, included that trio and the Belmondo brothers: Stephane on trumpet, Lionel on tenor sax. This is the quintet she brought to Carnegie Hall in the summer of 1995 for a twenty-minute appearance that announced her willingness to storm the boards stateside and demonstrated her theatrically and dazzling command. As her third Verve album, a collaboration of this sort might seem shrewd, but given the neglect accorded its predecessors, it limits the range of her appeal. There are telling moments: the scat solo on "Tokyo Blues," the elegant balladry of "You Happened My Way," the expected pleasure of "Song for My Father," the revitalizing energy of "Doodlin'" (different from Sarah's, which boasted words to Silver's piano solo), and "The Jody Grind." But the inescapable sameness of the material is underscored by the periodic dryness of her voice.

No record can convey her greatest gift, which is to electrify the air where she sings. In this, she shares with a select few performers the ability to resist the containment of technology. One night at the Vanguard, I sat with a soldier on leave, who came by the late show to see the famous jazz club, not the performer, whose name he didn't know. Within ten minutes, he was elated. A few songs later, she dedicated "A Child Is Born" to the Vanguard brethren who were there twenty-one years ago: Lorraine Gordon, Mickey at the bar, Katy at the door, the shades of Thad and Mel. Neither the soldier nor most of the rest of the house knew what she was talking about, but as she inched through the song, the place was quiet as a church. It occurred to me that Dee Dee Bridgewater—who at the time was a year older than Billie Holiday was at her death—is still the one indisputably great jazz singer of my generation, and one of only half a dozen under sixty.

62 ❖ Julius Hemphill
(Gotham's Minstrel)

It's twilight of a Sunday afternoon in 1977, and the usual suspects are arrayed in front of the glass-enclosed Bowery bar at Second Street, smoking and kibbitzing and taking measure of the event inside: the debut of the Real New York Saxophone Quartet. A year earlier, Ed Jordan, Southern University's music department chairman, had invited four hot new saxophonists—Julius Hemphill, Oliver Lake, Hamiet Bluiett, and David Murray—down from New York to New Orleans for a concert, backed by a local rhythm section. The four liked the gig, but with the kind of bluff audacity that typified that lovely time, they jettisoned the rhythm section. Now arrayed under a willfully provocative name (another New York Saxophone Quartet, which played written music, preceded them), they take the stage at the Tin Palace and, with a gasp of four-part disharmony, unleash a furious carnage of sound, occasionally clarified by the emergence of a solo, but not by the voicings or compositions.

The splendor of the moment was less musical than psychological, less a consequence of contemplation or for that matter rehearsal than of a new generation's stubborn devotion to self. Except for Murray, not yet twenty-two, the players were anything but wet behind the ears. Hemphill, Lake, and Bluiett, comrades from the St. Louis collective BAG (Black Artists Group) before descending on New York, were in their mid- to late thirties. They had all scuffled on the city's mean streets for between one and four years, and if they seemed to work a lot—albeit chiefly lofts and gallery concerts, some recordings—they remained greatly distanced from the middle-class security of mainstream jazz clubs and little known above Fourteenth Street or beyond Europe.

Yet they had such ambitions: Hemphill with his theatrical presentations and one-man audiodramas; Lake shuttling between solo sax recitals and his disco jump band; Bluiett and Murray organizing orchestras. During that same period in 1977, Hemphill and Abdul Wadud played duets at Elsom Gallery; Murray and Lake (along with Henry Threadgill, Muhal Richard Abrams, Don Pullen, Lester Bowie, Chico Freeman) appeared in a Bluiett band at the Brook; Lake had a trio with Fred Hopkins and Michael Jackson at the Palace, as did Hemphill's Roi Boyé and the Gotham Minstrels; Hemphill and Lake duetted at Axis in Soho; Hemphill played three nights at UTO Theatrical Center with a quartet, had larger ensembles at the Brook and the Palace, and appeared in big bands led by Charles Tyler and Bluiett, who briefly developed an ongoing big band workshop at Environ (one night Bluiett had more people on the bandstand than the floor), while Murray released his first two records (simultaneously, of course), and so forth. The joint was jumping. During one Sunday break outside the Palace, an older musician coached a newcomer about the sharks at the record companies then courting him. "I'm covered," says the kid, "I got my piece," and he folds back his jacket to reveal a pistol.

So we're all feeling good about the Real New York Saxophone Quartet that afternoon, better perhaps than we should, because of the daring, the meeting of minds, the promise. But I don't think anyone suspected what would come of it, not even when the first album, recorded that summer in Germany, appeared. By that time, a lawsuit had convinced them to trade in "New York" for the "World," but little on the World Saxophone Quartet's *Point of No Return* suggested serious absorption in exploring the potential of a renegade sax section (Murray's hurly-burly "Scared Sheetless" pointedly fills most of the play time), and that little bit was by Hemphill, who always preferred group conception to workaday nightly improvisation.

Within three years, WSQ (now signed to Black Saint) was one of the most prominent ensembles in jazz, concertizing everywhere, and securing a measure of critical consensus that achieved epiphany when cautious Martin Williams added its 1981 Zurich recording of "Steppin' " to the *Smithsonian Collection of Classic Jazz*, the only selection recorded after 1966. It's unfair to see Hemphill as the sole compositional brain behind WSQ; even on the follow-up album, *Steppin'*, which Hemphill dominates, "P.O. in Cairo" demonstrates Murray's growing confidence as a composer and several of Bluiett's early pieces—"Suite Music," "I Heard

That"—are masterly. But if Hemphill's role wasn't analagous to that of John Lewis in the MJQ, it mirrored and surpassed that of Gil Evans in the Miles Davis Nonet. He had the firmest grasp of big band conventions, the surest sense of what had been done and could be expanded in saxophone voicings, and the deepest commitment to write for the quartet's instrumentation. He was so prolific that his sound came to embody the WSQ approach, but his special talent—a clarity of purpose that made every piece singlar, vividly indicative of a specific mood or idea—influenced the other members as well. By 1980 and *Revue*, he had earned comparison with every orchestrator from Benny Carter and Duke Ellington on who devised a trademark sound for saxophones. Significantly, WSQ played opposite the Four Brothers—Stan Getz, Zoot Sims, Al Cohn, Jimmy Giuffre—at Kool Jazz in 1982.

And yet WSQ is only a part, maybe not the best part, of what Hemphill achieved before his death at fifty-seven on April 2, 1995, after years of illness—diabetes, heart disease, cancer—that had robbed him of a leg and years of music making. Saxophonist Marty Ehrlich, who along with Tim Berne is Hemphill's most steadfast disciple, pointed out "He got lumped in with the avant-garde, but he was really his own academy. One mark of his genius is that he found his own musical language at a really young age—it's pretty much all there in 'Dogon A.D.' "

Hemphill traveled a road similar to that of many musicians of his generation. Born in 1938 in Fort Worth, he was less than a decade younger than the trio of reed players who personified the Fort Worth mythography, Ornette Coleman, Dewey Redman, and John Carter, with whom he studied. He apprenticed in r & b bands, but relocated at twenty-eight to St. Louis, where he discovered other irreverent musicians weaned at the nexus of blues, jazz, and pop, as well as multimedia artists, among them BAG cofounder Malinke Robert Elliot, with whom Hemphill collaborated on various works.

In 1972, he formed a label, Mbari, and recorded four pieces, three of them released as *Dogon A.D.*, and the fourth, "The Hard Blues," issued three years later on *'Coon Bid'ness*. How startlingly fresh that music remains: the sinuous, sensuous, riveting directness of his blues is at once fiercely elemental and engagingly modern. On "The Painter," each of four players fills a discrete role suggesting the part-writing of a chamber group or a microcosm of a big band's antiphonal section work. Hemphill plays ardent, piping flute on the sixteen-bar theme, marrying ingenuous lyricism and purposeful dissonance, accompanied by Philip Wilson's spare brushwork and Abdul Wadud's Delta cello. Those records have lost nothing to time. And *'Coon Bid'ness*'s "Skin 1" and especially "Skin 2," with Hamiet Bluiett, prefigure his penchant for close saxophone harmonies. At a time when solo and duo wind recitals were commonplace, he collaborated with Oliver Lake on one of the best, *Buster Bee*, showing his strong yet uncompromisingly individual link to Charlie Parker.

Hemphill had a powerful theatrical streak: he performed hairless or hirsute in extravagant dashikis, gold lame, a variety of hats and earrings. His dramatic collaborations included *The Orientation of Sweet Willie Rollbar* in 1973 and *Long Tongues: A Saxophone Opera* in 1990. But his most memorable character was alter ego Roi Boyé, leader of the Gotham Minstrels, featured on two 1977 double-albums, where he solved the problem of sustaining a working band by overdubbing all the parts himself. *Roi Boyé and the Gotham Minstrels*, with its vocal deadpan and static rhythms, is often bleak and affectless, but *Blue Boyé*, an autobiographical jaunt through his southwestern boyhood, is a lark, from the alarming counterpoint of "Countryside" to the disarming gospel lament of "C.M.E." Everyone who's heard it enthusiastically recalls that album's "Kansas City Line," a ten-bar blues (at the end of every chorus you feel as if he might go over a cliff, but he always grabs the tonic in time) in which he descries the spirit and fiber of Parker without reiterating his actual phrases, an effect achieved by muting notes and twisting figures that are almost but not quite generic.

Parker's impact on Hemphill's playing is one of its primary delights because his take is so clear and yet so oblique. You can't miss it, but if you are a moldy bopper you might not accept it. Hemphill never plays a shell game with his music; originality indemnifies him against his influences, allowing him to borrow freely and transform accordingly. One of his most poignant compositions, "Bordertown," suggests the mariachi melody Copland borrowed for *El Salon Mexico* and is transfigured no less economically and movingly. He didn't make as many records as others in his generation, in part because of illness, but also because of a disinclination to accept conventional blowing sessions. Marty Ehrlich notes that he practiced constantly, yet had little interest in playing as an end in itself.

So we have a succession of projects, and among those, one of the finest is the 1988 *Julius Hemphill Big Band*, which takes the typical tack of opening with a few seconds of menacing dissonance before giving up a tidewater of opulent melody. Another is the Julius Hemphill Sextet, an ensemble of saxophones that didn't care to advertise its instrumentation in the name and didn't need to. *Fat Man and the Hard Blues* and *Five Chord Stud* are among his most decisive works, affording excellent solos by Ehrlich, Tim Berne (whose *Diminutive Mysteries*, with David Sanborn, is an elaborate interpretation of Hemphill's music), Andrew White, and the then little-known James Carter, while subordinating them to the collective scheme to a degree the WSQ members generally resisted.

Yet despite his focus on saxophones, I wonder if his truest soul mate wasn't cellist Abdul Wadud, who twanged and plucked in collusion with Hempill's alto, soprano, and flute in a variety of contexts for more than twenty years, from *Dogon A.D.* to *Julius Hemphill Trio* (a de facto greatest hits recital with "Georgia Blue," "Dogon A.D.," "Floppy," and "Bordertown") and the more exuberant *Oakland Duets*, a 1992 concert at which they rouse each other in colloquies of impressive concentration and rare candor. For all his enterprise and flamboyance, that honesty was Julius Hemphill's primary claim on our loyalties.

63 ❖ *Don Pullen*
(Last Connections)

Charles Mingus told of all-night rehearsals in which bassists slit their fingers with razors, played through the pain to build up calluses, and then slit them again. Don Pullen, whose second coming in jazz was signaled by service in Mingus's Jazz Workshop, had scars on the backs of his hands from raking them across keys to effect aggressive glisses and clusters on the piano. The expense of blood in pursuit of technique is generally considered unnecessary, but Pullen's hands graphically express his triumph in forging a unique, radiant style at a time when innovation, technical or otherwise, had been stalled in the backwater of traditionalism. Pullen, it needs hardly be said, did not arrive at the summit overnight. He was thirty-eight when he organized his breakthrough quartet with George Adams in 1979, and for more than a decade after that, he was stigmatized in some quarters as a knotty and inaccessible musician, an avant-garde refugee from the '60s. Yet after the band with Adams folded, his many solo performances and a first-rate album, *New Beginnings* (Blue Note), showed he had achieved something more lasting than brazen technique.

During the height of the New Thing in jazz in the mid-'60s, an exhilarating stream of new musicians came on the scene, most of whom were trying to play something no one had played before. One forgotten benefactor of that period is the saxophonist and pianist Giuseppi Logan, who had studied at the New England Conservatory and participated in the

1964 Bill Dixon concerts known as the October Revolution. Health problems caused his swift disappearance from music, but not before he demonstrated his ability to nurture talent with a 1964 quartet that included Milford Graves, Eddie Gomez, and Pullen.

Pullen's recorded concerts with Logan on (ESP-Disk) and his 1966 duets at Yale with Graves (released on their own label, S.R.P.) got him unfairly typed as an apprentice Cecil Taylor. The comparison wasn't entirely off the wall. In those years and even in the mid-'70s, Pullen employed a stop-and-go rhythmic attack, short and acerbic motifs, and bass-clef bombast set against intemperate sprinklings of notes in the treble—gambits associated more with Taylor than his own emerging approach, which is based on scrupulous harmonic control and countable rhythms. Pullen had studied previously with Muhal Richard Abrams in Chicago, but Abrams himself was little known then, so if you played clusters, you were measured against Taylor. Pullen himself soon disappeared.

In February 1973 at the Village Vanguard, Mingus held an open rehearsal for a Carnegie Hall concert. Many of us in attendance were delighted to find Pullen at the piano. During a break, he mentioned that he'd been Nina Simone's musical director for the past year and that Roy Brooks, Mingus's drummer, had recommended him for the Jazz Workshop. We commiserated about the passing of the avant-garde scene, and he asked, "What ever happened to Byron Allen?" I told him, "I don't know, I was wondering what happened to you." His playing that day, lithe and impeccably fingered, broken up by prearranged sequences of fierce glissandi, suggested enormous strides since the concerts with Graves and Logan. He spent two stormy years with Mingus, but the records were invariably disappointing. Only the double-album set, *Changes*, by which time Dannie Richmond had returned and George Adams and Jack Walrath shared the front line, show what the band could do. When he went on his own, Pullen embarked on a prolific recording regimen, albeit for small foreign labels, that showed he was a man of more parts than we knew.

His first album, a 1975 solo recital on Sackville, found him assembling his own style in response to the styles of his immediate predecessors. Indeed, it's difficult to listen to the four selections without discerning the shadows of Randy Weston ("For Richard"), Bill Evans ("Suite Sweet Malcolm"), Horace Silver ("Big Alice"), and Cecil Taylor ("Song Played Backwards"). His next recital, on Horo, consisted of two lengthy meditations—reminders of the impact Keith Jarrett had in the '70s with his solo concerts and gospel vamps. Yet as beholden to Jarrett as the title piece, "Five to Go," occasionally is, the flip side, "Four Move," though long-winded, is a definite advancement, combining the sublimated romance and bridled euphoria that are emblematic of Pullen's mature playing. That same year, there were quartet sessions with George Adams for Horo and a smashing quartet on Black Saint, *Capricorn Rising*, with Sam Rivers and Bobby Battle: the pointillistic yet fluent motion of his vamp-anchored solo on "Joycie Girl," his ferocious interaction with Battle on "Fall Out," the tempo changes on the title piece, and his quicksilver responses to Rivers on "Break Out" point the way to an assertion of self that moots the issue of influence.

In 1979 Pullen and Adams organized a full-time quartet with Dannie Richmond and bassist Cameron Brown, and if records only intermittently capture the steam the group regularly worked up in concert (the Adams vocals, often amusing live, stand up less well on records), they suffice to insure the band's standing as one of the best of the '80s. Not the least of its accomplishments was a book of originals that obviated any need for standards, though a few were played anyway. Pullen's "The Necessary Blues," "Samba for Now," and his Alice cycle grew in stature over time. Adams, the showman, would conduct with a finger or windmill arms or knee-bends; during solos, he would roll his eyes until only the whites showed. If you could get close enough to the keyboard, Pullen's physicality was no less occult. In one passage, his third and fourth fingers were bent down so that the fingers connected with the keyboard at the joints; in another, his four-finger clusters were arched so as to resemble goose shadows. Scar tissue discolored his knuckles and wrists pink and white.

Though Pullen played with percussive abandon, the rhythms were foursquare and countable. Though the sides and backs of his hands washed back and forth in a blur, the colors he produced supplemented the preset harmonies—at times, they were like an extension of Tatum's speed-of-light arpeggios. He could make those washes do anything he wanted, make them sound tumultuous or lyrical. He could tighten them into acerbic glissandi that filled out the chords with radiant color. He had become an undeniably recognizable stylist; suspicions of influence disappeared. Cecil Taylor's name was invoked only to underscore the differences between them. Taylor himself became an avowed fan. Pullen had rehabilitated harmony without sacrificing knuckle-busting brawn. He began to favor sambas and calypsos and flamenco, as well as ballads and blues, and he could lead you with inspired tenacity and the kind of offhanded good humor that virtuosity breeds in wise musicians from idyllic themes into the woods of squally variations and back again.

Pullen was beset by an inability to find and keep fitting accompanists, however, especially drummers—he would attain blistering cohesion with Bobby Battle in one performance and methodical dialogue with Ben Riley at another. On *New Beginnings*, in 1988, he worked with meticulous if occasionally busy response from Tony Williams and outstanding work from bassist Gary Peacock. The album, brimming with generous impulses and substantial variety, is virtually a résumé of how far Pullen had come as composer and pianist. The opener, "Jana's Delight," is a buoyant vamp tune, measured in eight-bar sequences and spelled by a lyrical twelve-bar bridge and a four-bar chordal finish; not until his third chorus do rapid washes enhance the efficient solo. The waltz "Once Upon a Time" counterposes eight bars of carnival sweetness with eight of jittery response in a performance of anarchic precision.

The terpsichorean "Warriors," which originally appeared as a half-hour rampage on a Black Saint recording of the same name, is now a contained vignette, the theme bobbing and weaving down the keyboard with exuberant sass. "At the Cafe Centrale" is a flamenco toe dance. Pullen's legato single-note inventiveness is handsomely represented on the title piece, but perhaps his most dynamic performance is "Reap the Whirlwind," its clusters suggesting a rhythmic power borne on the joy of thoroughgoing confidence and sustained in a martial drum solo and a bass solo in which the strings snap rhythmically against the wood. The one unaccompanied performance, "Silence = Death," is suitably introspective. Here, in full flower, embracing the slogan of the AIDS awareness group ACT-UP, Pullen limns a meditative ballad with tender clarity, altering his dynamics so that the piano sounds like chimes, extending the piece to the point of abstraction. Two-thirds through, he weds trebly clusters to midregister tones, producing mixed hues with a fixed palette.

New Beginnings is marred by fade-outs on "Jana's Delight" and "Warriors" that are inimical to the rush of excitement the pieces generate, a rush gratifyingly reinforced in Pullen's live performances of those pieces. Tony Williams occasionally sounds thin and/or busy, and the frequent drum and bass solos portend star power more than musical necessity. But the record was not a culmination of Pullen's work on those pieces. On the contrary, he outstepped his records as soon as they were released. At a subsequent set at the Village Vanguard with Ben Riley and Santi DiBriano, "Once Upon a Time" was bolstered with a more rugged bounce and the introduction of swing rhythms enforced a barrelhouse ebullience. "Ellington's Sound of Love," a romantic invocation by Mingus, was dramatized with pointed rests and ringing digital precision. "Warriors," in which dissonance is brought a bold step beyond Monk's minor seconds, closed with a big finish sorely missing from the record. At the time, it was possible to think of *New Beginnings* as merely a terrific souvenir.

❖ ❖ ❖

In fact, it was the beginning of a slow fade. Pullen's final years were death-ridden. The quartet with George Adams enjoyed an improbably successful run of nearly ten years, but was halted in 1988 when drummer Dannie Richmond died. Pullen's trio recordings of the early '90s were marked by ominous, even morbid titles: "Silence = Death," "Reap the Whirlwind," "Endangered Species: African American Youth," and "Ode to Life," a memorial suite. He was shaken by Adams's death in 1992, shortly after Pullen organized the African-Brazilian Connection and just before he instigated a collaboration between that group and Montana's Chief Cliff Singers. Within a year of the first African-Brazilian CD, Pullen was diagnosed with the lymphoma that would end his life at fifty-three on April 22, 1995. The CD he was working on in his last weeks was issued a year later as *Sacred Common Ground.*

Perhaps it's a mistake to read too strong a connection between intimations of mortality and the musical alterations that define Pullen's final works. But I can think of no musician of Pullen's stature whose art took so radical a rightward swing. At his best, his music possessed a heedless vivacity that matched the reckless raking of his knuckles and wrists over the keyboard. The chilling glissandi he generated, usually performed palms-up, made your hair stand on end. His reticence to use those painful techniques late in his career may simply reflect an acknowledgement of their toll. A cynic might speculate that he was simply opting for a more commercial formula in which chilling glissandi were best polished off in small doses. Yet in the end Pullen's last phase doesn't feel meretricious, medical, or ideological. Indeed, if his six Blue Notes—two trios, four African-Brazilian Connections—tip the scales a touch lite at times, their melodic invention is admirably steady. Something new has visited his music: on occasion the lyricism is so focused and unadorned that it seems scarcely possible that the theme is his own or that the variations will be sustained.

Pullen's piano style was a composite of at least three discrete approaches. The first to reach his audience was free or semifree, with short asymmetrical building blocks in the treble, great liberal washes over the keyboard, and jagged walks in the bass. The second (surely the first he perfected) was a straight-ahead attack based scrupulously on chords, with touches of gospel and blues, and a ringing percussive touch. The third, but first in importance, was his trademark attack, a wonder of jazz innovation that married the traditions of several homespun keyboard players, from Henry Cowell and his clusters to Jerry Lee Lewis and his glisses to Cecil Taylor and his tattoos, and came up with an original assault of his own. His control over a technique in which groups of keys were manipulated for whooping, laughing, cackling sounds was so precise that he could interpose them in decorous harmonic patterns without stretching a measure.

In the notes to the first Blue Note trio, *New Beginnings*, Pullen said he hoped to rekindle the spark of playing with Milford Graves in his avant-garde days. But if his neglected *Milano Strut* (Soul Note), a 1978 duet with Famoudou Don Moye, found him disporting with that kind of abandon, the trio album was marked by devotion to form, longing for melody, and at times a laconic distrust of his own strength. *New Beginnings* and its follow-up, *Random Thoughts*, with its contained expression and extended solemnity, were among his best, suggesting a new path, quite unlike those taken with Mingus and Adams. At the same time, he unveiled his smoky organ playing on David Murray's irresistible *Shakill* sessions (DIW), apparently primed to go in any number of directions. The direction he was planning became evident in 1992 when the first African-Brazilian Connection CD, recorded a year earlier, was released.

Kele Mou Bana, at best a Latin groove fest, remains the most stifled of Pullen's records, replete with the fugitive alto theme or piano vamp or percussion interlude, but rarely delivering on the promise of the mix, which involves saxophonist and flutist Carlos Ward in a role reminiscent of the one he played in Abdullah Ibrahim's Cape Town band, percussionist and singer Mor Dhiam from Senegal, and percussionist Guilherme Franco and bassist Nilson Matta from Brazil. When on the opening "Capoeira" Pullen enters with a stormy downward gliss, your ears perk but the blurs are too controlled, too contained. And that's how it goes on most tracks, a seductive smooshing of keys followed by a retrenchment. There are exceptions. He may hold back on "Yebino Spring," but the solo is charged and sustained, building to an exultant return by the alto. Best is the closing three-minute piano solo on "Doo Wop Daze," a churning invention reminiscent of Cecil Taylor in its jagged left-hand figures.

Pullen had opted for a light pop melodicism, but the next CD, *Ode to Life* (dedicated to George Adams), suggests he wasn't entirely satisfied. Restraint rules the day, but the composition is knottier, the lyricism more intense. The three glisses Pullen plays in all of "The Third House of the Right" are teases in a piece (forty measures with five nonrepeating sections) that promises more than the players deliver. But the five/four "Paraty" needs no glisses to help Pullen develop a scalar motif into an insistent, meditative variation. He skillfully extends the flamboyant "El Matador" (drawn from a tradition of Spanish pieces, including his own "Indio Gitano" from *Random Thoughts*), bounding between a scraping of the keys and a conventional if hesitant single-note approach that suggests typing. "Ah George, We Hardly Knew Ya," his most durable melody, is a sinuous waltz with a Spanish cast, expanded by Pullen's tapping, melancholy piano; it's amazing how *little* he plays in this mode while still holding the stage.

He is no less fastidious on "Anastasia/Pyramid," a seven-bar theme in eight, played twice, with a kinetic solo that is far too short, a glimmer of what he might have done with it years before. More frustrating is "Variation on Ode to Life," a work that accrued some urgency in concert, but in the recorded version is sapped by a protracted ending and a patterned and formulaic piano solo that keeps rushing to a climax it never quite reaches. I'm of two minds about it. The sadness is palpable, and sometimes it seems that instead of transforming that solemnity, Pullen bows to its crushing weight. On other occasions, I'm impressed by the sober, stubborn meticulousness of solo and arrangement.

The most exciting performance by the Connection is the version of "Yebino Spring" on the 1993 Montreux Jazz Festival CD, *Live . . . Again*, released while Pullen was in the hospital. A better showcase for Carlos Ward than the studio sessions, it presents a Pullen who can still summon his chops when needed, but also gives us second versions of simpler tunes that didn't offer as much the first time. The long gestating and posthumously released *Sacred Common Ground*, on the other hand, suggests another beginning in which the guttural a cappella singing and rhythmic chanting of a northwestern American Indian tribe is used as a template for jazz combo arrangements (the Connection is augmented by trombone and string bass). The compositions are by Pullen and Mike Kenmille, lead singer of the seven-member Chief Cliff Singers. At no time, it seems to me, do the two factions really blend. Nor does the record convince me that they are equals. Nevertheless, something remarkable happens. Pullen absorbs their strength and is provoked to the most delicate level of lyricism he ever achieved.

The highlight of the album—and in its very uniqueness an essential work in Pullen's canon—is "Common Ground," a piece that, significantly, opts not for a bonding format but for a sequential one: Kenmille (a cappella); piano trio; choir and drums. The trio melody is introduced with a tinkling sound born of the nursery or a music box. The thematic approach is a development of the trio version of "Ode to Life," but this particular solo is all Pullen, an organization of material that owes nothing to Bill Evans or Keith Jarrett or others associated with protracted song or gyrations of euphoria. The other key selection is "Resting on the Road," a waltz based on a repetitive eight-bar phrase and shaded with a subtle gospel hue. The second and third choruses of Pullen's solo employ his trademark accents with the precision of a surgeon. Other savory moments include concerted attempts to integrate the ensembles on the episodic "River Song" and the explosive "Message in Smoke." When I want to be sated by Pullen, I return to the earlier records. When I want to be moved by him, I stick right here.

64 ❖ Gary Bartz
(The Middle Passage)

The worst affliction that can befall a jazz musician is to turn thirty-five. At that point career winds are so light he or she might as well go to law school or try for a studio job, because the terrifying thing about these particular doldrums is that they are harnessed to time rather than space and can last as long as twenty-five years. Jazz is supposed to be a sophisticated, serious music in which apprenticeship and maturity count for something, but record contracts and critical enthusiasm are so wedded to youth that jazz musicians routinely spend their most accomplished years floating in the nether regions of middling Eurasian labels and obscure gigs. The gratifying news for the hardiest of players is that at the age of sixty a tempest of renewed interest will sweep them back into the mainstream, whether they are playing especially well or not. For at sixty, any musician who has weathered twenty-five years of benign neglect, having earlier enjoyed the enthusiasms rained upon callow youth, can now bank on rediscovery in the role of (flourish of trumpets, please) a Living Legend.

That's the way it is, and nothing can be done about it. Nor does the situation apply more to second-level artists than to the centrifugal forces of genius. Charlie Parker knew it—he lived long enough to see Armstrong, Ellington, and Young all taken for granted—and bailed out just in time. In his last years, Dizzy Gillespie found rose petals strewn in his path, as indeed he should; twenty years before, when he could wipe out all other trumpet players, he was the invisible man. The invisible woman was Sarah Vaughan, who went six years without a recording contract. Ben Webster was the holy ghost: gorgeous, sage, pugnaciously lyrical Webster, who gave up on America at fifty-five and settled in Copenhagen. Ten years later he was a dead legend. At a time when RCA signed Christopher Hollyday but not Jackie McLean, when Columbia set its sights on Joey DeFrancesco but not Jimmy Smith, when Blue Note flaunted Joey Calderazo and ignored Tommy Flanagan, it was apparent that living-legend status had its limits at the major labels. Yet each of those acknowledged masters is now recording after long cycles in still waters. American jazz lives are spilling over with second acts. The musicians who really deserve our compassion are those in their forties and fifties, who steadfastly persevere until the day when intermission is over. By the '90s, Gary Bartz had less than a decade more to endure.

Bartz is the Baltimore-bred saxophonist, schooled in his father's jazz club and Juilliard, who made a splashy debut on the New York scene in the mid-'60s, quickly establishing himself as perhaps the most promising new voice on alto since Cannonball Adderley. His career began with Max Roach and Abbey Lincoln in 1964, followed by a term with Art Blakey. In 1966, he made a test recording (never issued) with three other unknowns: John Hicks, Mickey Bass, and Ronald Shannon Jackson. A year later, he signed with Milestone. Bartz was a representative figure of that era, caught between the new thing and the old verities. Beyond his technical aplomb, which was and is considerable, he radiated raw energy. Bartz blew with such force that his intonation often threatened to veer flat or sharp, though he usually managed to stay in tune. He shared with Sonny Rollins a predilection for Louis Jordan, and though his playing was never as elemental as Jordan's, he did proffer a gritty, soaring lucidity of purpose.

The primary challenge, then as now, for a young musician entrusted with the responsibility of leading a band was to find an agreeable form. In that regard, as well as in his playing, he located two North Stars in John Coltrane (inevitably) and Jackie McLean. Bartz's much underrated and long unreissued second album, *Another Earth* (1968), tells the story. The title side is a suite of themes explored by a front line of Bartz, Pharoah Sanders, and Charles Tolliver. The harmonic underpinning is firm, but the force of the soloists is allowed to take the music outside. The voicings are slick and alluring, far more contained than Coltrane's, but full and bracing in a way that reflects the revels of the new music. "Dark Nebula," on the other hand, is lyrical hard bop in the mode of McLean, who spent the '60s mapping out his own turf as the boundaries were changing. Bartz's performance of Weill's "Lost in the Stars," an ardent duet with Reggie Workman that is a benchmark recording for both men, exemplifies his ability to bond rude power and constraint in the service of a standard.

His next album, *Home*, remains one of the headiest hard bop albums of that period, and it is quite likely to find an appreciative audience today, if Milestone gets around to reissuing it. Recorded live in Baltimore, this band (a quintet with Woody Shaw and Rashied Ali, another example of reaching inside and out) was the first of several that Bartz called his Ntu Troop, after a Bantu phrase for spiritual and physical unity, a big concern in the '60s. In 1970, Bartz toured with Miles Davis (*Live-Evil*), and though his initial response to that experience was not to go electric, he did embark on an ambitious multicultural project of his own late that year, first sampled in *Harlem Bush Music*. He wrote lyrics, sometimes in collaboration with his wife, Maxine Bartz, as well as narration. Initially, he had Andy Bey sing his songs; eventually—on the 1973 *Singerella: A Ghetto Fairy Tale*—he sang them himself. He also issued the usual denial of being a jazz musician. This was right after Miles had declared that calling him a jazz musician was the same thing as calling him the *n*-word.

Returning to those records for the first time in twenty-five years, I found they struck me exactly as they did then. Bartz's playing and writing are often compelling, but the songs and vocals are dispiriting. In a strange way, power won out over lyricism to the detriment of both. Although the records are a focused attempt to expand the jazz audience, to appeal even to children, the natural humor and occasional warmth of the earlier records is vitiated by the message. Other than a strong concert performance at Montreux in 1973 (*I've Known Rivers*), Bartz was leaning toward fusion, trying to make a sophisticated political statement within the context of synthesized trendiness. Soon the whole band was electric. When he returned to a modified jazz setting for the 1976 *Ju Ju Man* (Catalyst), his work sounded taxed beyond belief. The sustained clarinet notes on "Chelsea Bridge" wavered awkwardly, and his alto was often out of tune—he sounded cold, even brutish. The title selection, an adaptation of *A Love Supreme*, broiled under a hideous overdubbed vocal; on "My Funny Valentine," a singer indulged in what could pass as a parody of melisma run amok. In Raban's *Jazz Records 1942–90*, the listing for *Ju Ju Man* is followed by the ominous note: "Additional recordings by this artist are not included."

And, in fact, Bartz was not included in many discussions of alto sax players during the next fifteen years. In 1991 he came back on two records that are very good, though not good enough: they aren't consistently up to Bartz's playing on them. On *There Goes the Neighborhood!* (Candid), he fronts the Candid All Stars: Kenny Barron, Ray Drummond, and Ben Riley, a better rhythm section than he used in the Ntu days. He plays with the same explosive radiance that made his first albums so startling, but with far more skill, drive, wit, and warmth. On the opener, "Racism (Blues in Double B-flat Minor)," he rampages through nearly twenty choruses in under three minutes, and though the Coltrane influence is apparent in all its unbridled glory, Bartz fully personalizes that first solo with dynamic details, including growls and hollers, a range that encompasses three octaves, and elaborate turnarounds that run the choruses together. It's a brainy, flamboyant tour de force.

Surprisingly, it's also the only Bartz original on the session. Excepting the closer by Barron, the rest of the program draws on the era between "Laura" (1944) and "Impressions" (1961), including two Tadd Dameron tunes and the unlikely Frank Loesser song "I've Never Been in Love Before," once mocked by Lenny Bruce and here kidded by Bartz: he tweaks the key melody with a whimsical glissando, but lays evocative claim to the release and transforms the whole song in the melodic bebop variations that follow. In Dameron's "On a Misty Night," he sets up his second solo with a high-note drone and the pebbly arpeggios that lead to it. He quotes Bird in a "Laura" turnback (the horn is filled to bursting here and you half expect him to go dramatically flat) and his bruising escapade on "Impressions" erases all memory of "Ju Ju Man." The drawbacks reveal the problems of recording an underrehearsed band live (at Birdland), which include the absence of all form other than round-robins of solos and, in this instance, an undermiked piano.

A more studied Bartz emerges on *The Legacy* by The Reunion Legacy Band (Early Bird), which brings together six of those once promising young players of the '60s, some of whom have been long lost among the jazz diaspora. The ties run deep. The session was produced by Mickey Bass, who appeared on Bartz's unreleased first session along with John Hicks, who is also present. Hicks was a member of Music, Inc., the cooperative band created by Charles Tolliver that eventually led to the formation of the influential record label Strata-East. Tolliver shares the front line with Bartz and trombonist Grachan Moncur III, who through his '60s' association with Jackie McLean and two celebrated Blue Note albums of his own was an admitted influence on Bartz. The drummer is Billy Hart, the only member of the group who didn't contribute a composition or arrangement; Bass wrote three.

Moncur presents a problem; he beefs up the ensemble but is weak and ineffectual in his solos. He did contribute one of the more savory pieces, though, "A for Pops," which evokes Blue Note glories more than it does Louis Armstrong, and the record might better have employed his resources by including more of his writing and less of his playing. Tolliver appears ill at ease at the opening of "I'm Getting Sentimental Over You" (an efficient Bass arrangement), but it's a momentary lapse: for the most part his playing is robust, as is most of the session. The rhythm section is buoyant, the writing incisive, though in a couple of instances additional takes would have made for a stronger album. Bartz contributes one of his best pieces, a Rollinsesque calypso called "Do a Funny Dance," and is overall the most forceful soloist. On "Brother Rick," he opens with short bluff figures and is soon winging his way through the changes in the kind of hot pursuit that defines bop alto at the edge of a storm—the very storm that should blow him and many of his contemporaries back to the center of jazz consciousness. By 1998, Bartz stood incontestably among the finest alto saxophonists in jazz. But while several Bartz-wannabes half his age were recruited by major record labels, he was routinely passed over. As a result, his club and concert appearances were criminally infrequent.

65 ❖ David Murray
(Profuse)

American middlebrows have always been quaintly susceptible to the spell of virtuosity, a subset of Europhilia that believes anything requiring spectacular physical skills, as opposed to primarily imaginative ones, merits respect. Every boomtown affirmed its status by erecting an opera house, while much of the local talent was mocked, mimicked, or enslaved. Educated music versus homegrown; music you can't do versus music you can, only somehow it never occurs to you. But left to our own devices, we almost always prefer the musician next door, the crooner who sings like we do or whom we can easily imitate. The triumph of the blues, and of all the musics that partake of it, lies in a technical threshold so low that creativity has full parity with virtuosity.

That makes us suspicious of the blues and pop traditions, although it tends to exempt jazz, where virtuoso abilities are a given. I can't carry a tune across the street without risking a double hernia, but I can play a blues in C, as almost anyone can. Unfortunately, I can't think of anything original to do with that blues. Put another way: Elvis has a zillion impersonators (those who make a living at it and those who think they're Elvis when they listen to him), but it took Elvis to invent Elvis. His artistry, such as it was, lay less in his technical skill (he had a pretty way with a ballad) and genetic luck (he had a pretty face) than in the imaginative use to which he put those assets.

In classical music, where technique is an unbridgeable gulf for most people, it assumes outsized proportions, which is one reason the middlebrows instinctively trust a Horowitz or Heifetz. But in jazz, technique holds a middle ground. We can't do it, but we don't feel so remote from the possibility of doing it that the virtuosity alone intimidates us. Even an Art Tatum or Sonny Rollins seem somehow accessible, despite a technical mastery as far beyond our ken as Horowitz's, while the less flashy Miles Davis or Thelonious Monk, whose impact is more emotional than technical, give the illusion that they're downright reproducible—you only have to play a minor second to feel a tad closer to Monk. Nevertheless, technical aplomb seems to validate jazz, which is one reason Armstrong the inimitable trumpeter has always gotten more respect than Armstrong the imitable singer. When Artie Shaw or Benny Goodman or Keith Jarrett or Wynton Marsalis successfully broaches the classical repertoire, cultural arbiters clap their hands as if a horse were doing card tricks. But those arbiters are evidently unaware that no classical virtuoso—not Iturbi or Stoltzman, not Nigel Kennedy, no, not you either, Andre Previn—has played jazz of any distinction. Jean-Yves Thibaudet can read transcriptions of Bill Evans, but can't ad-lib twelve bars.

That sense of validation may be one reason jazzmen usually provoke critical suspicions when they marry their technique to pop, from Armstrong covering "Body and Soul" to Parker harboring strings to Davis brewing fusion. The last was especially troubling because it bred compromise: great soloists desperately lending themselves to the meretricious designs of producers; terrible soloists achieving numbing success with an elevator music that the trades inexplicably designate Contemporary Jazz. Yet the presumed dumbing down of jazz chops to suit elemental blues archetypes has produced a fairly broad range of durable music, from Basie editing away his New York polish to Gene Ammons hooking up with juke-joint fundamentals to Davis's *Jack Johnson* to Coleman's Prime Time and almost anything by Ronald Shannon Jackson. In the mid-'90s, David Murray leaped into those waters and the controlling rigors of rhythm and blues served to heighten the stupendous density of his bravura attack.

It began in May 1994 with four days in a Chicago studio that produced enough material for two DIW CDs intended to sate basic appetites. The satisfaction of these albums derives from a naturalness of expression that doesn't call attention to itself except to make you wonder at the paucity of records this good. By jazz standards, Murray is nothing if not a virtuoso—the pleasure of his company has always been underscored by his willingness to ride the whirlwind every time out. He's an aerialist, an acrobat, a quick-change artist, a bamboozler who moves the pea so quickly that you relish the con more than the outcome. Yet if the setting is in flux, Murray himself is resolute; like Miles Davis, he's a hedgehog who believes in being a fox. He alters the context, the instrumentation and style, but he himself is constant, a curious mix of aggression, caprice, and tenderness. His improvisations billow out to fill whatever setting he's contrived for them.

Working with rock musicians is nothing new to him. He started out in soul, gospel, and pop bands. When he travelled from Pomona College in California to New York in 1975 at the age of twenty, his association with the second—or was it third? or fourth?—generation avant-garde represented more of a break with his apprenticeship in gospel and r & b groups than the 1994 Chicago sessions do with his extraordinary body of work over the preceding two decades. Old jazz hands have compared his recording life with Sonny Stitt's, but the analogy is somewhat wide of the mark beyond the inability of either to say no to a recording session. Stitt became a have-sax-will-travel loner, working with every kind of pickup band, occasionally bestirring himself to glory (*Constellation!*), but often playing by the numbers. Murray seemed headed for that kind of prolificity in the late '70s and early '80s, but has countenanced relatively few throwaways, keeping himself fresh by sustaining several parallel bands and routinely adding new challenges, including regular big band sessions with Butch Morris at the Knitting Factory and elsewhere.

Electric backbeats have occasionally inspired him before, for example, "Gospel Medley," from his 1991 Jazzpar commission; the Music Revelation Ensemble sessions, particularly the 1990 *Elec. Jazz*; Kip Hanrahan and Ishmael Reed's *Conjure*; and the seductive *Shakill* albums, with Don Pullen on the Hammond organ. After he gigged with the Grateful Dead, that band's newsletter dubbed him the "Jimi Hendrix of the tenor saxophone," an odd tribute that speaks more to the issue of virtuoso technique than historical placement. How fitting that he should broach white rock through the incense of eternal hippiedom. One quality that has always distinguished Murray is his insistence on performing with old masters as well as contemporaries, not to mention his circumvention of avant-garde influences with elders from deep in the tradition. Inevitably, he recorded an entire album of Grateful Dead material, *Dark Star*, reconvening his great octet, which dutifully slogs through parched themes before sipping at the well of improvisation.

Not so with the Chicago albums, *The Tip* and *Jug-a-lug*, a musical concord involving Kahil El'Zabar of the Ethnic Heritage Ensemble, Robert Irving III and (Rolling Stones bassist) Darryl Jones of the last Miles tours, guitarists Daryl Thompson (son of Lucky and little heard in jazz beyond a 1989 Sam Rivers album) and Bobby Broom, and in what amounts to a guest appearance on two tracks, Olu Dara. Homages are offered to Miles, Ornette, and Sly Stone. Murray also renews his Bobby Timmons-inspired soul ballad, "Morning Song." His reggae—or is it

Cape Town?—strut version of "Flowers for Albert" feels less like a tribute to Ayler than to Murray himself, who introduced it at his first performance in New York and has revived it numerous times since, a theme as versatile as its composer. Recalling Ayler's own dismal efforts to wed free jazz to hippie rock (his titles telegraphed his desperation, *Love Cry* and *New Grass*), its inclusion makes for a rather piquant closing of an old circle.

Despite two didactic vocal tracks—by "wordist" G'Ra and El'Zabar, whose voice is not unappealing—*The Tip* has the edge over its mate due to a leisurely but never dreary twelve-to-the-bar cover of Sly Stone's "Sex Machine" that can stand with Murray's finest recorded performances. Thompson's guitar solo is incisive and impeccably paced, and Irving's organ sustains the mood until Murray enters: low, almost evasive, muttering his first phrases before moving quickly into a blistering midrange assault, forcing his riffs through crazy rhythmic hoops and landing on cat feet. Murray does away with the vocal shtick, fuzz, and prophetic funk of the Sly original, but in turning Stone's riff into a vehicle for theme-and-variations, he intimates how exciting it must have been for him to hear it back in 1969.

In carny-speak, a "tip" is the audience at an opening midway bally. Murray probably had a more contemporary meaning in mind, but on the title selection, which begins with an organ splash, and just about everywhere else, the vamps and riffs are slick enough to draw you into the tent. "M. D." opens with ominous accents on the first two beats of the eight/four scheme that ready you for dark Milesian ecstasy, and almost delivers. On occasion, the bally is too slick: "Kahari Romare," despite an impressive passage on kalimba, is mellow to a fault, and Murray sounds sedated. *Jug-a-lug* is smoother, more conventional, more of a swinger, especially the title track, yet in this context that's a problem. The more this band swings and the less it rocks, the more staid it becomes; the leanness it bring to stark riffs gets flabby when marking four. The improvisations remedy the deficit: Murray's bass clarinet spurs his rakish "Acoustic Octo-Funk," and Daryl Thompson's caustic guitar helps "Morning Song," replacing the less decisive Bobby Broom, whose solos spell Murray on other tracks.

In 1996, Murray relocated to France, and the following year introduced a band and an album on Enja called *Fo Deuk Revue* (the title is Senegelese for "Where are you from?") The ensemble spans the globe and would like to do as much for time. In combining American and Senegelese musicians, it aims, in Murray's words, "to fuse ancient music to the music of the future." The large cast includes Doudou N'Diaye Rose, a drummer born in Dakar in 1930, who composed Senegal's national anthem and is said to know more than a thousand rhythms; trumpeter Hugh Ragin and trombonist Craig Harris from Murray's big band; Robert Irving III and bassist Jamaaladeen Tacuma from his electric band; a six-piece Senegelese group called Dieuf Dieul, which combines African and Western rhythm instruments and vocals; and two Senegelese rappers known as Positive Black Soul. The lyrics in English are by Murray and Amiri Baraka. All things considered, the band sounds neither ersatz nor eclectic. Murray accurately points out that it "has certain elements of all my previous bands," and the wonder is how easily the big band riffs, blues licks, verbal riffs, and multiple rhythm sections mingle. Murray goes on being Murray, his tenor saxophone and bass clarinet ripping through the storm—the new scenery mirrors his controlled garrulity.

Yet because the setting breaks precipitously with orthodox jazz, it divided his audience. Those who prefer to hear him pure and without voices can hardly find themselves bereft. He has averaged at least three albums a year (discographers better start now it they are ever to catch up), and hardly a motif can have crossed his mind that wasn't preserved for posterity. Like Art Tatum, he has recorded many pieces in many versions, the instrumentation ranging from solo tenor saxophone to big band, the rhythms and tempos changing constantly. His development from the twenty-year-old college dropout cautiously finding his technique in downtown New York lofts to a forty-something expatriate commanding musical armies with implacable authority is minutely traceable.

Murray has always summoned his predecessors. At his New York debut, the program included homages to Louis Armstrong (by Bobby Bradford) as well as Albert Ayler, and among his finest compositions are tributes to other tenor saxophonists, from Coleman Hawkins and Lester Young to Paul Gonsalves and Dexter Gordon. The jazzcentric view practiced by Murray, along with Arthur Blythe, Butch Morris, James Newton, and other Californians who arrived in New York in the mid-'70s, seemed novel at the time. Most of the more interesting young musicians were fusing jazz and new music (European division) or jazz and pop (funky metal division). While countless saxophonists purchased sopranos and pretended Coltrane had nothing to do with it, Murray was contriving great fog banks of notes in the manner of Gonsalves and doubling bass clarinet so subjectively that no one bothered to ask if Eric Dolphy had anything to do with it. Today some of his early work sounds relatively naive, as Hawkins's early work does—pieces from 1976–77 indicate received emotions and even posturing, an affected free-spirited cool.

Compare the 1977 and 1986 versions of "Santa Barbara and Crenshaw Follies," and you can't miss the assumption of mastery in the latter, yet you might miss the extroverted precociousness of the former. Some of his solos on originals that became familiar anthems in the '70s and '80s (by Butch Morris as well as Murray) are phrased in a kind of nod-time, a slouching legato. Next to the masterful recitals of the mid-'80s and after, they sound shy, innocent, as though he were unwilling to apply the full measure of spiritual fury that makes his mature work riveting. Murray's lodestar role in jazz owes as much to his constant evolution as a soloist as it does to his capacious qualities as a bandleader. He was the representative tenor saxophonist for the '80s because he combined all the influences of the church (the Murray Family Band played Sundays at the Missionary Church of God in Christ), rhythm and blues, free jazz, and pay-as-you-go jazz into a convincingly integrated whole. He represented a revitalization of the classic tenor saxophone sonority—the Hawkins-Webster-Rollins line. Yet he sounded personal and urgent; no matter how furious the surface of his music, a subtext of clarity and discernment could be found in the details.

He is right to insist that the blendings incarnated in *Fo Deuk Revue* extended proclivities that were apparent all along. Consider the makeup of an album as characteristic as *I Want To Talk About You* (Black Saint, 1986): "Morning Song" is his soul anthem, the gospel according to Bobby Timmons; "Red Car" (Morris's answer to "Night Train" and the subject of at least two Murray recordings) rocks and rolls; "I Want To Talk About You" is classic jazz balladry, with a lineage of Billy Eckstine and John Coltrane. One of Murray's accomplishments, linking him to Ayler, is his ability to retain the rhythmic and emotional rush of church music when playing r & b, blues, or free jazz. Yet for Ayler, the transition from free jazz to r & b involved an awkward welding of backbeat rhythms, as though a steady downbeat pounding would make his glossolalia and variable timbre more accessible. Murray hasn't had to revise his basic approach. The gospel-propelled aspects of his music were already in place, authentic and decisive.

And yet Murray is a schooled and sophisticated improviser who flourishes under the pressure of rigorous musical structures. One of his best recordings is *The Hill* (Black Saint, 1986), a consistently provocative trio session with superb work by bassist Richard Davis and drummer Joe Chambers. Nowhere is Murray's disarming authority more forceful than on "Fling," a Butch Morris infrastructure of melody and rhythm that's coolly lyrical on the surface and tricky at the core. It's an enigmatic double-tiered piece in seven/four, with an ascending seven-measure episode of chromatic whole notes in the middle. The performance is five choruses long, including the statements at the opening and close, and Murray sails through the unusual meter and phrase lengths as though they were no more difficult than a waltz. He double-times the third chorus and follows with rugged permutations accenting the upbeats; articulates staccato high notes and legato slurs; brushes over one of the whole-note passages with fluttery arpeggios; and retards the closing theme so that the piece runs to ground like a glider.

Ellington's "Take the Coltrane" (from the same album) is a basic twelve-bar blues, but Murray's performance is another coiling tour de force, suggesting—in its affirmative spirit, speed, and aggression—Paul Gonsalves's immortal moment at Newport in 1956: Is it mere coincidence that Murray, like Gonsalves in his interlude to "Diminuendo and Crescendo in Blue," improvises precisely twenty-seven choruses? Ben Webster's influence, which shaped Gonsalves, is broached directly on "Chelsea Bridge," to which Murray brings increased vibrato. This tripartite invention for tenor, bass, and vibes (Joe Chambers) is one of the most persuasive reclamations of an Ellington-Strayhorn warhorse in a decade besieged by them. In the same recital, he switches to bass clarinet (which he has almost singlehandedly revived since the passing of Dolphy) for a consummately polished work of free association, "The Hill," and in an empathic duet with Davis called "Herbie Miller."

An ideal introduction to Murray's versatility are two ventures recorded for DIW in 1991: *David Murray Big Band*, an uneven but often exhilarating tour de force conducted by Butch Morris, and *Shakill's Warrior*, a diverting quartet session, with Don Pullen making an understated but highly effective appearance on the Hammond B3 organ. On the latter, everything works: Andrew Cyrille maintains a clean chomping backbeat, guitarist Stanley Franks adds brittle counterpunching, and Pullen and Murray explore a low-down, heads-up midnight groove. The opener, "Blues for Savannah," complements the big band's opener, also a blues, called "Paul Gonsalves." Murray's muscular eleven-chorus improvisation on the former reveals how much he learned from Gonsalves and how far beyond him he can go. This is "inside" Murray: gritty, vocal, chromatic, swinging—it's practically walking-the-bar Murray, in an irony-laden sort of way, and he retains interest chorus after chorus. As does Pullen, who whirls and flutters, setting up expectations he often foils in upholding the dark of night glow. Pullen's "Song of the Old Country," previously recorded with George Adams, is pleasantly revived as a blue ballad with Middle Eastern spice. "High Priest" is eleven minutes of foreplay, spurred by the guitarist. The promise is rendered in "Shakill's Warrior," a trite melody wed to a tricky blues configuration with modulations; "At the Cafe Central," an island song for which Pullen's organ replicates a set of whistles that Murray mimics at the end of his rigorously dynamic solo; Butch Morris's "Black February," a measured and spacious blues-driven work; and even a dramatic, worldly psalm, "In the Spirit."

David Murray Big Band gets off to a dazzling start with three performances that obliterate memories of the disappointing orchestra albums Murray and Morris recorded several years earlier at Sweet Basil. "Paul Gonsalves" is a seventeen-minute synthesized field holler that pays homage to the Ellington veteran who, in Murray's words, "opened the door for extended tenor saxophone solos on record." Murray orchestrated a transcription of the twenty-seven-chorus solo from "Diminuendo and Crescendo in Blue," which he intersperses throughout in a performance abundant in clashes between brasses and reeds. "Lester" is a high-cholesterol tribute to the dry lyricism of Young, whom Murray doesn't echo in timbre or phrasing (his sound is strictly his own with Websterian antecedents) but invokes in feeling and melodic line. His scoring for flute is admirable, as are Sonelius Smith's piano washes. "Ben" evokes Ellington in its muted brasses and blues riff. "David's Tune" is notable for its elegant precision, and "Istanbul" is a rhapsodic mood piece that features Murray's bass clarinet. Other pieces, with voices raised in poetry and song, are less enchanting, but then I'm not as multicultural as I should be. In this area, at least, Fo Deuk is a distinct advancement.

A year later, in 1992, Murray recorded a more consistent if less flamboyant big band album that DIW was unable to distribute in the United States for several years. *South of the Border* is contained, but rigorously executed. Butch Morris's "conductioning," a method (antecedents include Basie and Mingus) of improvising composition on the spot, is impressively realized in roundhouse glissandi and quizzical riffs he instigates in support of the terse soloists, among them James Spaulding, Don Byron, Frank Lacy, and Graham Haynes. It is a spiky, exuberant piece of work, notably so in an episode by the dual tenors of Murray and Patience Higgins on the dreamily enticing adaptation of "St. Thomas," in the aristocratic swing of "Happy Birthday Wayne Jr.," in the spiraling determination of "Fling," and in the full-blown bender of a solo by Murray on yet another definitive revision of "Flowers for Albert."

In 1997, Murray convened an extraordinary 22-piece big band plus the String Orchestra of the Conservatoire National de Paris for a Paris concert that his producing company (3D Family) edited for release the following year as *The Obscure Works of Duke Ellington & Billy Strayhorn*. Conducted by Murray (Butch Morris did not participate), it is his most expansive homage—not only to the venerated composers, but to his collaborators over twenty years and the generation they represent in jazz history. Murray also uses four musicians who made their marks earlier and, though it may be coincidence, three of them incarnate associations with the leading figures of the '60s avant-garde: trumpeter Bobby Bradford formed a quartet with altoist John Carter in the style of Ornette Coleman; bassist Dr. Art Davis played with John Coltrane; drummer Andrew Cyrille worked with Cecil Taylor for eleven years. The fourth, saxophonist James Spaulding, is a stand-in for the key mainstream alternative in that era, hard bop, which he helped forge in collaborations with Art Blakey, Freddie Hubbard, and Hank Mobley. The band is dominated, however, by important players who came up with Murray in the '70s and '80s, notably flutist James Newton; trumpeter Hugh Ragin; trombonists Craig Harris, George Lewis, and Ray Anderson; saxophonists Arthur Blythe, Hamiet Bluiett, Ricky Ford, Charles Owens, and John Purcell.

Newton, a fine but elusive musician, has mastered a technique made famous by Roland Kirk, requiring him to make kindred, guttural sounds at the same time he strenuously blows into his instrument, as heard here in an affecting version of Strayhorn's "Blood Count" and "African Flower," an adaptation of "Fleurette Africaine," the guileless theme Ellington introduced at a 1962 session with Max Roach and Charles Mingus. "African Flower" is a rangy work that begins with bass clarinet and percussion and enlarges with the addition of strings, a bass vamp, and stop-time into an elaborate fantasia; at times, especially during a stellar, undulating violin solo by Regina Carter, it suggests something of Randy Weston's Africanisms. Murray closes with popping sounds on bass clarinet against discretely deployed strings. "Love You Madly" is not one of Ellington's better songs, but Murray enlivens it by focusing on the main hook, treated as a shout riff; Carmen Bradford does much of the shouting and she sounds more adept than she did as a generic soul singer with the Basie band. Murray's tenor saxophone and the strings offer a lavish "Chelsea Bridge," with cadenza. "Northern Lights," deftly adapted from *The Queen's Suite*, has fine baritone-heavy writing for the reeds and a passage that meshes swirling strings, brass glisses, and epic percussion in a manner that recalls a favored gambit of film composer Bernard Herrmann.

The climactic piece is a protracted arrangement of Murray's "Paul Gonsalves," rendered as a chain of robust solos by Anderson, Ford, Carter, and others, none of whom are more prepossessing than Murray's enormously promising protege, D. D. Jackson, one of the most stimulating of the many gifted pianists to come along since Geri Allen opened the floodgates. Unlike Jacky Terrasson, who keeps his equally ebullient technique buttoned down with formalistic mazes, Jackson can hardly contain himself. Like Don Pullen, with whom he studied, Jackson inclines to huge woolly gestures containing the entire keyboard, which he smashes with a gleeful precision. Murray, who recorded with him on several occasions (most successfully on his own 1996 album, *Long Goodbye: A Tribute to Don Pullen*, on DIW, and as a guest on Jackson's two-volume 1997 *Paired Down*, on Justin Time) has called him "the most innovative musician of his generation," and he may be right. But the outstanding aspect of "Paul Gonsalves" is the sheer delight in swing, as the ensemble, mobilized by Cyrille, drives home the climactic choruses and Murray rides over it, using his tenor in the traditional role of a high-note trumpet. Here are musicians who postured for many years about the tradition, sampling it or parodying it or refurbishing it, burning up a swing vehicle for real, for fun, using everything they picked up in their long adventure in the parallel universe of avant-garde jazz. As Edward Albee once wrote, sometimes you have to go a long way out of the way to come back a short distance correctly. This is Ellington the hard way, earned and not memorized.

Murray's discography gives new meaning to the phrase "an embarrassment of riches." Several of his recordings, in addition to those mentioned, are among the benchmark achievements in the postmodern era, and others attest to a consistency that is rare in any era. They include the most durable of his early albums, *Live at the Lower Manhattan Ocean Club, Volumes 1/2* (India Navigation, 1977); sideman appearances on World Saxophone Quartet's *Revue* (Black Saint, 1980), Clarinet Summit's *In Concert at the Public Theater* (India Navigation, 1982), and Jack DeJohnette's *Album Album* (ECM, 1984); any and all octet recordings, but especially *Ming, Home, Murray's Steps* (Black Saint, 1980–82), and *Picasso* (DIW, 1993); collaborations with Jack DeJohnette (*In Our Style*, DIW, 1986), Randy Weston (*The Healers*, Black Saint, 1987), Milford Graves (*Real Deal*, DIW, 1991), Sonny Murray (*A Sanctuary Within*, Black Saint, 1991), and McCoy Tyner (*Special Quartet*, DIW, 1991); *The Jazzpar Prize* (1991, Enja); any and all recordings with Dave Burrell, especially *Ballads, Tenors, Spirituals* (DIW, 1988), *Brother to Brother* (Gazell, 1993) and *Windward Passages* (Black Saint, 1993); Bobby Bradford's suite *Death of a Sideman* (DIW, 1991); *Ballads for Bass Clarinet* (DIW, 1991); *Live '93 Acoustic Octo-Funk* (Sound Hills, 1993); *Love and Sorrow* (DIW, 1993); and *Quintet with Ray Anderson, Anthony Davis* (DIW, 1994). No musician personifies better than David Murray the dilemma of reconciling jazz's family values and the claims of autonomy.

66 ❖ Dave Burrell
(Brotherly Love)

First impressions can be foolishly decisive: my assessment of Dave Burrell was for several years fixed by his sololess contribution to the first and best of Pharoah Sanders's Impulse albums, *Tauhid* (1966). Submerged (with Sonny Sharrock) in the foggy bottom of a rhythm section that bided its time with tinkling vamps as Sanders prepared to unleash his omnivorous shock tenor, Burrell seemed perfectly content compiling tremolos and glissandi. I ignored the contrary evidence of his own 1968 debut album, which offered a not unexpected freebash (his collaborators were Sonny Murray and Sirone), a medley from *West Side Story*, and ragtime. Nor did I properly consider the 1980 release of his piano recital *Windward Passages*, perhaps because he was by then so firmly associated with Archie Shepp that his own lyricism seemed to me a minor and even self-conscious diversion.

Throughout the '90s, Burrell has given me immense pleasure, yet the earlier prejudice has held force to the degree that I am newly surprised every time out by his range and wit and deep—sometimes solemn—gift for melody. Those attributes are more apparent in his achievement as a composer than as a pianist and are best realized in his exceptionally rewarding association with David Murray. Since Murray makes records about as frequently as the sun rises, his marathon DIW sessions of January 1988 took a while to get released. But the eventual appearance of *Ballads*, *Deep River*, and *Spirituals* established Burrell's role as more than that of just a sideman.

Burrell's piano inspires and restrains Murray; his compositions add a collateral weightiness to Murray's rigorous writing in such pieces as the pensive tango, "Valley Talk," and the elegantly raucous conga-line blowout, "Abel's Blissed Out Blues." During the recording of *Ballads*, producer Kazunori Sugiyama suggested they try a duet, and Burrell revived "Sarah's Lament" from his unproduced opera, *Windward Passages*. A year later they made a duet album, *Daybreak*, for Sam Charters's label Gazell. After that, Burrell appeared on Murray's DIW performance of Bobby Bradford's *Death of a Sideman* and greatly augmented his own slim discography as a leader with two Gazell albums: his first piano recital since *Windward Passages*, *The Jelly Roll Joys*, and a second album of duets with Murray, *Brother to Brother*.

In September 1993, following engagements in Europe, Canada, and Oakland, California, Murray and Burrell debuted in New York at a short-lived club called Yardbird Suite. It was the kind of smash that begins moderately and spreads through word of mouth, answering a need no one knew existed until it was filled. Midway through the first number on opening night, the audience responded with the kind of approving shouts and laughter that underscore a playful spontaneity you won't find on the records, good as they are. In the studio, Burrell and Murray attend the music; live, they attend each other.

On "The Box," a blues configured over a comically striding two-beat, Murray displayed the timing of a master monologist, pitching his shrieks for maximum effect in a solo that otherwise exhibited his gruff Coleman Hawkins tone and tonguing a written transitional passage with a precision worthy of the legendary vaudevillian Rudy Wiedoft. On "Brother to Brother," they shifted from gospel tremolos to a strangely pellucid, free-form fury, and on "Abel's Blissed Out Blues" they took turns firing up the conga line, Burrell egging Murray on with razor-sharp glisses. Burrell's originals gave way to two Billy Strayhorn classics—"Lush Life," for solo piano, and "Chelsea Bridge" (a highlight of Murray's Black Saint album, *The Hill*), complete with tenor cadenza.

No aspect of Murray's playing has matured with greater rigor than his approach to timbre. His resonance and control can suggest the sonorities of a cello (opulent triple stops), a swing tenor's nostalgia-heavy vibrato, and the multiphonics of New Wave tenors, though with a discriminatory discipline that measures the space between the '90s and the '60s. More than most of his contemporaries, Murray paints in sound. Burrell's quietly focused pieces underscore that aspect of his virtuosity; small wonder Murray derives so much pleasure from playing them, sneaking in one of his own tunes occasionally, but with a modesty exceedingly rare in jazz. Burrell's thematic organization offers forms that allow Murray to concentrate on sound, timing, and responsiveness. In short, he can function primarily as an interpreter.

Burrell was outed as an eclectic of capacious tastes some twenty-five years ago, only to be held back by the kind of assumptions that are as self-defeating on the left as on the right. From the time he arrived in New York in 1965, after four years at the Berklee College of Music, he experimented with rags. He couldn't get them recorded, in part because they were considered musically and politically regressive. Few people heard his 1968 album, *High*, yet in retrospect it places him in the forefront of a small school of modernists who employed such venerable keyboard techniques as stride and boogie. In addition to the extroverted "East Side Colors," he introduced "A.M. Rag" (originally called "Margy Pargy"), based on a G-flat pentatonic scale and still his best known piece, and the medley from Leonard Bernstein's *West Side Story*, conceived as a response to the conventional version as recorded by Oscar Peterson. Before Burrell, the only pianist—after Monk himself—associated with new music in the '50s and '60s who routinely varied his solos with allusions to earlier styles was Jaki Byard. Soon the club would expand to include Muhal Richard Abrams and Don Pullen.

Burrell's approach was distinguished by the fact that his primary influence in the realm of striding bass lines was the last rather than the first titan in the New York lineage. "I listened to Monk all day, every day," he said in a conversation, " 'Don't Blame Me,' 'Just a Gigolo,' 'Lulu's Back in Town,' all the standards he interpreted with stride." Later he discovered Jelly Roll Morton, whom he venerates, and James P. Johnson. His long association with Archie Shepp was pivotal; as the one post-Trane saxophonist who regularly played standards and folk themes and called to mind the then-neglected Ben Webster, Shepp was open to infusions of tradition. "When I played 'A.M. Rag' with Archie, it was appropriate, it fit in." That association also led to one with Beaver Harris that produced the 360 Degree Music Experience, which stumped for a comprehensive interpretation of the past in works like *From Ragtime to No Time* and Burrell's *In: Sanity*.

Yet another defining association came in 1979 when Burrell played the entire summer in a duet with the Ellington drummer Sam Woodyard at a club in Montparnasse. They were billed as "The Old and the New." From Woodyard, he learned the importance of clear melodic statements and the advantages of taking the music outside in incremental steps, chorus by chorus. His most intimate collaboration, however, is with the Swedish poet Monika Larsson, his wife and the librettist for his opera *Windward Passages;* on the basis of the piano reduction (performed in Switzerland in 1979 and released by Hat Hut), the work has garnered a formidable underground reputation. The arias are at once severe and inviting. The subject is cultural dislocation. Based on Burrell's own experience, it concerns a black family that moves to Hawaii after the Second World War and settles in a valley of mixed ethnicities. The love of the black protagonist for a Japanese woman is set against the struggle for statehood.

The challenge posed by the unproduced *Windward Passages* is its partnering of opera singers and jazz musicians. While teaching for two years at Sweden's University of Gothenberg, Burrell used the school's orchestra to perfect and edit the score. Bridging the "social problems" between singers and improvisers, however, has proved far more difficult. Unsuccessful in securing funds for a showcase performance, Burrell draws on the opera for most of his projects. He has performed excerpts with Kenny Burrell (no known relation, though they are exploring the possibility of a Mississippi connection several generations back), which he also employs in his albums.

Jelly Roll Joys (1991) is aptly titled, an application of brisk two-beat rhythms to themes by Charlie Parker and John Coltrane, as well as Morton. Burrell tends to voice the bass tight, more in the style of James P. Johnson than the swaggering stride of Fats Waller, and he places his solos in the higher register, producing an effect that used to be tagged tickling the ivories. His buoyant adaptation of "Giant Steps" gives that fearsome harmonic raceway an unprecedented, convincingly sunny disposition. His thumping treatment of the trio strain in "The Pearls" and his authentic tango feeling on "The Crave" are testimony to his close study of the source material (as is the involvement of Sam Charters, who wrote the illuminating 1984 "imaginary memoir" *Jelly Roll Morton's Last Night at the Jungle Inn*).

The 1993 partnership with Murray, *Brother to Brother*, is a more emotionally complicated piece. It begins irresistibly with "The Box," a whimsical minor blues with an eight-bar transition and a couple of amusing hesitations. Equally light and refreshing is Morton's "New Orleans Blues," which Murray invigorates with a well-placed holler and Burrell stamps with the requisite Spanish tinge. "Brother to Brother" proceeds from violent dissonance to gospel resolution, employing *A Love Supreme*-era vamps learned from Jimmy Garrison (another close associate of Burrell's) to pace the mayhem of free episodes: Murray's tones explode like gunshots. The opening measures of "What It Means to a Woman" recall "Lazy Afternoon," but the song takes on a more expansive and vocal lyricism. Murray's "Icarus," previously arranged for orchestra and quartet, produces an air of suspense by counterposing a bass clarinet melody against an Alberti bass (broken triads). "Dancing with Monika" meshes triplet and duple rhythms, as well as saxophone and piano. Lacking the madness that made their live sets boisterous fun, *Brother to Brother* establishes a dramatic spell of its own.

67 ❖ *Abbey Lincoln*
(Strong Wind Blowing)

The reemergence in the early '90s of Abbey Lincoln as a queenly jazz singer and the simultaneous rediscovery of the long retired Doris Day prompted my thoughts about parallels and distinctions between them.

In 1991, each was the subject of documentary films: Gene Davis's *You Gotta Pay the Band: The Words, the Music, the Life of Abbey Lincoln*, which was initially broadcast overseas only, and Jim Arntz's *Doris Day: A Sentimental Journey*, which was shown on PBS. Day was the quintessence of blonde: even her golden album covers reflected the sunshiny chirpiness of an unaffectedly sexy voice and approach to song. Lincoln had carried the banner for ebony since the '50s: "A strong black wind blowing/ Gently on and on," Nikki Giovanni wrote of her.

That both women are uncommonly beautiful is a salient issue in their careers, though more so in the case of Lincoln, who was beautiful when Caucasian pop-cult assumed a Lena Horne or Dorothy Dandridge to be subversive flukes while all other black women were issued from the same mold as Louise Beavers. Her 1956 debut album was called *Abbey Lincoln's Affair . . . a Story of a Girl in Love*. On the cover, she was posed à la Julie London (she recorded it for London's label, Liberty), lying abed in a flimsy white dress, her cleavage roundly centered in the photograph.

Bob Russell, the lyricist who produced the album and gave the former Gaby Wooldridge the most durable of her several stage names, began his liner blurb by noting her "lines, curves, arcs and semi-circles in the tradition of the classic beauty." (He didn't bother to identify the arrangers—Benny Carter and Marty Paich.) Earlier that year, Lincoln appeared as a guest act in *The Girl Can't Help It*, earning coverage in *Ebony* for the way she filled out a red gown previously worn by Marilyn Monroe. Even when she signed with the much hipper Riverside label (where her allies included Kenny Dorham, Sonny Rollins, Wynton Kelly, and Max Roach), producer Orrin Keepnews felt obliged to point out Lincoln's "singular good fortune not only to sound beautiful but to look beautiful too."

All of which is agreeable enough, except that her beauty was hastily reassessed when in the early '60s she began to wear her hair natural, wrote songs with socially conscious lyrics, and let it be known that she was no one's Barbie doll. Concerning her natural hair, she expresses in the documentary her astonishment at how much it riled people. Yet something else needs to be said about good looks and their Hollywood potential. Lincoln's two important film roles, in *Nothing But a Man* and *For Love of Ivy*, came in the mid-'60s, but if a studio had been inclined to go the distance in making her a film star, the obvious time would have been her cover girl days in the '50s. Only a few major singers have enjoyed box-office clout in the movies, and only one—Day—was a woman. (Some would argue for Barbra Streisand, but even if you think she's an important singer, her hit records followed her stage stardom.) The other women vocalists who had the best chance of crossing over, albeit in a nonracist America, would have been African American: Ethel Waters in the '30s, Lena Horne in the '40s, and Lincoln in the '50s. By the time she began wearing her hair natural, Lincoln knew full well the obstacles she faced.

The big kick in the Day revival is that people who saw her films as kids in the '60s now found the character she perfected in some twelve movies, from *Teacher's Pet* in 1958 through *Send Me No Flowers* in 1964, to be virtually the converse of what it seemed. "I knew her before she was a virgin," Oscar Levant said of the former Doris Kappelhoff, setting the parameters for the sort of derision that plagued the last years of her career (she was forty-six in her last film). Yet it isn't her virginity that's at stake in *Teacher's Pet*, *Pillow Talk*, and *Lover Come Back*, but rather her independence and integrity. She always ends up in bed; she simply insists on getting there on her own terms. Those films lack the maturity and charm of Lubitsch, to say the least, as well as the incendiary erotic glow that makes Day's best records sizzle. But her kewpie-doll prettiness helps to distinguish the kind of steadfastness she represented from the muscular redefinition of the sexes enacted by Katharine Hepburn or Barbara Stanwyck. The fact that her films were marketed (and consumed) as a smarmy pursuit-and-conquest series is as telling an indication of Camelot's waning years as Day's version of a brave new autonomy.

Lincoln herself has been subject to a peculiar derision. After recording *We Insist! Freedom Now Suite* with Max Roach and her own *Straight Ahead*, she was branded "a professional Negro," which is quite true, if not in the sense intended. She remains unaccepted by many critics who complain of her pitch, attitude, and daring. I understand the reservations, having shared them for years: the distant, plangent quality of her voice attracts or repels; it's too unusual to permit indifference. What I initially heard as an off-putting flatness is now the aspect of her work I find most dramatically satisfying: a sometimes chilling willingness to let the lyrics and emotion control the phrasing, not at all surprising in a singer who is also a songwriter. Beyond that, I suspect that one reason Lincoln has found a new audience parallels a reason for the renewed interest in Day. The bristling feminine independence that marks her singing was ignored in the '50s and '60s, but is unmistakable now.

Early on, Lincoln performed many songs associated with Billie Holiday, with whom she is often linked, though she rarely offers the remotest shade of imitation. Her first of three Riverside albums (*Abbey Lincoln* in 1957, *It's Magic* in 1958, *Abbey Is Blue* in 1959) includes three of the man-obsessed songs Holiday recorded. Lincoln's interpretations are pointedly different. With Paul Chambers providing a rich arco bass, she sings "My Man" with a clarity and defiance completely shorn of the wistfulness and regret instilled by Holiday. On "Don't Explain," she intones the lyric over a bass vamp with Kenny Dorham's obbligato boosting her into something akin to a march. A still more surprising transformation is "I Must Have That Man," a lyric she ultimately changes to "I will have that man." She makes the verse a duet with drums and, after Roach establishes a rapid tempo, dashes through the chorus without a hint of despair.

One last comparison. Day was a marvelously sultry big band singer who found her true metier in pop. There is hardly a touch of jazz phrasing in her best work, which is nonetheless richly communicative. In this regard and in every other, she became a far more compelling singer than Ruth Etting, whom she so nervily played in *Love Me or Leave Me*. Lincoln made the opposite journey, starting out as a supper-club pop star who found her identity at the epicenter of jazz, interacting with an unexampled roster of instrumentalists and imbuing every phrase with the expressive urgency of the idiom. Her resurgence speaks to the renewed hunger for jazz singing, an idiom that flourished in the decades when pop songs were perfect vehicles for emotive improvisation but became at once freer and more insular in the barren environment of rock. The ecstatic swing of Ella Fitzgerald and virtuoso embellishments of Sarah Vaughan are gone, and only a hardy few seem eager to try and carry on the mantle. Yet lo, here in our midst, after thirty-five years on the fringe, is Abbey Lincoln: strong, vibrant, individual, with a carefully selected and largely self-composed repertoire, including the canny Rodgers and Hart lament "Ten Cents a Dance" (sung by her on Frank Morgan's Antilles album, *A Lovesome Thing*), which was introduced by Etting and apotheosized by Day.

No jazz vocal album in years was more favorably received than *The World Is Falling Down* (Verve), in 1990, in which gospel ardor enhanced her songs as well as her singing, and none was more eagerly awaited than *You Gotta Pay the Band* (Verve), which followed in 1991. The title selection of the former was her most indelible act of words and music to date, paced over a decisive backbeat with a deep blues undercurrent, a churchlike stoicism; it's about defying the ravages of time. Yet it's also a glittering jazz performance with surprisingly laconic, thoughtful solos by Jackie McLean and Clark Terry, who avows the songfulness of the performance by beginning his solo with a lick from Schubert. Like Holiday, Lincoln doesn't use many notes, and she chooses them with care, savoring long, open vowels, using blues shadings with telling subtlety, and savoring her rare and ravishing high notes. *The World Is Falling Down* also offers a novel approach to the overexposed "How High the Moon," a little noticed Morgan Lewis–Nancy Hamilton Broadway show tune that became a bop anthem when Charlie Parker, Dizzy Gillespie, Nat

King Cole, and other modernists recorded countless variations on it. Lincoln sings it in French and English and in waltz time, and revives the rarely heard verse, but what makes her interpretation fresh is her attention to the cresting loveliness of the melody.

You Gotta Pay the Band is a more intense, accomplished, and unified album. All the voices complement each other: Stan Getz's passion and Hank Jones's cool provide a tertiary level of drama; Getz and Lincoln are the secondary stage; the primary stage is reserved for Lincoln's interaction with her own arrangements for the ensemble. She also wrote six of the songs, and they provide most of the album's highlights. Her voice is primed, the midrange where she does most of her work is earthy yet removed, echoing from some place far away yet poised and pressing; higher notes have a throaty, tensile character.

"Bird Alone" is a 32-bar song with an insistent, repeating strain and a subtle modulation of harmonies in the release. Stan Getz's solo is exemplary: the first eight bars hew to the melody line; the second eight soar at first, then finish in a fiery turnback; on the bridge, Getz emotes in tandem with Jones, who backs him with powerhouse chords; the closing eight are given to a riff that breaks into double time before coming to ground. After Jones plays a chorus and a half, the singer returns with just Charlie Haden (cagey effect). Maxine Roach's viola amplifies the head. On the title track, the best of the originals, Jones opens with sixteen bars peculiarly suggestive of "Just a Gigolo" on a tune that recalls Freddie Hubbard's "Up Jumped Spring," which is also included here, and has a twelve-bar set-up for a sixteen-bar chorus. Lincoln and Getz mine it for everything.

The strongest of the Lincoln-Getz collaborations is Joan Griffin's "I'm in Love," which may remind you of "Bei Mir Bist Du Schoen." It's the one performance in which he chaperones the vocal in true Billie Holiday–Lester Young fashion. Getz smartly chooses the melody notes, adjusting the dynamics, and sculpts a meticulous, absorbing solo as though he had been chiseling away at it for years. Lincoln's "When I'm Called Home" is a sensitive rubato reading of an unusual song (three ten-bar stanzas), accompanied much of the way by Jones's piano and Mark Johnson's drums. For his twenty-bar interlude, the ailing Getz—what must he have been thinking playing this lyric?—is at his most fervid, his sound here and throughout the album heavier than usual, the notes always weighted. Lincoln matches him in her coda, with a big sustained final note.

The rest includes two Johnny Mandel tunes, of which "A Time for Love" is especially well realized; the aforementioned Freddie Hubbard waltz; a modest new bossa nova (Getz's closing note seems to have been mangled by an editor); a whimsical recitation with bass and overdubbed humming; and the matchlessly relevant choice of Yip Harburg's "Brother, Can You Spare a Dime," which has proved to be a song for all seasons. Just as Bing Crosby's sonorous cry claimed the song in 1932, Lincoln's stalwart execution is the right reading at century's end. She gives as much thought to Harburg's words as she does her own, underscoring a theatrical immediacy that would become more and more apparent in her concert performances.

Within a few years, Lincoln had found the will to turn a nightclub set into an eerily personal seance. A memorable performance at the Blue Note in 1995 put me in mind of seeing Jason Robards in *After the Fall* at the provisional ANTA Theater on Washington Square Park in the mid-'60s; the stage was three-quarters in the round, and the play began with the Robards character alone, walking out from the back and greeting a psychiatrist who isn't actually represented—who, in effect, is the audience. Minutes into the performance my attention was nailed by the realization that Robards was addressing his lines at me! Not too surprising, I surmised. We had good centrally located seats—maybe he liked playing to an adolescent. Fine. Every so often he'd look at me, and I'd hold his eye, as though doing him a service. As soon as intermission began, however, my companion expressed a sort of pleasurable embarrassment that Robards had addressed his lines to her. Before I could beg to differ, we heard someone nearby say, "God, I felt he was talking to me the whole time." We heard similar remarks out front.

That was the first time I'd ever seen a performer give an audience the delusion that he was speaking individually to each member, and I've only seen two others achieve the same effect. One is Frank Sinatra, on several occasions. The other is Abbey Lincoln. That kind of bond between performer and onlooker exemplifies a collaborative subversion of reality and common sense. Sure enough, at intermission the first two people I spoke to mentioned, offhandedly and with unmistakable pride, that she was singing directly to them, and indeed, I had thought she was focused on me.

How is it done? I'm not certain. Most performers gaze into the middle distance or over the heads of customers or move around too much or close their eyes. This trick requires the desire to make contact, to freeze time and aim each line—each word—at an individual and, then (instead of averting the returning look as one might when in a restaurant), hold it long enough to ignite a spark or pose a dare. Still, if that were all there is to it, the effect would be more frequently achieved. Relaxation plays a part: the performer must be very sure, unruffled, her concentration absolute, focusing all the energy in the room, setting up a kind of time warp so that we're all breathing at the same tempo. As her eyes lock into yours, even though only for seconds, the connection seems longer and somehow intimate. You're still wondering at it even after she looks away, and when she returns to you thirty minutes later, no one else in the room exists—your special relationship is reaffirmed. Pure illusion: examine it closely and it will disappear.

Most everything else in Abbey Lincoln's set can withstand a more mundane examination. Having been encouraged by the success of her recent albums to write more songs, she emerged as a figure with little precedent in jazz—an autobiographical diva, though like Billie Holiday or Edith Piaf (Lincoln has a taste for French *chanson,*) she was no less urgently personal in singing standard songs. With this difference: they sang of survival while faltering; Lincoln presents an image of revitalization and strength. Serenely beautiful in her middle sixties, dressed head to toe in black with sprinklings of glitter, her cornrows hanging from a high-top broad-brimmed hat that has become her trademark, her marvelously square jaw jutting just enough to establish infinite poise, she is a woman who has all but jettisoned the one subject that has sustained every other woman singer. As she has written, her producer Jean-Philippe Allard observed of *Devil's Got Your Tongue* (1992), "It was probably the only album of music he'd heard without a love song for a man and a woman." And that cycle of celebrational and plaintive arias was notably autobiographical. The children's choir on three virtuous selections is a bit too civic-minded for my taste, but Lincoln's knack for combining measured control with declamatory urgency never fails her, and, as usual, the album is graced by superb veteran and apprentice musicians, including trombonist J. J. Johnson and a young pianist named Rodney Kendrick, who augurs a promising career with his austere, deliciously lithe solo on "Evalina Coffey (The Legend of)," a panagyric for Lincoln's mother.

Lincoln's most expressive tour de force was to come, however, in 1995, with *A Turtle's Dream*: nine originals, plus "Nature Boy" and "Avec Le Temps." Allard once again found a fresh means of presentation, combining stellar soloists from three generations (Kenny Barron, Pat Metheny, Roy Hargrove, Lucky Peterson, and tenor saxophonist Julien Lourau, who has listened well to Joe Henderson and Stan Getz), top-drawer rhythm sections, and a few strings. At this stage, no one was likely to miss the generic quality of an Abbey Lincoln song, words or music. With rare exceptions, Lincoln writes songs of a woman alone, dispensing advice about cycles and acceptance that might seem trite if not for the enormous emotional resources she draws on as a singer and her ability to intensify lyrics with details that shake up clichés.

"Throw It Away," a canny variation on the theme that nothing is more completely yours than that which you give away, has a distinctive melody I expect other singers will cover. "Down Here Below," an original and expansively imagined song about faith, has two choruses with completely different lyrics, including a sixteen-bar B-section with four perfect couplets tied to a repetitive tenacious melody that is one of the finest examples to date of Lincoln's craftsmanship as a songwriter. The performance is exemplary: violin and cello are voiced and miked to do the work of a chamber orchestra, and Kenny Barron's piano improvisation is righteously graceful. The give-a-cheer sentiment of "Should've Been" is countered by a plaintive melody; on the other hand, the genuinely cheerful "Storywise" dispatches the awareness that "life has lost its cheer" in a swinging hymn (it has a fine Roy Hargrove solo) to universal love.

A self-described turtle, Lincoln does come down to earth in a couple of less cosmic love songs of a sort. Most rewarding and erotic is "My Love Is You," in which she enters in a vein somewhat reminiscent of Holiday, expressing longing for those moments of "tender awfulness." (Lourau handles his part capably, but it's hard not to think of what Stan Getz's searing decisiveness might have brought to this performance.) "Hey, Lordy Mama" is a low-down, violent blues that gets surprisingly specific about the retributive nature of breakups.

Lincoln is most eloquent in live performance, taking the measure of her audience. On record, the songs often suggest the consequence of loneliness; in concert, they are enlivened by the relief of shared experience. The long, sustained notes, often hit at a pitch just lower than what you anticipate, have the quality of elated drones. Give yourself up to them, and you are lost to her timbre and intonation and then to the world from which they derive. During one not untypical club set even she appeared surprised at how driven her music could be. After an instrumental interlude on "I've Got Thunder," during which bassist and drummer doubled time, she asked them to do the same for her, and as they complied she pushed the song to a frenzy. At the close of "Down Here Below," she had tears in her eyes, and on "Wholey Earth," she used swing devices to turn each phrase, employing unladylike growling in the manner of Cootie Williams. Yet she made of her encore, Hoagy Carmichael's "The Nearness of You," a lullaby.

Lincoln's music continues to deepen: "Street of Dreams" has never sounded more fateful than on the 1997 installment, *Who Used To Dance*, a characteristically spellbinding album, for which her rotating accompaniment includes six saxophonists—three prominent (Frank Morgan, Oliver Lake, Steve Coleman), three up-and-coming (Julien Lourau, Riley

T. Bandy, Justin Robinson)—and tap dancer Savion Glover, who provides sandy obbligato with his feet on the title piece, one of several originals about Lincoln's preferred theme, the weight of time. She also sings "Mr. Tambourine Man," which sounds a lot more earned in her interpretation than when introduced by the young Bob Dylan. It's as if she is saying that the struggle out there changes but the one in here is constant; in the end, the political is always personal.

PART EIGHT

❖

A Traditional Music

68 ❖ Randy Weston
(Afrobeats)

In the educated European tradition, great composers mine their own ethnic backgrounds as a matter of course: Beethoven appropriates a drinking song, Liszt cavorts with gypsies, Bartok adapts the folk songs of Hungary and Ives those of America. And in the early decades of this century, many composers, including Debussy, Ravel, Stravinsky, and Milhaud, made a show of their demotic wit by borrowing from jazz. Copland opined that jazz's primary value was as source material, Paul Whiteman was praised for having made a lady of jazz by introducing Gershwin's *Rhapsody in Blue*, and Gershwin himself called jazz a "very powerful" American folk music. Now, however, jazz's favorite dictum is that it is American classical music—not an ethnic or folk foundation for art but the thing itself.

So the question arises: If jazz is so cultivated, how does it explore its own roots? One obvious answer is via the songwriting fellowship that sprang from Tin Pan Alley. The irony here—predominantly white songwriters viewed as a kind of folk source (if you can imagine Jerome Kern as folk) for black performers—is bizarre, given who gets the money. A more obvious answer is via the blues: the only musical form to develop in the United States, a product of the African American experience, an apparently bottomless reservoir of inspiration for jazz musicians.

Even so, blues in jazz is primarily structural, not emotive. Those occasions when jazz embraces its rural roots, from Louis Armstrong recording with country shouters to Hannibal Peterson interpolating rural blues into his symphonic pageant, are rare. And although gospel is embedded in jazz's call-and-response, rarer still is the use of other African American folk musics, from work songs to spirituals (whose novelty appeal is surely one reason Charlie Haden's and Hank Jones's *Steal Away* found a receptive audience). White musicians are more likely to explore black musical traditions than their own. A few Jewish players have milked their ethnic backgrounds, from Benny Goodman's "And the Angels Sing" to John Zorn's band Masada, but a black musician, Don Byron, fully explored klezmer in a jazz context. In recent years, Asian American jazz musicians have begun to recover their own. But have Italian or Irish jazz musicians ever thought to exploit or interpret opera or reels as jazz?

The most wide-ranging and influential alliance between jazz and another musical culture is the Afro-Cuban movement, pioneered by Dizzy Gillespie and others in the '40s. Yet Latin jazz is an alloy, and while

Chico O'Farrill is undoubtedly correct in observing that jazz influenced Cuba more than the reverse, it remains something of a third stream, that is, Latin clave and percussion aren't tangential influences, but partners in the mix. Another example of ethnic borrowing was Stan Getz's bossa nova. In a similar way, the worldbeat movement of the past twenty years has flavored jazz with a vast array of international fillips. In the early '70s, Ellington wrote a piece about the didjeridoo; a few years later, Craig Harris was playing one. For a while, tablas were almost as popular as congas, and there was an invasion of flutes and whistles and gourds, as well as kalimbas and bandoneons and other instruments with exotic names.

Not surprisingly, Africa exerted the most appeal by far. Always a part of jazz in song titles and vague musical references, it became a genuine musical influence, especially after its own pop music was successfully exported. Africa provided numerous allusions for jazz in the '20s, when it was widely considered the adventurer's last playground and Marcus Garvey's last hope. In New York, Ellington's Jungle Band indulged in faux Africanisms with growly brasses and sexy dances; in Paris, Josephine Baker, nude but for a string of bananas, incarnated the fabled lure of primitive eros. If Gillespie looked to Africa by way of Cuba in the '40s, the following decade produced real interest in the mother continent. Folkways and other companies released field recordings, musicologists traced the African influence on blues, and Afrocentric pride was reasserted.

Randy Weston once observed that it was Thelonious Monk who alerted him to the link. But it was Weston who developed it. And though he didn't travel to Nigeria until 1961, he was premeditating an African American alliance much earlier, before he began recording. Born in Brooklyn in 1926, he witnessed firsthand the development of jazz's Afro-Cuban nexus, which jibed with the Afro-Caribbean rhythms and melodies that flourished in his neighborhood and were part of his own heritage. In the mid-'40s, he forged lasting relationships with musicians who would appear on his recordings a decade later, including baritone saxophonist Cecil Payne, trumpeter Ray Copeland, and bassist Sam Gill, who made a serious study of African and Middle Eastern musics and, in the '50s, adopted the Muslim name Ahmed Abdul-Malik. In those apprenticeship years, Weston became fascinated with Monk, whom he heard with Coleman Hawkins. After he was discharged from the army in 1947, he visited Monk at his home and began to spend time with him, absorbing his spare and percussive attack and his devotion to the blues. Weston was the first pianist to craft a distinctive keyboard approach that derived from Monk.

He was also the first modern musician to record for Riverside Records. At his second Riverside session, in 1955, he debuted "Zulu," a percussive riff that might have been called "Thelonious," and in 1958, he followed with "Bantu Suite" and his breakthrough composition, "Little Niles," a piece actually written in 1952, in which an engaging jazz waltz is given a North African twist with an undulating figure that reappears in much of his music. Weston's '50s recordings for Riverside (expertly supported by Cecil Payne), Dawn, Jubilee, Metro, and United Artists are among the most charmingly anomalous in the postbop era. His penchant for triple time, pentatonic melodies, and a shrewdly rhythmic piano attack, heavy on bass, was established before he went to Africa and developed further during the course of two tours of Lagos, Nigeria, in 1961 and 1963, and a 1966 state department visit to fourteen African countries. By 1969, he had settled in Morocco, living in Rabat and Tangier, where he operated the African Rhythms Club. At the same time Weston's South African counterpart, Abdullah Ibrahim, was bringing Cape Town rhythms to the United States, Weston was bringing jazz to Africa.

Weston recorded sporadically after 1960, mostly for independent and obscure labels (when American musicians relocate abroad they become invisible no matter how widely acclaimed they were before the move); the theme of Africa remained resolute in his music. A couple of his pieces, "Hi-Fly" and "Little Niles," had become jazz standards, and Weston, who has always been community minded, performed in schools, libraries, and churches. A towering and congenial man, he offered workshops and musical lectures. But now he sought a larger musical canvas that combined jazz, poetry, African song, and rhythmic pageantry. The result, in 1960, was *Uhuru Africa* (Roulette), a collaboration with the poet Langston Hughes, employing a griot-like narrator, trained concert singers, a big band, and an international percussion section including Olatunji, Candido, Max Roach, and others. The work feels dated now, its exuberance ersatz, its ambition didactic, except when the jazz elements take over (as in "Kucheza Blues"). It proved most significant in affirming Weston's flair for large ensembles and his musical bond with arranger and trombonist Melba Liston. Liston had previously arranged a sextet and trombone choir for Weston, but *Uhuru Africa* was the first of their many big band projects (they revived it at a 1998 concert in Brooklyn). A former writer for Gerald Wilson and Dizzy Gillespie, she was ideally suited to expand Weston's engaging themes for a full complement of brasses and reeds.

A second, less flamboyant big band album, *Music from the African Nations* (Colpix, 1963, reissued as *Highlife* on Roulette), received less attention but is the more rewarding work, and the more important compositionally: several pieces became standard in his repertory, including two by African composers (Bobby Benson's "Niger Mambo" and Guy Warren's "The Mystery of Love") and his own "Congolese Children" and "Blues to Africa." Liston's seductively dissonant arrangements are layered over buoyant rhythms that were way ahead of their time and sound surprisingly fashionable today. Weston's anchoring piano is well recorded, and the soloists, especially the great tenor saxophonist Booker Ervin, are less forced and more forceful than those on *Uhuru Africa*. Still, it stirred little interest. A year later a frustrated Weston went into the studio on his own and self-produced an irresistible album, *The Randy Weston Sextet*; finding little interest in the industry, he created a mail-order label, Bakton, to release it. With excellent playing by Ray Copeland and the urgently distinctive Ervin, the band offers defining performances of two signature Weston themes, "Berkshire Blues" and "African Cookbook," and engendered enough enthusiasm for the Monterey Jazz Festival to book the sextet plus Cecil Payne in 1966.

Weston's career should have taken off; instead, he took off for Africa, a timely flight considering the dark days that lay ahead for jazz as the rock juggernaut flattened even its most celebrated musicians. During the next eight years, he recorded hardly at all: two 1965 sessions (solo and trio) were released by Arista Freedom in 1977; the 1966 Monterey set was not issued until Verve bought the tape in 1996. The occasional albums he recorded in Europe had titles like *Afro-Blues* and *Randy Weston's African Rhythm*, as did most of his new compositions. After six years, he returned to the United States and enjoyed an improbable hit with *Blue Moses* (CTI), a funky big band compromise, arranged by the meretricious Don Sebsesky with Weston on electric piano. He returned to form in 1973 with *Tanjah* (Polydor), reuniting with Liston, resurrecting "Hi-Fly" and "Little Niles," and introducing notable new pieces, including "Tanjah" and "Sweet Meat," the latter featuring altoist Norris Turney. An Ellingtonian flavor is palpable not only in the specifics—Turney's appearance, Jon Faddis's high-strung, high-note trumpet, the undulating melodies—but in the broader achievement of tackling and extending what Ellington coyly described as the Afro-Eurasion eclipse.

Again his career should have taken off, but while *Tanjah* enjoyed respectable sales, Weston's big band projects were put on hold for the next fifteen years while he recorded almost exclusively as a piano soloist, mostly for exceedingly obscure labels (Cora, Arc), until 1987, when he and David Murray attained a meeting of minds on *The Healers* (Black Saint). Two years later he was signed by Antilles/Verve, and for the first time in two decades he came fully alive as a recording artist, making up for the lost time with one or more releases a year throughout the '90s.

These records are among his best and they represent a remarkable accomplishment: the crafting of a Brooklyn-Moroccan connection that is now as natural as any idiom in contemporary jazz.

In 1989, he recorded three volumes of "portraits" with a quartet (piano, bass, two percussionists). The subjects are Ellington, Monk, and himself, and taken together they acknowledge his primary influences and illuminate what he has made of them; on the Monk especially, he manages to be radical and reverent at the same time, though there are passages where the extra percussion sounds more like a gratuitous overlay than an integral component. Two enormously satisfying albums with Melba Liston led to the brilliant small band, African Rhythms, which is a culmination of everything he has achieved. *The Spirits of Our Ancestors* (1991) introduces the musicians who would make African Rhythms one of the most exciting touring bands of the day: the seasoned trombonist Benny Powell and tenor saxophonist Billy Harper and Weston's prize discoveries, alto saxophonist Talib Kibwe and bassist Alex Blake. Once again he recycles his repertory, salvaging "Blue Moses" from the fusion era and refashioning "The Healers," "African Cookbook," and others.

Weston never made a more blithely entertaining record than *Volcano Blues* (1993), on which he and Liston finally share equal billing. (Jazz arrangers, like Hollywood screenwriters, get only as much respect as they can wrangle. Benny Goodman's tributes to Fletcher Henderson were unusual in their day; Gil Evans never did split a marquee with Miles Davis until he was dead.) With a cast ranging from veteran Los Angeles tenor saxophonist and composer Teddy Edwards (who is masterful on a definitive trio performance of Guy Warren's "Mystery of Love") to urban blues singer and guitarist Johnny Copeland (on a revival of Basie's "Harvard Blues"), Weston presides over a chameleonic celebration of the twelve-bar sonnet that provokes and amuses and deepens with every hearing. But *Volcano Blues* could only exist as a record. *Saga* is an accurate reflection of the African Rhythms septet Weston debuted in New York in 1995.

Coming after its rousing predecessor, *Saga* may seem relatively staid, but its power emanates from the casualness of its virtuoso cultural blend. The balance between ensemble—arranged by musical director Talib Kibwe—and soloists is riveting and the rhythm section flawless, with guest Billy Higgins on drums, Neil Clarke on percussion, and the remarkable bassist Alex Blake, who pushes the beat with robust double-stops. Weston's piano is at the center, binding all the elements, and his playing is imbued with an unmistakable sense of delight. As usual, many of the compositions are old, reworked to suit this band and these rhythms.

Unlike a good many Afrocentric musicians, Weston never changed his name, and a similar lack of camouflage graces his musical borrowings. Some of his rhythms are so familiar one doesn't necessarily think of them as African, and that may be his point: a link exists, the family is more closely settled than previously thought. Nor does he fold in African instruments or chanting. In short, he hasn't gone native; he's taken what he can use to amplify his own music. That consists chiefly of African rhythms that lend a vivacious spark to jazz rhythms without overpowering them. On *Saga*, Weston plays in three, four, five, six, and eight—Africa accommodates him.

"Loose Wig" originated as a trio on the 1956 LP *The Art of Modern Jazz* (Dawn) and is given a ravishing face-lift in the 1995 septet version, with an extended bridge and unison scooped notes; its rhythms are heightened at every turn by Blake, who has developed a strumming/slapping/plucking technique that rocks the ensemble, and Billy Harper plays with impregnable authority. The classic swinging poise of "Saucer Eyes," a better-known piece from the '50s, is now underpinned by carnival rhythms and unfolds as a saxophone battle. One of Weston's most attractive melodies, "Tangier Bay," was a memorable piano solo on *Blues to Africa* (Arista Freedom, 1974); with Kibwe playing the seductive forty-bar theme over a jubilant vamp, it is completely refurbished. Perhaps the most impressive revision of all is the piano treatment (he's recorded it at least twice before) of "Lagos," in which Weston works in and out of rubato with unswerving equilibrium, lending the piece a rare and stately enchantment. More recent pieces include "F.E.W. Blues," a piano-trombone dialogue with an introduction that leads you to expect an old-fashioned blues, though Benny Powell and Weston use altered changes and textural devices to circumvent every expectation, and "The Three Pyramids and the Sphinx," a piano-bass duet with a strong, piquant melody.

Not everything is equally successful, but *Saga* is a formidable addition to a canon that, after more than forty years, is still subject to neglect. At New York's Iridium, with slightly altered personnel, Weston played to a full and eager house, yet he often seems an outsider, showing up in clubs sporadically, whether he is domiciled in Brooklyn or Morocco. Perhaps his most distinctive quality also undermines his appeal and that is his temperance. Weston's powerful hands relish the ringing of overtones between notes. Like Monk, he plays rests. *Saga* is a beautiful example of his restraint. Colorful, melodic, rhythmic, it borrows merely the seasonings of ethnicity to define Randy Weston's own archetypes.

69 ❖ Rosemary Clooney
(Going Her Way)

It's only a theory, but the period for the filtering and recycling of pop culture in the technocratic age seems to average about thirty-five years: the time necessary for the generation for whom it was created to reach the far shore of middle age, and the children of that generation to attain maturity and their own checking accounts. For example, the '20s revival peaked between the mid-'50s and mid-'60s and encompassed the Fitzgerald, Hemingway, and Hammett cults, as well as nostalgia for Prohibition and gangsters in representations as diverse as *The Untouchables* and *Some Like It Hot*. The reappearances of big bands, bebop, noir movies, and Second World War fashions, not to mention unlimited interest in the sex lives of the Roosevelts, were rife in the '70s and early '80s. If these calculations hold, the '90s should be knee-deep in hard bop, pre-rock pop, and lounge music. Voila!

Eisenhower-era middle-of-the-road pop was reproached not too long ago as the very stuff rock and roll was designed to ravage. Yet suddenly there is a full-blown renaissance of traditional pop singing and standard songs, not from the '70s singer-songwriters who are looking for an entrée to Vegas, but from the '50s icons themselves, living and dead. People now pronounce the name Nelson Riddle with a slight tremor of awe: beyond the community of singers and arrangers, he was less widely celebrated during his peak creative years than he is now, posthumously. Nat Cole sells more records as his daughter's overdubbed ghost and as the toast of reissues than he did as a corporeal megastar. All of Sinatra is indiscriminately in print. Jackie Gleason and Les Baxter are offered as kitsch classics. After decades of neglect, the Capitol catalogue, once the bluebook of jazz-influenced pop singers (Cole is said to have had a rare moment of pique when he called his office and a receptionist answered, "Capitol Records, home of the Beatles"), is now elaborately revived. Les Paul and Mary Ford are embraced as innovators. Tony Bennett, dropped by Columbia in the '70s, is twenty years later the same label's Grammy-monopolizing poster boy, an antidote to Michael Jackson. Peggy Lee, Kay Starr, Jo Stafford, Sylvia Syms, Margaret Whiting, Shirley Horn, Chris Connor, June Christy, Johnny Hartman, Jeri Southern, Della Reese, Annie Ross, and many others are eagerly rediscovered. Doris Day, who embarrassed us in our adolescence, is rightfully proposed for sainthood. Everything but sing-along-with-Mitch and coonskin caps is on the comeback trail. But then, as noted, time not only recycles, it filters a little bit, too.

And at the heart of it all is Rosemary Clooney, who for twenty years has rather quietly but persistently turned out the finest and most consistent series of recordings by any singer who came to prominence in the '50s. In a reversal of fortune too slick for fiction but just right for reality, she picked herself up after years of despair and inactivity to appear on Bing Crosby's final tour, which she greatly energized during their duet of "On a Slow Boat to China." As the tour ended, she signed with Concord Jazz and began recording annual thematic albums, usually accompanied by a small jazz ensemble. To those of us who knew her only from such Mitch Miller–produced novelties as "Come On-a My House" and "Mambo Italiano," the Concord Jazz series might have been a revelation, except that in that same period Columbia prepared us by rereleasing her collaboration with Duke Ellington, *Blue Rose*. Obviously, hers was a voice and style that transcended pop fashion; but the ease with which she drifted into the role of a quasi-jazz matriarch was as unexpected as it was uncalculated.

The makeover was in large degree circumstantial. She worked with a small combo because—until her renewed career was in full throttle—Concord could not afford to buffer her with a full orchestra. She sang a choice repertory of great songs because she was of an age and disposition when anything less would have been unthinkable. She made exclusively musical decisions because she was free at last from the blandishments of star-making machinery, a trade-off she accepts:

> Few of us were doing what we wanted to do in [the '50s], so I was never far away from the rest of the pack. When you had a difference with the company, the company won. I didn't feel I had that many choices. Now it's so luxurious because I can really think all year long about what I want to do for the next album. That's a big consideration in my life.

She is now a more expressive singer because an increased attention to lyrics and meaning and feeling is one of the ways an artist of her stature makes up for the inevitable loss in range and lung capacity. She is able to swing because like Crosby she has superb time, but she now swings with greater ease and confidence because . . . who knows? Perhaps she simply feels more in control of her talent. One has merely to switch from Clooney circa 1951 to Clooney circa 1998 to appreciate the gain in sage authority.

One durable lesson about American music imparted by Crosby and Louis Armstrong, underscored by their synchronous contracts with Decca and their appearances together in movies and on radio and TV, is the potentially easy mutuality between the jazz and pop spheres. Clooney has long been able to inhabit both worlds without belonging entirely to either. In 1951, the year "Come On-a My House" put her at the head of the Hit Parade, she recorded radio transcriptions backed by a studio orchestra playing standard bop-inflected arrangements, and the vivacious command she brought to songs like "You Make Me Feel So Young" (five years before Sinatra and Riddle made it a '50s anthem) or "My Old Flame" show that she had the makings of a good jazz singer from the start. Improvisation wasn't her forte, but an irrepressible rhythmic charm and the ability to read a lyric for meaning were. Those attributes were also present in her best studio hits, like "Tenderly" and "Half as Much," and in her resonant 1953 treatment of "You'll Never Know" with Harry James.

But Gresham's law is inviolable in popular culture, and as Clooney's novelties increased her price, her uncommon abilities were undervalued—though not by everyone. Ellington and Strayhorn recognized her expressive range, and all three had reason to be pleased with the 1956 *Blue Rose*. Scheduling problems necessitated her dubbing the vocals, a process supervised by Strayhorn, yet she rendered a matchless "Grievin'" and one of the finest versions of "Sophisticated Lady" on record. Clooney's mastery of tempo gives her the latitude to try any kind of song, but it is through the affective gravity of her voice that she makes them her own. Her instrument is a wonder: the throaty, sensuous, unmistakably plangent timbre conveys rueful intimacy and great intelligence of a kind that is read by some as wisely maternal and by others as wryly alert. She is a skilled actor in and out of song. If she hadn't decided to focus on her family—five children is quick succession—her Hollywood career might have evolved from cliché nice gals to character parts of the sort she has played on television. Like Sinatra, she inhabits her songs, addressing the lyrics as narratives. *White Christmas*, the top-grossing movie of 1954, is Crosby's show (and Irving Berlin's), but Clooney steals it in the sequence where she sings the smoky ballad "Love, You Didn't Do Right by Me," adducing a candor and dimension the film never regains.

Clooney was born in Maysville, Kentucky, in 1928 and began singing with her younger sister Betty at local events and amateur contests. In 1945, the two school girls auditioned on station WLW in Cincinnati, and won a nightly radio spot at $20 a week. Within a year, bandleader Tony Pastor (himself an Armstrong-influenced singer) heard them and took them on the road. After more than two years of travel and one-nighters, Betty went home and Rosemary settled in New York, determined to have a career. Musicians knew how good she was. She became friendly with

Sarah Vaughan. Billie Holiday paid her the ultimate compliment, considering the source: "You're a good singer," she said. After Rosemary sang "Taking a Chance on Love" on Tallulah Bankhead's radio extravaganza, *The Big Show*, Art Tatum sent her a dozen roses. In 1950, Clooney and the equally little-known Tony Bennett were hired as panelists for the TV show *Songs for Sale*, which required them to perform submissions by amateur songwriters. No songs were discovered, but the panelists were. Mitch Miller, who joined the show the next season, signed them to Columbia, where Bennett went from "Rags to Riches" and Clooney, an Irish-Catholic southerner, sang—reluctantly and under threat from Miller, who was ready to kill her contract if she refused—an Armenian folksong in an Italian accent, backed by harpsichord. "Come On-a My House" was the number one record in the summer of 1951. In short order, Rosemary was signed to Paramount, made the cover of *Time*, and landed her own TV show (no panelists, but lots of potted plants, half-open door frames, and wheelbarrows to camouflage her pregnancies).

Her singing underwent something of a transition in the years 1958 to 1961 as the novelty era faded and she focused on albums. She maintained a close friendship with Crosby (they taped a fifteen-minute daily syndicated radio show from her Beverly Hills home), and the first and best (by far) of their two duet albums, *Fancy Meeting You Here* (arranged by Billy May), in 1958, captures their poised interaction. Two years later, she and Nelson Riddle conjured an equally upbeat collection, *Rosie Solves the Swingin' Riddle*. Riddle had been music director for her 1956 TV show (Clooney and her present pianist and music director John Oddo transcribed and recreated sixteen of the arrangements he wrote for the show for the 1995 album *Dedicated to Nelson*). By 1960, they had fallen in love, and in the following year, he chose to commemorate their secret romance (they were married to others) by writing her a sumptuous album of lavish arrangements called *Love*.

It should have been her breakthrough record: it documents her most mature work to that date in a highly personal selection of songs, some of them fairly obscure, each treated with suitably diverse interpretations. Her rendering of Mark Blitzstein's "I Wish It So," for example, makes the most of the song's Irish air and diction in a rare and elegant expression of youthful erotic longing. No one has realized as well as she the desire and frustration at the core of Burke and Van Heusen's "Imagination" or emphasized as clearly the contrast between the light sauciness of the verse and the womanly daring of the chorus in Cole Porter's "Why Shouldn't I?" She was just thirty-two and serving notice of how much command she had. But RCA inexplicably refused to release the album. In 1963, Sinatra acquired it for Reprise, but the public was unresponsive, and it soon disappeared, never to achieve proper recognition until Reprise reissued it in the more receptive clime of 1995. The failure of *Love* boded ill; a dour follow-up with the pessimistic title, *Thanks for Nothing*, was less enchanting. The '60s proved as dark for her as the '50s had been bright. Her marriage fell apart, a longstanding dependency on pills took its toll, and the assassination of Robert Kennedy, a few feet from where she stood, sent her reeling into despair and, ultimately, an isolated cell in a psychiatric ward. The details are set forth in her 1977 memoir, *This for Remembrance*.

Clooney credits Crosby's 1976 invitation to join his show at New York's Uris Theater and London's Palladium with reviving her career and life. Crosby also wrote the introduction to her book, but he could scarcely have imagined the extent of her achievement in subsequent years. The most telling evidence is the series of albums for Concord Jazz. At first, she paid tribute to others—to Crosby, Holiday, Berlin, Arlen, Mercer, Van Heusen, Porter, Ira Gershwin, Rodgers and Hart. The singing is remarkably assured, as though nothing had been amiss—the timbre is richer, the rhythms more pointed. Clooney is the queen of vowels, and unlike most singers, she can mine a long *e* as handsomely as a short *a*. She lands on them with emphasis, draws them out with a slight shiver, imbues them with feeling as though they were midword oases. An ideal example is the verse on "But Not for Me" or the balladic reading of "Strike Up the Band" on the superior Gershwin entry. Only in collaboration with Woody Herman, oddly enough, did she attempt au courant '80s material and arrangements (*My Buddy*) that didn't suit her; otherwise, with little fanfare she produced the classiest shelf of songbooks since Ella. Still, she was a decade ahead of the curve—the cycle hadn't come around yet. Not until the early '90s, when she began appearing annually at New York's Rainbow & Stars and mounted unusually enterprising Carnegie Hall concerts, did a new generation seek her out.

The revival of interest in Clooney and other performers of her generation owes much to the realization that the songs they sing—beyond the once fashionable hits that made them stars—are an indispensable treasure that no one else can mine as well. The jazz bias for music over words probably begins with the idea that lyrics are conveniences with which improvising singers manipulate melody, a prejudice that resulted from the drivel many early jazz singers were forced to salvage. Antipathy toward classic lyrics is also entrenched in early rockcrit, which, born in the era of singer-songwriters, when Broadway and movie musicals were dying on the vine, sneered at the alleged profusion of "June/moon" images and rhymes. June/moon? In the work of Lorenz Hart, Cole Porter, Johnny Mercer, Johnny Burke, Hoagy Carmichael, Yip Harburg, Sammy Cahn, Dorothy Fields, Ira Gershwin, Andy Razaf, Alan Jay Lerner, Oscar Hammerstein II, Mitchell Parish, or Irving Berlin? Not likely, except as an inside joke. Some of the derision was plain ignorance. (In a TV interview on the occasion of Elvis Presley's death, a critic remarked on his innovative use of "ain't" in a song title; Kinkle's *Complete Encyclopedia of Popular Music and Jazz 1900–1950* lists forty-six songs from those years in which the first word is *ain't*, in addition to numerous songs in which "ain't" figures as the second or third word, as in "I Ain't Got Nobody" or "It Ain't Necessarily So.")

But a more potent factor was also at work, a defensiveness against the manifest adultness of great lyrics, which invariably deal with sex, love, loneliness, and sex. Many of us in our forties found ourselves responding to singers in a different way than we had a few years earlier, attending not only their timbre and melody, but the stories they tell. Paul Mc-Cartney, for example: they hadn't met, but when Clooney turned sixty-four in 1992, he sent her a framed, inscribed copy of his song "When I'm Sixty-Four." For some reason, few postrock singers can mine the meaning of prerock songs. Is it the often literary and metaphorical language that is alien to them or the rhythms on which the songs are dependent or the required subtlety in phrasing? Those with a theatrical background tend to overemote in a nonswinging Streisandarian bellow, as if determined to clobber the songs before they can clobber them back. Clooney instructs by example.

By the early '90s, Clooney had become something of a minimalist, exacting greater yield with less exertion from songs as familiar as "A Foggy Day" or "How Deep Is the Ocean?" or "Don't Fence Me In." At the same time, she became a candidly autobiographical singer. Few performers can make of their lives mirrors for the lives of their audiences, distilling their experiences into truths of universal application, while keeping safe distance from self-indulgence and nostalgia. She turned her attention to her own history in a series of increasingly evocative meditations on music of the Second World War, her sister act with Betty, the long road of a girl singer, the spell of New York, her love for Nelson Riddle, and her demicentennial as a pro. In every instance, her voice, with its brawny edge, heady vibrato, subtle throb, and unequivocal humor, reclaimed the material as a shared musical past. Never has her singing been more scrupulously under control—her near-parlando way of hitting a note and then nudging it up or down a tone or halftone, her foursquare phrase endings, her unostentatious cresting of high notes, and not least, her distinctive grip on sibilance. Billie Holiday justifiably observed that no one sang the word *love* like she did. No one sings the word *kiss* like Rosemary Clooney.

❖ ❖ ❖

The Concord Jazz project itself is unprecedented. On *For the Duration*, she cuts through the melodrama of such songs as "These Foolish Things," "The White Cliffs of Dover," and "I'll Be Seeing You," performing them straight up with spare and efficient arrangements by John Oddo, who adds strings to the quintet on a few selections. Among the pleasures of these records is the increasing closeness between Clooney, tenor saxophonist Scott Hamilton, and trumpeter Warren Vaché, which recalls the Holiday–Teddy Wilson sessions of the '30s. On "I Don't Want To Walk Without You, Baby," a song that can easily be overdramatized but which she treats at a medium-up roll, Hamilton's tenor issues forth in obbligato, contrasting his robust timbre with hers and accentuating her interpretive rigor. On *Girl Singer*, she prefaces "Straighten Up and Fly Right" with the audition tape she and Betty made of the Nat Cole novelty back in the '40s. She is at her best sailing into the verse of "More Than You Know," illuminating the lyric of "Autumn In New York," turning "Miss Otis Regrets" into a well-bred swinger, and uncovering an obscure gem by Richard Rodney Bennett and Johnny Mercer, "Lovers After All." On *Still on the Road*, she is supported by a first-rate Los Angeles big band of the sort that disappeared with movie musicals.

Nowhere is the earthy, almost chilling directness of her voice better captured than on *Do You Miss New York?*; turn up the volume, and it's as though she were in the room, the declarative phrasing shaded by a breathy echo that suggests the recitations of Ben Webster, whose tenor saxophone similarly echoed out of a fund of experience and emotion. Webster's shade is invoked more directly by Scott Hamilton and by the close-knit support of the sextet. The ballads, all from the top shelf, are the soul of the album: "Gee Baby, Ain't I Good to You," "A Beautiful Friendship," "I Ain't Got Nothing But the Blues" (originally slated for but not used on *Blue Rose*), "I Get Along Without You Very Well," and "We'll Be Together Again." She so persuasively imbues the last with maternal assurances that under her spell one recalls only with effort the very different interpretation by Sinatra. Her version is additionally graced with an expert half-chorus by guitarist Bucky Pizzarelli and a sensational full one by Warren Vaché that stands with his best work (and makes up for his coy gliss at the close of "Gee Baby"). On *Demi-Centennial*, Clooney revisits various stages in her life and finds an unlikely common ground on which to renew a motley of songs that could appear on no other singer's album, among them "Danny Boy," "I'm Confessin'," "Sophisticated Lady," "Mambo Italiano," and "White Christmas."

During these same years, she presented hugely successful and uniquely ambitious concerts at Carnegie Hall: one a tribute to arrangers (Riddle, Strayhorn, Peter Matz, Percy Faith, Meredith Willson, Cal Tjader, and

Johnny Mandel, who wrote her a gorgeous setting for his "The Shadow of Your Smile"); another a tribute to Crosby (she sang the entire medley, several dozen songs, he used to close his 1976–77 shows and told masterful anecdotes); and a retrospective that included a surprise appearance by Harry "Sweets" Edison, whose delicately precise obbligati and featured solo had the audience leaning forward in hushed suspense.

Perhaps her recovered place in American music at century's end was best indicated by two events in 1996. In June she was inducted into a Tampa-based International Jazz Hall of Fame, along with a dozen or so other living eminences, including Benny Carter, Lionel Hampton, Al Grey, Harry Edison, Ray Brown, Dave Brubeck, Illinois Jacquet, Ella Fitzgerald, and James Moody, and as many posthumous inductees, including Sarah, Billie, Dinah, Nat Cole, Billy Eckstine, and Cab Calloway—and no one in the audience or the press or among the musicians questioned the appropriateness of her inclusion. Indeed, her segment was a highlight of the evening. That simply couldn't have happened in 1950 or 1960 or 1970 or 1980. Then, in December, she was the final performer in a long Carnegie Hall salute, *Ira Gershwin at 100*. Most of the singers and dancers were from Broadway or cabaret, though a couple (Ruth Brown, Vic Damone) were veteran entertainers. Hardly any of them were able to make the lyrics seem anything more than clever, if that. After three hours, Clooney was introduced, and before she had sung eight bars of the verse to "A Foggy Day," the air was palpably altered. For the first time all night, one found oneself thinking about the song and remembering the tribute was to Ira, not George. Backed by a big band, she was also the only performer who injected the serene lilt of jazz, substituting the spaciousness of swing and her particular veracity for the rampant narcissism that preceded her. The audience roared.

Humbert Humbert, dining with Lolita in jukebox heaven, commented on the "nasal voices of those invisibles serenading her, people with names like Sammy and Jo and Eddie and Tony and Peggy and Guy and Patty and Rex, and sentimental song hits, all of them as similar to my ear as her various candies were to my palate," adding that Lo herself was a "disgustingly conventional little girl." He didn't count Rosie in his rosary, but he might have—back then. Not even Humbert could hear in the Rosemary Clooney of the '90s anything remotely like sentimentality, anonymity, or convention.

70 ❖ Joe Henderson
(Tributes)

Trummy Young's old axiom, " 'Tain't what you do (it's the way that you do it)," helped to define the jazz aesthetic in the classic age, when Louis Armstrong and Billie Holiday were constrained to record Carmen Lombardo songs and somehow made great works of them. But that's all changed. Today what you do counts for a lot. Contemporary records are evaluated as much by considerations of repertory as anything else. How could it be otherwise? In dreams come responsibility, and the dream of repertory freedom—realized incrementally since the days when producers insisted on originals (or new riffs on old chords) from which they could shake down the publishing rights or assembled jazz alloys from Beatles ballads and worse—has led to a more inventive and discerning approach in choosing material. No longer can the strongest of improvisers get by with the old formula of blues, rhythm changes, and a couple of standards.

In the '70s and '80s, the deaths of Ellington and Monk led to countless inquiries into their catalogs, while Jimmy Rowles initiated an exploration through the jungles of forgotten movie tunes (continuing safaris begun in the '50s by Ahmad Jamal and Red Garland), repertory ensembles scavenged the dark corners of swing, bop was apotheosized, and young players finally began panning the hard bop period for worthy compositions by Jimmy Heath, Kenny Dorham, Randy Weston, Sonny Clark, Wayne Shorter, Gigi Gryce, and several others, not least Joe Henderson, whose 1963 "Recorda-Me" has become a workshop favorite. So Henderson's 1992 breakthrough album, *Lush Life: The Music of Billy Strayhorn* (Verve), was more symptomatic than innovative. Yet any album done this well and met with such global enthusiasm could only bolster jazz's strangely neoclassical contribution to the fin de siècle.

In the early '60s, when jazz knew something about end-of-era decadence, Henderson emerged, along with Shorter and Booker Ervin, as one of the most original mainstreamers on tenor sax. Countering the deluge that followed John Coltrane's "Chasin' the Trane," they represented a post-Coltrane modernism that nonetheless held close to the verities of harmonies, bar lines, and the tempered scale. Ervin, perhaps the most aggressively individual of them, died young, and Shorter detoured to the land of fusion. Henderson kept plugging, but only rarely (for example, his Vanguard recordings on Blue Note) produced a satisfying representation of his mature playing style, a beguiling amalgam of varied tonal and harmonic approaches. The composer of such enticing riddles as "Isotope" and "The Bead Game," he is also an irresistibly lucid player, whose adroitness in conjuring stark and swirling riffs contributed immeasurably to two of the most durable jazz hits of the '60s, Horace Silver's "Song for My Father" and Lee Morgan's "The Sidewinder." Henderson's ability to suggest incantation in his more elaborate solos is magnified by a bewitching tone that can be both gruff and tender, virile and hollow, in the space of a phrase. In Billy Strayhorn he found a model collaborator.

A composer and arranger of genius, a lyricist of precocious charm, a pianist of elusive but unmistakable skill, Strayhorn as a recording director never seemed to get it quite right when producing his own albums, though he spent twenty-eight years as Duke Ellington's other self. Ellington himself fostered a reassessment of Strayhorn's abilities with the 1967 masterwork, *And His Mother Called Him Bill*. The intensity of Johnny Hodges's solo on "Blood Count" and of Ellington's stirring end-of-session "Lotus Blossom" were its two peaks, but those performances posed a situation it has taken more than two decades to resolve: How shall anyone else interpret them? Henderson does not play many of the ten selections on *Lush Life* as though he had a lifelong familiarity with them. What gives the record its piquancy is the suspicion that he is measuring himself against the material, testing himself in its rigors, enjoying the dangers as they unfold.

Another good decision was varied instrumentation. The full complement of five musicians appears on three selections, but the players are relayed on each of the remaining seven. The selection of tunes is shrewd. Though focusing, with three exceptions, on themes introduced before 1950, the program alternates swingers and ballads, famous and neglected pieces. The absence of space-breaks between the dirgelike "Blood Count" and the steaming "Raincheck" and between the even more steaming "Take the A Train" and the aptly named "Drawing Room Blues" underscores continuity. But I do wish they had substituted natural fade downs for board fades in the two instances where the latter are employed.

"Isfahan," from the 1966 *Far East Suite*, is treated as a duet for tenor and bass. The exceptionally gifted young bassist Christian McBride paces Henderson's theme recitation with double-stop chords on varied beats, as the intimate recording setup agreeably brings the clicking of keys and the whoosh of strings into the mix. Henderson remains cagily close to the underlying chords in two improvised choruses, deftly handling the turnbacks and occasionally doubling the time, but he is most impressive in his return to the theme, sustaining key notes with tremolos and producing a light yet cavernous sound that underscores the song's fragile beauty. "Blood Count" is less successful because Henderson's attempt to expand the melody with a chorus of improvisation merely diffuses it. He is undeniably persuasive on the theme, invoking an aching vulnerability in place of the high drama favored by Hodges and Stan Getz, but the expansion is muddled, and one is relieved when, after an astute eight-bar transition by pianist Stephen Scott, Henderson restores the magic of the melody. Drummer Gregory Hutchinson's gently firm backbeat helps hold the performance together.

Wynton Marsalis completes the quintet on three numbers, and his lissome trumpet complements the tenor, especially on a riveting uptempo "Johnny Come Lately," one of three pieces from the incredibly copious period of 1940 to 1942 when Strayhorn first put his mark on the Ellington orchestra, and the dreamy and chromatic ballad "A Flower Is a Lovesome Thing," which along with "Lotus Blossom" (originally called "Charlotte Russe") was introduced on the 1947 small-band sessions Strayhorn produced for Hodges. They treat "Johnny Come Lately" in call-and-response fashion, but go separate ways in their solos, Marsalis engineering a ripe maneuver to get from his first chorus to the next and Henderson recalling the robust and clear-eyed sailing of his Silver days. On "U.M.M.G.," a test pattern for trumpet players, Marsalis suggests the open, airy sound of Willie Cook.

Henderson is at his blowout best on the 1941 "Raincheck," which has attracted tenors since Ben Webster essayed the original solo (notably Sonny Rollins and Al Cohn), and "Take the A Train." Henderson tackles the former as a homage to Rollins, girding it with a powerful calypso rhythm in a stark setting of bass and drums and employing a couple of Rollins gambits, notably at the outset of his second and third ad-lib choruses. The strangely conceived piece—the release is placed near the end—is performed here with an opening vamp and closing coda and is happily rambunctious. "Take the A Train," which opens with a tenor sax adaptation of the famous Ellington piano vamp, is bolder still. Accompanied only by Hutchinson's elegant, dancing drums, Henderson chortles through nine choruses, the two men suggesting something of the drama of the John Coltrane–Elvin Jones collusions, but never straying from the changes or trampling the bar lines. Yet as a tour de force, it, too, is trumped by the album's closer, the title selection.

"Lush Life" is an unaccompanied tenor solo—nearly five minutes in duration, though only one chorus long. Henderson's rubato phrasing is so personal as to be practically a species of free jazz. He tags every element of the melody (another odd construction with its inseparable twenty-eight-measure verse and twenty-measure chorus), but flits loosely between passages, speeding some transitions and retarding others. It takes him nearly a full minute to wend his way through the last four measures, as though he can't bear to say good-bye to the song. His timbre throughout is malleable and ever changing, profoundly human in its candor, warmth, and resourcefulness. The achievement of this album is not merely the combination of the right musician with the right composer, but that musician's willingness to meet the challenge of provocative music as a way to get to places he might otherwise never go.

The extraordinary response to Joe Henderson's *Lush Life* was only partly attributable to its musical achievement. The gentle balm of the tenor saxophone—nurtured in a hothouse tradition in which individual timbre counts for as much as harmonic, melodic, and rhythmic polish—has been a stable repository for jazz's soul since 1929, when Coleman Hawkins figured out how to play a ballad ("One Hour"). Yet by the early '90s, a hole as large as that in the ozone layer opened up as Sonny Rollins persistently failed to record on a level commensurate with his genius; Wayne Shorter circled the lost isle of Atlantis; Branford Marsalis, who probably couldn't have claimed the mantle yet anyway, stopped trying; and David Murray operated mostly in the cold climes of culthood. And here, standing firm after a checkered career of more than thirty years, a screen against the rumble of chaos, was Henderson, a classicist in need only of the right project. The music of Billy Strayhorn and a mutable cast of young lions answered the need.

It also challenged him to follow up with another project of commensurate worthiness. He did just that, anticipating the slew of Miles Davis tributes to follow with *So Near, So Far (Musings for Miles)* (Verve). In some respects, this was a more impressive achievement. Because the entire recital is performed by a quartet of musicians who worked with Davis, a familial intensity was established with the soufflé timbre on the opening "Miles Ahead" (with minimum meddling, coproducer and transcriber Don Sickler parsed the Gil Evans masterwork into a song) and sustained for most of a very long CD. Though Henderson is a matured player, he has nonetheless found a way to recapture his Blue Note effusions of the '60s—those barely restrained circular riffs that revved up his solos—in such performances as "Teo," with its fairground theme, and "Side Car," happily reclaimed for a thematic excavation in which a single idea is worried for nearly two choruses before he climbs to the next stage of engagement.

Yet Henderson's an unlikely heir to the tenor throne: his style is intellectual and often introverted. Not since the days of Charles Lloyd's *Forest Flower* has a tenor saxophonist explored at such length the instrument's potential for flute sonorities in the upper range. No one has done so with greater effect, at least not since those keening penthouse cries of Ben Webster, as witness the lyric flowering of Henderson's readings of "Miles Ahead" and "Flamenco Sketches." But the introverted character of his playing is no less marked in his fast, occasionally diffuse improvisations, where fragmented phrases seem to bounce between the bar lines like furiously driven ping-pong balls. The sheen of aggressive euphoria that is the mark of Rollins and in a different way Coltrane becomes in Henderson a shy doggedness.

Two performances are especially notable. When the woman who inspired the punning title of "Pfrancing" disappeared from Miles Davis's life, the piece was occasionally called "No Blues," but the old adage definitely applies: if it looks like a blues, plays like a blues, and sounds like a blues, it's a blues. Paced every measure by the admirably responsive rhythm section, Henderson *builds* a solo of thirteen choruses, sauntering at first with caution and economy, sustaining his ideas from tier to tier, and finishing with a rattling two-chorus climax. Dave Holland follows with an uncharacteristically Mingusian bass solo, fleet and sure yet each note and phrase weighted, swinging. On "Flamenco Sketches," Henderson crests an affecting rhythmic vamp with his otherworldly, flutelike tone and mines the scalar development of the piece in a manner reflecting his lyrical kinship to Davis in its general parameters, never in the specifics. At other moments in the same piece, Henderson and guitarist John Scofield put aside linearity, indulging a strangely static beauty—broad, colorful brushstrokes that rise and fall with a rare mutuality of insight.

On the subject of empathy, particular mention must be made of Al Foster, whose work on drums is startlingly effective. His unfailing ken for anticipating a soloist's caesuras and responding not only with the right figure, but with a distinctively appropriate sound, has established him as one of the most forceful drummers of the modern era. He sparked Dexter Gordon on one of his best late recordings, *Biting the Apple,* and Davis on *Star People* and in various other performances; his appearance at a Sonny Rollins concert is a kind of insurance of high times. He listens and acts instinctively and aggressively. His reactions on "Pfrancing" and "Swing Spring" shake you up in their enhancing expediency and must make Henderson feel very, very secure.

That seemed also to be the case at a Blue Note engagement when the Henderson quartet shared a double bill with Red Rodney's robust quintet, offering a yin/yang of introversion/extroversion. Compared to Henderson's ricocheting shards of melody, Rodney's bebop fluency seemed buoyantly open. The one change in Henderson's personnel was the substitution of Mike Stern for Scofield; for anyone whose ears are still ringing from his years as Davis's ambassador to heavy metal, Stern's development as a sensitive jazz guitarist (a change enticingly announced on Harvie Swartz's memorable 1990 *In a Different Light* [Bluemoon] and underscored by his own uneven but often impressive *Standards (and Other Songs)* [Atlantic])—is welcome and unforeseen relief. In concert and on the record, Henderson performs not the classic modal "Milestones" of 1957, but the 1947 harmony-fraught bebop "Milestones." Holland's resounding tone was like a heartbeat, setting up ostinatos and walks with supple grace. Shadowed by Foster's hi-hat and Stern's chords, his "Milestones" episode became less a solo than a heated rhythm section interlude, prolonging the intensity established by Henderson. One reason the Blue Note set was so riveting was its human length: Henderson left you wanting more. That cannot be said of the CD, which, at a dense seventy-three minutes, could not have been performed at a single session and should not be force-fed in one sitting.

71 ❖ Tommy Flanagan
(Standards and Practices)

In the early '80s, amid a flurry of quietly astonishing albums and jazz club appearances, Tommy Flanagan's ascension to the Olympus of jazz classicism was acknowledged by nearly all critics and musicians. Which suggests how little critics and musicians count for in the jazz business. For despite the high marks accorded his most recent recordings then (*Giant Steps, The Magnificent Tommy Flanagan*) and the lucid, flat-out elegance of his trio appearances, he recorded almost exclusively for minor labels, most of them in Europe. Since that time, his work has continued to represent an unrivaled oasis of creative understatement. A veteran musician, born in Detroit in 1930 and bred in bop, he is arguably the premier mainstream pianist of jazz's tenth decade (if not him, then Hank Jones, who was born twelve years earlier in nearby Pontiac). But while every twenty- or thirty-something tyro—most of them undoubtedly *promising*, though none quite finished—was signed to a major record company (for example, Cyrus Chestnut, Rodney Kendrick, Danilo Perez, Stephen Scott, Renee Rosnes, Brad Meldau, Jacky Terrasson, Marcus Roberts, Benny Green), Flanagan wasn't until 1998, when Blue Note announced a one-shot deal. He had not had a prominent American affiliation since a one-shot for Galaxy (duets with Hank Jones) in 1978, and he usually records for German, Dutch, and Japanese companies with limited or no U.S. distribution. This is worse than scandalous. It's madness.

Since 1978, the year he returned to the fray after ten years as Ella Fitzgerald's accompanist, Flanagan has blossomed like a flower in one of those accelerated-motion nature documentaries, greatly exceeding his own considerable promise in the '50s when he was hired for such seminal recording dates as Sonny Rollins's *Saxophone Colossus* and John Coltrane's *Giant Steps*. For twelve years, he developed an extrasensory bond with the virtuoso Czech bassist George Mraz. His subsequent trios included the excellent young bassist Peter Washington and one of several front-rank drummers, including Kenny Washington and, in interim stays, Elvin Jones, Billy Higgins, and Al Foster. His primary drummer, and the musician who most closely matches Mraz in anticipating Flanagan's every move, is Lewis Nash, a young player of flawless taste and unerring empathy. With that kind of support, Flanagan has reclaimed the piano trio as one of jazz's most gratifying chamber units, filling a void created when Bill Evans—his senior by one year—died in 1980. It's not supposed to happen like that: the banner is supposed to be picked by the next generation, not a contemporary, especially one with as low-key a profile as Tommy Flanagan, the perennial sideman.

The whys and wherefores of his preeminence and that of his trio aren't easily explained. You can list his potential rivals and note that either they are involved in groups of another size or work irregularly. But Flanagan's position is less a matter of besting the competition than in bringing his own powers to a peak where competition is irrelevant. The inclination to classify him as a bebopper, though understandable (critics like to have everything labeled), must be resisted. His approach to the piano is as individual as his repertory, which is as distinctive as that of any musician in jazz. Like Jim Hall or Milt Jackson, he's perfected his own niche, a style beyond style, where the only appropriate comparisons are between his inspired performances and those that are merely characteristic.

Flanagan's dominance of the piano trio came at an odd and propitious time for him and for jazz. In the '60s, when trios enjoyed renewed popularity, thanks chiefly to Ahmad Jamal, Oscar Peterson, and Bill Evans, Flanagan was all but invisible, spending nearly fifteen years as a music director for singers, mostly for Ella but also for Tony Bennett. His re-emergence as a participant in dozens of sessions as leader and sideman answered the need for a deep lyricism that eschewed sentimentality and for a purposeful dedication to craft. No less rewarding than his inventiveness was his immersion in the classic jazz repertory. Flanagan played a significant and generally unheralded role in defining the postmodernist's fake book. He not only revived neglected works by Ellington, Strayhorn, Monk, Coltrane, and Thad Jones, but showed how they could be reinvigorated. He made a virtue of harmonic variety, preferring the colors of chords to the black and white of scales, and focused on nuance and touch and melodic variation to get to the core in each selection. His technique is unassuming, never calling attention to itself, as though the gems he uncovers were there all the time, waiting for him to bring them to light.

Billy Strayhorn's "Raincheck," with which he opens his 1989 album *Jazz Poet* (Timeless), dramatizes Flanagan's strengths and demonstrates precisely why genrefication is unfair to him. First of all, he arranged the piece for trio, so that Mraz's bass figures and Kenny Washington's brushes are essential components; never for a moment do you think you're hearing piano and accompaniment. His unusual up-tempo arrangement incorporates, in Ellington fashion, a scene-setting eight-bar transition before and after solos, as well as variations in the written material for all the players. The resourcefulness of his solo is underscored by repeated hearings and is inseparable from its rhythmic lilt, a lilt that has little to do with bop. For two choruses, Flanagan deftly strings pearls of notes, buffers them with chords, probes on and ahead of the beat, doubles the tempo, and fine-tunes his ideas. The heady optimism of the improvisation is faithful to the rhythmic feeling of the written material.

His resplendent chords and steely melodic figures combine in the quietly assured phrasing of "St. Louis Blues," where the bop rhythmic trope is prefigured in a Charlie Parker quote woven into the rubato opening. His pacing, economy, and harmonic sense inform a captivating "Willow Weep for Me," phrased at first behind the beat for a deep blues groove, then tossed in the breeze of a sparkling, double-time improvisation. On J. J. Johnson's "Lament" and the Rodgers and Hart standard, "Glad To Be Unhappy," any and all received ideas about rhythm are submerged in sheer poise. On the latter, especially, he merely grazes the keys at first, building tension as he increases the pressure of his attack. This is Flanagan the romantic, a side of the man rarely evoked as clearly as here.

"Willow Weep for Me" and "Caravan" aptly illustrate the smooth mechanics of the trio; in each, Flanagan provides transitional chords to set up the bass solos. On the latter, Mraz takes up where the piano leaves off. A problem with the later editions of Bill Evans's trio was the surfeit of bass solos, each plucked near the bridge and usually beginning with a squeaky glissando. The preponderance of Mraz solos were less predictable: they are played midregister, crafted with a melodic austerity that enhances Flanagan's own approach, and rarely exceed a chorus or two. Kenny Washington, a protege of Mel Lewis and Philly Joe Jones, uses brushes more frequently than most drummers, and he has developed a powerful, snapping style with them. On his featured piece, a furiously paced Flanagan original called "Mean Streets," he begins his solo with a spare figure on the snare and holds to it as he brings in the other accoutrements and switches to sticks. Even at that tempo and at that length, he sustains the poised elegance that is the trio's hallmark. A selection that typifies Flanagan's gift for finding overlooked songs is Matt Dennis's "That Tired Routine Called Love," which has become a standard part of his concert sets, highlighted by his transition from a featherlight rubato verse to a storming chorus that takes the piece increasingly far afield from the version on *Jazz Poet*. It's one he needs to record again.

The honor roll of jazz standards by mainstream composers is not necessarily identical with that of pop standards by the same composers. Jazz musicians have been responsible for keeping so much of the established catalog in the chips that we forget the distinction. We forget also that the musicians who first claimed pop songs for jazz often had to make an imaginative leap beyond that required of their successors. Anyone undertaking "Body and Soul" in the '90s can draw on more than sixty years of ingenious variations for inspiration. Louis Armstrong, on the other hand, had merely the song itself: the lead sheet for a torchy ballad written for a stage revue with no jazz connections or ambitions. Yet if a jazz musician can't make a standard sound new and even urgent, there is no point in playing it. Flanagan is an exceptional interpreter of both the jazz and pop traditions; he has adapted Ellington's "Sunset and the Mocking Bird," from *The Queen's Suite*, as a kind of intermezzo meditation, and he has enlivened Monk's "Friday the 13th" with a jaunty disposition that is entirely his own. He is no less persuasive with standards, and one could hardly ask for a better example than his 1992 version of "Yesterdays," the great ballad by Jerome Kern and Otto Harbach.

"Yesterdays" illuminates the different values gleaned in pop songs by jazz and pop performers. It was written for the 1933 musical *Roberta* and introduced by Fay Templeton, the nineteenth-century prima donna best remembered for her association with George M. Cohan in *Forty-Five Minutes from Broadway*; at sixty-eight, she was making the last of her fabled comebacks. Though the song provided a personal triumph for Templeton and a hit record for the Leo Reisman orchestra, it ran a distant second in popularity to the show's other ballad, "Smoke Gets in Your Eyes," introduced by an actress from Ukraine named Tamara (better remembered members of the cast included its star, Bob Hope, and Sydney Greenstreet, George Murphy, and Fred MacMurray) and successfully recorded by Reisman, Ruth Etting, Paul Whiteman, and others. With that kind of send-off, "Smoke Gets in Your Eyes" was inevitably taken up by jazz orchestras of the '30s (Artie Shaw, Benny Goodman, Tommy Dorsey), but despite its abiding success as a pop standard—one of Kern's most lucrative—the song had minimal impact in jazz. Among the few modernists who performed it at all are Thelonious Monk and Sarah Vaughan.

"Yesterdays" has had a very different life. Though largely ignored for several years, it became part of the jazz repertory in the late '30s after first Artie Shaw and then Billie Holiday (one of her greatest Commodore recordings) put earthy spells on a tune that had previously seemed intimidatingly wistful. Jimmie Lunceford worked up an extended version that, in its broadcast recording, preserves the most expansive trumpet solo by Freddie Webster, the transitional mystery man who influenced Miles Davis. That was fitting because as a jazz standard "Yesterdays" owes most of its renown to postwar modernists. Coleman Hawkins chose it for the "Woody'n You" session that helped to establish Dizzy Gillespie; shortly thereafter, Gene Krupa arranged it for his orchestra. Lennie Tristano demonstrated the flexibility of the chords; Miles Davis and Lee Konitz collaborated on a reclamation of the melody; and numerous soloists found the song a challenging fund for variations, among them Bud Powell, Stan Getz, and Hank Jones. Gerald Wilson and Bill Holman refurbished it for the supersonic bands of the '50s. Art Tatum recorded half a dozen versions in that same era.

A nine-minute version of "Yesterdays" that never relaxes its drama or interest yet never breaks the thread of the constantly recapitulated melody is the centerpiece of Flanagan's *Beyond the Bluebird* (Timeless). In a welcome change of pace, his trio (Mraz and Nash) is augmented by guitarist Kenny Burrell, a fellow Detroiter in whose group Flanagan worked back in 1954. They are roughly the same age—the pianist is a year older—and their shared background gives the album its theme. The Bluebird was a famous Detroit jazz club that served as a training ground for players and listeners of the postwar generation. The first five of ten selections are tied to that era: two Charlie Parker blues ("Bluebird" and "Barbados"), Thad Jones's "50-21," Benny Carter's "Blues in My Heart" (which predates *Roberta* by two years), and one memento from the jazz/ pop nexus, "Yesterdays."

Flanagan's version of Kern's artfully arpeggiated melody begins with a surprise: a verse. All the reference books, including the one by Alec Wilder, say the song doesn't have a verse—a point several listeners made in response to Flanagan's recording, among them pianist David Lahm, whose mother, Dorothy Fields, was Kern's most gifted lyricist (pace Hammerstein II fans). Flanagan explained that he learned the passage from Al Cohn, who thought it was the unpublished verse. He has no idea where Cohn got it. The passage, an alluring enigma, is firmly voiced and urbanely played as an unaccompanied prelude to the main attraction.

The first half of the theme is treated as a duet for guitar and piano and the second half as a guitar solo, boldly phrased in the higher frets. The division of responsibility is one of the album's constant delights; as with the trio, Flanagan's arrangements maximize the interactive canniness of his musicians. The next chorus is another surprise, a reharmonization of the theme by Flanagan alone, a thirty-two-bar tour de force of substitute chords. Only then, midway through the performance, do bass and drums kick in for two choruses of embellishments by Burrell and Flanagan, the latter inserting bluesy variations with customary wit and finesse. In the last improvised chorus, before the theme, the two Bluebird grads converse, feeding each other phrases. It's a true communion, comparable to those by John Lewis and Milt Jackson or Stan Getz and Kenny Barron.

The melody of "Yesterdays" is, like that of Ellington's best ballads, difficult to shuck off even in the throes of inspired improvisation. It combines a spare opening phrase—a three-note figure played twice—with grand arpeggios and encourages passing chords with its frugal harmonies, invariably managing to hold its own whatever the renovation, unlike, say, Kern's "All the Things You Are," where the harmonies engender variations on variations that leave the original melody far behind. On the other hand, "Yesterdays" shares with "All the Things" and virtually all ballads that have been adapted to the standard jazz repertory a fraternal feeling for the blues. *Beyond the Bluebird* is a disarming album because the blues-and-ballads surface is so familiar you don't expect to be jolted. Yet good jazz resides in the details, and the details here stem from companionable precision.

A supreme confidence in the chosen material is required to close an album with two pieces as formally parallel as Flanagan's "Something Borrowed, Something Blue" and Burrell's "Bluebird After Dark." Each is essentially a blues with a bridge (albeit a sixteen-bar blues in the Burrell piece) but are fully complementary: the first lyrical and smart, the second driven and robust. Both offer absorbing changes. Again, the foursome is enterprisingly deployed. "Something Borrowed" begins, after an eight-bar introduction of solo piano, with the first chorus, treated as a duet (twelve bars by piano and guitar), quartet (twelve bars), trio (the eight-bar release, without Burrell), and quartet (twelve bars). The tempo is brightened consistently throughout the performance, and the quartet goes out embellishing a vamp. Burrell's riff-laden "Bluebird After Dark" opens with drums; after the piano and guitar choruses (Burrell finishes his with a flourish), parallel episodes find Mraz's solo paced by piano and Nash's by guitar.

The Charlie Parker, Benny Carter, and Thad Jones pieces unfurl with force and refinement. More unexpected are three newer pieces. "Nascimento," by another Bluebird alumni, Barry Harris (who is three months older than Flanagan and whose definitive version of the song is found on his 1989 Xanadu recital, *The Bird of Red and Gold*), is an engaging ABAB bossa nova with a six-bar extension that serves the purpose of an increasingly bluesy turnback. Flanagan, who dazzles with his octaves and sweeping arpeggios, extends the extension into a rhythmic coda. Dizzy Reece's "The Con Man," previously orchestrated for Clifford Jordan's big band, is a breakneck blues that opens with what amounts to a six-chorus theme traded among the members of the Flanagan trio. The title selection is one of the most distinctive tunes Flanagan has written. "Beyond the Bluebird" has the conventional chorus length of thirty-two measures, but the phrases are oddly parsed (twelve/eight/twelve, though you can subdivide them further)—changeups in the melody demand scrupulous care in the embellishments.

Flanagan has recorded fairly prolifically in the two decades since he left Ella, though, as noted, many of his best albums are virtually impossible to find. Among the very best, in addition to the two discussed, are *Tokyo Recital* (Pablo), *Montreux '77* (Pablo), *Eclypso* (Enja), *Giant Steps* (Enja), *Thelonica* (Enja) and *Nights at the Vanguard* (Uptown). The last, an exploration of Monk, represents the apex of Flanagan's give-and-take with Mraz (recalling the pinnacle of Bill Evans's work with Scott LaFaro)—they went their separate ways at the summit of their association. The trio with Peter Washington and Lewis Nash is superbly represented on the 1997 *Sea Changes* (Evidence). Its much anticipated Blue Note album was recorded at the Village Vanguard, where Flanagan had not recorded since 1988 and where he routinely operates in an apparent state of grace.

72 ❖ Joe Lovano
(The Long Apprenticeship)

One indication of the capriciousness of the jazz community—or rather the Baltic states that constitute the alleged jazz community—is a presumption on the part of critics, the public, and record producers of the marginality of musicians who faithfully serve in big bands. This is strictly a postwar phenomenon. Before the war, a spot in a major big band made your career: to confine the issue to saxophonists, it was in roving reed sections that we first acclaimed Coleman Hawkins, Lester Young, Johnny Hodges, and Charlie Parker. After bop, small bands were where you looked for innovators. Big bands were home to solid professionals who were often faulted for a lack of originality—if not explicitly, then by the general assumption that a major player would be leading or co-starring in a hot combo. Count Basie himself argued that it would no longer do to fill the band with star soloists who might take off and leave him high and dry. The new stars of big bands were arrangers, who might take off but left their scores behind. Audiences no longer demanded epiphanies of big band soloists, but rather a steady competence. A generation of saxophonists, from the posthumously celebrated Paul Gonsalves to the still unsung Kenny Hing, were taken for granted if at all.

For example, Joe Lovano, who labored mightily with Woody Herman in the '70s and with Mel Lewis and the Vanguard Jazz Orchestra in the '80s. Practically every time he answered the conductor's call, he played something worth hearing. The audience, in the immediate blush of enthusiasm, responded accordingly. But that didn't get him many gigs on his own or an entry in Grove. Musicians knew he had something, and kept pushing him into the spotlight. Not until fifteen years after he joined Herman, having logged time with Charlie Haden's Liberation Music Orchestra and Elvin Jones, did he emerge front and center. After recording for several European companies, his first leadership session on a prominent American label (Blue Note) was released in the fall of 1991, a few months after he debuted his own band at the Village Vanguard. His long apprenticeship was over.

The turning point was not the release of his own albums on Soul Note (*One Time Out* and *Village Rhythm*, from 1987 and 1988, are the ones to look for) but the three he made in that same period with Paul Motian for Soul Note (*Misterioso*) and JMT (*Monk in Motian* and *Paul Motian on Broadway, Volume 1*). If those records had been released on a major label, no serious jazz lover would be unfamiliar with them—especially *On*

Broadway. In a program of standards by Gershwin, Arlen, Porter, and Kern, Lovano's tenor sax is intricately interlocked with Bill Frisell's guitar, Charlie Haden's bass, and the leader's drums, and in nine out of nine cases highly familiar songs are reborn. The arrangements, presumably by Motian, are deft and surprising, making the most of instrumental textures, which are ideal for a quintessentially textural player like Lovano, who is as expressive in his use of timbre as in his choice of notes.

How to place him: my first thought is to suggest Hank Mobley coming of age in the era of Ornette Coleman, but that might lead one to conjure Dewey Redman. Well, fine; now imagine Redman with an inclination less to Coleman than to Sonny Stitt and Sonny Rollins. Lovano is a bop player with a predilection for free jazz. Because he shares with Redman a warm and woolly sound, a throaty timbre that negotiates the tenor's entire range and often subsumes quicksilver phrases in a generously whirring vibrato, one can safely locate Ben Webster in his ancestry as well. One benefit of a big band apprenticeship is that you learn to make the most of every bar; another is that you are encouraged to feed on several generations of stylists.

As an example of a perfect Lovano improvisation, the kind of performance that has had fellow musicians raving about him, consider "My Heart Belongs to Daddy," Cole Porter's most cantorial sex song, as interpreted on *On Broadway*. After stating the theme, he has but one additional chorus to put his mark on it. His first four measures may seem a relatively tentative beginning, but they finish on an admirably lyrical plateau and the next four convey supremely confident davening. In the eight that follow, he doubles time, picking up speed and using timbre to underscore an ardent resolve. The final sixteen make for a literally breathtaking (he pauses for air only once in the last eight bars) payoff in which witting passion and emphatic high-note cries trump virtuosity. After Frisell's solo, Lovano returns in a passage that consists of overtones and low notes that at times blend into a methodical fuzz and high notes that fuse almost imperceptibly with the guitar. At such moments, texture is all: feeling, acumen, and motor nerve. Similarly, "Last Night When We Were Young" opens with a thematic paraphrase in which his resonant tone cloaks the notes—he sounds as though he were sighing the melody.

Lovano is a prolific and inventive composer, but not a distinguished melodist. Like almost every other gifted soloist, he is a better improviser than arranger and better arranger than composer. Thus his two simultaneously issued albums of 1991, which consist with one exception of originals, deprive the listener of that most fundamental pleasure, the spectacle of an imposing stylist transforming customary material. This seems to me an especially misguided decision in the case of his Blue Note debut, *Landmarks,* a generous showcase for his playing that nonetheless succumbs, in the absence of familiar anterooms, to teeming density. The intimacy he suggests on the Motian records is here, but one step removed. Tin Pan Alley, a designation I use in its broadest possible meaning, should be a fount for albums like this—and not just the usual standards; I won't complain if jazz musicians declare a five-year moratorium on "Lady Be Good" or " 'Round Midnight." Dozens, possibly hundreds, of worthy, little-known songs await excavation, as Red Garland and Jimmy Rowles used to routinely demonstrate.

That said, *Landmarks* is a handsomely crafted quintet session (with guitarist John Abercrombie, who plays a fine solo on "Dig This," pianist Kenny Werner, bassist Marc Johnson, and drummer Bill Stewart). I'm not sure I'll ever be able to tell the head on "Landmarks Along the Way"from the one on "Street Talk"—each a stop-and-go invention that recalls Rollins—even if the former has an expansive bridge, but those performances and the others on the album reward scrutiny. The bump-and-grind undercurrent of "Here and Now"; the diffuse, Deweylike energy of "Emperor Jones"; and the welcome balladic respite of "I Love Music" (by Emil Boyd and Hale Smith), in which Lovano demonstrates his intrepid willingness to let his tone spread and shimmer, are convincing points of reference. The thoroughly characteristic opener, "The Owl and the Fox," is a pithy summation of Lovano's prowess, most alive in his interplay with Marc Johnson's fleet bass and in his own posh timbre, which makes high notes howl and mercuric arpeggios cascade with pearly articulation.

Lovano's tour de force concert at the 1989 Amiens International Jazz Festival, *Worlds* (Label Bleu), though fitfully available as an import, was a better indication of Lovano's skill as a composer and arranger. In deleting piano and adding trumpet (Tim Hagans), trombone (Gary Valente), and voice (Judi Silvano née Silverman), Lovano makes a septet (with Motian and Frisell) sound at times like a far larger ensemble. The range, from the cellar notes of trombone and bass (Henri Texier) to the stratospheric pitches of Silvano (a soprano and Lovano's wife), and Frisell's guitar provides supple and shifting textures. The seven selections were preformed as continuous movements in a single work. A couple of the freer episodes sound like makeshift transitions, but succeed in a concert setting, eliciting support from the audience and underscoring contrast with segments in which the group barrels forward like a big band. Lovano is heard on soprano sax and alto clarinet, but reveals less confidence on those refractory instruments. He returns to tenor for his neo-bop anthem, "Spirit of the Night," which he treated on soprano on *Vil-*

lage Rhythm, and though the first notes of his solo suggest a Coltrane lick, the bravura texture with which he plays them and the ranging swing that he generates go way beyond the obligations of influence.

Still, a warhorse standard—"Body and Soul," no less—on his second Blues Note album, *From the Soul* (1992), cemented not only his major league prowesses as an improviser, but indicated the true domain of his gifts. He could play free or semi-free, but he was most inspired on jazz's home turf, which was just fine with his label. Lovano proceeded to earn for himself a large enough following to qualify for the oxymoronic status of jazz star. And at this point he proved himself an uncommon and knowing artist by taking risks with his records, albeit within the province of core modernism. His albums, which are artist- and not producer-driven, imply a high regard for his audience that the audience gratefully reciprocates. That he can appear as often as he does without wearing out his welcome (two examples: his "Somewhere" on Mike Manieri's uneven but generally fascinating *An American Diary* on NYC and his contributions to Bill De Arango's inventive *Anything Went* on GM) says something about how unassuming and consistent he is. He's one of those old-time cats who comes to play, no bull. That he is also one of the few musicians whose albums engender loyal expectations says something about his initiative, drive, and sense of history. While others mourn the absence of big projects that abounded in the age of Miles and Gil, Lovano commissioned Gunther Schuller to write the engrossing *Rush Hour* (1994), followed it with an impressive double take on quartet music, *Quartets* (1995), then joined the parade of those saluting an ailing Sinatra with an intriguing venture that targeted his abilities as an interpreter of unhackneyed standards.

If Frank Sinatra indulged himself in fantasies of attending his own funeral, all he needed was a ringside seat at his favorite record emporium. Premature eulogies ranged from the slickly conventional (Mike Smith's *Sinatra Songbook*) to the hard-bopping confrontational (Per Goldschmidt's *Frankly*) to the whimsically hip (James Moody's *Young at Heart*); from the fraternally respectful (Tony Bennett's *Perfectly Frank*) to the maternally devout (Carol Sloane's *The Songs Sinatra Sang*) to the dreamily reverential (Joe Lovano's *Celebrating Sinatra*). Preceding them was the elegantly musical *Very Sinatra,* recorded by Ruby Braff in 1981, before Sinatra even got sick. Songwriter catalogs have been plundered for decades, so a spate of collections fixed on performers makes sense, and Sinatra is an ideal choice—his zeitgeist is receding into the mist, and the songs most associated with him are rarely associated with anyone else.

Lovano's *Celebrating Sinatra* (1996) is the most unbounded and aspiring of the lot. With that respect for size and history instilled during his years with big bands, Lovano rescued from undeserved obscurity the prolific arranger Manny Albam to fashion arrangements that seem to have been conjured in the wee hours of the morning. My initial response was mixed, confounded by Albam's use of Judi Silvano in the scoring. The wordless harmonizing seemed effective enough, but I cringed at the fugitive bits and pieces of lyrics that float in and out of sight, distracting attention from the soloist and orchestra—especially the coyly repetitive fade-out on the phrase "and repeats" on "I've Got You Under My Skin." No reflection on Silvano, who handles a difficult role with skill: I don't think Leontyne Price could make it fly.

Those doubts were confirmed by a live performance at the Blue Note, where Lovano presented qualified versions of Albam's arrangements, retaining four high-pitched reeds and cello but not the strings and French horn that brace them on the disc. In that context, the soprano voice exacerbated a trebly imbalance that approached a screech, as on "Fly Me to the Moon," where a delicate ensemble interlude written in contrapuntal form suggests the foursquare plod of Swingle singing. On the other hand, Lovano offered a version of "South of the Border" with bass and drums in which he allowed his respect for Sonny Rollins an unrestrained liberty that, abetted by George Mraz and Al Foster, was uncannily accurate and quite thrilling. You have to have a strong sense of self to indulge a communion that deep.

On the record, Lovano's master is not Rollins but Ben Webster, whom he can summon with great tenderness, for example his reentry after the interlude on "I'll Never Smile Again." But he has long since arrived as his own man, and his individuality is emphasized by the familiarity of the material. Accentuating his higher register, he aims for speechlike precision in his theme recitations while his improvisations press at the edges of the harmonies without breaking ranks, resulting in a kind of reflective effusiveness, as on a quartet rendering of "Imagination." The small-group pieces, including "South of the Border" and a "Chicago" duet with drums, are fine, as expected. But *Celebrating Sinatra* is a summit for Lovano on other fronts. It elaborates his affection for woodwind voicings, ranging from a swift four-brothers swing ("I've Got the World on a String") to the abstractions of *Rush Hour* ("Someone To Watch Over Me"). And it brings to a new level his harmonizations with Judi Silvano.

Maybe as a result of numerous hearings, and a consequent expectation of the intrusive lyrics, I let down my guard and began to hear the record as more radical—well, maybe not more radical, but certainly more hallucinogenic. Albam's instrumentation flies in the face of contemporary tastes in Sinatra-style arrangements, which tend to revolve around the augmented big band approach of Nelson Riddle and Billy May. He evokes instead the packed-house romance of Axel Stordahl and Gordon Jenkins, while thinning out the strings (he uses four plus harp), and sharpening the edges with dissonance, tempo alterations (he plots "I've Got You Under My Skin" in three), and melodic digressions that would have herniated Stordahl. The soprano voice additionally hones those edges, and the excerpted lyrics emphasize a sense of dreamy late-night musings on songs that have long since escaped Sinatra's hold and made their way into the collective nervous system. Admittedly, this is a programmatic interpretation, but then listening is an art, too.

73 ❖ Geri Allen/Jacky Terrasson (The Parameters of Hip)

Two trio albums released simultaneously by Blue Note in 1995 have a lot to say about the recent state of jazz piano—the influences that bind, the increasing rapprochement with classic pop songs, the dictates of careers, the changing parameters of hip. Passages on Jacky Terrasson's *Jacky Terrasson* are so stylish, so cool, so brainy that you may at first find yourself yawning in self-defense. Yet Terrasson's technical assurance and the unmistakable pleasure he takes in it are contagious—what he shows off is generally worth showing off. Geri Allen's *Twenty One*, in contrast, is a mature work by a performer no less adept at musical gamesmanship who was repositioning herself as a jazz centrist. The effort wasn't a sellout but a display of strength.

Terrasson is hardly unseasoned. Born in Berlin in 1966 and educated in Paris and at Berklee, he arrived in New York in 1990. Within three years, he won the Thelonious Monk Competition and, amid various sideman engagements, organized a trio with bassist Ugonna Okegwo and drummer Leon Parker that reflects the principles of contrary rhythms and dynamics and the kind of group discipline associated with Ahmad Jamal. Jamal was a great favorite of Miles Davis's, though they never worked together, so it makes sense that the other pianistic influences evident on Terrasson's American debut constitute something of a Davis roll call: Garland, Evans, Kelly, Hancock, Corea, Jarrett. His associates know their Ron Carter and Tony Williams, too—Parker has his own version of Williams's patented hi-hat attack, only he does it on the ride cymbal (he doesn't use a hi-hat).

Terrasson also follows Davis's lead in renewing standard tunes, though where Davis would claim an unlikely song with his personal timbre and a meditative tempo, Terrasson prefers a hide-and-seek face-lift in which the melody is redesigned to suit his restructuring of the song's foundation. And where Davis developed an elastic approach to time, Terrasson usually cleaves to a steady beat, but gives the illusion of discrete tempos and even rubato by altering the rhythmic patterns played over the beat. One way or another, he succeeds in renewing the material, including three ballads famously performed by Davis. The price he pays for his sleight-of-hand, though, is a flipness that sometimes undermines the music's substance. Closer to Jamal than Davis in temperament, he rarely settles for one groove when he can motor between two.

For example, he neatly bisects "I Love Paris," pounding the first half of each chorus to a mildly funky long-meter beat and lightly dusting the second half to a standard swing-time four. The harmonic rhythm remains constant throughout, but the to-and-fro gives the impression of radical discontinuity. The arrangement is rendered yet more enigmatic by the telescoping of the last two measures of each chorus into transitions of varying length. Once you get past the general design, you can more fully appreciate the discursive details: the sudden feathery arpeggio, the extract from "As Time Goes By," the blues locutions, the wide-interval voicings, and a surprise ending that recycles the two-bar break in the first chorus.

Terrasson uses the same device (okay, it's a silent break) for the ending of "Just a Blues," but he turns the screw—and loosens it, too. The challenge is to uphold the harmonic rhythm of a conventional blues through five choruses, while piano and drums double time (in the fourth chorus) or incrementally retard it (in the fifth). Even with Ogekwo's metronomic bass to anchor them, this is pretty slick. I'm reminded of Davis's 1954 "The Man I Love" (take two), in which Monk tried to restrain the melody and got hopelessly lost. For Terrasson, it's a piece of cake. Hairier still is a rendering of "My Funny Valentine" in which an evenly maintained fast tempo is all but disguised by the pulseless, pianissimo statement of melody at the beginning and end. By now, the game is a bit more familiar: he begins with a minute or so of C-pedal deliberations (à la Keith Jarrett), which are recycled for telescoped transitions between choruses. The change-ups in dynamics and metrical figures are effortless; they may dispel the spell, yet the pianistics are robust and they get better in the album's middle passage.

The key to a rambunctious "Bye Bye Blackbird," which also begins with a pedal tone, is the steady bass walk (Keith, meet Paul Chambers) because until the final half-chorus Terrasson doesn't come within hailing distance of the melody. The 1926 ditty restored by Miles with a dreamy hipster's detachment is ignored here for a romp through the changes, but it's one helluva romp—fast and nervy, with fusing turnbacks, blistering riffs, waves of funk, thunderclap chords, and a nod to Harold Arlen. Even so, Terrasson will not go quietly into the groove. In the middle of the fifth chorus, the trio accelerates, the drums trade eights, and you can almost see the skid marks as they wind down for the finish.

Now comes a switch. "I Fall in Love Too Easily" and "Time After Time," two Styne and Cahn songs associated with Sinatra (the former with Miles as well), are taken disarmingly straight. Terrasson lingers lovingly over the first in a deft theme statement and a cannily spare variation. "Time" is all melody, but Terrasson isn't grounded by it; he seems genuinely to relish it. Rhythmic patterns wax and wane as Parker switches back and forth between brushes and sticks, Okegwo is buoyant (and not above a we-want-Cantor jape), and the pianist retards the melody for the finish. The slow motion "What a Difference a Day Made" is self-conscious and dull, but "For Once in My Life," introduced with a diabolic ostinato and laden with the standard reversals, includes an episode—as Parker exchanges brushes for sticks—when Terrasson seems insuperably nimble.

Geri Allen, at thirty-seven, was in the throes of midcareer in 1995 and not yet the reflexive catcher in the wry of Ornette Coleman's 1996 piano quartets. Having recorded for a decade, she had already produced a body of identifiable originals and a piano style that could be cut to fit most points in the mainstream, from standards to pedal-point modality to funk to free. Her most distinctive and original recordings include interpretations of Charlie Parker and Coleman. Yet because of her work with such left-of-center figures as Oliver Lake, Dewey Redman, Steve Coleman, John Stubblefield, Andrew Cyrille, and especially Charlie Haden and Paul Motian, the team that helped confirm her reputation, her decision to make an album that feels at first blush as decorous as *Twenty One* may be regarded with suspicion. That would be a mistake, because it was her most accomplished showcase since *Segments* (DIW) and the outstanding *Etudes* (Soul Note) from the late '80s.

The obscure title, she says, referred to the recommitment she made to goals she set for herself at twenty-one to extend the tradition of the masters. So there are allusions to Powell, Monk, and Mary Lou Williams. The presence of Ron Carter and Tony Williams, at the top of their game (this was one of Williams's last great recorded performances), points up yet again the immense influence of Davis's '60s quintet, specifically the tremendous achievement of Herbie Hancock in the years before he went pop. (If Hancock had gone to the great beyond in 1968, he would now be solemnly regarded as a jazz god.) Before Davis's band, a rhythm section was evaluated for its tightness; his young players showed you could be in sync and unraveled at the same time. Listeners could get caught up in the punishing sibilance of Williams's hi-hat or Carter's angular counterpoint or Hancock's impressionistic chords. They were three rowers pulling together, yet apart, in unison but not in unison.

That kind of interaction, despite an un-Milesian avowal of stable tempos, is apparent throughout *Twenty One*. This is a trio fearsomely alive. On the opener, "RTG," Williams's timekeeping frees Carter, whose timbre here and elsewhere often assumes vocal qualities, and Allen, who despite her ferocious attack begins her solo with a melodic figure and maintains an elegant attention to detail through four engaging choruses. Like Terrasson, she is practiced in juxtaposed rhythms and odd phrase-lengths. On the highlight of 1992's relatively languid *Maroons* (Blue Note), she energetically superimposed diverse patterns over four in "Number Four." She is no less unruffled here, playing three against four in the intro and coda of "If I Should Leave You" or improvising in four against an ostinato in six, played by the left hand in the treble, on "Drummer's Song." The fervor of her signature theme, "Feed the Fire," a woolly ten-bar blues, is such that the bass solo (with double stops and triplets) is a welcome respite.

Allen's bows to tradition are nothing if not heady. She has fastened together the two 1947 Monk pieces that have thirty-six measures, albeit in different configurations: "Introspection" is eight/eight/eight/twelve and "Thelonious" is eight/eight/ten/ten. Allen plays the heads consecutively and then alternates the grids in a fluid improvisation. Her acknowledgment of Powell is made via one of his most exhilarating displays, "Tea for Two." Replacing the verse with an intro on drums, she rampages through seven choruses, as Powell did, and though her touch is harder and far more uniform (supple dynamics have never been her long suit) she achieves a comparable elation. Compare the two versions (Buddy Rich backed Powell) for a concise lesson on the evolution of jazz percussion.

Perhaps she is paying homage to Nat Cole in her Styne and Cahn selection, "A Beautiful Friendship," but it's an opaque tribute. Beginning with a pedal-tone intro, she takes the tempo way up, essaying the melody with smartly voiced chords, but after four choruses dispatches the harmonies for modal meditations. She is most incisive on "Lullaby of the Leaves." Allen credits an arrangement by Mary Lou Williams in her notes, but if she has the 1944 recording in mind—with Frank Newton's incomparably soulful trumpet solo—the connection is once again obscure, except perhaps in the soulfulness of her own solo, which is measured and enthralling. When Allen finds a groove, she knows better than to deflate it with effects. (For a radically different voicing of the tune, listen to Jimmy Rowles's glinting transformation on his *Lilac Time*.)

Allen's playing can seem mechanical. On "In the Middle," her reliance on an ostinato and contrary rhythms results in a ten-finger exercise; and at her Vanguard engagement in late 1994, the maddeningly stilted drumming of Lenny White backed her into a barrage of chords. The triumph of *Twenty One* is in the certainty with which Allen's individuality asserts itself in a setting that might have neutralized her. It's the kind of album Terrasson will make when everyone stops calling him a genius and he can start breathing again.

74 ❖ *Joshua Redman*
(Tenor of the Times)

When I was asked to serve as host for the semifinals of the Thelonious Monk International Jazz Saxophone Competition in 1992, I accepted in almost complete ignorance of what the competition was all about, lured as much by the promise of a good party and the chance to see old friends as by the prospect of hearing the future of jazz. Truth be told, I had found the best-known previous finalists—Marcus Roberts and Joey DeFrancesco in the piano contest—underwhelming and had yet to hear the most recent victor, trumpeter Ryan Kisor. But something memorable took place at the November competition in Washington, D.C.: a tenor saxophonist named Joshua Redman made himself known.

Redman, who prevailed on an exceedingly fast first ballot, was at the time a twenty-two-year-old Harvard graduate, who though raised in California by his divorced mother was usually referred to as the son of saxophonist Dewey Redman. He had previously received two Leonard Bernstein Music Scholarships and a Joseph L. Merrill Scholarship and spoke of going after another degree. As the twentieth of the twenty-five semifinalists to perform, he distinguished himself instantly, with his gruff attack on "Woody'n You." Maturity in a fledgling is easier to recognize than to analyze. Buddy Tate once identified the first task of a jazz musician as the fulfillment of an individual sound, an observation that virtually defines the gap between the American jazz aesthetic, on the one hand, and the standards of European fiat and African communalism on the other. Redman had a sound. It might not be the sound he would have the next year or the year after that, but it pealed with personality and utterly subsumed his ample technique.

At an earlier point during the semifinals, a member of the rhythm section (pianist Richard Wyands, bassist Peter Washington, and drummer Kenny Washington) argued that the participants hadn't listened sufficiently, if at all, to Don Byas and other classic tenors whose personalities are divulged through timbre. A judge complained of all the Charlie Parker clones. Redman was not the only contestant who broke the mold, but he did so with the most poise, direction, and wit. No one was surprised that he made the finals, and his performance in that last round, when the competitors had been narrowed to six, decisively ruled the day. He began with the Earl Hines riff, "Second Balcony Jump," which he said he had learned from the Dexter Gordon version, but, notwithstanding a song quote or two, Redman's interpretation owed nothing to Gordon's tone or temper. He claimed the number with a vigorous yet evenly articulated double-time phrasing that growled and guffawed in a manner both edgily contemporary and classically robust. His other selections—Mal Waldron's "Soul Eyes," Monk's "Evidence"—were no less venturesome. During his performance of the last, the wife of one of the judges observed, "He reminds me of Clifford Brown." She was referring to both musicians' youthful maturity.

Other players also distinguished themselves. Eric Alexander, a twenty-three-year-old winner of the Notre Dame Jazz Festival and other competitions, made a vivid impression with performances of "Oleo" and " 'Round Midnight," demonstrating a command of the materials and a big, authoritative sound that won him second place. Third place was split when the judges found it impossible to choose between Chris Potter, a twenty-year-old New Yorker who has played with Red Rodney's band for two years, and Tim Warfield, Jr., a twenty-six-year-old Pennsylvanian who works with Marlon Jordan and made his mark earlier in 1992 with the Tough Young Tenors on the album, *Alone Together* (Antilles). The contest was nothing if not daunting. Each player was given ten lead sheets (mostly bop, only two ballads—at the end of the weekend everyone present would have voted a moratorium on "Cherokee" and "Sophisticated Lady") and allowed to choose his first selection; the second was requested by the five judges. An imposing panel was convened to render the verdict. Consider the pressure on a saxophonist coming on stage to withstand the scrutiny of Benny Carter, Jimmy Heath, Branford Marsalis, Jackie McLean, and Frank Wess. Not surprisingly, a few players choked. Some had trouble navigating varied tempos; they'd skid felicitously along the edges of "Confirmation" but bog down in the sloughs of " 'Round Midnight."

In the absence of a vast network of big bands and specialty labels, not to mention public jam sessions and the apprenticeship loft scene, the Thelonious Monk International Jazz Competition answers a need in motivating, gathering, and introducing young jazz players. But what a strange and troubling paradox that this event should boast the posthumous imprimatur of the High Priest, as well as the full and active support of his family. No one could fail to notice that if such a competition had been held in the '40s and Thelonious Monk had submitted an application, he would almost certainly have failed to make the semifinals, unless Mary Lou Williams and Duke Ellington were on the committee, and even then he would have been a decided long shot for the finals. We revere Monk for his originality, courage, and genius, three qualities of less consequence in a competition than conformity to established standards. That's the way it must be. A genius competition would become a political event: By what objective standards would the judges debate, for example, the merits of Albert Ayler or Cecil Taylor?

Which is one reason Joshua Redman walked away with the prize and the audience. He knew the changes, but played them from inside. He had the demeanor of a musician who has transcended the need to merely show off his speed or his circular breathing or his multiphonics. He played music instead of technique. But now he would face a very different sort of challenge: facing down the lure of the star makers. In less than three years, he would move in circles as foreign to most jazz musicians as the Arctic Ocean.

Hype is always someone else's enthusiasm, usually for something about which you are, at best, ambivalent. Hype is a frenzy of media hacks carrying water for a multinational corporation, usually a motion picture studio or record company. Hype is never your own predilection or zeal. So Redman had to contend not least with the hypelike acclimation accorded him and his first two recordings. Like muggers, backlash keeps to the shadows until it's safe to strike; in this instance, cynicism found some comfort in the surprising news that Redman had signed with a big record label known for administering jazz with all the respect due a wracking cold. Still, during his triumphant engagements at the Village Vanguard (he was an instant draw), only a curmudgeon would have wanted to stand outside the charmed circle of self-discovery.

I took an almost irrational pleasure in his skill—it answered a need I didn't know I had. At a time when the tenor sax was enjoying something of a revival, Redman's voice stood out in its sobriety and centeredness. That his primary influences stem from the '60s may have something to do with my own response. His live improvisation on "Sublimation," a piece that takes as its foundation John Coltrane's "Resolution" (the second movement of *A Love Supreme*), albeit with the addition of an extended balladic release, prodded the memory of a moment previously lost to me. I spent the summer of 1967 studying in the south of France. On an afternoon when I was reposing with several embryonic artists at a cafe, another student came by with a newspaper that announced, on page one, Coltrane's death. At the time of his passing, Coltrane was more than a young musician at the pinnacle of his celebrity; he was the one figure to whom much of jazz looked for nourishment and guidance.

Stunned by the news, we began discussing his legacy, and we fantasized one idea specifically: What would a musician born today, with no political or emotional ties to Coltrane, make of his music? Now we know. Redman was born two years after Coltrane died. The past two decades have swarmed with Coltrane imitators and acolytes, but I can't think of anyone who assimilated the body and soul of his 1961–64 period with more composure, weaving it into the larger colloquial tradition of the tenor. Other influences were evident in Redman's playing: Sonny Rollins, unmistakably, and Joe Henderson and Wayne Shorter, and possibly Eddie Harris. Many artists do have an affinity for the world as constituted during the years they came into it. Yet two qualities made Redman stand out among those who absorbed the same tradition: One, when focused, he was his own man regardless of conscious or unconscious homages; his core sound remained stable and sure, and his mentors have been filtered by a certitude that is the primary mark of a superior player. Two, he evinced a deliberated sense of architecture, the need to make every chorus count for something; he knew enough not to indulge himself or patronize the audience. There were moments during his sets when it seemed as if we were live at the Vanguard, circa 1961.

Everything about Redman's 1993 Vanguard debut was propitious. He had a fine quartet in Christian McBride (the astonishing twenty-one-year-old bassist, whose standing in the current jazz scene is not unlike that of Redman) and two talented newcomers: drummer Brian Blade, whose reflexes are fast and motions wasteless, and pianist Kevin Hays, who escapes the shadow of McCoy Tyner by reaching back to the bluesier economies of Hampton Hawes and Horace Silver. Redman engaged the audience, announcing the tunes, which, in addition to originals included Kenny Dorham's "Straight Ahead" and Sonny Rollins's arrangement of Jule Styne's "Just in Time," complete with blustery two- and one-bar breaks. On the former, Redman's even-tempered doubling of the tempo (a favorite gambit of his) suggested Lester Young, but in the timbre of the Rollins-Coltrane nexus.

The most extraordinary quality of his solos was not their fluency, however, but the shifts in tone that underscore a single phrase or note. He has the familiar arsenal of devices: tremolos and trills, growls and squeals, hidden-register chords. On more than one occasion, he established parallel patterns, a midrange action interspersed with lower-register asides in the manner popularized by Eddie Harris on his 1967 album, *The Electrifying Eddie Harris*, though Redman did it without the electric Varitone attachment. He scooped and faded certain notes, and favored glissando modulations, sometimes as though squeezing an errant note into proper pitch. No matter what details he used to dress up his phrases, though, Redman's dominant vocabulary consisted of the basic building blocks of jazz improvisation, riffs. He uses them to raise and lower the intensity of solos, returning to them for sustenance after exhausting bouts of double time and containing in their buoyantly rhythmic well-being his penchant for high-note squalls.

Yet that containment also suggested a deficiency that grew pronounced in concert hall performances. Redman is so fastidious in his control of the saxophone that even when he appears to let go, as in the banshee brilliance of "Sublimation," you suspect he is all too practiced. The rectitude that is the soul of his sound and his gift for brevity is not only an editor but a censor; at times he gives more of an illusion of spontaneity than the real thing. This is an issue that perhaps can only be resolved by living, but it's one where the son might look with profit to his father, who from the time he recorded with Ornette Coleman demonstrated an instinctive understanding of letting go and holding back. As if to compensate for his natural constraint, he occasionally blew to the galleries, making starlike gestures of virtuoso *oblige*.

Joshua Redman (Warner Brothers), a most impressive debut album, serves as one measure of how quickly he advanced. Recorded in the fall of 1992, it suggested without quite capturing the full level of his authority. Yet the best of its eleven tidy selections are so good you might find yourself longing for their relative modesty if you have heard his later displays of saxophone grandeur. Redman has not excelled in melodic improvisation; his strengths are in pursuing form and function. Among the strongest performances are "Echoes," which contrasts passages written against time with a conventional middle section (Redman's solo climaxes with the third of his four choruses), and "Tribalism," which uncoils wittily, like a snake, through twenty-four measures of descending modulations. "Groove X" is a well-constructed, oddly parsed piece: his variations, complete with doubling and two-note chords, charge over a pedal point and alternating rhythms. "Sublimation" is as close to ecstasy as he permits himself, while "Wish" opens as a wistful ballad in the manner of "Naima" but takes on gospel overtones.

The five standards are a mixed bag. A trio performance of Monk's "Trinkle Tinkle" is exemplary, detailed, and incisively respectful of the theme. James Brown's "I Got You" is the most dated selection, very '60s— jazz recitations of pop tunes with what used to be called boogaloo rhythms sounded patronizing then and are insupportable now. Yet his solo is a handsomely mounted exercise in double time. The tenor and bass duet on "On the Sunny Side of the Street" gets off on the wrong foot with presumptuous hokum—McBride, who bounces the strings, and Redman surely know the '30s (cf. the Johnny Hodges–Lionel Hampton version) weren't that corny—but rights itself in the solos. "Body and Soul" is the primary testing ground for tenor saxophonists, and it will be fascinating to hear what Redman can do with it when he feels less respectful of the melody, which he intones handsomely but with a rather constrained gravity. "Salt Peanuts" is a quicksilver sprint into Dizzy Gillespieland.

Warners timed the release of his second album, *Wish*, with his second appearance at the Vanguard, but, in fact, the music was recorded before the debut was issued. Once again, the record only hinted at Redman's growth, so readily apparent in performance. He achieved a level of complicity from the audience that was nothing short of miraculous. Guitarist Pat Metheny, who backed him along with Christian McBride and Billy Higgins, may have been largely responsible for packing the place (every set was sold out), but Redman won and earned the clamorous ovations. He played originals by himself and Metheny, classics by Charlie Parker ("Moose the Mooche") and Ornette Coleman ("The Good Life"), and much blues. Even when he didn't play the blues, he played the blues— long, sexy, doubled-up phrases that resolved themselves in places that get crowds to roar. Radiant with joy, Redman looked the audience in the eye and played for its pleasure.

Redman's candid willingness to communicate his joy in playing is as enchanting as his extraordinary talent. In forging that communal glow, he makes it easy to forget that jazz is often characterized as an elitist music. But he also portends the thin line between expressiveness and flash. Redman is open to experience and has performed in a variety of formal and informal settings. He has worked with Milt Jackson, Paul Motian, and Clark Terry, among many others. He played with enormous verve and imagination in the quintet Chick Corea and Roy Haynes conceived to explore the music of Bud Powell. At the 1996 JVC Jazz Festival in New York, he and Corea locked horns in an extrapolation of Powell's "I'll Keep Loving You" that was at once epic and detailed, a thorough investigation of a song that kept him on point through a reflective cadenza. At previous JVC festivals, leading his own quartet, he had settled for the easier rewards of a groove, basking in a renown that has garnered him screaming admirers and an endorsement deal with a fashion designer. You blink and remind yourself that he is not yet thirty, and you remember how presumptuous it is to be presumptuous. In 1997, he returned to the Vanguard with Trio, a cooperative with Christian McBride and Brian Blade. The capacity audience that week consisted almost exclusively of people of his own generation. We'll be following his progress for years to come.

75 ❖ Stephen Scott
(Taking Time)

On the second night of Stephen Scott's July 1993 gig at the Village Vanguard, a few notes in the upper treble of the piano were (uncharacteristically) indisposed—nothing terrible, just a few slack strings. Yet instead of ignoring the guilty keys, Scott kept whirling into them, almost fetishizing the ringing flatness as if increasing conversance might make that which was out in. His apparent deliberation in almost every aspect of the performance suggested a happy, decidedly Monkian eccentricity that had not been much heard in jazz in recent years. Scott, like the lovers deified by old blues singers, is a man who knows how to take his time. He gives the impression of a musician so at home with his technique that he has no need to show it off; so at home with himself that the keyboard is a feast of choices and rhythm a sea to be navigated at will. He's cool and he's hip. And in 1993, he was just twenty-four years old.

Which means that the '60s were fading into the sunset of Kent State at the time he was born. Yet like many musicians of his age, given a leeway of ten years, he is enchanted with the music of that era—and not, need I say it, with the far-out stuff. In those days, the "mainstream" pianists you might encounter at the Vanguard were patently distinct: a blindfolded fan would have had no trouble at all in recognizing Monk or Evans or Silver or Byard or Tyner or Hancock or Garland or others. That changed in the '70s and '80s, exceptions stipulated, as first the field was flooded with derivative players (Evans, Tyner, and Hancock had the most followers) and then by returning classicists (preeminently the celestial Michigan brigade: Hank Jones, Tommy Flanagan, Barry Harris, and Roland Hanna) who replaced idiosyncrasy with familiarity.

Scott is as much of the '60s as his contemporaries Joshua Redman, Mark Whitfield, and Jesse Davis. No previous generation of jazz musicians, excepting Dixielanders of the '40s (a perverse group, to be sure), has been as captivated by the styles of jazz dominant before its birth: Miles Davis loved Louis Armstrong but he didn't play "Potato Head Blues"; Sonny Rollins recorded with Coleman Hawkins, but he tried to sound as unlike his idol as possible and still remain in tune. Yet it is also true that no earlier generation could look back on as capacious and arguably complete a cycle of achievement—nearly a century of primitives, classicists, romanticists, modernists, avant-gardists, neoprimitives, neoclassicists, repertory companies, not to mention middling establishment acceptance from the academy, government, arts malls, and that ultimate arbiter of prestige, the U.S. postal system.

Paradoxically, Scott and musicians like him represent something sort of new, a classicism that precedes neither from the intricate assurances of bebop nor the dominant influences of the past twenty years (for example, Evans, Tyner, Hancock), but rather from the intermediate generation of '60s eccentrics. The patron saint of eccentrics is, of course, the loneliest Monk, and Scott is acutely caught up in his later work. All the influences are on grand display on his 1992 album (his second as a leader), *Aminah's Dream* (Verve).

Consider the one solo piano selection, "The Pit and the Pendulum," a witty title for a piece that explores stride, though this isn't the conventional stride of the Harlem school or even the Monkian take on James P. Johnson represented by the 1957 "Functional." This is Scott's take on the high-flying stride of the 1964 *Solo Monk* (recall that the cover painting depicted T. M. in a cockpit). The piece is a twelve-bar blues, but dig the reverential details: the bent notes in the theme, the raggedy arpeggio that leads to the improvisation, the varied bass line (the chunky fourth- and first-beat accent chords in the fourth improvised chorus are more Scott than Monk), the minor seconds, the broken stride, the closing flourish.

Or hear what he's done with the whole Milesian tradition of streamlined harmony and earthy pianists in "L'il Bro' . . . Life Goes On," a modalized theme of thirty-three measures (the last quadrant's got nine—shades of Horace Silver) that begins with rubato whimsy, proceeds with big "Milestones" chords, and has two handsomely articulated solos by Scott and by Ron Carter, whose work throughout is strong. So is that of Elvin Jones. But Carter's strangely dormant reputation gets a huge boost here, especially among those who forgot why he was widely considered the premiere bassist of his time. His single chorus on "L'il Bro," sustaining Scott's fervor with buoyant double stops; his beefy four-beat on

"Young Confucius," a knotty piece with a ten-bar release that trips into the melody as precipitously as the six-bar release in Monk's "Criss Cross"; and his nearly subversive responsiveness on "When God Created Woman," a triple-meter vamp with a choir of four wind instruments in which he ultimately seems to be leading the ensemble on a leash, are emphatic highs amid a shining performance.

Scott's voicings for the winds on four of the selections are less appealing than the machinations of the trio, though even here the provenance is consistent. With the addition of tuba on "Aminah's Dream," the ensemble recalls the nonet McCoy Tyner organized for the 1967 *Tender Moments* (a lesser effort, I think, but Scott may revere it), as does the triple-meter theme, notwithstanding the quasi-"Sidewinder" beat. The writing on "Postive Images (Mother, Father)" is similar, but a few piano flurries recollect '60s Ellington. "Behind the Scenes" is breezily Brubreckian, albeit swinging. "In the Spur of the Moment" begins with eighty seconds of "Motherless Child" before jackknifing into what is essentially a sixteen-bar blues, in which Scott and Carter adroitly riff and retard the rhythm. Jones's brushes irradiate the one standard, "You Are Too Beautiful," which elicits from the pianist a respectful if cursory embellishment. Even so, the piano here is well tuned and Scott chooses his notes as though time were on his side. As indeed it is.

76 ❖ *James Carter*
(All of the Above)

During the golden age of golden oldies, when rock and roll was a music administered chiefly to children through the medium of midspeed platters with donut holes, the musical argument of each record had to be established immediately, in the first bar. "Maybelline" or "Hound Dog" just wouldn't be the same with eight-bar intros. Perhaps no one grasped the challenge better than Little Richard when he screeched, "A wop bop a loo bop a wop bam boom." The passage from "be bop" to "wop bop" was in part a journey through back alleys and unpaved roads, with Sunday morning stopovers at wooden churches, in an effort to reclaim the glories of the uneducated tradition.

James Carter, a tremendously resourceful saxophonist, knows exactly how to get your attention at the starting gate and did from the moment he started recording, at twenty-three, in 1993. But then he appeared to embody far more history than he'd lived, and in a way that made him stand out from a generation of comers, some of whom were more likely to be consumed by history. Carter's secret is that he's also unintimidated by the present. His is the school of whatever works, which, paired with prodigious virtuosity, can be unsettling—like the 800-pound gorilla who wants to sit in. He can raise the roof or bring down the house. He can generate excitement or ennui. What distinguishes him from the equally ardent David Murray to the left and the equally polished Joshua Redman to the right is his refusal to commit one way or the other. His is a kind of free-ranging brilliance in search of a calling.

For example, Carter doesn't just double on reeds; he finds a distinct way of expressing himself on each one, a style individual to himself and the instrument that posits an extraordinarily intimate knowledge of what's been done and what can be done. Yet he is almost too much of a good thing, demanding of his audience a proportionate amount of knowledge if it is to follow him from decorously romantic ballads to avant-garde gymnastics to the educated version of "wop bop a loo bop a wop bam boom." Historical allusion aside, the most provocative thing to say about Carter at an early stage in what promises to be a major career is that he owns his influences, they don't own him.

Carter plays jazz as though he thinks it's a popular (as opposed to a meretricious) music. In this, he furthers the reclamation effort of the '50s that resulted not only in hard bop and soul, conceived as alternatives to rather than repudiations of the learned formalities of the cool school, but in renewed esteem for the music's own poor relations. Ironically, the techniques of bump-and-grind found their fullest amplification not in the greasy-greens jazz of the soul players, but in the subsequent fires of the avant-garde, the least demotic and most durable movement in jazz history. A crossbreed was born: the virtuoso improviser who draws inspiration from techniques affiliated with gallery-pleasing vulgarity and then lends them to a music too rarefied to attract a gallery. John Coltrane may have disavowed his own bar-walking days, but the experience was hardly lost on him.

No musician embodied the cross fire between high and low better than Rahsaan Roland Kirk, the largely self-taught saxophonist and inventor, who came out of the r & b joints of Ohio and Kentucky and turned himself into a modernist of frightening aplomb, underscored by his ability to function as a one-man reed section. When he arrived in New York, Kirk confused everyone: Was he indigenous or avant-garde, blues or bop, or all of the above? He was a walking repository of jazz history, a saxophonist who had absorbed the saxophonists before him and to whom he paid generous homages long before it was fashionable to hoist the banner of Jazz Tradition. He was equally at home playing to the gallery or sitting in it—he was a fan, a historian, a critic. If there was a gripe, it was that he was too much of a muchness, overwhelming. He was only forty-one when he died in 1977, but it seemed as though he'd been around forever.

In James Carter, who began playing saxophone three years after Kirk's death, we have an heir to Kirk's scholastic understanding of the instrument's history, as well as his virtuoso exuberance and capacious spirit. Carter is neither afraid to play to the gallery nor to confound its assumptions. He can apparently play anything, projecting himself in timbres that range from plummy to guttural, from arch ripeness to unholy shrieking. On his first four albums, he plays tenor, baritone, soprano, and alto, but only one at a time, otherwise his debt to Kirk would be accumulating compound interest. As it is, the similarities are unmistakable: Carter's use of circular breathing recalls Kirk's, and his synchronous mining of different registers suggests Kirk's self-described "miracle" of playing contrapuntal melodies on two saxophones at the same time; his soprano distinctly evokes Kirk's manzello; his alto less decisively favors Kirk's stritch. His use of rhythmic or climactic reed popping and squealing often has the same effect as Kirk's siren, and his thorough command of split-tones produces an effect akin to what Kirk achieved on his multiple saxophones.

If there's a gripe, it's that Carter also is too much. But that's not a complaint you'll hear from me . . . yet. I like the view from the gallery when the moon is full and the wolfsbane nigh. And Carter's attention to detail, his capacity for vocalizing phrases or rediscovering meaning in familiar melodies, protects him—and us—from the relentlessness of his attack. On the basis of seeing him on a dozen or so occasions, I would suggest that he gets into trouble when he gives in to an inclination for showing off every trick every time. As a determined harmonic player, a musician who never departs from the harmonic script, Carter can wear you down in a way John Coltrane or David Murray do not. When they blast themselves into a frenzy, they quit the blueprint to blow off steam. Carter will ingeniously alter the chorus cycle, but he's disinclined to junk it, and the result can be relentless if not implosive.

So much for the bad sets. In every other instance, he varies the tableaux, emphasizes the details, and balances the virtues of rabble-rousing extravagance, purple romance, and discerning bite, as he does on his fairly sensational albums. Like Little Richard, or for that matter Kirk, Carter knows how to make an entrance. When *JC On the Set* (DIW) came out in early 1994, the title selection dared you to turn away from its montage of pops, squeals, and split-tones that somehow cohere into a jolting song. Not a trick you can get away with twice. Yet on *Jurassic Classics* (DIW), recorded a few months later, he devised an even more stunning opening for "Take the A Train": a two-note chord, like the screeching of wheels, kicking off a breathless ride that never leaves the harmonic tracks (not even for the interjections of "Royal Garden Blues" and "Sweet Georgia Brown") and crows with a blistering certitude that recalls Kirk's work on *The Jaki Byard Experience*.

Well, we hadn't heard nothin' yet. That fall, Carter signed with Atlantic and decided to change the pace and record an album of ballads, *The Real Quietstorm*. He leads off with a baritone sax and piano duet on " 'Round Midnight," the most overplayed jazz standard since "Satin Doll"—a selection almost arrogant in its obtuseness. Of course, Carter and his pianist Craig Taborn (something of an heir to Don Pullen) completely undermine that assumption. Carter's entrance on baritone catches you off guard, and the surprise factor loses nothing after repeated hearings, not only because he focuses on the barking low register exclusive to that instrument, but because his notes harmonically counter the expectations set up by Taborn's intro. A masterful editor, Carter kindles interest without veering from Monk's song, sonorously vocalizing some notes, sustaining one pitch (à la Kirk or Harry Carney) for twelve measures, doubling time.

Carter proved himself an exceptional interpreter of Monk on the previous album as well, in a richly intoned "Ask Me Now" and his tour-de-force reading of "Epistrophy," which opens with a swagger note that barrels out of the tenor and gives the piece a novel r & b groove, splendidly parried by the swinging release. Rarely has the piece sounded as earthy. The long performance is a series of surprises: blues shouts, tempo changes, circular breathing cum register hopping, inapposite quotations (notably Monk's "Green Chimneys"), and a split-tone close. Like Kirk, with whom he shares a particular admiration for Don Byas (whose momentous 1945 Jamboree sessions should be a priority for reissue in this country), Carter is generous with tributes: Byas, Monk, Rollins, Coltrane, Clifford Brown, John Hardee, the Ellington crew. The split-tones and arco bass at the head of "Caravan" recall the opening of Kirk's "Rip, Rig and Panic," but the rhythmic segue on baritone is something new, acid tearing through steel. Carter has lovingly illuminated two unlikely ballads from Sun Ra's book, most successfully "You Never Told Me That You Care," a possible precursor to Kirk's "Theme for the Eulipions."

Atlantic, with input from Carter, designed *The Real Quietstorm* with a rosy hued, high-fashion, romantic look as befits a rosy, romantic record—if jazz is to enjoy a genuine breakthrough beyond the nonimprovisatory kitsch that saddles the charts, here is music with rhythm in its feet, light in its eyes, and brains in its back alley soul. But just in case anyone thought Carter had channeled his chops in one particular direction, he followed it in 1996 with *Conversin' with the Elders*, the ultimate expression of his penchant for paying tribute. There has never been a jazz homage quite like it, with chosen elders who span the known universe, from Buddy Tate, the most eloquent of the classic southwestern tenors, to Lester Bowie, the most madcap of urban trumpets. The repertory similarly encompasses Bennie Moten and Anthony Braxton. The truly ingratiating numbers are those on the edge of mainstream respectability, yet what makes the album cohere is the antivirtuoso air of all his chosen partners. Tate and Harry Edison were masters of less-is-more in their prime, long before age encouraged the need to edit. Bowie and Hamiet Bluiett are eccentrics who prefer humor and surprise to steely constancy. Altoist Larry Smith is little known outside of Detroit and lacks Carter's centered intonation.

Carter honors these musicians as influences on his playing, and if, clinically speaking, he can skip rings around them, he understands the precarious challenge he has set for himself. He has to hold up his end of the conversations—this isn't a competition for jam-session trophies. Edison long ago mastered the art of the spare and understated phrase that annihilates unruly or, for that matter, ruly clamor. In his company, Carter can't rely on instrumental wizardry. With admirable insight into the limitations of unlimited technique, he has submitted himself to a far more difficult trial, and he has handled himself with assurance, undoubtedly learning something about the shortcomings of brawn and the quandaries of history. Where will Carter go from here? For a musician whose apprenticeship has included Julius Hemphill, the Mingus Big Band, and the Lincoln Center Jazz Orchestra, and who has scored four out of four as a recording artist and will be thirty in 1999, the answer has to be, wherever he pleases.

77 ❖ *Louis Armstrong/Nicholas Payton (Interpreted)*

A music by any other name would sound as good—as long as it isn't called Dixieland. The word reeks of condescension, bringing to mind a philistine portrait: middle-aged white men (amateurs as likely as not) in straw boaters and striped shirts, with sleeve garters on their arms and beer and peanuts on the table, playing a music that so dilutes its inspirational source—the art of Oliver, Morton, and Armstrong—as to be unrecognizable. Like certain southern statues and the Confederate flag, the word has too much history, which begins with a $10 bill issued in New Orleans engraved with the Latin DIX. Dixie originally referred to New Orleans, until the songwriter Dan Emmett wished he was there, at which time it became synonomous with the entire slave-trading empire. We now know (see *Way Up North in Dixie* by Sachs and Sachs for the details) that the melody was written by a northern black, an irony worthy of Thomas Pynchon. The song was so potent as propaganda that the blind abolitionist poet Fanny Crosby (ancestor of Bing) attempted to appropriate the song for the North with a new lyric, "Oh Ye Patriots in the Battle" (wonder why it didn't catch on).

In 1916, jazz was invented (or so the papers said) by five white guys from New Orleans who invaded the North as the Original Dixieland Jass Band, ditching the *ss* for *zz* after vandals began scratching off the *J* in their posters. The novelty-oriented ODJB was not much of a band, but their music was fresh and gay, and they put two words into pop currency, "Dixieland" and "jazz." That the leader of the group was a loud-mouthed racist didn't help the group's reputation over time. Yet for years, both terms were used by black as well as white bands: King Oliver went from Creole Jazz Band to Dixie Syncopators. Jazz eventually went its own way, or Louis Armstrong's way, as Dixieland was left to antiquarians and tourists. By the '60s, black musicians in the old polyphonic idiom described their music as "traditional" ("trad" in the U.K.) or New Orleans style. Emanuel Sayles called his band the Silverleaf Ragtimers. Most of its practitioners were old enough to have had parents or grandparents who didn't earn DIX. Younger musicians tended to avoid the idiom, no matter the appellation.

That began to change in the '90s as the first generation of musicians to grow up in the vacuum created by Armstrong's absence explored the implications of his legacy. One might argue that the death of Armstrong in 1971, followed three years later by that of Duke Ellington, were among the most significant events in jazz in that era, generating a long-deferred recognition that this young music would have to find a way to sustain its historic achievement or succumb to the tyranny of the new. If Armstrong and Ellington produced a classical American music, it ought to have a life beyond their recordings, their scores. In late 1974, months after Ellington's passing, the jazz repertory movement bounded onto the stage with the twin appearances of two short-lived but defining orchestras, the New York Jazz Repertory Company (founded by George Wein, with rotating musical directors) and the National Jazz Ensemble (conceived and conducted by Chuck Israels). Those organizations failed chiefly because audiences were not yet ready to listen beyond what were widely construed to be the definitive recorded performances. Yet one has only to compare half a dozen Ellington versions of the same piece or contrast improvised variations on Lester Young's alternate takes to test the chimera of definitiveness in jazz. If symphony conductors can interpret Stravinsky or Copland without feeling the hot breath of the composers' own performances on their necks, jazz ought to have equal latitude.

This was a radical idea. Jazz had always been thought of in terms of improvisation and composition. Adding a third term, "interpretation," to the equation meant rethinking its verities. "What thou lovest well remains," Pound wrote, "the rest is dross." The problem went beyond a stiff-necked audience; the musicians were just as mystified. Horace Henderson couldn't understand why anyone would demand readings of the "classic" arrangements he and his brother Fletcher wrote half a century earlier, especially when he was willing to revise and improve them. Sy Oliver saw nothing amiss in altering the voicings and rhythmic accents in a presentation of Ellington's music—the alternative was imitation, and wouldn't that be presumptuous, even unseemly? The sidemen had another problem. Raised to seek individuality as the primary jazz requisite, they were now asked to play in styles of other musicians. The ideal lead alto in a jazz repertory band, for example, would have to master more than one approach, depending on the music, Ellington or Basie, Goodman or Lunceford.

By the '80s, a new generation was in place, unfazed by the threat of jazz interpretation. Young musicians were enthusiastic about mastering the classics, and young audiences—often drafted from classical subscription lists—attended their interpretations with little prejudice. Standards in this new area would have to be uncovered through trial and error. Which scores stand on their own and which need help? Which solos are classic expositions and which can be discarded in favor of fresh ones? What are the variables in articulation? When should rhythm sections refurbish old and dated practices? By century's end, repertory was firmly ensconced in the wings of cultural malls, and a new kind of jazz musician existed: one who could express as much satisfaction in successfully navigating an Armstrong invention as making one up, perhaps more. Although jazz repertory is in its infancy, lacking an audience savvy enough to demand high standards and recognize when they are or aren't met, the concept of performing great orchestrations by such composers as Ellington, Gil Evans, or Thad Jones is no longer controversial. Even John Coltrane's collective blowout, *Ascension* (a kind of avant-garde Dixieland), was accorded faithful recreation by Rova, which recognized that every sequence or pattern of notes can be replicated and interpreted, it matters not whether the source is a score or a recording.

The question of how to build on the work of an improviser or a genre, however, is another matter, where style may precede composition. Dixieland, the first popular jazz style, had long been trivialized when a few black traditional New Orleans bands began energizing the form from the ground up in the '80s, among them the Dirty Dozen and Rebirth Jazz Bands. Emerging from that minor revival, much as Armstrong emerged from King Oliver, was an ambition to perform the music of its greatest practitioner. The variety of options were made evident during one month in 1997 when no less than three Armstrong-inspired recordings appeared, only one of which was a repertory or transcribed tribute. *Doc Cheatham and Nicholas Payton* (Verve) is a wonderfully unsentimental sentimental journey. The New Orleans front line is present on several tracks, but the main event and big surprise is the evenly matched protagonists. You expect twenty-three-year-old Payton, who offered a good deal of exuberant shouting on his previous CD, *Gumbo Nouveau*, to overwhelm ninety-one-year-old Cheatham, who sings as much as he plays on his final recording. What happens is they blend so well you may have trouble identifying who is playing what when. Cheatham, who subbed for Armstrong in a Chicago pit band in 1926, has the broader sound and wobbles a bit in comparison to Payton's tightly focused middle-range attack. But this is not one of those patronizing ploys to honor the aged; on "Star Dust," Cheatham cuts the younger man to ribbons. Payton is well-mannered and self-assured, underplaying his hand in favor of true colloquy and paying as much homage to Cheatham as to Armstrong.

They are at their best in counterpoint or trading eights and fours (note Payton's first exchange, eight bars in one breath, on "Jeepers Creepers" or the way Doc picks up the ball from him on "I Cover the Waterfront"). In one instance only do I wish Doc had laid out: Payton's stop-time solo on "Black and Blue," followed by beautifully shaped growls and smears, is rock solid, while Cheatham's late entrance sounds as if his chops are tired. Cheatham had the advantage of having previously recorded with the four-man rhythm section, but Payton appears no less comfortable. If the older man's timbre on "She's Funny That Way" and "Out of Nowhere" is time haunted, Payton's is unexpectedly seasoned. Without stepping on Doc's toes, he essays occasional Armstrongian bravura on "I Got a Right To Sing the Blues" (Cheatham, acknowledging his own parlando approach, makes the lyric "I got a right to say the blues") or in his stop-time episode on "Dinah" or his swinging '30s-style Louis solo at the close of "The World Is Waiting for the Sunrise." Yet it's Armstrong's melodious contemporary who lights up "How Deep Is the Ocean?" with lovely grace notes and finds craftier variations for "Star Dust."

Payton, Terence Blanchard, and Wynton Marsalis have all said they were influenced by Leroy Jones during their school days, and *Props for Pops* (Columbia) is an effective showcase for a local musician who embraces the traditional setting, notwithstanding some modern influences. (His "You Must Not Be Hearin' Straight," a one-bar phrase modulated twelve times in a blues, is a hipper take on Horace Silver than Silver's "The Preacher," which is also included.) His singing can be overbearing; he reminds me of a cross between the traditionalist Joe Watkins and the surreal Al Hibbler. But his trumpet playing is full of surprising ideas: his energetic, riff-laden, cannily dissonant solo on "Struttin' with Some Barbecue"; the long harmonically rich phrases on "Someday You'll Be Sorry"; his architectonic three-chorus solo on "The Preacher"; his inventive paraphrase of "Baby, Won't You Please Come Home," including an intepolated phrase from Armstrong's "Cultural Exchange" on the Brubecks' *The Real Ambassadors*.

Randy Sandke's *We Love You, Louis!* (Nagel Hayer, a German import) is the most ambitious and rewarding Armstrong repertory recording since Dick Hyman's 1974 New York Jazz Repertory Company presentation. The seventeen numbers, from Oliver's "Mabel's Dream" to Handy's "Ole Miss," offer plenty of improvised solos, including three gems by the clarinetist Kenny Davern. But the most dramatic moments are the transcriptions from Armstrong, played by Sandke or in unison with Byron Stripling. I know of no better realized examples of interpretive drama in jazz repertory than these reading of "Potato Head Blues" and "Basin Street Blues," where you sit in agony waiting for the inevitable mistakes . . . and there aren't any, he makes it! It feels no less victorious than if he were pounding his way through the *Hammerclavier*. On these and the two-trumpet versions of "Struttin' with Some Barbecue" and "Swing That Music" (only the very last phrase lapses), the interpretive performances underscore the miracle that Armstrong spontaneously invented those solos.

Jones is an agreeable if minor product of his generation, imbued with the New Orleans idiom. Sandke is a gifted repertory performer and arranger. But Payton is something else, a musician whose playing implies less a reverence for the past than an assumption that the past will serve his future. He has been an irresistible anamoly ever since Doc Cheatham introduced him at a concert, "Trumpets for Dizzy," at the 1992 JVC Jazz Festival. "He reminds me so much of King Oliver," Cheatham said of the eighteen-year-old, and since Cheatham was the only person in the room who had ever heard Oliver in the flesh, that was a mouthful.

In the '50s, when jazz was rich in kings, George Wein could present its diversity exclusively in terms of royalty and stars, from Armstrong and Ellington through Coleman and Taylor. Young players were often relegated to student bands, which produced remarkably few musicians of consequence. By the '90s, jazz and Wein could no longer afford to marginalize youth. The tribute to Gillespie combined established trumpeters (from Harry Edison to Jimmy Owens to Jon Faddis, who directed the show) with young ones who were invited to prove themselves in proximity to the masters. They did: Roy Hargrove demonstrated his fire and Ryan Kisor his penchant for rhythmic displacement. Payton, however, encouraged proprietary feelings not only because he was the youngest, but because there is something uncanny about a teenager traversing bop chord changes with a punchy bravura and sound associated with an era that faded before Gillespie ever set foot in New York.

Payton's affinity for Armstrong was put to the test a few years later when Jazz at Lincoln Center presented an ambitious double-concert program of some thirty-six pieces, with four trumpeters in rotation. Good intentions were everywhere but musical command was in short supply, a consequence of bad casting in a few key roles and inadequate rehearsal. Payton approximated Armstrong's sound, but he (along with Wynton Marsalis, the musical director and primary soloist), was undone by clams and throttled notes that ruined the illusion. The best intentions simply won't do if the result is merely a close-enough-for-jazz rendering of music that must be played with studied accuracy. To the degree that Armstrong lives beyond his recordings, the question of improvisation versus composition is irrelevant. His "Muggles" invention is a perfect thing, and a botched performance is no more acceptable than a recitalist who plays *ff* where a composer marked *pp*. Payton and pianist Marcus Roberts worked so diligently at a transcription of "Weather Bird" that they managed to leach out all the joy.

At the second concert, a much emboldened Payton accurately emulated the Armstrongian glisses, the great slabs of sound, and convincingly accounted for "Wolverine Blues." Yet the concert was made memorable by the surprising triumph of Jon Faddis, a Dizzy Gillespie man, who, relaxed and funny, captured Armstrong's mocking splendor with his own impetuous bravura. He took "Swing That Music" at an appropriately ferocious tempo and triggered every firecracker in the climax; he opened "I Got a Right to Sing the Blues" with a sustained glissando of the sort that befuddled Armstrong's rivals. Faddis does not have

Armstrong's sound (Payton is much closer), but he found the music in the notes and the concomitant spirit in himself.

Payton got another chance, at the 1997 JVC Jazz Festival, in a program devoted to Armstrong and Bix Beiderbecke directed by Randy Sandke. This time he was ready, and indeed he emerged as the most inspiring musician of the week if for no other reason than that he made you wonder about his future. Sandke and others (going back to eighteen-year-old Taft Jordan in the Chick Webb band of 1938) have learned to reproduce Armstrong's solos and manner with reasonable authenticity, but Payton now used Armstrong's music—the broad range of his style—to enhance his own, much as Faddis had, but with that glimmering Orleanian sound that so impressed Cheatham. This puts him closer to musicians like Cootie Williams or Buck Clayton or Ruby Braff, who created individual styles on Armstrong's foundation, than to the tribe of repertory players. The fact is, after half a century of bop-inflected improvisation, the Armstrong model can serve as a new and provocative resource.

Payton made his mark on "fantasy" pieces, like a version of Don Redman's arrangement of "Stampede" in which Payton and Sandke represented a coming together of Louis and Bix, as well as adaptations of King Oliver's Creole Jazz Band numbers with two-trumpet breaks. ("Weather Bird," though, was left to Sandke, who restored a secondary strain Armstrong wisely left off the record, yet interpreted the solo with beauty and energy as substitutes for the mad humor of the original.) Perhaps inadvertently, Payton offered proof of how profoundly he had assimilated Armstrong's language at another concert, where he led his modern quintet in a generic post-bop original and an acceptable reading of "How Deep Is the Ocean," before essaying a roaring "Wild Man Blues." In that improvisation of rips, slurs, and sighs, building to an out-chorus saturated in euphoria, he sounded most like his own man.

How he will ultimately amalgamate a prewar style with an acceptable modernism was about the only interesting question raised by the festival. Nothing can replace or excel the exquisite power of Louis Armstrong in full flight, captured for all time in numberless recordings, but Armstrong's vision was not limited to his own prowess. It was broad enough to inspire an entire art, and is durable enough to withstand homage, revision, parody, modernization, neglect and even interpretation.

78 ❖ *Cassandra Wilson*
(A Different Songbook)

Repertory is the problem and the answer. It bedevils jazz singers today more than ever before. In the '30s and '40s, the jazz singers' complaint was that they got bottom-of-the-barrel material, while the big pop stars got the cream of Broadway and Hollywood. That wasn't entirely true, but then it wasn't really the issue. The jazz singer was renowned for nothing if not the ability to manufacture silk purses in quantity: 'tain't what you do, it's the way that you do it. Besides, numberless good songs were available for the picking. Besides besides, all those songs—the good, the bad, and the novelty—were in the language of the day. A singer *in* 1938 was a singer *of* 1938.

True, singers then, like now, ventured beyond genre and contemporaneity. Bing Crosby and the Mills Brothers weren't the only performers who husbanded assets by exercising the public domain. In the '40s, Sinatra demonstrated a marked affection for songs of the '20s. Raiding parties routinely returned from Nashville with country or cowboy songs; blues also were brightened for mass consumption. Spirituals were adapted and so were arias. But above and beyond all the exceptions was a songwriting factory that provided songs for singers, just as movies and plays provided roles for actors.

That changed as the juggernaut of rock pushed through the entertainment world, crushing the American version of operetta and the freelance vocalist. Songs were now conceived for (and by) particular performers or particular performances. In 1950, if a song like "Mona Lisa" made money for one singer, a dozen others took their turns and as many as half might actually score modest hits. Before the decade was up, not even number one records were covered. Pop was transformed, and jazz singers were in a quandary. What were the repertory choices? Jazz instrumentalists would occasionally nab material from the pop charts, but with such infrequent success—name four in the twenty years between Wes Montgomery covering the Mamas and the Papas and Miles Davis covering Cyndi Lauper—that the result was more a hand-wringing news story (gentlemen, what stand shall we take on this?) than anything suggesting casual assimilation. The jazz singer was no more flexible, finding no inspiration in Andrew Lloyd Webber or Bruce Springsteen and looking quite foolish trying to make sense of "Feelings." As musicians of the '90s increasingly looked aft for stylistic inspiration, singers were adrift in a Sargasso Sea of becalmed traditions, forced to revisit songs of forty and fifty years ago, the turf of the elders: Ella, Sarah, Frank, Rosemary, Carmen, Joe, Peggy, and Tony. The jazz singer in 1988 was still mining 1938.

For a long stretch, jazz singing was widely written off. The sanguine Dee Dee Bridgewater moved to Europe, and those who came after her couldn't really get started. Into the breach came rehabilitated veterans—albeit modernists—who had created their own songbooks. Betty Carter and Abbey Lincoln, plugging away since the '50s, emerged as the most provocative, inspired, and innovative singers in a generation: Carter for harmonic resourcefulness and improvisational flair, and Lincoln for attitude and interpretive power. Shirley Horn, after a hiatus of decades, came into renewed prominence as a saloon crooner of exceptional warmth and grace. Suddenly, the door was open, and a crowd of singers rushed in. This time they had an audience, but repertory remained the central issue.

Cassandra Wilson leads the younger pack by seniority and by the unexampled success of her first two Blue Note albums: *Blue Light 'Til Dawn* and *New Moon Daughter*, canny amalgrams of classic pop, modern pop, originals, and—pieces of resistance—treasure found where others failed to look, from Robert Johnson to the Monkees. She had been a decade in the wilderness, trying to figure out what to sing, a decade when she appeared stubbornly indisposed to open herself to an audience that was in desperate need of a singer as promising as she undoubtedly was. *Blue Skies* in 1988 augured an answer if only because the material was familiar and she put her mark on it, though she didn't see it that way.

Wilson, who comes from Jackson, Mississippi, moved to Brooklyn in the early '80s and became part of a circle of musicians with saxophonist Steve Coleman as its center. They were busy writing new music that crossed the jazz and pop divide, and they were onto something. Wilson was instantly tagged as the utility singer for a new movement: she had a smoky contralto, good looks, a sense of adventure, and originality. Her first album, *Point of View* (on the German label JMT), was recorded in 1985 and displayed her distinctive vocal mask without letting her take off. The disc was mixed to make the singer sound like one of the team, not the star—a ploy better realized through arrangements than the equalization of voice and instruments. Only rarely does she assert herself: on a Jean-Paul Bourelly rocker, "I Thought You Knew," and in her bravely individual reading of "I Wished on the Moon," a song associated with Billie Holiday that best suggested her potential as a fresh stylist in a now bereft tradition. The band includes Coleman, who coproduced, and trombonist Grachan Moncur III (she sings his "Love and Hate," well remembered from a 1963 Jackie McLean album). Too often the ensemble floats into a vague portentousness, robbing the singer of the sly intensity she portends but never quite delivers.

An excellent 1986 album by Air, *Air Show No. 1* (Black Saint), was a better showcase, though Wilson sang only three selections. For a singer blessed with an unmistakable timbre and attack, she took few pains in disguising her influences. Her wordless improv on "Side Step" is right out of Betty Carter, though she embellishes the sighs with growls and easily parries Henry Threadgill climax for climax. On Threadgill's delightfully quirky song, "Apricots on Their Wings," she swings the difficult piece, negotiating a neat change in meter and displaying an approach to range, dynamics, and phrasing mothered by Sarah Vaughan. Wilson's models are muted in the extended, brooding vowels of "Don't Drink That Corner My Life Is in the Bush," but the material, her own, is less convincing than the interpretation. *Days Aweigh*, her 1987 album, represented an advance in its assimilation of soul and pop conventions and in its more confident reading of "Apricots on the Wings" and two well-chosen standards: "Some Other Time" (with pianist Rod Williams) is unsteady, but "Let's Face the Music," in an arrangement that waltzes the release, is animated and sure.

Blue Skies is an album of ten standards, and Wilson is backed with cautionary care by a good trio: pianist Mulgrew Miller, bassist Lonnie Plaxico, and drummer Terri Lyne Carrington. Wilson covers nearly thirty years of songwriting, from the title selection (1927) to "I've Grown Accustomed to His Face" (1956), and about half of her selections were established by Frank Sinatra, though Wilson doesn't make you think of him. Notwithstanding the shadows of Vaughan ("I'm Old Fashioned") and Carter ("I Didn't Know What Time It Was"), she has reimagined these songs on her own sumptuous terms. Her most curious choice is "Shall We Dance?" (Rodgers and Hammerstein, not Gershwin), and she makes it work by the same savvy process with which Miles Davis reclaimed "Bye Bye Blackbird": an adjustment of tempo, an injection of blues. When she glides from an airy introductory scat figure into the melody, she makes it her own. Altering just a few notes, she turns the commonplace into the unexpected: on Burke and Van Heusen's "Polka Dots and Moonbeams," the telling phrase is "words ever after," pitched in a husky terrain that turns light pop into something dark and personal.

Wilson demonstrates improved articulation, a quality only intermittently displayed on her first record or her work with Steve Coleman (for example, his album, *Sine Die* [Panagea], a well-played pastiche of current jazz and funk mannerisms, where she sounds as though she had second thoughts about her original pieces). Every lyric on *Blue Skies* is interpreted for meaning. In this, she has much in common with Holiday, who also put her mark on songs by altering select melody notes but invariably made you believe the words were worth something. Nor do pronouns get in Wilson's way. It's a kick to hear a woman sing "Gee Baby, Ain't I Good to You," Don Redman's 1929 classic, definitively rendered by Hot Lips Page and popularized by Nat Cole in the '40s, then reestablished in the '60s by Joe Williams and Ray Charles. She intrepidly slips "Sweet Lorraine" into the second person ("you just found joy") and makes that work, too. Wilson is no belter, especially not on "Blue Skies," which has long been murdered by belters, preferring to keep her energy on reserve. She sustains interest because she knows these songs, knows how good they are—or appears to.

Like the gifted cabaret singer Mary Cleere Haran, who is at once more forthright and theatrical, Wilson doesn't pay contrived homage to standard songs, but rather earns her proprietary rights by reanimating them. Yet she expressed dissatisfaction with the album, and her response to its enthusiastic reception was to turn her back on the standard repertoire in favor of songs of her own composition, many of them oriented around obscure science-fiction themes. Despite her reservations, *Blue Skies* was a record with consequences. Doomed to narrow distribution in the United States, it went far in confirming the possibilities of classic songs among young jazz singers. In her intense originality, Wilson showed that songs worn to the bone through deadening lounge acts might just be the undying American lieder their admirers always said they were. In dusting off the middlebrow pieties that clung to them like barnacles, she claimed them anew.

The JMT albums that followed were dispiriting and, at best, uneven. *Jump World* is unconvincing fusion. *She Who Weeps* is bland and diffuse, even in a wordless "Chelsea Bridge" and a protracted "Body and Soul" that is built on a sleek vamp Dexter Gordon introduced. A more focused performance of the arrangement is heard on *Live*, and it's the audience's obvious favorite (sometimes the audience is right). *After the Beginning Again* indicates a regression: deep in the spell of Betty Carter, Wilson is mired in prosaic material and accompaniment. Yet she comes exotically alive in a protracted reading of the unlikely standard, "Baubles, Bangles and Beads," taken slow as if in a nearly inebriated trance, which suits the balmy lyric. *Dance to the Drums* (DIW), recorded in early 1992, is more predictive of where she was heading. Despite overdubs, heavy synth, and middling material, Wilson's individuality asserts itself with renewed conviction and an evocative finesse she would bring to a better menu of songs later in the year for Blue Note.

❖   ❖   ❖

Blue Light 'Til Dawn was a breakthrough, announcing the arrival of an accomplished stylist and a genuinely daring approach to repertory. Its casual authority and the enthusiasm with which it was received all but consigned the earlier work to designation as a lengthy apprenticeship, though the new album kindled a consensus of retrospective affirmation about the promise of *Blue Skies*, now fulfilled. To be sure, the strength of Wilson's trolling alto had never been captured as well as in the sophisticated rusticity of Brandon Ross's affecting arrangements, which encircle her with steel guitar, accordian, percussion, and violins, as well as the usual jazz instruments, in settings that are attentive, reserved, and singular. Produced by Craig Street, the album opens with a compelling "You Don't Know What Love Is" (once the property of Billy Eckstine), then mines the cavernous id of two Robert Johnson blues, songs by Joni Mitchell and Van Morrison, and originals, including a more forceful reading of "Redbone," introduced on *After the Beginning Again*, and the highly successful "Blue Light 'Til Dawn," which makes the best case to date for her claim to the mantle of songwriting jazz diva cornered by Abbey Lincoln and Betty Carter.

Unexpectedly, Wilson's New York JVC appearance in the summer of the album's release indicated ambivalence about the songs and her increased stature. In a set that included carnal performances of "My One and Only Love" and especially Johnson's "Come on in My Kitchen," she displayed the appropriate body language to back up the sighing intervals that are her imprimatur, while hiding in a maddening echo chamber of undigested sound, partly the result of an overamplified electric bass. Demonstrating neither microphone technique nor articulation, she allowed the words to bleed into the soup, raising the question of why she bothered to write lyrics if she didn't want them understood. The last best hope for jazz singing held herself one step back from success, as though she still hadn't decided if she really wanted to communicate with the strangers arrayed before her.

By 1996, with the release of *New Moon Daughter*, she had made the leap. She was still sultrily aloof, but smiled more easily, projected well beyond the ensemble, and focused on meaning, an ability now so rare it has emerged as the decisive sine qua non in the singer's trade. Wilson is the best known member of a new generation of singers who have made a point of doing what Lester Young and Dexter Gordon advised as an essential task even for instrumentalists, understanding the words. Jeannie Bryson, Denise Jannah, Kevin Mahogany, Densil Pinnock, and others have been around, but only now is anyone listening to those words.

New Moon Daughter is essentially more of the same—same instrumentation, producer, and arranger, though this time Wilson herself assumed chief responsibility for the charts. Perhaps it isn't as strong as its predecessor. Always given to back-of-the-beat nod-time, Wilson is sometimes self-indulgently languorous. Her treatment of Hank Williams's great ballad "I'm So Lonesome I Could Die" fails the melody, and the originals are flat, except for "A Little Warm Death," which is sexy and funny—qualities that have not appeared in her work in great quantity. But there are wonderful things here, some as good as anything she has done, including Son House's "Death Letter," a distinctively plaintive "Skylark," an improbably bright "Last Train to Clarksville," and a "Strange Fruit" that throbs with contained irony, and releases the song from Billie Holiday's grip as no one else has been able to do. Wilson bends notes as though they were made of shoe leather, and she nails them, especially low ones, with deft resolve. At times she grinds a phrase with a serrated cry that recalls Richie Havens. In coming to terms with the varied musics she has enjoyed, she is expanding the playing field.

79 ❖ Don Byron
(Musically Correct)

With instrumentalists skipping in and out of provincial musical neighborhoods, Don Byron's impending tribute to Mickey Katz should not have seemed quite so startling. Jews, after all, have played black music—folk and ethnic as well as America's Classical Music—throughout this century and before. Why shouldn't a black musician investigate Jewish ethnic music? Still, a dreadlocked klezmer promised something of an illicit thrill, and the audience at the Knitting Factory for Byron's triumphant debut in September 1989 tittered nervously through the opening numbers, until doubts about his dedication were allayed. Perhaps if Byron, who played seven years with Hankus Netsky's Klezmer Conservatory Band, had announced an evening of traditional klez, the persiflage would have been kept to a low roar. But Mickey Katz?: the jug-eared Yiddische parodist, who posed elflike on the cover of *Mish Mosh* with clarinet and salami; the Spike Jones alum, who recorded "Tico Tico" as "Tickle Kitzel" and "Shrimp Boats" as "Herring Boats," not to mention "Don't Let the Schmaltz Get in Your Eyes" and "Schlemiel of Fortune?" What's next? Cyrus Chestnut plays the Jimmy Durante songbook?

I'd have thought you had to be Jewish to enjoy Katz's wry. It turned out that Don Byron knew his man, and we—who remembered Katz's LPs as suburban predecessors of the *First Family* and Allen Sherman—didn't. Working chiefly from Katz's largely instrumental album, *Music for Weddings, Bar-Mitzvahs, and Brisses*, Byron fashioned an exhilarating and often moving evening, followed in 1993 by his recording *Don Byron Plays the Music of Mickey Katz* (Nonesuch), that restored Katz to the pantheon of diaspora klezmorim. Of greater consequence, Byron proved himself to be a seductive bandleader, genial, funny, and in command of a difficult book that demands disarming skills, rhythmic panache, and orchestral precision of an illusory sort—his ten musicians and singer had to sound as if they'd never seen a score. I don't know how much of the arranging style is unique to Katz, but the spectrum Byron's ensemble limned was lustrous in its meshing of clarinet, three brasses, violin, and percussion (with xylophone). In the fashion of klez, the band swung. Before one number, Byron instructed the audience, "Go against your Afro-American orientation and clap on the one and three, but don't do it outside this room." Most of the time, though—notably the serpentine "Mendel" and the patter-filled, dancing "Trombonik"—the beat was planted on the afterbeats. Either way, the pulse was airborne.

A few years earlier, at a Cooper Union series that presented new bands, Craig Harris introduced Tailgator's Tails, a quintet that allowed the trombonist to develop extended, often socially conscious pieces with an unusually broad range, from didjeridoo on the bottom to clarinet on top. Byron's clarinet that night was memorable, inventive and sure, as it is on Harris's JMT albums, especially "Cootie" on *Shelter* (1986) and "Dingo" (1987) on *Blackout in the Square Root of Soul*, on both of which he phrases on and against the beat, displaying full confidence in his intonation. At a 1984 Hamiet Bluiett concert, subsequently released on Black Saint as *The Clarinet Family*, Byron proved distinctive in the company of several gifted clarinetists; on his original, "For Macho," he worries riffs with the piping confidence one associates with the klezmer style. When those records came out, few of us knew of his involvement in the klezmer revival that began in the '70s.

Byron was born in 1958 and studied at New England Conservatory, matriculating around the time that Hankus Netsky of the school's Third Stream department set about organizing the Klezmer Conservatory Band. As he told the audience at the Knitting Factory, Byron went to a rehearsal, "heard one note of 'Dreidel' and was instantly into it." He stayed with KCB for seven years and credits it with keeping him on clarinet when there wasn't much call for it in jazz. The KCB recorded for Vanguard, and they show how quickly Byron mastered the klezmer language—the vocalized intonation, ardent wailing, and tortuous glissandi that, when secularized, found their way into the introduction of *Rhapsody in Blue* and the occasional *freylekh*-inspired improvisations of Benny Goodman. He is heard on Sam Musiker's "Der Nayer Doyne/ Sam Shplit" on *Klez!* and on Musiker's "Freylekhs" and Katz's "Mazel-tov Dances" on *A Touch of Klez!* In the same period he worked with the KCB, he also performed in several neighborhoods of jazz with, among others, Mercer Ellington, David Murray, John Hicks, Tom Pierson, Gerry Hemingway, Butch Morris, and Geri Allen.

That klez has some elemental resemblances to jazz has often been noted. Like the blues, Jewish dance music is based on the pentatonic scale, is highly rhythmic, and partly improvised. Even those who know Jewish music only as filtered down through Carla Bley's borrowings from Kurt Weill are likely to hear in klez uncannily familiar vamps and voicings. The klezmorim (the name is derived from the words *keley zemer*, Hebrew for musical instruments) draw on a tradition of itinerant musicians going back to the Middle Ages. Their legends, like those of early jazz, are full of stories that presume an inability to read music and are surely unrepresentative of their true abilities. Katz's arrangements, certainly, demand rigorous instrumental skills, though, like jazz, they aim for the mirage of improvisational ease. His bands employed several famous musicians rendered almost incognito by their Jewish names, including Mendel (Mannie) Klein and Shimshin Chaim (Sy) Zentner. The klezmer influence made its boldest incursion onto the pop charts in 1938 when Sholem Secunda's "Bei Mir Bist Du Schon" was domesticated for the Andrews Sisters—a huge prewar hit.

Yet unlike jazz, klez was a folk music, a community dance music, proudly insular and unable to withstand the forces of secularization. Assimilated Jewish musicians moved quickly into Tin Pan Alley or jazz or both. Between "Bei Mir" and "And the Angels Sing," the Yiddische estuary in American pop was virtually exhausted. Soon forgotten were such legendary klezmorim as Abe Schwartz, who contracted numerous klez recording sessions for Columbia, and the most celebrated New York klezmer, Dave Tarras, who exemplified that curious breed of ethnic geniuses (Celia Cruz and Skip James are others) who play for decades, win international renown, yet remain unknown to Americans who aren't of the same ethnic background. Even Mickey Katz, with several hits under his belt, was usually introduced as actor Joel Gray's father in the years before his death in 1985.

For all its constraints, though, klezmer is a ripe music, richly intoned and a bit outrageous in its elemental, driving, rhythmic lilt. Byron's band, an assemblage of New York-based players of various backgrounds, does it full justice, avoiding—for all its scholarly exactitude—any trace of solemnity. Lorin Sklamberg, as "the voice of Mickey Katz," cheers on the musicians like a Jewish Bob Wills and produces a judicious combination of twinkle and sigh in his extended number, "Litvak Square Dance," supported by xylophone, a vestigial reminder of what Katz likely borrowed from Spike Jones. In concert, Byron once told the band before giving the downbeat for "Litvak," "Just play D minor and you're safe." Bob Wills's Texas swing is also suggested in Mark Feldman's lusty tribute to Katz's violinist, Burrell Gill, in the way the fiddle rips through the space between clarinet and brass section.

Authenticity by bloodline was provided by Lee Musiker, a pianist usually heard accompanying singers (Mary Cleere Haran for a time). His uncle was Byron's favorite klezmer clarinetist, Sam Musiker, whose "Tsiviler" Byron regularly performs, but who is remembered by most as a tenor saxophonist and arranger with Gene Krupa's big band. Uncle Sam's father-in-law was Dave Tarras himself; his brother, Lee's father, is clarinetist Ray Musiker, who appeared on a 1963 Terry Gibbs (née Gubenko) album called *Jewish Melodies in Jazztime*, an appealing combination of klezmer bravado and bebop cool. Jewbop never quite became a recognizable genre, but Gibbs's record, which earned an additional footnote in jazz as the debut recording of pianist Alice Coltrane (née McLeod), points up by comparison one of the self-imposed limitations in Byron's klez. In choosing to play the Katz arrangements as recorded (a true jazz repertory decision, with which I often disagree), he doesn't allow enough of his own personality to billow through.

Time and again, I wish Byron would open the charts for an another chorus, but even his originals—including the delightfully racing "Bar Mitzvah Special," with a Spanish-sounding release (another pentatonic cousin: Sketches of Klez!)—cleave to the authenticity of short solo bites. That's one reason "Tears," which he composed on learning of Katz's death, stands out. A duet for clarinet and piano, it allows Byron to unveil a fuller range of tone colors and improvisational tropes. Beginning and ending with cadenzas over close, dark piano chords, it resolves pungent dissonances in pockets of minor-key radiance.

Byron has said, "Mickey Katz was one of my great influences and led one of America's great bands," an encomium that must confuse anyone clinging to the assumption that the whole thing is some kind of jape. When a Jewish colleague remarked after a Byron performance, "You know I grew up around this music and was always a little embarrassed by it," I was reminded of something B. B. King told me in 1969 when he was first beginning to play the white college circuit. He spoke of how black people who'd made it into the middle class were embarrassed by him and the blues. He frequently encountered an attitude that vaunted Duke Ellington as a classic and the Supremes as healthy new role models, he said, but that dismissed him and his music as something to be left behind. Similarly, the old-world rhythms and fixed minor-key melodies of klez cut too close to the bone of assimilated Jewish experience, with its reminders of urban shetls and rube accents. I'm sure it was the last thing on his mind, but Byron made it okay for a number of Jews to enjoy Jewish music again.

The price Byron paid was the inclination of critics to type him in that one mode. He burst free by issuing as his album debut not the Katz recital (that came next), but the charming motley of his 1992 *Tuskeegee Experiments* (Nonesuch). The opening melody intoned by clarinet in triple meter may recall the andante from Mozart's Sinfonia Concertante, but "Waltz for Ellen," like everything else on that eagerly awaited disc has an ironic tang of its own. The sense of humor that allowed him to make a splashy bow playing the music of Mickey Katz is discernible in everything Byron plays. Superficially, his album wears the veneer of Musical Correctness, the au courant equivalent of political correctness among young jazz producers and musicians. That is, personnel and instrumentation differ from track to track, repertory is diverse and surprising. You get a dirge, a poem, a jazz classic, a swinger, a solo, a duet, and (a signature surprise) Schumann's "Auf einer Burg." The ballast for it all is the soloist's diverting personality, his robust energy, his strangely demure swagger.

Byron is very much the contemporary clarinetist; his timbre can be as acerbic as that of John Carter and as airy as that of the overindulged Richard Stolzman. His approach to improvisation is rooted in hard beat/soft beat jazz phrasing, leavened by a penchant for schmaltz and a terrific ear for the pleasures of dynamics and the inflected squeak. As a composer, he offers a persuasive mixture of tradition and moxie, favoring tight unison voicings—so compact, indeed, that the blend of clarinet and guitar on "Tuskegee Strutter's Ball" sounds like a reed instrument you pluck and the pizzicato bass girding him on "In Memoriam: Uncle Dan" is like a leathery coat. He mixes familiar chords with vamps, as on "Next Love," and with his heads-up ability to subvert his own orthodox structures, seduces you into forgetting how bound to tradition he is. Which is in itself ironic because Byron is a straightforward player.

There is magic in the clarinet, as every survivor of the swing era knows, and Byron has found the right sound to let it flourish in a modern setting. After Bill Frisell's rigorous solo on the alluring "Tuskegee Strutter's Ball," a piece that opens with triplets and superimposes a melody in four, Byron plays a stunning, kindred solo of his own, making his instrument bleed and bend and rock as much as Frisell's guitar. Always engaged, piercing yet supple, he makes the clarinet sing, even shout. His hesitations and tempo changes all but disguise the conventional AABA form, and his invention holds you with its wry combination of forceful swing and klez-inspired burbling. His two-chorus solo on "Next Love" combines intensity and whimsy in the details, yet resounds with a cumulative force, and when he retards the second bridge, you wonder for a fleeting moment if he'll come out okay. There is no art without suspense.

"Next Love" also provides an agreeable introduction to a pianist named Edsel Gomez, who in a brief space corrals rhythm riffs, clusters, space chords, speedy runs, and off-center textures, avoiding clichés and retaining a relaxed sense of time. Ralph Peterson, Jr., sounds at times like a battalion of drummers, yet avoids unseemly clutter. He keeps time even when he breaks it up, sustaining intricate patterns and working closely with the marvelous bassist Reggie Workman, who flourishes his dexterous technique on "In Memoriam." Frisell and Byron have an especially empathic relationship that suggests even more than they have time to deliver on this disc. On "Tears," the quintet gets its most challenging workout because the point of this lament is addressed in ever expanding dynamics; as in all compelling chamber music, everyone has to breathe together.

Perhaps the best indication of Byron's shrewdly wry disposition is found in "Main Stem" and the title piece. "Tuskegee Experiment" is a linear and exceedingly rare example of poetry and jazz that works. The subject is horrific—barbaric experiments in which black men were used as a control group and denied treatment for syphilis. The performance, however, is no rant and is given a polished, even droll reading by Sadiq, whose poem is handsomely integrated into the music. Most of the poetry encountered in such settings is oracular or angry. Here, the primary impression is of a candid intelligence, the contiguous lesson of Byron's music.

You expect the Ellington selection also to be linear, but Byron's adaptation is arrestingly unpredictable, a kind of avant-klezmer deconstruction in which the melody intermittently pokes its way to the surface. This piece pointed the way to the still more assured *Bug Music* (Nonesuch) in 1996, in which his genre-busting sense of irony and adventure bloomed in an unlikely anthology of Ellington, John Kirby (the bassist whose sextet popularized the fashion of "jazzin' the classics" in the '30s), and especially Raymond Scott. A more assimilated Mickey Katz, Scott made his living working for the networks from the '30s on, while also leading integrated jazz combos and writing aberrational novelties that were routinely adapted for Warner Brothers cartoons. His music was rediscovered in the '90s as a precursor of every untrammeled musical id from Leroy Anderson to Spike Jones to Frank Zappa and perfectly suits Byron's penchant for an ensemble sound that is at once brightly humorous and fastidiously deployed.

Jazz hungers for new material beyond its own ever receding traditions and the parallel world of pop standards that nourished them for so long. Byron is in the vanguard of those locating and exploring the possibilities. If the search leads him into avenues where jazz ceases to be jazz, only a frazzled and increasingly irrelevant jazz purism is any the worse for it. Byron knows what he knows, and a sensibility that levels Ellington and Schubert and gives no less care to Mickey Katz's "Litvack Square Dance" and Raymond Scott's "Powerhouse" is no less valuable than that of the hedgehogs who know one big thing.

Byron isn't alone, of course; Bill Frisell, of *Tuskeegee Experiments*, unfurled his own map of Americana in 1993, *Have a Little Faith* (Nonesuch), with the clarinetist's participation. Here the angle is more Lisztian, consisting of transcriptions and adaptations of music by Aaron Copland, Bob Dylan, Muddy Waters, Sonny Rollins, and others, reconceived for guitar, clarinet, accordian, bass, and drums. Most strenuous is the seven-part suite Copland made of his ballet *Billy the Kid*. Frisell conflates a couple of sections and splits up some others, but this is withal a remarkably faithful rendering. Opening the prairie to the reediness of an accordian (played by Guy Klucevsek) and making the gun fight a barrage of drums (Joey Baron) might seem an invitation to banality, but the performance is too discerning to lapse into posturing. Electric bass (Kermit Driscoll) prods the first movement with a jaunty highstep, and the voicings throughout are fresh. Only an excess of spacy dissonance in "Mexican Dance" (from "Street in a Frontier Town") misses the mark.

Frisell achieves equally intriguing effects in some of the shorter pieces, voicing Byron's clarinet in unison with guitar to simulate the high scratchy sound of Muddy Waters's "I Can't Be Satisfied" and examining, with surprising conviction, the balladic quality of Dylan's "Just Like a Woman." Byron's filigree overlay in the second of two excerpts from Charles Ives is consistently absorbing, and in embracing the poignance of Stephen Foster's "Little Jenny Dow" instead of merely succumbing to its faded charm, he freshens Foster's melody. A shift from Sonny Rollins's "No Moe" to John Philip Sousa's "Washington Post March" echoes similar transitions in Rollins's own 1962 album *Our Man in Jazz*, as well as the more recent and deliberated pastiches of the Dutch bandleader

Willem Breuker. What Frisell and Byron bring to these works is a genuine affection that transcends eclectic mockery.

Yet the search for repertoire is perilous: I think specifically of Byron's Semaphore, an ensemble he introduced at a 1993 concert at Weill Recital Hall. Too much of his hour was given to J. D. Parran's "Proclivity," a finicky setting for a poem written and read by Shirley Bradley LeFlore that was, to borrow her own phrase, "sentimental and exclamatory." Self-consciously epic experiences generally require more tolerance than they get—when you live by the audience, you die by the audience. But the more modest pieces demonstrated how rich a vein for new material is new composition: notably a moody quintet for strings, piano, and two clarinets by Anthony Coleman; a duet written by Byron for piano (Uri Caine, another astute collaborator) and violin (Wonju Kim Malkin) that the composer said was partly influenced by Spike Jones; and a short diatonic waltz written by Byron to accompany a silent film, performed by clarinet and piano in a style generally reminiscent of the music Carl Davis writes for silent films and specifically obliged to Noel Coward's "Some Day I'll Find You."

Best of all was the historic ringer: Webern's 1930 Quartet for Violin, Clarinet, Tenor Saxophone, and Piano, op. 22. Jazz? Leave me out of it, though the instrumentation certainly suggests what the composer was listening to when he wrote it. Listening to Byron's performance, it occurred to me that swing, no less than melody and harmony, can be atomized. In the first movement, the quartet poked about in the usual pointillistic way, balancing the fragments. In the more audacious second movement, the rondo form provoked increased tension as the players employed body language to pitch their notes in the right places. The resulting suspense, as each note nervously precipitated the next, could be deciphered as swing in search of itself. No, Webern isn't jazz, but in this context the audience was open to anything with a head on it.

Byron appears to have discovered something important about jazz and swing and improvisation: their significance will atrophy if taken for granted. They must constantly be reassessed, rediscovered, reimagined, reclaimed from the larger musical turf. In the past, jazz was young enough to renew itself from inside. Perhaps that is no longer possible or desirable. Jazz is everywhere.

Acknowledgments

In a book that attempts to spot check a hundred or so years of jazz, I begin with two blackface comedians and conclude with a jazz clarinetist playing Webern. Need I add that at no time in this work's long gestation was it conceived as a conventional critique or history? Thus it required an unconventional editor: Oxford's illustrious Sheldon Meyer, who saw possibilities in the early stages of the project I did not and convinced me to forge ahead with an opus that may not be magnum in the critical sense but is undoubtedly so in the doorstop sense. Let it be said that even he turned a worrisome shade of carmine on weighing the completed draft; yet he unhesitatingly went to bat for it. In his acknowledgments to *The Jazz Tradition*, Martin Williams wrote of Sheldon: "He saw what sort of book this could be and encouraged me to revise the material and make it that sort of book." Now I know what he meant.

My thanks to the splendid staff at Oxford, especially Joellyn Ausanka, a jazz enthusiast herself, who shepherded the manuscript through all the stages that lead to publication; Brandon Trissler and Susan Day for various kindnesses; and Catherine Clements, a scrupulous, take-no-prisoners copy editor who saved me a thousand humiliations.

Much of this material germinated or simmered over time in Weather Bird, the column I have written for the *Village Voice* for twenty-four years; I thank Robert Christgau, who has edited me most of my adult life, the *Voice* staff, and its laissez-faire rulers—editor-in-chief Don Forst, managing editor Doug Simmons, publisher David Schneiderman—who allowed me to work half-time during the years I wrote *Visions of Jazz* and another book that is (I swear) nearing completion.

My thanks to Fred Kaplan and Jon Valin at *Fi: The Magazine of Music and Sound*, which published adaptations of the chapters on Vaughan, Basie and Young, and Sinatra; *Antioch Review* and Mark Lane at *The Oxford American*, which published the chapters on Hawkins and Clooney; Dave Oliphant at *The Library Chronicle of the University of Texas at Austin*, which commissioned and published an early version of the Parker chapter, providing the transcriptions; Jean Stein at *Grand Street*, which commissioned part of the Gillespie chapter, making those transcriptions possible; and John Lewis and Didier Deutsch of Atlantic Records, for whose record anthology *MJQ40* I originally developed the material on the Modern Jazz Quartet. My thanks to Thomas Owens and Jon Schapiro for the use of their musical transcriptions. I am, as ever, delighted to be represented by Georges Borchardt, Inc.; my thanks to Georges and Anne, Denise Shannon, and DeAnna Heindel.

I thank my assistants, Mary Beth Hughes and Chuck Bock, who take time from their own writing to help me with mine, and the many friends and colleagues from whom I am forever learning about music, particularly my brilliant mentors Dan Morgenstern, who will blanch at my failings but will also see his fingerprints on much of what is right and true; and Albert Murray, who will disagree with many of my conclusions but is himself partly to blame for keeping me focused on the larger canvas. I am ever grateful to my family: my mother, Alice, Helen and Norman Halper, Donna and Paul Rothchild (and Lee and Jenny), Ronnie Halper and Mark Donner (who has kept my computer humming while I gazed nostalgically at an abandoned 1957 Royal manual that never did me harm or lost a single byte of information), and Scotty the hamster. Above all, I honor my beloved wife, Deborah, who lives my work and helps make it possible, and my daughter, Lea, who, at nine, has been growing only slightly longer than this book and who made available to me her complete stock of blue pencils, without which *Visions of Jazz* could not have been completed.

G.G.
April 1998

Index of Names

NOTE: This index consists exclusively of musicians, composers, and songwriters.

Index of Songs and Selected Albums

NOTE: Entries in italics indicate albums.